D1325623

LIBRARIES IN BRITAIN
AND IRELAND

*

VOLUME III
1850–2000

The period covered by this volume of *The Cambridge History of Libraries in Britain and Ireland* presents challenges of a kind and on a scale not found in earlier volumes. Since the mid-nineteenth century an unprecedented expansion and diversification of library activity has taken place, which is reflected in the range of topics covered in this third volume. Libraries have become an industry rather than a localised phenomenon, and librarianship has developed from a scholarly craft to a scientific profession. The complexity arises in part from the place of libraries within a society that has seen itself as increasingly 'modern' in its commitment to public knowledge, education and democracy, and also to organisational efficiency and economic advance. Obviously it is libraries and librarianship that take the central position, rather than the wider scene which can be studied in depth elsewhere; however, it is not possible to provide a satisfactory account of library developments without a full appreciation of the social, economic and political environments that have produced and sustained libraries, and a proper balance between the two aspects must be maintained.

The types of library studied go well beyond the obvious categories of public, national and academic libraries, for each of which extensive coverage of the genre and of particular specialities is given. Education reached far into new social areas, with the aid of self-help institutions like the South Wales miners' libraries as well as the ubiquitous Carnegie Free Libraries (and the People's Network of the late 1990s). Scientific, medical and industrial libraries strongly influenced attitudes to information, not only in the library world but much more widely, particularly as pioneers in the technology of information which has led to the Internet. The needs of the professions, and other special-interest groups, have also influenced the libraries that serve them. At another extreme, the commercial lending libraries of the nineteenth and early twentieth centuries directly affected the style of the English novel – and perhaps moral attitudes. Subscription libraries have survived possibly rather better than their commercial rivals, and the phenomenon of book-collecting, the 'private library', is not neglected.

Although the volume covers a much wider selection of libraries than has to date been attempted in a single volume, it is clearly not possible to cover every library (or indeed every type of library) in the space available. Nor is it possible to deal with every activity connected with librarianship, the boundaries of the various sectors being decidedly permeable. But the picture that emerges is one of great diversity, with ramifications reaching between sectors and internationally.

ALISTAIR BLACK is Professor of Library and Information History at Leeds Metropolitan University.

PETER HOARE was formerly Librarian of the University of Nottingham. He was a founding member of the Library Association's Library History Group, of which like Alistair Black he is a former chairman.

LIBRARIES IN BRITAIN AND IRELAND

General Editor
PETER HOARE

Libraries pervade the culture of all literate societies. Their history illuminates that culture and many of its facets – the spread of literacy, the growth of scholarship, changes in educational practices – as well as reflecting changing social and political philosophies and practices. As a result, they have often developed in ways which could not have been foreseen by their founders.

The fundamental principle, of collecting for immediate and future use and enjoyment, has usually been combined with a social aim, the sharing of books and information among a wider group, which has become one of the characteristics of libraries today. This is one reason why libraries cannot simply be seen as a discrete phenomenon: throughout their history they must be considered part of the society they serve. This context includes the whole reading environment, the vital connection of libraries with social or cultural development, and the political framework which has become increasingly important in the past hundred years; economic and commercial aspects have also become more significant, as they have for the history of the book. The profession of librarianship has matured, especially in the last century, and has in turn affected the development of libraries: indeed it is the interaction of librarians and users that has provided much of the dynamic for that development. Changing methodologies of scholarship and the vicissitudes of private reading, too, affect the way libraries have developed.

Libraries vary enormously in form, in size and in purpose, and their nature has inevitably changed over the fifteen centuries encompassed in these volumes. In consequence the three volumes have different emphases and reflect different approaches to the historical record, but they share a common theme. This has inspired the project since its first inception on the initiative of Professor Robin Alston (whose library history database has been invaluable to many contributors), and under the aegis of the then Library History Group of the Library Association and its former Honorary Secretary Graham Jefcoate. Notwithstanding these differences in approach, the history of libraries is a continuum, and the divisions between the three volumes of what is essentially a single work are less precise than the volume titles may indicate. Developments for some years around the mid-seventeenth century may be treated in both Volume I and Volume II, though often in different contexts; and a similar overlap for the mid-nineteenth century exists between Volume II and Volume III. Readers concerned with these periods should be sure to consult both volumes.

The Cambridge History of Libraries in Britain and Ireland does not set out to be an exhaustive history of individual libraries: it is, rather, a general history charting the various trends and patterns of development, which studies different types of libraries and individual libraries as part of that broader view. In this way it aims to illuminate not only libraries and their users but also the wider history of the British Isles. Only in understanding their purpose and their context can the role of libraries be properly comprehended.

THE CAMBRIDGE
HISTORY OF
LIBRARIES IN BRITAIN
AND IRELAND

⋆

VOLUME III

1850–2000

⋆

Edited by

ALISTAIR BLACK

and

PETER HOARE

CAMBRIDGE
UNIVERSITY PRESS

CAMBRIDGE UNIVERSITY PRESS

Cambridge, New York, Melbourne, Madrid, Cape Town, Singapore, São Paulo

Cambridge University Press
The Edinburgh Building, Cambridge CB2 2RU, UK

Published in the United States of America by Cambridge University Press, New York

www.cambridge.org
Information on this title: www.cambridge.org/9780521858083

First published 2006

Printed in the United Kingdom at the University Press, Cambridge

A catalogue record for this book is available from the British Library

ISBN-13   978-0-521-78097-1   hardback
ISBN-10   0-521-78097-7   hardback

Only available as a three-volume set
ISBN-13   978-0-521-85808-3   three-volume set
ISBN-10   0-521-85808-9   three-volume set

Contents

vii

PART SIX

THE RISE OF PROFESSIONAL SOCIETY:
LIBRARIES FOR SPECIALIST AREAS

Contents

Tables

Contributors

CHRIS BAGGS was formerly a Senior Lecturer in the Department of Information and Library Studies, University of Wales, Aberystwyth.

ALAN BELL was formerly Librarian of the London Library.

ALISTAIR BLACK is Professor of Library and Information History, Leeds Metropolitan University.

B. C. BLOOMFIELD (died 2002) was formerly Director, Collection Development, Humanities and Social Science, The British Library.

RODNEY M. BRUNT is Principal Lecturer in the School of Information Management, Leeds Metropolitan University.

ANTONIA J. BUNCH was formerly Director, Scottish Science Library.

LIZ CHAPMAN is Deputy Director of Library Services, University College London.

IAN CORNELIUS is College Lecturer in the Department of Library and Information Studies, University College Dublin.

JOHN C. CRAWFORD is Research Librarian, Glasgow Caledonian University.

JOHN C. DAY was formerly in the Department of Library and Information Studies, University of Northumbria, Newcastle-upon-Tyne.

DEBBIE DENHAM (now Mynott) was formerly Reader in Children's Libraries and Literature at the University of Central England.

BOB DUCKETT was formerly Reference Librarian, Bradford City Libraries.

ALISTAIR S. DUFF is a lecturer in the School of Communication Arts, Napier University, Edinburgh.

SIMON ELIOT is Professor of the History of the Book, University of London.

GEOFFREY FORSTER is Librarian of the Leeds Library.

P. R. HARRIS was formerly Deputy Keeper of Printed Books, British Museum, and the British Library.

MARTIN HEWITT is Professor of Victorian Studies, Trinity and All Saints, University of Leeds.

PETER HOARE was formerly University Librarian, University of Nottingham.

GUY HOLBORN is Librarian of Lincoln's Inn Library, London.

JOHN HOPSON was formerly Archivist of the British Library, London.

ERIC HUNTER is Emeritus Professor of Information Management, Liverpool John Moores University.

GRAHAM JEFCOATE is Director of the University Library, Radboud University Nijmegen, and was formerly at the British Library.

REVD ALAN F. JESSON was formerly Bible Society's Librarian at Cambridge University Library.

PHILIP HENRY JONES was formerly in the Department of Information and Library Studies, University of Wales, Aberystwyth.

EVELYN KERSLAKE was formerly in the Department of Information Studies, Loughborough University.

GERARD LONG is an Assistant Keeper at the National Library of Ireland, Dublin.

JULIA TAYLOR MCCAIN is a research assistant at Bournemouth University.

IAN MCGOWAN was formerly Librarian, National Library of Scotland, Edinburgh.

LIONEL MADDEN was formerly Librarian, National Library of Wales, Aberystwyth.

JACK MEADOWS was formerly a Professor in the Department of Information Studies, Loughborough University.

CATHERINE MORAN is in the Music and Drama Library, Dublin Institute of Technology.

IAN R. M. MOWAT (died 2002) was formerly University Librarian, University of Edinburgh.

DAVE MUDDIMAN is Principal Lecturer in the School of Information Management, Leeds Metropolitan University.

CHRISTOPHER MURPHY is an independent researcher and consultant.

BERNARD NAYLOR was formerly University Librarian, University of Southampton.

DAVID PEARSON is Director of Research Library Services, University of London.

SIMON PEPPER is Professor of Architecture, University of Liverpool.

PEARL QUINN is in the RTE Stills Library, Dublin.

F. W. RATCLIFFE was formerly University Librarian, University of Cambridge.

ROBERT SNAPE is Tutor/Librarian, Myerscough College, Preston.

PAUL STURGES is Professor of Library Studies in the Department of Information Studies, Loughborough University.

FRANK WEBSTER is Professor of Sociology, City University, London.

Preface to volume III

Since the middle of the nineteenth century an unprecedented expansion and diversification of library activity has taken place, which is reflected in the range of topics covered in this volume. Similarly library history, though a specialised subject, has attracted a substantial and varied literature over the years. In setting the scope of this volume we have above all been aware of the wide array of library types and library themes that need to be included in a history of libraries in the last century and a half.

Something of the eclectic nature of library provision in this period can be gleaned from the particular example of the historic (but also industrial) city of York, as presented in O. S. Tomlinson's chapter on libraries in the book *The noble city of York*, edited by A. S. Stacpoole and others (York, 1972). In addition to the continuing growth of the ecclesiastical and scholarly York Minster Library, the city saw the development of more social library provision in the form of commercial circulating libraries. Ten of these existed at the start of our period; then from about the time of the First World War library services were provided by the stationers W. H. Smith and Boot's the Chemists, and by a sprinkling of 'twopenny libraries' established between the wars. Other libraries have included the York Subscription Library, the Mechanics' Institute and the Railway Institute; religious libraries, from the Society of Friends to the Bar Convent; professional libraries like the York Medical Society and the Yorkshire Law Society; the libraries of the confectionery manufacturer Rowntree and Company; educational libraries such as the two Anglican teacher-training colleges from the 1840s (now reunited as York St John College), the University of York, founded in 1961, and various school libraries; and, of course, from 1892 the municipal public library. York is also only a dozen miles from Boston Spa, one of the two main sites of the British Library and a major library force locally, as well as nationally and internationally. All these types of libraries command our attention.

Thus for the uninformed reader, unaware of the variety and depth of library provision in the modern period, a first visit to the contents pages of this volume would possibly spark surprise. A popular expectation, we speculate, is that a history of libraries will merely address the topic of public libraries; but we must also address the huge range of other libraries, not forgetting the context in which they developed – not least the implications of Betjeman's ironic remark in his poem 'In Westminster Abbey':

> Think of what our Nation stands for,
> Books from Boots' and country lanes . . .

The lush texture of modern library history required a rigorous structuring of the varied types of libraries to be described in this volume. However, to give lengthy attention to every single type of library is an impossible task even in a volume of this size: for example map libraries, music libraries and newspaper libraries (all with holdings and services often significantly different from those of the traditional book-centred library), not to mention other multi-media collections, have not been given particular attention, though references to them will be found in more general chapters.

The volume is divided into nine parts. The headings of some parts present themselves readily, thanks to the homogeneity of the chapters they contain. Introductory chapters consider the sources and methodologies appropriate for the study of library history in the modern era, in some cases quite different from those needed for earlier periods, and the place of the library in the modern world (the contextual introduction to the contributions that follow). There are discrete accounts of public, national and university libraries, and a section on the development of the library profession. All these divisions are relatively predictable.

The arrangement of the rest of the material is perhaps less obvious. We were aware that, like the modern age itself, library development occurred at a different pace and in different ways in different places. Hence we have a section presenting the reader with national perspectives – from England, Ireland, Scotland and Wales – that cross-cut the wide variety of library experiences described in the volume.

In contrast to the libraries of the state and the establishment, a significant amount of effort has been expended, over the past century and a half, by people establishing, or supporting, libraries *for themselves* – often, though by no means always, in the context of recreational reading. It is particularly important therefore to acknowledge this autonomous social enterprise, which we mark out under the heading 'The voluntary ethic'.

Equally unobtrusive, though at the other end of the spectrum, is the panoply of libraries created and used by the professions and 'experts' – in a wide variety of fields – that so defined the rise of the modern age. Some of the major manifestations of this 'special library' phenomenon are presented in a separate section.

Finally, no volume on the library in the modern era would be complete without paying appropriate attention to the implications for libraries of the competing and enabling information technologies of the digital age. While electronic developments permeate the whole recent history of libraries, we have provided space for a discussion of the issues more generally, opening the way for future historians of libraries to take up the continuing story.

Abbreviations

AACR	*Anglo-American cataloguing rules*
ABA	Antiquarian Booksellers' Association
ABTAPL	Association of British Theological and Philosophical Libraries
ACSP	Advisory Council on Scientific Policy
AIL	Association of Independent Libraries
ALA	American Library Association; Associate of the Library Association
ANSLICS	Aberdeen and North of Scotland Library and Information Co-operative Service
ASHSL	Association of Scottish Health Sciences Librarians
Aslib	Association of Special Libraries and Information Bureaux
AUT	Association of University Teachers
BAI	Book Association of Ireland
BAILER	British Association for Information and Library Education and Research
BBC	British Broadcasting Corporation
BC	Bibliographic classification
BETH	Bibliothèques Européenes de Théologie
BFBS	British and Foreign Bible Society
BIALL	British and Irish Association of Law Librarians
BIDS	Bath Information and Data Services
BIOSIS	[service offering bibliographic references for life sciences research]
BL	British Library
BLAISE	British Library Automated Information Service
BLDSC	British Library Document Supply Centre

BLCMP	Birmingham Libraries Co-operative Mechanization Project
BLCPM	*British Library catalogue of printed music*
BLPC	*British Library public catalogue*
BLPES	British Library of Political and Economic Science
BLRDD	British Library Research and Development Department
BM	British Museum
BNB	*British National Bibliography*
BNBC	British National Book Centre
BOT	Board of Trade
BRASTACS	Bradford Scientific, Technical and Commercial Service
BUCOP	*British Union Catalogue of Periodicals*
CAG	Cooperative Automation Group
CBI	Confederation of British Industry
CCL	Catholic Central Library (Dublin)
CD-ROM	compact disc – read-only memory
CHILDE	Children's Historical Literature Dissemination throughout Europe
CICRIS	Co-operative Industrial Commercial Reference and Information Service
CILIP	Chartered Institute of Library and Information Professionals
CIPFA	Chartered Institute of Public Finance and Accountancy
CLS	Central Library for Students
CMS	Church Missionary Society
CNAA	Council for National Academic Awards
COCRIL	Council of City Reference and Information Libraries
COM	computer output microform
CONARLS	Circle of Officers of National and Regional Library Systems
COPAC	*CURL On-line Public Access Catalogue*
COPOL	Council of Polytechnic Librarians
CSL	Circle of State Librarians
CUKT	Carnegie United Kingdom Trust
CURL	Consortium of University Research Libraries
DCMS	Department for Culture, Media and Sport

DDC	Dewey Decimal Classification
DENI	Department of Education, Northern Ireland
DES	Department of Education and Science
DHSS	Department of Health and Social Security
DNB	*Dictionary of National Biography*
DSIR	Department of Scientific and Industrial Research
DTI	Department of Trade and Industry
DTP	desk-top publishing
DVD	digital versatile disc
EARL	Electronic Access to Resources in Libraries
EDI	electronic data interchange
ERIC	Educational Resources Information Center
ESTC	*Eighteenth-century* [later, *English*] *short-title catalogue*
EU	European Union
FCO	Foreign and Commonwealth Office
FID	Fédération Internationale de Documentation
FLA	Fellow of the Library Association
FO	Foreign Office
GEAC	(proprietary name)
GKII, GKIII	*General catalogue of printed books*, 2nd (3rd) edition (British Museum)
GUI	graphic user interface
HATRICS, Hatrics	(originally Hampshire Technical, Research, Industrial, Commercial and Scientific Information)
HEFCE	Higher Education Funding Council (England)
HEFCW	Higher Education Funding Council (Wales)
HERTIS	Hertfordshire Technical Information Service (now simply Hertis)
HLC	Hospital Library Council (Dublin)
HMSO	Her (His) Majesty's Stationery Office
HULTIS	Hull Technical Information Service
IAC	Irish Advisory Committee (of Carnegie UK Trust)
IATL	International Association of Theological Libraries
ICI	Imperial Chemical Industries
ICT	information and communications [or computer] technology
IFLA	International Federation of Library Associations and Institutions
IIS	Institute of Information Scientists

INSPEC	*Information Services: Physics, Electrical and Electronics, and Computers and Control*
IPCS	Institution of Professional Civil Servants
IOLIM	International Online Information Meeting
ISBD	International Standard Bibliographic Description
ISBN	International Standard Book Number
ISTC	*Incunabula short-title catalogue*
IT	information technology
JANET	Joint Academic Network
JISC	Joint Information Systems Committee
JRLUM	John Rylands Library of the University of Manchester
JSCAACR	Joint Steering Committee for Revision of AACR
KCL	King's College London
LA	Library Association
LADSIRLAC	Liverpool and District Scientific, Industrial and Research Library Advisory Council
LAI	Library Association of Ireland (An Chomhairle Leabharlanna)
LAN	local area network
LAR	*Library Association Record*
LASER	London and South East Region
LAUK	Library Association of the United Kingdom (later simply 'The Library Association')
LCC	Library of Congress classification
LCSH	Library of Congress subject headings
LIC	Library and Information Commission
LINC	Libraries and Information Council
LIP	Library and Information Plan
LISA	*Library and Information Science Abstracts*
LJMU	Liverpool John Moores University
LLU	Lending Library Unit [of DSIR]
LOCAS	Local Cataloguing Service (British Library)
LSE	London School of Economics and Political Science
MANTIS	Manchester Technical Information Service
MARC	Machine Readable Catalog[u]ing
MEDLARS	Medical Literature Analysis and Retrieval System
MEDLINE	(online version of MEDLARS)

MERLIN	Machine Readable Library Information Network (British Library)
MLAC	Museums, Libraries and Archives Council
MLS, MLIS	Master of Library [and Information] Studies (etc.)
MRC	Medical Research Council
NANTIS	Nottingham and Nottinghamshire Information Service
NBA	Net Book Agreement
NBC, NBL	National Book Council, National Book League
NCL	National Central Library
NeLH	National Electronic Library for Health
NHRU	National Home Reading Union
NHS	National Health Service
NLLST	National Lending Library for Science and Technology
NRLSI	National Reference Library for Science and Invention
NLI	National Library of Ireland
NLS	National Library of Scotland
NLW	National Library of Wales
OCLC	Online Computer Library Center (originally Ohio Colleges Library Center)
OPAC	online public access catalogue
OSTI	Office for Scientific and Technical Information
PC	personal computer (specifically IBM)
PRECIS	*Preserved context index system*
R & D	research and development
RDC	Rural District Council
RLIN	Research Libraries Information Network
RSM	Royal Society of Medicine
RSLP	Research Support Libraries Programme
SCOLCAP	Scottish Libraries Co-operative Automation Project
SCOLLUL	Standing Conference of Librarians of London University Libraries
SCOLMA	Standing Conference on Library Materials from Africa
SCONUL	Standing Conference of National and University Libraries [later, Society of College, National and University Libraries]

SCOTAPLL	Standing Conference of Theological and Philosophical Libraries in London
SCOTUL	Standing Conference of Technological University Libraries
SDI	selective dissemination of information
SERLS	South East Regional Library System
SINTO	Sheffield Interchange Organization
SHEFC	Scottish Higher Education Funding Council
SHINE	Scottish Health Information Network
SLIC	Selective listing in combination
SLS	(later name of SWALCAP)
SPCK	Society for the Promotion of Christian Knowledge
SRIS	Science Reference and Information Service
SSC	Society of Solicitors in the Supreme Courts of Scotland
STEIN	Short Term Experimental Information Network (British Library)
STM	Scientific, Technical and Medical (especially as a publishing category)
SWALCAP	South West Academic Libraries Co-operative Automation Project
TALIC	Tyneside Association of Libraries and Information Bureaux
TBC	The Times Book Club
TCD	Trinity College Dublin
TIDU	Technical Information and Documentation Unit
UCL	University College London
UDC	Universal Decimal Classification
UFC	University Funding Council
UGC	University Grants Committee
UKCIS	United Kingdom Chemical Information Service
UKLDS	United Kingdom Library Database System
UKOLN	United Kingdom Office for Library Networking
UKOLUG	United Kingdom Online User Group
ULL	University of London Library
UNESCO	United Nations Educational, Scientific and Cultural Organisation
WEA	Workers' Educational Association
WILSH	Welsh Information and Library Services for Health

Introduction:
sources and methodologies for the history of libraries in the modern era

ALISTAIR BLACK AND PETER HOARE

The history of libraries in the modern period is rich in the resources, both specific and more general, which are required to prosecute the subject.[1] More history has been written about the past 150 years – witness the explosion of studies on the Victorian period since its rehabilitation in the mid-twentieth century – than about any other comparable period. This means that library historians have at their disposal a considerable amount of contextual knowledge to help them situate and make sense of the subjects they research. Secondly, modern organisations – organisations forged from the bureaucratic efficiency of maturing modernity – have generated vast swathes of archival documentation. As solid administrators, librarians have been busier than most over the past century and a half in documenting the activities of their organisations. Hence we have been bequeathed an abundant store of primary evidence, a good amount of which, owing to librarians' penchant for preservation, has thankfully survived.

Sources for modern library history can be divided into two basic categories. First there are library-centred administrative sources, which are derived mostly from instrumental needs to manage and improve library services, and to which one might add, for many types of library, the archives of their parent institutions. Secondly there are sources generated outside the library profession or the administrative domain of the library by those who have had something to say about them, whether as users or non-users.

Library-centred and administrative sources are extensive. They include library committee minutes, rule books, printed catalogues, annual reports, financial reports, registers of borrowers and members, statistics of use and of stock, the contemporary library press, architectural plans and drawings, photographs, brochures and official reports, as well as a wide variety of ephemera,

---

1 For a succinct discussion of sources, see J. G. Ollé, *Library history* (London, 1969).

from everyday documents like library tickets and promotional posters, to objects such as the indicator boards common in closed-access public libraries before the First World War, and, of course, the extant built forms of libraries themselves. The archives of the parent institutions – whether universities or cathedrals, government departments or industrial concerns – may also shed light from an angle that is not always the same as the library's own view of its activities. This can be true in respect of buildings and accommodation especially, but also of the institutional policies (or external pressures) which libraries have to respond to.

Librarians have been enthusiastic autobiographers, eager to pass comment in written testimonies on the systems and users they have managed and on the contribution they have made to the profession.[2] Library historians have also at times used interviews and oral recordings to capture the history of the profession 'in its own words'. In the 1970s David Gerard and Mary Casteleyn conducted a series of interviews with prominent librarians, including Frank Gardner, K. C. Harrison and W. A. Munford.[3] Some studies have made use of career-history interviewing.[4] Tapping into this healthy tradition, in 1999 the Library History Group of the Library Association began constructing an electronic archive of professional reminiscences, now incorporating the professional memories of around a dozen librarians.[5] A similar archive, 'Pioneers of Information Science in North America', has been constructed by Bob Williams of the University of South Carolina.[6]

Turning to popular, user-centred sources generated outside the library domain, three types of documentary evidence are worth highlighting: fiction and narratives in other media; autobiographies and diaries; and newspapers. Libraries have frequently found their way into cultural and media

---

2 For example D. Gerard, *Shrieking silence: a library landscape* (Metuchen, NJ and London, 1988), or K. C. Harrison, *A librarian's odyssey: episodes of autobiography* (Eastbourne, 2000), both describing careers in English public libraries. Examples of autobiography from other parts of the British library scene are D. Urquhart, *Mr. Boston Spa* (Leeds, 1990) and B. Vickery, *A long search for information*, Graduate School of Library and Information Science, University of Illinois at Urbana-Champaign, Occasional Paper 213 (Urbana-Champaign, 2004).

3 *Librarians speaking* (London, 1974–6), 23 tapes (British Library National Sound Archive). In 2002 a similar but smaller exercise was mounted by the Health Libraries Group of the Library Association: *Health Libraries Group oral history project*, 5 tapes (also British Library National Sound Archive).

4 E. Kerslake, 'A history of women library workers in English libraries 1871–1974', unpublished PhD thesis, Loughborough University (1999).

5 www.cilip.org.uk/groups/lhg/e-memory.html.

6 www.libsci.sc.edu/bob/ISP/ISP.htm.

productions of various kinds, and these have proved useful primary sources for library historians. Libraries have often featured in contemporary imaginative literature.[7] Some recent studies have examined libraries through the lens of children's literature.[8] Comics and film have also been mobilised as sources.[9] Imaginative cultural and media productions reflect the 'reality' – or at least perceptions or dramatisations of reality – of the user's view of libraries at the time they were 'authored'.

Users' written accounts of libraries in autobiographies, diaries and social commentaries are invaluable sources in library history. Such accounts are an important primary source for historians seeking to learn about the part that events, people, social practices and institutions have played in people's lives, as well as the meanings that autobiographers attach to these. Libraries have also featured in users' life histories, a significant number written by members of the working classes.[10]

Notwithstanding these efforts on a 'domestic' scale, library historians have been largely inactive in capturing the history of libraries in the words of users.[11] Evidence of library use can be found in large-scale, general oral-history projects, but such references are extremely rare and difficult to detect. Unfortunately, despite the importance of the topic and the considerable potential

7 A. Black, 'Representations of the public library in Victorian and Edwardian fiction: assessing the semiological approach', in P. Vodosek and G. Jefcoate (eds.), *Libraries in literature / Bibliotheken in der literarischen Darstellung* (Wiesbaden, 1999), 151–66; J. W. Singleton, 'The library in fiction', *Library Association Record* 20 (1918), 210–18.

8 E. Kerslake, 'Angry sentinels and businesslike women: identity and marital status in 1950s English library career novels', *Library History* 17 (2001), 83–90; E. Yontz, 'Librarians in children's literature, 1909–2000', *The Reference Librarian* 78 (2002) (Special Issue: The Image and Role of the Librarian), 85–96.

9 Regarding comics see D. Highsmith, 'The long, strange trip of Barbara Gordon: images of librarians in comic books', *The Reference Librarian* 78 (2002), 61–84. Regarding film see J. Williamson, 'Jungian/Myers Briggs personality types of librarians in films', *The Reference Librarian* 78 (2002), 47–60, and M. Nagl, 'Stille, Ordnung, Katastrophen: Bibliotheken im Film – Bibliotheken aus männlichem Blick?' (which also covers television), in Vodosek and Jefcoate (eds.), *Libraries in literature*, 115–26.

10 B. Wiltshire, 'The public library in autobiography', unpublished MPhil thesis, CNAA, North London Polytechnic (now London Metropolitan University) (1982). Many instances of library use are indexed in J. Burnett, D. Vincent and D. Mayall (eds.), *The autobiography of the working class: an annotated critical bibliography*, 3 vols. (Brighton, 1984–9). See also J. Rose, *The intellectual life of the British working classes* (New Haven and London, 2001).

11 There are some exceptions, for example Alistair Black's use of the Mass-Observation Archive: see A. Black, 'The past public library observed: user recollections of the British public library recorded in the Mass-Observation Archive', *Library Quarterly*, forthcoming.

value of the evidence, no systematic oral-history study of library patrons has been attempted.[12]

Articles in newspapers, both local and national, often offer an 'outsider's view' of libraries. Care has to be taken, of course, to distinguish genuine, detached observation from that which has been inspired or moulded by librarians or those connected with the library movement. Library historians will continue to be indebted to those librarians of the past who demonstrated great diligence in extracting material about libraries from contemporary newspapers and magazines and organising the cuttings into files and volumes, such as those that form part of the archives of the Library Association, of the Carnegie United Kingdom Trust and of many local studies departments of public libraries.[13]

Methodological issues in library history

The growth and diversification of history generally in recent decades has proved to be a mixed blessing for library history. On the one hand, library history has benefited from the arrival of the 'new history' and 'history from below', where the traditional emphasis on the history of great individuals and events, and on military, diplomatic and political history, has been challenged by historians seeking to give greater attention to the history of ordinary people and to the perspectives of those not in positions of power: the history of people and practices previously hidden from history. In keeping with this shift of emphasis, the library, as an 'everyday', seemingly innocuous institution, has been retrieved from the archives of history and rightly written into the historical record. This is true not just of popular, 'social' libraries, but also of those in 'establishment' institutions like the church, government and the professions, where libraries and their staff have for the most part occupied a relatively low status in the hierarchy of power. Library history has undoubtedly been invigorated by increased activity in local history and in such 'modern' subjects as the history of women and the working classes, as well as by the growth and increasing sophistication of areas like architectural and management history.

On the other hand, it is probably fair to say that, while contributing to, and feeding off, the development and diversification of modern history, library

---

12 Some studies have incorporated interviews with users, for example N. Moody, 'Fashionable design and good service: the spinster librarians at Boot's Booklover's Libraries', in E. Kerslake and N. Moody (eds.), *Gendering library history* (Liverpool, 2000), 131–44.

13 At the time of writing, the archives of the Carnegie United Kingdom Trust are deposited in the National Archives of Scotland. Those of the Library Association are deposited in the archives department of University College London.

historians could have done more over the decades to integrate their field with other fields of historical study. In being less attentive than they might have been to 'mainstream' history, library historians have laid themselves open to the accusation – albeit an unfair one – that their field has not moved far enough away from its antiquarian past. As well as borrowing too little from the rich endeavours of 'other' history, library historians have also been sparing in their employment of theory drawn from other disciplines, whether from sociology or cultural studies, philosophy or architecture. There are, of course, many exceptions to this general observation – indeed, this volume is densely populated with them. It is also the case that the search for facts and evidence in library history remains crucial and should not be abandoned in any mad 'rush for theory'. However, it has to be said that the better library history is often that which is infused and illuminated in some way by knowledge and contexts extracted from outside the primary and secondary sources of the subject. Such discursive studies are characterised by a willingness of library historians to admit that they need something on which to hang their work.

During the course of its recent development a tension has emerged in library history between description and analysis, between fact-grubbing and theory. However, the tension is much less pronounced in some areas of library history than in others. In considering the relationship between fact and theory in library history, it is possible to construct a taxonomy of institutions that warrant varying mixes of factual and theoretical approaches. Theory-rich approaches have been relatively common in public library history and in the history of the profession of librarianship. Here, although there is always more to be discovered, the facts of past development are fairly well known and widely available in secondary sources. Hence, the emphasis is now more on the development of theoretical interpretations rather than on disclosure of fresh primary sources. Topics where the need for factual discovery and for theory are more or less equally weighted include libraries in higher education, middle-class subscription libraries and specialist libraries of various kinds. Finally, situated at the far end of the spectrum are libraries that we might include in a category labelled 'hidden': libraries of a marginal and often ephemeral nature.[14] Here, the general priority has been – and will continue to be – the gathering of raw evidence, although exciting theoretical perspectives and opportunities inevitably present themselves and should be encouraged.

Library history thus has the opportunity to display a wider conception of topics worthy of research than has been evident in the past. This is also the case

---

14 The concept of 'hidden libraries' is explored in chapter 1, below.

in respect of theoretical approaches. The history of libraries can be researched at a 'macro' level – at the level of general development, policy formulation, class use, professional expertise and religious, political or civic influence. The 'macro' level can also address issues arising from the multi-layered nature of libraries, which can respond to a kind of stratigraphic approach, revealing the different approaches to similar issues at different times. However, precisely because they are such highly textured, idiosyncratic worlds of cultural activity, they can also be studied at the 'micro' level, with researchers addressing questions, for example, of how people behaved in libraries, the nature of disciplinary controls imposed, the detailed motives underpinning specific instances of library use and the nature of interpersonal relationships, whether between user and user, user and staff, or staff and staff. As one of us has written elsewhere:

> The study of minutiae in library history provides ammunition for fresh theoretical perspectives revealing the meaning of common, microscopic social practices and beliefs leading to the decoding of the discourses and practices of librarians, readers, benefactors or promoters. Attempts might thus be made to obtain the meaning of opening ceremonies; or of architectural styles; or of the 'haven' or 'rural' and other metaphors employed in respect of libraries; or of the change in emphasis in public library hygiene in the late-Victorian age away from ensuring clean air and good ventilation, towards fears concerning the lending and circulation of supposedly disease-ridden books, thereby reflecting the medico-moral discourse concerning the source of disease – said to be foul air in the mid-nineteenth century, but Pasteur's germs by the late nineteenth century. Whether one spoke in a library, returned books late deliberately or queued quiescently for long periods at the closed-access counter or the open-access wicket gate can reveal much, for example, about issues of discipline and rebellion in both the library and wider social setting.[15]

The way in which these methodologies have been applied in this volume, explicitly or implicitly, will become apparent in the text, varying from chapter to chapter depending on the availability of sources and the approach dictated by the subject matter.

---

15 A. Black, 'New methodologies in library history: a manifesto for the "new" library history', *Library History* 11 (1995), 76–85.

I

Libraries and the modern world

ALISTAIR BLACK AND PETER HOARE

Libraries and modernity

The 150 year period that this volume covers witnessed the emergence and development of what can justifiably be referred to as the 'modern library'. It coincided with the maturation of modernity: a change of gear within the broad epoch of modernity that was set in motion by the scientific revolution of the seventeenth century and the intellectual revolution of the Enlightenment of the eighteenth century.[1] During our period, industrial production moved on to a more technical plane, and became irrevocably determined by the outputs of applied science (the 'knowledge economy', we might observe, existed for a century or more before its 'rediscovery' in the late twentieth century). Society underwent a process of massification. This was as much the case in terms of political arrangements (universal suffrage), communications (the mass media, including the book trade and newspapers) and social provision (education, welfare and housing) as it was in respect of production, consumption and advertising. The 'control' dimensions of modernity, such as surveillance, bureaucracy and standardisation, intensified alongside its liberating tendencies, such as the free flow of ideas and the operation of a public sphere, which was extended via a variety of rational and accessible institutions – although restricted, some would argue, by others, especially as the twentieth century progressed.

Libraries mirrored and influenced each of these aspects of a mature modernity. Indeed, library development after 1850 is best understood as a function of the 'modern' society that began to emerge from around the middle of the nineteenth century. Most library activity of the past century and a half, we suggest, can be viewed in the context of the changing contours of modernity. Modernity has not, of course, been a static phenomenon. Theorists point to

1 P. M. Heimann, 'The scientific revolutions', in P. Burke (ed.), *The new Cambridge modern history*, vol. 13: *Companion Volume* (Cambridge, 1979), 248–70.

various phases in its evolution.[2] Indeed, some believe we have recently witnessed the culmination of modernity's final phase. A shift to a post-modern world and an information society, in which the grand narrative of modernity has become irrelevant and outdated, has been widely discussed and accepted.[3] On the other hand, those suspicious of the post-modern and information-society propositions conceptualise instead merely a new phase of 'late', or 'high', modernity and justify their position by pointing to the unvanquished, and even strengthened, continuities of the 'modern project': a deep residual faith in progress, in critical reasoning, in the freedom of the 'self', in capitalist production and market economics and, despite the risks they reproduce, in science, technology and expert knowledge.[4] It is not hard to see how the enduring components of the modern mind and modern culture listed here have generated – and continue to generate – high levels of library activity.

Pre-modern societies are essentially 'stationary societies', characterised by a slow pace of cultural, technological and economic change. The accumulation of knowledge occurs at a creeping rate, and its dissemination is patchy and parochial. By contrast, modern societies are societies in a state of flux, where technologies, economies, cultures and cultural production develop and change rapidly. To counter the unsettling experiences and unpredictable effects of sudden change, modern societies instinctively generate 'strategies of stability' that seek to restore a measure of continuity. One such strategy, it might be argued, is an increased emphasis on preserving and organising recorded knowledge in libraries and other kinds of repository.

The organisation of knowledge, a key factor in the concept of modernity and linked to its 'control' dimension, is fundamental to the work of libraries – through their management of patterns of use and through the standardised

2 M. Carleheden, 'Rethinking the epochs of Western modernity', in M. Carleheden and M. H. Jacobsen (eds.), *The transformation of modernity: aspects of the past, present and future of an era* (Aldershot, 2001), 83–115.

3 D. Harvey, *The condition of postmodernity: an inquiry into the origins of cultural change* (Oxford, 1989); P. A. Rosenau, *Post-modernism and the social sciences: insights, inroads and intrusions* (Princeton, NJ, 1992); S. J. Grenz, *A primer on postmodernism* (Grand Rapids and Cambridge, 1996); D. Bell, 'The social framework of the information society', in T. Forester (ed.), *The microelectronics revolution: the complete guide to the new technology and its impact on society* (Oxford, 1980), 500–49; A. Toffler, *The third wave* (London, 1980); United Nations World Summit on the Information Society, *Declaration of principles. Building the information society: a global challenge in the new millennium* (Geneva, 2003), www.itu.int/wsis.

4 A. Giddens, *Modernity and self-identity: self and society in the late modern age* (Cambridge, 1991); A. Giddens, *The consequences of modernity* (Cambridge and Oxford, 1990); F. Webster, *Theories of the information society* (London, 1995); A. Duff, *Information society studies* (London, 2000); D. Muddiman, 'World gone wrong? Alternative conceptions of the information society', in S. Hornby and Z. Clarke (eds.), *Challenge and change in the information society* (London, 2003), 42–59.

catalogues and classification of their stock, but also through the efforts of librarians and 'information professionals' for greater effectiveness in that organisation. This has grown well beyond national boundaries in the past century and a half, with the establishment of bodies like the Fédération Internationale de Documentation with its concern for universal subject control of published information.[5] In the last quarter of the twentieth century popular, indeed almost universal, access to the Internet, and particularly the development of search engines, has raised in the public mind questions of information management that reflect much of what the library profession has seen as its primary role. How that will affect the libraries of the future it is too soon to say; but most of today's concerns about information retrieval, from the efficiency of natural-language use in search engines to the sheer bulk of the amount of information available, had been addressed in libraries many years before.

The purpose and role of a library will vary from one to another and will interface with the driving forces of the modern age in different ways. However, generally speaking two basic factors have shaped the 'modern library', one practical, the other intellectual. Addressing the Library Association in 1938, its then president W. C. Berwick Sayers proclaimed that a collection of books was 'a modern Delphi, as much an oracular shrine as it is a laboratory'.[6] In this brief sentence Sayers succeeded in crystallising the dual essence of a library: its spiritual and material functions. On the one hand, a library fulfils an idealistic, poetic and mystical role. A library represents 'holy ground' where the wisdom of the ages can be consulted and absorbed and where the inner self can be explored and developed – a role which can perhaps be stretched to include the recreational function which for many library users has long been a major element. On the other hand, of increasing importance in the modern period is the library's utilitarian role. A library is often a place of worldly discovery, a citadel of science, a practical workshop.

In the name of individual and social progress, libraries have invariably accommodated both material and spiritual functions but, depending on type, they vary in the extent to which these are prioritised. Multiplicity of function is a common aspect in many libraries, and in the way they are supported by their parent institutions. One of the most prominent examples of this is the 'Fiction Question' which dominated public library discussions for many years

5 W. B. Rayward, *The universe of information: the work of Paul Otlet for documentation and international organisation* (Moscow, 1975); and W. B. Rayward (ed.), *International organisation and dissemination: selected essays of Paul Otlet* (Amsterdam, 1990).

6 Sayers, W. C. B. 'Presidential address', *Library Association Record* 40 (1938), 291–6 (citation p. 291).

around the turn of the twentieth century, and which still recurs in political debate about the role of the library: How far should public funding support a purely recreational use of fiction? (The question can also be asked of music and other media.) Is there a distinction between 'good' fiction and the worthless, literally insupportable kind? In fact libraries have always faced such questions, which take different forms in different contexts. Should medical libraries in hospitals serve (and be accessible to) patients as well as clinical and nursing staff – and what alternative or recreational provision is needed for what has been termed 'bibliotherapy'? Should a factory or department store supply books for leisure reading by its employees as well as for technical use – and what is the cost-benefit analysis for this? What is the right balance in an academic library between provision for research and scholarship on the one hand, and student needs on the other? All these apparent dilemmas in fact beg the question, since borderlines can rarely be drawn precisely and the essence of a library will often be seen in its inclusivity.

The 'local' perspective: hidden libraries

We have noted in the preface to this volume the impossibility of covering the history of all libraries, of every type, within a single volume such as this. The growing diversity of forms over the past 150 years makes it worth dwelling for a moment on those libraries of one particular obscure kind that we have been unable to accommodate to the full, which seems to be especially a feature of the modern world, in this country as elsewhere, partly because of wider literacy and the explosion of print culture (though there are also plausible sociological explanations of the phenomenon). Under the broad miscellaneous description of 'hidden libraries' we might list those in prisoner-of-war camps,[7] army installations,[8] hotels,[9] the home,[10] launderettes, alternative communities,[11] holiday camps, community centres, pubs, restaurants, coffee houses,[12]

---

7 L. Newcombe, 'A prisoner-of-war library', *Library Association Record* 18 (September 1919), 271–83.
8 T. Koch, *War libraries and allied studies* (New York, 1918). A. Hepworth, 'Desert information room', *Library Association Record* 44 (September 1945), 175–7.
9 M. D. Lopez, 'Books and beds: libraries in nineteenth and twentieth century American hotels', *Journal of Library History* 9 (1974), 196–221.
10 P. S. Morrish, 'Domestic libraries: Victorian and Edwardian ideas and practice', *Library History* 10 (1994), 27–44.
11 P. Jackaman, 'The library in Utopia: libraries in nineteenth-century alternative communities in Britain and America', *Library History* 9 (1993), 169–89.
12 P. Kaufman, 'Coffee houses as reading centres,' in his *Libraries and their users: collected papers in library history* (London, 1969), 115–27.

accommodation and facilities for servants and workers,[13] lighthouses and sea-men's establishments,[14] prisons and asylums.[15] This is an extremely selective list, and numerous other types of place and institution could be included as sites where 'hidden' library collections have existed. Library historians are for-tunate in having such a wide range of library types to investigate, and more energy will undoubtedly be expended in seeking out evidence relevant to institutions of the 'hidden' kind.

An example of the kind of topic that can be pursued in this area is the past provision of libraries in connection with various types of modern transport: airliners, tramcars, railways, buses and ships – again, an area that has grown enormously, and involved far more people, in our period. As modes of transport have developed, libraries have emerged in some places to help relieve the tedium of travel. In the nineteenth century, some enterprising booksellers set up 'railway libraries' with the opportunity to exchange books at each end of a journey: W. H. Smith's enterprise in this field lasted well into the next century.[16] At the start of the twentieth century collections of books on tramcars were humorously (although perhaps not entirely unrealistically) suggested, a service that would no doubt have been welcome on routes clogged by the notorious traffic jams of the time.[17] During the Second World War libraries were often supplied in troopships undertaking long voyages (as they had been and continue to be supplied on cruise liners in peacetime). Those who ran them insisted on organising collections in a disciplined, library-like fashion, in keeping with the military setting in which they were housed and operated.[18] Described in 1938 as 'the most unusual lending library in the country', the collection of 150 books housed in the waiting-room of Garsdale Station, on the main line between Leeds and Carlisle, served mainly railway staff, the station master acting as ex-officio librarian. Apparently bequeathed to the station in the 1890s by two elderly women, the library was said to contain a mixture of Victorian 'improving' literature and modern fiction.[19] Investigating

13 F. Stimpson, 'Servants' reading: an examination of the servants' library at Cragside', *Library History* 19 (2003), 3–11; R. Price, 'The factory library', *Librarian and Book World* 30 (3) (November 1930), 43–4.

14 G. Hedges, 'For those in peril on the sea: the Deal Boatmen's Rooms', *Library History* 19 (2003), 35–8.

15 D. Boswell, 'Prisoner, seamen and military establishments', in H. A. Whatley (ed.), *British librarianship and information science 1971–75* (London, 1977), 297–301.

16 C. Wilson, *First with the news* (London, 1985), 358.

17 B. Pepcroy, 'Tramcars as travelling libraries', *Library World* 9 (1906–7), 323–7. See also K. A. Manley, 'The Munich tramcar library', *Library History* 10 (1994), 71–5, for an example that found its way off the drawing board.

18 S. Newman, 'A troopship library', *Library Association Record* 42 (September 1943), 155–7.

19 'An unusual library', *Yorkshire Observer* (20 July 1938).

such 'transport libraries' is full of possibilities for research framed by issues like control, cultural and class tension, technical training, social mobility and social space.

As research subjects, marginal, small-scale libraries are as important as the large-scale collections and operations of public, university and national libraries. James Duff Brown defined the small library as a

> select general collection of books numbering from 200 to 5,000 volumes, such as may be gathered by students, schools, churches, commercial and industrial organizations, and all agencies in which books are either tools, or a valuable means of affording recreation. As a rule, such collections are formed without much regard to order or care in selection, and, save in the case of private collectors who specialize, the majority of small libraries are frequently a miscellaneous assemblage of odds and ends organized on very primitive methods.[20]

These criteria for defining the nature of the small library map perfectly on to the meagre but critical collections of books assembled in the bases of the Falkland Islands Dependencies Survey (FIDS), later the British Antarctic Survey, in the 1940s and 1950s. One member of the Survey in the late 1950s has recalled how reading the books deposited in accommodation huts by successive residents helped to make life more tolerable in an isolated and challenging environment:

> We read, of course, but books were precious because we had so few. We only had a small library at Base 'O' because it was a new base and had no time to build up any number of books like the older bases . . . I cannot remember any of the titles except Alistair Maclean's 'HMS Ulysses', which I'm sure I read more than once . . . [At one hut] I read the whole of the Bible while we were snowed in on journeys.[21]

The international perspective: influences and counter-influences

The scale of 'hidden' libraries has invariably been small, their coverage local and specific. By contrast, libraries and library systems have also been conceptualised and constructed on a national and even an international scale.

It is one of the features of modernity that it is not confined by national boundaries.[22] For those concerned with the world of books and libraries, such

---

20 J. D. Brown, *The small library: a guide to the collection and care of books* (London and New York, 1907), 5–6.
21 Archive of the British Antarctic Survey, Cambridge (submission of Dick Foster).
22 P. Hoare, 'The development of a European information society', *Library Review* 47 (1998), 377–82.

boundaries have always been fluid – from the exchange of manuscripts between continental Europe and early medieval Ireland and Anglo-Saxon England, through the flow of Reformation and Counter-Reformation material across Protestant and Catholic Europe, and the interchange of scientific ideas in the seventeenth and eighteenth centuries, to the global publishing world of the present century (with the associated benefits and problems for libraries). The modern world, however, has brought new challenges and new opportunities for international activity, and while there are clear differences of approach in different countries and different socio-philosophical systems the interaction of the British library world with its counterparts elsewhere has had an effect on all sectors. References to these effects in specific areas will be found in appropriate chapters of this volume; but the phenomenon is one which has influenced all parts of the library world and deserves special attention here.

Librarians (and users) from immigrant communities have informed the British library scene through the whole of our period. In the mid-nineteenth century Italian political refugees, largely from a cultured background, brought a welcome leaven, like Andrea Crestadoro of Manchester Public Library or of course Antonio Panizzi, whose radical ideas modernised the British Museum. Later radicals like Herzen, Marx and Lenin, whose use of that same library (and others) helped to develop political ideas that had world-wide effects, were also from the same type of background.[23] The influx from Eastern Europe in the early twentieth century, mostly of poor and ill-educated workers, led to developments such as strong Yiddish collections in the public libraries of London's East End, and to an awareness of the educational possibilities available through the public library which were long remembered.[24] After 1933 the arrival of Jewish refugees from Germany provided many libraries with new demands and also with fresh expertise in the form of scholars and librarians eager to continue their professional activity in their new home (some of whom, like Willi Guttsmann, the influential first librarian of the University of East Anglia, made real contributions in their new home).[25] In some cases this even extended to the creation of whole important new libraries, such as the Wiener Library and the Warburg Institute.[26] Later waves of

23 *Lenin at the British Library* (London, 1990).
24 Many testimonies of this kind are given in J. Rose, *The intellectual life of the British working classes* (New Haven and London, 2001).
25 W. E. Mosse (ed.), *Second chance: two centuries of German-speaking Jews in the United Kingdom* (Tübingen, 1991). We are grateful to Stephen Massil for this reference, which he however considers to undervalue the contribution of Jewish librarians.
26 F. Saxl, 'The history of Warburg's library, 1886–1944', in E. H. Gombrich, *Aby Warburg: an intellectual biography* (London, 1970), 325–38.

immigration – from the West Indies, from the Indian subcontinent, from Africa, and more recently from other parts of the Third World – have in their turn presented challenges and have also provided libraries with new experiences and possibilities. The positive multi-cultural nature of many public libraries in Britain today (not matched in all other countries) and their use as centres of information by ethnic-minority groups are a tribute to the way these opportunities were grasped in the last third of the twentieth century.

At the same time British librarianship made its mark across the world. The influence of British ideas on libraries across the Empire has been traced in a number of works, for example on India and Africa.[27] Close links are still felt with many Commonwealth countries, both in the Old Dominions such as Australia and New Zealand and in the countries that achieved independence after World War II; these are due in no small part to the determinative efforts of British librarians who first established library systems and trained their successors. The relationships continue to be mutually strengthened by consultancies undertaken by British librarians, especially in the Third World, by the contributions of professionals working with VSO and other agencies, and by the large numbers of overseas students attending schools of librarianship in Britain and Ireland. (On the other hand English isolationism can be seen in some nineteenth-century libraries, for example the Nilgiri Library in Ootacamund, a subscription library restricted to white residents in this Indian hill-resort,[28] or the free lending library of the Florence English Church, whose rules forbade passing books to others, 'least of all to Italian subjects'.)[29]

Some of those expatriate librarians brought back new ideas based on their experiences abroad which in turn have enlightened the profession in this country; some of this international influence has returned in other ways. One notable example is S. R. Ranganathan (1892–1972), who having studied librarianship in Britain became university librarian at Madras and a major figure in the Indian library world before and after independence. His *Five laws of library science* had a significant effect on library thinking in Britain and elsewhere, and his ideas on classification and subject analysis had a great influence on the

27 Three quite different examples are A. M. Fazle Kabir, *The libraries of Bengal 1700–1947* (London, 1987), J. Harris, *Ibadan University Library: some notes on its birth and growth* (Ibadan, 1968) and G. Armstrong, 'The culture and history of South African public libraries: the experience of Durban library', *Library History* 16 (2000), 35–47.

28 M. Panter-Downes, *Ooty preserved: a Victorian hill-station* (London, 1967), 52–6. S. McClarence, 'The town the British left behind' (*The Times*, 21 January 2006, Books section, 6) is an account of the library's survival, now wholly under Indian control.

29 Books from the library containing the rules are extant in the British Institute in Florence and elsewhere.

(British-based) Classification Research Group, and on practices particularly in special libraries, from the 1950s onwards.[30]

Probably the most influential and certainly the widest-ranging international enterprise in the library sphere is the British Council, founded in 1934 to promote 'a wider appreciation of British culture and civilisation'. Its libraries have since the start provided experience of British books and professional methods in countries across the globe.[31] In post-war Germany its crowded reading rooms contrasted with the poverty of 'purged' and impoverished German libraries (something similar was initially seen in the libraries it opened in Eastern Europe after 1989).[32] In India the British Council developed what has been described as 'a surrogate public library system', with a far larger number of loans from its libraries than in any other country.[33] Such popular libraries are a feature of most Third World countries today and the British Council's library activity is one of the great successes of the twentieth century. It has also, going beyond its own libraries, been the catalyst for the development of indigenous public library systems, especially in many African countries. If its libraries have sometimes been attacked as symbols of Western imperialism,[34] and if the relevance of Western methods to developing economies has sometimes been questioned, the appreciation of the British Council's activities shown by huge numbers of librarians and library users in many countries is testimony to the vitality and flexibility of the UK tradition that its work has sprung from.

Many other examples of international contacts and influences could be given. The Select Committee on Public Libraries in 1849 drew evidence from many significant European libraries (even if the application of that evidence in its recommendations or in the developments that followed is less than obvious). The Library Association undertook an even more wide-ranging survey of libraries throughout Europe and North America in 1936–7 (supported by the Rockefeller Foundation), with the two main objectives of creating understanding and assembling information.[35] The resulting volume contains

30 S. R. Ranganathan, *The five laws of library science* (Madras and London, 1931). An interesting selection of material on him, including correspondence with Bernard Palmer and other British librarians, appears in the Ranganathan centenary issue of *IASLIC Bulletin* 37 (3) (1992).

31 D. Coombs, *Spreading the word: the library work of the British Council* (London, 1988).

32 P. Hoare, '"Hungry for reading": libraries in the British zone of occupation', in A. Bance (ed.), *The cultural legacy of the British Occupation in Germany* (Stuttgart, 1997), 205–22.

33 B. Naylor, 'British Council', in J. Feather and P. Sturges (eds.), *International encyclopedia of information and library science* (London and New York, 1997), 39–40.

34 A. Ochai, 'The purpose of the library in colonial tropical Africa', *International Library Review* 16 (1984), 309–15.

35 L. R. McColvin (ed.), *A survey of libraries: reports on a survey made by the Library Association during 1936–1937* (London, 1938).

some remarkable reports and interpretations of political attitudes that are particularly interesting when read with the hindsight of history.[36] Again, an assessment of the influence of the data collected is not easy to make – the events of 1939–45 undoubtedly lessened its impact – but the volume itself is a valuable historical document. Scandinavian ideas, which the *Survey* enthusiastically reports on, influenced public library thinking from the 1930s onwards, not least in the design of buildings, and also in the development of modern children's libraries (though these seem to have an indigenous origin in the nineteenth century).

The impact of Melvil Dewey, his Decimal Classification and his other contributions to modern librarianship, both practical and theoretical, cannot be overstated, and it is notable that Dewey was one of the American delegates at the International Conference of Librarians in 1877, which led to the establishment of the Library Association. It should not be assumed from this that British and American libraries have always followed parallel paths, as is seen for example in the history of agreement and non-agreement on cataloguing codes in the twentieth century.[37] There are however many examples of collaborative projects such as the English Short-Title Catalogue (ESTC), a bibliographical database of English-language and other printing in the British Isles up to 1800, now run from the British Library and the University of California Riverside as a development of the original eighteenth-century project. And such collaboration need not be only with the United States, as seen in the British Library's involvement with the Gabriel project for national libraries, which has a strong European element.

The effect of the European Union on British and Irish libraries towards the end of the twentieth century should not be neglected, though it is perhaps too early to give a historical overview. There are two main areas: the funding of joint projects based in more than one EU country, which has led librarians in the United Kingdom and the Republic of Ireland to seek out overseas partners offering new ideas and opportunities for co-operation, and the impact of European legislation, particularly in the area of copyright and intellectual property rights more generally. This has combined with a more aggressive attitude on the part of 'rights owners' world-wide, which leaves librarians less able to deal with reasonable and modest demands for copying from their readers. Here

---

36 S. Karetzky, *Not seeing red: American librarianship and the Soviet Union* (Lanham, NY and Oxford, 2002), 81–2, comments critically on the Library Association survey (especially H. M. Cashmore's 'quite positive' report on Russia) and the 'internationalist' attitudes it reflects, which Karetzky characteristically deplores.

37 See Rodney M. Brunt's chapter 45 on cataloguing, below.

too, globalisation can often have a negative effect on local good practice: but British librarians have recently begun to make common cause with their colleagues elsewhere in the world on problems such as periodical price rises and the licensing of electronic publications.

Finally, one area of international activity in which British practice has had a direct impact on local provision in other countries is 'document supply', the modern equivalent of inter-library loan.[38] The National Lending Library for Science and Technology at Boston Spa pioneered in the 1960s the practice of rapid provision of loans or photocopies from its own extensive stock, which has been continued and expanded by the British Library since the NLLST's absorption into the new body in 1973. This contrasts with the co-operative provision more usual in other countries – though it tends to cost more – and has led to a global network of customers who find Boston Spa's supply faster and more reliable than those in their own country. Interestingly, the Boston Spa initiative has not been a model for other countries, perhaps because of its own success as a direct supplier internationally; it has meant, however, a much higher profile for the British Library and for British librarianship across the world.

Conclusion

The modern world, with its new dimensions for nations, governments and individuals, and the new challenges to established practices and preconceptions, has inevitably had its effect on libraries – which exist within a society itself undergoing traumas both positive and negative. They reflect modernism while being part of it.

Whether for cultural self-realisation or material advance, libraries of all kinds have provided what Raymond Irwin referred to as a 'golden chain' of knowledge and learning, traversing space and time.[39] People have sought enlightenment through libraries for personal and social reasons. Libraries have been intrinsically dynamic in their encouragement of individualism and the exploration of the self in what is by definition a communal setting of shared resources. Building on the public-sphere, associational world of the seventeenth and eighteenth centuries, to which they contributed significantly, libraries in the modern period have acted more than ever as reservoirs of social capital, providing a kind of social glue that has helped individuals, groups and

---

38 For fuller treatment see Antonia Bunch's chapter 44, below.
39 R. Irwin, 'The golden chain', in his *The heritage of the English library* (London, 1964), 26–42.

communities in their pursuit of trust and co-operation, as well as of life-objectives that are materially and intellectually rewarding.[40]

Above all, over the past 150 years, libraries have served as long-term investments in the philosophy of progress and improvement that lies at the heart of the modern age.

40 P. Clark, *British clubs and societies: the origins of an associational world* (Oxford, 2001); A. Goulding, 'Libraries and social capital', *Journal of Librarianship and Information Science* 36 (2004), 3–6.

PART I

*

ENLIGHTENING THE MASSES: THE PUBLIC LIBRARY AS CONCEPT AND REALITY

2

Introduction: the public library in concept and reality

ALISTAIR BLACK

The appearance and growth of 'free' local libraries funded from local taxation, which for over a century we have referred to as public libraries, resulted from the Public Libraries Act (1850), which initially applied to England and Wales. The Act was extended to Scotland and Ireland in 1853. Contributors to this section deal largely with the history of the public library in England. Developments in Wales, Scotland and Ireland receive specific attention in a later section in the volume. However, it should be stressed that many of the motives, drivers and issues of past public library development in England were to be found, to a greater or lesser extent, elsewhere in the British Isles.

Before public libraries were formally inaugurated in 1850, there had developed a patchwork of libraries of various kinds – for example, endowed libraries, ecclesiastical libraries, subscription libraries, book clubs and collections in coffee houses – that could in some ways be described as 'public'. But these libraries normally involved some kind of payment, either directly for use of the library, or indirectly for the service, as in the case of coffee houses, to which the library was appended. Proposals for libraries free at the point of use and subsidised from the public purse appeared a number of times in the first half of the nineteenth century. The idea was raised by the Society for the Diffusion of Useful Knowledge (SDUK) in 1826 and by the Select Committee on Enquiry into Drunkenness (1834). The idea also formed part of an unsuccessful Public Institutions Bill (1835) and featured in the deliberations of the Select Committee on Arts and Their Connection with Manufactures (1835–6).

The chair of the 'Arts and Manufactures' Select Committee was the radical Member of Parliament William Ewart. In 1845 he successfully guided through parliament a Museums Act, the wording of which, imaginatively interpreted, enabled three towns – Canterbury, Warrington and Salford – to provide 'free' libraries attached to their local museums. Along with public museums and art galleries, Ewart viewed public libraries as a means of elevating public taste and of inculcating artisans with an appreciation of good design and the skills necessary to carry it out. This would contribute in a small but significant way to increased prosperity and a civilising of the masses. A similar mix of worldly knowledge and civilising culture was evident in the work, in 1849, of a Select Committee on Public Libraries, established to find 'the best means of extending the establishment of libraries freely open to the public especially in large towns in Great Britain and Ireland' (the Committee's report is an immensely rich document of value not just to library historians but to social historians and historians of reading also). The key witness called before the Select Committee was Edward Edwards, an assistant in the British Museum Library. Edwards had undertaken extensive research on free library provision in other countries, and in his various pamphlets and books had attempted to demonstrate how free access to libraries and artistic culture could enhance the emergent open, meritocratic and materially efficient society he wished to see flourish.

From the outset public libraries have made reality of these founding concepts and motives by serving, at once, as emporiums of culture and citadels of scientific inquiry, broadly termed. Public libraries have consistently positioned themselves as sources of both useful knowledge and rational recreation. Books, newspapers, periodicals and reference sources, as well as extension and outreach activities in the form of lectures, classes and links with museum and art provision, have been provided to support both serious study and leisure. Public libraries have sought to meet the educational and technical needs of an increasingly commercial and politically informed society. However, they have also made available the 'diversionary', imaginative literature required to help counteract the social stress, alienation and dehumanisation associated with an industrialised, urban and 'rushed' society.

Interest in the public library idea has noticeably quickened at times of national crisis, pointing therefore to its role as an institution of social control and cultural and political conservatism. Its recreational purpose, although given a rational justification, has not always been readily accepted by librarians; while politically, rarely has the public library easily admitted truly radical perspectives. In addition, the technical and bureaucratic methods and modes of management and control that librarians have developed have further contributed to an enduring, though not dominant, illiberal view of public library provision.

On the other hand, as prominent civic institutions commanding a firm and favourable place in the life of the nation, public libraries have operated as important agencies of modernity, fashioning alongside other rational institutions a public sphere of open, democratic discourse and social and individual progress. They have proved their relevance to the needs of a wide variety of client groups, including children and the disadvantaged, as well as the many ethnic-minority populations that have made use of them over the decades. The diversity of its usership, past and present, makes the humble public library a remarkably vibrant subject for research, as does the variety of its promoters, which have included not only librarians, but also local elites, politicians, benefactors and civil servants.

3

The people's university: models of public library history

ALISTAIR BLACK

Although traditionally termed the people's university, since its inception in 1850 the rate-supported municipal public library has by no means appealed to everyone.[1] Indeed, at times, and in certain places and various ways, its impact has been disappointing. On the other hand, who could deny that the public library has successfully emerged over the past century and a half as an integral ingredient of the social fabric of our villages, towns and cities. It is ingrained in our cultural folklore. Historians of the public library are consequently best advised to view their subject as a *part of*, rather than *apart from*, society. Yet, often popularly portrayed as an unremarkable, 'backwater' institution, its relevance marginal and its level of social engagement tending towards the passive, the public library has not always inspired studies that address the contexts in which it has been rooted. The temptation of narrowly conceived, descriptive research has often proved too strong for historians of the movement, many of them librarians eager to draw attention to an institution for which they have considerable intellectual and nostalgic respect and which they may have sought to promote in ways that are accessible, digestible and productive. No excuses are offered here for being similarly tempted and commencing this chapter with a descriptive account of the past legislative apparatus, 'official' efforts and fundamental development of the public library. These 'foundational' data not only serve to celebrate, as we should, the historic value of the public library, but also provide a sextant to those who are new to the subject.

Although important, coverage of the basics of public library history in this chapter is none the less brief. Most of the facts of public library history are readily available.[2] Hence, the greater part of the chapter is given over to a

---

1 This chapter is largely based on the following: A. Black, *A new history of the English public library: social and intellectual contexts* (London, 1996), and A. Black, *The public library in Britain, 1914–2000* (London, 2000).

2 T. Kelly, *Books for the people: an illustrated history of the British public library* (London, 1977); T. Kelly, *A history of the public library in Great Britain, 1845–1975* (London, 1977); W. A. Munford, *Penny rate: aspects of British public library history, 1850–1950* (London, 1951).

dissection of the public library's past into a number of approaches, or models. These models are essentially contextual lenses through which the evidence of public library history can be viewed, and by which the institution's far from simplistic story can be told. Public library history can be researched and written according to a wide variety of themes – from surveillance to technology, from gender to national identity – and by drawing on the full panoply of historical disciplines. Within the context of this brief assessment, however, there is room for discussion, once the bare facts of public library development have been laid out, of only a selection of staple perspectives: the philosophical; the professional-bureaucratic; and the societal (including cultural, political, economic, and class and control perspectives).

The empirical model

A narrative of Whiggish progress, with its emphasis on mostly positive institutional, technical and collections development, has been the dominant mode of discourse in public library history. The fortunes of the public library have frequently been revealed by reference to various basic indicators of success: for example, growth trends in numbers of libraries, librarians, users and loans, in the size of bookstocks, in levels of expenditure, and so on. Over time the institution's fortunes have fluctuated – certainly if measured by means other than the crude performance indicators noted above. However, the general picture often painted is one of satisfactory, sustained and gradual long-term growth and improvement, facilitated from above by a series of enlightened 'official' interventions in the form of enabling legislation and helpful inquiries and reports.

The Public Libraries Act (1850), though providing the bedrock for a later flowering of public libraries, was in reality a relatively limited, and therefore limiting, piece of legislation. It took four decades for the public library movement to move into top gear. The 1850 Act permitted (importantly it did not compel) any municipal borough with a population of 10,000 or more to become a library authority and establish a public library funded from local taxation (the rates). However, it could only do this if it: charged ratepayers no more than $\frac{1}{2}$d in the £ (one half-penny in the pound) for the purpose; spent the money only on facilities and staffing (books and other printed materials could not be purchased from the library fund); and received permission from ratepayers in a special poll (two-thirds, or more, of ratepayers voting were required to support the proposal). Only if each of these qualifications was met could the local authority open a library ('library' is deliberately used here in the singular, as the concept of the branch library, let alone a system of libraries in a particular administrative area, barely crossed early promoters' minds).

The Act was extended to Scotland and Ireland in 1853. The following year, legislation applying only to Scotland increased the maximum rate chargeable to 1d in the £ (one penny in the pound), and allowed expenditure on books and other printed matter, as well as 'specimens'. Adoption was to be by a vote taken at a public meeting of ratepayers (the requirement that a two-thirds majority of those voting be secured was retained). These improvements paved the way for similar changes in amending legislation in England and Wales in 1855. In addition, the minimum population was reduced from 10,000 to 5,000 and the legislation was extended outside municipal boroughs to include improvement boards and commissions, and parish vestries. The Act also permitted library authorities to use their funds to establish schools of science and art. An Act of 1886, applying to Scotland, England and Wales, brought further changes: the majority of ratepayers required to accept adoption proposals was reduced to a straightforward majority and the population limit was removed (although this made little difference to most small authorities which found it extremely difficult to contemplate, let alone establish, a viable library service).

Over the next century a number of other minor changes to the existing public library legislation were implemented. However, none made any notable impact on the pattern of development, with the exception of three important Acts. In 1893 (1894 in Scotland) local authorities were allowed to establish a library service by local authority resolution, without recourse to a special vote by ratepayers. The Public Libraries Act (1919) empowered county councils to become library authorities. It also abolished the limit on public library spending, thereby bringing to an end the era of the 'penny rate'. Finally, the Public Libraries and Museums Act (1964) brought a formal end to the permissive basis on which libraries had developed since 1850. Henceforth, library authorities had a *duty* to provide a library service, one that was 'comprehensive and efficient', moreover. Further, it was to be the responsibility of government to 'superintend, and promote the importance of, the public library service'.[3]

A number of official investigations and reports have informed the development of the public library, through reasoned argument or, more often than not, simply through weight of evidence, by merely surveying and describing the current status of services or the cultural and information practices and

---

3 Full details of the legislative history of the public library are given in R. J. B. Morris, *Parliament and the public libraries: a survey of legislative activity promoting the municipal library service in England and Wales 1850–1876* (London, 1977).

needs of the populace. The Select Committee on Public Libraries (1849) laid the foundation for the inaugural Act of 1850, following the pattern established in the 1830s and 1840s of legislative action founded on 'scientific' inquiry.[4] The Adams Report of 1915, commissioned by the Carnegie United Kingdom Trust, highlighted the paucity of provision outside urban areas.[5] Later in the First World War, libraries were included in the deliberations of the Ministry of Reconstruction, whose report on the question paved the way for the 1919 Act.[6] In 1924 the Carnegie United Kingdom Trust published a relatively brief sequel to the earlier Adams Report.[7] A much fuller investigation conducted by the Board of Education followed in 1927: the Kenyon Report stressed the importance of the public library as a national asset and recommended stronger co-operative networking by libraries.[8] The crisis of the Second World War produced the widely admired McColvin Report, which laid down the principles and pathways for a post-war expansion of the service.[9] A clutch of investigations in the late 1950s and early 1960s contributed to the momentum that eventually delivered the 1964 Act.[10] In the 1990s extensive and illuminating reports were issued by the Department of National Heritage and by the Comedia research group.[11] These, like their predecessors, will prove to be invaluable sources for the historian of libraries and culture.

The early development of public libraries was slow. By 1868 just twenty-seven local authorities in Britain had adopted the public library legislation. Around half of these were in the industrial and commercial centres of the midlands and the north. By 1886 the number of library authorities had risen to 125; by 1918 there were 566 in existence, many providing more than one library service point, of course. In Ireland, by 1880 only two libraries had been opened under the Public Libraries Acts.

---

4 Select Committee on Public Libraries, *Report* (1849).
5 W. G. S. Adams, *A report on library provision and policy to the Carnegie United Kingdom Trustees* (Dunfermline, 1915) (Adams Report).
6 Ministry of Reconstruction, Adult Education Committee, *Third interim report: libraries and museums* (London, 1919) (Cmd. 321).
7 J. M. Mitchell, *The public library system of Great Britain and Ireland, 1921–3* (Dunfermline, 1924) (Mitchell Report).
8 Board of Education, Public Libraries Committee, *Report on public libraries in England and Wales* (London, 1927) (Cmd. 2868) (Kenyon Report).
9 L. R. McColvin, *The public library system of Great Britain* (London, 1942)
10 Ministry of Education, *The structure of the public library service in England and Wales* (London, 1959) (Cmnd. 660) (Roberts Report); Ministry of Education, *Standards of public library service in England and Wales* (1962) (Bourdillon Report); Ministry of Education, *Inter-library co-operation in England and Wales* (1962) (Baker Report).
11 Aslib, *Review of the public library service in England and Wales for the Department of National Heritage* (London, 1995); Comedia, *Borrowed time? The future of public libraries in the UK* (Bournes Green, 1993)

London was particularly slow to develop public libraries, until, that is, a frenzy of foundations came about from the late 1880s onwards. In London, and elsewhere, this sudden upturn in foundations was due to a combination of various factors: celebrations in 1887 marking fifty years of Queen Victoria's reign, which encouraged many local authorities to adopt the library legislation in her honour; rising rateable values; the growth of state education; increasing literacy rates; and, above all, philanthropic gifts from a range of benefactors, most notably John Passmore Edwards and the Scottish-born American steel magnate Andrew Carnegie.

After 1919, from which date county councils were permitted to become library authorities, coverage was gradually extended to those who, by virtue of their residence in rural areas, had previously found themselves effectively disenfranchised from the nation's public library service. By 1931 Cheshire could boast 279 village branch libraries, most very small admittedly, often set up in a school or village hall.

The public library's most impressive leap forward came in the 1960s. Once the era of austerity immediately following the Second World War gave way to a new age of affluence, the public library benefited significantly from the welfare state's heavy investment in cultural and education services. The public library underwent a programme of modernisation that finally wrenched it clear of the Victorianism that had arguably characterised it well into the twentieth century. New buildings, many based on modern Scandinavian design, sprang up across the country. Expenditure on libraries more than doubled between 1961 and 1967. Looking back in 1999 on what some have seen as the 'golden age' of public libraries in the 1960s, one retired public librarian stated that:

> Thirty years ago was an exciting time in public libraries. Some of us were looking at different ways of presenting the stock to make it more accessible and aiming at book collections which met a wide range of needs. A big central library aimed at having a good stock across all subjects. All this seems to have gone. There seems no policy behind what is offered (except the dubious one mentioned below) and stocks often look little more than random collections of books . . . Some libraries seem to have given up being places of book-centred learning . . . and focus on being neighbourhood centres, choked with information of every kind . . . Most libraries seem to make little effort now to have trained staff available on a constant basis to the public.[12]

As this testimony indicates, the last quarter of the twentieth century was a period of mixed fortunes, to say the least, for the public library. Innovations

---

12 Contribution to a Mass-Observation Archive directive on 'Public Libraries' (1999).

appeared and initiative were taken. These included: a switch to computerised catalogues; the provision of access to the Internet and other personal computing services; an enhancement of the public library's information role; the procurement of exciting designs for new buildings; improved customer care; and new modes of service delivery, generically termed 'community librarianship', that sought to engage more intimately and effectively with disadvantaged client groups. On the other hand, libraries constantly found themselves under financial pressure. Basic services were in many respects reduced, such as book purchasing and the number of hours that libraries were open. There was downward pressure on staff salaries. Worryingly, in the 1990s there was a significant reduction in the number of books borrowed. At the end of the twentieth century the public library retained a strong foothold in national and civic culture. Even so, its future status was uncertain, its future existence not entirely guaranteed.

The philosophical model

Libraries have always commanded an intellectual foundation and justification, and so it is legitimate to point to the past and current existence of a 'library philosophy'. The public library is rooted in the ideas and values that informed nineteenth-century liberalism. The two main philosophical strands of liberal thought, utilitarianism and idealism, both featured prominently in the thinking of leading advocates of the early public library, and continued to influence public library development in the twentieth century, as the institution became part of the apparatus of the embryonic and fully implemented welfare state.

The public library drew its initial philosophical and ideological sustenance from Benthamite-inspired utilitarianism. Under the influence of John Stuart Mill, utilitarians from the 1820s onwards promoted the notion of 'good citizenship'. Good citizens recognised the utility of life's higher pleasures, which included the pursuit of useful knowledge and education ('base' pleasures brought only short-term happiness and often long-term misery). Good citizens were supporters of meritocracy (the cornerstone of which was education) and denounced the exclusivity of closed, corrupt societies. They also endorsed the doctrine of self-help. Utilitarians recognised that the state had a role to play in enabling good citizens to help themselves. The state could also interfere to maximise utility: money spent on libraries and other educational facilities would be turned into profit when set against the money that would consequently not need to be spent on controlling and containing immoral behaviour, including criminality. Utilitarianism posited individuals as mechanistic units that were shaped by the environments they experienced. Good environments – precisely like public libraries – were anti-exclusive, meritocratic, knowledge rich and conducive to self-betterment, and consequently productive of good citizenship.

Utilitarianism informed the thinking of the public library's principal parliamentary pioneer, William Ewart, the driving force behind the work of the Select Committee on Public Libraries in 1849 and the Act of 1850.[13] Ewart was close to the loose parliamentary grouping known as the Philosophic Radicals who, under the leadership of John Stuart Mill, attempted to transform utilitarian theory into practical reforms. Strong utilitarian credentials could also be found in the ideology of Edward Edwards, the British Museum library assistant who, because of his knowledge and enthusiastic support of libraries, was enlisted by Ewart to contribute crucial evidence to the Select Committee.[14] Edwards' numerous publications are replete with the anti-privilege, meritocratic and rational language of utilitarianism.

If utilitarianism provided the public library with strong philosophical foundations, the idealist philosophy that came to eclipse it in the decades immediately before the First World War provided the boost required to establish the public library as a national institution. Like utilitarianism, idealism was no coffee-table philosophy. Idealist thought was translated into tangible social and cultural policy and improvements. The vocabulary of library promotion bore close resemblance to the language of idealism and its evangelical influences.[15] At the opening ceremony of the Birmingham Reference Library in 1866, the Baptist minister George Dawson presented the public library as 'the largest and widest church ever established'; the civic entity of which the library was a part he described as a 'solemn organism' gifted by the 'Grace of God'.[16] Idealist supporters of libraries like Samuel Barnett, vicar of St Jude's, Whitechapel and first warden, from 1885, of the Toynbee Hall settlement house, believed it was the duty of the educated and better off to help the culturally and materially impoverished to 'realise' themselves; that is to say, to realise the inner potential existing in everyone, thereby contributing to the greater good, or in metaphysical terms the 'absolute truth' or 'the achievement of perfection'.

13 W. A. Munford, *William Ewart, M.P., 1798–1869: portrait of a radical* (London, 1960).
14 W. A. Munford, *Edward Edwards, 1812–1886: portrait of a librarian* (London, 1963).
15 Not surprisingly, religious influences on the development of libraries were strong. In this regard, see M. Hewitt, 'Confronting the modern city: the Manchester Free Public Library, 1850–80', *Urban History* 27 (2000), 62–88.
16 Borough of Birmingham, *Opening of the Free Reference Library . . . by George Dawson* (Birmingham, 1866).

Envisioning libraries as places of spiritual harmony, Barnett announced that: 'Books spoke alike to rich and poor.'[17]

In many respects the value systems of idealism and utilitarianism are closely aligned: they share a belief in self-help, moral action and educational endeavour. However, epistemologically, the two philosophies diverge. Whereas utilitarians argued that experience was the source of knowledge, idealism was based on a Platonic nativism that situated knowledge innately, in the intellect and human spirit. A further divergence is identifiable in the area of ethics. Idealism emphasised citizenship as duty. This contrasted with the utilitarian definition of the good citizen as an individual whose actions produced utility. Moral action, idealists countered, was defined by love, duty and charity, which may not necessarily deliver personal, tangible, material utility.

Throughout the twentieth century – not least in the context of the welfare state – the public library offered the perfect arena for idealist philosophy, with its emphasis on the sharing of duty and resources and on communal action, to be played out. On the other hand, library purpose has never disregarded the atomistic outlook. The philosophy of the public library has unequivocally admitted the importance of individual self-betterment, but in a setting of ideological commitment to collective action and spiritual fulfilment. Nor at any juncture did the public library threaten to throw out the utilitarian emphasis on 'useful knowledge' in favour of the imaginative literature that might be construed to conform to idealist notions of the spiritual enrichment of the inner self. Both perspectives have been accommodated, even if the tension between the two has not always been mild.

The professional-bureaucratic model

The historical paradox of librarianship is the ease it has displayed in combining cultural endeavour with the more worldly practice of bureaucratic management. Public librarians have viewed their institutions as leading engines of cultural enrichment and conduits of 'sweetness and light', but have at the same time taken great pride in the bureaucratic techniques and technologies they have developed to help manage the large bookstocks and populations of readers for which they have responsibility. The librarian of the modern age of libraries has been a person of both learning and method. Bureaucratic efficiency lies at the heart of professional librarianship. It has underpinned the need to control both internal library operations and the activities

---

17 Quoted in Black, *A new history*, 160.

of users, and has also formed the cornerstone of librarians' stated mission to organise and control knowledge. Public librarians, like their colleagues in other library sectors, have been consistently aggressive in their search for order.

Especially before the First World War, the quest for order was reflected in a concern for surveillance. First, librarians pursued surveillance in terms of the utopian, meta-scientific gaze that they focused on the world of knowledge. Librarians positioned themselves as meta-professionals, claiming authority in being able to organise, via classification, cataloguing and indexing, the knowledge base of other expert and professional groups. Secondly, they constructed a highly formalised set of operational procedures termed 'library economy', expressed in written internal documents and in published manuals. Long before the appearance of the term 'information management' in the late twentieth century, librarians were engaging enthusiastically in its practice. Librarians have been both prolific recorders and planners of procedure and method, as well as being well versed in the administrative requirements of committee work and report writing. Thirdly, librarians have successfully tracked and monitored users and recorded their activities in a range of documents, from bound membership registers to computer databases of loans and returns.

Documentary tracking of library users has been complemented by direct physical observation. The need to place users under direct surveillance was accentuated in the nineteenth century by the departmental structures that libraries implemented. Unlike in the mid-twentieth century, when some large libraries were subjected to departmentalisation according to a division of knowledge (technology, local studies, literature, business, social sciences, arts, pure sciences), in the nineteenth century the service structures of public libraries were determined by a strict classification and differentiation of user groups and types of reader. This gave rise to distinct departments for children, serious readers (reference departments), readers of fiction (who mostly populated lending departments), readers of newspapers (newsrooms) and women (ladies' rooms). Each of these departments required supervision, and some were deemed to require much more than others – for example, children's accommodation, for obvious reasons, and ladies' rooms where, according to some librarians, extensive pilfering of pages from the fashion magazines occurred. The operation of surveillance was sometimes masked and described as 'supervision' – meaning physical closeness to the reader in order to offer efficient service. In the twentieth century surveillance became less overt, forming a natural aspect of open-planned libraries that simultaneously fulfilled the function of 'supervision' in terms of assistance and of uninhibited lines of service to the user.

Finally, making use of the professional-bureaucratic model invites consideration of issues of gender and status. The changing status and stereotypes of the public library could be construed as related to the shift, during the course of our period, in the gender orientation of the profession from male to female, certainly in terms of numbers. However, it is misguided to explain status changes by reference to the profession's feminisation. Status change is more likely to have been a function of changing attitudes to book learning and education, or to the public services; or a function of the economics of the labour market for many of the simple clerical tasks that a good deal of library work has always entailed.

Whatever the reason for, or the actualities of, the shift in status of public librarianship, it is interesting to speculate on whether any of the leading public librarians of the last quater of the twentieth century will in the future find their way into the historical record in any meaningful way. It is highly unlikely that they will achieve the standing of the great pioneers, people like Edward Edwards, James Duff Brown, Marian Frost, J. Potter Briscoe or L. Stanley Jast; or even the status of certain members of the mid-twentieth-century generation of librarians, such as the 'heroic' figure of Lionel McColvin or, less prominently, consummate professionals like K. C. Harrison, E. V. Corbett, Edward Sydney and Frank Gardner.

The societal model

Throughout their history, public libraries have been deeply societal, in that they have reflected the natural tensions associated with social, economic, cultural and political change. Early promoters positioned libraries as non-partisan vehicles of social class mixing and pacification, and of political consensus. Culture, it was argued, would serve as a solvent for squalor and dissatisfaction; while the provision of vocationally relevant knowledge would help create the common prosperity that would heal social discord. However, behind this façade of neutrality and integration the public library in reality was to remain a crucible of contested ideas, values and cultures.

The economy

The ebb and flow of the economy has impacted considerably on the development of the public library. Early proposals for libraries were drawn up in the context of the first great crisis and economic depression of proto-industrialisation, a slump in prosperity that fuelled the fires of the political movement of Chartism. Libraries were seen as places where artisans could educate themselves in the knowledge and skills required to boost trade and fight off international competition. Library knowledge would help fashion the skilled and educated workforce required to underpin the move to a technologically rich economy. Of particular importance were design skills, which foreign artisans were said to command in abundance. Libraries would also help raise the general standard of public taste, thereby acting as a 'demand pull' force on the aesthetic quality and functionality of manufactured goods.

Anxieties about international competition resurfaced towards the end of the nineteenth century in the wake of the lengthy depression that arose in the mid-1870s, when the twenty-year mid-Victorian boom came to an end. A public library was proposed in Oldham in 1881 specifically to counter foreign competition, 'to keep pace with the intellectual progress of other manufacturing Towns on the Continent of Europe and America'.[18] In Manchester in 1907, in response to the German trade challenge in particular, the Chamber of Commerce urged the public library authority to 'establish a complete expert branch of the free libraries replete with up-to-date information on the position of all the industrial arts dependent upon scientific knowledge'.[19] During the First World War, pessimistic projections of a hostile post-war economic climate encouraged many large public libraries to establish, in the spirit of reconstruction, commercial and technical departments. Economic malfunction between the wars, and the cuts in public expenditure that this precipitated, resulted in a series of proposals and actions on library co-operation and networking ('library gridism') to help meet the technical needs of the nation. The most adventurous of these was the establishment of a National Lending Library in 1930, with a supporting network of regional library bureaux and 'outlier libraries'.

It can be seen, therefore, that economic crisis has been a prominent and frequent driver of library development. But development has also been a function of benign economic conditions. This was certainly the case in the late 1950s and 1960s when, despite a pattern of stop–go economic growth and repeated balance-of-payments problems, an age of affluence ushered in what was by any measure a highly successful period of public library expansion. Thereafter, however, economic instability and a retreat from Keynesian economics undercut the healthy funding that public libraries had for some years enjoyed, and

18 Oldham Free Library and Museum Committee Minutes (27 July 1881).
19 *Manchester Chamber of Commerce Monthly Record* 18 (1907), 288.

consequently seriously damaged the morale of the public library movement in the closing decades of the century.

Culture

The public library has always been a site of contested culture. The tension between the public library's educational and recreational roles has been an enduring feature of provision. Under the influence of its utilitarian pioneers, the dominant aim at the outset of the public library movement was to dispense only 'useful' culture, which meant a heavy emphasis on non-fiction reading. However, to retain any credibility as popular institutions, public libraries were forced to accommodate public demand and make available large amounts of imaginative literature. Not all librarians and library committees, by any means, were at ease with this populist course of action. The conflict between those in favour of a predominantly 'non-fiction' role and those supportive of a liberal provision of fiction – known as the Great Fiction Debate – raged for decades before the First World War.[20]

By the inter-war period, tensions had subsided considerably, although controversy never really disappeared. Even in the liberal, permissive decades of the late twentieth century, anxieties emerged concerning the appropriateness of such cultural products as romantic fiction of the 'Mills and Boon' variety, graphic novels and non-book formats for purely entertainment purposes, whether gramophone records (especially jazz), video tapes, CDs or DVDs. Criticism of such sources was lent extra weight by the argument that if people wanted such materials, they should pay for them at the full market rate and not receive what in effect amounted to a subsidy from the taxpayer.[21] Fears concerning moral degeneration forced Harrogate Public Library in 1960 to ban *Lady Chatterley's lover* – even from the 'hidden shelf' behind the library counter; although generally speaking the second half of the twentieth century witnessed a determined retreat by libraries from the moral straitjacket of the Victorian era.

Cultural attitudes have often been reflected in attitudes to public library provision. The appearance of new communication media enticed librarians to enter into debates over the wider value and impact of the content they conveyed. The librarianship press is littered with examples of librarians expressing

---

20 R. Snape, *Leisure and the rise of the public library* (London, 1995).
21 Adam Smith Institute, *Ex libris* (London, 1986). In the 1980s the Thatcher government produced a Green Paper which raised the question of privatisation and charging for services: *Financing our public library service: four subjects for debate* (London, 1988) (Cm. 324).

anxiety over the arrival of television entertainment for the masses (1950s), 'video nasties' (1980s) and, at the end of the century, the dangers and untrustworthiness of the Internet.

Politics

Nowhere has the public library's intersection with culture been more acute than in the area of censorship. The romantic, 'public sphere' view of the public library is of an open institution, receptive to cultural difference. In reality, and inevitably, censorship has rarely been absent from public library activity and debate.

Librarians and library providers have frequently had to take censorship decisions on political grounds – decisions on what political material should and should not be read and, especially in the institution's formative period, what the political ramifications would be of widening access to knowledge and information. These questions were vividly in evidence in the arguments mobilised both for and against libraries at their inception. The public library was proposed and initiated against a backdrop of Chartist agitation for political rights and reforms, including universal suffrage. Opponents of public libraries believed that libraries would become schools of political agitation and revolution, and that the lower orders had not yet displayed the social maturity and respectability to make best use of educational facilities for engagement in existing political arrangements.

Supporters, on the other hand, suggested that libraries would provide, in the words of the radical Joseph Brotherton, 'the cheapest police force possible', serving to civilise the lower orders, turning them away from dangerous demagogues and incorporating them into the established political system. Early public libraries certainly did not set out to supply anything approaching what one might call 'dangerous' reading, a policy underpinned by the stipulation in the 1850 Act (though dropped shortly afterwards) that public library stocks would be accumulated through donations, the majority of which would surely come from 'establishment' sources. Citizens enlightened by the public library and other educational and rational institutions, it was argued, would inevitably come to see the unquestionable value of the free market industrial economy that had emerged over recent generations. This same argument was mobilised in later efforts, in the years shortly before and during the First World War, to boost the public library's role as a disseminator of commercial information and as a bulwark against 'dangerous' and 'wayward' economic and political systems. Similarly, during the depression of the 1930s public libraries were promoted as calming influences, at a time when the spectre of mob action again reared its head.

By the second half of the twentieth century the threat of any revolutionary political upheaval had truly dissipated. However, fears of political radicalism, arising out of social liberation, industrial action and the environmental, peace and human rights movements, remained. In the 1980s, as a counterweight to Thatcherite conservatism, some libraries took on the role of radical information centre and defender of minority rights – to the delight of some and the annoyance of others.

The battle between promoters and opponents of the public library in the institution's formative period never mapped onto a simple left–right political antagonism. Those on the left have by no means always supported libraries. Those on the right have not been its consistent opponents. In the fight to establish a public library in Leeds in the 1860s, for example, Liberal was pitted against Liberal.[22] This is not to say that the public library has discouraged political engagement. Their early newsrooms, for example, were said to be indispensable to the political education of the masses and to the progress of the 'liberal' state. The generous and open display of newspapers of varying political colours in newsrooms testified to the public library's commitment to political discourse and exchange, albeit contained in a relatively narrow frame.

In assessing the political role of the public library outside the sphere of party politics, it is evident that it has long occupied a prime place in the nation's infrastructure of public services. By definition, it has acted as a collectivist institution. Joseph Chamberlain, speaking at the opening of the new library in Birmingham in 1882, viewed the public library as 'a kind of communism which the least revolutionary of all of us may be proud to advocate'.[23] George Dawson trumpeted that the public library was a 'Holy Communion, a wise Socialism'.[24] At times, the level of collectivism that the public library should occupy has been hotly debated – as in the 1980s; or in the context of McColvin's plan for central grants and a controlling ministry; or during the deliberations leading to the 1850 Act. However, generally speaking the public library's position as an effective state institution, providing political enlightenment within 'normal' political parameters, has rarely been forcefully challenged.

---

22 A. Black, 'Local politics and national provision', in M. Kinnell and P. Sturges (eds.), *Continuity and innovation in the public library: the development of a social institution* (London, 1996), 48–66.

23 Quoted in Black, *A new history*, 159.

24 Borough of Birmingham, *Opening of the Free Reference Library*.

Class and control

In analysing these cultural, economic and political contexts, as well as the philosophical and professional perspectives, it is relatively easy to draw the conclusion that over its 150-year lifespan the public library has acted as a regular and efficient mechanism of social control. While it is true that the institution has in various ways and at certain points in its history evinced a cultural and social conservatism, and adopted at times of crisis a posture of consensus, to position the public library as, historically, fundamentally a controlling agency would be misleading.

Contrary to past simplistic accounts concerning their control dimension, public libraries were never 'imposed' agencies, working to hegemonise a wayward working class. The idea that the lower orders did not attempt to get what *they* wanted from libraries, for their own enlightenment and social ends, is naïve. Despite a 'soup kitchen' image in places, public libraries originated and grew very much as middle-class institutions, not because they were instruments of dominant class control, but because they often satisfied middle-class cultural needs. The middle classes frequently promoted public libraries in order to satisfy their own cultural requirements. Working-class users may have outnumbered middle-class users in most places, but as a proportion of their incidence in the population as a whole the middle-class presence was higher. Even in its early decades, the public library was never simply a 'university for the poor', as it is sometimes depicted. In large towns, 'books on the rates' made good sense to middle-class readers, in terms of the economies of scale obtained from establishing what were, in effect, small-scale versions of the British Museum Reading Room. As the Report of the Select Committee on Public Libraries recommended: 'A great Public Library ought, above all things, to teach the teachers; to supply with the best implements of education those who educate the people, whether in the pulpit, the school or the press.'[25] Public libraries were one way that the middle classes found to further their own class formation and consciousness.

In 1937 the American librarian Lowell Martin argued that in the popular mind the public library has been seen to exist for two essential, contrasting purposes: to control and repress the person; and to provide individuals with freedom and opportunity for self-expression and self-fulfilment. Through its bureaucratic mechanisms and censorious activities, the public library has at times provided strict 'lanes of conduct' for the individual. It has patently acted as a socialising agency. But the public library has also consistently fulfilled

25 Select Committee on Public Libraries, *Report*.

a powerful individualising function. The 'socialisation' and 'individualisation' roles of the institution have been symbiotic rather than contradictory, in that through the communal structure of the public library every single one of its users, every 'self', has in some small way contributed to the social world.[26]

26 L. Martin, 'The American public library as a social institution', *Library Quarterly* 7 (1937), 552–3.

4

Libraries for leisure time

ROBERT SNAPE

Introduction

The first edition of Thomas Greenwood's *Free public libraries*,[1] published in 1886, featured a cartoon depicting two well-dressed gentlemen entering a Free Library. Adjacent to the library was a public house; the door of the library led to education and personal improvement, that of the Red Lion to drink and poverty. The public library was clearly a profitable and purposeful place in which to spend free time, while the portrayal of the public house warned of the perils of misdirected leisure. The illustration presents a classic image of the Victorian concept of rational recreation in its promotion of reading as a leisure time activity. Not everyone agreed that it was the role of the public library to provide recreational reading, particularly popular novels with little apparent educational or moral content. Nevertheless, the scale of public demand obliged libraries to provide fiction, thus provoking disagreement about the proper place of leisure in the public library service. The leisure dimension of the service was a contentious issue both within the library profession and in society at large in the period 1850–1914. Throughout the remainder of the twentieth century the public library's treatment of leisure changed as the social context of leisure changed. At its close, libraries provided a broad range of leisure services reflecting increased time and money for leisure, the social validity of popular culture and the introduction of new communications technologies. However, the old divergence between the public library's educational and leisure functions remained in evidence. At the end of the twentieth century the future of the public library service envisaged by librarians and politicians was of globally networked information transfer and lifelong learning. The strategic development of leisure aspects of the library service occupied a much lower priority. Even within the profession, there was not a unified view of the public library's leisure functions, because throughout its history the validity

1 T. Greenwood, *Free public libraries: their organization, uses and management* (London, 1886).

of leisure provision had been a topic of debate and disagreement. The roots of this situation can be traced not only to the development of the library service in the period between the first Public Libraries Act and the First World War but to the decades that preceded its introduction in 1850.

Histories of the public library movement have tended to attribute its origins and development to its educational antecedents, notably the mechanics' institutes, and more generally to the advance of technology and industry and the economic necessity of a literate and educated working class. However, the desirability of providing leisure opportunities was also instrumental in the introduction of libraries and the development of library practice. The industrial revolution and the growth of manufacturing towns, particularly in the north and midlands of England, profoundly changed the context of popular leisure. The new manufacturing towns were characterised by rapid growth and minimal provision for leisure. Public houses, the mainstay of urban leisure activity, were notoriously venues for violent and socially reprehensible activities such as gambling, cock fighting and prostitution, and contemporary reports provide graphic descriptions of the prevailing levels of drunkenness and immoral behaviour.[2] As concerns about the leisure activity of the urban working class intensified in the early decades of the nineteenth century, its reform became a social and political priority and from the 1830s onwards a number of parliamentary Select Committees investigated various aspects of the leisure 'problem'. Some politicians argued for repressive solutions though others adopted a more persuasive approach and campaigned for the provision of alternative leisure opportunities, of which the public library was one manifestation.

The concept of publicly available libraries as agents of leisure reform preceded the 1850 Act by several years. In 1824 Robert Slaney, in his *Essay on the beneficial direction of rural expenditure*,[3] advocated the philanthropic provision of public libraries for working class people as an alternative to public houses and theatres, and in 1834 a parliamentary Select Committee[4] also suggested that public libraries might help to reduce drunkenness. James Silk Buckingham's *Public Institutions Bill*[5] echoed this in 1835 in recommending the establishment of libraries, museums and reading rooms as recreational facilities for working-class people, though nothing material developed at this time. However, the notion of a public library with a leisure function, in contradistinction to a

---

2 F. Engels, *The condition of the working class in England in 1844* (London, 1892), 124–33.
3 R. Slaney, *Essay on the beneficial direction of rural expenditure* (London, 1824).
4 *Report from the Select Committee on Inquiry into Drunkenness* (1834).
5 Public Institutions Bill 1835, reprinted in T. Kelly, *A history of public libraries in Great Britain 1845–1975* (London, 1977), 458–64.

purely educational function, had been articulated and clearly informed the *Report from the Select Committee on Public Libraries*[6] in 1849. Witnesses to this committee described how public libraries would, through occupying time in reading, improve social behaviour and moral standards. They would, Edward Edwards maintained, displace immoral and dangerous recreations and make industrial towns more orderly, a sentiment famously summarised in Brotherton's observation during the parliamentary debate of Ewart's Bill that libraries would be the 'cheapest police that could possibly be established'.[7] The rationale for the introduction of public libraries in 1850 was complex, but it was clearly anticipated that they would have a role in the reform of popular leisure.

The beginnings and growth of leisure provision, 1850–1918

Public libraries were established without clearly formulated objectives, and operational practice evolved in response to public demand, which was mainly for recreational reading. The 1850 Act did not permit libraries to buy books and they initially relied on donations, many of which included substantial numbers of novels. Several public libraries inherited the bookstocks of defunct mechanics' institute libraries, which by the later nineteenth century had become largely recreational in nature, and it was common for a new public library to open with substantial proportions of fiction in its stock. Fiction and light reading were not confined to lending departments and the issue statistics of reference departments show that they too provided recreational material. For example, between 1852 and 1857 Manchester's reference issue included approximately 53,000 novels, while in 1868 alone Liverpool's reference library issued 189,841 novels.[8] However, the greatest demand for fiction was in lending departments, and the *Parliamentary returns of Public Libraries for 1876–7* showed that in the majority of libraries novels accounted for between 55% and 80% of the total issue.[9] In the following decade the demand for fiction grew apace, and in 1889 a comparative analysis of twenty-two public libraries published in the *Fortnightly Review*[10] revealed that fiction accounted for 60% of the total issue in over eighteen libraries and for more than 75% in nine.

6 *Report from the Select Committee on Public Libraries* (1849).
7 House of Commons, *Parliamentary debates*, 3rd series, 109 (1850).
8 E. Edwards, *Free town libraries* (London, 1869).
9 *Parliamentary returns of public libraries 1876–7*.
10 W. M. Gattie, 'What English people read', *Fortnightly Review* 46 (1889), 302–21.

The provision and borrowing of public library fiction became a controversial topic for many reasons, not the least of which was the cultural importance of Literature and the perception of a hierarchy in which popular fiction occupied a lowly position. In the later Victorian period the reading public expanded, publishing became a lucrative commercial activity and the production of cheap popular fiction increased, a trend reflected in the increase in the number of novels published annually from 381 in 1850 to 1,825 in 1899.[11] Successful novelists such as Mary Braddon, Mrs Henry Wood, James Payn and Rhoda Broughton enjoyed mass popularity on a previously unheard-of scale, their books being purchased in multiple copies by most public libraries. Distinctions between 'low' and 'high' culture in fiction were important to critics and librarians, and so too were those between readers of fiction. The assumption that sensational and allegedly immoral popular fiction was read predominantly by uneducated working-class readers provoked widespread concern, and as late as 1898 an article in the *Westminster Review*[12] argued that such fiction encouraged immoral and criminal tendencies. A further contributory factor to the controversy that surrounded public library fiction was the negative reaction of the press and the political right. This was particularly marked in the pre-1914 era when librarianship was seeking social recognition as a professional occupation, its cause not being aided by perceptions of public libraries as storehouses of romances and adventure stories.

The Great Fiction Question

The extent of the supply of fiction in public libraries led to accusations of their having abandoned educational objectives for the satisfaction of the seemingly never-ending demand for popular novels. The profession was divided, some librarians supporting fiction provision as a legitimate aspect of the service, others remaining antagonistic to it. Fiction became the subject of a prolonged public debate that was contested over many decades, most fiercely between 1890 and 1914. The Great Fiction Question, as this came to be known, was in essence two questions: should public libraries provide fiction, and if so, what kind of fiction?

There was a minority view that libraries should not provide any novels and although few advocated the complete abandonment of fiction, many argued for a severely restricted level of provision. It was virtually impossible

11 J. Gross, *The rise and fall of the man of letters* (London, 1969).
12 T. M. Hopkins, 'A protest against low works of fiction', *Westminster Review* 149 (January 1898), 99–102.

for libraries to withdraw totally from fiction provision, though as early as 1879 Taylor Kay proposed that a 'hard and fast line' should be drawn against fiction of any kind and that public money should not be used to fund private leisure.[13] This became a common argument in the following decades as general magazines and newspapers took libraries to task for providing fiction 'on the rates'. A particularly devastating critique appeared in O'Brien's portrayal of public libraries as a 'socialist's continuation school' serving the leisure interests of a minority: 'Are theatre-goers, lovers of cricket, bicyclists, amateurs of music, and others to have their earnings confiscated, and their capacities for indulging in their own special hobbies curtailed, merely to satisfy gluttons of gratuitous novel-reading?'[14] Extreme though this may now seem, it reflected a residual public opinion, and it was not uncommon for the adoption of the libraries acts to be rejected through opposition to spending ratepayers' money on novels.

One method of circumventing such criticism was to operate a subscription department in parallel to the free lending department to provide new books for readers able to pay a fee. Warrington, Wigan, Rochdale, Watford and Stockport amongst others adopted this practice. The income provided the funding to buy new books, which were later transferred to the free lending department. Subscription departments were stocked with ample amounts of popular and recreational literature to attract fee-paying members. One of the most successful subscription departments was that in operation at Bolton, which in 1883, for example, contained over 30,000 novels and 20,000 magazines and had an issue of 58,000 books. It was eventually able to transfer approximately one thousand books each year to the free lending department. Subscription departments were patronised mainly by middle-class readers, and the sense of exclusion from what was clearly a premier-level standard of service was often a source of discontent amongst members of the public unable to afford the fees.

Most librarians were not absolutely opposed to fiction and accepted that public libraries ought to provide fiction of literary merit, even if they were less enthusiastic about escapist novels and sensation fiction. Some were more liberal in approach and believed that the provision of imaginative literature simply for amusement was in itself a valid public library function. Thomas Greenwood summarised the consensual view in stating that while there was no

13 J. T. Kay, 'The provision of novels in rate-supported libraries', *Transactions and proceedings of the 2nd annual meeting of the Library Association of the United Kingdom, Manchester* (1879), 42–6.

14 M. D. O'Brien, 'Free libraries', in T. Mackay (ed.), *A plea for liberty: an argument against socialism and socialistic legislation* (London, 1891), 329–49.

widespread desire to prevent the library from satisfying the recreational needs of the public, light readers ought not to stand in the way of solid ones.[15] In other words, popular fiction was acceptable, but was of less importance than literary fiction and educational work. Some critics were concerned about women's reading and their supposed addiction to romances, but as James Duff Brown observed, the barely literate shop girl was unlikely to read classical works of literature in preference to popular novels.[16] Greenwood too was sympathetic to working women finding escape in the novels of Mary Braddon, Mrs Henry Wood and Rosa Carey.[17] A substantial proportion of public library members were young adults, and pragmatic librarians, realising that they were unlikely to be attracted by serious literary works, understood the necessity of providing suitable fiction to retain their patronage. However, the influence of librarians on the range of books provided was limited as decisions on the selection of stock were usually made by a sub-committee of the library committee.

Book selection, open access, and guidance and advisory work

Following the 1855 Public Libraries Act, which permitted libraries to spend money on books, thereby reversing the legislation of 1850, it became the normal practice to delegate responsibility for selection to a sub-committee of the library committee. Librarians might attend book selection meetings and submit lists of suggested purchases, but decisions on what was to be bought or rejected lay with the committee. Not infrequently quantity and cost, rather than literary merit, were the criteria by which committees decided upon their purchases, a practice scathingly criticised by both James Duff Brown[18] and Ernest Baker.[19] Book selection committees comprised not only elected members but also co-opted persons whose literary knowledge and social status were, in theory, of assistance in stock selection. These men were described by one writer as 'gentlemen of literary ability and taste, who are not connected with the Council',[20] though James Duff Brown had a somewhat contrasting view of them as 'cocksure local notables' whose main aim was to fill the shelves at the lowest possible cost.[21]

15 Greenwood, *Public libraries*.
16 J. D. Brown, 'In defence of Emma Jane', *Library World* 3 (1900–1), 215–19.
17 T. Greenwood, 'The great fiction question', *Library Year Book* (1897), 107–16.
18 J. D. Brown, *The small library: a guide to the collection and care of books* (London, 1907).
19 E. Baker, 'Standard of fiction in public libraries', *Library Association Record* 6 (1907), 70–80.
20 J. Hanson, 'Free public libraries', *Westminster Review* 98 (1872), 333–77.
21 Brown, *The small library*.

Book selection was also a vehicle for covert censorship. There are numerous examples of public libraries refusing, on moral grounds, to buy specific novels, such as at Beverley, where the library committee withdrew H. G. Wells' *Ann Veronica* in 1910, and Doncaster, where Fielding's *Tom Jones* suffered a similar fate in 1913 when the committee decided it was not a 'suitable' book for a free library.[22] A less direct form of censorship was to put certain novels on restricted access, such as occurred in Birkenhead where novels by Fielding and Smollett were kept in a locked cupboard and issued only on request.[23] Some libraries experimented in delaying the purchase of new novels until a period of time after their publication in the hope that borrowers would lose interest, though this strategy carried the risk of decreasing issues.

The most significant development in the Great Fiction Question was the introduction of open access by James Duff Brown at Clerkenwell in 1893. Although initially received with scepticism, by 1901 it had been adopted by approximately thirty public libraries and gradually became the norm. Various arguments were voiced against open access, particularly that it would increase the borrowing of fiction through obviating the borrower's reliance on the catalogue when choosing books. By the last decade of the century the first children to benefit from the Elementary Education Act (1870) formed a substantial proportion of the reading public which was well served by the publishing industry's steady supply of cheap fiction. This expanded mass readership knew how to read, but not, in the view of some critics, what to read. Ernest Baker summarised the view of most librarians when he wrote of readers 'dissipating their intellectual energies on trash because the road into the true world of literature has never been pointed out'.[24] The realisation that there was a lack of direction in choosing what to read led to the development of advice and guidance in the choice of books. This was welcomed in the national and provincial press, one newspaper acknowledging it to be a timely initiative in an age in which people had forgotten how to choose what to read.[25]

Librarians approached guidance and advisory work through the two themes of systematic reading and literary merit. The period between 1893 and 1914 saw the emergence of several schemes to encourage library users to choose wisely and to read progressively. Ernest Baker argued that fiction offered an

---

22 A. H. Thompson, *Censorship in public libraries in the United Kingdom during the twentieth century* (Epping, 1975).

23 W. A. P. Johnman and M. Kendall, *Report of the commission appointed to enquire into the condition and working of free libraries of various towns in England* (Darlington, 1869).

24 E. A. Baker, 'Direction for popular readers', *Contemporary Review* 89 (1906), 498–504.

25 *Manchester Evening Chronicle* 3 April 1903.

opportunity to librarians to substantiate their claim to professional status by actively promoting and intervening in reading.[26] In 1903 he published his *Descriptive guide to the best fiction*,[27] with the stated object of providing

> a fairly complete list of the best prose fiction in English, including not all that interests students, but all that the ordinary reader is likely to come about, with as much description of matter and style for the guidance of readers as can be condensed into a few lines of print for each book.

The Guide was an invaluable model of fiction categorisation and the practice of producing lists of recommended books became widespread, resulting in a plethora of library readers' magazines such as those produced in Manchester, Leeds, Kingston upon Thames, Wigan, Chorley and Accrington. These magazines aimed to guide readers to new additions to the library, especially non-fiction books, and to encourage educational and improving reading. Fiction classification was a further method of providing guidance to readers, Baker once again propounding this on the grounds that a structured arrangement of novels might encourage borrowers to try novels by authors with whom they were unfamiliar.

Open access also reinvigorated interest in the use of library lectures to provide guidance in reading. Many libraries entered into co-operative schemes in conjunction with the National Home Reading Union, an organisation founded in 1889 by John Brown Paton to promote systematic reading. The Union encouraged the establishment of local reading circles under the direction of an educated person with literary knowledge and the ability to lead a discussion. It issued lists of recommended books, and circles were able to choose from these the titles they would read and discuss. Initially many circles were based in churches, or operated as private circles meeting in members' homes, but the close affinity between the aims of the Union and those of public libraries eventually led to collaboration. The first National Home Reading Union circle to be established in conjunction with a public library was in Stepney in 1903 in order to 'encourage systematic reading and profitable use of the libraries by drawing attention to the best authors and suggesting and providing interesting courses of reading'.[28] Circles were established in five Stepney libraries, and although attendances were at first high, public interest waned. Nevertheless Stepney maintained a programme of reading circles for many years, albeit with relatively low numbers in attendance.

---

26 E. A. Baker, 'Wanted – a guide-book to books', *Library Association Record* 2 (1903), 89–97.
27 E. A. Baker, *A descriptive guide to the best fiction: British and American* (London, 1903).
28 Borough of Stepney, *Public libraries committee report* (1904).

Many librarians were sympathetic to the aims of the Union, but practical support was slow to materialise, partly because of the additional workload involved. The Library Association officially approved collaborative work with the Union in 1904, and in 1907 the Union, which realised the benefits of working through public libraries, undertook to find circle leaders for any library interested in establishing a Union circle. However, further development was hampered by the residual resentment of some librarians who felt the Union was usurping their role in the provision of guidance in matters related to reading.

Despite these initiatives to reduce the issues of popular fiction and promote the reading of literary fiction and non-fiction, the demand for fiction remained undiminished. The unofficial movement to effect policy changes in the selection of fiction reached an unsuccessful climax at the Library Association's 1908 conference. This was not the first occasion that fiction provision had been discussed, but the introduction of open access and the lack of progress in securing professional standing for librarians, itself largely due to the fiction question, combined to make the discussion one of great significance. A controversial paper on library fiction proposed that the expenditure of public money on books whose only purpose was to amuse the reader could not be justified, and that a national selection policy of excluding ephemeral novels should be adopted. The proposal is worth quoting in full:

1 That the function of a public lending library is to provide good literature for circulation among its readers, and that the same test must be applied to its works of fiction, as to the books in its other departments, – they must have literary or educational value.
2 That every public lending library should be amply supplied with fiction that has attained the position of classical literature, such as the works of Scott, Dickens, Thackeray, George Eliot; and among the more modern writers Stevenson, Kipling, Meredith, Hardy. These names are, of course, merely given by way of illustration, and each library must be allowed to make its own rules as to the admission into the charmed circle, provided that it can satisfy its conscience that the suggested test has been applied.
3 That the purchase of mere ephemeral fiction of no literary, moral, or educational value, even if without offence, is not within the province of a public lending library.[29]

The strength of feeling about the demand for fiction was reflected in the fact the motion received almost unanimous support, though it had little practical

29 A. O. Jennings, 'Fiction in the public library', *Library Association Record* 10 (1908), 534–41.

effect other than to provoke a body of broadly supportive correspondence in professional journals. This marked a turning point in the fiction debate and the beginning of a realisation that the public demand for popular fiction could neither be ignored nor significantly moderated. By the outbreak of the First World War the Great Fiction Question had lost much of its impetus. Occasional anti-fiction outbursts continued to be encountered, but they increasingly expressed a minority viewpoint only.

Smoking, billiards and newsrooms

The provision of fiction was the principal form of leisure provision, but many other aspects of pre-1914 library practice had a distinctive leisure appeal. Some libraries housed games, smoking and conversation rooms, most of which were inherited from parent institutions, usually mechanics' institutes, though some were purpose built. When Fleetwood public library was established in 1887 in the Whitworth Institute it retained the Institute's billiards and chess room for a number of years. A billiards room sub-committee of the library committee was formed and a billiard marker was employed between six and ten o'clock each evening except Sunday. Its popularity led to the opening of a further room for draughts and dominoes, though persistent gambling led to the closure of both rooms in 1892. Similar examples of games and recreation rooms in libraries based on former institutions were to be found in Cirencester, Lockerbie, Dumbarton and Alloa. A few libraries adopted a positive approach to games rooms, and although few survived for any significant length of time, they embodied a modern approach to leisure that was rarely encountered again until the 1970s. When Manchester's Openshaw branch was opened in 1894 it incorporated recreation rooms and a coffee room, and although the latter was short-lived, the games, smoking and billiards room was still being maintained in 1907, largely for the sake of the income it generated. Chorley's new library opened in 1899 and included a smoke room, which, unlike its conventional newsroom, provided seating. The experiment was unsuccessful, the librarian recording that the room had been patronised by the 'roughest of people' whose conversation could be heard from a distance.[30] Not surprisingly, public library games and recreation rooms aroused strong opposition, reflected in Thomas Greenwood's observation that a billiard room would always exercise a stronger attraction than a reference library or a newsroom.[31] The legality of funding such rooms through the library rates was also doubtful.

30 *Library Association Record* 3 (1901), 125–7.
31 Greenwood, *Public libraries*.

A notorious aspect of public library leisure practice in the late nineteenth and early twentieth centuries was the obliteration, or 'blacking out', of betting news from newspapers. The first public library to obliterate the betting sections of the newspapers was Aston Manor in 1893 on the grounds that 'rough and ill-behaved fellows' were deterring the general public from using the newsroom. Other libraries adopted the practice, though a survey of blacking out undertaken by Folkard, the librarian at Wigan, revealed that several did so for moral rather than pragmatic reasons. Conversely, some libraries rejected blacking out as a form of censorship likely to generate negative publicity. As one librarian commented, the issue was little more than a pedantic fad pursued by the ultra-righteous.[32] Although most libraries abandoned the practice after the First World War, a few continued it and in at least one authority it was still in operation as late as 1968.[33]

1918–1945

During the inter-war decades the development of leisure provision was restricted through underfunding and insufficient money for stock purchase. Some libraries were forced to resort to the second-hand market for fiction, a practice that could hardly have contributed to satisfying the perennial demand for newly published novels. Although open access to the fiction shelves eventually became the norm, lending departments in the 1920s and 1930s were characterised by dull buildings and unappealing stock. A Library Association survey published in 1938 presented a depressing image of fiction shelves with drab and unattractive arrays of shabby books, filthy volumes and much-handled rebinds.[34] Public library subscription departments survived in some areas until at least the middle of the 1930s, an anachronism compounded by the fact that their stock was not transferred to the free lending departments for many months. This practice, where it existed, must have exercised a detrimental impact on the general standard of fiction provision to the non-fee-paying member.[35]

The Great Fiction Question was no longer debated as heatedly, though few volumes of the professional journals of the period were without at least one letter or article railing against fiction. The residual antagonism to popular

---

32 A. J. Philip, 'Blacking out', *Library World* (1905), 261–3.
33 Thompson, *Censorship in public libraries*.
34 L. R. McColvin (ed.), *A survey of libraries: reports on a survey made by the Library Association during 1936–37* (London, 1938).
35 McColvin (ed.), *Survey of libraries*.

fiction was evident in the deployment of subtle methods of regulating access to it such as the issue of tickets for non-fiction only, or of allowing extra tickets to the normal allocation to be used only for non-fiction. Other methods included the arrangement of fiction shelving in alternation with the non-fiction and positioning fiction at the far end of the library, thus forcing novel seekers to walk through the non-fiction shelves to reach their goal.

The beginnings of a modern approach to the public library's leisure function were heralded by the publication of the Kenyon Report[36] in 1927 which stated its belief in the validity of the use of libraries for recreational purposes, even if this were to be found in 'literature which does not appeal to more highly cultivated minds'. Nevertheless the Report did approve the practice of delaying the purchase of new popular fiction. Referring to the spread of the county library service into rural areas, the Report was unequivocal in its affirmation of recreational reading for its own sake, stating that a library should aim to 'relieve the tedium of idle hours quite irrespective of intellectual profit or educational gain'. Elsewhere the demand for fiction remained buoyant. A survey of sixty urban lending departments undertaken in 1924 showed that novels accounted for 80% and over in thirty-four libraries and for less than 70% in only six.[37] Although the Public Libraries Act of 1919 placed the responsibility for the county library service with Education Departments, the new libraries established were far from exclusively educational in nature. Indeed, the County Librarian of Fife alleged that at least 80% of the books issued by all lending departments were sensational, sentimental and sordid fiction.[38] A survey undertaken in Fulham in 1935 yielded more detail about the type of fiction borrowed.[39] Of the thirty-eight most popular novelists, all except Dickens were modern authors, and included P. G. Wodehouse, Edgar Wallace, Warwick Deeping, Zane Grey and Jeffery Farnol. The preference for modern popular fiction was accentuated by the complete absence of literary yet readable authors such as Hardy, George Eliot, Thackeray and Scott. With the advent of the BBC a number of libraries, notably those at Coventry and Sheffield, initiated library-based wireless discussion groups to promote education through leisure time. Many libraries developed extensive music collections of multiple copies of scores, band parts and choir music for bulk issue to local music groups.

36 Public Libraries Committee, *Report on public libraries in England and Wales* (London, 1927).
37 *Report on public libraries*, 251.
38 W. Boyd (ed.), *The challenge of leisure* (London, 1936).
39 F. E. Hansford, 'What adults read', *Library World* 38 (1935–6), 229–32.

1945–2000

The major post-war developments in the leisure aspects of public libraries occurred from the 1960s onwards, and prior to this there was only modest progress. Patterns of use did not change significantly, and Rowntree and Lavers, in their study of leisure in England, reported that a considerable proportion of the fiction borrowed from public libraries was not of a 'first-rate quality'.[40] Librarians maintained however that an increasing proportion of people were reading serious fiction, which may also have been true in view of the more widespread availability of readers' advisers. In the immediate post-war years a surge of interest in the uses of libraries resulted in a number of readership surveys which once more indicated that fiction remained the most popular element of the service. The 1964 Public Libraries Act confirmed that the provision of recreational facilities was a valid library function, and should have brought to a close the moribund debate on library fiction, but the minority anti-fiction lobby still continued to express itself on occasion. The leisure role of the library was later amplified in the Library and Information Services Council's national mission statement for the public library service which committed libraries to active participation in cultural activities and to the promotion of a positive use of leisure time.[41]

The removal of the ban on *Lady Chatterley's lover* in 1960 and the pervasive influence of pop culture throughout the remainder of that decade brought the most profound changes in social attitudes to leisure that libraries had ever experienced. Novels became increasingly explicit in their treatment of sex and violence, and the view that English Literature, at least in its modern form, embodied consensual social and moral values virtually disappeared. Most libraries abandoned the practice of keeping books in a restricted cupboard, and overt censorship was rarely reported although it was certainly not extinct.[42] The dilapidated and dirty fiction shelves of the pre-war era were gradually replaced by bright and well-lit areas, and the introduction of protective transparent bindings enabled novels to retain their colourful and usually illustrated dust covers, thereby creating a much-improved overall appearance. Fiction categorisation by genre became commonly practised and paperbacks in reinforced bindings added to the informal appeal of the modern lending department. When obliged to deal with controversial novels, of which, following the

---

40 B. Seebohm Rowntree and G. R. Lavers, *English life and leisure: a social study* (London, 1951).

41 Library and Information Services Council, *Setting objectives for public library services: a manual of public library objectives* (London, 1991).

42 Thompson, *Censorship in public libraries.*

Chatterley trial, there were many, most libraries abided by the Library Association's 1963 policy document on censorship which stated that material that had not incurred any penalty under the law should not be excluded from libraries on moral, political, religious or racial grounds.

The provision of recorded sound began in the later 1930s but remained relatively rare until after the Second World War. By 1954 approximately fifty library authorities had record collections, and from the 1960s onwards records were more and more commonly available in libraries, followed in later decades by the new media of cassettes, compact discs, videos and software packages. As had occurred with fiction, the diminishing influence of Arnoldian concepts of culture on stock selection had an impact on the types of recorded music provided. Whereas in the late 1960s it was rare to find any form of recorded music other than classical, with the occasional exceptions of jazz and folk, by the 1980s it was equally rare to find a collection that did not feature substantial proportions of popular music in all its guises.

The local government reorganisation of 1974 created new and larger authorities and comprehensive leisure departments. This trend placed the management of library services within an overall leisure context, and had implications for the leisure dimension of the library service. In 1991, to take a sample year, ninety-one library authorities were in leisure departments, twenty-six in cultural services departments, thirty-one in education departments (these being mainly in Northern Ireland) and only eight in an autonomous libraries department. One effect of this was a rekindling of the professional debate as to whether the library was essentially an educational or a leisure service. However, in practice it meant that many libraries operated in a leisure context in which customer orientation and an egalitarian approach to readers' choices resulted in book selection policies that were responsive to community demand. In many authorities this was based on a greater awareness of the complexity of urban community structures and an active interest in the provision of fiction for ethnic minorities, teenagers and other specific social groups. New library buildings were designed to accommodate a range of leisure functions and usually included comfortable reading areas, music departments and children's play areas; some went further and incorporated coffee bars, theatres, exhibition rooms and social centres. Towards the close of the century there was a resurgence of interest in public library reading circles.

In the 1980s the Conservative government subjected certain local authority leisure services to competitive tendering, and in 1986 a report from the Adam Smith Institute proposed that library services should be included within this framework.[43] Specifically the report suggested the introduction of a premium book subscription scheme through which those willing and able to pay a fee would have priority of access to newly published novels and biographies. The profession's response was overwhelmingly antagonistic, and this together with support for the status quo from influential public personae ensured that the proposal did not become practice. However the introduction of privatisation and competition in local government operations had the effect of making services, including libraries, more aware of private sector practice in marketing and promotion. In the 1980s several library authorities launched fiction promotion schemes which aimed to reinvigorate demand for contemporary fiction. Many such schemes were successful in generating interest in new fiction and often achieved significant increases in the issue of promoted titles. The demand for fiction remained high until the end of the century and although overall there was a decline in borrowing from public libraries, more fiction was borrowed than any other type of book.[44]

Conclusion

At the close of the twentieth century the place of leisure in the public library service could be summarised in the phrase *plus ça change, plus c'est la même chose*. The 'golden age of leisure', a concept that emerged in the post-war period when it seemed that computer technology would reduce the length of the working week and herald a new era of cultural renaissance, was not realised. Instead there was economic recession and increased global competition, both of which elevated the status of work in society and in the lives of individual people. For most, leisure remained residual and complementary, and passive cultural consumption continued to fulfil functions of relaxation and escapism – functions to which genre fiction, recorded music and film videos were perfectly suited. Although there were notable improvements in leisure provision in public libraries, for example the enhanced standards of library building, the introduction of recorded sound and vision and the adoption of less censorious selection policies, a passive reaction to leisure demand remained a defining theme. In essence, the library at the end of the twentieth century provided cultural materials, principally books, to be taken home for recreational purposes in much the same way that it had done a hundred years earlier.

43 Adam Smith Institute, *Ex libris* (London, 1986).
44 L. England, *The library user: the reading habits and attitudes of public library users in Great Britain* (London, 1994).

If the public library did not develop an overall policy or vision of its role in leisure, this reflected the general treatment of leisure in parliamentary politics; it was not until the establishment of the Department of National Heritage in 1992 that a government department had anything resembling an overall responsibility for leisure and culture in the widest sense. Nevertheless, the public library has been extensively used for leisure purposes throughout its existence. Its survival as a leisure institution is a reflection of its popular appeal, a fact continually affirmed through customer surveys. Despite the repeated criticisms of fiction provision, the professional disagreements about the use of libraries for leisure and the recurrent underfunding, the public library has continued to provide free public access to books of all types without obliging the reader to justify his or her choice. By the end of the twentieth century very few, if any, libraries restricted access to published fiction; neither did librarians attempt to impose literary fiction upon readers. The history of the provision of leisure through public libraries suggests that whenever librarians or library committees have interfered with readers' freedom of choice, the results have been unproductive and negative. Conversely, public library leisure services have been most successful when they have reacted positively to public demand, be this for sensation novels, genre fiction or popular music.

5

High seriousness: the reference and information role of the public library 1850–2000

BOB DUCKETT

The role of the new public libraries which were established under the Public Library Act of 1850 and subsequent legislation was discussed at length in the debates and commissions that preceded the Act. It was clear that the new public libraries would have a role in education and cultural affairs. However, the agenda, and the means to achieve it, were not clear. Experience with earlier 'public' libraries, and the varied range of subscription and circulating libraries, mechanics' institute libraries, newsrooms and reading clubs, all had an influence, as did the character of the librarians appointed to run these virgin institutions. Controversies over reference versus lending use, public instruction versus leisure provision, self-help versus librarian mediation, were a feature of early public library history.

Collections of quality

An early model for the new public libraries was that of the British Museum Library and other libraries of national renown such as the university libraries of the time. Hence we see broadly custodial policies adopted whereby the 'best' literature was collected and made available for consultation in reading rooms. A study of the early printed catalogues (again using British Museum practice as a model) of libraries such as Manchester, Liverpool, Bradford and Sheffield shows scholastic aspirations and competence.

At Manchester, W. R. Credland's impressive 283-page *The Manchester Public Free Libraries: a history and description, and guide to their contents and use* (1899) tells us that the Reference Library catalogue was published in 1864, listing some 30,000 books in author and title sequences. In the chapter on 'The Reference Library: guide to its contents and use' there are sections on Specifications and Patents, Directories, Newspaper Files, Parliamentary Papers, Reviews, Magazines and Newspapers, Early Printed Books, Manuscripts, Rare or Curious

Books, and Bibliographies. In a table provided we learn that 61,080 books were used in the first year of the Reference Library (1852–3), rising to 440,442 forty-six years later (1897–8). Stock rose in those years from 15,744 to 114,630. Contents listed range from the nine-volume catalogue of Trinity College Dublin and *Pictorial Art of Japan* (1866), to a 1561 'black letter' edition of Chaucer and the *Proceedings of the Society of Biblical Archaeology*. (The place of rare books in public libraries is one that has changed with the rise of Special Collections departments in university libraries; few public libraries are still active in this field.) An item of interest in Credland's work is that hundreds of periodicals were provided in branch libraries.[1] The Reference Library at Bradford published several subject-based catalogues, the one for textiles being particularly notable; while the much smaller library at nearby Keighley published a *Catalogue of books in the Lending Library other than fiction* (1913–14).

A special category of 'literature' is archives, and in the foreword to *Guide to the manuscript collection in the Sheffield City Libraries* (1956), the Librarian tells us that 'The care and collection of archive material in the West Riding of Yorkshire has devolved mainly upon three institutions – the Leeds and Sheffield City Libraries and the Yorkshire Archaeological Society.' The guide itself is an impressive work of scholarship by the Librarian of the Department of Local History and Archives.[2] Responsibility for archives is another function once undertaken by public libraries that has been transferred to other organisations, although in some cases the archives are still located in public libraries, for example, Halifax and Birmingham.

Such catalogues represent a rich bibliographical heritage, much of which has now disappeared. In a survey of public libraries undertaken in 1993, many of the librarians who had day-to-day responsibilities for reserve and reference collections reported that those historic collections still surviving were under threat.[3] Such collections played a decreasing role in twentieth-century public librarianship and even just maintaining these mini-BM libraries was a financial burden.

Not all libraries during the nineteenth century were able to develop collections of quality. The Kenyon Report of 1927 is a useful 'snap shot' of what the situation was at that time. A distinction is made between the urban library service and the county library system. The section covering the former divides

1 R. Credland, *The Manchester public free libraries: a history and description, and guide to their contents and use* (Manchester, 1899).
2 Sheffield City Libraries, *Guide to the manuscript collection in the Sheffield City Libraries* (Sheffield, 1956).
3 R. J. Duckett, 'Reference libraries today', in *Encyclopedia of library and information science*, vol. 54 (New York, 1994), 305–36.

the public library into four sections: (a) reference department; (b) lending department; (c) reading and newsrooms; and (d) branch libraries, delivery stations and travelling libraries. Comments on the standard of reference departments are not favourable: lack of funds, overreliance on donations, lack of a collection policy, unsuitable classification and cataloguing, poor quality of staff. 'The stock should include the best and latest encyclopaedias, dictionaries, and other quick reference books; bibliographical indexes; editions of the classic works of literature, and the like. Authoritative works on other subjects . . . To these should be added a supply of books dealing with subjects of local importance.'[4]

The quality and content of reference stock was later featured in the 1962 'Bourdillon Report', *Standards of public library service in England and Wales*.[5] Reference books were better covered in municipal libraries than in county libraries. 'Apart from books on subjects of special local interest, libraries serving less than 100,000 population appear to concentrate on quick reference material and standard works.' Unsatisfactory was the extent to which all but the largest libraries were stocked with specialised bibliographical tools such as abstracts, bulletins, and indexes to periodical literature, 'without which they cannot do their job adequately'. The committee were also critical of the provision of periodicals. Every library giving a basic library service should, regardless of size, provide a basic selection of at least fifty periodicals, including some foreign language titles. 'Our survey indicated that reference libraries were well used . . . There was little discrepancy between county branch and smaller municipal libraries, but large municipal libraries handled many more enquiries as a whole', wrote the committee. The imbalance between the riches of the large municipal libraries, with their standards, patents, government publications, census returns, newspaper files and quality book collections, and the smaller libraries without, continued to be a cause of concern, particularly to those larger libraries who stocked them. 'Too many people from outside the local authority', so the argument ran, 'who paid nothing towards maintaining these expensive services, were using them: their own authorities were getting something for nothing.'

In response to the problems that these *de facto* regional reference libraries such as Birmingham, Manchester, Leeds and Liverpool had in providing a regional service on a sub-regional rate base, there was established the Council

---

4 Board of Education, Public Libraries Committee, *Report on public libraries in England and Wales* (The Kenyon Report) (London, 1927), 60 (Cmd. 2868).
5 Ministry of Education, *Standards of public library service in England and Wales* (The Bourdillon Report) (London, 1962).

of City Reference and Information Libraries (COCRIL). A survey by the Centre for Research on User Studies commissioned by COCRIL in 1983 confirmed the situation: 75% of the enquiries received by personal visits, 40% of the phone enquiries and 20% of postal enquiries to city centre libraries came from the cities' own population, and 25% of the visits, 60% of the phone enquiries and 80% of the postal enquiries came from another local authority.[6]

Collection policies later became standard, and stock revision and disposal better planned[7]. Even so, it is a sobering exercise to compare the quality and level of non-fiction acquisitions of public libraries at the end of the nineteenth century with those at the end of the twentieth. As a look into the surviving stacks of the long-established municipal libraries will testify, collections of quality were built up. But other agencies had arisen to cater for medium- and high-level non-fiction and research collections in the universities, colleges and special libraries. There was less need now for the public library to be the 'poor man's university'.

Since Bourdillon, the book has taken an ever-decreasing share in public library activity. Indeed, the APT Review (of library and information co-operation) in 1995 'takes the view that a public library system which remains predominantly based on printed text is likely to become more a museum of an obsolescent culture than the core of an information system which addresses the emerging needs of the general public'.[8]

The cultural dimension

The early public library was seen to be a force for education and culture, and it was often by means of the librarian's personal contacts, private benefactors and public appeals that these collections were established. Greenwood, in his *Free public libraries*, has a chapter entitled 'What private munificence has done for free libraries.' In the second edition of 1887 he estimates that during the first thirty-six years since the passing of the 1851 Act, no less than £600,000 had been given to Free Libraries in the form of buildings, sites, gifts of books or money.[9] This development was paralleled by the establishment of art galleries, museums and other civic amenities. Librarians were often curators of museums and directors of art galleries. In his 1881 book, *Notes on free public libraries*

6 C. Harris, *The use of reference services in large city libraries: the CRUS study* (Sheffield, 1983).

7 See, for example, ARLIS/UK and Ireland, *Guidelines on stock disposal* (Bromsgrove, 2000).

8 Apt Partnership, *The Apt review: a review of library and information co-operation in the UK and Republic of Ireland* (Sheffield, 1995).

9 T. Greenwood, *Free public libraries: their organisation, uses, and management*, 2nd edn (London, 1887), 147–69 (specifically p. 147).

and museums, James Hibbert follows his plea for private generosity to make good the paucity of income raised from the rate, by the need to cater for art, and gives advice on how to obtain prints, paintings and statues. He concludes his book, 'The work of the Free Libraries will lie in helping to educate the higher classes, and in continuing for the labouring classes the training of the elementary schools. By their means the treasures of literature, art and science will be free to all.'[10]

In an age when the quality of a library's collection was proclaimed by the quantity of incunabula, hand-painted books on natural history and fine bindings owned, quality of scholarship also featured. The role of the public library in supporting local scholarship should be recognised. Support for local historical and parish record societies in their endeavours to transcribe, publish and research local records was invaluable, and many a chief librarian featured as a subscriber, or even a committee member. This support often went wider afield, as runs of *Surtees Society*, *List and Index Society*, *Navy Records Society* and other societies' transactions and proceedings still residing in bookstacks today testify.

After the 1939–45 war this antiquarian tendency lessened, but the public library continued to be a buyer of local publications, accepting the role of an archive for local publications. Many libraries were, indeed, publishers themselves, filling a gap where mainstream commercial publishers fought shy of small print runs of local interest material. The quality and quantity of publications submitted for the annual Alan Ball library publishing awards was impressive. Purchase and publication apart, public library support for local literature festivals, writers and poets in residence, creative writing workshops, reading groups, desktop publishing facilities, and giving advice on publication and copyright matters was commonplace.

Bibliography and access

One particular spin-off from this scholarly tradition was the concern with bibliography. We have already mentioned the printed catalogues that public libraries produced. These were particularly necessary in the days of closed access when books were fetched on request from book stores and remote shelves. A development of this was the practical problem of identifying stock and locating it. Much attention was paid to descriptive cataloguing and filing rules, and it is at this time that card and sheaf catalogues made their

---

10 J. Hibbert (ed.), *Notes on free public libraries and museums* (Preston, 1881), 106.

appearance. The need to locate requested books and journals resulted in a number of union catalogues and centralised collections. Before the days of formal inter-library lending – an initiative that came from the public libraries via the Workers' Education Association with the establishment of the Central Library of Students in 1916 – the local librarian was a useful person to know. In the archives at Bradford is correspondence from the London-based journalist Clement Shorter, editor of the *Tatler* and *Sphere*, asking his friend Butler Wood, Bradford's Chief Librarian, to obtain books for him.[11]

An interesting post-war example of this concern with bibliography was the Background Materials Scheme, in which the larger municipal public libraries co-operated with university libraries to ensure that early printed books coming on to the market were purchased by libraries, and so keep them in the public domain. By 1954, twenty-four public libraries were co-operating with nineteen university libraries and ten special libraries. These libraries reported holdings of 4,982 works published before 1640 and 5,399 published between 1640 and 1700.[12] The Background Materials Scheme petered out in the 1950s but the same altruistic co-operative policy and desire for national bibliographic control can be seen in the rather larger and higher profile Regional Subject Specialisation schemes, whereby public libraries throughout the UK took responsibility for acquiring books on specific subjects based on the coverage and classification of the *British National Bibliography*. The initiative here had come from the public libraries in London which lacked the large central lending collections and well-stocked reference libraries of the provincial cities. For serials, the rich holdings of periodicals in public libraries were a feature of the *British Union Catalogue of Periodicals* (BUCOP), begun in 1944.

From the 1950s there had been much debate over what stock a public library should have, particularly as other, non-book, services developed. Another change was the increase in the number of formats in which information and literature could be acquired or accessed. Not only could large documentary resources be tucked away in a microfilm cabinet or a tray of CD-ROMs, but they could also be accessed electronically from distant databases. The Reference Library at the end of the twentieth century needed, some claimed, to be little more than a computer terminal mediated by the computer literate, person-friendly, information officer. The holdings strategy of the nineteenth-century librarian-custodian was giving way to the 'virtual library', the 'library without walls', 'the joined-up library'.

11 West Yorkshire Archive Service, Bradford Office, Butler Wood papers.
12 K. G. Hunt, *Subject specialisation and co-operative book purchase in the libraries of Great Britain*, Library Association pamphlet 12 (London, 1955).

Scholars, instructors, educators

In his autobiography *Tuppence for the rainbow*, published in 1990, Leslie Sands recalled his use of the local reference library as a young student:

> The Ref. Library, as it was always known, was my regular evening habitat from six p.m. until the Central Library closed its doors. There I would sit, entrenched in my notebooks and texts, catching up on the last year's work and coping with current homework, revision and preparation. At half-past seven prompt I would leave my books where they lay and go downstairs and outside into the fresh air, to enjoy a short stroll and a cigarette. Then it was back to work until the bell went, when I would walk home with my studies still spinning and weaving through my brain.[13]

Reference libraries have always exuded an air of scholarship. As we have seen, the early librarians often had scholarly backgrounds and pretentions. A look at the backgrounds and careers of the early public librarians shows that it was common for the chief librarian to be a man of letters and to write articles, essays, and even books[14]. Many a chief of this time was styled FRSA (Fellow of the Royal Society of Arts), RSL (Royal Society of Literature) or similar. Our scholar librarians, our committed men of letters and learning, were also active in the intellectual life of their community and gathered round them a number of like-minded people.

These same chiefs and their senior staff were also active in the development of professional affairs, for as well as the role model of the scholar librarian, there was also the less exalted role model of the library clerk. Practices and procedures had to be established and these same imaginative minds were pioneers in library economy. In the annals of the national and regional library associations we see a constant stream of papers and discussions on topics ranging from the practical and the political to the topographical, literary and cultural. Thus at meetings of the Northern Counties Library Association in 1901–2, topics ranged from 'The library income and the library rate', 'Some remarks on book classification' and 'English and American Public Libraries: a comparison', to 'The history of printing as told in the books in the Reference Library', 'The literary and historical side of Harrogate', and 'The importance of collecting local literature'. There was also a paper on 'Does open access extend the educational influences of a library?'[15]

---

13 L. Sands, *Tuppence for the rainbow* (Bradford, 1990), 187.
14 W. A. Munford, *Who was who in librarianship* (London, 1987).
15 R. J. Duckett, 'Friend or foe? The Northern Counties Library Association, 1900–1920', *Library History* 12 (1996), 155–70.

As the size and complexity of their libraries increased, librarians become more concerned with library policies for education and in the professional activities necessary to bring about these aims. Librarians such as Berwick Sayers, Ernest Savage, Stanley Jast and Lionel McColvin before the 1939–45 war, and K. C. Harrison, A. W. McClellan, E. V. Corbett, William Munford and George Chandler afterwards, not only wrote extensively on professional affairs, but also wrote texts on how to find and organise knowledge. These often had a practical application in assisting staff to pass their chartership examinations, but they also developed into guides for library staff and their public to find books and information, and hence further the educational and informational role of the public library. Often these were works of great detail and required prodigious industry to compile – Cotgreave's *Contents-subject index to general and periodical literature* (1900) was a case in point. The volunteer-compilers of the Library Association's *Subject Guide to Periodical Literature* (later *British Humanities Index*) were other exemplars of this altruistic bibliographic tradition.

Services

Since 1912, the Reference Library, with its quiet and pleasant atmosphere, has offered excellent facilities for study and research purpose, and a Study Room is available for students working for long periods. The bookstock has steadily risen over the years, and today there is an excellent collection of finely produced books and standard works covering a large variety of subjects. The books in the Reference Library supplement those in the Lending Library, and the student who works in the Library can call on the book stocks of both departments. There is an extensive collection of purely reference works such as dictionaries, encyclopaedias, atlases, maps, gazetteers, guide books, directories and year books . . . Learned and specialist periodicals are also displayed in the Reference Library.

This account, in a commemorative booklet *The public library service in Keighley, 1904–1954*, then itemises some special collections, extols the excellent lighting of the Reference Library reading room, and notes that it is used for occasional art exhibitions and lectures.[16]

The reference made earlier to the provision of journals in branch libraries in Manchester prompts mention of the importance of newsrooms in public library history. Often the butt of jokes about the smelly inhabitants and the blacking of betting news in the papers, it was one of the aims of public library

16 Keighley Corporation, *The public library service in Keighley, 1904–1975* (Keighley, 1954).

legislation to enable all classes of people to have access to news and information. Newsrooms were popular *before* the 1850 Act, many towns having more than one – to reflect different political persuasions – and they remained a major part of public library provision until the 1980s.

The development into new areas of service was seen in the move towards 'community information' in the late 1970s. A tract for the times was *Libraries are ours: the public library as a source of information for community groups.*[17] The changing reference ethic was neatly encapsulated in the range of policy statements prepared by members of the newly formed Public Libraries Research Group in 1981. Under Adult Reference Services (the use of 'reference library' was by now becoming outmoded) the policy statement declares that 'Reference and information services exist to provide, directly or as a referral point, for the information needs of the community.' Five objectives are listed:

1. To select and make available to all sections of the community material relevant to their information needs;
2. To co-operate with other information-providing agencies to provide a flexible network of information provision for the community;
3. To provide public awareness of the service;
4. To train users to exploit the service;
5. To provide special support services where appropriate (e.g. technical, local government information, local history, etc.).

There were, in addition, separate policies and objectives for Adult Lending Services, Commercial and Technical Information Services, Library Services to Ethnic Communities, and so on.[18] The change to 'information needs', community groups, and a proactive stance is clear.

The service ethic, so forcefully championed in the late nineteenth century, was tested at the end of the twentieth by government policies of privatisation. Pressure was put on local government to make their services more responsive to consumer needs. A government 'green paper' *Financing our public library service: four subjects for debate*, was published in 1988.[19] The four subjects were:

Wider charging: the means to attract new money for growth?
Joint ventures: the means for better and more effective services?
Contracting out: a means to better and more cost-effective services?

17 B. Darcy and A. Ohri, *Libraries are ours: the public library for community groups* (London, 1978).
18 P. Heeks and P. Turner (eds.), *Public library aims and objectives: policy statements prepared by members of the Public Libraries Research Group* (Brighton, 1981).
19 Minister for the Arts, *Financing our public library service: four subjects for debate: a consultative paper* (London, 1988).

Anomalies: inconsistencies and limitations in library authorities' present powers to charge.

Many services were put out to tender. Information and reference services were not exempt and, notably in the case of Westminster, an internal market was created. In 1992 five library business units were established, of which the Westminster Reference Library, the Schools Information Service and 'Information for Business' were three.[20] 'Best value' and service standards were also introduced nationally, and a little earlier, 'core services' had been identified. One result of this, and the general tightening of finances from the late 1970s onwards, was the charging for services such as genealogical and research enquiries. The situation varied from authority to authority, with the situation nationally becoming confused.

Subject departments

Prior to 1920, the typical public library was small in scale, with the chief librarian often the only experienced professional; and he did almost everything to run the library – bookman and administrator. The readership was small and he knew the readers well. During the 1920s there was a period of expansion following the introduction of open access and the availability of greater funds, with larger libraries expanding with more service points, materials and staff. Some degree of division of labour was necessary. There was also a questioning of the traditional division into reference and lending libraries. In 1916, the Library Association established a committee to promote the idea that the public library, as the library serving all sections of interest in the community, could provide a service for technical and commercial information. Coventry had already established such a service in 1915, Leeds in 1918, and Birmingham, Dundee, Manchester and Wolverhampton in 1919, followed.[21]

Large libraries generally accepted the need for specialist subject divisions: music, commerce, science and technology, and local history were among the most common. An influential figure was A. W. McClellan, who advocated 'service in depth' whereby the professional librarian would come into more contact with the library user by developing subject specialisation and combining reference and lending stocks[22]. Many of these ideas were first developed

20 P. Cox, 'The Westminster experience' in M. Ashcroft and A. Wilson (eds.), *Competitive tendering and libraries: proceedings of seminars held in Stamford, Lincolnshire* (Stamford, 1992).
21 T. Kelly, *History of public libraries in Great Britain, 1845–1975*, 2nd edn (London, 1977).
22 A. W. McClellan, *The reader, the library and the book: selected papers 1949–1970* (London, 1973).

by Ernest Savage, Edinburgh's City Librarian before the Second World War, though he was only able to introduce three of his proposed nine departments because of building constraints. The deployment of staff developed by Mc-Clellan at Tottenham during the 1950s was taken up by Eastbourne, Harlow and Nuneaton in the 1960s. Later, Hertford's Stevenage library reorganised along subject lines and Bradford was the first purpose-built subject departmentalised central library in 1967. The much larger Birmingham (1972) followed, but still with a reference/lending split. Liverpool in the 1960s developed along somewhat different lines, with a Commonwealth and an International Library. In 1969, the Library Association published Michael Overington's *The subject departmentalized public library*.[23]

With the enlargement of public library authorities under the Local Government Act in 1974 (1965 in London), the time was ripe for further subject specialisation. Indeed, Bradford did increase the number of subject departments and Glasgow reorganised its Mitchell (reference) library into ten subject departments in 1981, but suddenly, subject departments were passé. Birmingham reduced its ten subject departments to three 'faculties' and Bradford scrapped its in 1985, returning to a traditional reference/lending split. A major motive for this turnabout was financial. Numerous separate departments were expensive to administer, subject specialists were expensive to employ, and in-depth stock was expensive to purchase.[24] The early eighties were a time of recession and such expensive services were under threat.

There were other factors at work. The rapid expansion in higher education – new universities, colleges of advanced technology and polytechnics – diverted much of the need for specialist stock, services and subject experts away from the public libraries. There was also something of a backlash against such 'elitist' services to the cultured and educationally privileged minorities. New policies of 'positive discrimination', targeting specific social groupings, drew resources away from traditional reference libraries with their expensive non-fiction books, standing orders and periodicals. There were also new ideas of how best to provide information to these new constituencies. 'Community information' became fashionable and operated on quite different lines: leaflets and pre-packaged 'info' rather than monographs and serials; community 'drop-in' centres rather than hushed and intimidating reading rooms; and street-wise information advisers with CAB (Citizens' Advice Bureau) training rather than the academically literate subject specialist. Indeed, the role

23 M. A. Overington, *The subject departmentalized public library* (London, 1969).
24 Duckett, 'Reference libraries today'.

of librarians as advocates and activists was seriously debated. No longer did subject specialists with their roots in traditional academic disciplines seem appropriate to the modern-day community-orientated library service. The abandonment of the Dewey classification system, tied into an anachronistic 1878 knowledge structure, was common about this time, being replaced by broad stock categories such as those common in book shops. Many reference libraries and reference sections disappeared, with reference and lending stock being integrated. Expenditure on bookstock and journals was reduced; reserve stocks were weeded and the space vacated used for new services. Attention was now paid to identifying collections on a regional level, and beyond, where knowledge of the location of material was more important than having the material itself. Up to a point this was a development of the union catalogue principle, but with the added bite of planned development. The 1980s was the era of LIPs – Library and Information Plans, in which government funding was available for research and producing lists of resources, but not for implementation.

Answering questions

One of the hallmarks of public library service has been that members of the public can go to any library and expect to find the answer to their information needs. Traditionally, the answer has lain in the bookstock. There is no clear evidence that the early public librarians saw it as their job to answer the public's questions themselves. Their job was to select and provide books and other printed material, catalogue and classify them, produce catalogues, fetch and replace requested items, and otherwise curate their stock. It was up to the public to use the resources and find the answers for themselves. By the second half of the twentieth century, however, 'reference' or 'enquiry' work had become a standard service offered by public libraries. This combined the bibliographical expertise of traditional reference work with the 'Readers' Advisors' work that was developing in the lending libraries. The regular column in the *Library Association Record* by Herbert Woodbine of Birmingham Reference Library, from 1936 to 1944, is still regarded as the pinnacle of 'good' reference practice. In these columns, the aspiring librarian was introduced to the value of the various books in the reference library during the course of answering questions, guided by the experienced Woodbine.

When the Library Association was an examination board, papers on information sources featured. In a 1976 paper on Bibliographical Control and Service, we find questions such as 'Why are directories and yearbooks of importance in reference work?'; 'What are the main types of reading lists which are compiled by librarians to aid readers?'; and 'Describe the sources of biographical information you would use to trace information about British persons who died in the second half of the nineteenth century.' In the harder, Part Two examination, there were three papers on bibliographical organisation, one for the humanities, one for the social sciences and one for science and technology. A sample question from each is 'How far does the nature of the library material in your chosen field need specialized staff to exploit it?'; 'State why periodicals are important in the social sciences. How, as a librarian, would you exploit fully their control?'; and 'Describe the information retrieval services useful for searches in patent literature.' (The questions have been abbreviated.)[25]

It is a moot point how successful reference work has been. A rash of studies in the 1980s using unobtrusive testing techniques were not impressed with the success rate,[26] but enquiries continue to be a feature of public library service. In 1997 the Department of National Heritage estimated 53 million requests for information a year.[27] Questions abound at this point over the definition of an enquiry, and indeed CIPFA (Chartered Institute of Public Finance and Accountancy), who organised the collection of annual statistics from public libraries, abandoned counting enquiries because of the lack of consistency.[28] The problem is still unresolved, and the weaker measures of 'library use' or 'reader contacts' have tended to be used instead.

Nowadays, questions can be asked of any public library from around the world via the Internet.

Information

No statement of public library aims and objectives, services and achievements, would have been complete at the end of the twentieth century without copious references to 'information', and what were once called 'Reference Librarians' and 'Reader's Advisors' became 'Information Managers' and 'Information Resources Officers'. Yet the word 'information' was not a feature of the 1850

25 The Library Association, *Examination papers set for Summer 1976* (London, 1967).
26 See P. Hernon and G. R. McClure, *Unobtrusive testing and library reference services* (Norwood, NJ, 1987) for a comprehensive review. K. Whittaker, 'Unobtrusive testing of reference enquiry work', *Library Review* 39 (6) (1990), 50–4, has a UK test.
27 Department of National Heritage, *Reading the future* (London, 1997).
28 J. Sumsion and others, *The CIPFA enquiry count* (Loughborough, 1994); N. Blake, *Enquiry statistics: an analysis of enquiries asked at selected public and special libraries in the UK*, LISU Occasional Papers 11 (Loughborough, 1995).

public library legislation and it is not listed in the indexes of Greenwood's *Public library yearbooks* in the 1890s and 1900s. Quite when the Information Age started is a matter of debate, but as far as public libraries are concerned a broad generalisation would be that it started with the specialist services provided by the larger city libraries in the 1920s, of patents, trade directories, industrial standards and other commercial 'information'. An impetus to this was given during the 1914–18 war when it was discovered that many of our industries could not provide the products needed for the war effort. In 1919, a Ministry of Reconstruction report proposed an elaborate scheme for providing techni-cal information based on the newly created Department of Science, Industry and Research (DSIR) associations and stations which were to be established (rather than public libraries, as was the hope of the Library Association).[29] Nevertheless, many of the larger libraries went ahead with specialist services and adopted some of the information techniques being developed. The devel-opment of sophisticated indexing techniques, close classification, trade and report literature, and SDI services – selective dissemination of information – were all techniques which found their way into the reference services of public libraries.

A boost was given to such specialist services during the 1939–45 war when public libraries took on a number of information roles for the government such as casualty information, ration book distribution and Citizens' Advice Bureau work. This overt information role continued and was accelerated in the technological 1960s after the Russians, heralding a new age of communication, put their Sputnik satellite into orbit and specialisation became the fashion (reflected in the development of subject departments).

The work of Aslib (Association of Special Libraries and Information Bureaux), founded in 1924, and the special libraries themselves, are outside the scope of this chapter, but many co-operative ventures were formed at this time involving both public libraries and industrial information services. Two of these were SINTO (Sheffield Interchange Organization), founded in 1939, and MANTIS (Manchester Technical Information Service) in 1948. The new discipline of 'information science' was popularised in the library world by books such as Jack Burkett's *Special library and information services in the UK*, 1961[30] and Douglas Foskett's *Information service in libraries*, 1958.[31] Many

29 Ministry of Reconstruction, Adult Education Committee, *Third interim report on libraries and museums* (London, 1919).
30 J. Burkett (ed.), *Special library and information services in the United Kingdom* (London, 1961).
31 D. Foskett, *Information services in libraries* (London, 1958).

other post-war developments in librarianship were having an effect on public library information services, not the least of which were the new management philosophies of team working, management by objects and corporate business plans.

Local government reorganisation in 1974 (1965 in London) created larger library authorities which not only facilitated greater specialisation, but, under the influence of the Bains Report into local government management, caused to be set up several information, intelligence and current awareness services for local government.[32] Particularly important was the Greater London Intelligence Unit which led the way in this field. By now, online and teletext services were available and public library staff added these to their armoury of information aids.

The shift from 'reference libraries' to 'information services' is highlighted in the second edition of R. N. Lock's *Library administration*, published in 1961. Given the impossibility of having large traditional reference libraries in the majority of authorities, and since it is 'essential that accurate knowledge be provided by competent staff', it is, therefore, 'better to aim at what is generally regarded as an "information service", that is, the provision of answers to enquiries not needing prolonged search into a great variety of sources'. Lock also identifies 'the "quick reference service": the provision of directories, annuals, guides, and so on, for the use of the casual enquirer. This service is again a valuable contribution to the community, but should not be confused with the reference library ideal.'[33] The different-levels-of-reference-service scenario is repeated by Royston Brown in 1979: 'Access to relevant information is one of the most important requirements for the individual . . . The provision of information has traditionally been a part of the public library service, usually centred on the reference library, but in the modern public library increasing importance is being placed on this aspect of the service. The concept behind the reference library is that it will be stocked with material which will not be lent and will, therefore, always be available.'[34] The decline of the reference library ideal is chronicled in this author's 'Paradise Lost? The retreat from reference'.[35] This is not to say that public libraries ceased to answer questions, but the depth of stock which underpins research and 'high seriousness' no longer had the priority it once had.

32 Department of the Environment, *The new local authorities: management and structure* (The Bains Report) (London, 1972); L. Grayson, *Library and information services for local government* (London, 1978).
33 R. N. Lock, *Library administration*, 2nd edn (London, 1965), 43–53.
34 R. Brown, *Public library administration* (London, 1979).
35 R. Duckett, 'Paradise lost? The retreat from reference', *Library Review* 41 (1) (1992), 4–24.

The Internet and other developments in communications are having a profound effect in libraries. 'E-reference' is developing and EARL's (Electronic Access to Resources in Libraries) *Ask a Librarian* service is just one successful development at the start of the new millennium.[36] Public library provision of free public access Internet terminals is another. In 1997, the Library and Information Commission (LIC) published *New library: the people's network*, setting out a strategy for a radical transformation of the public library service. 'It proposed that they [public libraries] should be connected to a national digital network, giving them a fundamentally new role as managers of electronic content and gateways to a vast wealth of online information.'[37] In 1998, the LIC proposed 'to develop a New Library Network which will initially be based on the Internet but which is capable of evolving into a dedicated broadband network . . . [and] is compatible with the process being developed by the UK education departments for the National Grid for Learning'.[38]

Despite the long road travelled from reference library to information terminal, the need for a person-friendly intermediary to the information and knowledge jungle remains. The vision is still the same.

36 http://www.earl.org.uk/ask.
37 Library and Information Commission, *New library: the people's network* (London, 1997).
38 Library and Information Commission, *Building the new library network* (London, 1998).

6

Extending the public library 1850–1930

MARTIN HEWITT

From 1850 to 1900 the public library movement was dominated by the struggle for 'extension' in the sense of new adoptions of the Library Acts, and for the expansion of existing library systems and provisions. Late nineteenth-century librarians were quite capable of conceiving of library 'extension' entirely in such terms. This chapter considers extension in its later sense, which, to avoid systematic anachronism, we might term library 'outreach'.

We still know relatively little about library outreach before 1930. Thomas Greenwood's accounts of the history and current condition of the public library movement, which commenced in 1886,[1] provide us with scraps, and once the British library press was established coverage became fuller. But much of the early literature on library outreach is exhortation rather than description, and the coverage of outreach in existing library histories is rather sketchy.

This is not surprising, because outreach activity for much of this period was itself patchy and uneven. Of course the circumstances of the movement as a whole were not propitious. Given that many libraries were struggling just to stay afloat, the idea of actively increasing demand could quite naturally seem unattractive. In any case, the process of achieving necessary support for the adoption of the Library Acts almost invariably involved a considerable campaign of publicity, and it was tempting for promoters to feel that the library was already, at its foundation, enshrined in the communal consciousness.

Early writers on library issues, especially Edward Edwards, Greenwood and James Duff Brown, concentrated on providing guidance on internal management, and any wider ambitions were limited to encouraging existing readers to 'serious' reading. In outreach thus conceived, pride of place went to the catalogue, the touchstone, before 1900, of librarianship. Essential, of course, in the era of closed stacks, once enthroned the catalogue was not easily deposed.

---

1 T. Greenwood, *Free public libraries: their organisation, uses and management* (London, 1886).

The experience of Manchester, the first library opened under the 1850 Act, is typical in many respects. The poll was carried after a vigorous publicity campaign. Once the library was opened, a handful of lectures on the bookstock were delivered, but not repeated until the later 1880s. Instead, the energies of a succession of chief librarians were directed at pioneering expansions of the branch library system, and designing and preparing comprehensive catalogues. In the 1870s and 1880s regular weekly lists of new accessions were published in local newspapers, but there was no sustained utilisation of the press for promotional purposes.

Of course, for the nineteenth-century library, each local history was unique; nevertheless, the story always has the same smattering of action confined by a desultory interest in outreach. In the years before the 1890s effort was largely restricted to annual reports, classes and lectures, but in all three cases progress was undramatic. Annual Reports may have served as a significant channel of communication between library and public, but most were fairly barren lists of statistics and administrative detail, and there is little evidence that they were widely circulated or read, even if by the Edwardian period some libraries were attempting to enliven them with illustrations and a more informal text. Likewise, although in the early years classes were relatively common, especially in the midlands, where Wolverhampton in particular built up an extensive provision, few libraries conceived of classes as a means of expanding library usage, and their number waned rapidly in the years immediately following the passing of the 1890 Technical Instruction Act. Wolverhampton hived off its classes in 1902. Watford, where the system survived until 1919, was one of the few exceptions.

This left lectures as the one genuine outreach activity that obtained any significant importance in the first forty years of the public library. The fullest development of library lecturing occurred at Liverpool where, explicitly empowered by a local act, the library built up an impressive programme in the years after 1865. In the 1890s annual attendances at the lectures in the central and branch libraries reached over 50,000. Liverpool was exceptional: elsewhere lecturing was often attempted but rarely sustained.

Around 1890 there are signs of a shift in temper, heralded by Peter Cowell's essay, 'How to popularize the library', published in the *New Review* in October 1893. Cowell advocated a range of activities which neatly encompassed the elements of outreach that dominated the ensuing twenty years: lectures (and library lecture halls), contacts with local associations (and the provision of meeting space for them), specialised catalogues and handlists, distribution of leaflets and circulars, attention to favourable press coverage and (albeit obliquely) library exhibitions. The subsequent two decades saw the unsure and uneven transformation of attitudes, prompted perhaps by the emerging sense of professional solidarity encouraged by the Library Association in the 1880s, and increasing awareness of the American revolution in outreach. Even so, suspicion of 'new-fangled' ideas of librarians as missionaries of the book remained entrenched in many quarters. Librarians of the prestigious non-municipal institutions and of many municipal libraries shared the unease of A. Capel Shaw at Birmingham, that the librarian was, as he put it, being converted into a 'jack of all trades' by what James Duff Brown termed in 1904 'the craze for magic-lantern entertainments, lecturettes, reading circles and so forth'.[2]

Nevertheless initiatives did begin to multiply. Library lectures spread rapidly and by the early 1900s had become a staple of outreach activity, mostly in miscellaneous single-lecture courses, occasionally through more specialised Gilchrist Trust or university extension courses. Local variations emerged, such as the 'half-hour talks', informal, conversational and focused directly on literary topics, common in the east midlands. It became customary for new library buildings to include a lecture hall. Even so, various practical problems, especially relating to the legal powers of libraries to subsidise lectures, meant that in the twenty years before 1914 probably less than half the municipal libraries at any one time were organising library lectures, and it may not have been much more than a quarter.[3]

One advantage of lectures was that they raised the general profile of the library. It was common for handbills or even lecture syllabuses to be not only placed in shop windows, but circulated to local places of employment, and even via house-to-house distribution. Outside larger cities, a public lecture remained sufficiently newsworthy to attract press notice. At the same time, lectures on library matters became one means by which more enterprising librarians (such as W. E. A. Axon and Charles Sutton at Manchester, J. Potter Briscoe at Nottingham, W. H. K. Wright at Plymouth and Butler Wood at Bradford) promoted their libraries. But in general, lists of new accessions apart, before World War I, few librarians appear to have found the time for anything more than the very occasional article on library matters in the local press, and lecture publicity only occasionally developed into more general promotional efforts. In the 1890s and 1900s Cambridge library undertook a series of house-to-house leafleting campaigns. In the years before World War I Nottingham

---

2 *Library Association Record* 6 (1904), 472; T. Kelly, *A history of the public library in Great Britain, 1845–1975* (London, 1977), 201, citing unsigned article in *Library World* 6 (1903–4), 76.
3 More than fifty in 1900, according to Kelly, *A history of public libraries*, 199, citing T. Greenwood, *British library year book 1900–1901* (London, 1900), 269.

published a pseudo-newspaper, the *Lenton News*, exclusively for the purposes of promoting the branch library. At Leeds and elsewhere, priority was given to circulating information on the advantages of the library to school-leavers. But pure promotion of this sort remained unusual.

In general, libraries sought to reach out to new readers by providing concrete assistance. The lecture often provided the impetus for the production of relevant bibliographies or small book displays, which in many cases were part of a more sustained effort to provide a selection of reading lists, as an alternative to bulky catalogues and annual updates. By the end of the 1880s Nottingham already had an elaborate set of single class list catalogues. The phenomenal success of the Wigan class list covering the library's especially strong collection of technical and mining subjects alerted librarians in the early 1890s to the potential of such lists. Otherwise, an important pioneer, here as elsewhere, was John J. Ogle of Bootle, who by 1890 had a growing series of small pamphlets entitled *Our town reading lists*. In the quarter-century before the outbreak of World War I librarians produced a wide number of variants on this theme. Many libraries (fifty in a 1903 Library Association survey[4]) issued occasional topic lists; some posted lists on topics of the day on library notice boards. At Wandsworth, the librarian went as far as to offer to furnish board school teachers with bespoke reading lists.

Many libraries were content with this, but the more dynamic usually progressed to a local library periodical. In the Edwardian period the 'bulletin' challenged the lecture as the most widely adopted outreach activity. Bulletins, like nearly all outreach activities, had already been widely adopted in America. In Britain the first seems to have been Duff Brown's *Clerkenwell Quarterly Guide for Readers*, dating from the early 1890s. Brown viewed the bulletin predominantly as a means of catalogue updating and of communicating rules and administrative arrangements to library users, and lists of recent accessions remained the central justification of many of the numerous bulletins launched before 1914. Nevertheless, many librarians seized enthusiastically on the potential of the bulletin for attracting new readers. Topical booklists, chatty jottings on library and book topics, even original articles on literature and local history abounded. Alfred Cotgreave's *West Ham Library Notes* offered a varied content of new accessions, literary and historical articles and jottings, to which was later added the not uncommon local Notes and Queries section.

Many libraries found that it was possible to obtain sufficient advertising matter to allow the bulletins to be distributed free. Hence from 1895 Brentford

---

4 The survey was conducted by the Library Association's Committee on Public Education and Public Libraries: see *Library Association Record* 7 (1905), 611–15.

produced 1,000 copies of *The Brentonian*, a twenty-page bulletin with seven pages for cataloguing purposes, and four pages of historical articles, financed by nine pages of advertisements. Some bulletins were sold. Norwich sold 12,500 copies of the first number of its bi-monthly guide in 1911, although such numbers were not easy to achieve or to maintain, and by 1914 it appears that the bulk of library magazines were free.

To lectures and magazines were increasingly added displays and exhibitions of various sorts. By the 1890s specially installed display cases, in the entrance or adjacent to the borrowing counters, seem to have been becoming common. In this 'domestic' setting such book displays were hardly outreach, although some libraries, such as Newark in the 1920s, had display cases installed outside the building. However, where libraries attempted to make exhibitions into more of an event, they became a recognisable feature of purposeful outreach activities. The precise history of these initiatives is particularly difficult to uncover because library and municipal gallery were often combined in a single institution. As a result, library services often had exhibitions and displays that had little connection with the library. In other places, such as Birmingham, an organisationally distinct gallery or museum was housed within the library. In either case such collections did little to attract readers, and were often just one more drain on the stretched resources of the penny rate. Exhibitions as a deliberate element of outreach tended to appear only gradually from the early 1890s. The widely publicised success of book exhibitions at St Helens given not in the library itself but in the Town Hall gave them a new impetus, especially in the larger provincial centres and in London. Nevertheless, they remained much less prevalent than the library lecture. The Library Association survey of 1903 suggests that 38 libraries held occasional exhibitions, although they do seem to have become more widely used thereafter.[5]

For outreach purposes book exhibitions seemed particularly appropriate. There were numerous variations on the theme – book cover design, typefaces, the history of book production, book illustration or specific types of literature. Commemorations inevitably provided a ready excuse for exhibitions of the works of prominent writers, and these were often fleshed out with illustrations, letters and other appropriate memorabilia. Stoke Newington's 1908 tercentenary commemoration of Milton included an entertainment, with recitals and an appreciation of Milton, and a large exhibition of Miltoniana. The other main exhibition staple was local history, with collections of paintings and prints, old photographs, or maps and plans. Norwich possessed a separate exhibition

5 *Library Association Record* 7 (1905), 611–15.

hall, but few libraries had space for lengthy occupation, and exhibitions often lasted only a few days (three days for the Stoke Newington Milton exhibition). Hence perhaps the low attendance figures often quoted: fewer than 4,700 for an exhibition of watercolours at the central library and two branch libraries in Woolwich in 1911; a mere 'some hundreds of people' for the six-day exhibition of pen and ink sketches of the highways and byways of Northampton, in that town in 1919.[6]

Exhibitions or displays were often associated with schemes to draw particular groups of potential users into the library. At Cardiff in the later 1890s, John Ballinger invited local societies to spend an evening in the library, with an address and a book display. This sort of direct contact with local associations was part of a much wider impetus, inspired by the vision of the library as the hub of the literary and intellectual life of a community, providing meeting space for local associations, a venue for conversaziones and other public meetings. Despite the powerful advocacy of Cowell and others, in the pre-Carnegie years this aspiration presented particular problems for cramped libraries and overworked librarians. As a result, effort was uneven and intermittent. In a very few cases enthusiastic librarians went one step further and established societies of their own: Wolverhampton had a Field Club and a debating society in the 1880s, and the Passmore Edwards Library, Plaistow, sponsored a literary and debating society in the mid-1890s. Occasionally librarians sought to promote a particular literary interest, as in the Shakespeare circles formed at Worcester and Dundee.

It often appeared easier to work in co-operation with the various national movements, such as the National Home Reading Union (NHRU) which had analogous aims. By 1903 thirty-three libraries had NHRU circles, and in the following years various reports and manifestos advocated the strengthening of such links. In a few cases very close co-operation developed, with librarians undertaking the role of local organisers. However, for a number of reasons relations between the public libraries and the NHRU never really gelled, and most librarians contented themselves with providing accommodation, or liaison over the supply of books. There were complications in linking a subscription-based organisation with the free-to-user public libraries. There was also a certain resentment at the implication that librarians were not entirely competent in matters of book selection. Similar tensions also inhibited closer co-operation with the Workers' Educational Association, despite enthusiastic support from some quarters (for example, Edward McKnight, librarian at Chorley). During

6 *Library Association Record* 13 (1911), 475 and 21 (1919), 36.

World War I the library movement was not well pleased with vocal WEA support for the transfer of libraries to local education authorities, and James Stewart's London survey of 1924 showed only ten of the seventy-seven libraries included providing rooms for WEA classes.[7]

The patchy record of the public libraries in embracing these opportunities for co-operation is symbolic of the limited achievement in the outreach field in the quarter-century before 1914. The mythic transformation from the librarian-as-conservator to the librarian-as-missionary was widely celebrated. An accepted canon of activities was sanctified by endless repetition in the library press. But the concept of outreach had ossified, a conservative cast of mind persisted, and the movement failed abjectly to mount any concerted campaign to defend its reputation or to challenge the financial restrictions of mid-Victorian library legislation. In 1912 it was still necessary, as Stanley Jast put it, to 'arouse librarians to the absolute necessity of scoring the mission and ideal of the public library as deeply as may be in the mind of the average man'.[8]

The war changed everything, and its shadow stretches right through to the end of the period under discussion here. On the one hand, frenzied attention to recovery, reconstruction and the post-war economic struggle prompted renewed interest in the potential of the library, and brought the abolition of the penny rate limit. On the other, the disruptions and legacy of the war rendered the new vistas of 1919 a delusion. Not until the later 1920s was it finally possible to discern a new sense of dynamism; no dramatic transformations, but a ferment of minor innovations and experimentation, both in the larger libraries but also in the smaller services.

Outreach activities were hit hard by the war. Lecture halls were requisitioned, librarians volunteered or were conscripted, funding was cut, and all forms of publication, annual reports, catalogues and occasional lists were severely curtailed. Outreach activities which remained often acquired a distinctively wartime flavour. Even the preparations for peace brought little respite. As librarians were carried along by the new fears of technological and economic backwardness, libraries were reconceptualised as mechanisms of business and industrial education, 'arsenals in which the producers may forge their implements of knowledge', as the Library Association Record rather unfortunately expressed it in 1918.[9]

---

7 J. D. Stewart (ed.), Report on the municipal library system of London and the Home Counties (London, 1925). See also Library Association Record NS 3 (1925), 141–3.

8 L. S. Jast, 'The library outlook: an address to municipal library assistants', Library Association Record 14 (1912), 35–6.

9 Editorial, Library Association Record 20 (1918), 5.

For a while, new forms of library service, science and technical libraries, commercial libraries and information bureaux, stimulated some outreach developments. It suddenly became *de rigueur* for librarians to be out addressing businessmen's associations on the services the library could offer. The exclusive preoccupation with economic development soon ran its course, and by 1920 the backlash had begun. Some semblance of pre-war 'normality' returned, albeit a strained normality. Libraries struggled to restore suspended outreach efforts, and the movement as a whole toiled to regain the sense characteristic of the pre-war years of being on the verge of new opportunities. Some activities, such as published annual reports, never really reappeared. Catalogues were often superseded by single sheets, short select class lists, or pamphlets like the much-praised Leeds *What to read* series. Re-establishing library bulletins was painfully slow: only from the mid-1920s was the trickle of reappearances swelled by a flow of new launches. Links with local associations creaked back into life. The London survey of 1924 suggested that of seventy-seven libraries, sixteen provided for university extension lectures, eighteen for local societies and twenty for other bodies.[10]

Exhibitions were the aspect of library work that perhaps recovered most. Space was still a problem (the London survey indicated that while twenty-nine libraries held exhibitions, forty-nine did not, mostly through want of space[11]), but by the mid-1920s the London libraries were once again a hive of exhibition activity, and the provincial centres and the new county library services were following suit. As before the war, topics and approaches were extremely varied. Half-centenary anniversaries of the establishment of municipal libraries provided one new theme. Exhibitions were contributed to local events, civic weeks or health weeks. Some localities sought to establish a more regular cycle of exhibitions, such as Walthamstow's annual book cover exhibition, or experimented with coupling exhibitions with high-profile public lectures.

The 1919 Act did not change the legal position of library lectures. Nevertheless, lectures made a relatively rapid comeback, developing in those places where they had been maintained through the war, being reintroduced where they had temporarily been abandoned, and also expanding into fresh territory, including the new county library services. By the later 1920s the survey for the Public Libraries Committee indicated that lectures were provided in over half the metropolitan boroughs, and in between a third and a quarter of county or municipal boroughs and urban districts (in all 111 authorities out of

10 Stewart, *Report on the municipal library system.*
11 *Ibid.*

375). Many of these were substantial courses, with admission of one shilling or sixpence, aimed attracting an educated middle-class audience. Islington had four lecture halls generating an income of over £1,000, and at Coventry the library progressed from co-operating with a local society to inaugurating its own successful series. However, notwithstanding healthy initial surpluses, by the later 1920s more and more were slipping into deficit.

By this time a major competitor to lectures had appeared in the form of radio 'talks'. However, despite the enthusiastic advocacy of close co-operation between libraries and radio from figures such as R. S. Lambert of the BBC Adult Education Section, the radio had relatively little impact on library outreach before 1930. Croydon and Liverpool pioneered broadcasts of radio transmissions within the library in the early 1920s, and a handful of libraries organised radio discussion groups. Indeed, by 1930 Coventry was hosting seventy-eight post-talk discussions, with an aggregate attendance of 1,047. But, practical problems apart, there was a good deal of resistance to the kind of centralised provision inherent in such initiatives. In many respects, therefore, perhaps the most significant impact radio had on outreach in the twenties was in the opportunities it created for library propaganda. As the 1920s progressed, Library Association nominated speakers began to appear with increasing frequency.

The LA's links with the BBC indicate that it was finally reacting to one of the most enduring criticisms of it, its failure to operate as a campaigning organisation. Although before 1914 it kept outreach on the agenda, the Association had been extremely tardy in taking positive action. The only real pre-war development was an attempt in the mid-1900s to encourage individual librarians to intervene more actively in the press. It was not until 1921 that the LA finally established a Publicity Committee, and even then it did so rather reluctantly. Thereafter, the Association did finally begin, slowly, to address the public relations needs of the movement, mounting, for example, a 'press campaign' on the importance of libraries for education, and publishing propaganda leaflets for bulk purchase and distribution by libraries. Press cuttings on library issues were monitored and responses from the library movement organised where this was deemed appropriate.

This activity did reflect a broader shift in attitudes in the 1920s. Promoted by events like the 1921 LA 'Publicity Exhibition', 'Advertising', a concept hitherto almost entirely absent from library outreach, became almost a watchword. In 1925 Bolton Public Library distributed 20,000 bookmarks advertising library services. By this time several libraries were clearly developing a kind of 'wayside pulpit', with posters presenting quotes of key supporters on the value of the public library. Nevertheless, before 1930 such activities were the exception not the norm.

Overall, the 1920s brought a broader commitment to library outreach only half pushed through. Despite the developments discussed above, the library movement was never able to establish itself as the acknowledged centre of communal intellectual life. Enquiries and reports continued to be preoccupied with questions of internal administration. Indeed it is hard to avoid a sense that as the twenties progressed there was an inexorable narrowing of the dominant conception of the role of the library to an element in a system of education, especially adult education. Certainly, just below the surface lurked a profound unease at the demands of library outreach, nicely encapsulated by the concluding phrase of the *Library Association Record*'s grudging review of Lionel McColvin's *Library extension work* (1927)[12] – 'publicity can be overdone'.[13]

12 L. McColvin, *Library extension work and publicity* (London, 1927).
13 *Library Association Record* NS 5 (1927), 135.

7

Public library outreach and extension
1930–2000

DAVE MUDDIMAN

Although by 1930 the building blocks of the British public library were well in place, many questions remained about the level and extent of its social engagement. Traditionalists argued against an overt societal role: in their view, the public library should remain a limited, passive, book-based service aimed at the individual reader, 'without the clutter of social reform, moral reform, literary reform and all the other reforms'.[1] Progressives, in contrast, envisaged a wider public library: in 1927 the authors of the Kenyon Report urged that libraries should become an 'engine of great potentiality for state welfare' and 'the centre of the intellectual life of the area which [they serve]'.[2] *Outreach* (the provision of services beyond the physical entity of the library building) and *extension* (the development of library-related activities over and above the core provision of books)[3] became important mechanisms in this progressive project. Over time they came to embody the ambitions of those librarians committed to harnessing the public library to bring about the good society in twentieth-century Britain. This chapter thus examines the ideas, practices and influence of outreach and extension, and it assesses the degree to which they have been accepted as legitimate models of public library service. It seeks to explain why the wider public library has never been fully realised and it considers the consequences of this failure for the social identity of the public library movement.

---

1 W. A. Munford, 'The public library idea', *Library Association Record* 57 (1955), 350.
2 Board of Education, Public Libraries Committee, *Report on public libraries in England and Wales* (London, 1927), 37–9 (The Kenyon Report).
3 Straightforward definitions of outreach and extension are adopted here for purposes of clarity. However, historically, the definition of each term has led to much confusion: writers have tended to include outreach within their definitions of extension and vice-versa. See A. Black and D. Muddiman, *Understanding community librarianship: the public library in postmodern Britain* (Aldershot, 1997), 19.

Libraries for all: outreach, special services and the welfare state

Outreach has always enjoyed a wide measure of support among public librarians when it has been presented as a means of overcoming physical impediments to voluntary library use. Writing in 1927, McColvin argued that the developing public library service could be much improved by the delivery of books to readers unable to reach library buildings; for example the geographically remote, those who worked long hours, and the sick and the disabled. He claimed that 'it does not matter how we get books to [such readers], and no possible means of distribution should be overlooked', and proposed measures such as delivery to homes by tramcars; the use of outside volunteers and 'distributing agencies'; deposit collections in guilds and workplaces; and reading aloud to the sick and the blind.[4] Many librarians supported these views. The 1933 Library Association Conference at Harrogate was marked by a series of debates about services beyond the walls of the library – to hospitals, prisons and seafarers, and 'the distribution of books through voluntary bodies.'[5] Pioneering initiatives were inaugurated. In 1927 Worthing public library introduced a hospital deposit collection and by 1933 this practice had been taken up by thirty authorities nationwide.[6] In 1931 Manchester commissioned a 'bibliobus', the first truly mobile service targeted at poorly served areas of the city, and five such vehicles were in service in England by 1939.[7] In 1938 the first public library prison service – at Mollesby Bay, Suffolk – was opened.[8] In 1940, County Durham initiated the first deposit collection in a local authority elderly people's home, although it was left to McColvin's own authority – Westminster – to develop the first comprehensive housebound readers' delivery service in 1947/8.[9]

In the 1950s and 1960s such initiatives multiplied and, attaining some kind of critical mass, they coalesced into the 'mobile and special' services which became a common feature of the public library scene. Development took time. Basic standards of services in these fields were slow to develop: they were, ironically, almost completely ignored by the McColvin Report, and the

---

4 L. R. McColvin, *Library extension work and publicity* (London, 1927), 55.

5 See *Library Association Record* 3rd ser. 3 (1933), Conference Supplement.

6 R. Sturt, 'Hospital libraries in England and Wales: a history', in M. Going (ed.), *Hospital libraries*, 2nd edn (London, 1973), 31.

7 C. R. Eastwood, *Mobile libraries and other library transport* (London, 1967), 36.

8 G. Bramley, *Outreach: library services for the institutionalised, the elderly and the physically handicapped* (London, 1978), 62.

9 M. J. Lewis, 'History, development, change', in J. Ryder (ed.), *Library services to housebound people* (London, 1987), 5.

1964 Public Library Act established only a general duty to provide a 'comprehensive' service. Turf wars with voluntary agencies, social services, the prison service and health authorities over responsibility for both the financing and the operation of outreach services also hindered development. Nevertheless, by the 1960s, a majority of public library services had incorporated into their mainstream provision a series of mobile services, prison and hospital services to local institutions and a housebound reader service, usually operated in part by volunteers. By 1962 there were an estimated seventy-nine urban and 199 county mobile vehicles in the UK;[10] a 1966 survey found that 67% of public library authorities provided deposit collections at elderly people's centres;[11] a 1968 survey of prisons in Scotland found that all were supported by local authority libraries.[12] Only in hospitals did little progress appear to have been made: a King's Fund survey in 1959 found that in only thirty out of 157 hospitals in north-west England did patients receive services from the public library, and it highlighted major problems of lack of co-ordination and unevenness of provision.[13]

In general, the final thirty years of the twentieth century saw the increasing institutionalisation and professionalisation of this mode of outreach. Legislation such as the Chronically Sick and Disabled Persons Act of 1970 and the Prison and Borstal Rules (1964) has underpinned the permanence and funding of special services. By 1999 all UK prisons were served by local library authorities and 93% of UK local authorities offered housebound reader services.[14] At national level, librarians developed special interest groups relevant to these services, and some journals, such as *The Book Trolley*, became key organs in the dissemination of information and expertise. In addition, the Library Association was instrumental in developing a whole series of guidelines and standards for good practice in these areas of outreach. Some of these, such as those relevant to prisons, are subsequently being utilised in the implementation of service level agreements with the Home Office, local authority Social Services departments and Health Authorities.[15] Moreover, in recent years, mounting concern with the social exclusion of disabled and elderly people and the need to respond to the Disability Discrimination Act (1995) have resulted in a revival

10 Eastwood, *Mobile libraries*, 38.
11 Lewis, 'History, development, change', 10.
12 M. Hunter, 'Libraries in Scottish prisons', *The Book Trolley* 2 (1968), 58–60.
13 Sturt, 'Hospital libraries', 55–7.
14 See the survey in D. Muddiman *et al.*, *Open to all? The public library and social exclusion*, 3 vols. (London, 2000), vol. 2, 8–32.
15 See R. Collis and L. Boden (eds.), *Guidelines for prison libraries*, 2nd edn (London, 1997); and L. Hopkins, 'Prison library services: the public library authorities perspective', *Public Library Journal* 9 (1994), 159–61.

of innovation in the shape of partnership projects designed to overcome inter-agency barriers as well as those of access.[16]

Nevertheless, the claim made by Lewis that 'welfare library services . . . are often regarded as the Cinderellas of public library provision'[17] clearly has some elements of truth and is still reflected, as she suggests, in poor resources, status and transport facilities. Services to some disadvantaged social groups, such as people with mental handicaps, remain seriously underdeveloped[18] and prison and hospital library services remain hampered by difficulties of funding, professional perception and inter-agency co-operation. Many deposit collections and housebound services still depend disproportionately on philanthropy and volunteer support through agencies such as the Women's Royal Voluntary Service, and the services provided to most physically disadvantaged readers are less than comprehensive. In this sense, public library special services typify many other peripheral areas of the British welfare state: they are only marginally established as core service provision. In the year 2000 'special' services remained just so, and McColvin's vision of access for all had only been imperfectly realised.

The good citizen: library extension, education and culture

Although equality of access preoccupied the developers of UK library systems throughout the twentieth century, it left unresolved many questions about the range of services to be offered, their purpose, and the extent of take up and usage. In the 1930s, a significant number of reformist librarians, dissatisfied with low usage levels and a narrow range of book-based services, began to advocate a major *extension* of the scope of library activities in order to reach out to the perceived 60% of the population who were non-users.[19] To some degree, these librarians took their cue from the Kenyon Report, which had argued that 'the principle underlying the library service is that it exists for the training of the good citizen'.[20] For Eric Leyland, writing in 1938, this necessitated the creation of a 'wider public library', where books were a means rather than

16 A well-documented example is the Gloucestershire Visually Impaired People's Service, a partnership between the County Library, *Share the vision*, and the RNIB. See Capital Planning Information, *The Gloucestershire project: services for visually impaired people* (Stamford, 1998).
17 Lewis, 'History, development, change', 17.
18 D. Strong, 'Services to people with mental handicaps', in J. Ryder, *Library services to housebound people* (London, 1987), 160–84.
19 The figure is used by E. Leyland, *The wider public library* (London, 1938), 6.
20 Board of Education, Public Libraries Committee, *Report*, 39.

an end and the library adopted an educative rather than a passive stance. This approach would involve the transformation of the library into a 'cultural centre, which would include lounges, meeting rooms, lecture theatres with projection facilities, a local information bureau and a local collection and/or museum'.[21]

Perhaps the most successful practical exponent of this vision was Edward Sydney, Librarian of the London Borough of Leyton between 1928 and 1956. In an area Sydney himself described as a 'lower middle class to working class East London dormitory with few slums, no mansions and a steady and sturdy collection of ordinary folks', Sydney set about transforming the library services of the borough. In 1934 a new library and 'cultural centre' was opened at Church Lane, Leytonstone, which was 'planned and equipped to provide a library service and meeting place for local cultural and educational activities'.[22] The library almost exactly prefigured Leyland's vision of the wider public library – it contained a lecture hall and two other meeting rooms, and was equipped with the latest state of the art film, audio-visual and exhibition equipment. Almost immediately, and surprisingly to some traditionalist librarians, the integrated library and cultural centre developed into an enormous success. The library developed into a centre for discussion groups and lectures, drama, concerts and gramophone recitals, film and exhibitions. As Sydney's cumulative figures, produced in a report of 1948 show, over a thirteen-year period average attendances at these events were very high – around thirty per discussion group and eighty per film show, even though many events were subject to problems and cancellation during the wartime blitz.[23] In addition, by 1939, some two dozen independent local organisations were regularly using the library, including the WEA, Essex County Council for adult classes and the 'electricity department for the demonstration of electrical cookery equipment'.[24]

Sydney's innovations were replicated after 1945 in locations such as Dagenham, Leicester, St Pancras and Sheffield, and especially in Swindon under another enthusiast, Harold Jolliffe.[25] In the 1950s 'extension activities' became part of the normal practice of some UK library authorities, although they undoubtedly remained marginal in a lot more. In terms of their content, library extension programmes were usually a hybrid mix of liberal adult

21 Leyland, *Wider public library*, 184.
22 E. Sydney, 'Adult education and the public library' *Library Association Record* 48 (1946), 275–9.
23 London Borough of Leyton Libraries Department, *Opportunities 1948–9* (London, 1948).
24 Sydney, 'Adult education', 275–9.
25 Jolliffe went on to write a widely read manual on the topic. See H. Jolliffe, *Public library extension activities* (London, 1962).

education, populism, high-minded citizenship and, perhaps most strongly, cultural enlightenment. Lecture and film programmes usually adopted the formula of blending topics of contemporary interest and popular appeal with others which opened up the world of academia, high culture and the arts.[26] Sydney's account of wartime drama at Leytonstone, for example, tells of the middlebrow world of amateur dramatics spiced up with a Shakespeare season in 1942/3 sponsored by the Council for Encouragement of Music and the Arts.[27] Music, however, seems to have been almost entirely dominated by an agenda which sought to bring classical music to the masses – it was not until the 1960s that 'jazz, folk and popular' music began to appear in programmes of recitals or concerts. However, high culture was to some degree counterbalanced by worthy manifestations of popular culture – exhibitions and displays, for example, often linked reading and popular practical activities such as do-it-yourself.[28]

Sydney himself argued that public libraries needed to adopt an active and educative stance and 'eventually provide training for every citizen to make his fullest possible contribution to the common welfare'.[29] However, such benign public service evangelism was not always what it seemed. Its 'goal was to wean the public away from the pub; Hollywood films; cheap detective fiction and popular songs'.[30] It never sought to engage with and support popular culture on its own terms: in the end, it sought to control and improve it. For this reason, perhaps above all, the 'extension' project of the mid-century public library was doomed to fail: librarians and educators were, in the end, powerless in the face of the commercial cultures of ITV, Hollywood, and rock and roll. Extension activities were gradually, as a result, scaled down, and although they continued to be popular in localities like Swindon, attendances never again attained the levels of the Leytonstone experiment. By the 1970s, with the notable exception of children's events, they had in the main been redefined as 'cultural' activities and become largely the preserve of middle-class provincial elites.

In spite of this, a number of contemporary librarians have continued to emphasise the educational mission of the public library and have attempted to develop initiatives shorn of the baggage of middle-class culture. In the 1970s, for example, a majority of public library authorities participated in adult literacy campaigns organised by the BBC and the government's Adult Literacy

26 Ibid., 92.
27 Sydney, 'Adult education', 277.
28 Jolliffe, Public library extension activities, 267–91 and 175.
29 E. Sydney 'The future public library service: paragraphs 1–11 of the proposals', Library Association Record 48 (1946), 120.
30 G. Mulgan, 'Culture', in D. Marquand and A. Seldon (eds.), The ideas that shaped post-war Britain (London, 1996), 197.

Unit, and although activity in this field declined in the eighties, some individual authorities continued to develop services.[31] More recently, attempts have been made to link libraries closely to government policies which promote lifelong learning and the 'learning society', for example through the development of open learning packs, open networks and ICT study support centres.[32] The 'People's Network' programme for providing internet access in all public libraries takes this further by envisaging for the 'transformation of libraries' and their repositioning at the centre of a lifelong learning revolution.[33] However, recent survey evidence suggests that this will not be easy to achieve: study support centres and other library-based educational initiatives appear to remain hampered by familiar problems of short-termism, poor funding and shortage of skilled staff.[34] Even in the information age, the wider public library remains a transient and marginal phenomenon.

Libraries for social change: outreach, community librarianship and social exclusion

Although outreach was by the mid-twentieth century widely accepted as a means of overcoming physical impediment to library use, the public library movement was much more circumspect about reaching out to those excluded by class or culture. It is true that in the 1930s the Library Association had participated in a National Book Appeal for the Unemployed and helped disseminate some 100,000 donated books to 300 centres for the unemployed; moreover a small number of librarians and library authorities had organised deposit collections and even special extension classes.[35] However, the dominant professional sentiment was undoubtedly resistant to treating the unemployed as 'a special and inferior class' and argued that unemployed people 'should be encouraged to use branch libraries and centres'.[36] This view was applied, in the 1950s and 1960s, to many other marginal social groups for whom the public

31 See G. Bramley, *Adult literacy, basic skills and libraries* (London, 1991).
32 See L. Greenhalgh and K. Worpole, *Libraries in a world of cultural change* (London, 1995), 100–11.
33 Library and Information Commission, *New library, the people's network* (London, 1997), 2.
34 See Muddiman *et al.*, *Open to all?*, vol. 2, 8–32 and 107–27.
35 See 'The national book appeal for the unemployed. A review of the first year's work', *Library Association Record*, 4th ser. 2 (1935), 471–3; and the reports in *Ibid.*, 156–7.
36 This comment was made by a Miss Browning at a County Libraries section meeting at the Library Association Harrogate Conference in 1933. See *Library Association Record*, 3rd ser. 3 (1933), conference supplement xvii. Similar sentiments are expressed by library staff in J. Barugh and R. Woodhouse, *Public libraries and organisations serving the unemployed* (London, 1987).

library provided little of interest, such as poorly educated industrial workers, people with reading difficulties and newly arriving immigrants. Such social groups tended to be ignored by libraries and regarded as invisible in the public library universe. The result, by the late 1960s, was a disturbingly low level of library use in working-class areas, with membership figures as low as 8% in some localities for unskilled manual workers and their families.[37]

Partly as a response to this state of affairs, in the 1970s attitudes began to change. A significant minority of public librarians – some influenced by American developments in the 1960s and others responding to the general *Zeitgeist* – recognised the need to 'add their expertise to the struggle against those social ills which beset society – the evils of poverty, discrimination, inequality and crime'. They began to criticise the status quo and advocate a proactive and socially engaged 'community' librarianship. A series of landmark texts and reports argued that the disadvantaged were the problem of the library and that public libraries urgently needed to adopt a community rather than an institutional orientation.[38] A Library Association 'Community Services' group was established in order to focus attention on 'the development of appropriate library and information provision in deprived areas'.[39] Outreach and extension were both seen as a key means of operationalising this new 'community' approach. Writers on community librarianship argued that mobile services, deposit collections and educational and cultural activities should no longer be restricted to the disabled, the institutionalised and children, but that they should be extended to all who experienced social and cultural barriers to library use. Outreach was argued to be an appropriate method of service delivery for social groups as diverse as Black and ethnic minorities, single homeless people, and gay men and lesbians. Indeed, some went on to argue, as a logical extension of these ideas, that outreach might ultimately constitute the *dominant* mode of delivery of library services, largely replacing a buildings-based operation. The public library would, as a consequence, become 'deinstitutionalised' and much more closely in tune with the needs of its community / communities.[40]

---

37 See, for example M. Devereux, 'Libraries in working class areas', *Assistant Librarian* (1972), 170–172; and P. Jordan, 'Social class, race relations and the public library', *Assistant Librarian* 65, no. 3 (1972), 38–41. The survey figure is from B. Luckham, *The library in society* (London, 1971), 26.

38 See in particular: Department of Education and Science, *The libraries' choice* (London, 1978); and P. Coleman, *Whose problem? The public library and the disadvantaged* (Newcastle under Lyme, 1981).

39 Library Association, Community Services Group, 'Group rules (constitution)', *Community Librarian* 3 (1986), 18–19.

40 See W. Martin, *Community librarianship: changing the face of public libraries* (London, 1989); and J. Vincent, *An introduction to community librarianship* (Newcastle under Lyme, 1986) for the clearest statements of these ideas.

In practical terms, these ideas did result in significant shifts in the orientation of library services in some local authorities. From 1970 in the London Borough of Lambeth, branch libraries were progressively reorganised into 'neighbourhood groups' and librarians given responsibility for services to neighbourhoods rather than the administration of buildings. Outreach, including urban mobiles, deposit collections and associated educational activities, were rapidly expanded and offered to myriad community groups and meeting places. Outreach became in Lambeth the preferred mode of delivery: by 1977 the borough was offering outreach collections and activities to over 500 community groups and locations.[41] Other urban authorities developed variations on this model: Manchester remodelled its inner city branch libraries as community resource centres and meeting places, and replaced branch with community librarians, set up a special fund for outreach initiatives and developed outreach collections targeted at Black and ethnic minority communities. Such initiatives were replicated, in diluted form, in many locations in the early 1980s – Bradford, for example, operated a high-profile refurbished double-decker bus which brought children's books, books in Asian community languages and a rights and advice service to deprived inner city estates. Progressive county authorities such as Leicestershire and Derbyshire developed a range of initiatives targeted at rural deprivation, and a range of service innovations, especially targeted at unemployed youth, were inaugurated in urban Scotland.[42]

Initiatives such as these have undoubtedly left their mark on the public library movement. In 1997, a study of the work of over a hundred public library outreach projects concluded that they represented a growing awareness on the part of the public library of its community development role.[43] However, the weight of evidence suggests that community librarianship was (and is) an uneven and limited phenomenon. Even when they were most numerous in the early 1980s, many public library outreach initiatives were time limited, funded by grant aid and operating relatively independently of the core book-lending services and, most importantly, the mainstream library service budget. After

---

41 For discussions of outreach in Lambeth see J. Hill, *Children are people: the librarian in the community* (London, 1973); and J. Armour, 'The why and how of outreach: reach out or be forced out', in W. Martin (ed.), *Library services to the disadvantaged* (London, 1989), 83–94.

42 For a good overview of the range of activity developed in the early 1980s see R. Astbury (ed.), *Putting people first: some new perspectives on community librarianship* (Newcastle under Lyme, 1989). A. Hasson, 'Reaching out', in M. Kinnell and P. Sturges (eds.), *Continuity and innovation in the public library: the development of a social institution* (London, 1996), 148–66, provides an overview of outreach in Scotland.

43 F. Matarasso, *Learning development: an introduction to the social impact of libraries* (London, 1998), 23–26.

1985, financial cutbacks together with a new ideological focus on 'heritage', the core service, marketing, and performance measurement severely constrained innovation targeted at the disadvantaged. Even in Lambeth, outreach was heavily curtailed in the late 1980s and early 1990s, and by this time it was clear that 'community' librarianship was being used as a label for any and every form of library community contact.[44] In 1999 a survey of all UK library authorities estimated that only 16% of them had developed consistent and comprehensive responses to the problems of disadvantage and social exclusion.[45]

Conclusion

It is currently fashionable to promote the public library as an institution of social inclusion on the assumption that it provides free and universal access to recorded knowledge. However, this review of twentieth-century outreach and extension activity suggests that a more realistic appraisal of the public library's social identity is needed. Although progressive librarians have successively articulated visions of a 'wider public library', by and large these have failed to gain the support of the whole public library movement. Except briefly in the most progressive periods of twentieth-century British history, outreach and extension have as a result been confined to the periphery of the public library service, especially when their purpose has been social or cultural change. Outreach has only ever been fully accepted by the library profession as a means of ironing out obvious physical and geographical inequities of access, and it has been regarded with circumspection when it has threatened significantly to extend the library's public or change its institutional culture. This marginalisation of an 'extended' public service is undoubtedly symptomatic of what Dunleavy conceptualises as a 'low welfare state' in twentieth-century Britain: the limited provision of uniform and heavily formalised public services.[46] More specifically, it clearly reflects the identity of a public institution which, contrary to popular myth, is at root socially conservative and culturally constrained.

44 See Black and Muddiman, *Understanding community librarianship*, 93–129.
45 See Muddiman *et al.*, *Open to all?*, vol. 2, 24–7.
46 P. Dunleavy, 'The United Kingdom: paradoxes of an ungrounded statism', in F. G. Castles (ed.), *The comparative history of public policy* (London, 1989), 242–91.

8

Public library services for children

DEBBIE DENHAM

... we must produce original thinkers. School and college education train the mind so that it becomes an efficient machine for the *purpose* of thinking. The process is, however, more or less a compulsory one and reading done during its course is done for the most part as a task. This is not the kind of reading conducive to original thought, for that must be voluntary, even as thought is voluntary. All our great thinkers have been great readers, – voluntary readers.[1]

Introduction

This chapter considers the development of public library services to children and young people, paying particular attention to staffing, the provision of resources, teenage library users and links between libraries and schools. The provision of public library services to children, particularly in the early days, is well documented. Two key texts which have proved to be useful sources of anecdotal and statistical evidence are Gwendolyn Rees's *Libraries for children: a history and bibliography*[2] and the more recent *Library services for young people in England and Wales 1830–1970* by Alec Ellis.[3] Since 1971 there have been few monographs that document the recent development of services except for *Focus on the child* by Elkin and Lonsdale,[4] which covers issues such as child development and literacy as well as providing examples and commentary on recent library developments. The dichotomy between the role of public libraries in education and their place as a provider of entertainment is considered throughout.

1 G. Rees, *Libraries for children: a history and bibliography* (London, 1924), 10.
2 Rees, *Libraries for children*.
3 A. Ellis, *Library services for young people in England and Wales 1830–1970* (Oxford, 1971).
4 J. Elkin and R. Lonsdale, *Focus on the child: libraries, literacy and learning* (London, 1996).

Pioneering libraries for children

Prior to the passing of the 1850 Public Library Act few children had the opportunity to use a library, either for borrowing books or for reference purposes. Those libraries for children which were in existence were to be found in schools or Sunday schools and were supported by donations from agencies such as the Religious Tract Society or the Society for the Promotion of Christian Knowledge (SPCK). The children of the middle and upper classes who attended private schools would have had access to collections of books and other material to support the curriculum but children from the poorer classes of society had little chance of finding materials to support their intellectual development. There were examples of mechanics' institutes operating in the metropolitan districts which provided books for the children of their members, but high fee levels restricted membership to skilled craftsmen and the 'middle and respectable classes'.[5] The development of 'ragged schools' in the early part of the nineteenth century began to provide some opportunities for young children to undertake formal education, although the disappointing statistics testify to the fact that the majority of children (60%) were not able to attend and of those who did a considerable proportion did not attend for more than a year. Such short periods of schooling were unlikely to have a significant impact on these children. Many of these schools made some library provision but the Sunday schools of the early nineteenth century had collections which were generally superior to those held by day schools. During the 1850s the increasing number of secular schools began to mark the decline of the Sunday schools.

The 1850 Public Library Act provided the opportunity for local councils to make books available to children and young people as well as adults. Early provision in a limited number of authorities consisted of small collections of books for children in the main adult library. It was not until 1861 that the first separate children's room was opened, in Manchester, although for reference purposes only and for the exclusive use of boys. This was during the time of the cotton famine and may well have been a response to large numbers of destitute children with time to fill. Chroniclers of the early development of children's libraries, such as Gwendolyn Rees, provide evidence of libraries with an array of services and resources which were used by large numbers of children. Particularly evocative is Rees's picture of children queuing outside the library, waiting patiently until there is sufficient room for them to be allowed

5 Ellis, *Library services for young people*, 1.

entry. This picture was nowhere near as idyllic as it might appear at first, for until 1919 these services were largely limited to the metropolitan districts. The exemplary services noted by Rees were those which stood out. They represented a relatively small number of, admittedly high-quality, examples and were by no means widespread even in metropolitan districts. The resources available for children were also severely limited and the number of volumes retained by individual libraries was insignificant in relation to the total number of children living in any borough. In 1871 Birmingham's collection of 456 books for children was woefully inadequate for the population of about 69,000 children living in the city at the time.

Reading accounts of these early services it is evident that they were the result of the social and political concerns of the time; they were part of the middle-class effort to enlighten and educate the working classes, coupled with a desire to ensure that they learnt correct behaviour. A considerable number of rules concerning cleanliness, behaviour and the appropriate way to handle books were of real concern to the providers of the early library services to children. The rules on cleanliness could have made it difficult for children from poorer working-class backgrounds to avail themselves of the libraries' facilities; there were enlightened authorities which provided sinks and overalls for children's use.

A raft of legislation designed to protect children, particularly the offspring of the poorer, working classes, supplemented the public library and education legislation of the second half of the nineteenth century. The middle classes and religious organisations had long been concerned about the fate of young children working in the industrial cities of England, and the development of a public library system and a formal education system occurred at a time when legislation was developed limiting where and for how long children could work, through a series of Factory Acts.

The children's public library agenda in the early years was largely focused on the provision of a range of material to support children in their educational and intellectual development. Despite this, there is evidence that children were encouraged in the basics: to become life-long readers and to gain all-important literacy skills. Much of the early provision was undertaken in conjunction with schools, with teachers helping in the selection of suitable books for the library and through close work with school boards, which in many instances provided some funding to support the work of the public library.

It is important to remember that access to libraries was limited to children in the immediate local area, with the difficulties of travel in the Victorian period making it impossible for children to go far in the evenings. Although many metropolitan authorities had exemplary library services for children these were often confined to the central library and larger branches; the provision was by no means widespread throughout the authority. Other restrictions based on age and gender also applied in the early years of library services to children. All the early services required children to be of an age where they could read before they were allowed library tickets, so children were expected to be at least seven or eight before it was felt they could benefit from the provision made by libraries.

The restrictions of the rate allocation held back the development of libraries in the Victorian period, although significant educational legalisation and the laws designed to protect children had provided some initial impetus. The rate limit affected all public library provision; many authorities benefited from the philanthropic grants from Andrew Carnegie in order to erect vast new library buildings, but did not have sufficient funds to equip them with a wide range of books and other material. Children's libraries suffered in particular, because they were generally perceived as the 'Cinderella' of the library service, a luxury. Service developments had to be rooted within the mainstream of the adult public library service before similar provisions were seen as necessary for children. This perception of children's libraries continued well into the twentieth century. By the end of the nineteenth century forty libraries in England and Wales had separate children's rooms and an additional sixty or so of the hundreds of libraries in existence had some provision for young people. The slow growth in literacy rates during this period may further have impressed on public library service providers that there was little to be gained from expanding services to include children, although the exponential growth in school attendance and the raising of the upper age limits for school attendance in the last thirty years of the nineteenth century ensured a growing market for children's library services.

The early years of the twentieth century saw a 'mushroom growth' in the provision of library services to children and young people.[6] By 1914 it was maintained that 62% of the population in England had access to public library facilities and 46% in Wales.[7] There was still considerable resistance within the public library movement itself to the establishment of separate children's libraries, even though there was little desire to cater for children within the main adult library where minimum age limits of sixteen years were not uncommon.

---

6 Rees, *Libraries for children*, 9.
7 Ellis, *Library services for young people*, 43.

The First World War severely curtailed the development of public libraries for adults and children. The commandeering of public libraries, the enlisting of male members of staff in the armed services, the need for economies in book funds and severe paper shortages making it difficult to acquire adequate books for the service all played their part in reducing service provision, including children's services, in the majority of authorities. Throughout the 1920s and 1930s the development of children's libraries continued to be haphazard. Innovative service developments were taking place but these were within individual authorities and it was unusual for ideas to be shared between authorities. The abolition of the penny rate in 1919 had provided opportunities for increased expenditure on libraries, but following the devastation of the First World War it is easy to envisage that services for children would not have been the first priority of the majority of library authorities. However, a growing interest in children's libraries and librarianship in the professional press was evident during the 1920s. Rees published a thesis on libraries for children,[8] and articles in significant journals such as *The Librarian and Book World* and *Library World* appeared in 1924.

Services to children in rural areas became more common from about 1915 onwards with a number of county schemes making books available to small, isolated rural communities, despite the fact that this was a time of war and services in metropolitan districts were contracting. It is evident that the number of books available in individual communities was very low: 'at Bulley, 27 books were provided for 57 villagers, 17 of whom were children'.[9] After the First World War increasing numbers of authorities provided lending facilities for children and separate libraries or reading rooms, and it was finally becoming common for children to have free access to the book collections, although this did cause some problems in the supply of adequate materials for the needs of all children. Open access proved to be an important promotional tool considerably increasing the use of the collections. The growing number of open access collections also stimulated interest in how these books should be arranged and catalogued for children's use. The Dewey Decimal System became the norm for the classification of non-fiction books for children and there were many examples of the categorisation of fiction, where schemes tended to focus on organising fiction into subject and/or age-related groupings. It was uncommon to find books arranged in alphabetical order until the later decades of the twentieth century.

8 Rees, *Libraries for children*.
9 Ellis, *Library services for young people*, 48.

Although affected by the economic stringencies of the 1920s and 1930s, public library services to children advanced throughout this period. A significant development was the growing numbers of librarians who were employed to work with children. This presented opportunities for increased co-operation with schools and for additional outreach and library-based activities to become the norm rather than the exception. More children were being reached by the library services of the day; it was estimated that, by 1926, 96.3% of the population of England and Wales lived in authorities that had elected to make library services available within their areas.[10] The 1930s saw a continuation of the lecture programmes and storytelling sessions that had been initiated in earlier decades, and reading circles for children were introduced with the purpose of further instilling a love of reading amongst library visitors. The need for an informal and welcoming environment was recognised from the earliest days of public library provision to children, when considerable attention was paid to providing the right atmosphere and furniture. Later in the 1920s areas were provided for smaller children and picture books stocked to cater for their reading needs.

The Second World War had a considerable impact on public library services for children: the obvious effect of paper shortages was a rise in the price of new books at a time when many authorities were, of necessity, cutting bookfunds and when there was a growing demand for reading materials because of the imposition of the blackout laws. There is considerable evidence of co-operation between library authorities, with books being moved from the inner city areas to county authorities to provide resources for the migration of evacuees moving from urban to rural areas. During this period children's librarians became increasingly keen to determine what children would like to read and there are examples of surveys of children's reading interests. These surveys tended to argue that different choices of reading materials were enjoyed by girls and boys, the former tending more towards school and domestic stories and the boys towards adventure stories.

The 1940s saw an increased interest being taken in the preservation of children's books. Although this work had been mooted at the end of the nineteenth century it was the 1940s that saw a number of important collections being presented to public libraries. This interest has taken on an increased significance today, with growing numbers of scholars working in the field of children's literature. Questions of access and preservation have led to projects

10 Ellis, *Library services for young people*, 61.

like CHILDE, which use technology to digitise collections and make them available via the Internet[11].

Towards a modern library service for children

Library provision for children in the 1950s was fraught with arguments about the detrimental effects of television and the cinema on reading, and more particularly attributing falling issues and library use to these competitors. This was a time of rebuilding and regeneration and it took until 1950 before the majority of authorities were equivalent to their pre-war status. Few new libraries were built in this post-war period but attempts were made to encourage library use by removing some of the membership limits which had previously been imposed. It also became increasingly common for branch libraries to make provision for children.

The Public Library and Museum Act of 1964 enshrined the principle of library provision for children within a legislative framework; however, it proved difficult to determine what constituted a 'comprehensive and efficient' level of service provision for children's libraries or indeed for public libraries in general. The haphazard and varied development of children's libraries over the previous hundred years had provided some exemplars of both good and bad practice but this variation did not lend itself to a definitive notion of the core and additional services which should be provided by any individual borough.

The reorganisation of local authorities which began in the 1960s with the foundation of the Greater London Authority and continued into the late 1990s at sporadic intervals had various effects on the provision of library services to children. Early reorganisations tended to allow for economies of scale, with larger boroughs being made from smaller ones, and in London the added advantage of the Inner London Education Authority allowed for a good system of school libraries and support for their operation to be set up. The 1960s also saw considerable library development in the county councils, with new libraries being opened in a number of authorities and an acceptance that children's libraries were a natural part of any new developments. County councils still experienced difficulties in providing sufficient materials for children during school holiday periods; a number of large county authorities took this opportunity to instigate holiday mobile services to small village communities.

The development of new libraries during the 1960s was often led by the architectural tastes of the time; this was a period of large open-plan buildings.

11 *CHILDE* http://www.bookchilde.org (accessed on 24.01.01).

This did allow for children's library services to be fully integrated and to aid the removal of barriers within service provision but did not make it easy for activity sessions and group meetings to be held. The furniture and décor within children's libraries became increasingly tailored to the specific needs of children, particularly the under eights who had only recently been more actively encouraged to make use of libraries by the wide scale, though by no means total, eradication of lower age limits for library membership.

The concept of providing rewards to children for their reading achievements gathered momentum in the 1960s, with a number of authorities providing badges and certificates to children upon reading an agreed number of books or answering questions about their reading choices. At the end of the 1990s LaunchPad, an advocacy group for children's libraries, developed the first national event of this type, The Reading Safari. The 1960s also bore witness to growing numbers of local and regional book fairs and art festivals in which libraries took part. These activities have now become part of the mainstream of children's service provision.

The key targets for service provision in the 1960s were perceived as: the children of working-class families, who were less likely to borrow library books or be library members than the children of professional and middle-class parents; children in rural areas, who were still far behind the more innovative and widespread provision made in urban boroughs; and teenagers, particularly those who were less likely to continue at school beyond the compulsory leaving age. There was a general consensus that any of the added value services needed to be either educational or cultural in their focus. The production of in-house magazines and publicity materials continued in a number of authorities, and story hours were proving increasingly popular. It was during the 1960s that libraries first began to make a concerted effort to attract the under fives into libraries with a number of authorities offering storytimes for this target group.

The 1970s were years of exponential growth for children's library services. This was a time – the early 1970s at any rate – of reasonable economic stability and relatively high levels of funding for library services. The effects of such reports as that of the Bourdillon committee in 1962, which had made a clear case for children's services and the need for children's librarians, and of the various educational reports which had been produced during the previous decade, were at last bearing fruit. The number of children's librarians was growing and the extension activities undertaken by libraries were becoming increasingly diverse. Janet Hill's seminal work *Children are people*[12] described a plethora of

12 J. Hill, *Children are people: the librarian in the community* (London, 1973).

activities undertaken by staff at Lambeth libraries with children in a range of venues. The concept that the library should be taken to children and be firmly anchored in the local community, rather than the expectation that children would come to the library, took root. This concept of library work with children laid the foundations for a much more child-centred approach to this area of work that was to become a feature of the next thirty years of development. The 1970s witnessed considerable advances in service provision to a number of targeted groups, particularly teenagers, under fives, children with special needs and children from diverse cultural backgrounds. An increased range of multi-media resources was also being provided by libraries, and growing interest in resource-based learning within education provided the impetus for public libraries to provide additional resources to support book provision.

The 1980s was a time of economic recession and cutbacks in public library services. Children's libraries experienced significant reductions in staffing and resource budgets at a time when there was considerable educational reform which impacted on children's service provision. The advent of the GCSE examination in 1986 and the Education Reform Act of 1988, which introduced a National Curriculum, continued the move way from textbook teaching to more student-centred learning. This made considerable demands on the declining budgets of children's libraries. The Children's Act of 1989 also demonstrated the important role public libraries have to play in information provision to parents and carers as well as to children themselves. The siting of a childcare information bureau within the newly created Centre for the Child at Birmingham Central Library in the mid-1990s was an example of how seriously some authorities took this role.

The 1990s saw a significant pattern of local authority reorganisation and internal restructuring which again had a significant impact on public libraries. In particular the break up of large county authorities into smaller administrative districts, with larger towns and cities being made into individual authorities, caused a weakening of centralised services. The advantages of economy of scale were lost in many areas and this caused a decline in service provision in some cases. In spite of this, children's libraries continued to perform well. Loans of books continued to increase year on year until the year 2000.[13] This increase was set against a background of significant and long-term reorganisation, a period of declining book budgets, reductions in opening hours and falling numbers of staff working with children (down from 633 in 1998–9 to 617

13 *Library and information statistics unit*, http://www.lboro.ac.uk/departments/dils/lisu/list01/ (accessed on 24.01.02).

in 1999–2000). This occurred at a time when there was greater concern about standards and measuring the quality of service provision. It is difficult to assess the value of children's library services. Qualitative as well as quantitative data need to be gathered and evaluated.

From the mid-1980s onwards there was an exponential growth of the use of Information and Communications Technology (ICT) in libraries. The factors responsible for this growth included the introduction of increasingly cheap personal computers, a significant increase in the number of electronic resources available and the acceptance of the Internet as both a potential source of information and a communication medium. Children's librarians were amongst the first to see the potential of ICT within the public library service and there are a number of examples of libraries using BBC microcomputers in the mid-1980s. Growth in ICT provision in public libraries was steady throughout the 1990s but the implementation of the government-funded people's network led to an increased emphasis being placed in this area of service provision. There are many innovative examples during the 1990s of ICT use in children's libraries but they are by no means widespread. A survey carried out in 1997 found that there was 'disappointingly little use of ICT as a means of promoting literacy in public libraries'.[14] A further survey in 2000 identified that there had been little significant improvement in this although it was acknowledged that the lottery-funded training programme and grants for content development were likely to change this situation over the next few years. This is not to suggest that there are no examples of good practice in the use of ICT. The *Stories from the Web* project provided an innovative example of the full potential that can be achieved by ICT, as did the European-funded projects *Verity* and *Chilias*.[15] The problem as demonstrated by the *Chilias* project was sustainability in an era when much of the funding was project based and, therefore, by its nature for a limited period.

A new era for children's services dawned in the 1990s with the government's agenda for multi-agency working and social inclusion. Many multi-agency initiatives were designed to reach those on the fringes of society and, in the case of libraries, those who were non-traditional users. This made it increasingly possible for children's librarians to work with other local council departments, particularly education and social services. Libraries and education departments had a changing relationship throughout the twentieth century, and in the latter

14 D. Denham, 'Promotion', in J. Elkin and M. Kinnell, *A place for children* (London, 1997), 93.
15 G. Mynott, D. Denham and J. Elkin, 'A place for children revisited', *Journal of Library and Information Science* 33 (2001), 133–44.

half of the century many opportunities for collaborative working were missed. Although libraries generally had good links with local schools there was little opportunity for inter-departmental working at a strategic and policy level. This fact was highlighted by a survey of children's libraries carried out in 1995[16] which resulted in a renewed affirmation of the value and role of children's libraries whilst noting the inequitable provision made around the country. The findings of this were supported by the *Review of public library services in England and Wales* completed in the same year,[17] which, although not directly concerned with services to children, underlined the high value both the general public and library staff placed on library provision for children.

Staffing

The staffing of children's libraries came under consideration in the late nineteenth century. Early children's libraries were often staffed by janitors but it became increasingly evident that this was unsatisfactory, and there was a general recognition of the need for qualified staff who were interested in children and young people and could provide them with the support they needed in the use of resources. Libraries may have had separate rooms for children and a growing range of well-catalogued resources available but it is questionable how much use the majority of children could make of these without the expert guidance of a trained professional because the majority of collections were closed access.

As children's libraries developed, calls grew for trained staff to operate the service, a recognition by many that specialist skills were required, although the desire to appoint such staff was hampered by the lack of training courses available in Britain at the time. The children's librarians who were appointed continued to provide educational talks in addition to the selection of material and advice on its use. A few tentative storytelling sessions were begun in the most enlightened authorities. Many of these storytelling initiatives were planned events; however there was also a desire to offer impromptu sessions whenever a group of children were receptive to such an event.

Criticism has been levelled at the children's librarians of the mid decades of the twentieth century. As their numbers increased it was perceived that they

---

16 Department of National Heritage, *Investing in children: the future of library services for children and young people*. Library and Information Services Council (England) (London, 1995).
17 Aslib, *Review of the public library service in England and Wales for the Department of National Heritage*, Final Report (London, 1995).

were losing sight of their fundamental educative role as defined in the early days of service provision and were much too fond of the overly saccharine approach to their job which resulted in a perceived over-concentration on storytelling.[18] It was during the 1940s, however, that work with children became increasingly accepted as a viable and vital part of public librarianship. Yet despite a growing membership of the Association of Children's Librarians, rising from 600 in 1952 to 1,000 by 1959, there were few opportunities for training and development for children's librarians. By the end of the 1950s there was still a considerable proportion of authorities, almost 50%, which did not provide specialist children's librarians.

The 1960s were years of intense shortages of qualified staff in children's libraries, with few training opportunities available to those who wished to specialise in this field. In some cases this was attributed to the fact that posts were available but there were no suitable candidates to fill them. The first degree course for librarianship was accepted by the Council for National Academic Awards, at the Liverpool Polytechnic School of Librarianship, in 1970. This course included the study of children's libraries and literature, and child development. Many of the other library schools were to follow suit but from a period of relative strength at the beginning of the 1990s the study of children's librarianship and literature in the redefined schools of information studies began to decline. A new emphasis on the management of information and a crowded curriculum which needed to take account of technological developments linked to the decreasing number of posts available in the public library sector were important factors that contributed to a decline in education and training for children's librarianship at university level.

Reading for pleasure or for instruction? Children's fiction, non-fiction and other resources

The advent of the first 'Golden Age' of children's books in the 1860s, with authors such as Lewis Carroll, Charles Kingsley and George MacDonald, made available a growing body of high-quality imaginative literature. Libraries also had access to the growing numbers of non-fiction books that were being published, particularly in response to the widening school curriculum resulting from the 1870 Elementary Education Act. This did not mean, however, that there was enough material for librarians to be spoilt for choice. The difficulty in finding sufficient high-quality material for purchase meant that attention

---

18 Ellis, *Library services for young people*, 89.

was turned to the selection process, and bibliographical tools that could help in this process were actively sought. The dearth of printed books did not extend to the field of magazine publication for children, however; there were numerous titles on the market. During the 1930s children's libraries supplemented the numerous commercially available magazines by publishing their own: this was the advent of publications such as *Junior Bookshelf* that continued in publication until the early 1990s. Increasingly those working with children also produced their own booklists to aid children, parents and teachers in their selections.

The 1950s saw an exponential growth in the number of titles published for children, virtually doubling from fewer than 1,000 per year in the 1940s to nearly 1,800 in the 1950s. Throughout the 1960s the publication of children's books continued to increase, averaging over 2,000 volumes per year, in this the 'Second Golden Age' of children's book publishing in the UK. This was the time of authors such as Joan Aiken, Alan Garner and John Christopher, and also a period when there was considerable talent working in the picture book industry: Victor Ambrus, Charles Keeping and Brian Wildsmith, for example. Attempts were made to introduce early readers to help children in the move from picture books, and reading schemes, to the array of fiction available for the more competent reader. This period also saw the phenomenal rise of the paperback and in particular Puffin, a publisher of high-quality paperbacks that began to be bought in large numbers by public libraries because of the cheapness. The issue of durability was raised in this period but the advantage of price outweighed most librarians' reservations. Towards the end of the twentieth century a number of authorities instituted reviewing systems for the selection of books. Today this must be a formidable task when faced with more than 8,000 titles per year.

The increase in immigration from Commonwealth countries during the 1960s necessitated a growing awareness of the special needs that children of these families might have. The focus of library services, as with other areas of educational and social provision, was on enabling the integration of these children into British society. There was no attempt at this time to provide books in mother-tongue languages, the belief being that this would be detrimental to the educational development of the children and would undermine their progress in learning to speak and write English. The 1980s saw a number of publishers who produced high-quality dual language and mother-tongue storybooks. Although some small publishers such as Tamarind have survived into the twenty-first century there is less dual language and mother-tongue publishing than in earlier years.

The 1990s witnessed a return to what to many had been the real strength of public library services to children: the support of reading and literacy. A range of initiatives on national and regional levels were implemented during this period. The central government's funding of the National Year of Reading (1998–9) provided an impetus for a number of reading-related activities in public libraries. However, children's libraries have always provided materials in addition to books. In the early days of children's services, illustration collections were the most common form of audio-visual material provided. Ray[19] acknowledged that although public libraries were slowly accepting the need for a mixed media approach and had a role to provide information and entertainment in a variety of formats including records and audio cassettes, this provision was not being readily made for children, and any children's material was maintained within the main collection. Increasingly during the 1980s and 1990s public libraries provided a range of multi-media resources for children. Originally only resources which could be proved to have an educational value were provided. By the end of the twentieth century, however, libraries were increasingly prepared to provide the full range of resources, including in some instances videos and playstation games.

Services to schools and school libraries

From the earliest days of public library provision there was collaboration between the school boards and local libraries, particularly in rural areas where public library services were sparse and underdeveloped. The 1902 Education Act disbanded the school boards and gave the task of running schools to local education authorities. This provided an opportunity for greater co-operation between schools and public libraries, both now run by the same local authority (except in London). Although many saw the benefits of close collaboration there were those detractors who felt that the public library service should not have close links with any one particular section of the community. In areas where close collaboration existed class visits from local schools were a regular feature of the public library routine. These visits were not solely for the purpose of selecting and changing reading materials but were also designed to promote the library by introducing children to the resources and expertise which would be at their disposal should they choose to visit outside of school

19 C. Ray, 'United Kingdom', in C. Ray (ed.), *Library service to children: an international survey* (New York, 1978).

hours. In addition to these programmes of visits many schools benefited from loans of books to support the curriculum and to provide additional reading material for school pupils.

Relationships between schools and public libraries were extremely varied. Some public libraries provided bulk loan collections either on a permanent basis or on long-term loan. Many of these services were funded by the education authorities, which would make annual payments to the public library to administer the services. There were also early examples of exhibition collections of selected books at Manchester and Sheffield. In Scotland early experiments at the end of the 1920s and during the 1930s set up dual-use libraries within schools. As has often been a feature of school library services, the majority of the work undertaken was with primary schools. There was far less contact with secondary schools, which were much more self-sufficient. Although the 1940s saw the production of a wealth of recommendations and suggested standards by a range of interested bodies, and although agencies such as the School Library Association accepted these standards, it is difficult to find many examples of school libraries that fully implemented the recommended levels. There was a recognition by the newly formed Ministry of Education that the resources in school libraries should support children's individual needs rather than become an additional source of textbook material that should already be available in the school classrooms. It was not until 1954 that it became generally accepted that a professional librarian was a more appropriate appointment for managing the school library than a teacher librarian. Training for school librarians and teacher librarians became more common, both as part of the curriculum in teacher training colleges and as short courses for teachers who were already fully qualified.

By 1959 less than 50% of library authorities provided school library services and many were severely underfunded. The commitment of the local education authority had a significant impact on the size of grants made to operate these services, which could vary from tens of pounds to tens of thousands per year. The relationship between public libraries and schools was generally good during the 1960s. Virtually all library authorities had some links with the schools, usually through the loan of books and arranged class visits. Some authorities continued to provide more substantial services in the form of advice and exhibition collections. In one authority an early example of a school library service was developed, whereby books bought by individual schools were acquired and processed, and thus the books arrived at schools ready to be unpacked and placed straight onto shelves. Although the majority of schools made some school library provision the quality of this varied considerably and there was little consistency of standards.

The social agenda, particularly in poorer working-class areas, benefited school library provision. The school and, to a lesser extent, the public library were seen as being able to compensate for the poor home environment by the provision of adequate study space and a wide range of up-to-date books. The Inner London Education Authority was one of the few authorities which wholeheartedly embraced the concept of professional librarians operating school libraries. The Education Reform Act of 1988 had a significant impact on school library services. The decentralisation of funding from the local education authorities to individual schools meant that many school library services struggled to survive. Many schools were unwilling to buy into services they had previously enjoyed for free.

The development of homework clubs in libraries during the late 1990s was part of the movement to support children's learning with book and ICT resources. Children's librarians had been supporting children's homework needs since the early days of public library provision and this was a period when this informal support was formalised into timetabled clubs with appropriately trained staff. In some cases the services operated with the support of youth workers or teachers, another example of collaborative working across a number of interested agencies.

Libraries for teenagers

It was in the 1920s that fledgling services to teenagers were started. As already demonstrated, there were close links between public children's services and local secondary schools but there was growing concern that children above the age of fourteen, having left school, might well lose interest in the library and therefore in reading. The perennial questions about service provision to this group, which are still being addressed today, are rooted in the early, if limited, provision of the 1920s. In many cases the inclusion of a teenage room was undertaken as an expedient to satisfy adult users who felt the presence of twelve to eighteen year olds to be disruptive. There was also considerable support during the economically poor years of the 1920s and 1930s for the argument that children's library provision could be best served through schools and that public libraries should concentrate their services on those who had left the formal education system. This view was supported by the report of the Kenyon Committee in 1927, and Alex Philip went so far as to suggest that the key time for reading development was between the ages of twelve and twenty.[20]

It was not until the mid-1930s that the first dedicated teenage library appeared, at Walthamstow. This lack of provision was perhaps a result of the arguments which still resonated within the profession about how best the needs of this group of library users could be met. It was far more common to find library services concentrating their efforts on younger children, a more easily defined and accessible group than adolescents who left school at fourteen and were more difficult to track down and attract into library buildings.

In the 1950s there was particular concern about the low numbers of secondary modern school pupils who continued to make use of the library after leaving the formal education system. The low rates of continued use do not come as a surprise when the picture of provision for young people is examined; Walthamstow was still the only borough to offer a separate library for young people. It would have been hard for library staff to press for separate provision in the face of the Library Association's well-publicised belief that adolescents should be allowed to make use of both the children's and adult sections as they saw fit, but that it was unnecessary to make any separate provision for this group of users. In total only 18% of libraries maintained teenage sections for libraries by 1949.

The 1960s witnessed a growing demand from youth groups to be able to make use of libraries, particularly with late-night opening opportunities for teenagers. The staff shortages that were being experienced at the time, however, meant that the potential of this early example of cross-agency working could not be exploited to the full. Although separate library facilities for teenagers were rare in the 1960s there were increasing numbers of authorities which made teenage collections available either in the adult or the children's library. The majority were placed in the latter, a sign that it had not yet been recognised that teenagers were likely to feel diffident about using facilities in a place frequented and designed for much younger children. A particularly innovative example of a teenage club which included dancing and the availability of coffee-making equipment opened in Lincoln in 1968. Ellis in his account of library provision for children published in 1971 was optimistic that the type of provision made at Lincoln and in some parts of the United States was likely to become much more common after that date.[21] This did not prove to be the case, however, despite some innovative examples in the 1980s and 1990s, such

20 Ellis, *Library services for young people*, 56.
21 Ellis, *Library services for young people*, 146.

as Xchange at Bradford and the Teenage Reading Groups of Southwark. This type of provision was by no means widespread. By the end of the twentieth century, collections of books for teenagers were standardly provided by the library authorities, but there were few examples of separate rooms being made available for teenagers. The problems of siting collections for this age group were often overcome by the simple expedient of providing two collections, one in the adult library and one in the children's library.

Conclusion

This chapter shows the development of children's libraries from the earliest days in the middle of the nineteenth century to the beginning of the twenty-first century. It is possible to see that many of the current developments are based on the solid, and often ground-breaking, work of the early pioneers of services to children. It is easy to forget that services to teenagers, under fives and collaboration with local schools had developed long before current terminology had evolved to provide names for these services. Much of the development which has taken place can be attributed to the pioneering spirit of many children's librarians over the decades and their firmly held commitment to the ideal of serving children as individuals. A time of change and development faces children's services. The full potential of ICT developments need to be realised. ICT may well change the face of children's library provision but will not alter the concepts underlying that provision. There are increased opportunities for collaborative working both with other departments within local authorities and with other children's library services and, of course, with age-old partners such as local schools.

9

Public library people 1850–1919

PAUL STURGES

Histories of libraries have tended to focus on buildings and books, with people mainly introduced in the character of librarians. However, it could be argued that public libraries are much more about people than they are about books. Few British public libraries have sought to develop 'great' collections in the way that research libraries have, the majority of the buildings make small claim to importance, and public libraries have generally defined their mission as a response to the needs of people. The nineteenth-century promoters of the public library idea, such as James Silk Buckingham, William Ewart and Edward Edwards, definitely saw libraries as a mechanism for social improvement rather than as monuments to scholarship. This meant institutions open to all. As Edwards put it,

> They [public libraries] must contain, in fair proportions, the books that are attractive to the uneducated and the half-educated, as well as those which subserve the studies and assist the pursuits of the clergyman, the merchant, the politician, and the professional scholar. They must be unrestrictedly open to every visitor.[1]

At least four main categories of people connected with public libraries deserve discussion. These are: the local campaigners and politicians responsible for setting up and guiding the libraries; the community of actual and potential users; the librarians; and the benefactors whose gifts played an important role in raising the level of activity in public libraries. This chapter will concentrate on the period 1850–1919 during which the character of the British public library was formed. It will do so by looking at each of the four groups in turn, but some aspects of social change and its consequences from 1919 to 2000 will also be outlined.

---

1 E. Edwards, *Memoirs of libraries*, vol. 1 (London, 1859), 776.

Promoters and politicians

The Act of 1850 said that the councils of towns with a population of over 10,000 could provide a public library if the ratepayers (local taxpayers) consented.[2] In the early years this was decided by a poll of ratepayers, in which a majority of two-thirds was needed for adoption of the Act to take place. The amending Act of 1855 altered the population limit to 5,000 and required a public meeting, rather than a poll. The need for a majority of two-thirds remained. The effect of these provisions was to guarantee a public debate in every community where the idea of a public library was suggested. This debate took place in meetings, pamphlets and the columns of newspapers. It provides a good indication of the nature of public opinion in relation to libraries community by community, and identifies many of those individuals who felt that libraries were important in some way or other. The division of opinion was basically between those who felt that libraries were a benefit to society and those who saw libraries as not merely another demand on the public purse but an expense that would not be repaid by positive public response.

A flavour of the debate in one of the earliest communities to adopt the Act, Leamington Spa, indicates the type of arguments that were typically marshalled by either side. At public meetings in January 1856 and December of the same year, the supporters of a library spoke of the needs of 'industrious artisans', 'the working man', 'the masses' and 'the industrial classes'. The scheme for a library was presented entirely in an adult education and social improvement context: 'The more we educate the masses, the better members of society they become.'[3] The opposition argued that: 'At present there is almost an entire absence of disposition for reading amongst them [the working classes], if we are to trust to past and present appearances.'[4] Letters to the local press purporting, not totally convincingly, to be from workers asked, 'Stead of fine books and fine rooms, lets have decent comfortable houses to live in.'[5] Nevertheless the December meeting passed the necessary resolution and a public library was opened on 16 March 1857.

Progress was not necessarily so smooth in other communities. The City of Leeds followed other big cities, Manchester (1852), Liverpool (1852), Sheffield (1853), Birmingham (1860), in adopting the Act. However, the debate there

2 R. J. B. Morris, *Parliament and the public libraries* (London, 1977).
3 *Leamington Advertiser* (3 January 1856).
4 *Leamington Advertiser* (16 December 1856).
5 *Royal Leamington Spa Courier and Warwickshire Standard* (5 January 1856).

showed opposition to a library in the ascendant for a while. In 1861 a petition to the Town Council with 600 signatures called for a public meeting to discuss the adoption of the Public Libraries Act. The grounds for this were that: 'A free library, where men of all grades might resort, and from which books of an instructive and elevating tendency could be circulated without charge, would greatly improve the social, moral and intellectual condition of this populous and important borough.'[6] The Council rejected this by a majority of nearly five to one, mainly on the grounds of the expense involved, in relation to what was alleged to be working-class indifference towards a library. Not until 1868 did the Council agree to call a public meeting, which passed the necessary resolution in favour of a library by a small and unenthusiastic majority. The Council avoided action for some time, and only in August 1869 did it set up a committee to implement the Act.

The division between the two kinds of opinion on public libraries was broadly on a liberal–conservative axis, but in few cases was the library idea openly opposed on the grounds that it would make subversive ideas available to the workers. In later years, although the division of opinion in most towns continued to be broadly on left–right lines, it was not always quite as simple as that. On occasion, councillors from all parties competed to show their commitment to popular institutions, such as the library, and to introduce prestigious projects that might win them credit and attract votes. In general, Usherwood concludes that the British library has not been a political institution, and nor has it been a focus of political dispute.[7]

The public

The promoters of the public library idea felt that there were sufficient numbers of people in the country who could and would use libraries. The evidence of use of libraries that were broadly accessible to the public, such as those of the mechanics' institutes, had tended to bear this out. As we have shown, there were local campaigners and councillors willing to support the setting up of libraries under the 1850 Act. Nevertheless the question as to whether the supporters of libraries were right about the public remained to be answered. Some indication of the readiness of the population for libraries can be derived from

6 T. Kelly, *A history of public libraries in Great Britain 1845–1975*, 2nd edn (London, 1977), 28.
7 B. Usherwood, 'Public libraries and political purpose', in M. Kinnell and P. Sturges (eds.), *Continuity and innovation in the public library: the development of a social institution* (London, 1996), 189–209.

three sources: rates of literacy, access to schooling and, finally, the availability of leisure hours and quiet spaces in which to read.

Literacy, schooling and leisure

National rates of the ability to sign one's own name in a marriage register provide the crudest, but most widely available, indication of changes in general literacy. They correlate well with other more reliable, but less widely available, indicators, and their steady improvement from 1839 onwards is free of the erratic fluctuations that might cast doubt on the trends they reveal. Throughout the second half of the nineteenth century they suggest a steady and quite swift increase in the basic literacy of the population at the age of marriage.[8] This increase was such that for both men and women the rate of ability to sign reached well over 90% by the end of the century. This point had been reached from rates of something over 50% for women and nearly 70% for men in 1850. The general trend and narrowing gender difference are swifter continuations of the trends that are observable throughout the period since 1754 when marriage registers first contain signatures. Despite the strong reservations about the precision of such figures that are appropriate, it is still reasonable to see the period as one in which the population was in the later stages of a process of achieving some form of near universal literacy.

Woven in inextricably with the spread of literacy is, of course, the spread of schooling. In England in excess of 30,000 schools, ranging from the great endowed and fee-paying 'public' schools through to small and rudimentary schools provided by parishes, charities and private proprietors (the so-called 'dame schools'), were available at the mid-point of the century. There was no national system of schooling, but in 1833 the government had allotted public funds to education for the first time. This took the form of grants to the British and Foreign School Society (supported by the nonconformist Protestant sects) and the National Society for the Education of the Poor in the Principles of the Established Church in England and Wales. Between them they set up thousands of schools, and by 1858 a total of 2,500,000 children were enrolled across the range of private and publicly supported schools. Of these, 636,000 were in government-inspected schools.[9]

The Public Libraries Act actually pre-dated a genuinely national system of schooling by twenty years. It was not until 1870 that an Elementary Education

8 L. Stone, 'Literacy and education in England 1640–1900', *Past and Present* 42 (1969), 61–139.
9 R. Schofield, 'Dimensions of illiteracy 1750–1850', *Explorations in Economic History* 10 (1973), 437–54.

Act was passed. By the provisions of this the government took up the responsibility for providing education wherever voluntary effort was insufficient. The effect of the Act was to carry the basic educational programme into those communities too poor or too isolated to benefit from the system then in force. It extended rather than replaced the existing effort, and it is quite clear from the progress of the literacy statistics that it made no dramatic difference to the continuing rate of improvement in the years immediately after it was passed. Compulsory education was not introduced until 1880, and not until 1891 was education made, in a limited sense, free. In the second half of the nineteenth century the crucial phase had been reached in the process of Britain becoming a fully schooled society.

If literacy suggests the simple ability to read and schooling suggests some grounding in concepts which might give reading meaning, then there is still the need for time to read, a place to read, and the resources to acquire reading matter. The possession of these further requirements was also becoming available in some degree or other to the masses of the British population at this time. This was not, however, a happy or comfortable process. Since the sixteenth century the agricultural population had largely been shifted off the land into the towns, where its members sought other forms of employment, many of them in industry. Urban life was frequently brutally hard, but legislation began to be introduced to ameliorate some of the worst conditions. Factory Acts were slowly and grudgingly voted in by parliament. In the 1860s a Saturday half-day holiday was added to the Sunday break more or less universally allowed to workers. Gradually a little leisure time became the norm for the urban population and whole new leisure industries (professional sports and music hall for instance), and self-help, public or charitable provision of leisure facilities (parks, galleries, social clubs, etc.), appeared to serve those freed for inexpensive enjoyment. During this same time an improvement in the economic condition of the bulk of the population provided the improved incomes from which something could be spared for more comfortable home life and for leisure pursuits. Between 1850 and 1900 average money wages increased steadily, whilst average retail prices, after some fluctuation, were lower at the end of the period than at the beginning.[10] Many people began to obtain living conditions with access to light and perhaps a quiet space in which reading was possible. Not everyone who could read wanted to read, but certainly a proportion of those who could read did wish so to do.

10 B. R. Mitchell, *Abstract of British historical statistics* (London, 1962), 343.

Library use

Did the newly literate and schooled use the little leisure granted to them to make use of public libraries? The evidence is that some of them did. Take, for instance, a rather superficial analysis of the membership records of the first year of Doncaster library in 1870.[11] This shows that there were 1,210 members, out of a population of 18,768, of whom 8% could be called professional, 25% were tradesmen and clerks, 30% were skilled workers, 12% labourers and servants and 25% revealed no occupation (suggesting that they were probably dependent members of families). The proportions of members of the middle and working-classes here are fairly typical of those derived from a number of such lists by Kelly,[12] although his interpretation of them is that this represents a predominantly working-class membership. Another view of the figures suggests that library membership did not appeal to many members of the most prosperous part of a community, who might be expected to have access to reading material already, or to a high proportion of the working masses. The dynamics of this can be illustrated by a comparison of two communities: Leamington Spa and Oldham.

These were, and still are, towns of differing character. They have been selected to provide contrast, on the basis of Post Office figures, published in 1863, of the rates per capita of letter deliveries across the country.[13] These figures represent a powerful expression of the rates of genuine literacy in individuals, since receipt of a hand-written, personally addressed letter is not a casual or random event. The highest level of deliveries was, with little exception, experienced in resort towns, and the lowest, with odd exceptions, in northern industrial towns. Leamington Spa, with an average of fifty-seven letters delivered to each resident during the year, had one of the highest national rates, and Oldham with six was one of the lowest. Both were, nevertheless, towns that set up libraries under the provisions of the Act. The interesting thing is that the size of the libraries and the rate of use were not so dissimilar as their populations and other aspects of their demography.

Leamington when it set up its library in 1857 had a population of about 16,000, whilst Oldham when its library began in 1883 had about 110,000. A comparison of the two libraries in 1901 shows that Leamington had a collection of about 20,000 whilst Oldham had 58,000. Leamington had an average daily issue of about 200 and Oldham about 570. Thus activity in Oldham was at about three

11 A. J. Smurthwaite, 'An occupations list of 1870', *Library History* 1 (1969), 192–4.
12 Kelly, *History of public libraries*, 81–4.
13 Postmaster General, *Ninth report* (London, 1863).

times the level of that in Leamington, but the population of the town at the turn of the century had become about six times as great. What made the difference in the two populations were Oldham's 30,000 cotton workers and 8,000 other industrial workers. In terms of their leisured, professional and skilled classes the two towns were broadly similar at the time they obtained their public libraries. Each had a middle class of something like 2,000–3,000 people. That of Leamington was dominated by those who sold goods and provided services for the resident gentry and visitors, whilst that of Oldham consisted of business people, clerks and officials. These were the types of people whom evidence from other towns, like Doncaster, shows to have been the members of public libraries. It was not the total population of a community that mattered in library terms, it was the number whose lifestyle had readied them for library use. Although a large proportion of members might be workers, these members did not represent a large proportion of the urban masses that public libraries had been supposed to serve.

Librarians

The larger cities were able to appoint experienced librarians and scholars to take charge of their new services. Manchester chose the library campaigner Edward Edwards himself as its first City Librarian, and Birmingham Public Library employed J. D. Mullins, the experienced librarian of the Birmingham [subscription] Library in 1865. Such people were not numerous, however, and smaller communities made what seem bizarre appointments. For instance, Martin Finnigan, a former policeman, was appointed at Bolton, and Chester-field chose Dennis Gorman, whose qualifications or experience were not felt worth recording. Other communities achieved acceptable compromises, Oxford appointing Benjamin Blackwell, former bookseller and father of the founder of Blackwells, in 1854, whilst Cambridge had, in 1853, appointed the twenty-two-year-old John Pink, a bookseller's assistant. Significantly though, Pink's strongest competitor was Thomas Cross, a retired stagecoachman.

Only after the passage of some decades did the apprenticeship schemes in some of the better-run library systems begin to produce significant numbers of librarians grounded in the basics of the work, some of whom could then take their knowledge and experience on into the service of other employers. Some of the more notable figures of British public librarianship emerged from this background. Ernest Savage, though he left school at the age of twelve and had worked in a printing shop before joining Croydon Public Libraries, was able to build a successful career at Birkenhead, Coventry and

Edinburgh on the basis of his training there. Other entrants had a better educational grounding: Stanley Jast, for instance, when he joined Halifax Public Library as an assistant in 1887 had studied, unsuccessfully, for the Civil Service examinations. John Potter Briscoe, later City Librarian of Nottingham, had at least continued his schooling until the age of eighteen when he joined a Bolton Public Library system which was beginning to gain a reputation for high standards. Other systems, such as those of Leeds and Newcastle upon Tyne, gained the reputation of producing the type of librarian whom other communities might see as a very desirable potential employee.

Thus librarians without either suitable educational background or appropriate experience were steadily replaced by successors whose training in the routines of library work was sound. At the end of the nineteenth century the Library Association tried to confirm this trend of improvement by introducing programmes of education and training for librarians, at first with little success. A system of examinations, introduced in 1904, and the register of librarians, begun in 1909, gradually produced results and an identifiable profession began to emerge. The system of private study for professional examinations remained important for the public libraries until after the Second World War, as the Library School set up at University College London in 1919 mainly served the academic library sector. Whilst study for the Library Association qualifications undoubtedly improved the quality of professionalism in public library work, it also tended to lock it into established ideas and practices. Only with full-time education for librarians at the Library Schools that were set up first as a temporary measure to cope with post-Second World War professional shortages did a more open-minded vision of the public library emerge from the educational process.

Philanthropists

It is arguable that without the stimulus provided by philanthropic gifts to public libraries, the movement would have developed much less fast and at lower levels of provision. The number and scale of gifts not only benefited the recipient communities, but excited emulation elsewhere. On examining the progress of public libraries in Britain in the last decades of the nineteenth century, it becomes clear that philanthropy did not merely provide buildings and books. The hope or expectation of private financial assistance was the main stimulus for some communities to vote public funds for a library service in the first place. Andrew Carnegie's gifts, amounting to £1,750,000 distributed to 295 libraries between 1897 and 1913, totally dominated library giving. Indeed, it is sometimes suggested that his buildings burdened communities with monuments they could not maintain effectively, let alone use for good library services. Second to Carnegie for number of library donations in Britain, was the publisher John Passmore Edwards (1823–1911), who gave fifteen libraries in London and nine in Cornwall and Devon. There were others. In 1886 Greenwood[14] could already cite the Edward Pease Library in Darlington, the Nicholson Free Library at Leek, the Brunner Free Library at Northwich and the Harris Free Library and Museum at Preston as examples of recent 'worthy munificence' and others followed in numbers during the following years.

Carnegie gave for museums, parks and other public institutions, but libraries were his chief concern. This he explained by his own early access to the books of a local benefactor. Passmore Edwards also traced his interest in libraries to his joy in having access to books as a child, and had clear arguments to support his expenditure. For most donors, however, it seems to have been a rather imprecise sense that a library could play a positive role in society, whilst providing a lasting monument to their memory, that led them to give. For instance, the brewer Michael Thomas Bass had nothing at all of any interest to say about his gift of a library building to Derby in 1879.[15] In this case his library philanthropy seems to have been just one of a series of gifts of different kinds to various communities in which he had a stake.

The role of philanthropy seems to have been most important during the first seventy or so years of public libraries, when a stimulus to growth was most needed. The twentieth century was not a particularly important age for public library philanthropy in Britain, partly because effective funding of library systems by local councils gradually began to be the norm rather than the exception. However, the concept has achieved something of a return with the stress on commercial sponsorship introduced in the 1980s. This has continued to be a significant means for introducing change into systems.

Change after 1919

In the period following the Public Libraries Act of 1919, library service was extended to those towns that had not introduced it, and to the rural areas, in the form of county libraries. Gradually it became possible to look at the overall impact of the libraries on the population, and during the mid-century

14 T. Greenwood, *Free public libraries: their organisation, uses and management* (London, 1886).
15 P. Sturges, 'Beer and books: Michael Thomas Bass, Derby Public Library and the philanthropy of the beerage', *Libraries and Culture* 31 (1996), 247–71.

a consistent pattern of library use developed, with roughly speaking one third of the population regular users, one third occasional users and a final third non-users. Furthermore, as Black argues, the committed users were by then predominantly from the middle classes.[16] However, by the end of the century and after 150 years of public libraries in Britain, a new watershed was reached in the public's relationship to its libraries. For the first time there was a serious decline in what has usually been seen as the key aspect of library use, with book issues falling by 20% in the 1990s. The number of posts in the public library sector for professional librarians also fell in the 1990s, by 15–20%. In the late twentieth century levels of use other than borrowing increased greatly, but the figures suggest that the type of public library that was created in the 1850–1919 period, and which flourished between 1919 and 2000, had by the latter date reached the end of its lifespan.

Demographic trends are a significant part of this. Lower birth rates and increased life expectancy are creating an older population with a low worker/pensioner ratio. The nature of employment has changed enormously, with a high proportion of jobs less than full time, and a smaller proportion not in any sense permanent. The evidence is that those in employment in Britain devote increasingly long hours to their work and suffer greatly increased stress as a consequence of their working environment. Despite this, leisure time is abundant. To fill this space a myriad of leisure activities, travel opportunities and communication technologies have emerged. The long-term trend of population shift reflects the British preference for suburban life. People have moved in great numbers from the centres of cities to the suburbs and nearby small towns or villages. This has effectively depopulated the business districts of towns where nineteenth-century central libraries were built, and reduced the population density of the old working-class inner city areas which had well-used branch libraries. The future of the public library depends on how effectively it responds to changes in the age patterns, employment, leisure preferences and location of the people who are its reason for being.

16 A. Black, 'Skeleton in the cupboard: social class and the public library in Britain through 150 years', *Library History* 16 (2000), 3–12.

PART II

*

THE VOLUNTARY ETHIC:
LIBRARIES OF OUR OWN

10

Introduction: libraries of our own

ALISTAIR BLACK

An historic suspicion of the centralised state, combined with the rise of the free market and a supporting ideology hostile to extensive state intervention and friendly to self-help, meant that voluntary action remained as important an aspect of library provision in the decades immediately after 1850 as it had become in the 'associational' society that had emerged during the Enlightenment and early industrial revolution.

As towns and cities grew, social intercourse intensified. Equally, to counter the anonymity inherent in urban living, citizens became increasingly more 'clubbable'. The emergence of communities of shared interest – at times, as in the case of mining communities, spatially coherent also – fed through into the establishment and continuing existence of a variety of 'social libraries', based on the payment of a subscription or a long-term proprietary investment. Libraries as different as the private and prestigious London Library and the relatively marginal libraries established in working men's clubs would correspond equally to this description. Many social libraries satisfied the credentials of the pure public sphere institution theorised by the German sociologist Jürgen Habermas in his *Structural transformation of the public sphere: an inquiry into a category of bourgeois society* (1989): rational, open, democratic, independent of the state and commercial interest, and supportive of the free expression of ideas and of scientific and intellectual discovery.

As publicly funded libraries developed and became more accessible (whether in the form of municipal public libraries, university libraries, national libraries or government repositories of various descriptions) social libraries relying on independent sources of income inevitably declined. However, in the pluralistic post-modern, or late-modern, world, niche cultures found room to flourish, and this has ensured the survival, albeit not permanently guaranteed, of the voluntary social library in one form or another.

Other kinds of social library have been based less on public-sphere values than on commercial interests. After 1850 circulating libraries like Mudie's

Library, W. H. Smith's and, later, the Times Book Club and Boot's Booklover's Library tapped into the opportunities offered by a deepening commercial society. They also offered an alternative to what some saw as the unrespectable and unhygienic service offered by public libraries. But again, as publicly funded libraries expanded, commercial library ventures found their profits squeezed and were eventually forced to withdraw from the market.

In the early part of our period, and in the context of relatively meagre public alternatives, private collecting continued to have relevance. However, as time went on, large private collections became increasingly rare, their fabric broken up and absorbed into more accessible libraries. Yet the decline in the cost of books relative to increasing incomes has once again, in recent decades, led to a renaissance of the personal library – and on a scale, moreover, far in excess of the modest household libraries of the nineteenth century.

II

Circulating libraries in the Victorian age and after

SIMON ELIOT

Introduction

Circulating and subscription libraries overlapped and frequently shared many characteristics, so the distinction between them is often rather arbitrary. Indeed, occasionally circulating libraries referred to themselves as 'subscription' libraries, and vice versa. Nevertheless, most subscription libraries had a different origin from circulating libraries. Many evolved out of small, private book clubs during the eighteenth century and shared many of their characteristics. They tended to have rather high annual subscriptions, they sometimes required subscribers to take a share in the library and they frequently concentrated on 'serious' subjects (theology, philosophy, history, biography, travel, etc.) to the exclusion or underrepresentation of fiction. However, with the growing production and consumption of fiction – particularly in the form of the novel – such libraries were never going to satisfy what many would have regarded as a vulgar demand. This was left to commerce, and commerce was what circulating libraries were all about. The circulating library was certainly a success in its time: the *Library History Database to 1850* currently lists 5,481 circulating libraries or 44.5% of all the institutions recorded.[1]

It is no coincidence that circulating libraries and the novel rose together. As commercial organisations, their subscription rates were closely tailored to their market. One might subscribe on a yearly, quarterly or monthly basis. Some libraries allowed shorter subscription periods offering a weekly or even a daily rate; these shorter subscriptions could be frequently found in small circulating libraries serving poorer areas or in libraries with a distinctly seasonal trade (such as spa towns and seaside resorts). Some circulating libraries charged by the volume borrowed (with or without a security deposit). Most circulating libraries, of whatever size, were general in content, that is, they stocked

---

1 As at 19 August 1998, see http://www.r-alston.co.uk/stat.htm.

fiction and non-fiction; additionally they commonly had some reference works, newspapers and magazines on offer.

But the generality and the commercialism of circulating libraries often went further. It has been remarked that specialised book shops were rare in the past, most selling many more things than books. Similarly, circulating libraries were a focus for other forms of commercial activity, often but not always print related. Sometimes the library was the main focus of activity, with other sales being added to it; in many other cases the circulating library was simply an appendage to other, and probably more profitable, activities. Suppliers of stationery, printed forms, books, newspapers and magazines could also advertise a circulating library on the premises but in practice this might be no more than a few shelves of miscellaneous titles. This was even more likely to be the case if the shop sold items more remote from those of the book trade: groceries, patent medicines, musical instruments or fancy goods. Even the largest circulating libraries offered other services. Lovejoy's library in Reading was, by 1887, performing many roles: insurance agent, publisher of an 'Estates Register', seller of board games, stationer and newsagent, seller of leather goods, seller of maps and travel guides, bookbinder, printer, engraver, die-sinker and relief-stamper – and running a rare-book finding service.[2] Advertisements for businesses for sale in the book trade journals of the later nineteenth century frequently mentioned a circulating library as part of the business, though often it was placed rather far down in the list of attractions.

One of the reasons for this diversity – and it is something of a paradox for libraries of a commonly commercial character – was that it seems to have been difficult over most of our period for circulating libraries to generate sufficient profits to be stand-alone enterprises. Partly this was due to the problem confronting any commercial library that was trying to satisfy two rather different sorts of customer: those who were essentially wanting to read the latest fashionable and popular books (commonly novels), and those who wanted to read canonical works of fiction and/or non-fiction. Holding the balance between a rich stock of books always available for borrowing and

2 *A catalogue of the books in the General Subscription Circulating Library at Reading* (Reading, [1887]). The library had been established by George Loveday in 1832 and in its mid-Victorian heyday attracted the likes of Thackeray, Wilkie Collins, Charles Kingsley and Charles Dickens through its doors. A feature of the library was its collection of 'rare and valuable Editions of Mr Ruskin's Works' which, by 1887, had been turned into a reference collection.

a large enough range of multiple copies of currently in-demand titles was a tricky business. However, it needed to be done efficiently and continuously if the library were to satisfy a diverse range of readers and make them think it worthwhile to renew their subscriptions.

Most circulating libraries were not as well founded or as large as those described below, and this fact of scale is important. Most users of small circulating libraries would have experienced both a quantitative and a qualitative difference. Obviously there would be fewer books to borrow, fewer copies of popular works and a longer delay in getting the most recent books (indeed, many would have had to wait until surplus copies from larger libraries began to filter down or cheap reprints were produced). But a recent analysis has suggested that smaller libraries tended to stock conservatively: in such libraries the percentage of canonical works went up and the proportion of less-well-known titles went down. In libraries with between 2,000 and 3,000 titles 40–60% might be canonical. In libraries with fewer than 500 titles that percentage might be as high as 70–90%.[3]

It is likely that the circulating libraries that got closest to independent profitability were those that serviced specialist markets. There were circulating libraries such as Lewis's Library at 186 Gower Street devoted to scientific and technical books.[4] There was the Universal Circulating Musical Library at 86 Newgate Street, established early in 1853 and run first by C. J. Graue then by Gustav Scheurmann & Co., and Novello's Music Library at 1 Berners Street, both lending printed music.[5] In the 1930s there was the Circulating Library of the Children's Book Club at 17 Connaught Street.[6] There were also libraries that offered exclusively foreign texts such as Rolandi's at 20 Berners Street that in 1849 stocked over 1,400 books in Italian and Spanish.[7]

Libraries in special locations catering to a transient but affluent clientele, such as those in fashionable seaside resorts or spa towns, would also be in

---

3 F. Moretti, *Atlas of the European novel 1800–1900* (London, 1998), 144–8.

4 For example, *Catalogue of Lewis's Medical & Scientific Library [. . .] New edition revised to Midsummer 1887* (London, 1888).

5 Graue published the *Catalogue of the Universal Circulating Musical Library* (London, [1853]), describing it as 'Importers of Foreign Music, and Publishers'. A later catalogue 'including the Supplements of 1855 & 1856' was published by Scheurmann, and claimed that the library contained 'upwards of 50,000 distinct works'.

6 *Catalogue of the Circulating Library of the Children's Book Club* (London, April 1933). The library was opened in December 1931.

7 *Libri italiani & spagnoli: Catalogue of Italian and Spanish Books with a few in Portuguese, lent to read by P. Rolandi, at his French, Italian, German, and Spanish Circulating Library* (London, 1849).

an advantageous position. For instance, in Scarborough in 1868 there were at least nine libraries of a commercial character, five of which were located in booksellers' and stationers' shops, for a population of around 18,000 people.[8] In Bath in 1852 there were thirteen circulating libraries and two specialising in music; despite the growth of public libraries there were still eleven in 1902 and four as late as 1952.[9] Circulating libraries abroad stocking English books and catering to a transient population by offering subscriptions on a weekly, fortnightly or monthly basis, such as B. Maurer's circulating library in 'Trinkhalle 1' at Bad Schwalbach, would also be in an advantageous position.[10]

Small circulating libraries remote from other forms of textual competition might also flourish. In 1865 the Bala Circulating Library had around 448 titles (some 330 in English, 118 in Welsh) which were overwhelmingly non-fictional with strong religious content; subscription was just two shillings a year but the library was only open 8.00–9.00 pm on a Monday.[11] In the mid-twentieth century, at a time when most large circulating libraries were closing, small circulating libraries survived, commonly in working-class areas and often called 'twopenny libraries' from the cost of hiring a book, offering westerns and formula romances of the Mills and Boon type (a similar phenomenon could be found in Australia in the 1930s and 1940s).[12]

Such specialist institutions had a number of economic advantages over more general and larger circulating libraries. First, they served a well-defined and homogeneous market whose needs and wants might be easier to anticipate. Second, being specialist they bought from a smaller range of publishers and thus found it easier to be comprehensive within their narrower range. Third, they dealt in materials that users commonly would not wish or need to own, so borrowing was a first, not a second choice of the library's subscribers. Fourth, in the case of the specialist middle-class libraries, many of these publications were not likely to be subject to rapid cheap reprinting that might incline the user to wait to buy rather than to borrow. In the case of small and or

8 *A directory of Scarborough & Falsgrave 1868* (Scarborough: S. W. Theakston, 1868).
9 *A directory for the city and borough of Bath, and its environs* (Bath, 1852); *The Post Office directory 1902* (Bath, 1902); *Kelly's Directory of Bath and neighbourhood* (London, 1952).
10 *List of English books B. Maurer Circulating Library* (Bad Schwalbach, c. 1900). This list had many novels listed in two-volume form which suggest a strong dependence on Tauchnitz editions. Peter Hoare has also drawn my attention to the Gabinetto Vieusseux in Florence, 'much used by expatriates in the season in the nineteenth century', and to a D. R. Marx who ran a 'British & Foreign Circulating Library and Reading Room' in Baden-Baden (*Catalogue of English books*, 1864); he also ran a German and a French circulating library. See A. Martino, *Die deutsche Leihbibliothek* (Wiesbaden, 1990), 992.
11 *Catalogue of the Bala Circulating Library* (Bala, [c.1865]).
12 M. Lyons and J. Arnold (eds.), *A history of the book in Australia 1891–1945* (St Lucia, Queensland, 2001), 191–9.

local libraries, there was often an additional advantage: they offered a flexible payment system which allowed hire of individual volumes for short periods (even just over-night) with no formal subscription.[13]

How did a normal circulating library make its money? A consistent and, if possible, growing subscriber base was vital in order to provide a library with a reliable, long-term income. Take the one guinea a year charge by Mudie's which entitled a subscriber to borrow one volume at a time. This annual subscription rate represented an income to the library of 0.69 of an old penny (d) per day or 4.85d a week per subscriber. Roughly speaking, therefore, a borrowed volume in the hands of an average subscriber was earning the library 0.69d a day. Higher subscriptions that allowed the borrowing of more than one volume at a time represented better value for the subscriber but less income per volume borrowed for the library.

Books varied substantially in price but, for sake of argument, let us take a book that cost the library 5s or 6od. Given the trade practice of offering thirteen copies for the price of twelve, this unit price might be reduced to 55.25d. Ignoring all other costs, the library in question would therefore have to lend that volume for a minimum of eighty subscriber-days (or eleven weeks three days) to recover its bare costs before any profit could be generated.

But it is not enough to get books off the shelves and into the hands of borrowers. Any library worth its salt has to have a large quantity of its stock available on the shelves for borrowing. This means that a high proportion of books bought by a library was, at any given time, not earning its keep by being loaned out. This put more pressure on the volumes that were borrowed and extended the time before they began to make a profit. Of course, there would be subscribers who did not borrow all the time, and for the times they were non-borrowers they represented income with very little cost to the library.

The calculations above ignore a number of factors, the most important of which would have been running costs (including rent, interest payments, heating, lighting, etc.) and labour. Work in a closed-shelf library is labour intensive. At the height of his activities Mudie, for instance, was employing some 250 people in his library, very few of whom were casual labour.[14] Labour costs in the nineteenth century were much lower than now, but nevertheless such a workforce must have represented a significant and regular drain on the

13 The *Catalogue of J. Marston's Circulating Library, Mosley Street, Newcastle-on-Tyne* (Newcastle, 1858) offered 2,325 titles which could be borrowed at the rate of 'one penny per volume each night'. In *A Catalogue of F. T. Vibert's Circulating Library, Market Place, Penzance* (Penzance, [185?]) non-subscribers were offered a rate of twopence per volume for four days.
14 G. L. Griest, *Mudie's Circulating Library & the Victorian novel* (Bloomington, IN, 1970), 31.

resources of any middling-to-large circulating library. Given all these additional costs, it is unlikely that a volume could make much profit unless it circulated for between nine months and a year.

In order to reduce the time before profits were made on a given volume, a circulating library needed to buy its books as cheaply as possible, either by buying titles at a substantial discount from publishers or, in the case of a smaller or more remote library, buying second-hand copies from larger, metropolitan libraries. For this reason, although we shall mostly be looking at the larger libraries, we need to think of the post-1850 circulating libraries not as individual units but as part of an interdependent system. The large libraries such as Mudie's and Smith's could negotiate substantial discounts which, for instance, might reduce the unit cost of a three-decker novel from 31s 6d to 15s or 16s (stronger or better-healed publishers could hold out for much more).[15] Even so, many copies were not circulated for long enough to make much of a profit, even at a discount. The big libraries therefore turned themselves into second-hand book dealers selling on stock at significantly reduced prices. Some copies would no doubt be bought by private individuals, but most multi-volume works, particularly novels, would be bought by smaller or provincial libraries for recirculation. Even in the main catalogues of books for loan there were notices for 'Twelve volumes of Recent Political Biography Demy 8vo newly bound in cloth' (at 40s) and 'Selections of one hundred volumes of popular novels, in sound condition for Library use, are offered for fifty shillings net cash'.[16] No doubt the libraries that bought these job lots would, after exhausting their smaller and less fashionable market, sell the volumes on to still smaller libraries or into the second-hand book trade to be sold for a few pence from a street barrow. In the nineteenth century books, like clothes, went through many owners as they steadily descended the socio-economic ladder.

The circulating library system also had drawbacks for the user. First, as in any rental system, the reader's money did not buy the goods, simply a temporary right to use them. Second, unless the user paid a substantial subscription, users might find that they were only able to borrow part of a work at a time; thus necessitating multiple trips to the library. Third, given the limited number of copies of popular works stocked by a library, readers commonly had to devise

---

15 Blackwood, publisher of George Eliot's *Mill on the Floss*, was able to hold out for a price of 29s for 3,000 three-decker sets of the novel in 1860; see Griest, *Mudie's Circulating Library*, 145.

16 See, for instance, *Catalogue of the principal Books in circulation at Mudie's Select Library*, *January, 1891*; the supplement bound in at the end of the British Library copy also offers 'A Parcel of one hundred volumes of novels, Our own selection is offered for THIRTY SHILLINGS net Cash.'

a list specifying alternative options if the first choice were not available.[17] Fourth, and finally, circulating library users were haunted by the fears of infectious diseases and the threat of them being spread by contaminated but still circulating books:

> 7. No subscriber shall return to the Club any book which has been exposed to infection from any CONTAGIOUS DISEASE. THE CLUB WILL BEAR THE LOSS. (A doctor's certificate will be required before any further book is issued.)[18]

For the middle-class borrower there was one more drawback that had its roots in the fear of infection, though here the fear was of moral rather than physical corruption. The larger libraries, and the smaller that wished in the English fashion to ape their betters, viewed themselves as having a moral function and did not offer books, particularly works of fiction, that might corrupt the reader. Mudie's desire, in his own words, to run a 'select' library ensured that authors such as Charles Reade (with *Cream*), George Meredith (with *The ordeal of Richard Feverel*) and George Moore (with *A modern lover, A mummer's wife* and *Esther Waters*) found it difficult or impossible to have some of their works circulated by Mudie's or Smith's.[19] In the librarians' defence, however, one might say that on occasion the decision may have been as much an economic as a moral one. Libraries needed a large subscriber base, and anything that might have made their collections less suitable to females (commonly regarded as the more vulnerable) would have seriously reduced the size of the market.

Why then, given all the drawbacks and limitations for both proprietors and subscribers, did circulating libraries flourish in the period after 1850? One answer is that they had been part of the British way of books since the early eighteenth century, and the book trade was a very conservative one. Fundamentally, however, the reason was economic. Britain had traditionally been a

17 Many libraries included in either their rules or their advice to users clauses such as: '2. – In order to avoid disappointment, and to facilitate the exchange of Books, it is necessary that Subscribers should name at least double the number of Volumes required for each exchange, and the selection should consist entirely of Books actually published and in circulation at the Library' (from *A catalogue of the books in the General Subscription Circulating Library at Reading*, [1887]). In smaller libraries the need to offer a range of alternatives was that much greater: in Vibert's circulating library in Penzance, which had just 582 titles on offer, the catalogue noted that in order 'To prevent disappointment, subscribers are requested to send a list of four or five sets from the catalogue.'
18 *Catalogue of the Circulating Library of the Children's Book Club* (London: April 1933).
19 George Moore's retaliation in the form of a pamphlet *Literature at nurse, or circulating morals* (1885) was one of the most incisive attacks on Mudie's position, though its results were much less than Moore claimed for it. (A facsimile edition of this pamphlet, with an introduction by Pierre Coustillas, was published by the Harvester Press of Hassocks, Sussex, in 1976.)

high-price culture as far as books were concerned. Although the average price of books was beginning to fall by the 1850s,[20] most new books still represented a significant investment for the average book-buyer. For someone on a good working-class income of 30s a week, a 3s 6d book might represent the whole of their disposable income for that week. Even higher up the social and income scale, at the level of many of the users of the larger circulating libraries, books were costly. To someone earning £200 a year, a 6s book might represent about a third to half of the week's disposable income.[21] Despite an industrial revolution that brought cheapening of raw materials and mass production to books, as late as 1895 10% of the books listed in the main trade journals cost more than 10s. Many of these books were of the sort that were in high demand at the counters of circulating libraries, in particular the three-decker novel costing a guinea and a half (31s 6d) and in which, it was claimed, Mudie's specialised.

Mudie's Select Library

The library that more than any other meant 'circulating library' to the Victorians and post-Victorians was founded by Charles Edward Mudie (1818–90) in 1842 in a stationery, newspaper and bookselling business he ran at 28 Upper King Street (now Southampton Row), London. Ten years later he moved to larger premises at 510 New Oxford Street. He expanded on this site and on 17 December 1860 opened a major new gallery and library.

With its stuccoed exterior, round hall whose lantern roof was supported on Ionic columns that were echoed by pilasters, the 1860 library was neoclassically grand. Despite this, we should think of Mudie's circulating library more as a great warehouse, rather like an Argos store today. The books were not browsed but ordered from a catalogue and brought to the borrower waiting at one of a number of semi-circular counters, each one dedicated to surnames that began with a letter within a specified alphabetical range (say 'L to R') by a library assistant. Behind the scenes the system employed all the latest technology: iron staircases, lifts and communication via speaking tubes. Books are bulky, and Mudie's needed to despatch and receive huge quantities daily. Borrowers who could not attend in person, and who could afford a minimum two guinea subscription, could be served by a second part of Mudie's lending system, the London Book Society, which would receive written orders and dispatch

20 The 1850s marked the first decade in which books priced at 3s. 6d. or under were the predominant category in the titles listed in the *Publishers' Circular*. See S. Eliot, *Some patterns and trends in British publishing 1800–1919* (London, 1994), 61–8.
21 S. Eliot, '"Never mind the value, what about the price?" Or, how much did *Marmion* cost St John Rivers?', *Nineteenth-Century Literature* 56 (2001), 164–7.

them by special vans within a 20 mile radius of Oxford Street.[22] Mudie's third section was the Country department, which dealt with the rest of the UK and the world beyond. Mudie was early into containerisation, having brass-bound, tin-lined boxes of various sizes (holding from ten to a hundred volumes each) made to transport books in bulk to the provinces, Europe, the Empire and beyond. Some of these were sent to individuals, but many went to supply local book clubs and libraries. At Mudie's height in the later nineteenth century up to 1,000 boxes might be sent out every week.[23]

Supporting this distribution system were a number of branch offices: 281 Regent Street and 2 King Street, Cheapside in London, and in Birmingham and Manchester as well. Beyond these were the many small local circulating libraries that took out an institutional subscription to Mudie's, and displayed the yellow Mudie's sticker – which adorned the cover of every loaned book – in their windows. Many of these, no doubt, were bought in bulk from Mudie's catalogues that announced 'Selections of one hundred volumes of popular novels, in sound condition for Library use, are offered for fifty shillings net cash.'[24]

Apart from the technology of supply, Mudie's innovation was fourfold. First, he offered a new and attractively low annual subscription rate of one guinea.[25] Second, in order to make this low rate profitable, he conducted the library on a grand scale. Third, as we have seen, the Library was a 'select' one, that is, its stock was actively managed morally to ensure an acceptable range of books to as wide a range of borrowers as possible. Fourth, in order to guarantee the demand, he advertised widely, listing the latest books on offer and suggesting that large numbers of copies were available.[26] In this he was not exaggerating. Mudie's was commonly the best single customer that Victorian publishers had. In 1855 the library bought 2,500 copies of the third and fourth volumes of Macaulay's bestseller the *History of England*, in 1857 3,250 copies of Livingstone's *Travels* and 1859 1,000 copies of Tennyson's *Idylls*.[27] Even when not ordering on this epic scale, Mudie's could make the difference between profit

22 In 1857 the scheme went as far as Hampstead in the north, Mile End in the east, Notting Hill in the west and Peckham in the south; it was later extended.

23 Griest, *Mudie's Circulating Library*, 29.

24 See, for instance, the back pages of *Catalogue of the principal books in circulation at Mudie's Select Library, January, 1891*.

25 By the standards of the time this was a ruthlessly competitive rate. Those libraries that tried to undercut it, such as the Library Company Limited of Pall Mall in the early 1860s with its 10s 6d rate, quickly failed. See Griest, 23.

26 Mudie's advertised relentlessly; in *The Athenaeum* in 1880, for instance, Mudie advertised in the issues for 10 January, 13 and 27 March, 3 and 10 April, 15 May, 31 July, 28 August, 2 and 9 and 16 October, 6 and 13 and 20 November, 25 December.

27 Griest, *Mudie's Circulating Library*, 20–1.

and loss on the publishing of a novel. A first, three-decker edition of an average novel might well have a print run of no more than a few hundred sets. An order from Mudie's for between 100 and 200 sets – not uncommon – could push the novel into profit even if no further edition were published.[28] In the case of a popular novelist such as Walter Besant, the order from Mudie's alone could amount to 500 sets, one third of an uncharacteristically large first edition.[29]

It is noticeable that some of the largest individual orders were for non-fiction works. Mudie's is so closely associated with the three-decker novel that we are in danger of forgetting that the library's stock was a broad one, with a preponderance of non-fiction. Using a crude but consistent criterion – the number of pages that Mudie's catalogues devoted to non-fiction and fiction – we can trace an interesting trend. In 1857 75% of the pages were devoted to non-fiction, 25% to fiction. By 1869 the balance had shifted to 65% non-fiction, 35% fiction. By 1891 the proportions were 57% and 43%. This represented the highest point for fiction, for by 1899 non-fiction was at 58% and fiction at 42%. The period when fiction was at its greatest proportion ran from 1884 (42.8%) to 1891 (43.1%). By 1931, although the layout of the catalogue had changed and therefore direct comparisons are not easy, the balance was closer to Mudie's earlier years: 67% non-fiction, 33% fiction.[30] Mudie's advertisements, certainly in the later nineteenth century, favoured non-fiction.[31]

Perhaps the apparent predominance of fiction in the Mudie list was due to the fact that works of fiction sometimes took the form of three-decker novels, and therefore one title would be represented by three volumes on the library's shelves. Between January 1858 and October 1859 Mudie claimed to have added 391,083 volumes to the library, 165,445 being fiction.[32] Here fiction represented 42% of the total volumes (as opposed to titles). In the ten years between 1853 and 1862 Mudie claimed to have added 960,000 volumes to the Library, nearly half of which were fiction.[33] However, despite fiction never being more than half in bulk – and probably about one-third in terms of titles – of Mudie's lending stock, in terms of public perception, then and since, it is fiction in

---

28 Griest quotes a list of orders from circulating libraries for Mrs Annie Edwards's *Leah* in 1875: Smith's: 25, Day: 13, Cawthorn: 13, Mitchell: 6, Mudie: 125 (*Mudie's Circulating Library*, 25).

29 Letter from Andrew Chatto to Walter Besant, 18 October 1883, Chatto & Windus Letter Book 17, fol. 290; Ledger Book 3, fol. 775.

30 A similar balance can be found in larger provincial circulating libraries: in *Jolly's Circulating Library general catalogue* (Bath, 1909) non-fiction is listed in single column between pages 1 and 563, fiction in double columns between pages 565 and 673.

31 Of the fifteen advertisements in *The Athenaeum* in 1880, for instance, eleven were exclusively of non-fiction.

32 Griest, *Mudie's Circulating Library*, 38.

33 Griest, *Mudie's Circulating Library*, 21.

general and the three-volume novel in particular that loom largest on Mudie's shelves.

Scholars have commonly assumed that the three-decker novel was, if not actually created, then certainly encouraged and sustained by Mudie and his ilk as the form that particularly benefited the circulating system based on the borrowing of one volume at a time. Historically and logically this is a somewhat difficult view to sustain. Mudie can certainly be exonerated from the guilt of creating what many came to regard as a monster. The three-decker had emerged at the beginning of the nineteenth century as one of the preferred forms for the respectable novel, but it only achieved its fully inflated price of 31s 6d (a guinea and a half) in 1821 on the publication of Scott's *Kenilworth*, a full twenty-one years before Mudie established his library. It was Mudie's, along with its major rival Smith's, that issued the ultimatum to publishers in 1894 which killed off the form. After the First World War Mudie's contracted and moved premises, but it survived to the mid-1930s: forty years of life after the death of the form that was supposed to have sustained it.

If the novel was a compelling one, then clearly the demand for volumes 2 and 3 would be strong. If it was not, then the later volumes might languish on the shelves earning the library nothing. A circulating library's economy depends on the unit cost of the book and the number of days it is out on loan; it does not matter whether the book is the third volume of a three-decker or a single-volume novel unless the unit price is different. The very best discount Mudie's could negotiate might reduce the per volume cost to just under 50% of the notional price, meaning that each volume of a three-decker would cost it about 5s. By 1842 Bentley and others had established 6s as a standard price for the first single-volume reprint of novels. Even with a much less generous discount, the unit cost for such a reprint would be significantly lower than 5s. If the single-volume book was popular, Mudie's could buy three copies for less than the price of a discounted three-decker; if it was not, there would be only a single volume, not three, taking up room on his shelves. A single-volume novel, having much more matter in it than a volume of a three-decker, would not have to be returned so often, thus reducing both the borrower's and the lender's costs.

From the 1860s onwards, Mudie's and all other circulating libraries buying the three-decker novel were under growing pressure from the publishers. As has been established, it was difficult for a library to make a profit on a volume in less than nine months to a year. By the late 1860s single-volume cheap reprints of three-deckers were being issued less than a year after their first edition. By the 1880s this reprint gap could be as short as three months. Over the same period the price of these reprints fell from 6s to 3s 6d and then in some cases to 2s.[34] This meant that it became more and more difficult to make a profit from three-deckers and then sell them on. By 1884 Mudie was admitting to George Bentley that: 'we find by careful analysis of figures extending over 2 or 3 years that not one in twelve of the 3 vol novels pays its way. We are not alone. Other libraries feel the difficulty arising from the over production and over pressure of this class of book.'[35]

With more and more uncirculating and unsellable novels accumulating in the basement of Mudie's building (ominously named 'the Catacombs'), the Library had to find alternative methods of lending texts to its readers. As many novels were serialised in monthly magazines prior to book publication, it was sometimes possible for a circulating library to wait until the annual volume of the magazine was produced and then buy that instead of, or in addition to, the three-volume version. In October 1883, for instance, Mudie cut his initial order for Walter Besant's *All in a garden fair* from 500 sets to 300 because he was offered the annual volume of *Good Words* in which the novel had been serialised.[36] But such tactics were never going to be enough. On 27 June 1894 Mudie's and Smith's issued circulars which, among other things, required publishers to offer multiple-volume novels at no more than 4s a volume less discounts and insisted that there be a whole year's grace before cheaper editions were issued. Although presented as a way of saving the three-decker, it was in practice its death-knell. Despite this, some publishers, notably Chatto and Windus, did make an attempt to sustain the form over the next two years. In November 1895 the firm was still advertising four new novels in three-decker form, although now priced at 15s the set.[37] In October 1896 just one three-decker was on offer from the same publisher.[38] Only one conclusion is possible from this: Chatto and Windus tried to carry on because it was profitable to do so. This implies that, one, the profit margins for a publisher were very large when the cover price was 31s 6d for they were large enough to carry on at 15s; two, a publisher might well be able to make a profit on the most mediocre of novels as long as he sold a goodly part of the first, and possibly only, print run to the circulating libraries. It appears that the inflated price of the three-decker may well have been of more advantage to the publishers than to the libraries. If this was so,

---

34 S. Eliot, 'The three-decker novel and its first cheap reprint, 1862–94', *The Library* 6th series, 7 (1985), 38–53.
35 Griest, *Mudie's Circulating Library*, 168.
36 Andrew Chatto to Walter Besant, 18 October 1883, Chatto & Windus Letter Book 17, fol. 290. Novels by Thomas Hardy and R. D. Blackmore suffered the same fate.
37 *Publishers' Circular*, 2 November 1895, 497.
38 *Publishers' Circular*, 3 October 1896, 329.

Table 11.1. *Multi-volume works in relation to*
Mudie's total stock (%)

	>3 vols.	3 vols.	2 vols.	1 vol.
1857	0.49	21.71	10	67.8
1865	0.47	31.63	14.11	53.8
1869	0.49	34.15	20.1	45.26
1872	0.13	37.37	18.22	44.28
1881	0.17	34.95	13.62	51.26
1884	0.23	38.86	14.65	46.26
1889	0.1	40.24	12.34	47.32
1890	0.1	34.45	14.24	51.2
1891	0.2	34.33	13.34	52.13
1892	0.22	33.93	11.91	53.91
1893	0.16	29.72	11.94	58.19
1894	0	28.94	11.94	59.12
1899	0.04	22.5	8.55	68.9

it would go a long way to explain why, in the period 1861–4 when Mudie's was in severe financial difficulties with many large debts owed to the major publishing houses, those houses propped Mudie's up, and why many became major shareholders when in July 1864 the Library was converted into a limited liability company.[39]

For a commercial library one of the most accurate accounts of its nature is to be found in its catalogue. We have already seen that fiction was never the predominant presence in Mudie's, despite its reputation. However, what remains unanswered is how important was the three-decker within Mudie's fiction stock. Table 11.1 is based on sampling every fifth page of a number of catalogues between 1857 and 1899 and converting the numbers into a percentage share of the whole fiction stock.

What is striking is that before the crisis of 1861 three-volume novels constituted just under 22% of the fiction titles. Two-volume novels provided 10% of the share and single-volume fiction accounted for more than two-thirds of the titles. In the 1860s and 1870s three-deckers accounted for just over a third of the titles; this increased to 39–40% between 1884 and 1889. At the very point that Mudie was complaining about the Catacombs filling up with three-volume novels, the three-decker was significantly increasing its share. Nevertheless, even at its height, Mudie's had more one-volume titles (46–47%) than three-volume titles. It is equally clear that Mudie's was doing something

---

39 D. Finkelstein, "'The Secret': British publishers and Mudie's struggle for economic survival 1861–64', *Publishing History* 34 (1993), 21–50.

to correct the problem four years before the 1894 ultimatum. Between 1889 and 1894 the three-volume novel share dropped from 40% to 29%. By the end of the century the three-decker novel was back to around one-fifth of fiction titles, much as it had been in 1857. It is striking that the despised two-volume novel always had a firm place on Mudie's shelves, despite what publishers told writers about the need to bulk two volumes up to three. Certainly, three volumes would take up more shelf-room and sometimes (but not always) Mudie's might order more copies of sets than of one-volume titles,[40] but nevertheless the single-volume work of fiction, which was supposed to have triumphed in the circulating libraries only after 1894 was, in fact, a very significant presence in the catalogues from the very beginning.

Mudie's survived into the mid-1930s partly because it was never as dependent on fiction or on the three-decker novel as historians have suggested, and partly because it followed the pattern of most other circulating libraries in diversifying within and beyond the book trade. It had, for instance, very large bookselling and bookbinding departments which issued monthly catalogues to be sent 'Gratis and Post Free to any address'.[41] These catalogues consisted of '1. Recent Popular Books at Greatly Reduced Prices', '2. Works by Popular Authors in Sets or Separately' and '3. Books in Ornamental Bindings, for Presents, Prizes, etc.'. Any large circulating library would need a bindery to repair or replace bindings of loan books and bind up the tens of thousands of catalogues produced annually, but Mudie's made a virtue out of necessity by producing fine and lavish bindings to satisfy the carriage trade and – as the educational system expanded – the growingly important 'prize book' market.[42]

The most significant catalogue was '1. Recent Popular Books at Greatly Reduced Prices'. This was where Mudie's attempted to increase profits or recoup loses on non- or no-longer-circulating books. The catalogue issued on 15 May 1878 is typical. It was forty-eight pages long ('Works of History,

---

40 Using the data provided by Finkelstein, 'The Secret', it is possible to calculate average order sizes for one-volume and three-volume titles (not all fiction) from some publishers' order books. On average Mudie's ordered 181 copies of one-volume titles and 269 sets of three-volume titles from Smith and Elder between 1858 and 1865. However, from Bentley between 1857 and 1859 he ordered an average of 421 copies of one-volume titles and only 325 copies of three-volume sets. Significantly, in both cases Mudie's orders represented a higher proportion of the average total sales for three-volume titles (Smith and Elder 40%, Bentley 60%) than single-volume titles (Smith and Elder 32%, Bentley 56%).

41 *Catalogue of the principal books in circulation at Mudie's Select Library*, April 1888, verso of second leaf.

42 In April 1888, for instance, the buyer was offered a set of seventeen volumes of Besant and Rice's complete novels in a bewildering array of options: Half Roan £46; Half Persian £54 6s. 0d.; Half Morocco £68; Imitation Whole Morocco, marbled edges £76 6s. 0d.; Whole Calf, marbled edges £102; whole Morocco, gilt edges £144.

Biography, Travel, &c.' covering pp. 1–31 and 'Works of Fiction' pp. 32–47) and offered books at substantial discounts. *Daniel Deronda* (1876) could be had in four volumes for 14s, Hardy's *Hand of Ethelberta* (1876) in two volumes for 3s 6d, Ainsworth's *Chetwynd Calverley* (1876) in three volumes for 3s. Ouida's *Ariadne* published in June 1877 at 31s 6d was being offered at 5s; R. D. Blackmore's *Erema* had been published at 31s 6d in November 1877 and Mudie's was discounting it to 6s just six months later. Most extraordinary, Braddon's *An open verdict*, which had been published in three volumes in April 1878, was being offered just one month later by Mudie's at 9s. One suspects that some of these were new, uncirculated copies. Certainly by January 1913 Mudie's discount list had forty pages devoted to 6s novels mostly discounted to between 1s 6d and 2s and at least 6% of these were described as being 'new'. After the formalisation of the Net Book Agreement in 1901 such discounting became much more contentious, as the Times Book Club was to discover. On the corner of the New Oxford Street building and running three-quarters of the way down the four-storey building was advertising text that summarised Mudie's functions. Above 'Theatre Ticket Office' was the legend 'Books on Loan & for Sale'; both 'loan' and 'sale' were given equally heavy weighting.

Finally even this diversification was not sufficient to protect Mudie's from a world changed beyond recognition since 1842. As in the 1860s, attempts were made to enlist the publishers' financial support but on this occasion to no avail.[43] Mudie's was finally closed by a court order on 12 July 1937.

W. H. Smith and Sons

Smith's had an origin very similar to Mudie's. It was initially a 'newswalk' (essentially a facility for selling, hiring and distributing newspapers) established in the early 1790s in Mayfair, which had become a 'Newspaper agents, Booksellers and Binders' business by 1818. By 1821 the firm had opened a reading room in the Strand in which subscribers (by the month or year) could read a wide range of newspapers and magazines.[44] We should not forget the important role periodicals played in circulating libraries, large and small: Mudie's certainly had magazines for loan, and not merely because they contained serialised novels; and bound volumes of periodicals featured commonly in its clearance catalogues.

Between 1848 and 1860 W. H. Smith was establishing bookstalls in most of the major, and quite a few of the minor, stations springing up on the rapidly

---

43 See, for instance, the letter from Fairbairn, Wingfield and Wyckes to Chatto & Windus (Chatto & Windus archives, general correspondence, E–G 1936).
44 C. Wilson, *First with the news* (London, 1985), 9–17.

expanding railway network. The bookstalls sold newspapers, books, maps, guides and travel accessories such as rugs and candles. Apart from the purchasing and housing of stock, the greatest cost for a large-scale circulating library was distribution. In the emerging network of manned bookstalls supplied by steam trains Smith's had an ideal supply system for a circulating library. In November 1859 Smith's offered to act as Mudie's agents, using the bookstalls as library outlets. Mudie refused (possibly because the fee offered, estimated at £1,000 per annum, was too low) and, as a consequence, Smith's proceeded to set up their own library in the first half of 1860.[45]

Smith's subscription rates were almost identical to those offered by Mudie's (including the one guinea per annum for one volume) but its dependence on many small outlets rather than a few large ones made the library rather different from Mudie's. The subscriber registered at one of the major bookstalls and could borrow from its stock of books but had to return the volume to the same stall. This implies that the majority of frequent users were commuters who naturally passed the same bookstall each working day. By 1861 there were no fewer than 177 bookstalls from which books could be borrowed.

Even the largest stalls were pressed for space, so most books would be ordered from printed catalogues, delivered by train, and be available for collection the following day. In the early decades the main library stock was centralised on Smith's London offices at 186 Strand, which also dealt with subscriptions and the disposal of surplus stock.[46] By the early 1880s there were over 12,000 subscribers to the Library.[47] By 1908 it was calculated that the central depot had over a million volumes in stock, and by 1949 more than 500 of Smith's bookstalls and book shops were functioning as branches of the circulating library.[48]

Pressure on space led to Smith's being less enthusiastic about three-decker novels. Smith's did order sets, but not on the scale of Mudie's. For display, distribution and ease of reading on journeys, the cheap, single-volume novel

45 G. Clear, F. E. K. Foat and G. R. Pocklington, *The story of W. H. Smith & Son* (London, 1949), 16; Wilson, *First with the news*, 355. In 1848 Smith's had proposed a circulating library specifically to serve the customers of the London and North Western Railway (Wilson, *First with the news*, 358).

46 By 1920 the Library Department had moved to Smith's new Strand House, Portugal Street, and by 1949 it was located in Bridge House, Lambeth.

47 For instance, in 1881 there were 12,298; in 1882 12,199.

48 L. M. Griffiths, 'W. H. Smith & Son's Circulating Library', unpublished MLS dissertation (Loughborough University, 1981), 44, 78; Clear, Foat and Pocklington, *Story of W. H. Smith & Son*, 69. For further information on the library and bookstalls of W. H. Smith see S. Colclough, '"A greater outlay than any return": The library of WH Smith & Son, 1860–1874', *Publishing History* 51 (2003), 67–93; S. Colclough, '"Purifying the sources of amusement"? The railway bookstalls of WH Smith & Son, 1855–1860', *Publishing History* 53 (2004), 5–30.

was to be preferred. It is not insignificant that it was in the decade following the establishment of Smith's Library that publishers began to issue one-volume cheap reprints of three-decker novels soon after the first edition.[49] By the mid-1850s publishers such as Routledge and Chapman and Hall were producing single-volume novels bound in a glazed, often yellow, board with an illustration on the front cover and selling at 1s, 2s or 2s 6d. Smith's themselves, using Chapman and Hall as agents, produced such 'yellowbacks' in the late 1850s and early 1860s.[50] In other words, Smith's station bookstalls represented an important outlet for both bought and borrowed one-volume novels. Long before the ultimatum of 1894, Smith's circulating library was rehearsing the role of a library without the three-decker.

As we have seen in Mudie's, lending and selling were not opposites, they were both in the continuum of a successful circulating library's activity. Smith's too had to get rid of non-circulating titles and had done so since the Library's inception by issuing catalogues of 'New and second-hand books at greatly reduced prices'. The importance of this process was made clear in Smith's training literature: 'the revenue return from subscriptions is so inadequate to produce a substantial profit that the disposal of the books may justly be coupled with the other issue – obtaining subscriptions for their use'.[51] By May 1881 you could buy Disraeli's *Endymion* (published in December 1880 at 31s 6d) for 7s 6d and Braddon's *Just as I am* (October 1880, 31s 6d) for 4s 6d.[52] It is clear from the accounts of the Library that it was only returning a modest annual profit in the 1880s because resale of books compensated for the losses made on circulating them. Significantly, by 1893–4 even this was not enough and Smith's library made a loss in that year.[53]

After 1894 the Library's profits increased. However, it was never more than a minor adjunct to Smith's main activities of newspaper and book selling and distribution. For instance, between 1 October 1899 and 30 September 1900 the firm's total profits were £189,243 4s 4d; the Library contributed £6,333 0s 2d to this, just 3.4% of the total.[54] The liberals in the Smith empire liked to think of the Library as a form of service to the community; those of a more

49 Eliot, 'The three-decker novel and its first cheap reprint', 38–53.
50 C. W. Topp, *Victorian yellowbacks & paperbacks 1849–1905*, vol. 3 (Denver, Colorado, 1997), xxiii–xxiv.
51 *A guide for the use of managers of W. H. Smith & Son's Bookshops* (1908, for private circulation) quoted in Griffiths 'W. H. Smith & Son's Circulating Library', 78.
52 W. H. Smith & Son Archive, ccc424, 49–50.
53 S. Eliot, 'Bookselling by the backdoor: circulating libraries, booksellers and book clubs 1870–1966', in M. Harris and R. Myers (eds.), *'A genius for letters': bookselling from the sixteenth to the twentieth century* (Winchester, 1995), 159.
54 W. H. Smith & Son Archive, x.121.

hard-headed disposition probably regarded it, particularly after Smith's moved into high-street shops in the first decade of the twentieth century, as a loss leader. However, even a loss leader can lose too much. In the 1950s the Library may have been losing up to £50,000 per annum;[55] its closure on 27 May 1961, nearly a generation after Mudie's had folded, marked the beginning of the end for large commercial circulating libraries.

Boot's Booklover's Library

A number of large commercial circulating libraries were founded on the cusp of the nineteenth and twentieth centuries, after the watershed of 1894 and, one might say, as new attempts at solving the problems raised by Mudie's and Smith's. When Boot's Booklover's Library was founded in 1898 at the instigation of Florence Boot (the wife of Jesse Boot, the founder of the Nottingham-based chain of Boot's Cash Chemists), there was a narrower and sharper idea of what such libraries should be.[56] Unlike its older, mid-Victorian models, Boot's was overwhelmingly a fiction-based library, much of its original stock being derived from the surplus lists of those older institutions.[57] Its 1905 catalogue, for instance, had some 841 pages; 269 were devoted to non-fiction, thirty to juvenile works and no fewer than 534 pages to fiction.[58] It was highly competitive, its annual subscription rate of 10s 6d being half that of its main rivals, and non-subscribers were welcome to borrow individual books at 1d or 2d a time (with a 2s 6d returnable deposit), a pattern of subscription more common to small local libraries than national ones. National, however, it was, with 256 branches by 1907, matching Smith's nation-wide chain of high-street shops. Unlike Smith's, books could be exchanged 'at any branch in the kingdom'. Although still there, the moral filter function celebrated by Mudie was slowly being relinquished. The catalogue for 1905 reluctantly conceded:

> Whilst we do not pretend to dictate to our readers as to either the quality or range of their reading, we realise fully the duty we owe to the Public and the State in the facilities that, through our large Circulating Library, we afford for the perusal of all literature, including some books that, personally, we regret

55 Griffiths, 'W. H. Smith & Son's Circulating Library', 111.
56 R. E. Theobald, 'Boot's Booklover's Library 1899–1966', unpublished MA thesis (Loughborough University, 1988). A very brief, web-based account of the Boots Library can be found at: http://www.boots-plc.com/information/info.asp?Level3ID=39. For information on Boots librarians see N. Moody, 'Fashionable design and good service: the spinster librarians at Boots Booklovers Library', in E. Kerslake and N. Moody (eds.), *Gendering Library History* (Liverpool, 2000).
57 Griffiths, 'W. H. Smith & Son's Circulating Library', 76.
58 Boot's Booklover's Library, *A catalogue of modern English literature* (Nottingham, 1905).

to see published, but which in common with other Libraries we are bound to supply on demand. If we may not dictate in this matter to our readers, we can at least take particular pains not to catalogue any books that appear to us unsuitable for general circulation.[59]

As with more august catalogues, what was listed and what was available were rarely quite the same thing. Perhaps because Boot's was aimed at a socially lower market, its early catalogues also performed an educational function. Entries for the 'best known books' were augmented by plot summaries derived mostly from Baker's *Guide to the best fiction*. Thus Boot's could be seen as contributing to the process of canon definition and stabilisation occurring in the wake of educational reform in 1870 and later, and the creation of literature as a university subject.

What was implicit in Smith's was explicit in Boot's: the library was a loss leader whose most important function was to draw customers into the shop. For this reason the library was always located at the back of the premises or on its first floor so that borrowers had to run the gauntlet of consumer temptations both there and back. Even a loss leader, however, needed to be capable of delivering some sort of a return, and Boot's too issued lists of library books for sale.[60] Books with its distinctive label may still be found in second-hand and charity bookshops, and even in private libraries of the aristocracy, nearly forty years after the closure of the libraries in 1966.

The Times Book Club

The last decade of the nineteenth century and the first of the twentieth witnessed a transformation in the book production industry, the result of which was a huge increase in book and newspaper production, a dramatic fall in book prices and fierce competition selling textual materials to a market that was fully literate by 1913.[61] The arrival of cheap mass-circulation daily newspapers, the first being the *Daily Mail* launched in May 1896 by Alfred Harmsworth (later Lord Northcliffe), put pressure on traditional newspapers such as *The Times*. By 1905 it was devising a system to boost its circulation: anyone paying an annual subscription of £3 18s 0d to *The Times* automatically became a member

---

59 Boot's, *A catalogue of modern English literature*, 1905.

60 These secondhand copies could on occasion threaten the success of cheaper reprint editions. Writing to his publisher Edward Arnold on the subject of a cheaper edition of one of his novels E. M. Forster observed: 'Unless one undersells secondhand library copies it would not be any good' (letter dated 29 March 1911, Berg Collection, New York Public Library).

61 S. Eliot, *Some patterns and trends in British publishing, 1800–1919* (London, 1994), 13–14.

of the Times Book Club (TBC) and entitled to borrow three volumes at a time. The library was based at 93 New Bond Street and would deliver and collect the books weekly, free within the London postal district; for country subscribers special rates were negotiated. The first catalogue, compiled in September 1905, covered 891 pages with its author and title listing alone. As Boot's had done, the Times Book Club catalogue synopsised many of its entries, using Baker but supplementing him with material from the *Times Literary Supplement*.[62]

'The Times' Book Club . . . is at once a circulating library and a bookshop' asserted the introduction to the first catalogue.[63] Each catalogue entry had a 'published price' and an 'our price' printed next to it; net books had just one price. This approach proved influential. Even as far away as Plymouth, Pophams Circulating Library, which stated that it was 'In connection with the Times Book Club', published an undated catalogue in which every single item had a 'lowest cash price' attached to it.[64]

The books for sale were classified by the TBC into four categories:

Class A 'Absolutely new': 25% off list books, 'publishers' price if net'.

Class B 'Clean and uninjured', 'in circulation about a month': 35% off list books, 20% off net books.

Class C 'Sound copies of three months' use': 50% off list books, 33.33% off net books.

Class D Six months' use: 70% off list books, 50% off net books.

Class A seemed to suggest that the TBC was trying not to infringe the Net Book Agreement that had come into force in 1900 after ten years of negotiation and experiment and which forbade selling new books below their published price. The provisions of Class A may well help to explain the common assumption among publishers and booksellers in 1905, namely, that the TBC had signed the Net Book Agreement. Class B, however, should have given them pause: the difference between absolutely new and 'clean and uninjured' might be very difficult to establish and, in any case, offering a 20% discount on net books a month after publication clearly was a direct challenge to the new alliance formed between the booksellers and the publishers.

The Book War, precipitated by the arrival of the TBC, was messy and long drawn out and included a general agreement among publishers, reached in October 1906, not to supply books to the TBC for circulation, or to *The Times* or

62 *A catalogue of the most important books available for free circulation among subscribers to The Times* (London, 1905), verso of titlepage.
63 *A catalogue of the most important books* (1905), 1.
64 *Catalogue of the principal books in circulation at Popham's Library* (Plymouth, n.d.), v.

the *Times Literary Supplement* for review. There was also a civil action between *The Times* and the publisher John Murray which Murray won with £7,500 damages in 1907. The Book War precipitated the very thing that the TBC was designed to prevent, a financial collapse of *The Times* and intervention by an outside purchaser. In 1908 Harmsworth took over the sorry mess, signed the NBA and by doing so withdrew the challenge to the book trade that the TBC had represented.

One cannot but think that the TBC was a victim of its own publicity. In order to create a public stir *The Times'* manager, Moberley Bell, and his advertising manager, the American Horace Hooper, had to sell hard, and to sell hard they had to be up-front. The TBC was doing very little in 1905 that Smith's and Mudie's were not doing in the 1890s. The major difference was that *The Times* did it loudly and the older circulating libraries did it quietly.

Despite the set-back, the TBC survived and continued to innovate. In 1911 the library became available to the general public and in 1914 the borrowers were given direct access to the shelves, an innovation rare even among public libraries until after the First World War. By the time the library moved into new premises in Wigmore Street in 1922 it was a profitable concern.[65]

Conclusion

Mudie's went into liquidation in 1937; W. H. Smith's Library closed its doors in 1961, and the Times Book Club in 1962; Boot's Booklover's Library followed suit in February 1966. The repercussions spread out through the subtle network of dependency to the smaller and local libraries. Bath, which had had fifteen circulating libraries in 1852, saw its last, owned by Ulrico Maurice, close in 1966. The factors that caused these failures were many. As we have seen, many larger libraries had functioned, covertly or openly, as discount sellers of new or nearly new books. The 1930s saw the first of the modern book clubs founded in the UK and Penguin began issuing its first sixpenny paperbacks in 1935. In 1966 Smith's in association with Doubleday & Co. set up Book Club Associates which now dominates the UK book club market. All these events effectively undermined the system by which the circulating libraries could turn a potential loss into a modest profit by reselling cheaper books. Smaller and working-class libraries, particularly in the midlands and the north, survived for longer, but the spread of television in the 1960s, particularly commercial television with its diet of westerns and soap operas, provided an easier source of escapism.

65 I. Norrie, *Mumby's publishing and bookselling in the twentieth century* (London, 1982), 74.

Public libraries, theoretically a threat to commercial libraries from the later nineteenth century onwards, expanded rapidly after the First World War and commonly became open access. In the 1960s and 1970s, with less concern to promote education over entertainment, public libraries began stocking in large quantities the sorts of fiction once only available in the twopenny libraries. In essence, in the later twentieth century the various markets once served so extensively by the circulating libraries found freer, cheaper and easier sources of supply, and economic natural selection did the rest.

However, a faint echo of those circulating libraries that charged by the volume and did not exact a subscription can be found in the early twenty-first century: the video – and now DVD – rental shops that are offering cheap, use-once access to the electronic equivalent of the three-decker novel.

12

The subscription libraries and their members

GEOFFREY FORSTER; AND ALAN BELL

It is remarkable that the 1849 report of the Select Committee on Public Libraries makes little reference to the vast number of subscription libraries that existed in Great Britain and Ireland by the middle of the nineteenth century.[1] In the days before rate-supported public libraries, these libraries were a crucial source of reading matter for a significant proportion of the literate population. In a trade directory of 1853 for the West Riding of Yorkshire, no fewer than twenty-three libraries were listed for the town of Leeds – a town that was not to provide a rate-supported library until 1872. Of the libraries listed, fifteen were commercial circulating libraries. Two others held theological books (respectively 'Catholic' and 'Methodist', the former being described as a subscription library); the remaining six were all described as 'subscription libraries'. Two had a specific professional interest (law and medicine), two were part of mechanics' institutes and two were 'middle-class' subscription libraries (Holbeck and Leeds).[2] Even such a long list omitted several other subscription institutions providing libraries (for instance, those of the Philosophical and Literary Society, the Church Institute, the Literary Institute and the New Subscription Library).

Subscription libraries had emerged in significant numbers in the latter half of the eighteenth century, a more formal version of the book clubs or reading societies that had flourished during the same period.[3] Like the reading societies,

---

1 For general treatments of the history of subscription libraries see T. Kelly, *Early public libraries: a history of public libraries in Great Britain before 1850* (London, 1966); F. Beckwith, 'The eighteenth-century proprietary library in England', *Journal of Documentation* 3 (1947), 81–98; P. Kaufman, 'The community library: a chapter in English social history', *Transactions of the American Philosophical Society* new series 57 (7) (1967), 1–65, reprinted in abridged form in his *Libraries and their users*, 188–222 (which also contains other relevant papers).
2 W. White, *Directory and gazetteer of Leeds, Bradford, Halifax, Huddersfield, and the whole of the clothing districts of the West Riding of Yorkshire* (Sheffield, 1853), 255.
3 T. Kelly, *Books for the people: an illustrated history of the British public library* (London, 1977), 64–5.

Table 12.1. *The number of subscription libraries in Great Britain*[a]

	Total founded		Number remaining active		
	before 1850[b]	1850	1900	1950	2000
England	274	105	44	15	10
Scotland	266	79	38	7	2
Wales	5	1	0	0	0
	545	185	82	22	12

[a] I am grateful to Dr Keith Manley for access to his extensive data on libraries up to 1850 (cited as Manley database), and to Professor Robin Alston for the information in his massive database of libraries before 1850 (www.r-alston.co.uk). All library historians of the earlier nineteenth century are deeply indebted to their efforts.

[b] At least fifty-seven subscription libraries had been founded in Ireland by 1850, but comparable data on the later situation there cannot be provided at present and they are therefore omitted from this table.

they were created by and for communities of local subscribers. Unlike the reading societies, subscription libraries tended to occupy separate premises rather than relying on the homes of their members and aimed to establish permanent collections rather than selling off their books annually. They relied, as did the circulating libraries, on the regular payments of their subscribers, and these subscriptions were, at least initially, their only source of income. However, subscription libraries differed from the circulating libraries in being essentially democratic in nature. Their books (and their librarians) were chosen by committees elected by the subscribers. Their collections were aimed in the main at a general readership rather than at a particular religious, political or professional group.

The heyday for the creation of subscription libraries was during the first quarter of the nineteenth century. The momentum had eased significantly by mid-century, though one founded in 1841 has become the most renowned of English subscription libraries – the London Library, which is treated more fully at the end of this chapter. As Table 12.1 shows, many earlier libraries were no longer operating by 1850; few examples of later creations are known, even though provision of public libraries under the 1850 Act was in many places very slow.

Subscription libraries were not evenly distributed. In England, most appeared in the industrial towns of the northern and midland counties, though there was also a high concentration in the south-west. Several large towns, like Leeds, were able to sustain more than one subscription library. Most of these

English subscription libraries were of the proprietary type where a subscriber would pay a capital sum on admission and, additionally, an annual subscription. Shares in such institutions were usually the property of the subscriber and were transferable by sale, gift or bequest (though some, such as the Portico Library in Manchester, required subscribers to pass their shares back to the institution[4]). It is not surprising, considering the fees charged, that the proprietary subscription libraries were populated largely by members of the middle classes.

In Scotland, the largest concentrations of subscription libraries were to be found in the agricultural and industrialised lowland counties, though extending to Fife and Perthshire. It has been said that, thanks to their libraries, the populations of Ulster and the lowlands of Scotland were the best informed in the whole of Europe. Proprietary libraries were numerous in Scotland as they were in England (Kelso, at one time or another, possessing three). The early examples of the working-class libraries of the lead-mining communities at Leadhills (founded 1741) and Wanlockhead (1756) in Lanarkshire and the antimony mining community at Westerkirk (1792) in Dumfriesshire were all still flourishing in 1850 and still exist at the time of writing. Their foundation – and their survival – suggests a better level of overall general education in the parishes of Scotland than in those of England, where the development of working-class libraries came much later.[5]

In Ireland, there were fewer subscription libraries than in England and Scotland and most of those so far discovered seem to have come into existence somewhat later.[6] Many were located in the northern counties of Antrim (including Belfast), Down and Londonderry, though they appeared also in major towns further south such as Dublin, Kilkenny and Cork. Politics more generally seems to have concerned subscribers to such libraries – the radical *Northern Star* was being conducted almost exclusively by members of the Belfast Reading Society (later the Linen Hall Library).[7] There were a few working-class subscription libraries, for example the Four Towns Book Club in Co. Antrim, where an admission fee and annual subscription were charged but where subscribers had no share in the property of the library. A large number

4 A. Brooks and B. Haworth, *Portico Library: a history* (Lancaster, 2000).
5 J. C. Crawford, 'Historical models of library provision: the example of Scotland', 4 vols., unpublished PhD thesis for Glasgow Caledonian University (1993); P. Kaufman, 'Scotland as the home of community libraries' and 'Leadhills: library of diggers' in his *Libraries and their users*, 134–47 and 163–70. Cf. also chapter 13, below, on working-class libraries.
6 M. Casteleyn, *A history of literacy and libraries in Ireland: the long traced pedigree* (Aldershot, 1984), 89–119; J. Killen, *A history of the Linen Hall Library 1788–1988* (Belfast, 1990), 5–9.
7 Killen, *History of the Linen Hall Library*, 21.

of commercial circulating libraries (particularly in Belfast and Dublin) would appear to have made up for the lack of provision organised by and for local communities.[8]

Just six examples of subscription libraries have been identified in Wales: St Peter's Lending Library, Neath Library, Glamorgan Library (in Swansea), Newtown Library and Welshpool Reading Society were all proprietary; Wrexham Mechanics' and Apprentices' Library did not issue shares.[9] The urban readership that failed to sustain more than these few examples also failed to create a significant number of other societies providing a general library as part of their activities. The Royal Institution in Swansea with a library of 4,500 books in 1851 was exceptional. As in Ireland, there were commercial circulating libraries to help to make up for this lack of reading material. However, there was little library representation of this or any other kind in the rural districts of Wales and in the growing mining communities for much of the nineteenth century. Even after the Public Libraries Act of 1850, public library provision (that is, funded by local authorities) reached these areas only with the development of the county library system from the 1920s onwards. Some effort was made to provide some reading material for the working classes before this. The second half of the nineteenth century witnessed the creation of libraries by chapels for their congregations and, as the century came to an end, miners' libraries were being created, by the mining communities themselves, in large numbers.[10]

The number and type of subscriber could vary greatly between institutions. The Kelso ('Old') Library had begun with seventy subscribers in 1750 but had only sixty-five in 1857; at the other end of the country the Tavistock Library recovered from earlier losses and had 'well over a hundred' by the end of the nineteenth century.[11] Membership of the Guildford Institute (a mechanics' institute but with many characteristics of a subscription library) dropped from around 400 in 1875 to 250 ten years later.[12] On the other hand, the Edinburgh Subscription Library had over 400 members by 1880 and its local rival, the Edinburgh Select Subscription Library, had 300 subscribers by

---

8 See www.r-alston.co.uk.

9 See also P. H. Jones and E. Rees (eds.), *A nation and its books: a history of the book in Wales* (Aberystwyth, 1998); E. Rees and G. Walters, 'Swansea libraries in the nineteenth century', *Journal of the Welsh Bibliographical Society* 10 (1966–71), 43–57; K. Kissack, *Victorian Monmouth* (Monmouth, 1986), 128–32.

10 C. M. Baggs, 'The miners' institute libraries of South Wales 1875–1939', in Jones and Rees (eds.), *A nation and its books*, 297–305.

11 *The Tavistock Subscription Library 1799–1999* (Tavistock, 1999).

12 R. Chamberlin, *Survival: the rise, fall and rise of the Guildford Institute* (Guildford, 1997), 66.

1881.[13] Founding members occasionally included members of the landed gentry,[14] but very rarely artisans, requiring as they did an initial capital investment of a guinea or more and an additional annual subscription. Solicitors, doctors, merchants, manufacturers, bankers, schoolmasters, clergymen, grocers, politicians, printers, booksellers and in some libraries their wives and daughters formed the greater part of most lists of subscribers. And this situation had not changed in 1850 when the members of the libraries still surviving were mostly of middle-class stock, commonly sharing members with the local philosophical and literary societies but less commonly with the mechanics' institutes.

There was though an increasing concentration on exclusivity in some of the subscription libraries of the later nineteenth century which drew some criticism. The creation in Barrow-in-Furness of a 'public lending library' in 1864 was, in fact, an independent venture pointedly intended to improve upon the limited efforts and membership of the nearby Ulverston Library (founded in 1847);[15] the municipal library at Barrow was not opened until 1882.[16] The libraries in the larger towns were still solidly middle class. Their members, though, were living at an increasing distance from libraries founded in a semi-rural situation but which now found themselves in the middle of busy commercial or retail districts. The Portico Library in Manchester experienced these changes, and also introduced changes of its own with the first admission of female members in the 1870s and the families of members from 1904. Despite such changes, there is a suggestion in the report for the 1904 AGM that this library was failing to attract members from the city's new industrial and professional sectors and this suggestion is probably applicable to other surviving proprietary libraries: 'The Portico is a splendid place for retired Manchester citizens, who still reside in the neighbourhood, to spend a portion of their time in, and to meet their friends.'[17]

Despite their respectable middle-class constituency, subscription libraries were not always the places of quiet repose in busy town and city centres that they are often imagined to have been. This is most obviously revealed by the elections to their management committees. The Portico Library's committee

13 Manley database.

14 As at the Devon and Exeter Institution; see F. M. Drake, *A hundred years with the Devon & Exeter Institution* (Exeter, 1913), 20–2.

15 J. Gavin, 'Cumbrian literary institutions: Cartmel & Furness to 1900', in P. Isaac and B. McKay (eds.), *Images & texts: their production and distribution in the 18th and 19th centuries* (Winchester, 1997), 53–64.

16 T. Greenwood, *British library year book 1900–1901* (London, 1900), 76.

17 Brooks and Haworth, *Portico Library*, 29–36.

elections in the mid-nineteenth century brought about a shift from the 'quiet gentlemanly' medical men and clergymen previously dominant to what one contemporary commentator described as 'a junto of Leaguers, Papists and warehouse salesmen'.[18] Following on from the Tory-dominated committees of the 1830s at the Leeds Library, the committees of the 1840s were dominated by Puseyite supporters of the Vicar of Leeds, Dean Hook, to the chagrin of the liberal, dissenting *Leeds Mercury*. In 1853, a completely new committee was elected which was intent on introducing new practices rather than pursuing local politics. It immediately set about filling gaps in the collections, extending the opening hours and chasing outstanding subscriptions.[19]

Changes in committee membership could radically alter a library's outlook and character: those actually employed to run subscription libraries tradition-ally had less influence on a library's direction. Members were anxious to keep control of book selection and other matters in an institution that in many cases they actually owned. As the nineteenth century progressed, however, perma-nent staff were more commonly employed and given more responsibility, rather than the part-time booksellers and others engaged at the outset. There is some evidence that career librarians of quality were increasingly sought by the larger institutions, though the salaries offered were not always high. In 1853, the Leeds Library employed Robert Harrison as its librarian on an annual salary of £120; he moved on to the London Library in 1857 and twenty years later was one of the founders of the Library Association.[20] Also influential in the Library Association's early days was J. Y. W. MacAlister, librarian at Leeds 1881–7, recruited from the Liverpool Library and later librarian at the Royal College of Surgeons.[21] At Nottingham Arthur Lineker, librarian 1899–1926, became a Fellow of the Library Association in 1914 and encouraged his staff to take professional qualifications.[22] It must be said, however, that many sub-scription libraries continued to employ unqualified librarians – sometimes to good effect – well into the twentieth century.

From the very outset, the collections of the subscription libraries reflected a tension between the acquisition of material to meet the needs of contem-porary subscribers and the acquisition of material of lasting value outside

18 Brooks and Haworth, *Portico Library*, 32.
19 Beckwith, *Leeds Library*, 47–51.
20 Beckwith, *Leeds Library*, 51–3.
21 Beckwith, *Leeds Library*, 72–7; S. Godbolt and W. A. Munford, *The incomparable Mac: a biographical study of Sir John Young Walker MacAlister* (London, 1983).
22 P. Hoare, 'Nottingham Subscription Library: its organisation, its collections and its management over 175 years', in R. T. Coope and J. Y. Corbett (eds.), *Bromley House 1752–1991: four essays celebrating the 175th anniversary of the Nottingham Subscription Library* (Nottingham, 1991), 1–47 (particularly 41–2).

the immediate requirements of subscribers. Material in the former category, by virtue of being retained rather than discarded, might in due course form part of the latter category. The Victorian and Edwardian novels and periodicals and runs of eighteenth-, nineteenth- and twentieth-century travels common to many of the surviving institutions and now highly prized were acquired to satisfy previous generations of subscribers. Changes in the subject areas from which everyday acquisitions were made reflect the changes in the reading tastes of the subscription library members. Philosophy and theology were very popular in 1850 but much less so a century later. The same is also true of science and, in certain libraries, books in foreign languages. The subscription libraries at Hull, Leeds, Norwich, Nottingham and Plymouth all acquired substantial quantities of the latter in their early days.[23]

Several subscription libraries surviving into the twentieth century in the larger provincial towns held significant collections. Thomas Greenwood's *British library year book 1900–1901* gives the following figures: Belfast (Linen Hall Library) 44,000 volumes; Birmingham Library 80,000; Edinburgh Subscription Library 'over 43,000'; Hull Subscription Library 50,000; Leeds Library 60,000; Liverpool Library 98,400 (including the Lyceum; the Athenaeum had another 36,000); Manchester (Portico Library), 42,000. The subscription libraries in Leicester, Nottingham and Whitby all held 30,000, and even the Tavistock Library boasted 16,000 volumes.[24] Many of these subscription libraries were still aiming to add books of value to future generations. At Leeds, Nottingham and Hull, 'standard works' sub-committees were established to review the existing collections. At Hull, £25 was spent annually in the 1870s 'in the purchase of rare and valuable works, the worth of which is not likely to be affected by lapse of time, as is that of the ephemeral productions which are so eagerly sought after by the mass of readers'.[25]

The premises occupied had a direct impact on a library's development. The Portico Library in Manchester opened in 1806 in a magnificent purpose-built library and reading room where it still resides today, but most subscription libraries began in humble rented accommodation and only moved into grander and more permanent premises once the viability of the undertaking was established. In the later part of the nineteenth century further expansion was sometimes possible. In 1880–1 the Leeds Library built a major extension

23 See, for example, P. S. Morrish, 'Foreign-language books in some Yorkshire subscription libraries 1785–1805', *Yorkshire Archaeological Journal* 53 (1981), 79–92.
24 Greenwood, *British library year book*, 273–320.
25 *History of the subscription Library at Kingston-upon-Hull* (Hull, 1876), xvii.

to the rear of its 1808 building at a cost of £4,400.[26] The Plymouth Proprietary Library's 1812 building acquired a new frontage in 1850.[27] The Liverpool
Library and the Hull Subscription Library each shared newly built premises
with another institution. As early as 1802, the Liverpool Library had offered
a home to the Lyceum Club and continued to share its premises until the
Library closed in 1942, after being damaged by bombs.[28] In Hull the Library
and the Philosophical and Literary Society moved jointly into the new Royal
Institution building in 1855.[29]

Added space provided increased opportunities. In 1854, the Bradford Library
and Literary Society moved into new premises in order to make room for a
desired increase in membership.[30] Frequently, the library premises included
property to rent, providing an additional source of income. It is perhaps not surprising that several of the surviving subscription libraries have such premises:
the Leeds Library's building has two shops at ground level in a busy shopping
street, as does Nottingham's; the Portico Library rented its ground floor to a
bank in 1920 (in 1986 the area – with extra sound-proofing! – was leased for
use as a café-bar).[31]

Just twelve subscription libraries were still in existence at the end of the
twentieth century, and some of these were amalgamations of previously independent institutions. The Armitt Library (created 1909) was an amalgamation
of the Ambleside Book Club (1828) and the Ambleside Ruskin Library (1882),[32]
and the Birmingham and Midland Institute (founded 1854) incorporated in 1955
the Birmingham Library (1779), which itself had absorbed the Birmingham
New Library (1794) in 1860.[33] The fashion for creating subscription libraries
faded as literary and scientific institutions and mechanics' institutes, with
libraries of their own in addition to other facilities, began to appear in increasingly large numbers. A significant number of the disappearing subscription
libraries in fact amalgamated with these new institutions with which they frequently had a large number of members in common: for example the Chester
Public Library (founded 1773) had 120 subscribers in 1836, but only forty-four
in 1856, and was taken over the following year by the Mechanics' Institute.

26 Beckwith, *Leeds Library*, 22–4 and 64–72.
27 *Western Evening Herald* (1989), various articles.
28 N. Carrick, 'Liverpool Library in the eighteenth century', unpublished MA dissertation,
      University of Sheffield (1995), 50–1.
29 Victoria County History, *A history of the County of York, East Riding*, vol. 1, 425–6.
30 D. M. Roberts, 'The Bradford Library 1774–1974', unpublished MA dissertation, Univer-
      sity of Sheffield (1974).
31 Brooks and Haworth, *Portico Library*, 68–9 and 106–8.
32 E. Jay, *The Armitt story* (Ambleside, 1998), 1–8.
33 Parish, *Birmingham Library*, 63, 80.

The libraries of the rival institutions occasionally became the dominant feature. This was the case at the Literary and Philosophical Society of Newcastle upon Tyne.[34] Founded in 1793, this society began with an emphasis on research and education, concentrating particularly on science, local industry and local antiquities.[35] The first library acquisitions, not unnaturally, emphasised the sciences. But, by the middle of the nineteenth century, the book collections had broadened with the inclusion of reviews, magazines and more popular works. By 1891, the increasing demands faced from subscribers caused works of controversial divinity, novels and practical works on law and physics to be admitted for the first time. The specialist science collection was combined and then shared with that of the Mining Institute from 1870. Another original emphasis, the museum collection, had been disposed of some time before. However, the lecture programme, another original feature, continues vigorously to this day. Two further surviving examples where the library is the central feature of a more general institution are the Ipswich Institute (a mechanics' institute founded 1824)[36] and the Highgate Scientific and Literary Institution in London (founded 1839).[37]

Unfortunately, a large number of subscription libraries never attracted enough subscribers to sustain other than a small-scale operation. The Warrington Library, founded 1760 and one of the earliest in England, never had more than seventy subscribers and closed in 1848 when it was taken over by the local corporation (already responsible for one of the first public libraries). The proposers of the Leeds New Subscription Library (founded 1793), created in large part because of the overcrowding and difficulty of obtaining new books at the 'Old Library', imposed a limit of a hundred members: it failed in the 1860s. At the York Subscription Library, rising costs coupled with a falling membership (and a perpetually modest subscription) caused continuing problems. Membership had fallen from 487 in 1825 to 366 by the centenary in 1893, despite the population of York doubling during the same period (and even that marked a recovery from 284 in 1877).[38] Book purchasing suffered as a result: in 1825, £270 from a total income of £670 was expended on books, while by 1893

---

34 R. S. Watson, *The history of the Literary and Philosophical Society of Newcastle upon Tyne (1793–1896)* (Newcastle, 1897). A second volume by C. Parish covering 1896–1989 appeared in 1990.

35 Literary and Philosophical Society of Newcastle upon Tyne, *Bicentenary lectures* (Newcastle, 1994) concentrates on its involvement with a wide range of professions.

36 E. H. Hanson, *An historical essay of the Ipswich Institute 1925–1987* (Ipswich, 1989).

37 *Heart of a London village: the Highgate Literary and Scientific Institution, 1839–1990* (Highgate, 1991).

38 York Subscription Library, *Celebration of its centenary* (York, 1894).

the total income had dwindled to £496 and the expenditure on books to just £118. The library closed in 1917.

The creation of free public libraries and particularly the gradual appearance of local branch libraries was also considered by contemporaries to have had a detrimental impact on subscription libraries during the later nineteenth century. The chairman of the Portico Library in Manchester wrote in 1904: 'It is only necessary to remind the Committee that the multiplication of well-appointed free libraries . . . [has] neutralized to a large extent the advantages which the Portico possessed.'[39] Where closures occurred, the new local public library was often the obvious place to deposit the failed library's collection, thus ensuring that the subscription library's collection was kept together for the public good. The Kilkenny Library Society (founded in 1811) was approached by the local corporation in 1904 with the suggestion that its collection be absorbed within the new Carnegie free library: this duly occurred, though not until 1911.[40] More recently, the Montrose Subscription Library closed in 1975 when its collection was added to Montrose Public Library. Salvation by amalgamation did not happen in every case and many collections were simply sold by auction or to local booksellers.

In the case of subscription libraries that had been long struggling to attract subscribers and income, as in Kilkenny, their closure and their absorption by the new public library is understandable. It is a little harder to understand why the grander, middle-class institutions like the Portico Library should so quickly suffer from the free-library challenge. The collections of the larger subscription libraries were not to be surpassed in size for many decades. The Birmingham Library, which in 1860 merged with its local rival the Birmingham New Library, boasted as a result that it had the finest reference library in the midlands.[41] The Hull Subscription Library at its centenary in 1875 had, with 36,000 books, more than the combined collections of all the other libraries in Hull.[42] And those same larger libraries could offer social exclusivity in comfortable surroundings.

The removal of many subscribers to these larger metropolitan examples to homes in the suburbs has already been mentioned as one reason for declining levels of use. Another was said to be the growth of individual subscriptions to the large metropolitan circulating libraries such as Day's, Harrod's and Mudie's, which supplied customers throughout the country with popular reading. It is a little ironic that many subscription libraries turned to these same circulating

39 Brooks and Haworth, *Portico Library*, 58.
40 Casteleyn, *History of literacy and libraries in Ireland*, 117–19.
41 Parish, *Birmingham Library*, 71.
42 Victoria County History, *County of York, East Riding*, vol. 1, 425.

libraries. The reasons included pressure on storage space, their subscribers' seemingly insatiable demand for light fiction, and financial stringencies. For an annual subscription, the demand for large numbers of popular works in subscription libraries was satisfied by the temporary acquisition of borrowing copies from these companies. At the Birmingham Library in 1860, 'The Committee have felt compelled by the increasing competition of other libraries and book clubs to supply an unusual amount of light literature for the use of the large proportion of members requiring that class of books, though it is a subject of regret to them that it should be necessary to apply the funds of the Library to such a purpose.'[43] As demand was satisfied, the books could then be exchanged for others. The use of commercial circulating libraries dated from the mid-nineteenth century and lasted until recent times, the Portico Library's subscriptions only ending in 1969 and Nottingham's continuing until 1980.[44]

Despite the growing competition from public and circulating libraries, many larger proprietary libraries celebrating their first centenaries looked forward confidently to a further hundred years. At Hull, in 1875, the president said: 'Another jubilee will come; and another centenary. When such epochs arrive, the Library will still be in its youth, growing more rapidly than now, and rendering far wider and better service.'[45] Sadly another hundred years brought the library's final dispersal.[46] The Linen Hall Library in Belfast was forced from its original accommodation during its centenary year in 1888: instead of dissolving, however, it purchased its present home in Donegall Square. Earlier the same year, the Linen Hall's secretary stated that 'After a century of varied growth, the Society of today is able to claim the possession of one of the most important public libraries in Ireland',[47] a claim which is still valid today.

The subscription library was, at its outset, a place of innovation, with books on open access, printed catalogues and democratic selection procedures. As the nineteenth century closed, many libraries were looking to introduce card catalogues and modern conveniences such as electric lighting, typewriters and telephones. The Portico Library sent a deputation to the Leeds Library in 1902 to compare methods and to seek ideas for improving the home institution. However, the twentieth century began with a new wave of subscription

---

43 Parish, *Birmingham Library*, 71.
44 Hoare, 'Nottingham Subscription Library', 20–2.
45 *History of the subscription library at Kingston-upon-Hull*, xxiii.
46 J. Hooton, 'The Hull Subscription Library closure and sale', *Library History* 4 (1976), 11–12. The Leeds Library acquired 1,500 volumes at the sale.
47 Killen, *History of the Linen Hall Library*, 69, 65.

library closures.⁴⁸ As it progressed, those that remained faced threats both old and new and, as a result, declined still further in number. The Hull and Plymouth proprietary libraries lost their historic buildings and much of their historic collections to enemy action during the Second World War but continued to function. One casualty of the war did not survive: in 1942 the Liverpool Library closed its doors, in the face of competition from commercial circulating libraries and the evacuation of members from a city suffering heavy bombing. From 950 members at the end of the eighteenth century, the membership of the Liverpool Library had fallen to under 400 by the time of closure.⁴⁹

Those libraries that struggled on past the Second World War were faced with a variety of challenges: vigorous and expanding public library services, declining memberships, aging bookstocks, deteriorating and expensive buildings and new public charges. In the 1950s, the exemption from local taxation granted to many libraries under the 1843 Scientific and Literary Societies Act was removed, almost always precipitating a financial crisis. Additional financial blows were dealt by the combination of low rents from tenants and, from the early 1970s onwards, high inflation.

Despite being founded to collect books in perpetuity, the subscription libraries had always disposed of stock, not least because of restricted premises. Institutions removed unwanted material, frequently donating or selling it to other local libraries. Failing libraries, as a last desperate measure, sold items of value to raise much-needed funds; such asset-stripping became increasingly common in the twentieth century (even affecting the London Library in the 1960s). In the 1950s several libraries sold runs of periodicals when demand for them existed amongst the new university libraries, and fine illustrated books were sold in the 1970s and 1980s when that demand had waned. Rare-book collections were always vulnerable: the Portico Library sold a fourteenth-century manuscript and modern first editions for £103 in 1913, then sold a collection of eighteenth-century pamphlets to the John Rylands Library in 1928.⁵⁰ The disposals at the Nottingham Subscription Library were particularly severe: in 1926, 2,500 'old fashioned books' were discarded and a significant number of older books 'of comparatively little use in a General Library' were sold to Sotheran's for little over £500: they included a 1493 *Nuremberg Chronicle*, a

48 Examples from the Manley database, not mentioned above, include Cockermouth Library (1904); Lancaster Amicable Library (1905); Huddersfield Subscription Library (1906); Wolverhampton Library (1912); Whitehaven Library (1921).
49 Kaufman, *Libraries and their users*, 214; *Liverpool Daily Post*, 6 April 1942.
50 Brooks and Haworth, *Portico Library*, 66, 77.

1496 book of hours, three other incunabula and Speed's maps of 1676. In 1980, Nottingham was again forced to sell books for the sum of £24,786.[51]

The imperative to preserve as much as possible continued despite such desperate measures. At the start of the twenty-first century, as public and academic libraries themselves dispose of large quantities of stock, the collections of the larger subscription libraries are increasing in local and national significance once again. It would be an overstatement to say that subscription libraries at the start of the twenty-first century are enjoying a revival. There is no known recent example of a new subscription library being founded on the model of 200 years ago, and several of the surviving examples continue to struggle owing to a lack of income (and subscribers) and problems with ancient buildings. Nevertheless, from amongst the surviving examples, there are signs of increased activity and renewed interest. Not least of these signs is the existence of the Association of Independent Libraries (AIL) founded in 1989 with twelve members, rising to twenty-seven by 2003. The members include proprietary subscription libraries, mechanics' institute libraries and libraries of philosophical and literary societies, together with the London Library, an institution unlike any other. The aim of the AIL is to increase awareness of the buildings and collections of the member libraries as well as to provide a source of support for libraries and library staff often remote from other professional contact and expertise.[52]

The surviving subscription libraries have benefited by continuing to provide a traditional book-based service in comfortable and attractive surroundings. Many are custodians of listed buildings and of historic book collections of some antiquity; their memberships are relatively small, allowing a personal service from staff not possible in larger institutions; subscriptions have not risen in line with inflation, allowing a larger cross-section of society to afford them; and those with city-centre properties have been able to apply increased rents to the repair of their buildings and stock and to the purchase of new stock and of new technology. The success of the subscription library product is witnessed by increasing memberships in many of them. This has been encouraged at least in part by the development of a higher public profile. The AIL has assisted in this but the local loyalty, hard work and enthusiasm that preserved a few examples of a late eighteenth and early nineteenth century phenomenon are

---

51 Hoare, 'Nottingham Subscription Library', 18–19.
52 For further information about the AIL see G. Forster, 'Libraries for the few: the members of the Association of Independent Libraries and their archives', *Library History* 9 (1/2) (1991), 15–26; G. Forster, 'The subscription library in the twentieth century', *Library Review* 44 (6) (1995), 5–18; and its website www.independentlibraries.co.uk.

now developing the traditional services by extending opening hours, opening historic buildings to the public, putting on lectures, computerising catalogues and creating websites. That the proprietary libraries are gradually acquiring charitable status emphasises their desire to preserve institutions of great historical interest and collections of national importance and make them available to as wide a public as possible.

The London Library: a pendant by Alan Bell

Most of the libraries already discussed have Georgian origins. The London Library is an early Victorian foundation, atypical in this as in its size, and in its influence on the literary and cultural scene for more than a century and a half. While it shares some characteristics of its smaller sisters it deserves fuller treatment and consideration of its distinctive role.[53]

The puzzling thing about the foundation of the London Library in 1841 is that it had not taken place much sooner. At the beginning of Queen Victoria's reign the provincial cities of England could show several notable precedents for serious, purposeful subscription libraries, but in London it took the strenuous efforts of Thomas Carlyle to identify the need and to galvanise the vague intentions of metropolitan literary men into practical proposals.

Late in 1838 Carlyle began to use his widening range of literary acquaintance in London to agitate for a 'serious' lending library there. His own attitude to libraries was equivocal: they were essential to his historical work, but he found it inconvenient, even distressing (he wrote of the 'Museum headache'), to study in the British Museum's reading room when he could do the same work more efficiently at home. Carlyle's annoyance with the Museum fuelled his campaign on behalf of the London Library, and he enlisted in the cause the young Richard Monckton Milnes, William Dougal Christie (who became with Carlyle the joint secretary of the planning committee), and others. John Forster and others assisted in what Carlyle called 'working the great bellows-machinery of the Newspaper Press'.

In spite of the stress it occasioned he did not spare himself in the cause, even though he found public speaking a challenge. A public meeting was held in the Freemasons' Tavern on 24 June 1840, at which Carlyle followed Dean

---

53 See W. Baker, *The early history of the London Library* (Lewiston, NY, 1992), S. Nowell-Smith, 'Carlyle and the London Library', in C. B. Oldman and others, *English libraries 1800–1850* (London, 1958), and the amiably informal *Rude words: a discursive history of the London Library* by J. Wells (Macmillan, 1991). M. Grindea (ed.), *The London Library* (Ipswich, 1977) combines factual articles with members' reminiscences.

Milman and Lord Lyttelton with a brief but effective speech, not censuring the Museum but proposing an essential complement to it:

> Leaving all other institutions and the British Museum and the circulating libraries to stand, a deservedly good library of good books is a crying want in this great London . . . London has more men and intellects waiting to be developed than any place in the world ever had assembled. Yet there is no place in the civilised earth so ill supplied with materials for reading for those who are not rich. I have read an account of a public library in Iceland, which the King of Denmark had founded there. There is not a peasant in Iceland that can not bring home books to his hut better than men can in London. Positively it is a kind of disgrace to us, which we ought to assemble and put an end to with all convenient despatch.[54]

And so, with many sound-bites, much applause, and immediate administrative resolve, the Library was soon on the road. The principles of accessibility, availability for home study and low cost to subscribers, which have remained central to the Library's administration, were clearly identified in the earliest prospectuses. They were explicitly set out by W. D. Christie in an open letter to Lord Clarendon (who became the Library's first President), which includes a list of supporters who entered their names before 15 February 1841.[55]

Carlyle had identified as a potential librarian a journalist and former book-seller, John George Cochrane (1781–1852), who had edited the *Foreign Quarterly Review*, and in February 1841 edged him in (nine votes to eight) ahead of a somewhat limited field; doubtless Cochrane's connection with the cataloguing of Scott's library at Abbotsford also counted in his favour. His arrival freed Carlyle from the burden of joint secretaryship; and the founder (for so he is correctly regarded) became a deliberately non-participant member of the Library's committee. He was, of course, from the start a heavy user (291 volumes in eleven months of 1842), and his early borrowings included the Camden Society's *Chronica Jocelin de Brakelonde*, the Bury St Edmunds history on which his *Past and Present* (1843) was founded.

Rented premises were found in Pall Mall; then from 1845 a lease was taken of 12 (renumbered 14 in 1884) St James's Square. The stock, which Cochrane was able to assemble using special desiderata lists solicited from the subscribers (including, for example, Gladstone on ecclesiastical history and Mazzini on Italian history), grew rapidly. He was helped by purchasing

---

54 *Morning Chronicle*, 25 June 1840, and see *The collected letters of Thomas and Jane Welsh Carlyle* (Durham, NC), vol. 12, 174–5.
55 W. D. Christie, *An explanation of the scheme of The London Library, in a letter to the Earl of Clarendon* (London, 1841).

opportunities for older continental books still glutting the London market after the dispersals of the Napoleonic wars. The Committee and members urgently demanded a catalogue, which Cochrane was able to make available by mid-March 1842: 134 pages, giving titles of about 13,000 works. About 1000 volumes were being added each month while the Library was starting up, and supplements were printed in 1843 and 1844. By then Carlyle was able to urge on Edward Fitzgerald the convenience of being 'admitted freely to such an extent of book-pasturage',[56] and in November 1846 even the founder was able to admit to a complaining member that 'To me it yields on the whole tho' by no means what I wished, yet some average approximation to what I hoped'.[57]

In 1847 a second edition of the *Catalogue*, with 512 pages of author entries, was issued. Cochrane mistrusted subject indexes, which were indeed less necessary in smaller open-access libraries, and the Library ran tolerably well on such inadequate, cumulated author indexes until growth demanded an overall revision at the end of the century. The 1847 catalogue was able to list 119 life and 725 annual subscribers (at £20, and £2 p.a. respectively, with £6 entrance money). They include a good many with country addresses: the 'London Library' had been thought of from the start as being able to provide a postal service to those living far from the metropolis. It is not easy (then as now) to categorise the membership, who at that early stage included more of the nobility and gentry than in later years. Barristers, civil servants and clergy seem prominent, representing perhaps a 'reading' element, though it is of course the 'writing' element, including Dickens, Leigh Hunt, George Henry Lewes and Thackeray, who seem now to stand out among the roll of intelligent reading members for whom the Library was also created. Dickens himself, with Forster, George Grote, Henry Hallam and Monckton Milnes, was then among the twenty-four members of the Committee (of whom twenty-two are noticed in *DNB*: the two others were members of parliament). These twenty-four, along with the President, Vice-Presidents and Trustees, made up something of a *comité d'honneur*, but the governance of the Library was clearly in the hands of a smaller group (the quorum was only three). From the start, however, they all took a keen interest, and the first Patron, HRH Prince Albert, presented a quantity of recent German publications.

Cochrane, whom members much respected as what Carlyle called a 'bibliographer' (its modern equivalent might be 'reader services and acquisitions

---

56 Carlyle, *Letters*, vol. 18, 251.
57 *Ibid.*, vol. 12, 85.

librarian'), fell ill and died in 1852. Gladstone immediately tried hard to secure the post for the Neapolitan political refugee J. P. (later Sir James) Lacaita, but the Committee, to Carlyle's relief, overwhelmingly preferred William Bodham Donne (1807–82), a well-connected Norfolk *littérateur*, who held the post for five years and left to become Examiner of Plays without having made any special impression on the Library. A disappointed deputy, John Edward Jones, probably bore the brunt of the work under him (and long continued dissatisfied when Donne's successor was appointed). The Lacaita incident was to be Carlyle's last strenuous effort on behalf of his Library; in old age he became its (strictly non-participating) President, holding office from 1870 till his death in 1881.

Robert Harrison, who succeeded Donne in 1857, brought with him some relevant professional experience. Harrison was eventually indeed the first Treasurer of the Library Association, for which some preliminary meetings took place in 1877 at the London Library. He had worked in St Petersburg as a tutor and lecturer from 1844, returning to England in 1853 to become librarian of the Leeds Library. He was strongly recommended by his Leeds committee, and once in London rose to the challenge of arresting a sharp decline in both income and members. Membership at the start of his tenure stood at 970; when he left in 1893 it was 2,302. In spite of tensions such as disputes over *ex gratia* payments for use of his apartment in an already crowded building, Harrison produced a serviceable fourth edition of the catalogue (1875), and a fifth (1888) with a classified index, making a step in the direction of a subject index to the collections. In 1879 the building and site were secured for £21,000, raised on debentures; this was a precaution that had major consequences for continuity and development. By the 1890s, however, it was clear that a new hand was urgently needed, and Harrison was retired on an enhanced pension.

In 1893, a library that had become grossly overcrowded, its original rooms and even its corridors and staircases overflowing with books, welcomed a new Secretary and Librarian. C. T. Hagberg Wright (1862–1940) was of Irish and Swedish descent and a graduate of Trinity College Dublin. From 1890 he had worked at the National Library of Ireland (partly on the conversion of its stock to Dewey classification), and he was appointed to the London Library from a field of 253 applicants. Dr Hagberg Wright was to spend the rest of his working life at the Library. He had much to do, but had relative youth and boundless energy to do it. Harrison's contrarious deputy Jones had been disposed of in 1886, but there were other aged and limited members of staff for Wright to deal with. He had to advise his committee to provide the next generation of employees with improved salaries and suitable terms of service. With the Library's full backing, and money raised once more largely by debentures, Wright started planning a new building on the existing site. Construction started with a four-storey book stack at the rear of the house and then worked forward to the Square, where special additional contributions to the building fund allowed for the reconstruction of the façade in its present familiar form. The new buildings were formally opened in December 1898, during the energetic presidency of Sir Leslie Stephen.

By then Hagberg Wright had been busy, with very limited assistance, on an overall reclassification, and soon began a new author catalogue to replace the 1888 edition. A full stock census was taken, revealing a total of around 167,000 volumes. These were examined, marked, recatalogued (with special efforts made to check details of authors' names), and re-placed, in just over three years; revision and editing of the slips took a further three and a half years, and the new catalogue was published in 1903, supplemented by eight annual instalments. Next came the Subject Index, for which a graduate assistant was specially appointed; he was C. J. Purnell (1878–1959), trained in the Bodleian, who became deputy librarian and eventually Wright's successor from 1940 to 1950. The *Subject Index* appeared in 1909, with further volumes in 1923 and 1938; its size and concision have given it a utility well beyond the London Library's own stock. The author catalogue was then revised and published in two volumes (1913–14), to be further extended by supplements, all issued under Wright's supervision but with a major editorial contribution from Purnell, in 1920 and 1928. Here, too, the compilation soon enjoyed a circulation beyond the subscribers. Meanwhile the site was being consolidated by further freehold acquisitions to provide land for future growth, but more immediately (though delayed by war) a seven-storey extension of the rear book stack was erected in 1922. In 1934 – the year in which Wright received a knighthood – the next stage of development (which included much-needed new working accommodation for staff) was completed, filling the site almost though not quite completely. Membership figures rose, too, in line with the improved facilities: in 1893 the roll stood at 2,302; in 1920, 4,014; and in 1939, 4,410.

Even more than his predecessor Harrison, Wright had a special interest in Russian literature, having as a young man travelled in the country to learn the language. Their work has ensured for the Library a high reputation in the subject that has never been entirely overtaken by the later development of specialist research institutions. Wright had friends in Russian dissident cultural circles, and he also gathered 700 signatures of English admirers for an eightieth-birthday tribute to Tolstoy, which in 1908 he delivered personally at Yasnaya

Polyana. He was known, somewhat apprehensively, as a pursuer of benefactors, and became a respected figure in the world of rare books. He saw the special importance of well-chosen (though, in a library of this kind, less-used) additions to the antiquarian stock. In 1920–1, for example, he acquired intact from the Methodist Church the Allan Library, a substantial collection of historic texts of the Reformation period.

As Sir William Orpen's 1922 portrait at the library shows, Wright, with luxuriant Edwardian moustaches and velvet smoking jacket, cut a notable figure. Librarians should not expect the history of their institutions to be characterised by their own tenures, but Sir Charles Hagberg Wright's years in St James's Square must be an exception. He died in 1940, shortly before the Library's centenary. The members had been duly respectful, indeed increasingly in awe, of his achievements. During his tenure they seem to have been generally well heeled and well connected, if somewhat complacent, and they were able to enjoy the benefits of improved premises with an expanding and well-housed stock.

Purnell took up the librarianship and saw the institution through the Second World War. He had a hard time of it during the Blitz, especially in February 1944 when an incendiary bomb severely damaged the new building, leading to serious losses in the Religion section and a general reduction in services. For a time the Librarian, bombed out of his own home, took up residence in the basement. Membership was, to start with, badly affected by the war, but soon recovered; by 1944 the roll stood unprecedentedly at over 5,000. Many of the recruits, not least numerous temporary civil servants, remained in membership after 1945, and the average remained comfortably over 5,000 until the late 1950s.

Meanwhile Purnell was at work on further volumes of the *Author Catalogue* and the *Subject Index*. These were not published until after his retirement in 1950, but he was kept on to complete the task during the time of his successor, Simon Nowell-Smith (1909–96), who held office until 1956. Nowell-Smith was a bibliophile and former assistant editor of the *Times Literary Supplement*, who had spent the war as an Admiralty civil servant. His tenure was brief but he revived the Library, not least in giving its acquisitions a clearer focus and bringing an outsider's eye to what had become an administratively introverted organisation. 'Representative' (i.e. corporate) membership was introduced. Any discouragement to joining caused by rising subscriptions was largely offset by a new trust fund, which provides both half-fee grants to those who cannot afford the full subscription and a very useful supplement to the Library's annual book-purchase allocation. Staff salaries were brought more into line with those in comparable institutions, and were before long assimilated to university scales. War damage was made good and, following the then sub-librarian's sudden death, Stanley Gillam (1915–2004) was recruited from the Bodleian (where his career had started, coincidentally similar to Purnell's many years before) to take the deputy position.

Soon afterwards Nowell-Smith resigned in order to resume literary work, and Gillam succeeded him in 1956, serving until 1980. (He was in turn succeeded by Douglas Matthews (b.1927), who had been deputy since 1965 and served until 1992.) Almost immediately the Library's finances, in which the subscription income was inadequately supported by appropriate reserves, were put into turmoil by the Westminster City Council's summary withdrawal of a standing exemption under the 1843 Scientific and Learned Societies Act, and a full rate on the building was claimed. The Library strongly contested this to a point at which the costs of a further appeal would have been disproportionate, and members were generous in assisting the costs of the case. The President, T. S. Eliot, gave high mandarin testimony to the Library's cultural quiddity, but even he failed to convince the rating tribunal of the real extent of its cultural outreach.

A mood of barely redeemable penuriousness set in. There was a sale of specially donated books and literary manuscripts, which raised £25,000 in 1960, and another in 1966 (which then seemed essential, and lucrative), of the Library's eighty-eight incunabula, raising a further £67,000; these were large sums for the time, but could be no more than palliative. Committee minutes of this period make distressing reading, with unavoidable expenditure rising ahead of increased subscriptions, and rented-out property requiring substantial outlay. It was fortunate for the Library that a way was found, without undue complication, of securing registration as a charity.

Charitable status was essential, not only to secure rate and tax concessions and other fiscal privileges but more generally to demonstrate that this beneficent literary society was not some kind of exclusive private club. The membership had been broadening, not least with the rapid national postwar growth in higher education. University lecturers and their graduate students increasingly found that St James's Square was able to offer, at moderate fees, facilities that their own institutions could not always provide. For its part, the London Library was able, in spite of unpropitious financial indications, to expand its membership range without displacing its more general readership. (The Library has never been able to analyse its membership in much detail – 'scholars' need their 'general reading', and the 'general readers', surprisingly often, need works that would elsewhere be deemed strangely recondite.) The membership remains notable for its contingent of media personalities, as well as its larger group of literary and academic readers; they can all be guaranteed a discreet lack of recognition on the premises.

Faced on all fronts with rising costs (book prices, even at special discounts, were by 1971 six times their wartime equivalents), but with income largely restricted to subscriptions that could be raised only very gradually, it was clear that a finance policy based on something more than occasional general appeals was needed. From the early 1970s a committee chaired by the newspaper heir Michael Astor, assisted as Treasurer by a resolute accountant member, Lewis Golden, addressed the problem. An appeal substantially exceeded its £500,000 target, and helped to pay for urgently needed additional storage space and to start replenishing financial reserves. A long lease of rented domestic property was sold, the result producing a much higher yield in equities. Bequests and donations, with this careful financial planning, helped to ensure that a decade later the Library found itself on a very much firmer footing, with some of the resources that were needed to contemplate further physical expansion and – perhaps even more importantly – the inauguration of computerised cataloguing and circulation systems. Membership increased accordingly: an average of 6,109 in the decade 1975–84 became 7,509 in 1985–94, and has since stabilised at above 8,300. Expenditure on books and periodicals rose, too; in the same decades the average annual figures are £46,166 (1975–84), £116,333 (1985–94), and since 1995 £169,267; it is a matter for pride that budgets have each year allowed some increase in the allocation for acquisitions. The stock is currently reckoned at around a million volumes.

A further successful appeal, aimed at final expansion on the site and the gradual computerisation of the catalogues, commemorated the Library's 150th anniversary in 1991. By then it was clear that the London Library, through judicious husbanding of its financial resources, improved facilities for access, and the maintenance of provision for book purchase and of reader service standards, was able to offer its members something that is increasingly seen as entirely special in a rapidly changing world of libraries. The urgent need for further space continues to cause anxiety, and will inevitably dominate planning for future needs. Events of the last decade, in library technology, book conservation and improvement of services, have nevertheless been able to draw on the confidence that has developed from an improved financial situation. Additional rare-book storage was ingeniously achieved in the new 'Anstruther Wing' of the 1990s. Though expanding the Library's site is difficult in one of the highest-priced parts of London, it may not prove impossible, especially with some advantageous fiscal changes to encourage donations from a loyal membership. Behind all this discreet modernisation there is a sense that the Library is still developing its traditional accessibility – modem and mouse included – on lines of which even Carlyle himself could not have disapproved.

13

Radical reading? Working-class libraries in the nineteenth and early twentieth centuries

CHRIS BAGGS

Introduction

Had you conducted a library audit in many towns in the industrial North of England between 1860 and 1880, or the mining communities of South Wales between 1895 and 1914, you would have encountered numerous libraries, which were not part of the public library system, but instead belonged to the local Co-operative Society or Miners' Institute respectively. Why should that have been? Why, when the legislation allowing for local authority provision had been passed in 1850, should these alternative libraries not just be flourishing, but have been established in the first place?

This chapter investigates the phenomenon of independent working-class libraries in Great Britain in the nineteenth and early twentieth centuries, looking for broad explanations as to their origins. Were they a conscious attempt by this newly emerging and, then, increasingly self-confident class to break clear of middle-class hegemony? Could their existence in part be understood by the phenomenon of 'radical reading', i.e. that the reading practices of the working class involved materials that were politically, economically, socially and culturally radical in their outlook? Were there more mundane reasons for their existence?

The discussion concentrates on those libraries associated with working-class organisations and groups; libraries that arose from a collective response to reading needs based on either a common group identity or a shared ideological position. It does not attempt to deal with those countless libraries assembled by individual working people, acting on their own. These organisations and groups were many and varied, but to come within this chapter's parameters the libraries must essentially be self-administered and self-financed by the working class, and not provided for them via some external agency.

Establishing the themes

A distinct working class emerged in Great Britain towards the end of the eighteenth century with the spread of the industrial revolution and the rapid urbanisation of certain parts of the country. But what critical factors were required before this new class could move to establish its own libraries?

First, it had to be literate. Universal elementary schooling eventually came with the introduction of compulsory, free, state-run education in the decades following the 1870 Elementary Education Act, and this helped ensure that by 1900 the United Kingdom had a mass reading audience, with 97.2% of men and 96.8% of women considered literate.[1]

There also had to be sufficient printed matter at acceptable prices for this new reading public, and the nineteenth century witnessed the arrival of cheap, mass-produced books, newspapers, popular magazines and journals, whilst tracts and pamphlets were everywhere.[2] Cheapness allowed many working-class readers to buy printed materials, but access via purchase was still limited and reading remained a major drain on a working-class family's budget. For most of the nineteenth century, the working-class reader required other forms of access, most obviously via libraries.

Another factor can be described simply as a thirst for knowledge. Knowledge, via the printed word, might be power, as it gave the emerging working class some understanding of the natural world, and of the political, economic and social systems that impacted directly on their lives. But, they had to make a very conscious effort to overcome the many obstacles placed in their way. The desire for self-education and self-improvement was a vital characteristic shown by many working-class readers for much of the nineteenth century.[3]

Finally, there had to be sufficient self-confidence to believe that these problems could be overcome without the involvement of other groups in society. This assertiveness may have come from an awareness that the interests of all classes were not identical. In library terms this meant that middle- and working class reading tastes were not the same, and that it would be wrong to rely on the former to provide for the latter's reading requirements. The desire shown by working-class readers to control what materials were stocked in libraries would prove a strong motivating factor in setting up their own facilities.

---

1 R. D. Altick, *The English common reader* (Chicago, 1957), 171.
2 Altick, *English common reader*, 260–364.
3 J. Burnett (ed.), *Useful toil: autobiographies of working people from the 1820s to the 1920s* (London, 1974); and D. Vincent, *Bread, knowledge and freedom* (London, 1982).

Tracing the history of working-class libraries
pre-1850

The mid to late eighteenth century saw a major rise in the number of libraries theoretically open to the 'public': subscription, circulating and others linked to specific organisations.[4] But these facilities did not suit nineteenth-century working-class readers for various reasons. Many circulating libraries were little more than fashionable social and leisure accessories for their middle- and upper-middle-class audiences, and their subscription regimes were not generally attractive to working people. Subscription and other proprietary libraries were likewise normally beyond the reach of the working man's pocket, besides which their club-like procedures and atmosphere would not have appealed to 'men in fustian jackets', whilst the regular physical mingling of different classes was not a common feature of the early nineteenth century. Even mechanics' institutes, ostensibly developed for a working-class audience in the 1820s, did not provide free access to their libraries.

Thus in the pre-1850 period, one simple reason for establishing working-class reading facilities was financial. The individual 'common reader' did not possess the wherewithal either to use existing libraries or to purchase even the smallest sample of available publications. However, by pooling their limited resources, as they did with great success in Carlisle, working-class readers could significantly increase their purchasing power and choice of materials, and as a result develop collections.[5] Initially journals and newspapers, and then books, could be chosen to suit their reading needs, rather than having to read material bought for the very different clientele frequenting circulating or subscription libraries, or material chosen for them in the libraries of the philanthropically motivated mechanics' institutes. Other practical benefits followed such co-operation. Establishing their own reading facilities meant that rules and regulations could fit their living patterns, such as opening in the evening after work. Reading rooms could be located in congenial surroundings, as in Nottingham, where rooms were rented above public houses in working-class residential areas, making access easier.[6] But it was not simply a question of physical and mental comfort or convenience; there was much more at stake – control. The sentiment expressed in 1823 by Thomas Hodgskin, an

---

4 T. Kelly, *Early public libraries* (London, 1966), 118–51 and 185–240.
5 'The labourer's reading room', *Household Words* 3 (1851), 581–5; this anonymous article was written by Henry Morley.
6 P. Hoare, 'The operatives' libraries of Nottingham: a radical community's own libraries', *Library History* 19 (2003), 173–84; D. Wardle, *Education and society in nineteenth century Nottingham* (Cambridge, 1971), 183.

early advocate of independent working-class education, could easily be applied to library provision: 'it would be better for men to be deprived of education than to receive their education from their masters; for education in that sense is no better than the training of the cattle that are broken to the yoke'.[7] The selection policies of many mechanics' institute libraries were restrictive, with political and religious works, newspapers and even fiction being banned in certain instances. This discouraged or angered the targeted audience. The Artizans' Library, founded in Nottingham in 1824, failed because of 'its lack of appeal to the class for which it was intended'. Subscription rates were probably too high, but more crucially the library was dominated 'by members of the local "establishment"'. 'The more politically conscious working men probably suspected, with some justice, an aura of patronage about the library, and were at the same time suspicious of the political motives of the shareholders.'[8] By administering their own reading facilities, both financially and managerially, working-class readers gained that decisive element of control, as well as valuable experience in running their own affairs, at a time when the working classes generally were flexing their economic and political muscle, and acquiring that self-confidence essential to successfully do things for themselves.

William Lovett was one early working-class leader, who understood the value of organised reading facilities.[9] Library provision was an integral part of the London Working Men's Association that Lovett began in 1836, but he soon realised that what was needed was a national library service for working people. In the 1840 Chartist manifesto, *Chartism; a New Organization of the People*, Lovett, who gave evidence to the 1849 Select Committee on Public Libraries, called for 'circulating libraries, from a hundred to two hundred volumes each', that would be 'sent in rotation from one town or village . . . to another'.[10] The ultimate failure of Chartism meant that this plan was never realised on a national scale, although libraries were established in many Chartist and People's Halls in places such as Bradford and Keighley in the 1840s.[11]

Chartism was not the only working-class movement that saw the importance of providing libraries as part of their educational work. Some of the contemporary utopian socialist communities and 'Halls of Science' associated

7 B. Simon, *The two nations and the educational structure 1780–1870* (London, 1974), 215.
8 Wardle, *Education and Society*, 175.
9 W. Lovett, *Life and struggles of William Lovett* (London, 1967).
10 W. Lovett and J. Collins, *Chartism; a new organization for the people* (London, 1841; repr. Leicester, 1969), 25.
11 Simon, *Two nations*, 243–53.

with Robert Owen included libraries,[12] as did various bodies linked with the first phase of the Co-operative movement.[13] Very little documentary evidence has survived about these libraries, except to suggest that they were very limited in size and not very radical in content. They did however show that the Victorian mantra of 'self-help' could be pursued just as effectively by working-class organisations working entirely on their own.

Tracing the history of working-class libraries post-1850

The first major working-class movement to develop libraries in the post-1850 period was the Co-operative movement,[14] whose second phase began with the foundation of the Rochdale Pioneers in 1844. Within a few years the Pioneers had opened a reading room and library,[15] and as Rochdale acted as a model for the whole movement such facilities became an automatic part of many new Co-operative Societies. By 1879, there were scores of libraries in the northern heartland of English co-operation, with many others in Scotland, and isolated examples in Plymouth, Grays and Portsea.[16]

The libraries were limited in stock, the largest being Rochdale, which in 1879 had over 14,000 volumes. Regular finance came via either an annual grant from the local society, or a fixed percentage of its annual profits being devoted to reading facilities, which formed an integral part of general educational provision. Library usage could have been restricted to members only, but many societies opened their libraries to the general 'public', as the Co-operative Society library was, for much of the last third of the nineteenth century, the only generally available reading facility in many towns and villages. Indeed between 1850 and 1879 more Co-operative Society libraries were opened in England than public libraries.[17]

---

12 Simon, *Two nations*, 235–43.

13 E. Nicholson, 'Working class readers and libraries: a social history 1800–1850', unpublished MA thesis, University of London (1976), 80–99.

14 C. M. Baggs, 'The libraries of the Co-operative movement: a forgotten episode', *Journal of Librarianship and Information Science* 23 (1991), 87–96; and J. Everitt, 'Co-operative Society libraries and newsrooms of Lancashire and Yorkshire from 1844 to 1918', unpublished PhD thesis, University of Wales, Aberystwyth (1997).

15 A. Greenwood, *The educational department of the Rochdale Equitable Pioneers Society Limited* (Manchester, 1877).

16 E. Barnish, 'The Co-operative libraries of Lancashire, Yorkshire and Durham', in *Transactions and proceedings of the second annual meeting of the Library Association* (London, 1879), 61–4; Everitt, 'Co-operative Society libraries and newsrooms'.

17 J. Everitt, 'Co-operative Society libraries', *Library History* 15 (1999), 36.

These libraries were run, financed and controlled by the ordinary working members who constituted the local Society, and access to a library or reading room in a much-frequented shop was easy and comfortable. Larger Societies, such as Rochdale, Bury and Oldham, ran branch reading rooms as well as the central store library, adding to this sense of a genuine local community facility. As late as 1891–2 an advert for three Co-operative stores in London's East End highlighted the provision of a 'free library' as one of the advantages of using the local Co-op.[18] However by the early twentieth century many Co-operative Society libraries had merged with newly established public libraries, suggesting that their original *raison d'être* was waning.[19]

It might be expected that the growth of trade unionism post-1850, with its manifest interest in developing educational opportunities for the working class,[20] would have produced some library development associated with the movement as a whole or with individual unions. However, unlike Germany,[21] this was strikingly not the case in the United Kingdom. Apart from a few isolated libraries provided by small craft-based trades unions,[22] such libraries were not a widespread phenomenon, except in one small area of the country. This lack of interest in trade union run reading facilities did not just reflect individual trade union attitudes. In 1884 the national Trades Union Congress passed a motion calling for the establishment of public library services across the country.[23] This decision suggests that trade union leaders were satisfied that public library provision would meet the general reading needs of their members.

The major exception was in South Wales, where the closing decades of the nineteenth century saw local miners develop the most effective independent working-class library system in the United Kingdom.[24] The miners of South Wales have acquired a reputation as being 'great readers',[25] and from the mid-nineteenth century often had money deducted from their wages to pay for their

18 M. Ll. Davies, *Women's Co-operative Guild, 1883–1904* (London, 1904), 123.
19 Everitt, 'Co-operative society libraries', 36.
20 B. Simon, *Education and the labour movement 1870–1920* (London, 1965).
21 H-J. Steinberg, 'Workers' libraries in Germany before 1914', *History Workshop* 1 (1976), 166–76; and D. Langewiesche and K. Schönhoven, 'Arbeiterbibliotheken und Arbeiterlektüre im Wilhelminischen Deutschland', *Archiv für Sozialgeschichte* 16 (1976), 135–204.
22 D. Mayall, 'The library of the London Society of Compositors, 1855–1896', *Library History* 5 (1979), 55–60; and S. Shipley, 'The libraries of the Alliance Cabinet Makers' Association', *History Workshop* 1 (1976), 180–4.
23 J. J. Ogle, *The free library* (London, 1897), 66.
24 C. M. Baggs, 'The miners' libraries of South Wales from the 1860s to 1939', unpublished PhD thesis, University of Wales, Aberystwyth (1995); H. Francis, 'The origins of the South Wales Miners' Library', *History Workshop* 2 (1976), 183–205.
25 C. M. Baggs, 'How well read was my valley? Reading, popular fiction, and the miners of South Wales, 1875–1939', *Book History* 4 (2001), 277–301.

children's education.[26] When elementary education became free, this money was switched to providing Workmen's Halls and Institutes, which acted as social, recreational and educational centres for the local community. Amongst their facilities was invariably a library.

Some coal-owners provided limited financial and other forms of assistance, and other local residents could join (as 'outsiders'), but in the largely one-industry-dominated valley communities, these Institutes were funded, run and controlled by the miners. Between the 1870s and 1939, up to 200 miners' libraries and reading rooms were founded in the South Wales mining valleys, such that nearly every mining community, no matter how small, either had its own facility or was only a short distance away from one. In the Rhondda valleys alone, there were approximately twenty miners' libraries, offering more static library points than any subsequent public library service has provided.

Together, these libraries stocked nearly half a million volumes, as well as thousands of newspapers, magazines and journals. Tredegar Institute, whose Library Committee was chaired in the 1920s by future left-wing labour MP and minister of health Aneurin Bevan, represents the pinnacle of the Miners' Institute movement, and by 1923 its library held over 8,000 volumes.[27] From the 1920s Tredegar openly pursued a radical book-selection policy, with the library being seen as a major instrument in raising the class-consciousness of its readership.[28]

Economic recession in the mining industry in the 1920s and 1930s deprived many miners' institutes of the regular funding they needed to function effectively, whilst expanding county library services began nibbling away at their independent provision.[29] Nevertheless many Institute libraries continued until the second half of the last century, and in Mountain Ash a few surviving examples were held responsible for the local Urban District Council being the last authority to adopt the old permissive Public Library legislation in 1964.

Library and reading facilities can be found in other working-class institutions, such as working men's clubs.[30] This philanthropically motivated movement, begun initially in 1862 to provide somewhere for working people to

26 L. W. Evans, *Education in industrial Wales, 1700–1900: a study of the works school system in Wales during the Industrial Revolution* (Cardiff, 1971).

27 D. J. Davies, *Ninety years of endeavour: the history of the Tredegar Workmen's Hall, 1861–1951* (Cardiff, 1951).

28 Baggs, 'The miners' libraries', 259.

29 Baggs, 'The miners' libraries', 159–86.

30 J. Taylor, *From self-help to glamour: the working man's club, 1860–1972* (Oxford, 1972); G. Tremlett, *Clubmen: the history of the Working Men's Club and Institute Union* (London, 1987).

meet socially in a teetotal environment for recreation and limited educational advancement,[31] became a genuine working-class institution following a 'palace' revolution in 1884. Officially, most clubs contained a reading room with newspapers, periodicals and some reference works, whilst some clubs, including those in Swansea, Gainsborough and Sheerness,[32] had larger libraries, which loaned books. But the movement's educational side always came a distant second to its recreational function (aided by the provision of cheap alcohol), and despite the obviously convivial surroundings, the number and quality of the reading facilities quickly decreased as the twentieth century progressed.

Again, it might have been anticipated that the working-class political organisations, which developed in the last quarter of the nineteenth century, would provide examples of yet more libraries and reading rooms. Certain radical clubs in London organised small reference and lending collections,[33] as did branches of individual political parties, including the Socialist Labour Party and the Independent Labour Party.[34] Single- or limited-issue radical organisations, such as the Fabian Society and the women's suffrage movement, also put together book boxes that were circulated amongst interested groups.[35] Such more specialist provision could be investigated further, but overall there is little evidence to show much determined effort by working-class political organisations to establish general libraries and reading rooms (unlike their German counterparts).[36]

These later working-class political organisations (and the trade union movement) were probably not more actively involved in instigating general library facilities owing to the existence of the expanding, popular and essentially neutral public library movement, which could and did meet the general reading needs of a growing percentage of the British population, the working class included. Why should any working-class political organisation wish to compete? The British public library movement was in a much better position to provide a general service: it had reasonable and regular finance, growing

31 R. Price, 'The working men's club movement and Victorian social reform ideology', *Victorian Studies* 15 (1971/2), 117–47.

32 S. R. V. Lee, 'The development of libraries within the Working Men's Club and Institute Union', unpublished MLib thesis, University of Wales, Aberystwyth (1992).

33 S. Shipley, *Club life and socialism in mid-Victorian London* (Oxford, 1971); Taylor, *From self-help*.

34 *Labour Leader* (7 April 1894), 4; *The Pioneer* (10 June 1911), 2.

35 P. Pugh, *Educate, agitate, organize: 100 years of Fabian Socialism* (London, 1984), 61–2; E. Crawford, 'Libraries', in *The women's suffrage movement: a reference guide 1866–1928* (London, 1999), 343–9.

36 Steinberg, 'Workers' libraries', 166–76; Langewiesche, 'Arbeiterbibliotheken', 135–204.

experience and expertise and, following the 1919 Public Libraries Act, increasing geographical coverage.

So, why spend money on a Co-operative Society library and also pay rates to support a local public library? Why maintain a miners' institute library, when a better-funded county library service was available? Clearly one reason might be the strength of that sense of ownership or communal solidarity referred to earlier. But were these working-class libraries also still supplying a reading need by meeting a demand for radical literature? By the end of the nineteenth century, much radical literature was available in cheap pamphlets. This was eagerly bought at party political meetings by those interested in its message,[37] but was not normally stocked by libraries, whether public or otherwise. Was radical literature being deliberately withheld by public libraries from its working-class readers? What evidence is there that working-class reading was generally radical?

Radical reading?

Early nineteenth-century examples of working men pooling their resources or breaking away from the censorship practised by certain mechanics' institutes to build their own libraries suggest that controlling access to the materials they wanted to read was an important issue at the time. Similarly, in the early years of the co-operative movement one reason given for establishing their own libraries was that appropriate materials could be bought, that is to say materials that dealt with the principles of co-operation.

But unlike some of the other working-class libraries mentioned above, the miners' institute and Co-operative Society libraries were not one-issue libraries, frequented by a committed readership looking for radical reading material. These were general libraries, offering reading materials across the whole spectrum of fiction and non-fiction to a general reading audience of every age and every interest. The reading habits of the vast majority of this audience did not differ greatly from the reading habits of public library readers. Thus, with the spread of public libraries in the late nineteenth and early twentieth centuries, the development of the 'twopenny' circulating library, and the ready availability of cheap reading materials for purchase, many of the initial reasons for setting up alternative working-class libraries began to recede.

Issue statistics and library catalogues suggest that, no matter what the initial motivation for Co-operative and miners' institute libraries was, they

---

37 T. A. Jackson, *Solo trumpet: some memories of socialist agitation and propaganda* (London, 1953).

subsequently did not exist for radical reading. Much of the stock and the overwhelming bulk of the reading was non-controversial and largely fiction, and such material could be more effectively supplied by the public library system. Radical material *was* stocked in miners' institute libraries and *was* read by a small but vocal minority.[38] But even in the revolutionary hotbed of the South Wales mining valleys, reading was overwhelmingly lightweight, and the percentage of fiction read frequently rose to 80% or more between the two World Wars.[39] The novelist Rhys Davies wrote about one Institute library he used as a boy that books by Marx, Engels, Bakunin and Tolstoy 'looked as if they never went out'. By contrast books by 'Marie Corelli and Hall Caine were shabby'.[40] Even at Tredegar, despite buying everything by Lenin, 'nobody was interested' as 'the issue of books was by far and away fiction'.[41]

If contemporary public libraries were denying working-class readers access to radical material, then perhaps maintaining these alternative libraries had some justification. But there is little substantive evidence to support the claims of censorship made by certain hard-line proletarian publications, which themselves sought to steer public library purchases in the desired radical direction by 'besieging the libraries' and hijacking their suggestions boxes.[42] The lengthy existence of miners' institute libraries in South Wales had more to do with communal solidarity and local politics (plus weak and underfunded public library alternatives) than with a genuine need for a facility that gave its audience the radical reading material that would otherwise be denied them.

Conclusions

This chapter has suggested that various interlocking factors led to the emergence during the nineteenth century of independent working-class libraries, and there is little doubt that control and ownership were the critical factors. These libraries were essentially run, financed and staffed by their working-class members, and the feeling that the community 'owned' the facility was very powerful. As the former secretary of Barnsley Co-operative Society remarked on the eventual closure of its library in 1971: 'Well it was ours, wasn't it.'[43]

38 W. J. Edwards, *From the valley I came* (London, 1956); W. Paynter, *My generation* (London, 1972), 33.
39 Baggs, 'The miners' libraries', 402–43.
40 R. Davies, *Print of a hare's foot* (London, 1969), 78.
41 O. Powell, oral history tape, 29 November 1973, South Wales Miners' Library, University of Wales, Swansea.
42 *The Miner* 71 (8 October 1927), 8; 102 (12 May 1928), 12; *Plebs* 16 (March 1924), 161; 19 (April 1927), 151; 21 (May 1929), 115.
43 Everitt, 'Co-operative Society libraries', 40.

The idea of radical reading cannot justifiably be seen as a major, lasting or general cause, apart from during the first half of the nineteenth century, when there is clear evidence that working-class readers were denied access by certain libraries to the reading material that they wished to read. Even then that reading material was not always radical in nature. Later evidence from public libraries and Co-operative and miners' institute libraries confirms that the library reading habits of the vast majority of the working class were simply not radical in character.

14

Private libraries and the collecting instinct

DAVID PEARSON

This book, devoted to the history of libraries, primarily assumes an implicit definition of a library as a collection of books held in some kind of communal ownership, with rights of access and resultant benefits for a group of people. This may be a relatively small and well-defined group, such as the members of a university, or a much wider one like the citizens of a municipality or even a whole nation. In seeking to chart how libraries and their contents have influenced and helped to shape our social history, we must remember that books have come to people not only via public collections but also through direct personal ownership, and that books are objects (unlike some other historical artefacts) which it has long been feasible to own in considerable numbers. Private libraries are an important part of our cultural and intellectual fabric, and they have also played a significant role in developing public collections.

The title of this chapter brings together two concepts – 'private libraries' and 'collecting' – which are commonly yoked together interchangeably but whose interrelationship should be examined more carefully at the outset. Collecting, in the widest sense, is a topic which can be studied from a psychological viewpoint as a commonly manifested aspect of human behaviour, and it has generated a considerable literature in its own right.[1] Book collecting was memorably defined by A. W. Pollard as 'the bringing together of books which in their contents, their form or the history of the individual copy possess some element of permanent interest, and either actually or prospectively are rare'.[2] The collecting instinct as encapsulated here is akin to that which develops collections of art, or stamps, or railway tickets; the collection is something special rather than functional, the collector is a bibliophile and a connoisseur.

---

1 A good point of entry to this field is W. Muensterberger, *Collecting: an unruly passion* (Princeton, NJ, 1994), and its bibliography.
2 A. W. Pollard, 'Book-collecting', in *Encyclopaedia Britannica*, 11th edn (London, 1910–11), vol. 4, 221.

This analysis does indeed apply to many private libraries formed during the last 150 years, but it is not the only motive that has led people to assemble them. The existing literature in this field is dominated by the Pollard approach and it is important to recognise that the standard works – like Seymour de Ricci's *English collectors of books and manuscripts* or John Carter's *Taste and technique in book collecting* – give a one-sided view which fails to represent the larger picture.

In 1905 the books of Frederick Locker-Lampson (1821–95), a minor Victorian poet, were sold to the American collector E. Dwight Church. Locker-Lampson's collection, sometimes known as the Rowfant Library (the name of the owner's Sussex house), comprised about 1,230 volumes contained in two book-cases. Its aim was to contain the first editions of the masterpieces of English literature; each book was carefully selected and 'the compactness and unity of this small collection, in which every book appears to have been bought for a special reason and to form an integral part of the whole, gave it an artistic individuality which was a pleasant triumph for its owner'.[3] Although the collection was mostly dispersed soon after its acquisition by Church, the Rowfant Library is commonly cited as an important and trend-setting example of 'cabinet collecting' and Locker-Lampson's name will regularly be found in works about book collectors.[4]

Around the time that the Rowfant Library crossed the Atlantic, librarians at Cambridge University were coming to terms with the gift of Lord Acton's private library of 70,000 books. Acton (1834–1902), Regius Professor of Modern History at Cambridge, had inherited family libraries from both his father's and his mother's side, to which he added steadily throughout the second half of the nineteenth century. He acquired both new books and old books, from all over Europe, to develop a truly rich and profound research resource focused on European and ecclesiastical history since the Reformation. His motives had little to do with taste and bibliophily; his library was a working tool. It was one of the largest private collections of its time, or indeed of any time, and through its preservation at Cambridge it has served continuing generations of users, but Acton's name is rarely encountered in the literature of book collecting.[5]

---

3 J. Carter, *Taste and technique in book collecting*, 3rd impression with corrections and an epilogue (London, 1970), 20.

4 On the Rowfant Library see (as well as note 2) S. de Ricci, *English collectors of books and manuscripts (1530–1930) and their marks of ownership* (Cambridge, 1930), 174–6; B. Q. Schmidt, 'Frederick Locker-Lampson', in W. Baker and K. Womack (eds.), *Nineteenth-century British book-collectors and bibliographers* (Detroit, 1997), 258–64.

5 O. Chadwick, 'The Acton Library', in P. Fox (ed.), *Cambridge University Library: the great collections* (Cambridge, 1998), 136–52.

Locker-Lampson and Acton seem to stand at opposite ends of a spectrum, not only for size, but also for purpose: the former was motivated by the desire to create something iconic and exquisite; the latter wanted texts as a gateway to knowledge and understanding. If we are to take a balanced overview of private libraries, we have to consider all parts of that spectrum, not just one end of the rainbow. The dividing lines are not clear-cut, as Locker-Lampson was genuinely interested in the contents of his books, and the published catalogues of the Rowfant Library, with detailed descriptions of the books, were bibliographically useful in their day. Acton undoubtedly liked books as objects.

In approaching the subject of private libraries, therefore, it is important to recognise that there is a variety of motivating factors that have led people to assemble them. People may buy books because they wish to use them, for study or reference, as an integral part of their working lives. Acton's library is a particularly spectacular instance, but countless other collections with the same rationale have been formed over the years by academic and professional men. These may develop a critical mass with the potential to enrich the national pool of institutional collections: the 3,500 books of John Lightfoot, bishop of Durham (1828–89) which went to the Divinity School in Cambridge and the 9,500 Japanese books of the diplomat and scholar William Aston (1841–1911) which were acquired by Cambridge University Library are examples among many which could be chosen.[6] Collections are also formed around subject areas which may or may not be directly related to an owner's professional occupation, but which take his interest: he acquires because he wants to learn and study, or because he wants to preserve that which may otherwise be lost, but also because the collecting instinct kicks in, the desire to own. The collection of 200 books on bees and apiculture left to the parish of Frodsham by their vicar, William Cotton, in 1879 is a small example. Numerous local history collections have been formed in this way, and most public libraries have been enriched at some point in their history by the acquisition of material assembled by local antiquaries. Ilford Public Library bought 2,000 volumes on Essex and its history from the collection of Frederick Brand (1857–1939), compiler of the *Essex Index*; Emmanuel Green (1832–1919), who published the *Bibliotheca Somersetensis* (1902), bequeathed over 10,000 books on the history of Bath and Somerset to Bristol City Library. There are many other similar examples.

In collections like this we can see some stepping stones to link the philosophy of a library like Acton's with one like Locker-Lampson's: or, rather, we can

---

6 Information on these collections, and others in this paragraph, is taken from B. C. Bloomfield (ed.), *A directory of rare book and special collections*, 2nd edn (London, 1997).

see that individual collectors are likely to be driven by a mixture of subject interest, delight in ownership, desire to preserve and a vision of comprehensive coverage that will be present in different proportions from owner to owner. The ratio of that mixture, combined with the opportunities that are created by spending power and by the marketplace, will shape the profile of each collection formed. We must also recognise that other motives may influence the formation of private libraries: people have collected books because they perceived it to be fashionable to do so, or because a well-chosen library could enhance their status or image in society. The growing sense of a library as an appropriate accoutrement for respectable households, which developed throughout the nineteenth century, led to the creation of numerous country house and town house libraries where the books were essentially there as furniture. 'It would be an error, except in special circumstances, to design a library for mere study', wrote Robert Kerr in his influential book on *The gentleman's house*, published in 1864; 'it is primarily a sort of morning-room for gentlemen'.[7]

Books may also be collected for their investment value; or perhaps more accurately, the idea of books as an investment is one that has been a regular refrain and debating point throughout the period under discussion here. The prices raised by high-profile books and collections have always made good newspaper content, and booksellers have not been slow to exploit the popular perception of the investment potential of rare books. In the early 1980s the London bookselling firm of Francis Edwards formulated a scheme inviting people to invest in a carefully chosen portfolio of collectable books, whose value was reckoned to rise above the rate of inflation.[8] Such notions may be thought to be recent, but as long ago as 1877 Bernard Quaritch was corresponding with *The Times*, disputing a suggestion that books might not prove a good investment: 'A library formed by a shrewd, liberal-handed, well-educated collector is sure to realize ultimately a profit ... old books are as good an investment as anything else.'[9] In 1932, at a time of falling prices, Andrew Block felt that 'in spite of world depression books are still one of the safest investments'.[10] Prices for books have in fact fluctuated considerably over the years, affected by fashion as well as wider economic trends. Analysis of the investment potential

7 Cited in C. Wainwright, 'The library as living room', in R. Myers and M. Harris (eds.), *Property of a gentleman* (Winchester, 1991), 15–24 (citation p. 20); Wainwright's article contains more information on this theme. See also J. Ciro, 'Country house libraries in the nineteenth century', *Library History* 18 (2002), 89–98.
8 R. Harley Lewis, *Book collecting: a new look* (Newton Abbot, 1988), 60–4.
9 *The Times* (16 May 1877), 10.
10 A. Block, *The book collector's vade mecum* (London, 1932), 202.

of books suggests that a carefully chosen library can indeed outperform inflation, but this is only rarely the real driver for collectors, who 'should have a
much higher goal than investment return; namely the pleasure of conceiving,
buying and completing a collection in a particular field'.[11]

In a short narrative account of book collecting, it is hard to avoid concentrating on individuals who stand out as major figures, but it is important to
remember that private libraries are often multi-generational affairs. Many of
the significant British examples, in the houses of the aristocracy and gentry,
have been developed over long periods by successive owners, sometimes with
fallow periods between interested generations. The great library which two
successive earls of Crawford, the 25th (1812–80) and 26th (1847–1913), built up
at Haigh Hall in Lancashire in the mid to late nineteenth century was founded
on earlier collections passed down through the family and enhanced from the
late sixteenth century onwards.[12] The library of the duke of Devonshire at
Chatsworth House, now much depleted by sales but still an impressive collection, benefited from the interests of successive dukes, but particularly the 2nd
(1672–1729) and 6th (1790–1858).[13] The gradual dispersal of collections like this,
inherited by new title holders with less interest in books, or a need to raise
money for death duties or other debts, was a steady source of supply for the
book market throughout the period under discussion.

The second quarter of the nineteenth century is commonly regarded as a
period of retrenchment in British book collecting, a bear market after the bull
market of the earlier decades of the century and the *Bibliomania* so famously
hymned by Thomas Dibdin in his 1809 book of that title. In 1832 he was
writing rather about *Bibliophobia: remarks on the present languid and depressed
state of literature and the book trade*, and the death of Richard Heber the following
year has been said to mark the end of the 'Dibdinian age' of book collecting.[14]
Prices may have fallen for previously fashionable material (Heber's books were
sold for little more than half what he originally paid), but private collections of
all sizes were actively being formed from a generally plentiful market supply.

In 1850, the starting date for the present survey, several major British collectors were well into their stride and continuing to accumulate substantial
libraries. Bertram, 4th earl of Ashburnham (1797–1878) was a wealthy aristocratic collector in the classic mould, who assembled many thousands of

11 K. Hill, 'Rare books as investments', *The Book Collector* 47 (1998), 342–51 (p. 351).
12 N. Barker, *Bibliotheca Lindesiana* (London, 1977) gives a detailed account of the development of the Crawford Library; on the early foundations of the collection, see
pp. 13ff.
13 De Ricci, *English collectors*, 33, 78–81.
14 De Ricci, *English collectors*, 102.

manuscripts and printed books, strong in biblical and liturgical texts, incunabula and early English printing.[15] Alexander, Lord Lindsay, later 25th earl of Crawford (1812–80), had been building up 'a Library equally fit for the studious and the elegant squires' since the late 1820s and would continue throughout the middle decades of the century.[16] George Daniel (1789–1864), an accountant by profession and appreciably lower in the social and financial pecking order, was nevertheless successful in developing a substantial collection of early English books, including Shakespeare and other Elizabethan literature, which caused some excitement when sold at auction in 1864.[17] Thomas Corser (1793–1876), rector of Stand, near Manchester, was active particularly during the 1840s and 1850s in acquiring a similarly spectacular library of early printed books, strong in English material, which was dispersed in a series of sales between 1868 and 1876.[18]

Other collectors of similar mould, active around this time, include Edward Utterson (1776?–1856; sold at auction, 1852–7), Sir William Tite (1798–1873; sold at auction, 1874) and Alexander Dyce (1798–1869; 15,500 volumes bequeathed to the South Kensington Museum, now the Victoria and Albert Museum).[19] William Henry Miller (1789–1848), who bought many thousands of volumes at the dispersal of the Heber Library, had just died but his collection continued to be developed by his heir, Samuel Christie-Miller, from the early 1850s onwards; this became the Britwell Court Library, which released an outstanding collection of early printing onto the market when sold in the early twentieth century.[20] At the more scholarly end of the spectrum, Martin Routh, President of Magdalen College, Oxford (1755–1854), was still, in his late nineties, actively using his library of about 16,000 volumes, which on his death went to transform the bibliographical resources of the recently founded University of Durham.[21]

Another collector who was well established by mid-century, but whose library continued to expand right up to his death, was Sir Thomas Phillipps (1792–1872), a phenomenon in a class of his own who devoted most of his life,

15 P. F. Gehl, 'Bertram Lord Ashburnham', in Baker and Womack (eds.), *Nineteenth-century British book-collectors*, 10–20.

16 Barker, *Bibliotheca Lindesiana*, p. 71.

17 F. Herrmann, *Sotheby's: portrait of an auction house* (London, 1980), 50–2.

18 De Ricci, *English collectors*, 150; Herrmann, *Sotheby's*, 59.

19 De Ricci, *English collectors*, 139, 154–5; *Dyce collection. A catalogue of the printed books and manuscripts bequeathed by . . . Alexander Dyce* (London, 1875).

20 De Ricci, *English collectors*, 105–13; *The Britwell handlist or short-title catalogue of the . . . library of Britwell Court Buckinghamshire* (London, 1933).

21 R. D. Middleton, *Dr. Routh* (Oxford, 1938), 250–9; A. I. Doyle, 'Martin Joseph Routh and his books in Durham University Library', *Durham University Journal* 48 (1955–6), 100–7.

money and energy to assembling a collection of well over 100,000 items. On record as wishing to possess 'one copy of every book in the world', Phillipps amassed a huge library of printed books, but it is as a collector of manuscripts (a 'vello-maniac', to use his own expression) that he is best known. He developed a fascination for historical manuscripts of all kinds, including charters and deeds, and his manuscript collection ran to many more individual items than the 36,000 listed in his own sequence of numbering. He was a man of independent means, but not a particularly wealthy one, and he developed his library against a background of continuing financial struggle, further exacerbated by a tendency to make more enemies than friends. His story has been well told elsewhere; the collection was eventually dispersed, in sales stretching over a century. The effectiveness of Phillipps's life's work, and his reputation in posterity, would have been much enhanced if one of the numerous abortive attempts to find a permanent institutional home for his collection had come to fruition.[22]

The mid-nineteenth-century collections mentioned thus far have been large ones, running to many thousands or even tens of thousands of volumes. Previous writers in this field have identified this period as marking the rise of the kind of 'cabinet collecting' later exemplified by Locker-Lampson, of small but perfectly formed collections which reflect an owner's taste and style within limitations imposed by space or budget. The collection formed by the brewer Henry Perkins (1778–1855), comprising just 865 carefully chosen manuscripts and early printed books, raised £26,000 when auctioned in 1870 (nearly twice the sum realised by the much larger library of George Daniel), and is often cited as an early example of this trend.[23]

What is equally noteworthy, in the second half of the century, is the growth of significant subject-focused collections, not necessarily numerically huge but important within their scope, dealing with areas outside the fashionable circuits of fine and early printing, literary classics and illuminated manuscripts. William Blades (1824–90), printer and bibliographer, assembled a collection of 2,000 books and 1,500 pamphlets on printing and its history, recognised at the time as a unique and distinctive resource and purchased after a successful fund-raising campaign by the newly formed St Bride Institute.[24] Francis Fry (1803–86) specialised in English Bibles, and his 1,200 volumes were purchased for the British and Foreign Bible Society for £6,000; 1,500 early

---

22 A. N. L. Munby, *Portrait of an obsession: the life of Sir Thomas Phillipps* (London, 1967).

23 Carter, *Taste and technique*, 19.

24 S. Berger, 'William Blades', in Baker and Womack (eds.), *Nineteenth-century British book-collectors*, 21–7.

books on astronomy collected by John Couch Adams (1819–92), Director of the Cambridge Observatory, were bequeathed to Cambridge University Library.[25]

Collectors like this, developing significant libraries in defined areas distinct from what taste and fashion would dictate as the expected hunting ground of the bibliophile connoisseur, would become increasingly noticeable as time progressed, but there was still plenty of activity in the later nineteenth century in forming more general all-round libraries, like the 18,500 volumes bequeathed to the South Kensington Museum by John Forster (1812–76), embracing classics, history and travel as well as wide-ranging holdings of English literature.[26] On a larger scale, the library collected by Henry Huth (1815–78) and continued by his son Alfred (1850–1910) became, like the Britwell Court Library, a major repository of early printed books both British and foreign, as well as manuscripts and autograph letters.[27] Private libraries are developed through supply as well as demand, and the late nineteenth-century marketplace produced plentiful opportunities for British collectors to reharvest the fruits of earlier generations of library builders. The Settled Land Acts of 1882 and 1884 made it possible for trustees to sell property which had been passed on as heirlooms, irrespective of restrictions placed by earlier testators, which encouraged financially pressed estate owners, at a time of economic downturn, to look to their library shelves as realisable assets. The sale of the duke of Hamilton's library in 1882–4, including the library of William Beckford of Fonthill (1759–1844), was a direct result of this legislation; other major dispersals of the last twenty years of the century were the duke of Sunderland's library (1881), the Syston Park library of Sir John Thorold (1884), part of the library of Lord Crawford (1887–9) and the Ashburnham library (1897–9).[28]

Sales like these at the top end of the market provided opportunities for the most celebrated and iconic books to change hands – the Syston Park sale included a Gutenberg Bible, a Mainz Psalter and all four Shakespeare folios – and there was also a brisk trade, as there had always been, in regular offerings of less spectacular collections, the auctioneers' bread and butter. Sotheby's, the market leaders at that time, held 450 book sales in London between 1890 and 1899, a figure which is typical of the level of activity throughout the second half of the nineteenth century – the comparable statistic for the decade 1850–9

25 Bloomfield, *Directory of rare book and special collections*, 126 and 26.
26 *Forster collection. A catalogue of the printed books and manuscripts bequeathed by John Forster* (London, 1888); *Forster collection. A catalogue of the paintings, manuscripts, autograph letters, pamphlets, etc. bequeathed by John Forster* (London, 1893).
27 De Ricci, *English collectors*, 149–54.
28 Herrmann, *Sotheby's*, 70–84.

is 434. The differences between the run of the mill sales of the 1850s and 1890s lie not so much with quantity as with content, reflecting changes in taste and in attitudes to what the discerning private library owner had on his shelves. The titlepage of the sale of 'the valuable library of a gentleman deceased' held by Sotheby's on 7 January 1850 advertised 'Camden, Britannia . . . Ancient and Modern Universal History, 24 vol. . . . Picart, Religious Ceremonies 6 vol. . . . Rapin, History of England', and other standard historical and antiquarian works. When the 'select library of a distinguished literary character' was sold on 6 May 1850 the highlights picked out on the titlepage were 'Langebeck, Scriptores rerum Danicarum . . . Eusebius . . . Montfaucon . . . Auctores Classici Latini, 99 tom. . . . British essayists . . . Byzantinae historiae scriptores . . . Parliamentary History of England . . . Together with an excellent selection of the best editions of the Greek and Latin classics'.

By contrast, the titlepage of the 'Catalogue of the valuable and extensive library of a gentleman (removed from Yorkshire)', which came under the hammer at Sotheby's on 8 May 1899, reads:

> comprising standard works in all the various classes of literature (English and foreign), a number of sporting books, antiquarian, architectural, archaeological and topographical works, publications of learned societies, a large series of books illustrated by George Cruikshank, fine illustrated French books, extra-illustrated volumes, Charles Dickens' works . . . Ruskin's works, manuscript and printed books of hours, etc. Kelmscott Press publications and writings of William Morris, first editions of modern authors . . .

Historical, antiquarian and topographical books are still included here but there is a much greater emphasis on literature and contemporary books, as well as a rather more recreational and less scholarly flavour (sporting and illustrated books). An increasing interest in English literature, and in contemporary or near-contemporary authors, was one of the major developments in book-collecting tastes in the last quarter of the nineteenth century; 'first editions of modern authors' is not a phrase likely to be found in a mid-century sale catalogue, but is very much a selling point from a catalogue of the 1890s. People became keen to own not only Shelley, Dickens or Tennyson but also Ruskin, Swinburne, Kipling or Stevenson; William Morris, and his Kelmscott Press books, were also highly collectable. This trend was fostered partly by the growth of societies for the study and reading of modern authors, and partly by the publication of numerous lists and bibliographies of their works, offering signposts to collectors. The bibliographies of nineteenth-century poets produced by H. B. Forman and T. J. Wise from the 1880s onwards are among the best known, but as leaders of what was then a growing field.[29]

One other noticeable change between an auction held in London in 1850 and one in 1900 is that more of the books from the later sale would be likely to be travelling abroad, particularly to America. Book collecting and library building in America have a history stretching well into its colonial past, as does the transport of books across the Atlantic, and the later nineteenth century saw a steadily increasing demand from American collectors with broad visions and new money. Robert Hoe III (1839–1909), owner of a successful printing business, was particularly active during the last thirty years of his life in building up a classic bibliophile collection of illuminated manuscripts, fine and early printing, fine bindings and Americana, much of which came from England.[30] A generation later, three American names in particular rose to prominence in the Anglo-Saxon book-collecting world: Henry Folger (1857–1930), Henry Huntington (1850–1927) and J. Pierpont Morgan (1837–1913).[31] All three had considerable wealth derived from business, and they all established their libraries as permanently endowed foundations, to endure long after their deaths. Manuscripts and early printed books travelled across the Atlantic in great numbers during the late nineteenth and early twentieth centuries to build such collections, and the momentum thus injected was an important factor in sustaining competition and prices in the antiquarian trade. *The Times* noted in 1906 that 'the commercial value of Shakespeare quartos has increased to about ten times the prices paid ten or twenty years ago, thanks to the unlimited commissions of two or three American rival collectors. It seems hopeless for English collectors to attempt to enter the arena in the face of such odds.'[32]

There was nevertheless no shortage of native activity in the early decades of the twentieth century, either in the maturing of existing collections or in the forging of new ones. The donation of the Acton library to Cambridge in 1902 was mentioned earlier; other substantial collections which went to academic homes included the library of Richard Copley Christie (1830–1901), who bequeathed a carefully chosen collection of 8000 volumes focusing on

29 See M. Sadleir, 'The development during the last fifty years of bibliographical study of books of the XIXth century', in F. C. Francis (ed.), *The Bibliographical Society: studies in retrospect* (London, 1949), 146–58.
30 D. C. Dickinson, *Dictionary of American book collectors* (New York, 1986), 160–2.
31 Dickinson, *Dictionary of American book collectors*, 119–21, 171–3, 233–4; see also B. A. Kane, *The widening circle: the story of the Folger Shakespeare Library and its collections* (Washington, DC, 1976); D. C. Dickinson, *Henry E. Huntington's library of libraries* (San Marino, CA, 1995).
32 'Some recent phases of book-collecting', *The Times* (26 December 1906), 6.

the Italian and French renaissance period to Manchester University; 9,000 volumes of Judaica from the collection of Albert Lowy (1816–1908), presented to Jews College, London; 4,000 volumes of Slavonic works bequeathed to The Queen's College, Oxford, by William Morfill (1834–1909), Professor of Russian at Oxford; and the library of Ingram Bywater (1840–1914), Regius Professor of Greek, 4,000 volumes illustrating the history of classical learning, bequeathed to the Bodleian Library.[33] This was still a period during which large and specialised collections could be given to municipal institutions, a trend which diminished as the twentieth century progressed and the number of university libraries grew; in 1899 Henry Watson, professor at the Royal Manchester College of Music, gave nearly 17,000 volumes of music and books about music to Manchester Central Library, and in 1905 William Kelly, a prominent local member of the Plymouth Brethren, gave 15,000 volumes to Middlesborough Public Library, largely theological in content but including several thousand books of the handpress period.

Major collections of the bright, beautiful and rare which came onto the market during this period included the libraries of William Morris (1834–96) (largely bought *en bloc* by the Manchester collector Richard Bennett, but acquired by Pierpont Morgan just a few years later) and of William Amherst, 1st Baron Amherst of Hackney (1835–1909), an active collector of early English Bibles, incunabula and other early printing during the last four decades of the nineteenth century, whose books were sold between 1906 and 1921. These and other sales of this period were rather eclipsed by three huge collections which began to be dispersed during the second decade of the century: the libraries of Huth (1911–22), Hoe (in New York, 1911–12) and Christie-Miller (the Britwell Court Library, 1916–27). A much smaller but equally headline-grabbing library which came to the saleroom in 1919–21 was that of Henry Yates Thompson, a supreme example of cabinet collecting; Thompson began buying illuminated manuscripts in the 1880s and decided he would limit his collection to just 100 manuscripts, of the finest quality he could obtain. Through successive market opportunities, including the collections of Ashburnham, Morris and John Ruskin (1902), he bought and sold until deciding to part with them all. The first sale, just thirty lots, made £52,360 in an hour and a half, creating a new record for a single sale session at Sotheby's.[34]

33 Summary information on the collections mentioned in this paragraph will be found in Bloomfield, *Directory of rare book and special collections*.

34 B. Q. Schmidt, 'Henry Yates Thompson', in Baker and Womack (eds.), *Nineteenth-century British book-collectors*, 21–7; C. de Hamel, 'Was Henry Yates Thompson a gentleman?', in Myers and Harris, *Property of a gentleman*, 77–89.

Literary texts continued to be popular fodder, in the fashionable sense of book collecting, throughout the early twentieth century, and turn of the century enthusiasms for first editions of Kipling, Conan Doyle or Robert Louis Stevenson gave way to the likes of J. M. Barrie, John Galsworthy or George Bernard Shaw in the 1920s. John Carter spoke of a dawning interest in scientific books on collectors' horizons as a major development of that decade – 'the recognition that thought is as worthy of the general collector's attention as imagination', as he put it – but however elegant his phrasing, there were in fact important private collections of scientific books being developed well before then.[35] The astronomical books of John Couch Adams were noted above; twenty years before Adams, John Graves (1806–70), sometime Professor of Jurisprudence at University College London, bequeathed to the college his library of 14,000 books, particularly strong in mathematics but also embracing physics and other sciences. Received wisdom has it that scientists have always had libraries, but that until the early twentieth century, when the notion of collecting scientific books developed, they were essentially working tools which may subsequently have become historically interesting more or less by accident. Graves, however, whose library has been described as 'the most important private mathematical collection ever made', had extensive holdings of incunabula and other early printing, including 260 editions of Euclid, and his collecting vision clearly went beyond the purely functional.[36] The physicist Silvanus Thompson (1851–1916), Principal of Finsbury Technical College, formed a library of nearly 13,000 volumes, with particular strengths in the history of electricity and magnetism, which was purchased by subscription after his death for the Institution of Electrical Engineers.[37]

Medical men, likewise, have long been accumulators of books, which they have needed for professional use. The modest collection of 700 books owned by Charles West (1816–98), founder of Great Ormond Street Hospital and now preserved there, is typical of the working libraries of many successful late nineteenth-century physicians.[38] Other doctors of this period who took book collecting more seriously tended to expand their interests beyond the purely medical. David Lloyd Roberts (1834–1920), surgeon to St Mary's Hospital, Manchester, was particularly interested in Sir Thomas Browne, author of *Religio Medici*, and the 5,000 books he bequeathed to the John Rylands Library

---

35 Carter, *Taste and technique*, 53.
36 J. L. Thornton and R. I. J. Tully, *Scientific books libraries and collectors*, 3rd edn (London, 1971), 350; A. R. Dorling, 'The Graves mathematical collection', *Annals of Science* 33 (1976), 307–10.
37 Bloomfield, *Directory of rare book and special collections*, 258.
38 Bloomfield, *Directory of rare book and special collections*, 251.

included a fine Browne collection, but also major holdings of English and continental literature.[39] Sir John Williams (1840–1926), Professor of Obstetrical Medicine at University College London before his retirement in 1893, became the first President of the National Library of Wales, to which in 1909 he donated the Library's foundation collection of over 25,000 books, with a strong focus on Welsh interest.[40] The man generally credited with raising interest in the serious collecting of medical books, for historical rather than clinical interest, is Sir William Osler (1849–1919), Regius Professor of Medicine at Oxford, who assembled a collection of about 8,000 volumes, carefully chosen to represent the development of medicine from the earliest times; the books were bequeathed to McGill University in Canada and the catalogue published in 1929 (*Bibliotheca Osleriana*) became an influential guide for both collectors and bibliographers.[41]

Another great but rather different medical collection being formed around the same time was that of Sir Henry Wellcome (1853–1936), a successful pharmaceutical businessman (American born but London based) who devoted much of his energy and considerable fortune during the last forty years of his life to assembling a vast collection of books, manuscripts, pictures and artefacts around the general theme of medicine and mankind. Whether Wellcome fits in a roll call of private libraries is a moot point; his vision was to create a permanent public collection rather than one for his individual use or delight, although it was never formally open to the public during his lifetime. Collecting via a network of agents on an international scale, he bequeathed to his trustees not only 250,000 books but also 100,000 pictures and over a million museum objects, which have since become the public benefits their founder hoped for as the Wellcome Library in London, and in museum collections, not only at the Science Museum but also in galleries all round the world. Wellcome's collecting achievements mark him out as the Heber or Phillipps of his generation, though his name is less commonly encountered in the annals of book collecting than the likes of his compatriots Huntington or Morgan, whose libraries were more spectacular but significantly smaller. Wellcome may prove to be the last individual ever to create a collection of this physical magnitude: there has been nothing quite like it since his death,

39 J. R. Hodgson (ed.), *A guide to special collections of the John Rylands University Library of Manchester* (Manchester, 1999), 23.
40 D. Jenkins, *A refuge in peace and war: The National Library of Wales to 1952* (Aberystwyth, 2002), 143–6.
41 P. J. Matthews, 'Sir William Osler', in Baker and Womack (eds.), *Nineteenth-century British book-collectors*, 310–21.

and it seems unlikely that anyone today could assemble something on such a scale.[42]

Although many of the rare and desirable books dispersed through the great sales of the 1910s and 1920s went to America, there were still British enthusiasts with the money and the interest to assemble fine collections. The lawyer Sir Leicester Harmsworth (1870–1937) was one of the more significant rivals to the Americans when the libraries of Huth and Christie-Miller came to the auction rooms; in 1921 he forestalled the second portion of the Britwell Court Library sale (early English theological books) by purchasing it *en bloc*. When his own collection came in turn to be dispersed, it ran to thirty-five sales held at Sotheby's between 1939 and 1953.[43] A very different, but much respected collector of the time was Thomas James Wise (1859–1937), who concentrated on English literature and built up a particularly fine library of nineteenth-century English writers, with an emphasis on poets; his published bibliographies, as noted earlier, were also highly influential. His 'Ashley Library' (named after Ashley Road in north London, where he lived) was purchased for the British Museum Library after his death; its reputation was compromised by the recognition, shortly before Wise's death, that he had not only collected but that he had also forged fictitious pamphlets supposedly by Browning, Swinburne, Tennyson and other important authors, 'discovered' by the famous bibliographer and sold to unsuspecting libraries and collectors.[44] The book trade, like all other sectors of commerce, suffered from the slump in the world economy, and prices fell, particularly in the early 1930s. The January 1929 New York sale of Jerome Kern's collection, with high prices fetched for 'collectable' English literature, has been cited as a watershed after which 'the lights went out'.[45]

As the twentieth century progressed, the trend towards collecting in specialised areas became increasingly noticeable; to put it another way, the important collections are often those which focus on a particular subject, outside the well-trodden and the fashionable, and build up a particularly comprehensive

42 J. Symons, 'These crafty dealers: Sir Henry Wellcome as a book collector', in R. Myers and M. Harris (eds.), *Medicine, mortality and the book trade* (Folkestone, 1998), 109–30.

43 E. M. Dring, 'Fifty years at Quaritch', in R. Linenthal (ed.), *The Book Collector: special number for the 150th anniversary of Bernard Quaritch* (London, 1997), 35–52 (pp. 43–4); '£227,645 for a library: Harmsworth sales ended', *The Times* (2 December 1953), 4.

44 W. Partington, *Thomas J. Wise in the original cloth* (London, 1948); J. Carter and G. Pollard, *An enquiry into the nature of certain nineteenth-century pamphlets* (London, 1934; reprinted with additions 1983); J. Collins, *The two forgers: a biography of Harry Buxton Forman and Thomas James Wise* (London, 1992).

45 A. Freeman, 'The Jazz Age library of Jerome Kern' in R. Myers *et al.* (eds.), *Under the hammer: book auctions since the seventeenth century* (London, 2001), 209–30.

resource in that area. There was nothing new about academic and professional men developing collections in their field of interest, and the library of 6,000 volumes on economics and the history of thought which John Maynard Keynes (1883–1946) bequeathed to King's College, Cambridge is clearly in that tradition.[46] Less mainstream, but arguably no less valuable in terms of enriching the national reserves of research materials, are the 8,000 books on cricket, the combined collections of Frederick Ashley-Cooper (1877–1932) and Sir Julien Cahn (1882–1944), which the latter's widow gave to Marylebone Cricket Club in 1944, or the 10,000 books and pamphlets on magic which Harry Price (1881–1948) bequeathed to London University.[47] John Johnson (1882–1955), Printer to the University of Oxford, took an interest in printed ephemera, which gathered momentum through the acquisition of other existing collections, until the whole became the huge collection (over a million items) which is now one of the many glories of the Bodleian Library.[48]

These are all professional men developing private collections with an obvious relevance to their field of work, but their activities are in keeping with a general broadening and democratisation of the idea of book collecting which gathered pace in the second quarter of the twentieth century and has been a feature of the bibliographical landscape ever since. Guides for book collectors published around the turn of the twentieth century – of which there were several – commonly assume that their reader is a gentleman of means who is seeking advice on the best and most desirable books to buy. *The private library: what we do know, what we don't know, what we ought to know about our books*, by Arthur Humphreys (1897, with four subsequent editions) is primarily aimed at helping owners of large houses to make sound decisions in stocking their library shelves with good editions in suitable bindings. The main issues being addressed by Humphreys are set out in his preface:

> For many years I have had opportunities of inspecting and reporting upon collections of books in numerous country houses, and I must say that the condition of books in the greater number of them is chaotic. A man will talk about all his possessions – his pictures, his objets d'art, his horses, his garden, and his bicycle, but rarely will he talk about his books . . . There are servants in every house qualified to do everything except handle a book.

J. H. Slater's *How to collect books* (1905), whose decorated cloth cover imitates a sixteenth-century strapwork binding, is full of pictures of incunabula and

46 A. N. L. Munby, 'John Maynard Keynes: the book-collector', in his *Essays and papers* (London, 1977), 19–26.

47 Bloomfield, *Directory of rare book and special collections*, 294, 403.

48 Bodleian Library, *The John Johnson Collection: catalogue of an exhibition* (Oxford, 1971).

fine bindings, and its chapters are devoted to such topics as 'manuscripts', 'incunabula and the early printers' and 'some celebrated presses'.

Although this flavour is still present in some later guidebooks, a book published in 1934 on *New paths in book collecting: essays by various hands*, edited by John Carter, offered a different kind of vision. Carter and his co-essayists pointed out the new worlds to be explored in areas like detective fiction, yellowbacks (cheap editions of fiction published for Victorian railway-travellers), or books on the Great War – all fields in which it was then possible to develop significant and unique collections at relatively little cost, as the books involved were outside the existing bibliophilic circuits. Here was a way to spread the pleasures of book collecting more widely, with the prospect of achieving something distinctive. The same point was made by Iolo Williams in *The elements of book-collecting*, published in 1927: 'If [the collector] chooses to form his library round a subject that is little understood, and has been studied by comparatively few people, he will make his book-collecting all the more useful and . . . find it easier.'[49] Furthermore, as *The Times* pointed out, reviewing the exhibition which was mounted in London in association with *New paths*, 'it brings a rich man's hobby within the reach of every man'.[50]

Some of the more spectacular successes which this approach could bring can be seen in the field of children's books. This is a category of literature which was not traditionally very high on the agenda of bibliophiles or librarians, although its profile is much higher today than it was fifty years ago. The creation of collections like that of Fernand (1905–88) and Anne (d.1988) Renier, who assembled a library of over 80,000 children's books (mostly nineteenth and twentieth century, but with some earlier material), has been a significant catalyst in that raising of awareness and interest.[51] The Renier collection was given to the Victoria and Albert Museum in 1970; in 1988 the Bodleian Library purchased a smaller but equally celebrated collection of 20,000 children's books, built up by Peter (1918–82) and Iona (b.1923) Opie.[52] Working with steady and dedicated enthusiasm over several decades around the middle of the twentieth century, these two couples were able to exploit the opportunities created by being specialists in a generally neglected field, where material could

---

49 I. A. Williams, *The elements of book-collecting* (London, 1927), 95.
50 'New paths in book collecting: detective fiction and war books', *The Times* (30 October 1934), 12.
51 A selection of material from this collection is reproduced in L. De Vries, *Little wide-awake: an anthology from Victorian children's books . . . in the collection of Anne and Fernand Renier* (London, 1967).
52 'The Opie appeal', *Bodleian Library Record* 13 (1988), 5–7; I. Opie, *The treasures of childhood: books, toys and games from the Opie Collection* (London, 1989).

often be acquired relatively cheaply. It is doubtful whether a collector starting out today to acquire historic children's books, could match the achievements of the Reniers or Opies; the marketplace is more aware of the value of the material, and the opportunities are fewer.

For the same reasons, it is no longer possible for private collectors to assemble the kinds of libraries built up by Huth or Christie-Miller at the end of the nineteenth century, with their vast sweep and multidisciplinary coverage of early printed books. There is still an active marketplace for such books, and prices generally rise as the years pass, but collections like this are now found in institutional research libraries, from which they are only rarely released. There are only about 228 copies of the Shakespeare First Folio surviving in the world today, and when over eighty of them are locked up in the Folger Library, there are fewer available to purchase.[53] During the twentieth century, vast quantities of books moved from private to institutional ownership, to enrich university libraries on both sides of the Atlantic. The impetus of the big American collectors at the beginning of the twentieth century – whose books went to their own endowed foundations – was continued later in the century, on a more modest but steady scale, by American universities keen to develop their research collections. British universities have also been in that marketplace, often with less financial muscle but poised to welcome the achievements of private collectors. Important collections which have moved into university libraries during the later twentieth century include those of A. N. L. Munby (1913–74; library and book trade history, including over 7,000 booksellers' and auctioneers' catalogues), purchased for Cambridge University Library; Sir Geoffrey Keynes (1887–1982; some 8,000 volumes, a wide-ranging collection covering literature, medicine and science), bequeathed to Cambridge University Library; William Carlton (1886–1973; 12,000 books on all aspects of stenography), bequeathed to London University Library; and Walter Harding (1883–1973; over 100,000 items of music, ballads and songbooks), bequeathed to the Bodleian Library.[54] The foundation of new universities in the later part of the century has also created opportunities for more general private academic collections to find a good use in helping to create brand-new institutional libraries – the Library of

53 A. J. West, *The Shakespeare First Folio: the history of the book*, vol. 2: *A new worldwide census of First Folios* (Oxford, 2003).

54 D. J. McKitterick, 'The Munby Collection in the University Library', *Transactions of the Cambridge Bibliographical Society* 6 (1975), 205–10; D. J. McKitterick, 'Bibliotheca bibliographici', *Bulletin of the Friends of Cambridge University Library* 4 (1983), 7–9 (and see also Keynes's own published catalogue of his collection, *Bibliotheca bibliographici: a catalogue of the library formed by Geoffrey Keynes* (London, 1964)); Bloomfield, *Directory of rare book and special collections*, 405, 504; A. H. King, *Some British collectors of music c.1600–1960* (Cambridge, 1963), 82–3.

the newly founded University of Kent at Canterbury was enhanced in this way with the books of the Shakespearian scholar John Crow (1904–69).[55] The transfer of books from private to institutional ownership, where they are likely to be properly conserved and more widely accessible, is clearly of long-term benefit for society at large, but each such transfer diminishes the pool of material available for private collectors.

It has nevertheless still been possible for men of means to develop distinguished collections of rare and valuable books, taking a more focused stance than the likes of Ashburnham or Huth, and matching them in quality if not quantity. Several outstanding collections of fine and interesting bookbindings have been formed by British collectors during the twentieth century; that of William Moss, sold in 1937, was considerably surpassed by that of J. R. Abbey (1894–1969), who specialised not only in bindings but also in colour plate books and illuminated manuscripts.[56] Abbey's library was sold in a series of major sales held at Sotheby's between 1965 and 1978; Henry Davis (d.1977) established a more permanent footing for his no less remarkable collection of bindings by gifting it to the British Library.[57] The diamond merchant Albert Ehrman (1890–1969) collected fine bindings, as well as incunabula, type specimens and early book sale catalogues; his Broxbourne Library (named after his home in Hertfordshire) became another celebrated late twentieth-century collection, now partly distributed between the Bodleian Library and Cambridge University Library, although the incunabula, chosen to represent the spread of printing across Europe, were sold in 1977–8.[58] The collection of Sir Paul Getty (1932–2003), held in a purpose-built library at his estate at Wormsley in Buckinghamshire, shows that this kind of thing can still be done; principally a collection of fine bindings, from the middle ages to the present day, it also includes important illuminated manuscripts.[59]

It should be clear that the shaping of private libraries has been influenced over the years by a variety of factors, personal need or interest being perhaps the most obvious. Where books are being collected for direct academic or

---

55 Bloomfield, *Directory of rare book and special collections*, 107.
56 S. Gibson, 'Colonel William E. Moss', *Bodleian Library Record* 5 (1955), 156–66; A. R. A. Hobson and A. N. L. Munby, 'Contemporary collectors xxvi: John Roland Abbey', *The Book Collector* 10 (1961), 40–8; see also Hobson's notice of Abbey in E. T. Williams and C. S. Nicholls (eds.), *Dictionary of national biography 1961–1970* (Oxford, 1981), 1–2.
57 M. M. Foot, 'The Henry Davis Collection: the British Museum gift', in her *Studies in the history of bookbinding* (Aldershot, 1993), 355–83.
58 A. Ehrman, 'Contemporary collectors ii: the Broxbourne Library', *The Book Collector* 3 (1954), 190–6.
59 H. G. Fletcher (ed.), *The Wormsley Library: a personal selection by Sir Paul Getty* (London, 1999).

professional use, the owner needs little guidance in deciding what to buy, beyond the kind of information about available books to be found in catalogues and reviews. Those with less experience, or whose bibliophilic interests are less professionally focused, have been able to draw on a range of secondary literature offering advice on book buying, like the books by Humphreys, Slater and Carter mentioned above. Such books may be essentially lists of titles and editions considered desirable – examples, from various generations, include William Goodhugh's *English gentleman's library manual, or a guide to the formation of a library* (1827), Seymour de Ricci's *Book collector's guide* (1921) and F. Seymour Smith's *An English library: an annotated list of classics and standard books* (1943) – or they may be compendia of historical and practical information, mixing aspects of bibliography with advice on dealing with the book and auction trade. Henry Wheatley's *How to form a library* (1886), Iolo Williams's *Elements of book-collecting* (1927) and G. L. Brook's *Books and book collecting* (1980) are examples of the latter sort.

Successive generations have also had their own journals, geared to the interests of book collectors, which not only function as vehicles for the exchange of information and the publication of articles, but also help to create a sense of community: examples include *The Bookman* (1891–1934, when it merged with *The London Mercury*), *The Book Collector* (from 1952, originally founded as *The Book Handbook* in 1947) and *Antiquarian Book Monthly* (from 1979, originally *Antiquarian Book Monthly Review*). Some titles like this have been published by associations formed specifically for bibliophiles, which have also been instrumental in promoting interest in books and collecting: *The Private Library* (from 1956) is the journal of the Private Libraries Association, founded in 1956; *The Book-Collector's Quarterly* (1930–5) was the organ of the First Edition Club, founded in 1922. The oldest of these associations is the Roxburghe Club, founded in 1812, whose small and significantly aristocratic membership continues to publish facsimiles and bibliographical reference works based on the contents of their collections.[60]

The book and auction trade has naturally been a major influence in the formation of private libraries, not only as a reservoir of supply but also as a source of advice. Good booksellers have long established the kinds of relationships with their clients which allow them to guide the building of collections, and to steer purchasing opportunities towards those who they know will be interested. Another major factor in the shaping of interest and collecting fashion has

---

60 C. Bigham, *The Roxburghe Club: its history and its members 1812–1927* (Oxford, 1928); N. Barker, *The publications of the Roxburghe Club, 1814–1962* (Cambridge, 1964).

been the publication of bibliographies and catalogues, opening up awareness of new fields and providing checklists of material to be collected. The rising interest in collecting contemporary English literature in the later nineteenth century was fostered in this way, as noted above; since that time, the massive bibliographical advances of the twentieth century have seen the national, and indeed international, published heritage mapped in increasing detail. The short-title catalogues, which have produced definitive listings of the surviving output of the presses of the English-speaking world down to 1800, are much supplemented by a vast range of more specialised and detailed bibliographies in particular subject areas.[61] These allow owners to place their books in a wider context, to assess rarity and to identify gaps, with much greater accuracy than that which was available to nineteenth-century bibliophiles. Exhibitions can also have a catalysing effect. A major exhibition on *Printing and the mind of man* was mounted in London in 1963 and the expanded version of its catalogue, listing over 400 books from Gutenberg to the Second World War with a noteworthy impact on human history, became an influential guide for collectors; the abbreviation *PMM* is still commonly found in auction and booksellers' catalogues today.[62]

Collectors have themselves added significantly to this body of material, by issuing catalogues of their libraries; there may be a variety of motives behind such publications, including vanity, advance publicity for a forthcoming sale or the wish to leave a permanent memorial, but the advancement of knowledge can be a genuine factor too. When the five-volume catalogue of the Huth Library was published in 1880, long before the short-title catalogues or even the 1884 catalogue of pre-1640 English books in the British Museum, it was a genuine resource discovery tool for bibliographers and historians. The *Bibliotheca Osleriana* will still be found cited in catalogues today, partly as an accepted definition of the key books in the development of western medicine, partly because its bibliographical descriptions and annotations remain useful. Collectors who specialise in particular fields may themselves become the bibliographical specialists in those areas; Barry Bloomfield (1931–2002) was known not only for his authoritative published bibliographies of W. H. Auden

---

61 There are far too many of these to try to enumerate. A selective list of author bibliographies published in the twentieth century will be found in P. Bernard *et al.* (eds.), *Antiquarian books: a companion* (Aldershot, 1994), 413–39. See also T. H. Howard-Hill, 'Enumerative and descriptive bibliography', in P. Davison (ed.), *The book encompassed* (Cambridge, 1992), 122–9.

62 J. Carter and P. Muir (eds.), *Printing and the mind of man: a descriptive catalogue illustrating the impact of print on the evolution of western civilisation during five centuries* (London, 1967); revised edn (Munich, 1983).

and Philip Larkin, but also for his collections of their works and associated literature.

It is today generally the case that important texts, for study and research, are found in institutional libraries rather than private ones. In the era of Huth and Christie-Miller, books which either were, or were thought to be, unique might be found only in the libraries of great collectors. As stated above, the catalogues of such libraries could reveal texts not otherwise known, and late nineteenth-century editions and facsimiles of Elizabethan literature not uncommonly drew on originals held in private hands.[63] The movement of this sort of material into public collections, combined with the vastly improved catalogue access which we now have to these libraries, makes private libraries less significant in this regard. The counterbalance to this point is the increasing interest we have today in the unique, copy-specific aspects of early books, where the individual characteristics of privately owned copies have something to offer to the national record.

One change which did take place during this period, not already discussed, relates to the condition of books, and a growing appreciation of the importance of tampering as little as possible with their original physical state. Anyone reading through Locker-Lampson's Rowfant catalogue will be struck by the high proportion of the books, of all centuries, described as bound in gilt decorated morocco by late nineteenth-century binders. Collectors of his generation, and earlier, took it as read that desirable books were improved by being rehoused in new bindings according to the current taste, which is why so many early English books, which passed through the hands of Victorian collectors, have lost all trace of their original covers, together with endleaves, bookplates, and other evidence of early ownership and use which we now regard as important. An emphasis on the importance of original condition was one of the messages, and achievements, of the late nineteenth-century literary enthusiasts like T. J. Wise, although their concerns were originally focused only on nineteenth-century material.[64]

The major changes which have taken place in the book-collecting world during recent decades have been around the issues of supply and opportunity mentioned earlier. Regret for a lost Golden Age is a regular refrain among bibliophiles, of all periods – in the 1720s, Humfrey Wanley was lamenting

---

63 For example, editions of the works of Greene and Dekker were issued in the 1880s, edited by A. B. Grosart, under the title of *The Huth Library: or Elizabethan-Jacobean unique or very rare books . . . largely from the library of Henry Huth*.
64 Carter, *Taste and technique*, 28–30.

that the supply of good-quality old books was in decline[65] – but the transfer of vast quantities of books from private to institutional ownership during the twentieth century means that collectable books simply do not circulate on the market as they once did. Libraries do dispose of books from time to time, but the selling of material with any kind of heritage value can be very controversial, as the John Rylands Library discovered in 1988.[66] It has been observed that the momentum in book buying towards the end of the twentieth century swung away from the research libraries and back towards private collectors, as institutional budgets declined, but this affects demand rather than supply.[67] The business has not transferred to bookshops, as this is also a sector which has been diminishing; Lord Clark, opening the Antiquarian Booksellers' Association (ABA) Fair in 1978, lamented the decline of traditional antiquarian bookshops and the growth of sale by postal catalogue, a format which is now increasingly overtaken by sales through Internet websites.[68] However, none of these outlets handles the quantity of material that flowed through the marketplace a century ago.

A brief chronology like this is inevitably selective in its depth of coverage and cannot list all the countless book collections and private libraries which have been formed in Britain since the middle of the nineteenth century. The preceding pages have mentioned a number of the more famous names in the field, but a comprehensive roll call would be vast. The purchase of books for personal ownership, new, second-hand and antiquarian, has been a widespread social phenomenon for many centuries and at the time of writing shows little sign of decline. It is too early to tell whether, or when, the growing importance of electronic information and communication will affect this. Private libraries have taken many forms and sizes and they have been important in a variety of ways. Their potential for long-term benefit has been most obviously realised when they have become a useful permanent addition to a public repository, but their value as tools for the advancement of learning or professional activities must also be recognised; they have provided recreation and satisfaction for their owners, and sometimes fascination for the world at large. Collectors have

---

65 'The book trade in 1984 – and after?', *The Book Collector* 33 (1984), 417–30 (p. 417).
66 See 'The rape of the Rylands', *The Book Collector* 37 (1988), 169–84.
67 A. Rota, 'Bookselling in a changing world', in Bernard *et al.* (eds.), *Antiquarian books*, 1–6 (p. 2).
68 R. Taylor, 'Of dealers and collectors', in H. G. Fletcher (ed.), *A miscellany for bibliophiles* (New York, 1979), 1–13 (p. 10); 'over fifty percent of secondhand and antiquarian booksellers in the UK today do not conduct their business through a shop' – S. Miller, *Book collecting: a guide* (Royston, 1994), 173.

been important catalysts in opening up and generating interest in new fields of study, and in helping us to recognise that previously neglected areas of our documentary output deserve more attention. The nineteenth and twentieth centuries have seen the rise of municipal and institutional libraries, making private provision seem much less important than it was in earlier times; it is arguable that the balance is closer than we may think, and closer than the proportions of this book imply.

PART III

*

LIBRARIES FOR NATIONAL NEEDS: LIBRARY PROVISION IN THE PUBLIC SPHERE IN THE COUNTRIES OF THE BRITISH ISLES

Introduction: library provision in the countries of the British Isles

PETER HOARE

Library development occurred at a different pace and in different ways in different places: the various chapters on public libraries, subscription libraries and libraries in higher education make this plain. Many factors influenced the foundation and fortunes of libraries over the years, from local politics and economic cycles to nationalist movements and world wars.

In particular the existence of the 'home nations' in the British Isles, with Wales, Scotland and Ireland (North and South) all differing from each other as well as from England, and having at various times different relationships with the United Kingdom as a whole, has led to quite different library traditions reflecting the history and culture of each country. Each has a national library (except England, which as so often assumes it does not need to assert its own national identity within Britain). The position of each country on its 'minority' languages (specifically Welsh and the closely related Gaelic and Irish) has varied over time and again is reflected in library provision. Legal and educational systems have had their own influence, in both cases overlaid with questions of religious allegiance.

This section of the volume, therefore, presents the reader with national perspectives – from England, Ireland, Scotland and Wales – that cross-cut the wide variety of library experiences described in other chapters. A series of views of the library scene in a typical English city over 150 years sets the tone; sub-sections for Wales, Scotland and Ireland then survey library provision (particularly but not only public libraries) and the appropriate national library – with the following section of the volume dealing with the national library of the whole United Kingdom.

The library scene in an English city: Newcastle upon Tyne libraries 1850–2000

JOHN C. DAY

Whilst Newcastle upon Tyne has served as an important regional centre from medieval times, its rise to national dominance was particularly significant during the nineteenth century. As the coal exporting, heavy engineering, chemical and shipbuilding industries expanded, Newcastle became the commercial and social hub of Tyneside and its hinterland.[1] Most of the immediate industrial development was along the banks of the River Tyne in the suburbs of Scotswood, Benwell, Elswick, Byker and Walker, and in the surrounding coalfield. Like many northern manufacturing complexes, there was also a dramatic population influx particularly in these industrial suburbs. Indeed for the whole of Newcastle there was an increase from 70,504 in 1841 to over 274,900 by 1921, although in the last decades of the twentieth century there was a steady population decrease despite boundary changes. Likewise Tyneside's heavy industry fell away rapidly in the 1980s and 1990s, a decline that can be traced back to the beginning of the twentieth century, although there was some short-term revival during the two World Wars.

1850–1900

Newcastle's nineteenth-century industrial prominence was matched by civil and social change as the city was replanned and a wide range of Victorian social reforms were implemented. Much of this applied only to the more prosperous city centre and to middle-class suburbs, with the working-class areas having to rely on charitable and religious organisations for their initial social infrastructure. Library provision in 1850 in Newcastle was no exception in this regard.[2]

---

1 Authoritative accounts of nineteenth-century Newcastle can be found in S. Middlebrook, *Newcastle-upon-Tyne: its growth and achievement*, 2nd edn (Newcastle upon Tyne, 1968); and N. McCord, *North East England: an economic and social history* (London, 1979).
2 J. Knott, *Newcastle libraries in the early 19th century*, History of the Book Trade in the North Papers (Newcastle upon Tyne, 1973).

Neither the 1851 list of institutions in Hudson's *History of adult education* or the later 1854 *Education census* provides a complete picture of mid-nineteenth-century library provision in Newcastle.[3] However, both give brief details of the libraries of the city's Literary and Philosophical Society (established 1794) and its Literary, Scientific and Mechanics' Institute. The radical founders of the former were involved in a number of complementary educational and literary developments during the first fifty years of the century, including the establishment of the Mechanics' Institute.

The 'Lit and Phil' was dominated by the commercial and professional middle classes of Newcastle as the membership fee and annual subscription were prohibitive for potential working-class readers, even if they could obtain suitable nominees and proposers. Not that the bookstock would have attracted the casual reader, as it excluded novels, religion, politics and law, concentrating on history, biography and the sciences. By the early 1840s the library had over 750 members (sixty-one female) and a bookstock in excess of 16,000 volumes. Equally important were the series of demonstrations and lectures whose participants included George Stephenson, Thomas Sopwith, Joseph Swan, W. J. Hooker and W. G. Armstrong. By 1850 the Library possessed over 24,000 volumes, but its membership had dropped to about 530. Attempts to revitalise it in the next decade involved subscriptions to Mudie's Circulating Library in London for lighter literature – but not novels – and a reduction in the membership fee. As a result the Society prospered throughout the 1860s and 1870s, with membership exceeding 1,500, and book issues increasing threefold.[4]

For working-class readers the mechanics' institute movement in Northumberland and Durham had been particularly vigorous, with Newcastle leading the way in 1824.[5] Its utilitarian and radical founder members had strong links with the 'Lit and Phil', and, in keeping with the principles of Brougham and Birkbeck, excluded novels and newspapers as well as books on religion and politics. The annual subscription of twelve shillings was to be spent entirely on new books once the running costs had been met, and as a result a varied and attractive bookstock was soon accumulated. As a comparatively wealthy institute, the membership increased rapidly from 243 in 1824 to over 790 by 1837,

3 J. W. Hudson, *History of adult education* (London, 1851); and Census Returns of Great Britain 1851, *Education. England and Wales. Report and tables. 1854* (London, 1854).

4 R. S. Watson, *The history of the Literary and Philosophical Society of Newcastle upon Tyne 1793–1896* (London, 1897); and the second volume covering 1896–1989 by Charles Parish (Newcastle, 1990).

5 A number of detailed unpublished studies exist, e.g. J. C. Day, 'Library provision in nineteenth century Northumberland', unpublished MPhil thesis, University of Strathclyde (1987); and J. Knott, 'A history of the libraries of Newcastle upon Tyne to 1900', unpublished MLitt thesis, University of Newcastle upon Tyne (1975).

with a bookstock in excess of 4,000 volumes. Unfortunately, like most mechanics' institutes, the intended working-class membership was soon overtaken by clerks and shopkeepers, and both the lecture programme and the adult classes were only partially successful. By the time of the trade depression in the 1840s membership was beginning to decline and financial difficulties were emerging. The opening of a newspaper reading room in 1847, a revamping of the adult classes and, like the 'Lit and Phil', a subscription to Mudie's, together with regular book boxes from the Northern Union of Mechanics' Institutes Itinerating Book Box Scheme, saw a temporary revival with membership exceeding 900.

During the 1850s a number of alternatives to the libraries described above came into being in Newcastle. The Elswick Works Literary and Scientific Institute had been opened in 1848 for the betterment of the employees of what was later to become Vickers Armstrong Limited, and in similar vein the North Eastern Railway Institute was established in 1852 for the benefit of railway staff. In direct competition to the traditional mechanics' institute, which excluded religious literature, the Newcastle upon Tyne Church of England Institute opened in 1854, with a reading room, a ladies room and evening classes. All three libraries outlived the Newcastle Mechanics' Institute, surviving largely with recreational literature until the early 1950s.

As the Literary and Philosophical Library had specifically excluded legal and medical texts and did not purchase all of the newer scientific and technical works, a number of professional and academic groups in the city began to establish their own libraries. This variety of special professional libraries was indicative of Newcastle's rise to prominence in the nineteenth century. The earliest was the extensive collection of books on antiquities and archaeology begun by the Society of Antiquaries of Newcastle upon Tyne shortly after the Society was founded in 1813. This was followed by the beginnings of collections at the Natural History Society (1829), the Newcastle and Gateshead Law Library (1835), the Newcastle Farmers' Club (1846/7), the North of England Institute of Mining and Mechanical Engineers (1852) and the library of the Newcastle upon Tyne School of Medicine and Surgery (c.1834), later to become part of Newcastle University. Each of the above collections continued in one form or another into the twentieth century, with some attaining national importance, but all were essentially for members, although access was allowed to serious research workers.

As is apparent above, the working-class reader in Newcastle in 1850 had virtually no access to library facilities, but for those desirous of information on current events there existed a number of news and reading rooms where local and national papers could be seen, usually for a small quarterly or monthly payment. They included the Working Men's Reading Room and Library, the Royal Arcade Reading Room, Arthur's Hill Reading Room, the Chartist-supported Democratic Reading and Newsroom and the St Nicholas Library and Reading Room. For the middle-class reader who wanted similar access the more expensive Central Exchange Newsroom charged one guinea annually. All played an important role in disseminating current information but they were often short-lived establishments. The reduction in stamp and paper duty by the early 1860s, together with the establishment of a newsroom at the Mechanics' Institute and the opening of the public library in the 1880s, ensured that none survived into the twentieth century.

Often equally short-lived were the small commercial circulating libraries that attempted to supply the lighter literature supposedly in demand by the working classes. They had first appeared in Newcastle in the 1740s but early records for those in existence between 1801 and 1830 suggest that in some of the larger ventures non-fiction predominated over fiction. After 1850 most seemed to have concentrated on 'books of the day', with William Kaye's 1852 *Circulating Library Catalogue* clearly indicating a very large proportion of fiction. For that decade local directories list at least eight such establishments in operation, as well as a juvenile circulating library and two specialising in musical scores. If access to literature for the working classes was difficult in the 1850s – a factor not helped by its prohibitive cost – then the establishment of the free public library in 1880 went a long way to resolving the problem.

In Newcastle the initial proposal to adopt the 1850 Public Libraries Act was put forward by Dr William Newton, a radical councillor, who represented a populous working-class suburb. He suggested the appointment of a committee to consider the establishment of a public library in Newcastle, his case relying heavily on the temperance argument and on the benefits of educating the working classes; unfortunately the committee never seems to have reported formally. Some sixteen years later, in 1870, Newton's son Henry reintroduced a similar proposal that was eventually carried in July 1874. By May 1879, after the acquisition of the Mechanics' Institute building and library, the Corporation began a temporary lending library service in September 1880 with a stock of 19,000 adult volumes and 1,000 for junior readers. The interest shown by the reading public was amply demonstrated, with over 4,000 readers registering in the first week. By the end of the first twelve-month period nearly 14,000 readers had joined, of which just under a third were female and 4,413 were between the ages of fourteen and twenty. The range of occupations of readers clearly showed that all sections of the population were using the library, a success which was mirrored by the Reference Library when it opened in 1884 with an initial stock of 22,000 volumes. A Local History Collection and one of patent literature were equally successful. By 1890 custom-built library premises were completed, and as the public library gained in popularity the number of small circulating and subscription libraries in Newcastle declined, the local trade directories dropping the heading *Libraries* from their classified commercial section by 1888.

Pressure for branch libraries was resisted owing to the low income from the penny rate until Alderman William Haswell Stephenson, a local businessman, offered to build branch libraries at Elswick (1895) and Heaton (1899). Their existence became the catalyst for the Corporation agreeing to increase the rate to three halfpence in the pound. By the turn of the century Newcastle Public Libraries could be regarded as a considerable success. They possessed a large and varied lending stock, a scholarly reference collection and a well-staffed service, governed by a Library Committee that was both forward looking and comparatively censorship free. Readership figures were high and clearly represented a wide spectrum of readers of both sexes and all occupational and age groups.[6]

1900–1950

Success in the public sector continued into the next century despite financial restrictions. Between 1900 and 1940 a further six branch libraries (including the inevitable Carnegie edifice) were opened, although the general bookstock came in for much criticism for both its physical state and its biased non-fiction selection policy. Staff shortages during the war years allowed the authority to extend its policy of employing female staff and, as demand on the service continued, book loans topped the one million mark for the first time in the year 1938–9.

As the public library prospered so too the earlier 'professional' libraries began to expand. This was particularly the case at the Literary and Philosophical Society Library, where they had begun to adopt the new Dewey Decimal Classification and had at last to admit novels — though not more than 20% of the bookfund was to be spent on fiction. A further attraction was the opening of a music library in 1913. Membership of the 'Lit and Phil', Society of Antiquaries and the Natural History Society all increased dramatically during the First

---

6 J. Knott, *Newcastle upon Tyne City Libraries: the first 100 years* (Newcastle upon Tyne, 1980).

World War as other forms of recreation became limited. Indeed the membership of the 'Lit and Phil' peaked in 1919 with over 5,000 registered readers. The Depression years heralded a fall in membership for all of the institutions – a state of affairs not reversed until the late 1940s, once wartime hostilities had ceased.[7] As for other Newcastle libraries like the Elswick Institute, the Church of England Institute and the North Eastern Railway Institute, survival was only possible by dramatically increasing the amount of fiction. But as competition for recreational activities intensified, with the growth among other things of the workingmen's club movement, these libraries gradually stagnated as their membership dwindled.

Other major developments on the Newcastle library scene emerged during the first half of the twentieth century. As early as 1904 the Library Association held its annual meeting in the city, although of considerably more importance was the establishment of the Northern Regional Library Bureau in 1931. Perhaps the most significant event was the creation of a large academic library in the new Armstrong College building in 1926. It was formed by the merger of the libraries of the two Durham colleges in Newcastle, those of the College of Medicine and Surgery and of Armstrong College (formerly the College of Physical Sciences), which eventually became King's College Library in 1937.[8] Both the public library and the Literary and Philosophical Library donated substantial runs of little-used academic journals to the newly created college library.

The period also witnessed the growth of special libraries in the Newcastle area.[9] The early library of the Institute of Mining and Mechanical Engineers (est. 1852) continued to flourish, often in conjunction with its neighbour the 'Lit and Phil', and was joined by a similar collection in 1888 at the North East Coast Institution of Engineers and Shipbuilders. In both instances, as heavy industry declined on Tyneside in the period up to 1950, their national importance as sources of current information declined. On a less ambitious scale, and largely for their own employees and research needs, information units were established at internationally known companies such as Vickers Armstrong (now Alvis-Vickers), C. A. Parsons (now Siemens),

7 G. Jobey, 'The Society of Antiquaries of Newcastle upon Tyne', *Archaeologia Aeliana*, 5th series, 18 (1990), 197–216.

8 E. M. Bettenson, *The University of Newcastle upon Tyne 1834–1971* (Newcastle, 1971); E. M. Bettenson, *The University of Newcastle upon Tyne: after 1970 – a selective view* (Newcastle upon Tyne, 1987).

9 A. Wallace, 'The libraries, public, private, university and special of the city of Newcastle upon Tyne', typescript (1950).

Thomas Hedley & Co. (now Procter and Gamble) and British Paints (formerly International Paints, then Courtaulds and now International Coatings Ltd, Azco Noble), as well as at professional organisations such as the Northern Architects Association, the Newcastle Chemical Industry Club and what became the Department of Social Security (now the Department of Work and Pensions).

1950–2000

Following the years of penury during the Second World War, the next thirty years saw the rapid development of the public library in Newcastle as funds became more readily available and as newly qualified staff began to make an impact on the service. By 1950 the Central Lending Department had been refurbished and was now wholly open access – the last major public library in the country to be converted. Changes grew apace as a separate Commercial and Technical Department was opened in 1954 which eventually became the hub of a technical information co-operative with the acronym TALIC (Tyneside Association of Libraries and Information Bureaux), which was in turn superseded by NETWORK in 1977. As more funds were obtained a travelling library was instituted and four new branches were opened, including an award-winning circular building at Jesmond with 'saw-tooth' glass walls. At all the new branches reader demand was heavy and lending issues increased dramatically, while administratively the number of branches and services necessitated some devolution of authority from the Central Library.

Overdue refurbishment of some older branches was also carried out but no amount of modernisation could bring the old Central Library building wholly into the mid-twentieth century. After much political in-fighting, a new building designed by Basil Spence was completed in 1968. Unfortunately, four years before its opening the 1964 Public Libraries and Museums Act had laid down minimum standards for library provision which coincided with cut-backs in bookfunds and an increase in the price of new books. From 1965/6 the public service began to fail to meet the target figure for new book purchases, although this did not prevent the opening of four new branch libraries in the next few years.

A major revision of service provision was called for in 1974 when Newcastle became one of the new districts of the Tyne and Wear Metropolitan Authority. The neighbouring library services of two adjacent urban boroughs – Gosforth and Newburn – as well as two former Northumberland County branch libraries now came under the control of the City Libraries. The 1980s heralded further significant changes as the impact of budget reductions began to take effect and the authority had seriously to consider value-added services. As a result a cafeteria was opened; a self-financing computer software and cassette library was developed and, despite adverse publicity, some rare books were sold. To further bolster funds one of the earliest branches (Elswick) was closed and both library posts and opening hours throughout the system were reduced. Despite the stringent measures new services were still introduced with the creation of the Newcastle Business Library, replacing the former Commercial and Technical Department, and the emergence of a very success-ful publishing programme based on the Local Studies Department.

Conditions did not improve following the demise of the Tyne and Wear Metropolitan Authority in 1986, and opening hours were further reduced (a cut of 33% since 1980), as was the bookfund. The inauguration of the New-castle Libraries Agreement in 1989, a stock and collection policy co-operative between the public, academic and private sectors in the city, had little impact on the situation. It is not surprising to find that an analysis of the annual statis-tics shows a 6% fall in bookstock totals and a steady decline in issues over the decade.

The early 1990s witnessed even greater stress on public library provision although it was still maintaining services at all its branches, albeit with reduced hours. These financial problems were not unique to Newcastle as poll tax cap-ping on many local authorities was having a detrimental effect on the provi-sion of all council services. The threat of compulsory staff redundancies and a proposal to renegotiate staff salaries resulted in industrial action. Predictably reductions in the bookfund were soon reflected in a further fall in book issues, although the loans of non-book materials were increasing. Money was never-theless found to refurbish a number of branch libraries, now to be referred to as community libraries, and later as family learning centres, and the service began rather belatedly to introduce IT facilities to complement those already in use in the Business Library. Whilst mainstream revenue funding was restricted the library took advantage of Government Urban Programme grants to develop a Marketing Advice Centre, an Educational Guidance Unit and a Patents Advice Centre, and obtained other monies through Inner City Partnership funding. Further income to support ongoing development was raised by the sale of rare but little-used material of considerable bibliographical merit in 1997 and again in January 2000, although this did not prevent an announcement that no adult fiction would be purchased during the financial year 2000/1.

Other sectors of Newcastle's library world fared little better in the final decades of the twentieth century. The 'Lit and Phil', the Society of Antiquaries, the Natural History Society and the Institute of Mining and Mechanical Engineers all saw their memberships decline and had to resort to subscription increases and fund raising. As regional archive services developed, most were only too willing to deposit their manuscript materials, and to transfer older bookstock to local public and academic libraries. All four nevertheless survived, but not without some form of local co-operation, amalgamation or national funding.

In the industrial world, as firms were merged and headquarters transposed elsewhere, special library facilities in Newcastle also changed. Where earlier industrial information units had survived (Vickers, Siemens, Procter and Gamble) they frequently became branch sections of much larger international electronic research services. Newer and successful architectural, legal and newspaper libraries developed in Newcastle, as did information resources for the building trade and the glass, lead and chemical industries.

If public and private library development in Newcastle slowed down in the information technology age this was not the case with local academic libraries. King's College continued to grow throughout the 1950s and 1960s as both a teaching and a research institute, being elevated to full university status as Newcastle University in 1963. Despite financial stringencies in later years new premises in the form of the Robinson Library were completed in 1984. Grants and generous bequests have further enhanced its capabilities, which catered for in excess of 12,000 students by the end of the century.

To complement the more traditional courses offered by Newcastle University, the merger of three local colleges of higher education by Newcastle Corporation in 1969 to form Newcastle Polytechnic created another large academic library. Before educational cut-backs began to restrict capital expenditure the Poly completed the building of a new multi-storey library, and it too gained university status, as the University of Northumbria at Newcastle upon Tyne in 1992, with an annual enrolment of over 14,000 full-time students at its two campuses by 1999–2000. To add to the 30,000 students in full- and part-time higher education in the city, Newcastle College, formerly the College of Further Education, itself had over 30,000 students, using its own library and IT facilities.

Conclusion

Library development in all its aspects since 1850 in Newcastle upon Tyne has largely followed national trends. Owing to the city's prominence in the nineteenth century a number of collections of national importance evolved.

The public library service, which perhaps reached its zenith in the 1960s and early 1970s, has always been rated as one of the best public systems in England, and still gains many plaudits. So too the depth of research material and special collections at Newcastle University, the presence of a School of Informatics (the former Library School) at the Northumbria University, and the co-operation and support of Information North – a regional information development agency – which has now been subsumed, along with NETWORK, into two newly created bodies: LINK and NEMLAC. The latter co-ordinates the work of library, museum and archive services and continues to keep Newcastle at the forefront of library provision and development in the UK.

17

Public libraries in Wales since 1862

PHILIP HENRY JONES

Were it not for the challenge posed by the Welsh language to an ostensibly neutral (but in practice Anglophone and British) professional ideology, the history of public libraries in Wales – characterised by a preponderance of small and poor authorities – might be regarded as little more than a depressing coda to the English experience. The development of public libraries in Wales falls naturally into the same three periods as in England: slow but accelerating growth in urban areas up to 1914; the extension of the service to rural areas and the virtual completion of urban coverage during the inter-war years; and what may prove to have been the Golden Age of the public library from the late 1950s to the early 1970s. These periods also broadly coincide with a significant change in the attitude of many librarians to the Welsh language, from an almost total neglect of the needs of Welsh speakers to a commitment to provide as comprehensive a service as the economic limitations of Welsh-language publishing permitted – and, finally, to attempts to overcome these limitations by actions which went far beyond any earlier vision of the role of the public library.

Nineteenth-century Wales displayed little enthusiasm for public libraries. Between 1862, when Cardiff became the first local authority to adopt the Acts, and 1894 there were only twelve adoptions. At least six of these were prompted by the offer of a gift or the prospect of acquiring cheaply the assets of an existing institution. Although such inducements might help persuade ratepayers to adopt, they did not always work: Llandudno rejected adoption in 1889 despite being offered a library worth £2,000.[1] These early adoptions were in industrial or resort towns, most of which already possessed subscription or institutional libraries serving a middle-class and professional readership.

From 1895 onwards there was a marked increase in the number of library authorities. The 1894 Local Government Act enabled civil parishes to assume

---

1 T. Greenwood, *Public libraries: a history of the movement*, 4th edn (London, 1894), 279.

library powers, and by 1919 some twenty-seven Welsh parishes had done so. Several, fortunately, never operated a service; the remainder, their populations ranging from under 9,000 to a mere 613, were too small to be able to offer any significant service. The other incentive to adoption was the availability of Carnegie building grants from 1897 onwards. By 1914, twenty-six Welsh library authorities had received over £78,000 from this source.[2] As well as imposing standard conditions to ensure that the libraries he had built were adequately funded, Carnegie rejected requests from a few authorities (such as Llanidloes in 1902) where the income from a penny rate was wholly inadequate, or (as at Cricieth) required that authorities set up a maintenance fund.[3] Even so, by stimulating further adoptions his grants increased the number of small and impoverished authorities. As elsewhere, the upkeep of a Carnegie building often made it impossible for small authorities to develop their service, which all too often degenerated into a newsroom and a grubby collection of outdated books looked after by a caretaker 'librarian'. On the other hand, the poverty of most Welsh library authorities made it impossible for them to build libraries for many decades following the termination of Carnegie grants: Montgomeryshire's headquarters at Newtown, opened in 1963, was the first new library building in North Wales for half a century.[4]

By 1914 at least seventy-two local authorities in Wales had adopted the Acts. Erratic record-keeping in the smaller authorities makes greater precision impossible: Machynlleth, for example, adopted the Acts twice, in 1897 and 1912. Ten authorities never operated a rate-supported service and thus lost their library powers to counties following the 1919 Act. Since two other authorities had also vanished as a result of local government changes, by 1914 about sixty Welsh local authorities were offering some kind of rate-supported library service. The figure is again imprecise because of problems experienced by small authorities such as Penmachno, which opened a reading room in 1905 but was forced to close it by 1911.[5]

The Adams Report of 1915 showed that 54% of the population of Wales lived in areas which had not adopted the Acts. Even where they had been adopted, small authorities, limited resources and the penny rate restriction frequently prevented the development of any worthwhile service: twenty-one of the fifty-two authorities surveyed had an annual income of less than £100 in

---

2 J. Roe, 'The public library in Wales: its history and development in the context of local government', unpublished master's thesis, Queen's University of Belfast (1970), 214.
3 Roe, 'Public library in Wales', 67, 63.
4 *Library Association Record* 65 (1963), 510.
5 Roe, 'Public library in Wales', 49.

1910–11, and a further thirteen an income of less than £200. This was spent on buildings and staff, rather than books. Only six Welsh authorities met Adams's criterion for a 'moderately efficient' library of spending over £150 a year on books. Nineteen spent less than a pound a week, one parish, Llanuwchllyn, spending only a pound a year. Staffing was equally unsatisfactory. Only Cardiff and Swansea employed more than ten staff. A few small authorities, such as Aberystwyth and Holyhead, employed women because they could not afford male librarians.

Perhaps the most startling finding was that one authority, Cardiff, was responsible for almost a third of the total expenditure on libraries in Wales. With the enthusiastic support of Cardiff's council, which wished to gain city status and eventually recognition as the capital of Wales, John Ballinger, Cardiff's Librarian from 1884 to his appointment as the Librarian of the new National Library of Wales in 1908, was able to make the library one of the best in Britain. Cardiff's purpose-built Central Library, completed in 1882, was greatly expanded in 1896. To help meet the cost, Cardiff obtained a local bill permitting an additional halfpenny rate. In response to public demand five branch reading rooms with small reference collections were set up in 1889–91,[6] and a systematic branch programme was implemented from 1900 onwards. Ballinger was particularly interested in developing services for children by setting up Children's Reading Halls (as pioneered in the USA) and instructing children how to use a library. From 1899 onwards, in conjunction with the School Board, the library began to operate a service to primary schools which soon expanded to cover elementary schools and institutions for children with special needs. American influence may also explain Ballinger's readiness to pioneer schemes such as a telephone service for commercial enquiries in 1907. Cardiff also developed outreach activities, including library visits by groups of working men, branch lectures and the publication from 1904 onwards of a substantial periodical.

As part of Cardiff's campaign to ensure that it should be the home of the proposed National Library, the library built up a large and valuable Welsh collection, recorded in a 550-page printed catalogue published in 1898. The isolation of Welsh material – albeit in a rather splendid ghetto – is as indicative of the place of the language in late nineteenth-century public libraries as were the stained glass windows in Cardiff's library, which depicted English literary figures rather than representatives of Glamorgan's literary tradition.[7]

The needs of the million or so people in Wales (almost 50% of the population) who could speak Welsh, a quarter of a million of whom were monoglot Welsh,

6 Greenwood, *Public libraries*, 271–2.
7 Greenwood, *Public libraries*, 272.

were almost wholly ignored by public libraries. They continued a long-standing tradition, since earlier subscription libraries, catering for an Anglicised elite, had no reason to acquire Welsh material. Mechanics' institute libraries, even those serving predominantly Welsh communities, acquired few Welsh books. The 1870 Llanelli catalogue, for example, included about ninety Welsh books in its 2,000 titles.[8] The few public libraries, notably Swansea and Cardiff, which possessed scholarly Welsh collections viewed them as reference materials for antiquarian research and, increasingly, as counters in the game of deciding where the National Library of Wales should be located. Ironically, the 1905 decision to site the National Library in Aberystwyth was largely governed by the fact that key collections of Welsh manuscripts then in private ownership (the Welsh equivalent of the Cottonian collection) would be given only to a Library in Aberystwyth.[9]

The smaller urban libraries of South Wales made practically no attempt to include Welsh books in their lending collections. Although almost a third of the population of Pontypridd in 1901 could speak Welsh, the 1897 library catalogue listing 1,999 volumes included only two Welsh titles – duplicate copies of an outdated dictionary.[10] Even the most Welsh areas recorded a low proportion of Welsh titles. Blaenau Ffestiniog's 1906 catalogue listing 2,600 books included no more than 320 Welsh titles in an authority where almost 6,000 people (over 57% of the population) in 1901 were monoglot Welsh.[11] Past practice and the inferior status of the language meant that a low level of Welsh-language provision was generally accepted and that explicit complaints concerning the shortage of Welsh material, as at Aberdare in 1912, were extremely rare.[12]

The failure of the majority of Welsh public libraries to develop satisfactory services during the prosperous pre-1914 era was acutely felt during the Depression of the inter-war years. Long-term unemployment led to such a massive outflow of population that even in 1961 fewer people lived in Wales than in 1921. As rate income collapsed, the development of library services had to rely heavily on external funding, notably from the Carnegie United Kingdom Trust (CUKT), which between 1917 and 1940 gave Welsh libraries over £57,000.

Despite wartime problems, the CUKT decided to implement Adams's recommendation that it should finance experimental rural schemes. In 1917 it

---

8 Llanelly Mechanics' Institute, *Rules & catalogue* (Llanelly, 1870).

9 See Lionel Madden's chapter on the National Library of Wales, below.

10 P. F. Tobin, 'Pontypridd public library, 1890–1990', in P. F. Tobin and J. I. Davies (eds.), *The bridge and the song: some chapters in the story of Pontypridd* (Bridgend, 1991), 67–78 (citation p. 70).

11 Roe, 'Public library in Wales', 142.

12 *Aberdare Central Public Library: golden jubilee 1904–54* (Aberdare, 1955).

awarded Caernarfonshire an annual grant of £400 for a period of five years to set up the first such scheme in Wales.[13] The model – followed by all the Welsh experiments – was the Staffordshire scheme of a central repository circulating book boxes to centres in primary schools. Five other Welsh counties – Cardiganshire, Denbighshire, Brecon and Radnorshire (initially operating a joint service), and Montgomeryshire – eventually operated CUKT-financed experimental schemes. Following the passage of the 1919 Act, the remaining Welsh counties adopted the Acts and began to provide a library service, aided by CUKT capital grants to cover their initial costs. A major weakness was that when Glamorgan adopted the Acts in 1923 it excluded the Rhondda and Mountain Ash on the pretext that they were already being adequately served by miners' institute libraries. The County Council's understandable desire to minimise expenditure was matched by that of the two Urban District Councils, and reinforced by local opposition to competition with the indigenous institute libraries.[14] Following years of fruitless discussion which poisoned relations between Glamorgan, the CUKT and the two authorities, the Rhondda eventually adopted the Acts in 1933 (though it was not until 1939 that it began to provide a service) while Mountain Ash enjoyed the dubious distinction in 1963 of being the last authority in England and Wales to adopt.

While county libraries undoubtedly met a hitherto unsatisfied demand for books, severe problems soon became apparent. Securing satisfactory funding was the major difficulty. The 1919 Act made county libraries the responsibility of sub-committees of powerful education committees. Since he was not a chief officer, the librarian generally had little influence, and was further handicapped by the initial decision of the CUKT to stress the cheapness of county services. Although a few librarians, notably Owen Williams in Denbighshire, overcame these problems, several counties levied a wholly inadequate library rate. Caernarfonshire, for example, crippled its service during the inter-war years by levying only a farthing rate. The redoubtable Miss Jane Roberts, Librarian from 1926 to 1952, had to rely on CUKT book-purchase grants to keep the service alive in impoverished Merioneth.

The relationship between county libraries and existing library areas was often difficult. Although the 1919 Act allowed any library authority (other than a county borough) to relinquish its powers to a county council, authorities which were too small to fund an acceptable service clung to their independence. By

13 T. E. Griffiths, 'Caernarvonshire and its libraries: development of the first county library in Wales', *Transactions of the Caernarvonshire Historical Society* 33 (1972), 170–89.
14 C. Baggs, '"The whole tragedy of leisure in penury": the South Wales miners' institute libraries during the Great Depression', *Libraries and Culture* 39 (2004), 115–36.

1939, only six authorities had relinquished library powers to counties. Many survived by borrowing books from the county systems, generally paying a subscription based on the product of the county library rate for their area.

In order to provide an adequate service to densely populated areas where the system of book boxes to centres was clearly inadequate, several authorities (such as Pembrokeshire and Carmarthenshire) resorted to differential rating from the late 1920s to enable them to staff small urban branches.[15] In industrial South Wales, some public libraries attempted to use miners' institute libraries as service points. Supplying books financed by community taxation to private institutions which restricted public access[16] was questionable in principle and proved disastrous in practice: thousands of books entrusted by Glamorgan to institute libraries were stolen because of inadequate supervision.[17]

Since authorities could not be compelled to amalgamate, co-operation (as advocated in the Kenyon Report) was promoted as a panacea. From the mid-1920s, the CUKT pressed for the development of an inter-lending system. The obvious location for the scheme's bureau was the National Library of Wales, but suspicion of Welsh Wales amongst the urban librarians of Glamorgan and Monmouth, and a plausible claim that the problems of authorities in the industrialised south-east differed from those in other parts of Wales, led to two bureaux being established in 1931, one in Cardiff covering Glamorgan and Monmouthshire, while the other, at the National Library of Wales, covered the remainder of Wales. Despite repeated criticism, this inefficient arrangement remained in force until 1973.[18] Because of inadequate expenditure on books a low proportion of requests was satisfied by regional stock. Indeed some librarians criticised the scheme for tempting the weaker authorities to borrow books they should have bought.[19]

The National Library of Wales attempted to play a leading role in the development of Welsh libraries by hosting annual conferences from 1925 onwards. Although D. Rhys Phillips, Secretary of the Welsh Bibliographic Society, had

15 Roe, 'Public library in Wales', 105–6.
16 The aggressively exclusive attitude of many institutes is epitomised by a notice reproduced in the McColvin Report: 'This is NOT a Public Library. Any person other than a member found using it will be prosecuted' (L. R. McColvin, *The public library system of Great Britain: a report on its present condition with proposals for post-war reorganization* (London, 1942), 49).
17 S. Scott, 'Public library development in Glamorgan 1920–1974: an area study, with particular reference to Glamorgan County Library', unpublished FLA thesis (1979), 84.
18 National Library of Wales, *Annual report 1973–74* (Aberystwyth, 1974), 20.
19 E. Luke, 'The future of library co-operation in Wales', in *Conference of Library Authorities in Wales and Monmouthshire 1951. Report of the proceedings* (Aberystwyth, 1951), 24–38 (specifically p. 26).

advocated such a step in 1916,[20] it was not until 1931 that the Wales and Monmouthshire Branch of the Library Association was founded. The avoidance of the word 'Welsh' in its title indicated a reluctance to make any concession to alleged Welsh nationalism, and it was only the disappearance of Monmouthshire in the 1974 reorganisation of local government that made possible a change to the 'Welsh Library Association'.

In Welsh-speaking areas, the county library services initially recorded a considerable demand for Welsh books. Welsh-language publishers, however, were in no position to increase the number of new titles or even reprint established favourites, as wartime shortages and inflation had exacerbated the parlous state of the industry. For most of the 1920s fewer than a hundred Welsh titles were published each year. County Librarians, notably Saunders Lewis, Glamorgan's first County Librarian, repeatedly drew attention to the shortage of Welsh books.[21] Cardiganshire's Librarian complained in 1925 that 'the demand for Welsh literature, of the type of the Home University Library ... is greater than the supply available'.[22] In 1927 T. O. Jones, Caernarfonshire's first Librarian, requested a CUKT grant for publishing Welsh books. In rejecting his application the Trust pointed out that making such a grant would set a dangerous precedent for subsidising books in Irish or Scottish Gaelic.[23]

During the inter-war years library authorities in the resort towns of North Wales largely escaped the effects of the Depression and several made modest improvements in their services, most notably Llandudno and Rhyl, both of which appointed their first qualified librarians in 1935.[24] Prosperity may have bred complacency: in 1934 Conwy decided to respect the views of 'certain members of the committee' who felt deeply 'that anything dealing with Hitler, Russia or anything of that sort should be kept out of our library'.[25] In the industrialised areas of South Wales, libraries were very heavily used by the unemployed, mainly in a quest for escapist literature.[26] Although Cardiff still remained a centre of excellence, many municipal libraries fell into a semi-derelict condition. The dramatic effects produced by spending fairly small sums to remodel services in such areas were demonstrated at Pontypridd, where

20 D. R. Phillips, 'Public library policy and provision in Wales', *Library World* 19 (1916–17), 117–20, 147–52 (citation p. 120).
21 *Western Mail*, 21 February 1922.
22 D. G. Griffiths, 'Cardiganshire rural libraries scheme', in *Conference on libraries in Wales and Monmouthshire 1925. Report of the proceedings* (Aberystwyth, 1925), 26–9.
23 Griffiths, 'Caernarvonshire and its libraries', 182.
24 Roe, 'Public library in Wales', 124.
25 *Library Association Record*, series, 4, 3 (1934), 236.
26 W. B. Ready, 'Through depression in the Hayes: the hungry, the troubled and the studious', *Library Review* 31 (1982), 35–45 (specifically pp. 40–1).

a CUKT grant of £900 enabled the library to appoint its first professionally qualified librarian, remodel its interior and increase its stock by over 10,000 volumes.[27] Issues rose from 14,400 in 1930 to over 309,000 in 1933, but the authority's inability to sustain funding led to a considerable fall in issues by 1939. Even so, it did well enough to be praised as a 'really good' library in the McColvin Report of 1942.[28]

McColvin's report demonstrated the failure of Kenyon's belief in the force of example and exposed appalling failures in authorities such as the Rhondda and Aberdare. Its proposed reorganisation of Welsh libraries into five units was politically impractical and took as little account of poor communications in Wales as did the 1974 reorganisation of local government.

A survey of Welsh libraries carried out in 1948 outlined a dispiritingly familiar scene of poverty and uneven development. Some 400,000 people were still not receiving any kind of library service. Six of the thirteen counties had made little progress since the 1920s. Two-thirds of the lending bookstock of urban libraries was held by three authorities. While Welsh books represented a significant proportion of the stock of county systems, less than 3% of the lending stock of urban authorities was in Welsh.[29]

Although the problems facing the smaller authorities intensified, only eleven relinquished their powers between 1945 and 1955. Some county libraries tried to force the issue by cutting off the supply of books, as Denbighshire did to the parishes of Bersham and Esclusham Below in the mid-1950s. Both attempted to go their own way, but a ratepayers' revolt in Bersham led to its relinquishing its powers in 1956.[30] A unique solution to a common problem – a small town containing both a county headquarters and a municipal library – was arrived at in Aberystwyth in 1947, when the town (which possessed a half-empty Carnegie library and unspeakably grubby books) and Cardiganshire (which had cleaner books but was desperately short of working space) agreed to set up a joint library service. As well as rationalising the use of scarce resources, the agreement meant that the Joint Librarian became a chief officer who could argue the library's case in a Library Committee which was no longer merely a sub-committee of the Education Committee.

Cardiganshire set up the first mobile library service in Wales in April 1949, when a van costing £1,500 (paid for by the wife of a London-Welsh dairyman)

27 Tobin, 'Pontypridd public library', 71–2.
28 McColvin, *Public library system*, 42.
29 Library Association, Wales and Monmouthshire Branch, *Report on the municipal, urban district and county libraries of Wales and Monmouthshire, 1948* (Morriston, 1950).
30 Denbighshire County Library, *Librarian's annual report for the year ended March 31st, 1958*, 5.

began making monthly visits to villages. Considerable numbers of Welsh-language books were borrowed during the first year of the new service but demand then fell away sharply: as in the 1920s, borrowers had read every Welsh book of interest to them.[31] Since large mobiles failed to reach many potential readers in areas with a scattered population, in 1963 Cardiganshire introduced a service of small vans visiting individual houses, despite some initial opposition (one councillor denounced the scheme as 'extreme nationalism').[32] Following the success of the first van in south Cardiganshire, the service was extended to cover the whole of the county by the beginning of 1968. The vans reached many people who had never before used a public library, and initially recorded a high proportion of Welsh-language loans, partly because they did not carry light English fiction.[33]

From 1950 onwards, Alun Edwards, Cardiganshire's Librarian, began a prolonged and ultimately successful campaign to increase the supply of Welsh books. In 1951 Cardiganshire Education Committee set up a Welsh Books Committee, empowered to spend £2,000 a year to promote the production of Welsh books for children. Later guaranteed-purchase agreements by libraries were foreshadowed by an agreement that each school in the county would buy two copies of every suitable Welsh title.[34] The dire condition of Welsh-language publishing led to the setting up in October 1951 of an official investigation into its problems. Although the main recommendation of the Ready Report of 1952, that Welsh-language publishing should receive a government grant, was not immediately implemented, the Report prepared the way for the present system of subsidy. Initial efforts were directed towards securing a more adequate supply of Welsh books for children, but Alun Edwards, realising that adult light fiction accounted for a high proportion of public library loans, campaigned vigorously to improve the provision of such material in Welsh. The most important step was the establishment in 1961 of the Welsh Books Council, which was initially staffed by employees of Cardiganshire Joint Library.[35]

According to the Roberts Report of 1959, two-thirds of the fifty-two library authorities in Wales were below the minimum population (40,000) for an efficient library service and none met the committee's criteria for annual expenditure on books. More positively, Roberts was the first official enquiry to recognise the existence of the Welsh language by stating that all public libraries

---

31 A. Edwards, *Yr hedyn mwstard: atgofion* (Llandysul, 1980), 51–2.
32 Edwards, *Hedyn*, 127.
33 Edwards, *Hedyn*, 134.
34 Edwards, *Hedyn*, 53–4.
35 R. Llwyd (ed.), *Gwarchod y gwreiddiau: cyfrol goffa Alun R. Edwards* (Llandysul, 1996), 64.

in Wales (the 'all' was important, given attitudes in south-east Wales) should provide a 'comparable' service for Welsh and English speakers. Unfortunately, it failed to indicate how authorities could meet the extra cost. The Bourdillon report of 1962 set out for the first time quantitative criteria for the provision of Welsh-language material: for every 1,000 Welsh speakers served, fifty of the 250 volumes per annum per thousand population acquired should be in Welsh.

The 1964 Act led to a reduction in the number of library authorities as the last five parishes lost their library powers to counties and a number of small authorities decided to relinquish their powers. By 1967, there were thirty-nine library authorities in Wales: thirteen counties, four county boroughs, twelve boroughs, and ten urban districts (of which four depended on county systems for their stock). Great disparities in size remained, the largest, Glamorgan having a population of almost 400,000 and the smallest, Cricieth, just over 1,500.

The 1974 reorganisation of local government introduced a two-tier scheme of counties and districts. Library powers were to have been allocated to the eight new Welsh counties, but the day before reorganisation was implemented four districts (all Labour strongholds) were granted library powers. Several of the new county units were workable and offered worthwhile economies of scale – but none had a chance to prove itself fully during the inflation of the 1970s and institutionalised philistinism of the 1980s.

Further local government reorganisation in 1994–5 reversed the trend towards larger units by creating twenty-two library authorities, with populations ranging from 60,000 to over 295,000. The new authorities have had to grapple with significant new responsibilities deriving from legislation such as the Welsh Language Act 1993 and the Disabilities Discrimination Act 1995, as well as implementing initiatives such as the People's Network. From 1999 they have also had to come to terms with the existence of the National Assembly of Wales. Several developments – notably the promulgation of standards for public libraries in Wales and the requirement for authorities to produce three-year library plans – suggest that the Assembly firmly intends to improve services and break down barriers to access, while the establishment of CyMAL: Museums Archives and Libraries Wales is intended to reinforce the role of these institutions in improving the quality of life for people in Wales. Perhaps ominously, promoting what is described as 'Wales' cultural identity and bilingual heritage' (a significant form of words – the list nowhere specifically mentions the Welsh language) is placed halfway down the list of objectives in CyMAL's strategic agenda. As in the nineteenth century, utilitarian considerations ('High quality skills and education') appear to have triumphed over linguistic sentiment.

A shortage of professionally qualified library staff had always been a problem in Wales. D. Rhys Phillips was apparently the first, in 1916, to express the additional need for bilingual librarians, who would be 'at least equal in accomplishments and mental outlook to the alert bilingual villager-class'.[36] Some improvement came as several of the early county systems appointed Welsh-speaking graduates as librarians, often in the face of bitter hostility from the staff of municipal libraries. Following the Roberts Report's suggestion that Wales needed a school of librarianship, Alun Edwards and Cardiganshire's Director of Education, John Henry Jones, set in train a process which brought about the creation in 1964 of the College of Librarianship Wales, a finely nuanced title since 'Welsh College of Librarianship' would have been unacceptable to too many powerful bodies. Under the dynamic leadership of its principal, F. N. Hogg, it rapidly became a far more cosmopolitan and larger institution than was originally envisaged. Its internationalism helped to break down the Britocentric views of an older generation of librarians by emphasising the abnormality of the English monolingual model of librarianship. Its size permitted sufficient Welsh-speaking staff to be employed to develop a range of Welsh-interest and Welsh-medium courses. A significant proportion of the librarians currently employed in Wales passed through the college. Regrettably, following the college's enforced merger in 1989 with the University of Wales, Aberystwyth, a failure of vision and commitment at the centre meant that the initial contingent of staff was not renewed by fresh recruitment, and the future of the Welsh element is now at risk.

36 Phillips, 'Public library policy', 148.

18

The National Library of Wales

LIONEL MADDEN

It is not surprising that, despite occasional earlier calls by individuals to establish some sort of national collection, serious moves to create a national library for Wales should have coincided with the growing reassertion in the nineteenth century of the claim of Wales to be treated as a distinct nation and not a mere adjunct to England. An important meeting at the National Eisteddfod in 1873 expressed a strong aspiration to establish a national library. Interim accommodation for a 'Welsh library' was offered by the University College of Wales in Aberystwyth, itself newly founded in the previous year.

The argument was not easily won. The most persistent advocate was Sir John Herbert Lewis, MP for the Flint Boroughs, who from 1892 worked tirelessly to secure for Wales a fair share of the Treasury grant for national museums and libraries. The campaign eventually succeeded in 1905 with the announcement that the British government intended to establish a National Museum of Wales in Cardiff and a National Library of Wales in Aberystwyth.

The decision to locate the Library in Aberystwyth owed much to the town's central location within Wales, the existing Welsh collection in the university college, a successful appeal fund and a magnificent site donated by Lord Rendel, as well as to errors of judgement in Cardiff's presentation of its counter-claim. But the deciding factor was undoubtedly the magnificent collection of manuscripts and books built up by Sir John Williams, a retired physician and former medical adviser to the royal family. No national library for Wales could possibly have been created without his collection and he made it clear that he was not prepared to give it to Cardiff and that Aberystwyth was his preferred location.[1]

The Library was formally created by royal charter in March 1907. The charter defined in some detail what the library should collect. It required it to build

---

1 For the pre-history and first half-century see D. Jenkins, *A refuge in peace and war: the National Library of Wales to 1952* (Aberystwyth, 2002).

major collections of Welsh and Celtic materials but also to ensure holdings in all subjects that would be of service to higher education and research in Wales. It specified, too, that the collections should include not only printed and manuscript materials but also photographs, paintings, pictures and other visual items. A supplemental charter of 1988 added audio-visual materials to the list. Despite a consistently small purchase grant, good collections of British and Irish materials were ensured when the Copyright Act of 1911 granted the Library legal deposit status, albeit with some restrictions which were not finally removed until 1987.

Collections

From the beginning, until a radical restructuring in 2001, the Library was organised in three curatorial departments responsible for manuscripts and records, printed materials, and pictorial materials and maps. The foundation collections of each department owed much to the generosity of Sir John Williams.

Among the many outstanding private collections and individual items donated by Williams the jewel was the Hengwrt-Peniarth collection of manuscripts. This comprised over 500 volumes including the Black Book of Carmarthen, the Black Book of Chirk, the Book of Taliesin, the White Book of Rhydderch and the Hengwrt Chaucer. These, together with Williams's Llanstephan manuscripts and other collections acquired during the early years, ensured that the Library had an extraordinary wealth of Welsh and other manuscripts by the end of the first decade of its existence.

Williams was, too, a generous donor of printed materials. His extensive gifts included copies of the first three books printed in Welsh, the first Welsh translation of the New Testament and the first book printed in Wales. With the collection from the college and the acquisition of the libraries of E. H. Owen of Ty Coch, Caernarfon, and Principal J. H. Davies of Cwrt Mawr, Llangeitho, the Library could by 1926 claim to have a copy of almost every major publication in Welsh or relating to Wales up to the end of the nineteenth century.[2]

The Library's foundation collections of portraits, topographical drawings, prints and maps were based on a substantial donation of items by Williams. Subsequently, the maps collection has benefited from the legal deposit status. In its acquisition of pictures the Library has concentrated on portraits and landscapes and has the best Welsh collections in these fields. Photographs have been

2 R. G. Gruffydd, 'Wales, National Library of', in A. Kent (ed.), *Encyclopedia of library and information science*, vol. 41 (New York, 1986), 353.

actively collected and include the extensive and enormously important archives of the Victorian photographer John Thomas and the twentieth-century photographer Geoff Charles whose work covers the period 1939–79. The sound and moving-image collection, established in 1980, includes, together with many original items, an important archive of off-air recordings of television and radio broadcasts in Wales.

From the 1930s the Library developed as a national repository for Welsh records, acquiring large deposits of estate, denominational, institutional and personal records, as well as public records, including Court of Great Sessions records transferred by the Public Record Office and probate records deposited by the Church in Wales. In 1983 a Welsh Political Archive was established to collect relevant materials in any format.

Buildings

The Library opened in temporary accommodation in the old assembly rooms in Aberystwyth in 1909. Following a competition Sidney Kyffin Greenslade was appointed architect. His solid, white classical building set on the hillside was planned to dominate the town, though the spread of university buildings behind and above it since the 1960s has considerably diminished the impact desired by the architect.

Building began in 1911 but the total complex designed by Greenslade, albeit with some modifications, was not completed until 1965. From the beginning the Library faced financial difficulties which were only alleviated by the fortunate appointment of Lloyd George as Chancellor of the Exchequer in 1908. Much of the finance to support the building had to be raised by the Library itself and the building fund was considerably helped by private subscriptions, including many from working-class supporters. However, despite financial problems and the interruptions of war, the work went ahead. The first stage of the building was occupied in 1916, the front and the terracing forming the main approach were completed in 1937, and the central hall and main staircase were opened in 1955. Completion of the first bookstack in 1965 realised the Library on the scale originally envisaged. Two further bookstacks were opened in 1982 and 1996, and other buildings and infills of courtyards were undertaken over the years to meet developing needs.[3]

3 D. Huws, *The National Library of Wales: a history of the building* (Aberystwyth, 1994).

In 1938–9 a tunnel was dug into rock on library land. During 1940–5 items from several London institutions, including the British Museum, the National Gallery and Dulwich College, were housed for safety in the tunnel and also in the main library building.

Governance

The royal charter sets out a system of governance by court of governors and council. The court of governors has overall responsibility and elects the president, vice-president and treasurer who are the Library's principal officers, all serving in an honorary capacity. While the court exercises general oversight, regular guidance of the Library is carried out by the council, the majority of whose members are elected by the court. Council, operating through its standing and occasional committees, directs Library policy. Inevitably, a large burden of work and responsibility has always fallen on the officers.

The charter appointed Sir John Williams as first president and he moved to Aberystwyth so that he could participate fully in the development of the new institution. Despite his offers to retire because of increasing infirmity he was persuaded to remain in office until his death in 1926. His contributions to the collections and to the building fund during his lifetime and by bequest on his death made him the Library's most generous and visionary benefactor. In 1990 the Library instituted a Sir John Williams bibliographical lecture in his memory.

Day to day administration is undertaken by the Librarian, who is appointed by the council and works under its direction. One of Williams's first actions was to secure the appointment of John Ballinger as the first holder of the post. Ballinger took up office in 1909 and retired in 1930 at the age of seventy. A native of Monmouthshire, he had only a very limited knowledge of the Welsh language. He was, however, unquestionably the outstanding Welsh librarian of his day, having been the distinguished Librarian of Cardiff public library since 1884. He was a formidable figure, autocratic, single-minded and utterly professional. Essentially a printed-books man his public library background meant that he was well equipped technically to establish sound procedures for cataloguing and classification and to look for ways of serving the wider community. He believed firmly that the task of the librarian was not scholarship but service to users. His pugnacious character made him a formidable fighter for adequate resources for the new institution. Despite the difficulties posed by the outbreak of war within a few years of the Library's opening, he succeeded in setting the new institution on a firm foundation with a worthy building, strong collections and appropriate library procedures. He was knighted on his retirement and died early in 1933.[4]

Ballinger was succeeded by William Llywelyn Davies, formerly deputy librarian and keeper of manuscripts and records. Davies was the author of the first history of the Library, a project which Ballinger had himself hoped but failed to bring to fruition.[5] Davies strove to make the Library the central record repository for Wales. Following recognition in 1926 of the Library as an approved repository for manorial records, owners of estate records were increasingly encouraged to deposit. In his first annual report Davies appealed for an increasing use of the Library for the deposit of Welsh public records. Important agreements were reached with the Presbyterian Church of Wales and the (Anglican) Church in Wales for the systematic deposit of their records.

Davies died in office in 1952, having been knighted in 1944. Of the six succeeding Librarians (all male), one, like Davies, was previously Keeper of Manuscripts, two were Keepers of Printed Books, three were professors of Welsh, while the present Librarian, appointed in 1998, was Director of Information Services at the University of Wales, Swansea.

Staff

Until the 1970s the number of library staff was small. On the outbreak of war in 1914 there were fourteen staff, of whom seven enlisted within two years. During 1914–18, as during the 1939–45 war, the Library experienced considerable staffing problems. When Thomas Parry (1953–8) became Librarian staffing stood at forty-nine, and this had risen to sixty-nine by 1969 when his successor, E. D. Jones (1958–69), retired. (The figures for these years may, in fact, be a little higher since it is not clear from the annual reports whether they include manual workers such as electrician and carpenter.) During the librarianship of David Jenkins (1969–79) the Library, benefiting from increased public spending on higher education and research, saw a dramatic increase in its staff. This brought its own pressures, with a desperate need for more staff accommodation. The 1960s also saw the appearance of trade unions in the Library and a formal union complaint to the Treasury in 1968 about staff/council relations. In 1978 negotiating machinery on the Civil Service model was introduced and in 1979 staff participated in Civil Service strike action.

---

4 M. A. Bloomfield, 'Sir John Ballinger: librarian and educator', *Library History* 3 (1973), 1–27.
5 W. Ll. Davies, *The National Library of Wales: a survey of its history, its contents, and its activities* (Aberystwyth, 1937).

On the appointment of R. Geraint Gruffydd as Librarian (1980–5) the staff stood at 163 but the following years of increasing pressure on the public sector saw a marked decline and by 1988 the figure was down to 137. Numbers rose again significantly thereafter to over 200, but the government's insistence on fixed-term appointments and the need to seek outside funding make meaningful comparisons with earlier figures virtually impossible.

Nobody reading the annual reports and council minutes can fail to be struck by the clear evidence of increasing government control after 1980. An annual staff reporting system was introduced in 1983, the first corporate plan was presented in 1988, the Welsh Office carried out a staff inspection in 1989–90, a statement of the library's performance against targets was required in the annual report for the first time in 1995, and audits were conducted with increasing frequency throughout the 1980s and 1990s. In 1996 the practice of centralised pay negotiating across the United Kingdom was abolished and the Library, in common with other similar institutions, known at the time as non-departmental public bodies, was given responsibility for setting its own pay scales and conducting its own pay negotiations with staff and unions.

These changes had an inevitable effect on the business conducted by council and on the work of the librarian. They also led to a significant increase in administrative staff to cope with the requirements of central government. A revealing insight into the extent to which the librarian's post had changed is provided by Thomas Parry's description of his period as Librarian in the 1950s. According to Parry he had a small staff, did not need to attend more than about one committee meeting each month, and was only infrequently required to travel from home. As a scholar he had ready access to the collections, and ample time to read the output of other Welsh scholars and much else besides, and the found plenty of time for research. None of these statements could have been made by the Librarians in office from the 1980s onwards.[6]

The creation in Aberystwyth in 1964 of the College of Librarianship Wales, which in 1989 became the Department of Information and Library Studies of the University of Wales, Aberystwyth, produced a steady flow of bilingual qualified librarians. Hitherto, professionally qualified librarians had been a rarity in the National Library but the proportion steadily increased, particularly in the Department of Printed Books.

6 T. Parry, *Amryw bethau* (Dinbych, 1996), 64–5.

Library and nation

One of the distinguishing features of the Library has always been its location in mid Wales and its contact with a strong Welsh-speaking tradition. Because of this it has from the beginning been perceived as an unmistakably Welsh institution. Certainly it has for many years provided a model for a fully bilingual institution where it is entirely natural to hear Welsh as the language of the workplace. With the exception of Ballinger, all the senior staff have been Welsh-speaking. Yet, surprisingly, it was not until 1956 that it was resolved to record minutes of court and council bilingually rather than in English only and not until 1972 that the annual report was presented bilingually.

Until the creation of the Welsh Office in 1964 the Library was financed directly by the Treasury. Thereafter the Secretary of State for Wales assumed the responsibility, with the Welsh Office increasingly exercising a directing and monitoring role, particularly in the 1980s and 1990s. In 1999 funding and monitoring of the Library passed to the newly created devolved National Assembly for Wales.

From its foundation the Library has been involved in outreach activities for the benefit of the people of Wales. The charter provided for a duplicates section and this allowed the Library early to develop a book-loans system in conjunction with adult education centres and public libraries.[7] From 1933 to 1955 the Library acted as a clearing house for a scheme to supply books to tuberculosis sanatoria throughout Wales. For many years it provided the headquarters of the Wales Regional Library Scheme for inter-lending and other forms of co-operation between Welsh libraries.

The contribution to Welsh and Celtic scholarship has been enormous. The collections have, of course, provided the source material for research. In 1909 the Library began publication of *Bibliotheca Celtica* and other bibliographical tools have followed. The Library's *Llyfryddiaeth Cymru: a bibliography of Wales*, which superseded *Bibliotheca Celtica* and the *Subject index to Welsh periodicals*, is now available online. *Cylchgrawn Llyfrgell Genedlaethol Cymru: The National Library of Wales Journal* commenced in 1939 and is still published twice a year. University of Wales staff working on the standard Welsh dictionary, *Geiriadur Prifysgol Cymru*, were housed in the library from 1921 until they moved into the University of Wales Centre for Advanced Welsh and Celtic Studies when its purpose-built building was completed in 1992 adjacent to the Library. Staff

---

7 C. M. Baggs, 'The National Library of Wales book box scheme, and the South Wales coalfield 1914–1939', *National Library of Wales Journal* 30 (1997), 207–29.

of the Centre have special access to the collections and user privileges. Since 1997 the Library has been a partner in the Aberystwyth Centre for the Book which publishes the annual *Y Llyfr yng Nghymru: Welsh Book Studies*.

The first major exhibition of the Library's treasures in its main gallery was mounted in 1920. It set the pattern for a regular programme which has continued to the present. Exhibitions have celebrated events in Welsh national life, such as the four-hundredth anniversary of the translation of the Bible into Welsh in 1988 or the six-hundredth anniversary of the uprising of Owain Glyn Dwr in 2000. Others have displayed the Library's holdings, not least the numerous fine portraits and landscapes in the picture collections. Exhibitions have also been mounted regularly in galleries throughout Wales. As befits a major cultural institution, the Library has long had a significant regular presence at the annual Welsh-language National Eisteddfod.

Completion in 1996 of a large extension offered a welcome respite for several years from the overwhelming preoccupation with finding space for stock and staff. As a result the Library was able to embark on a very significant upgrading of visitor facilities to provide additional gallery space, a multi-media lecture theatre, a new education unit, shop and restaurant. An energetic digitisation programme ensures that increasing amounts of material from the collections are made available to remote users through the Library's website at www.llgc.org.uk.[8]

8 For details of recent work and plans see Andrew Green, 'Digital library, open library: developments in the National Library of Wales', *Alexandria* 14 (2002), 161–70.

19

The Scottish library scene

JOHN C. CRAWFORD

By the middle of the nineteenth century Scotland had enjoyed well over a hundred years of a distinctive library culture, reflecting its independent legal and education systems, its particular geography and sociology.[1] This culture derived partly from the foundations of the 'first endowment' period centred on the years 1680–1720, when endowed libraries such as the Innerpeffray Library and the Leighton Library at Dunblane were set up by individual benefactors in local communities, largely with educational or theological intent. The established Church of Scotland brought its own distinctive views of book use; its policy that library provision in the Highlands should be the product of intervention from the Lowlands was still being applied 200 years later. A final and most characteristic influence came from the climate of community-based activity, influenced strongly by the ideas of the Scottish Enlightenment, with its emphasis on social philosophy.[2] From these ideas, and earlier social thinking back to John Locke, had developed the concept of mutual improvement, which may be defined as the spiritual and intellectual improvement of the social individual through corporately organised intellectual activity.[3]

Scotland in the mid-nineteenth century had a wide variety of means of access to literature: book clubs and middle-class subscription libraries were widespread (circulating libraries were less common, and were largely concentrated in the towns of the east coast). It also had as many universities as the rest of the United Kingdom put together, and their libraries had long been rooted in the local community, unlike their English counterparts. Libraries for

---

1 J. C. Crawford, 'Historical models of library provision: the example of Scotland', unpublished PhD thesis, Glasgow Caledonian University (1993) (includes a comprehensive bibliography of primary sources).
2 A. Chitnis, *The Scottish Enlightenment: a social history* (London, 1976); J. C. Crawford, 'The origins and development of societal library activity in Scotland', unpublished MA thesis, University of Strathclyde (1981).
3 J. C. Crawford, 'The ideology of mutual improvement in Scottish working class libraries', *Library History* 12 (1996), 49–61.

the medical and legal professions also flourished (one of them, the Advocates' Library, eventually becoming the basis of the National Library established in 1925). One of the most significant ways in which Scotland differed was in a tradition of working-class subscription libraries dating back to the mid-eighteenth century which represented a strand of self-sufficiency and an urge to self-improvement not matched elsewhere. The Leadhills Library, founded in 1741 and visited by Dorothy Wordsworth (and surviving to the present day), was only the most prominent of these.[4]

The nineteenth century and middle-class intervention

New types of publicly available library appeared in the nineteenth century, all characterised by middle-class interventionism. The subscription library tradition enjoyed varied fortunes. The last middle-class subscription library was founded in 1826, by which time about seventy-three had been established. Poor administrative standards and falling book prices meant that many were already in decline. Some, such as Greenock and Langholm,[5] survived into the twentieth century by assuming a more popular character but many disappeared. There were twenty-five left by the end of the nineteenth century. Working-class subscription libraries suffered from small incomes, lack of resources, the inability to invest in development and vulnerability to the trade cycle. They were also unable to cope with the challenge of industrialisation and urbanisation. The movement survived successfully in the traditional heartland of the community library, the large village and the market town. By the end of the century there were eighty-three.[6]

Middle-class intervention had originated with the Scottish philosopher Dugald Stewart (1735–1828), who believed that libraries provided for the working classes would produce a more industrious and pliable workforce, an idea which led to the development of mechanics' institutes.[7] Complementing this was the rise of Evangelicalism. In Scotland religiously based libraries had originated with the Moderate clergy, some of whom pondered the growing

---

4 P. Kaufman, 'Leadhills, library of diggers', in his *Libraries and their users* (London, 1969), 163–70.

5 J. T. Hamilton, *Greenock libraries: a development and social history 1635–1967* (Greenock, 1967), esp. 54–63. For Langholm, see the historical account by R. McGeorge in *Supplementary catalogue of the Langholm Library* (Langholm, 1900), 1–12; cf. also C. M. Grieve ('Hugh McDiarmid'), *Lucky poet: a self-study in literature and political ideas* (London, 1943), 8–13, on his youthful use of the library.

6 Crawford, 'Historical models', 76–8.

7 Chitnis, *Scottish Enlightenment*, 174–5, 219–20.

working-class interest in books and reading and concluded that it should be both encouraged and controlled. However from the early nineteenth century onwards the initiative had shifted to the Evangelicals.[8] The middle-class promoters of mechanics' institutes and religious libraries saw little value in imaginative literature, and intellectual development was believed to be inseparable from manners and morals.[9] Both mechanics' institutes and religious libraries represented a direct attack on working-class intellectual independence, the former by limiting stocks to 'value-free' subjects, mainly science and technology, the latter by providing stocks of religious books favoured by Evangelicals. Both types were hostile to fiction and imaginative literature.

Mechanics' institutes had begun in the 1820s to provide working men with a background of technical education which would allow them to develop the new skills demanded by the industrial revolution. The first, the Edinburgh School of Arts, which had a library from the beginning, had been founded in 1821.[10] By 1851 there were about fifty in Scotland, mostly in the central belt. The largest, in Glasgow, had 6,000 volumes.[11] In terms of foundation the major impetus is usually thought to relate to the 1820s and 1830s but in Scotland foundation continued until the 1860s, at least ten being founded between 1850 and 1868.[12] Although the mechanics' institutes made a substantial addition to the facilities available to the reading public they were only moderately successful in appealing to the working classes and had a substantial middle-class following. Whatever their defects, they were the first form of library provision aimed at the working classes to invest heavily in buildings and equipment.

Church and religiously based libraries

Church and religiously based libraries were usually small and of short duration. The movement roughly paralleled the rise and fall of Evangelicalism and the founding of the Free Church of Scotland in 1843. As religious controversy declined in the 1850s and 1860s and the Church of Scotland reasserted itself, so the religiously based library declined and the large number of small libraries

---

8 J. C. Crawford, 'Denominational libraries in 19th-century Scotland', *Library History* 7 (2) (1985), 33–44.

9 J. V. Smith, 'Manners, morals and mentalities: reflections on the popular Enlightenment of early nineteenth century Scotland', in W. M. Humes and H. M. Paterson (eds.), *Scottish culture and Scottish education, 1800–1900* (Edinburgh, 1983), 25–54.

10 W. R. Aitken, A history of the public library movement in Scotland to 1955 (Glasgow, 1971), 39–41.

11 T. Kelly, *Early public libraries: a history of public libraries in Great Britain before 1850* (London, 1966), 229–30.

12 Crawford, 'Historical models', 81.

which had come into being rapidly disappeared. Religiously based libraries did attempt to expand user groups beyond the traditional male middle and upper working-class base and to include women and children. At the Free Church Library in Kirkcaldy, which functioned from about 1845 to 1855, women were always the majority of users.[13] About forty-six such libraries, all small, still survived in the mid-1890s.

Second endowment libraries

Although now largely forgotten, 'second endowment' libraries were the preferred form of publicly available library activity in Scotland between about 1850 and 1900 and form a strand in library provision that is particularly Scottish. (The term 'second endowment' distinguishes them from the 'first endowment' period of 1680–1720.)

The first viable example, the Campbell Library, was founded at Pollokshaws, near Glasgow, in 1844, the last being founded as late as 1929. They were founded by wealthy patrons and in funding, administration and standard of service provided represented a norm of publicly available provision. They combined the old strategy of community management with a new interventionist philanthropy which could define aims and values. Their philosophy was one of personal betterment, constructive recreation and community development in locations where this strategy was likely to work. They were rarely found in inner city areas. They were often housed in a community hall or recreational centre where good accommodation was cheaply or freely available. The best examples compared directly with rate-supported libraries (some later became part of the public library system) and represented a halfway house between the old world of voluntary community library provision and a new world of professionalism and regular funding. By the mid-1890s there were 107 of them and they were the largest class of libraries at the period to include major libraries. Representative examples were Baillie's Institution in Glasgow and the Chambers' Institution in Peebles, both with 17,000 volumes in 1900.[14]

Economics and infrastructure

Steam printing was introduced in the early nineteenth century, and by the middle of the century the bulk of printing was done by steam. The growth of

---

13 Kirkcaldy Free Church, 'Library book, 1845–55' (Kirkcaldy Central Library).
14 T. Greenwood, *British library year book 1900–1901* (London, 1900), 288 and 316.

the cities facilitated retail distribution, and the virtual completion of the main railway network by the 1870s lowered transport costs and speeded up distribution. The improved postal service made ordering, the dispatch of invoices and paying easier and faster. The number of publishers increased and most of the great publishing houses were formed by this time, including Routledge which specialised in reprints.[15] Reprints were important to libraries because book prices remained relatively high until the 1890s. Between 1828 and 1835 the average price of a complete book fell by half. From 1852 discounted book sales became common and by the late 1860s cheap paperback editions became available for as little as sixpence. Although five shilling reprints of novels had been available since 1829 it was not until the 1890s that hardback first editions became available at prices from five to six shillings.[16] Improvements in communications made it easier for booksellers to offer discounts. In 1879, because of the coming of the railway to the town, Robert Scott, bookseller in Langholm, was able to offer 15% discount and free delivery of books to Westerkirk Library, some 4 miles from Langholm.[17]

These changes effectively reversed the economics of the community library. Community libraries were originally founded because books were expensive and distribution networks were poor. By the late nineteenth century books were cheap and communication was better than ever before, which helped old patterns of library use to survive in a different world.

The problem of the Highlands

In the Highlands the preferred Lowland model of decentralised library provision, in communities united by a common ideology, did not apply. The centralised model, driven by intervention from the Lowlands, and proposed originally by James Kirkwood, an Episcopalian clergyman, at the end of the seventeenth century, survived as late as the early twentieth century. Between 1818 and 1824, a clergyman of the Associate Church, John Brown, had established twenty-four libraries of religious literature in the Highlands and in 1826 the Education Committee of the General Assembly of the Church of Scotland founded 'itinerating libraries' in the Highlands on the East Lothian model, an initiative which had run its course by 1840.[18]

15 J. Feather, *A history of British publishing* (London, 1988), 133–40.
16 R. D. Altick, *The English common reader: a social history of the mass reading public, 1800–1900* (Chicago, 1957), 280–312.
17 Minutes of Westerkirk Library, Dumfriesshire (held at the library), 3 November 1879.
18 J. C. Crawford, 'Policy formulation for public library provision in the Highlands of Scotland', *Journal of Librarianship* 16 (1984), 94–117.

However by the end of the century there was evidence of local initiative. Argyllshire had nine village libraries. Sutherland had five and Highland Perthshire, Ross and Cromarty, and Caithness had two each. This reflects decisive changes in the Highlands, notably in the last fifteen years of the century. By the mid-nineteenth century steamer services had penetrated to the northern coasts and to the islands. This was followed by the railways, reaching the sea at Thurso in 1874, at Mallaig in 1894 and at Kyle of Lochalsh in 1898. In the remote parish of Gairloch in Wester Ross serious road building did not begin until the 1840s and yet by the 1870s the parish boundary was only 4 miles from the nearest railway station at Achnasheen. This facilitated community development which included book and periodical use: Poolewe Public Hall, which included a reading-room, was opened in 1884 and by 1912 the parish had at least six Coats libraries and a reading room at Inverasdale on Loch Ewe side.

Two Acts of Parliament are fundamental to the development of community library activity in the Highlands. In 1872 the Education (Scotland) Act introduced compulsory elementary education. At this time sign-literacy in the Highlands was restricted to 65% of men and 49% of women as against national averages of 89% and 79% respectively, but by the end of the century illiteracy had virtually disappeared. Furthermore a network of elementary schools was built throughout the Highlands, providing many rural communities with their only public building where small libraries might be housed. The position in the Highlands therefore became similar to the prosperous areas of rural Scotland earlier in the century. Secondly, the Crofters' Holding Act of 1886, by guaranteeing security of tenure to crofters, had the indirect effect of creating settled communities in which community development of an educational and cultural nature might take place. The Education Act, by specifying teaching through the medium of English, represented an attack on the Gaelic language, an attack which contrary to popular opinion was supported rather than rejected by Highlanders. There can be little doubt that libraries took their cue from education and contributed to the decline of Gaelic. Such few printed catalogues as survive from the Highlands record few if any Gaelic titles. In 1887 Tongue Subscription Library, in Sutherland, had fourteen titles in Gaelic out of a stock of 2,623 volumes. Campbeltown (Ardesier) Public Library, near Inverness, had none at all nor did Salen Public Library in Mull. In the 1830s 10% of the stock of Kilbride Public Library on Arran consisted of Gaelic books. By the end of the century it was indistinguishable from any Lowland village library.[19]

19 Crawford, 'Historical models', 178–80.

An active, if unsuccessful campaigner against the promotion of English by libraries was James Coats Jr., an eccentric Paisley businessman whose family was noted for philanthropic activity. Between about 1903 and 1908 Coats distributed about 4,000 libraries, each of about 300 volumes, mainly in the Highlands and islands of Scotland.[20] Although the collections were too small to be of long-term value they did plug a gap in the Highlands, and because most of the libraries were sent to schools Coats can be claimed as the father of the school library in Scotland. Unusually the libraries contained Gaelic books, and because of the relative lack of Gaelic titles Coats even arranged for at least three English language titles to be translated into Gaelic.

Although the Coats libraries contained few religious titles, his initiative, like Kirkwood's, was a Lowland intervention into the Highlands and the last of its kind. The future lay with the implementation of existing legislation and the new county libraries.

Public libraries and a new world

When the first Public Libraries Act was passed in 1853 Scotland already had a rich, varied and largely voluntaryist library culture, based for the most part on community units. This partly explains the slow progress of the rate-supported movement and why it came to resemble what had gone before. The Act of 1850, which covered England and Wales only, was extended to Scotland in 1853 and was amended the following year by the Public Libraries (Scotland) Act of 1854 which raised the rate limitation from the product of a halfpenny rate to a full penny and allowed the money so raised to be spent on books as well as buildings, furnishing, heating, lighting and staffing. Although there was further legislation and a consolidating Act in 1887 the basic principles remained unchanged until 1919 when the rate limitation was raised to three pence.[21] Although the penny rate has been criticised as inadequate, for the most part it generated higher incomes than those available to the voluntary sector, so provision must have seemed reasonable to contemporaries when compared with what they had been used to. The penny rate did not generate sufficient income for initial purchase of plant and equipment and traditional philanthropic strategies continued. The Act applied only to cities and towns which were, for the most part, small. The movement made slow progress up to 1897 when Carnegie grants became available. Progress was made in two main

20 J. C. Crawford, 'The library policies of James Coats in early twentieth century Scotland', *Journal of Library History* 22 (1987), 117–46.
21 Aitken, *History of the public library movement*, 1, 52–5, 61, 65.

areas: in market towns where the 'free library' took on the traditional community character; and in large towns like Dundee, Perth or Paisley where local
philanthropists could compensate for resource deficiencies. By the mid-1890s
there were thirty-two free or rate-supported libraries. Patronage by minor
local patrons had been a key factor in bringing them into being. Although the
future lay with them they were, numerically at least, swamped by the voluntary
sector which still continued to survive and indeed expand. There were, at the
time, some 467 publicly available libraries in Scotland. Public (rate-supported)
libraries had a total membership of 105,402, about 2.5% of the population, and
they were more successful in recruiting women members than other types.
Because they were free their issues greatly exceeded all others and, in addition
to a lending service, they usually provided reference and newspaper libraries.
Only three, however, provided services to children.[22]

Thanks to the benefactions of Andrew Carnegie (and his special attention
to the land of his birth) most Scottish burghs had adopted the Acts by 1909.
The main period of adoption was the ten years 1899–1908, when forty libraries
were founded, compared with thirty-three in the period 1853–98.[23] Carnegie
patronised fifty-four local authorities in Scotland (65% of Scottish local authorities). Just as important, and hitherto disregarded, is Carnegie's patronage of
non-rate-supported libraries and reading rooms. These grants, mainly small,
were for the most part given to fund, partially or wholly, the erection and
stocking of small village libraries and reading-rooms. Some 118 of these grants
were made, of which eighty-eight (73%) went to Scotland.[24] This shows that
Carnegie retained some links with the old community tradition, despite his
commitment to rate-supported free libraries.

Carnegie's most significant legacy, however, was unintentional. In funding
the extension and consolidation of the rate-supported movement he brought
into being a network of small, under funded burgh library services which
became the basis of Scotland's public library system and effectively replicated
the old community tradition in a new administrative guise.

One of the key themes of the twentieth century was the link between
libraries and education. In the old community era there were strong if unofficial
links between libraries and education because local schoolmasters were often
intimately involved in library activity. However burghs were not education
authorities, this privilege being reserved for county councils, which were not

22 Crawford, 'Historical models', 87–8, 122–38.
23 Aitken, History of the public library movement, 76, 349, 79.
24 A. J. Smith, 'Carnegie library buildings in Great Britain: an account, evaluation and
survey', unpublished FLA thesis (1974), vol. I, 65, 107–21.

initially library authorities. The Education (Scotland) Act of 1918 created a county library service which provided a limited service to rural areas, replacing the old community-based services. This partially re-established the link with education but the new service was greeted with hostility by the burgh librarians who feared absorption. Although co-operation between burgh and county was possible it rarely happened in practice. The situation did not change until the second half of the twentieth century. The threepenny rate limitation was abolished in 1955 and for the first time a publicly funded library service became a statutory obligation. In 1975 local government reorganisation created two tiers of authority: a small number of large regional authorities providing all major services including education and forty-one second-tier authorities which administered 'local' services – including libraries.[25] School libraries, meanwhile, remained with education, with happy results, for by the early 1990s Scotland had as many school librarians as England. In 1996 local government was reorganised yet again and a new system of unitary authorities was created, thus allowing co-operation between library and education services.

Partly as a result of the growth of public expenditure in the 1960s, public libraries which had dominated the professional agenda since the beginning of the century fell into relative decline. In the early sixties professional librarians began to be appointed to further education colleges and central institutions (the Scottish equivalent of polytechnics) and, thanks to the Robbins Report, university library staffs expanded and more staff became professional librarians.[26]

Conclusion

Over a lengthy period libraries in Scotland have complemented and supplemented widespread, but limited, cheap education and given the average Scot opportunities to continue reading and book use after the conclusion of scholastic education. Libraries were based on small, inexpensive administrative units which were most effective outside major cities, much like the educational process itself. Scottish library history, apart from the period of middle-class intervention in the nineteenth century, has been marked by consensuality, among social leaders in the eighteenth and nineteenth centuries and among political parties in the twentieth. Libraries have supported key factors in Scottish intellectual life. They have encouraged all social classes to participate in

25 A. Midwinter and M. McVicar, *Public library finance: developments in Scotland*, Library and Information Research Report 85 (London, 1992), 20.
26 Crawford, 'Historical models', 283.

intellectual life and supported the Scottish rejection of a separate class of intelligentsia. Religion has been a major motivation to book use for all social classes, but especially for the working classes, in whose enthusiasm for controversial religion can be found the origins of working-class intellectual independence. Libraries also played an important part in developing educational and reading traditions in the Highlands over a relatively brief period between about 1880 and 1910.

20

The National Library of Scotland

IAN McGOWAN

Any consideration of the history of the National Library of Scotland must begin with the body from which the National Library was born, the Library of the Faculty of Advocates in Edinburgh.[1] Inaugurated in 1689 and given the privilege of legal deposit by the Copyright Act of 1709, the Advocates' Library was long regarded as Scotland's national library in all but name. Although a modest degree of financial support had been forthcoming from the Treasury to extend the storage areas of the Advocates' Library in the first half of the nineteenth century, the burden on a private body of maintaining a library with legal deposit status and a national role became increasingly difficult to bear.

The 1850s saw a growing feeling in Scotland that the country's cultural institutions were suffering undue neglect in comparison with the support offered by the government to bodies such as the British Museum, the National Gallery and the Royal Dublin Society. Such neglect was rectified in part with the opening of the National Gallery of Scotland in 1859 and of the Industrial Museum of Scotland, precursor of the Royal Museum of Scotland, in 1861. However, state assistance for the Advocates' Library remained elusive. The Faculty's appeal for an annual grant for the Library was met with the scepticism of the then Chancellor of the Exchequer, William Ewart Gladstone, who doubted the practicality of funding from the public purse a private body which already benefited from 'a tax upon authors'. Nevertheless, Gladstone did raise the possibility that 'it might be right to negotiate with the Advocates for taking over the whole property in the Library for public uses - under covenants securing to the Faculty any special privileges which might be useful to them and which without injuring the community might form an appropriate record of their former ownership'.[2] It appears that this radical solution was never

---

1 J. St Clair and R. Craik, *The Advocates' Library: 300 years of a national institution 1689–1989* (Edinburgh, 1989), 9.
2 W. E. Gladstone to Lord Aberdeen, 16 May 1854, MS 3581, fol. 145, National Library of Scotland.

translated into formal proposals, either to the Faculty or to the government, and in the continuing discussions the 'purchase' option found less favour than the suggestion of government aid in return for the Library becoming more a national and public institution, but without the transference of property. It was on this basis that a scheme was drawn up by a committee of local citizens for a 'National Library for Scotland'.[3] In spite of promises of serious consideration of the proposals by the Treasury, and the support of a wide section of the Scottish Establishment, the government remained unpersuaded and the scheme came to nothing. Rebuffed by the Treasury, the Faculty did not abandon entirely its hopes of government funding, although it viewed the prospects of success with a degree of pessimism.

The most celebrated voice raised in support of the Faculty's case was that of Thomas Carlyle, who praised 'incomparably the best of all the Libraries we have in Scotland' in a letter of 1874 to Robert Horn, later to be Dean of Faculty:

> My clear testimony therefore is, that it essentially belongs to Scotland at large, - such the liberal practice of the Honourable Faculty whose property it especially is, - and that it fairly deserves all reasonable help and support from whatever calls itself a Government in that country. I think you have a solid right to bring your claims before the Chancellor of the Exchequer.[4]

In spite of support from so distinguished a quarter, however, the prospect of substantial financial assistance from the government seemed increasingly remote.

In 1886 the City of Edinburgh received the offer of £50,000 from Andrew Carnegie for the establishment of a free public library. This initiative opened once more the question of a national library, and whether the new public library and a national library, based on the Advocates' Library, could in some way be combined. There were obvious difficulties in adapting the Advocates' Library to the functions and procedures of a municipal public library, and while discussions continued between the Faculty and the Edinburgh City Council for several years, the difficulties could not be overcome and the new Edinburgh Public Library came into independent being.

Others recognised that the matter was of wider concern than just to Edinburgh and the Faculty. For example, a statement was prepared in 1902 for the Convention of Royal Burghs by Robert Graham, a former Glasgow bailie (councillor and magistrate), which emphasised that 'the project is by no means

---

3 'Report by sub-committee', 7 February 1865, National Library of Scotland Archives.
4 T. Carlyle to R. Horn, 3 April 1874, MS 3706, fol. 89, National Library of Scotland.

one concerning the interests of Edinburgh solely, but is of national Scottish interest and importance'.[5] It was suggested that a new national library should be a wholly new institution, not one founded on an existing body or collection, particularly in the light of the failure over many years to convince the government that it should fund a national library based on the Advocates' Library. In 1905, the precedent set by the Welsh in campaigning successfully for the creation of the National Library of Wales encouraged Edinburgh Trades Council to send a resolution to the Secretary for Scotland, the Marquess of Linlithgow, calling for that example to be followed in Scotland.[6] The resolution gained a sympathetic response from some, if not all, senior officials of the Scottish Office, and over the next few years this sympathy turned into more positive support. This support, and that of influential public figures, such as the earl of Rosebery, supported in the editorial columns of the *Glasgow Herald*, came at a time when the financial burden of the Library was again being felt by the Faculty. The time was therefore propitious to think again of a formal approach to the government, and in January 1912 a committee of the Faculty, chaired by T. B. Morison KC, was appointed to consider the future of the Advocates' Library. The committee recommended that the Faculty should approach the government and ascertain 'upon what terms public funds might be afforded in order to place the administration and equipment of the Faculty's General Library on a level with the modern standard of the national libraries'.[7]

However, hopes that the creation of a national library was in sight were ended by the First World War. The end of the war left the Advocates' Library facing a financial crisis. The fees of intrants to the Faculty, traditionally used to fund the Library, had dried up, forcing the Faculty to seek a voluntary subscription from its members in order to replenish its reserves and to keep the Library going. Although £13,000 was raised by this means, stark choices were facing the Faculty: nationalisation, outside aid from the government or some other benefactor, or a dramatic reduction in the Library's scale of operations, with the possible surrender of the privilege of legal deposit. Outright nationalisation became the favoured option, and a scheme of transfer was devised and presented to the government in 1921. With the support in Cabinet of the Scottish Secretary, Robert Munro, the proposal for the creation of a national

---

5 R. Graham to the Convention of Royal Burghs, 'A National Library for Scotland', 1902, National Library of Scotland Archives.

6 Edinburgh Trades Council to Secretary for Scotland, 'Resolution', 1905, ED/6/1, National Archives of Scotland.

7 Records of the Faculty of Advocates, FR.10, pp. 277–83, National Library of Scotland.

library was agreed by the government, but only when financial conditions permitted the state to take on this additional financial responsibility. In the meantime, an annual government grant of £2,000 was awarded to the Faculty to support the Library.

Broadening the question of a national library to include the wider Scottish public, the Faculty embarked on a public appeal for support, and an appeal pamphlet was drafted by two Faculty members who played key roles in the negotiations for a national library, H. P. Macmillan (later Lord Macmillan) and W. K. Dickson, Keeper of the Advocates' Library from 1906. The pamphlet was given a rhetorical flourish by the addition of a concluding section by John Buchan, whose deputy Macmillan had been in the Directorate of Intelligence during the war:

> It must not be said that a nation, which above all others is tenacious of tradition and historic possession, permitted one of the chief of its heritages to decay, or a race which has carried the light of its learning throughout the globe suffered the lamp of its own citadel to grow dim. [8]

An Endowment Trust for a new national library was established in 1923 and a number of wealthy individuals were approached for support. An initial donation of £1,000 was received from Lord Rosebery, but this, and all other gifts to the Trust, was soon overshadowed by the generosity of Mr (later Sir) Alexander Grant, of McVitie and Price, biscuit manufacturers, whose offer of £100,000 removed any obstacle to the acceptance by the government of the Faculty's proposals for the transfer of the non-legal collections of the Advocates' Library to the nation to become the National Library of Scotland. On 26 October 1925, the day appointed for the transfer, the new Board of Trustees of the National Library of Scotland met for the first time in Parliament House, Edinburgh.[9]

The user of the Library would have noticed very little immediate change in the way the Library worked under its new designation. The staff and premises remained the same, the readership did not alter significantly, and legal deposit operated in much the same way as in the past. However, within a few years, significant differences began to emerge. The number of staff increased from six in 1925 to twenty-eight in 1934. The collections began to be enhanced by a series of generous gifts and bequests of books and manuscripts, such as the Rosebery collection of early Scottish books, stimulated by the creation

---

8 W. K. Dickson and H. P. Macmillan with John Buchan, *A national library for Scotland* (Edinburgh, 1922), 11.

9 P. Cadell and A. Matheson (eds), *For the encouragement of learning: Scotland's national library 1689–1989* (Edinburgh, 1989), 215–65.

of the new National Library.[10] The Glenriddell manuscripts of Robert Burns, presented to the nation by the American benefactor John Gribbel in 1914 and held in trust by Lord Rosebery pending the creation of a national library in Scotland, now found their proper home.[11] The Library also received gifts of money for the purchase of books and manuscripts, notably from Lord Rosebery and Mr and Mrs W. R. Reid of Lauriston Castle, and these funds remained the principal means of purchasing items for the collection until the Library's Purchase Grant from the government was substantially increased in the 1960s.

From 1925, the main task of the Trustees was to find more suitable accommodation for the Library than the labyrinth of rooms described by the 1928 Royal Commission on National Museums and Galleries as 'subterranean, maze-like and in certain cases not free from actual damp'.[12] There was general agreement that nothing other than a new building would meet the Library's pressing needs. Agreement on the site of such a new building was less easy to reach. After a long and sometimes acrimonious public debate, it was determined that the new National Library would be on George IV Bridge in Edinburgh, adjacent to the existing Advocates' Library, and on the site then occupied by the Sheriff Courthouse, itself scheduled for removal to more suitable premises. The government's commitment to the construction of the new building was encouraged by a further donation of up to £100,000 by Sir Alexander Grant, conditional on the government providing a matching sum, and on the building being located on George IV Bridge.[13] The protracted disputes about the relocation of the Sheriff Courthouse and the suitability of the rather cramped George IV Bridge site for the National Library meant that it was not until 1934 that Reginald Fairlie was announced as the architect selected to design the new Library. Plans acceptable to all parties were finally achieved in June 1936, and construction work began in November 1937. The outbreak of war led to the suspension of building work, which was not begun again on a large scale until 1951. The building was officially opened by Her Majesty the Queen on 4 July 1956.

10 G. Hogg (ed.), *Special and named printed collections in the National Library of Scotland* (Edinburgh, 1999).

11 National Library of Scotland, *Catalogue of manuscripts acquired since 1925*, 8 vols. (Edinburgh, 1938–92).

12 Royal Commission on National Museums and Galleries, *Interim report*, Cmd. 3192, Parliamentary papers, 1928–9, VIII, 43.

13 I. G. Brown, *Building for books: the architectural evolution of the Advocates' Library 1689–1925* (Aberdeen, 1989), 2.

The opening of the new building presented new opportunities for the development of services. It also reinforced the idea of the National Library as an independent institution, closely linked to its historic progenitor, the Advocates' Library, but now with a distinct and separate public face. The long and complex process of design and construction of the building left its mark with, by modern standards, inflexible and inefficient use of space. It did, however, give the Library greatly expanded reader capacity, dedicated exhibition space, and much-improved staff accommodation. On the other hand, nothing could disguise the fact that predictions about the ability of the building to cope with the intake of publications had been hopelessly optimistic. In the 1930s it had been argued that the George IV Bridge site would provide accommodation for the next hundred years. Even in 1956 it was still considered that the building would meet the Library's storage needs until the end of the century. It soon became clear that a crisis would be reached by the mid-1970s if extra storage space was not provided. This pressing need to obtain more space for the Library presented the Trustees with a dilemma. The possibilities to extend storage space in the George IV Bridge Building were being exhausted; either the Trustees could rely on the uncertain prospect of space for expansion becoming available in the vicinity of George IV Bridge, or they could move to secure a site some distance away, but immediately available.

As the need for additional accommodation became more urgent, and as space close at hand failed to materialise, the Trustees agreed to the acquisition by the government on behalf of the Library of a disused biscuit factory (pleasingly appropriate in view of the origin of the Library's endowment) a mile to the south of central Edinburgh in Causewayside. Part of the existing structure was converted into temporary storage for approximately 750,000 printed books. This also allowed the creation in 1974 of a new Map Room, which had previously been located in the George IV Bridge Building, and was replaced there by a Music Room. These measures provided some relief from the most pressing of the Library's space needs, as the planning proceeded for the construction of an entirely new additional library building on the newly acquired site. For practical and financial reasons, the construction of the building was undertaken in two phases. The part of the factory building not used by the Library for storage was demolished and the first phase of the building built, being handed to the Library in 1987. Material from the temporary store and the Map Library was transferred into Phase 1, and the store demolished to make way for the building's second phase, which was completed in 1994. The design team, led by Andrew Merrylees Associates, Architect, was able to provide over 19,000 m² of floor space in the building, incorporating stack floors, reading areas and staff accommodation.

As well as providing essential space for the expansion of the collections, the construction of the Causewayside Building made possible the development of important new services. The National Library of Scotland had been known primarily for its collections in the humanities and social sciences. However, the privilege of legal deposit had ensured that the collections also included significant scientific and technical materials, and the desirability of a national scientific library for Scotland utilising these collections had long been argued. In 1981 the argument was strengthened by the transfer to the National Library of Scotland of the important collection of the foreign periodicals of the Royal Society of Edinburgh. The new building could provide the space needed for a Scottish Science Library and Business Information Service. To enhance the legal deposit collections and the collections of the Royal Society of Edinburgh, for the first time the Library devoted a substantial proportion of its government grant for purchases to scientific material, initially books and periodicals, and increasingly electronic resources. The development of electronic delivery as the primary method of supplying information to the scientific community led to the decision to close the separate reading room of the Science Library at the end of 2001, and to provide access to printed scientific, technical and business material through the general reading room in the George IV Bridge Building. Subsequently, negotiations were successfully concluded with a range of information suppliers to allow access by the general public to a range of electronic resources previously available in practice only to the academic sector.

Also relocated to the Causewayside Building was the Library's Inter-Library Services, originally founded as the Scottish Central Library for Students in Dunfermline by the Carnegie United Kingdom Trust. In 1952 the Scottish Union Catalogue, based in Glasgow, merged with the Scottish Central Library for Students and the two bodies, renamed the Scottish Central Library, moved to Edinburgh. In 1974 the Scottish Central Library merged with the National Library of Scotland and as the NLS Lending Services became the first division of the Library to operate from the Causewayside Building. In 1998 Lending Services changed its name to Inter-Library Services to reflect the wider range of work for which it had become responsible.

Through the 1990s the Library undertook a complex programme of building work in the George IV Bridge Building. This was primarily aimed at the upgrading of the building's fire safety precautions to meet current standards, but also involved major renovation of outworn plant and fabric. However, in this period the Library's efforts were not only aimed at ensuring the physical preservation of its rich collections and providing access to them in its reading rooms. Increasingly the Library developed its services for those who could not use the Library in person. The Library's website[14] and its programme of travelling exhibitions, for example, sought to extend its activities beyond the confines of its buildings in Edinburgh.

From the 1970s the Library began to play an important role in stimulating and facilitating co-operation among library and information services in Scotland, notably through early collaborative ventures in library automation and the initiatives leading to the creation of the Scottish Library and Information Council and the Scottish Confederation of University and Research Libraries. By the beginning of the twenty-first century, the Library fully recognised that its function was not just to be a national library for Scotland, but to form an important element in the network of global information provision.

14 National Library of Scotland website: www.nls.uk.

21

The Irish library scene

CATHERINE MORAN AND PEARL QUINN

The first library legislation to apply to Ireland was the UK Public Libraries Act of 1850, which allowed town councils in Britain with a population of 10,000 or more to levy a rate of a halfpenny in the pound on property to support public libraries in their area. This Act was extended to Ireland in 1853 but was of little practical benefit, as municipal authorities of such size did not exist in Ireland at that time.

The principal Act which allowed the establishment of public libraries in Ireland was the Public Libraries (Ireland) Act 1855, which allowed municipal and town councils with a population of 5,000 or more to establish a library and levy a rate to a maximum of one penny to support it. A two-thirds majority of householders was required to pass the Act. In spite of subsequent amendments to the 1855 Act in 1877 and 1894, adoption of the Acts was slow. Dundalk was the first public library in the country to open under this legislation, in 1858. The city of Cork had been the first to adopt the Act in 1855, but a rate was not struck until 1892. Even by 1880 only Dundalk and Sligo had opened public libraries, though the 1880s saw some improvement with Belfast, Dublin, Kingstown (now Dún Laoghaire), Limerick and Rathmines (at that time a township just outside Dublin city boundaries) all adopting the Act. The situation in Dublin itself was unique: the first public libraries, in Thomas Street and Capel Street, both founded in 1884, and North William Street, founded in 1899, were funded not by the library rate but by a yearly grant of £500 to each branch as well as £300 for the purchase of books.[1] This money came from the Borough Fund which consisted of rents from lands, houses and estates. In 1908 a financial crisis precipitated by the Libraries Committee's funding of the new municipal gallery of modern art led to a week's closure of Dublin's public libraries, which by now included Charleville Mall and Kevin Street. Libraries in the capital were not funded from the rate until the passing of the 1911 Public Libraries

---

1 T. Greenwood (ed.), *British library year book 1900–1901* (London, 1900), 117–18.

(Art Galleries in County Boroughs) (Ireland) Act which raised it to a penny halfpenny ($1^1/_2$d).[2]

The reasons for this tardiness and haphazard development are not hard to understand. The 1855 Act had been introduced at a time when Ireland was still reeling from the devastating effects of the Great Famine. Prior to this cataclysmic event some impetus towards the establishment of a public library system had developed with the introduction of national (primary) schools in the 1830s. The Young Ireland Movement had founded Repeal Reading Rooms throughout the country in the 1840s, with the aim of promoting Irish literature and culture as part of their advancement of the cause of Irish nationalism.[3] Similarly in the 1890s, when literacy levels had improved and the impetus for a properly organised public library system had regained momentum, many figures prominent in the Gaelic Literary Revival became involved. Douglas Hyde (1860–1947), one of the founders of the Gaelic League,[4] and Padraig Pearse (1879–1916) were among the founders of Cumann na Leabharlann ('The Library Association' – not to be confused with the later Cumann Leabharlann na hEireann or Library Association of Ireland founded in 1928), set up to promote public libraries.

However, it must be acknowledged that some elements in many communities opposed the adoption of the Library Acts. The most serious opposition came from ratepayers, a situation certainly not unique to Ireland. A degree of clerical opposition was also apparent.[5] Further complicating the situation was tension between what could be seen as two contrasting elites – the old Anglo-Irish ruling class and the emergent Irish nationalist political and cultural groups, of which the Gaelic League was one. However it would be an oversimplification to suggest that self-appointed arbiters of contrasting cultures foisted public libraries on an uninterested populace. The Public Libraries (Ireland) Act 1902 allowed any rural district council to adopt the 1855 Act, and was the main impetus for the foundation of the Irish Rural Libraries Association in 1904 (this was nearly twenty years before rural districts in England were given this right). The primary objective of Cumann na Leabharlann was to make rural districts aware of the legal powers the 1902 Act gave them, which

---

2 M. Kennedy, 'Civic pride versus financial pressure: financing the Dublin Public Library Service, 1884–1920', *Library History* 9 (1992), 83–96.

3 The Young Ireland Movement was set up to support Daniel O'Connell's campaign for repeal of the Act of Union between Ireland and Britain. Its members founded the *Nation* weekly newspaper (1842) to further this objective.

4 Founded in 1893 primarily to promote the revival of the Irish language but also to preserve the traditional customs, stories, dance and costume associated with it.

5 B. Grimes, *Irish Carnegie libraries: a catalogue and architectural history* (Dublin, 1998), 21.

in addition to allowing adoption of the 1855 Act included the right to enter into agreements with school managers allowing the use of schools as libraries. Further major developments were to occur some twenty years later. The (UK) Public Libraries Act of 1919 which raised the permitted library rate from 1d. to 3d. also applied to Ireland. After partition, the Irish Free State's Local Government Act (1925) and the UK's Public Libraries Act (Northern Ireland) 1924 both made the county the basic unit of library administration.

One of the most important factors in expediting public library development in Ireland was the funding provided by the Carnegie grants. It is possible to divide the provision of these grants to Ireland into two separate phases. The first, about 1903–13, involved the allocation of individual grants by Andrew Carnegie to local authorities on the strict proviso that the authority concerned (Urban or Rural District Council) could obtain a free site for the library building. The grant covered the cost of construction only – no provision was made for buying books or employing a librarian. This lack of 'follow-up' was to have unfortunate consequences in rural Ireland where the yield from the penny rate was inadequate to maintain a decent level of service.[6]

The second phase began with the foundation in 1913 of the Carnegie United Kingdom Trust (CUKT), based in Carnegie's birthplace, Dunfermline, Scotland, with an income of some £100,000 per annum. One of its first acts was to commission a report by Professor W. G. S. Adams on the state of public libraries in Great Britain and Ireland. His report revealed the comparatively poor level of library service in Ireland at that time, with only 1,245,766 people living within a library district in 1911, that is 28% of the total population of Ireland, as opposed to 62% in England, 46% in Wales and 50% in Scotland.[7]

The most authoritative account of the situation in rural Ireland, which brought the harsh realities of Adams's figures to life, is to be found in a report for the CUKT Trustees, *Glimpses at the rural library problem in Ireland*, prepared in two parts (Part One by Cruise O'Brien, 1915, and Part Two by the playwright and author Lennox Robinson, 1917); Robinson had by then been appointed Organising Librarian in Ireland for the CUKT.[8] The preface to O'Brien's report outlined the difficulties faced in rural areas; Carnegie libraries were established in these areas 'without very complete local information. As a result these

---

6 For a thorough examination of the role of public libraries in rural Ireland during this period see F. Devlin, 'Brightening the countryside: the library service in rural Ireland, 1902–1935', unpublished PhD thesis, St Patrick's College, Maynooth, 1990.

7 W. G. S. Adams, *A report on library provision and policy to the Carnegie United Kingdom Trustees* (Edinburgh, 1915), 6.

8 Cf. M. O hAodha, 'Irish rural libraries: glimpses of the past', *Library History* 18 (2000), 49–56, which draws largely on this report.

benefactions have tended to create a wrong idea in the minds of the people as to the purpose the founder had in view.'[9] Essentially the small and badly financed local authorities in rural Ireland were unable to maintain what in some cases were rather elaborate buildings, with the result that the libraries were used for activities for which they were never intended. Many were used as makeshift village halls: in the case of Askeaton Carnegie Library in Rathkeale RDC (Co. Limerick) two rooms had been sublet, one to the local Temperance Society and the other to the village band. Lennox Robinson discovered similar situations in his travels throughout rural Ireland. In a 1916 letter to Sir Horace Plunkett, the Irish representative on the board of the CUKT in Dunfermline and an Anglo-Irish landlord active in agricultural reform, he wrote:

> A certain Father McCarthy . . . has just gone to Ballyhahill [also in Rathkeale RDC] and has created a transformation there; he is a splendid, energetic young priest – a tremendous Sinn Feiner as are most of the young priests, and I believe the first use the restored library was put to was a meeting at which Father McCarthy sang six rebel songs and enrolled 150 members in a Sinn Féin club. But we won't tell this to the other Trustees![10]

One could perhaps facetiously argue that this was community librarianship in a nascent form! Plunkett for his part had founded the Irish Cooperative Reference Library in Dublin as part of his agricultural reforms. It was furnished with a £10,000 grant from the CUKT but was moved to London in 1927 where it served as an outlier library of the inter-library loans system funded by the Trust. Plunkett's efforts were widely appreciated: for example Hubert Butler, the pioneer county librarian of Co. Londonderry, 'revered' Plunkett. He saw him and his associates

> at the centre of the movement to bring self-education within the reach of those who were too poor or too far away to reach it in the normal way. The library was to be the intellectual centre of the village, as the creamery was to be its economic centre. By means of books the animosities that arose from race and religion and class were to be dissolved.[11]

Lennox Robinson's wry humour could not disguise the inadequacy of Irish rural library service provision. On his recommendation the Irish Advisory

---

9 Carnegie United Kingdom Trust, *Glimpses at the rural library problem in Ireland*, 2 vols. (Dunfermline, 1915), preface.
10 L. Robinson, *Curtain up: an autobiography* (London, 1942), 89.
11 H. Butler, 'The county libraries: sex, religion and censorship', in his *Grandmother and Wolfe Tone* (Dublin, 1990), 50–63. This essay was amended from an earlier version 'The county libraries and the censorship', first published in *Irish Writing* 8 (July 1949).

Committee of the CUKT was established in 1921, and this committee followed the policy of encouraging the development of library services in rural areas (as recommended by Adams in his report). This prioritising of rural areas by the CUKT applied to both Britain and Ireland, but was particularly desirable from an Irish point of view, since Ireland's economy was based predominantly on agriculture, with high levels of emigration and little industrialisation. The exception was Belfast, more highly industrialised, and which had had a public library since 1888. Belfast also benefited from the presence of the Linen Hall Library, a subscription library with significant collections (which since the 1970s has developed into one of the major libraries of Northern Ireland).

The first meeting of the Irish Advisory Committee (IAC) took place on 11 July 1921, the same day that the War of Independence ended and treaty negotiations began in London. The resulting civil war between pro- and anti-treaty forces ended in defeat for the anti-treaty side in May 1923 and left a considerable legacy of bitterness and mistrust. It was against this background that the IAC undertook its work, with a good degree of success given the extraordinary circumstances under which it was operating. One of its principal achievements, over the three years of its existence, was the introduction of experimental county library schemes in Donegal, Wexford, Sligo, Kilkenny and Galway in the Irish Free State and Antrim, Derry and Fermanagh in Northern Ireland. The sum of £20,000 was allocated to Ireland (both North and South) by the CUKT between 1921 and 1922 out of a total library expenditure by the Trust for that period of £250,000.[12] The IAC administered the scheme in the following way: on receipt of an application for funding it would recommend to the CUKT that the proposed service should be financed for two years, on the proviso that the relevant county council would pass a resolution undertaking to maintain the scheme by striking a rate at the end of that period. Boxes of books were supplied to the main county town from a central repository in Dublin, for distribution throughout the county. The scheme had to be administered by a trained librarian. The Dublin Book Repository was run by Christina Keogh (1895–1963), an influential figure in the Irish library world, who remained in charge until 1960; in 1923 the Repository became the Irish Central Library for Students, serving as a supplier of books requested at local libraries. It was funded by the CUKT until 1947 when it was taken over by An Chomhairle Leabharlanna (The Library Council of the new Irish Republic).

At almost exactly the same time as the beginning of the county library schemes – an essentially secular enterprise – an important initiative aimed

---

12 Carnegie United Kingdom Trust, *Annual Report* (1920), 4.

at improving book supply was coming from a quite different source. The Central Catholic Library was founded in Dublin in June 1922, initially as a reference library,[13] by the Irish Jesuit priest, librarian, writer, bibliographer and university lecturer Fr. Stephen J. Brown SJ (1881–1962). Fr. Brown was a key figure in Irish library circles until his death in 1962. He was a member of the Council of the Library Association of Ireland, and a founding member of the School of Library Training at University College Dublin.[14] From its inception, the Central Catholic Library (CCL) was portrayed as a unique enterprise in Ireland, although Catholic lending libraries were administered by the Sisters of the Holy Faith at Clontarf and Haddington Road, Dublin in 1922 (another was planned at Glasnevin). However, these ventures were not conducted on the scale envisaged by Fr. Brown and his companions.[15]

Notably the CCL was a specialist library which was intended to supplement and not to supplant any existing libraries.[16] It was open to all genuine readers irrespective of class or religion. Ultimately, the key function of the CCL was the dissemination of Catholic literature, and by implication Catholic doctrine. Its stock was intended to encompass the entire Catholic *œuvre*, not just theological works, as it was intended that the library would become a centre of Catholic studies, as well as serving to introduce the general public to Catholic literature.[17] The CCL was in fact a library of its time, part of a wider Catholic library movement of which Fr. Brown was very much aware. The Dublin venture was therefore intended as a model for the establishment of other Irish Catholic libraries; another Central Catholic Library was established in Waterford in 1934.[18] Similarly reference is made in the sources to the Rex Library and Bookshop, Smithfield Market, Belfast, which was founded c.1936, and to a library modelled on the CCL which was opened by Fr. Brown in the Irish army training camp on the Curragh, Co. Kildare, in 1927.[19] Unfortunately,

13 *The Central Catholic Library: the first ten years of an Irish enterprise* (Dublin, 1932), 36.
14 C. Moran, 'Fr. Stephen J. Brown, S.J.: a library life 1881–1962', unpublished MLIS thesis, University College Dublin (1998).
15 S. J. Brown, 'A new storehouse of Catholic thought', *The Month* 141 (1923), 410; S. J. Brown, 'The Central Catholic Library: an apologia by the Hon. Librarian', *Irish Ecclesiastical Record* 24 (1924), 391; M. H. MacInerney, 'Catholic lending libraries', *Irish Ecclesiastical Record* 19 (1922), 577.
16 Brown, 'New storehouse', 410; Brown, 'Central Catholic Library: an apologia', 389; R. Walsh, 'Libraries', *Saorstat Eireann Irish Free State official handbook* (Dublin, 1932), 209; S. J. Brown, *Libraries and literature from a Catholic standpoint* (Dublin, 1937), 35–6.
17 S. J. Brown, 'Jubilee of an Irish library of Catholicism', *Catholic Library World* 19 (1948), 157.
18 Brown, *Libraries and literature*, 30–1; M. O'Sullivan to C. Moran, 19 August 1997.
19 Central Catholic Library, *Annual Report for 1938–39*, 16. The Curragh camp library was founded by the chaplains and officers: cf. Brown, *Libraries and literature*, 30–4, and *Central Catholic Library: the first ten years*, 45.

little information concerning these libraries appears to have survived. Interestingly, the CCL applied twice to the Irish Advisory Committee of the CUKT for funding in the early 1920s; sadly their appeal for funding was rejected, after careful consideration, owing to the denominational nature of the library. The library was, however, permitted to obtain books on loan from the Dublin Book Repository.[20]

The momentum of the CUKT-supported developments in public library service provision very nearly stalled as a result of what became known as the 'Carnegie Row' in 1924. As Lennox Robinson himself put it, his work with the Irish Advisory Committee 'was to come to an abrupt and painful end'.[21] Robinson had published a short story, 'The Madonna of Slieve Dun', in the short-lived literary journal *To-morrow*, about a girl who is raped and believes herself to be the Virgin Mary as a result of her consequent pregnancy. One of the IAC members, Fr. T. A. Finlay, found the story offensive and tendered his resignation. Although the committee split on whether or not the story should have been published, this did not occur along strictly denominational lines. At the time of this dispute its members included Lady Gregory (who knew Lennox Robinson through the Abbey Theatre); Thomas Lyster, Librarian of the National Library; James Wilkinson, Librarian of Cork City Carnegie Library; George Russell (the writer and artist 'AE'); and Christina Keogh of the Dublin Book Repository. One of Robinson's most vocal supporters on the committee was Thomas O'Donnell, a Catholic from Co. Kerry who stated that his sisters, who were 'pious Catholics . . . thought it a beautiful story'.[22] By contrast the Provost of Trinity College, Dr J. H. Bernard, objected strongly to the story on grounds of sexual decency, a delicious irony not lost on Lady Gregory – 'If the Provost intends to see eye-to-eye with the Catholic Church he is not a Protestant.'[23] The Provost also tendered his resignation from the committee and the dispute eventually ended with the dismissal of Robinson and the suspension of the IAC by the Trustees in Dunfermline.

This dispute is not widely known about even today, but its ramifications were to last a long time in the Irish library world. Twenty-five years later Hubert Butler lamented the loss of independence that resulted from the committee's suspension (he believed Robinson should have resigned from the committee) and the breaking down of 'the last cultural bridge between the Twenty-six

20 Carnegie United Kingdom Trust, *Minutes of meeting of the Irish Advisory Committee*, 12 April and 9 November 1923, 16 January and 9 April 1924. National Library of Ireland, MS 10,542(1).
21 Robinson, *Curtain up*, 135.
22 L. Robinson (ed.), *Lady Gregory's journals 1916–1930* (London, 1946), 279.
23 Robinson (ed.), *Lady Gregory's journals*, 281.

Counties and the Six'.[24] Butler, a Southern Protestant from Kilkenny, had trained in Ballymena, Co. Antrim, and served as county librarian in Co. Londonderry, so was in a better position than most to judge the effect this row had on cross-border relationships. In truth the IAC had never been independent in the way that really mattered – the distribution of money. It was not free to award grants to county library schemes without first submitting any requests it approved of to the Trust for clearance. Lady Gregory noted Sir Horace Plunkett's dissatisfaction with the CUKT committee, and the feeling that it was 'especially prejudiced against Ireland'.[25] Be that as it may, the CUKT continued to fund county library schemes on an all-Ireland basis after the suspension of the IAC (but, it must be stressed, administered directly from its headquarters in Dunfermline). In 1927 the CUKT published a pamphlet by Robert Wilson, county librarian of Sligo,[26] which aimed to give guidance to the new county library authorities (again both North and South) on their powers and responsibilities under the recent Public Libraries and Local Government Acts. This pamphlet revealed that since the inauguration of the county schemes in 1922 fifteen counties in the Irish Free State and four in Northern Ireland (Antrim, Londonderry, Fermanagh and Tyrone) had availed themselves of them. By the time the Carnegie county library grants ran out in 1930 a further seven counties in the Irish Free State had adopted the scheme, with the encouragement of the new Library Association of Ireland (founded in 1928).

The Cork-born novelist Frank O'Connor has written very amusingly if somewhat acerbically about his days as a librarian during this period. He started his library career in 1924 as a trainee in Sligo under Robert Wilson and saw at first hand the operation of the county library scheme. After completing his six months of training, O'Connor was next posted to Co. Wicklow, where the county library had been established in a rather unusual manner. The Carnegie row had erupted while O'Connor was in Sligo, with the result that a local Catholic parish priest on the Wicklow library committee was resolutely opposed to a library. To get around this problem O'Connor persuaded Seamus Keely, a local Irish teacher and nationalist (and later a judge) who had recently been released from an internment camp, to masquerade as a representative of the CUKT at the library committee meeting. The presence of such an exemplary Irishman with impeccable nationalist and Catholic credentials appears to have assuaged the priest's fears. In the words of

24 Butler, 'County libraries', 56.
25 Robinson (ed.), *Lady Gregory's journals*, 274.
26 R. N. D. Wilson, *The county library service in Ireland* (Dunfermline, 1927), 7.

O'Connor, 'Wicklow County Library owed its existence to a shameless piece of gerrymandering.'[27]

In the light of this remarkable account by O'Connor it is tempting to speculate on the origins of other county library schemes. While one must assume such incidents were most unusual it can be said with certainty that, given the raw nature of political feeling in the Free State after the civil war, the Carnegie schemes must at the very least have aroused suspicion. In Northern Ireland sectarianism played its part too; a 1938 Library Association publication reported that a Co. Tyrone librarian had found Catholic opposition to the county library scheme because many centres were run from Protestant schools.[28] On the other hand Hubert Butler tells of the objection by a Protestant committee member in Coleraine, Co. Londonderry, to 'political propaganda from Dublin' in the form of the scholarly Irish Texts Society being present in a rate-supported library.[29] Such attitudes however were not confined to the North: Letitia Dunbar-Harrison's appointment as county librarian in Mayo in 1930 was strongly objected to by the local library committee on the grounds of her Protestant religion and Trinity College education. The dispute was not finally resolved until 1940 when Dunbar-Harrison was appointed to a position in the Department of Defence.

The role the Carnegie grants played in expediting the development of public libraries in Ireland, particularly in rural areas, was considerable, but other even more imaginative initiatives took place in the 1930s and 1940s without the CUKT's financial aid. The establishment of an Irish Free State hospital library service for patients in the 1930s was largely due to the characteristic enthusiasm of its key founder, the aforementioned Fr. Stephen Brown.[30] Fr. Brown's desire to set up such a service, a new departure in Free State library practice, appears to have stemmed from his attendance at the annual conference of the Library Association in Cambridge in September 1930. He contended that the provision of a definite hospital library service would have a therapeutic effect. Significantly, he felt that hospital patients should not be excluded from public library services in the Free State.[31] Inevitably, he was concerned, in accordance with Irish cultural concerns of the time, that the chosen books would be morally

27 F. O'Connor, *My father's son* (Belfast, 1994), 22.
28 L. McColvin (ed.), *A survey of libraries* (London, 1938), 32.
29 H. Butler, 'County libraries', 55.
30 The development of the service can be traced in the annual reports of the Hospital Library Council, and in the special report *The Hospital Library Council 1937–1958* (Dublin, 1958).
31 S. J. Brown, 'Library service for hospitals', *An Leabharlann* 3 (1933), 112; M. E. Going (ed.), *Hospital libraries and work with the disabled* (London 1963), 17–31.

desirable as well as possessing literary merit. Fr. Brown, however, exhibited a complex attitude towards censorship, and his views on this topic require careful interpretation within the context of the predominantly Catholic cultural norms of the Irish Free State (and subsequently the Irish Republic), coupled with his membership of the Jesuit order.[32]

After a lengthy battle a committee was appointed early in 1937 by the Minister for Local Government and Public Health (and future President of Ireland) Sean T. O'Kelly, to organise and administer a hospital library service. This committee, which Fr. Brown chaired until 1943, was afterwards called the Hospital Library Council (HLC); before it had its own headquarters in Dublin the CUKT had permitted the Council to meet at the Irish Central Library for Students. The service was formally declared open in October 1937.

From the outset the Council was aware that an efficient scheme would have to be administered on technically sound lines, flexible enough to cope with the needs of each type of hospital, and that the operation of the service could not run counter to normal hospital activities. Because the Council would not take a direct part in the actual working of the service within the hospitals, it was evident that the success of the scheme largely depended upon the extent to which the hospital authorities co-operated 'by ensuring that the regulations laid down are observed'.[33] Although it was realised from the start that the majority of hospitals would be obliged to rely on volunteers to run the Library service, it was hoped that in the larger hospitals a trained library professional would be hired to administer the service. A watchful eye was kept on proceedings by the Council's organising librarian, who paid periodic visits to participating hospitals.[34]

Owing to financial constraints only hospitals classed as voluntary or semi-voluntary, and TB sanatoria, were included in the scheme.[35] The books were supplied in proportion to the number of beds, at no charge to the participating hospitals, though they remained the property of the Council. Naturally, the book stock was subject to the approval of the Council's Book Selection Committee, aided by a panel of readers, which would have operated in accordance with the stringent state censorship laws. Non-fiction was classified by Dewey, while fiction, the most popular form of reading material, was simply arranged

32 Brown, *Libraries and literature*, 37–68.
33 J. Barry, 'Policy of the Library Association of Ireland: a paper read at the Cavan Conference', *An Leabharlann* 7 (1940), 71–8; S. J. Brown, 'The Hospital Library Service', *Irish Library Bulletin* 11 (1950), 208–10.
34 Brown, 'The Hospital Library Service', 209.
35 The service provided by the HLC was never extended to hospitals operated by health boards.

under ten subject headings (Adventure, Biographical, Collections, Detective, Humour, Ireland, Love, Nature, Religious and Sport). The procedures for issuing books conformed as far as possible to those in public libraries, and patients were not charged for the use of the books. The popularity of certain kinds of books among hospital patients was seen, unsurprisingly, to resemble borrowing patterns long established in the public library system. The Council was concerned at the possibility of infection and advocated that each patient be supplied with specially made cellophane book covers which would be exclusive to the inmate of each bed and slipped on and off each item as it was issued and returned.

While the scheme apparently became an accepted part of Irish hospital life, it nevertheless encountered many difficulties. Damningly it was not always 'evident to patients in hospitals that books are available for their use': the Council therefore supplied display cards to hospitals with the request that a copy be placed in each ward in order to alert the patients to the library facilities available to them.[36] In 1975 the Department of Health commissioned an evaluation of the work of the HLC and concluded that the service it offered was 'totally inadequate and sub-standard'; as a result the service was abolished in 1977.[37]

The ubiquitous Fr. Brown was also involved in the formation of the Book Association of Ireland (BAI) in 1943, an organisation which aimed to bring together groups and individuals in Ireland involved in book distribution and interested in promoting reading. Fr. Brown was Chairman of the Council of the BAI, and Christina Keogh, of the Irish Central Library, was its Honorary Treasurer. Preliminary steps for the establishment of the BAI had been taken by the Library Association of Ireland.[38] The premises for the new Association were at 38 Westmoreland Street, Dublin, which also happened significantly to be the premises of the booksellers James Duffy and Co.[39] The BAI, like the London-based National Book Council,[40] was eager to promote book reading and the wider distribution of books of all kinds, but with an Irish emphasis. In addition, the BAI was intended to create and maintain contact between the Irish book world, Irish expatriates and the foreign market generally. Furthermore, Fr. Brown hoped that the new association, like the NBC, would now bring

36 *Hospital Library Council 1937–1958*, 13–15.
37 Thomas Armitage to Miss N. Hardiman, Honorary Secretary, Library Association of Ireland, 24 November 1975 (An Chomhairle Leabharlanna archival material).
38 'Editorial Notes', *An Leabharlann* 8 (1943), 68; 'An Leabhar Chumann The Book Association of Ireland', *Irish Library Bulletin* 6 (1945), 21–2.
39 S. J. Brown, 'New Irish Book Association', *An Leabharlann* 8 (1943), 79.
40 Subsequently the National Book League, now the Book Trust.

together all who were interested in books in Ireland, from publishers to book lovers. Both personal and institutional membership were available.[41]

In addition to publishing lists of Irish publications, the BAI organised events like the Children's Book Week held in May 1944, a venture promoted in the *Irish Library Bulletin* as one which could avoid the penalties of censorship.[42] Moreover, like hospital libraries, children's librarianship was an innovation which clearly demonstrated the utility of librarianship in the public sector. This first Children's Book Week was opened by the Minister for Education, a welcome official endorsement of the BAI's objectives. The location of the event in the Bernadette Hall, Rathmines, was particularly significant since the Rathmines Carnegie Library was the first public library in the country to provide a separate department for children, as well as being one of the first libraries in Ireland to adopt open access.[43] By all accounts the event was a success with the children for whom it was intended, and the Council of the BAI were satisfied that by organising this kind of event they had taken a step in the right direction, 'towards the realisation of one of their most cherished aims, i.e. the creation of a generation of book-lovers, who will know books for what they are, an essential equipment for the business of living.'[44] It is certain that the BAI lasted into the mid-1950s, though the exact date of its demise remains elusive.[45]

Despite such initiatives public library development in the Republic of Ireland stagnated in the period immediately following the discontinuance of the Carnegie grants in the late 1940s, in spite of the formation of An Chomhairle Leabharlanna (the Library Council) in 1947 as part of that year's Public Libraries Act.[46] This lack of development may be partly explained by the rather hasty introduction of the Act, which was formulated partly in response to the Carnegie Trust's offer of the Irish Central Library for Students, and was consequently too focused on that objective.[47] It was not until the more

---

41 'An Leabhar-Chumann, The Book Association of Ireland: objects, advantages and conditions of membership', *Irish Library Bulletin* 6 (1945), 64.

42 'Prohibition and propaganda', *Irish Library Bulletin* 5 (1944), 37.

43 C. A. Keogh, *Report on public library provision in the Irish Free State, 1935* (Athlone, 1936), 5.

44 C. Meehan, 'An Leabhar-Chumann – The Book Association of Ireland Children's Book Week', *Irish Library Bulletin* 5 (1944), 71–3.

45 Catholic Central Library, *Minutes of Council Meeting*, 1 June 1951 and 3 July 1953, Central Catholic Library Archival Collection.

46 M. Casteleyn, *A history of literacy and libraries in Ireland: the long traced pedigree* (Aldershot, 1984), 220.

47 D. Ellis-King, 'Decades of aspiration: public libraries 1947–87', in An Chomhairle Leabharlanna, *The university of the people: celebrating Ireland's public libraries* (Dublin, 2003), 43–55. See also D. Ferriter, 'The post-war public library service: bringing books "to the remotest hamlets and the hills"' (*ibid.*, 67–77), for a more detailed look at the socio-political context surrounding the introduction of the 1947 Act.

favourable economic circumstances of the 1960s, following reports by An Chomhairle Leabharlanna on the inadequate stocking and funding of the Republic's libraries, that any significant post-war expenditure took place. Since then public libraries in the Republic have generally enjoyed increased levels of funding, albeit suffering some cut-backs during the recession of the 1980s. Since 1973 libraries in Northern Ireland have been organised differently, through five Education and Library Boards rather than by county authorities, an initiative designed to raise the educational role of libraries and to overcome sectarian problems. A large degree of co-operation on public library and other matters exists between the North and the Republic: a North–South Liaison Committee consisting of members of the LAI and the Northern Ireland branch of the Library Association (now CILIP) meets several times each year, publishes the journal *An Leabharlann*, and organises an annual joint conference.

The establishment and maintenance of a public library service in Ireland was a remarkable achievement, considering the enormously difficult economic and political circumstances, particularly in the early years of the Irish Free State. Irish librarians and library users owe a great deal to the early instigators of the public library service, many of them prominent in literary and other fields, who created the basic infrastructure which allowed future investment and development to take place.

22

The National Library of Ireland

GERARD LONG

The origins of the National Library of Ireland may be traced back to a private society. 'The Dublin Society for improving husbandry, manufactures and other useful arts and sciences' was founded in 1731. A royal charter was granted in 1749. The Royal Dublin Society, as it became, was concerned with improvement of the country in matters such as agriculture, manufactures and art.[1] The government acknowledged the Society's usefulness by an annual grant. The use of public funds to help support a private institution was likely to lead to controversy. Membership applications were decided upon by ballot of the members, which included liberal and conservative elements. In 1835, Daniel Murray, Roman Catholic archbishop of Dublin, applied for membership; his application was contentiously rejected.[2] This incident presented an opportunity to William Smith O'Brien, Conservative MP for the County of Limerick, who, in 1836, proposed to the House of Commons that a Committee be appointed 'to inquire into the administration of the Royal Dublin Society, with a view to the wider extension of the advantage of the annual parliamentary grant to that institution, without reference to the distinctions of party or religion'. The Select Committee, under the chairmanship of Smith O'Brien, prepared a *Report* on the Society, which recommended that:

> the Library of the Dublin Society ought to be considered as intended, not solely for the advantage of a comparatively few individuals who belong to the Society, but as a National Library, accessible under proper regulations to respectable persons of all classes, who may be desirous to avail themselves of it for the purpose of literary research.[3]

---

1 For a general survey of the Society, see J. Meenan and D. Clarke (eds.), *RDS: the Royal Dublin Society 1731–1981* (Dublin, 1981).
2 Regarding Dr Murray's failed application, see W. Meagher, *Notices of the life and character of His Grace Most Rev. Daniel Murray, late Archbishop of Dublin* (Dublin, 1853), 69–70.
3 *Report from the Select Committee on Royal Dublin Society* (1836), xii (H.C. 1836 (445)). See also G. Long, 'The foundation of the National Library of Ireland, 1836–1877', *Long Room* 36

The Society's Library had previously been available to the public in a very limited manner, and from 1836 onwards it became more accessible, largely as a result of the efforts of the Society's Library Committee to provide increased accommodation and longer opening hours. The Library stock in 1836 was largely scientific and technical, reflecting the Society's aims, but over the following decades the acquisitions policy became more general, and an emphasis was placed on acquiring material of Irish interest. For example, an important collection of pamphlets dealing with seventeenth-century Ireland was purchased from the London bookseller Thomas Thorpe in 1840. Official publications were also acquired. In 1852, the Library was described as 'containing about 22,000 volumes at present and receiving accessions at the rate of 500 volumes a year'.[4] By 1862, the Library contained 'about 30,000 volumes'.[5] Thus when in 1863 the Library received a donation of approximately 23,000 volumes from Jaspar Robert Joly (1818–92), this gift not only added significantly to the Irish holdings of the Society, it virtually doubled the size of the collection. T. W. Lyster described the collection thus:

> The Joly collection contains 23,000 printed volumes with a large mass of unbound papers and prints and a fine collection of Irish and Scottish song music. Its selection of Napoleonic literature is the most excellent in the three kingdoms, and that dealing with the French Revolution is not less extensive. But the chief interest lies in the quantity of books dealing with Irish history, topography and biography; the valuable collection of periodicals; and the portraits of the worthies of Ireland and views of Irish scenery classified and arranged in alphabetical order.[6]

The collection was given to the Society on condition that 'if at any time hereafter a public library should be established in the city of Dublin under the authority of Parliament . . . analogous to the library of the British Museum in London'[7] the Joly Library would be transferred to it. An increased emphasis on acquiring Irish material is evident. In 1863, Frederick J. Sidney told the

---

(1991), 41–58. For an overview of the National Library and its collections, see N. Kissane (ed.), *Treasures from the National Library of Ireland* (Drogheda, 1994) and G. Long, 'The National Library of Ireland', in N. Buttimer and others (eds.), *The heritage of Ireland* (Cork, 2000), 305–12.

4 Royal Dublin Society, *Library Committee Minutes*, 30 March 1852.

5 *Thom's Almanac and Official Directory* (1862), 794.

6 T. W. Lyster, 'Great Irish book collectors: Jaspar Robert Joly', *Irish Book Lover* 5 (12) (1921), 99–101. See also P. Henchy, 'The Joly Family and the National Library', *Irish University Review* 7 (1977), 184–98 (vol. 7 no. 2 was the 'National Library of Ireland Centenary Issue').

7 *An Act to authorise the Commissioners of Public Works in Ireland to acquire from the Royal Dublin Society and others lands for the erection of a science and art museum in Dublin, and to establish a national library in Dublin; and for other purposes* (1877), 10. Short title: *The Dublin Science and Art Museum Act*.

Select Committee on Scientific Institutions (Dublin) that 'One principle that guides us in the purchase of our books is, we consider that books written by Irishmen have a particular right to be placed in that library.'[8] The 'Minute of 1865' of the Lords of the Committee of Council of Education[9] severed the private and public funds of the Society and the government undertook the complete support of several departments, including the Society's Library. The *Report from the Commission on the Science and Art Department in Ireland* (1868–9) recommended the formation of a General Industrial Fine Arts Museum in Dublin, the central group of institutions to include 'a Science and Art Museum, a Public Library, a Museum of Natural History, a Museum of Irish Antiquities, a National Gallery and a School of Art'.[10]

Following protracted negotiations between the Royal Dublin Society, the Department of Science and Art (London) and the Commissioners of Public Works (Ireland), the *Dublin Science and Art Museum Act* of 1877[11] was passed, establishing a National Library and National Museum. This Act enabled the transfer of most of the Society's Library, and the Joly Library, to the new National Library (the first explicitly 'national' library in the United Kingdom of Great Britain and Ireland, preceding the establishment of the Free State by over forty years, and arguably a sop to the Home Rulers). The Library was funded by, and reported to, the Department of Science and Art (London) until 1900, when it was transferred to the administration of the Department of Agriculture and Technical Instruction for Ireland. It formed part of the Dublin Institutions of Science and Art, which comprised the Library, the Museum, the Natural History Museum, the School of Art and the Royal Botanic Gardens, all of which originated in some degree in the Royal Dublin Society, and all of which, except the Gardens, were located around the Leinster House headquarters of the Society. The Director of the Science and Art Institutions (in practice, the Director of the Museum) was responsible for care of the Library building and certain administrative duties; this situation obtained until the retirement of G. T. Plunkett in 1907. (There are no longer any formal links between the two institutions.)

The Library was superintended by the Council of Trustees, eight of whom were appointed by the Society, and four by the Department. The Council of Trustees held its first meeting on 21 February 1878, and appointed as the

8 *Report from the Select Committee on scientific institutions (Dublin)* (London, 1864), 117 (H.C. 1864 (495)).
9 *Report from the Commission on the Science and Art Department in Ireland*, 2 vols. (H.C. 1868–69 (4103, 4103–I)) (minute from vol. I, vi–ix)
10 *Report from the Commission on the Science and Art Department in Ireland*, vol. I, xxxvi.
11 Cf. footnote 7.

first librarian William Archer (1830–97), librarian of the Royal Dublin Society since only 18 January 1877. Until 1890, the collections of the National Library remained in Leinster House along with the Society's own library. Under Archer, it was among the first libraries to implement the Dewey Decimal Classification system. In 1881, an architectural competition took place for the design of the Museum. A controversy ensued when the shortlist of five contestants was found to contain no Irish firm (all were English). A second competition, this time to include the Library, was won by the Dublin-based firm of Thomas N. Deane and Son, the winning entry strongly influenced by Archer's pamphlet *Suggestions as to public library buildings.*[12] The Library was built by the firm of P. and D. Beckett (P. Beckett was the grandfather of Samuel Beckett).

Archer, who retired in 1895, did much valuable work in the field of natural history, an interest he shared with Robert Lloyd Praeger (1865–1953), appointed Assistant Librarian in 1893 to replace Charles Theodore Hagberg Wright who had left to become Librarian to the London Library. Praeger's contribution to Irish natural science is immense, including *Irish topographical botany* (1901) and *The way that I went* (1937), a classic work on the Irish landscape. He became Librarian of the NLI in 1920, and was elected as the first President of the Library Association of Ireland in 1928.[13]

The new library proved very popular, as the figures for annual returns of readers indicate. However, the *Trustees' Reports* continually refer to the space shortage, noting particularly that the East Wing as planned by the architect was unfinished. The annual purchase grant (1878–97/8: £1,000 per annum; 1898/9–1919/20: £1,300 per annum, reduced to £900 during the war years) gave cause for concern, as did the staffing levels.

In April 1900, responsibility for the Library was transferred to the Department of Agriculture and Technical Instruction, under which the Library remained until 1923/4. T. W. Lyster described the Library in 1902:

> The Library is open from 10 a.m. to 10 p.m. daily, except on Sundays and on three weekdays at Christmas, four weekdays at Easter, and twelve weekdays in August. The attendances of readers in 1878 numbered 27,452. In 1900, the

---

12 W. Archer, *Suggestions as to public library buildings: their internal plan and construction, best adapted to effect economy of space (and, hence, saving of cost), and at same time most conducive to public, as well as administrative, convenience, with more especial reference to the National Library of Ireland* (Dublin, 1881). Regarding the architectural competition, see R. Lohan, *Guide to the Archives of the Office of Public Works* (Dublin, 1994), 43–8. See also F. J. Burgoyne, *Library construction: architecture, fittings and furniture* (London, 1897), 153–8, and Frederick O'Dwyer, *The architecture of Deane and Woodward* (Cork, 1997), 393.

13 T. Collins, *Floreat Hibernia: a bio-bibliography of Robert Lloyd Praeger* (Dublin, 1985); S. Lysaght, *Robert Lloyd Praeger: the life of a naturalist* (Dublin, 1998).

twenty-third year of the Library, the attendances numbered 148,405. . . . The Library is still the only considerable popular Reference Library in Dublin . . . It is the State Library – the tiny British Museum of Ireland.[14]

The staff in 1903/4 consisted of the Librarian, three assistant librarians, twenty attendants and two temporary cataloguers. The reports occasionally make comparisons, in areas such as funding and staffing, with their London counterparts. The Library served as 'the only State-supported Public Library in Ireland'[15] and, to an extent, the reluctance of Dublin Municipal Council to establish a central reference library was due to the popularity of the national institution.[16]

The Library transcended political and sectarian divides and was popular with both conservative and radical elements in Dublin.[17] To some degree, this was due to T. W. Lyster, who succeeded Archer as Librarian in 1895. A founder member of Cumann na Leabharlann in 1904 and the Irish Rural Libraries Association in the same year, he was described as 'the most zealous man I know' by W. B. Yeats,[18] who from his student days in the adjacent Metropolitan School of Art frequently read in the Library. Lyster also encouraged the students of the nearby University College Dublin to use the Library, though after his time, in 1923/4, their access was restricted because of pressure on space and 'upwards of 700 standard text books used by students were . . . transferred to the Library of University College Dublin'.[19] The *Catholic Bulletin*, frequently critical of the Royal Dublin Society and the Trustees, noted that the opening hours had been shortened, and that 'It appears that their High Mightinesses have dumped four or five hundred text-books, more or less antiquated, into the College Library at Earlsfort Terrace, and told the Irish University students to go there after them.'[20] (The largely Protestant students at the even more

14 T. W. Lyster, 'The National Library of Ireland', in Department of Agriculture and Technical Instruction for Ireland, *Ireland industrial and agricultural* (Dublin, 1902), 302–3.
15 *Report of the Librarian of the National Library of Ireland, adopted by the Council of Trustees, and forwarded to the Department of Science and Art as their Report 1896*, 469.
16 M. Kennedy, 'Civic pride versus financial pressure: financing the Dublin public library service, 1884–1920', *Library History* 9 (1992), 83–96; M. Kennedy, 'Plans for a central reference library for Dublin 1883–1946', *An Leabharlann*, 2nd series 7 (1991), 113–25.
17 A. Mac Lochlainn, '"Those young men . . .": the National Library of Ireland and the cultural revolution', and A. Sheehy Skeffington, 'A coterie of lively suffragists', in their *Writers, raconteurs and notable feminists: two monographs* (Dublin, 1993), 5–33 and 35–52. As well as James Joyce and George Moore, notable figures who read in and wrote about the Library include Oliver St John Gogarty, Arthur Griffith and Desmond Ryan.
18 J. Kelly (ed.), *The collected letters of W. B. Yeats*, vol. 3 (Oxford, 1994), 438. See also P. Donlon, 'Lyster, Thomas William', in *Oxford dictionary of national biography* (Oxford, 2004), vol. 34, 946–7.
19 *Report of the Council of Trustees National Library of Ireland 1923/4*, 1.
20 *Catholic Bulletin* 14 (1924), 362.

adjacent Trinity College had use of a library which had, since 1801, benefited from British legal-deposit legislation.)

As well as serving as a reference library, the Library displayed a specific interest in Irish bibliography. Richard Irvine Best, the first Celtic scholar on the Library staff, was appointed Third Assistant Librarian on 25 March 1904; his *Bibliography of Irish philology and of printed Irish literature* (Dublin, 1913) and its companion volume covering 1913–41 (Dublin, 1942) are standard bibliographies of the subject.[21] Best and his colleagues Lyster and William Kirkpatrick Magee appear in the 'Scylla and Charybdis' episode (set in the Library) of James Joyce's *Ulysses*, set in Dublin on 16 June 1904. Magee, a schoolfriend of W. B. Yeats, was appointed Assistant Librarian in 1895; he is better known as the essayist 'John Eglinton', a perceptive and trenchant critic of the Literary Revival, and appears in George Moore's trilogy *Hail and Farewell*.[22]

Lyster retired in 1920, and was succeeded as Librarian by Praeger. The Library was closed during the Civil War, from 28 June 1922 until 13 February 1924. Praeger retired in February 1924, under the provisions of the *Government of Ireland Act* of 1920, which offered certain Civil Service officers the possibility of early retirement on pension. Under the same Act, W. K. Magee retired in January 1923.[23]

In 1921, the new state had purchased Leinster House from the Royal Dublin Society. In 1924/5, after the foundation of the Irish Free State, the Library was transferred to the Department of Education, under which it remained until 1986. The annual purchase grant was doubled to £2,600 in 1922/3 (backdated to 1920/1). Staff levels improved, and women could now apply for posts as assistant librarians and library assistants.

Best became Librarian in 1924. His efforts ensured that the collection of Gaelic manuscript material grew significantly, many important items coming from the Sir Thomas Phillipps collection. Between 1898 and 1936, E. R. McClintock Dix presented the main part of his collection of early and provincial Irish imprints to the Library, amounting to some 8,000 volumes.[24] The cultural introspection associated with the Free State was not particularly evident in the Library, though a gradual shift towards almost exclusive specialisation in

21 Seán Ó Lúing, 'Richard Irvine Best: librarian and Celtic scholar', *Zeitschrift für Celtische Philologie* 49–50 (1997), 682–97.
22 'John Eglinton' described some of his contemporaries in *Irish literary portraits* (London, 1935); see also A. Frazier, 'Magee, William Kirkpatrick', in *Oxford dictionary of national biography* (Oxford, 2004), vol. 36, 113–15. See also G. Long, *A twinge of recollection: the National Library in 1904 and thereabouts* (Dublin, 2005).
23 *Report of the Council of Trustees National Library of Ireland 1923/4*, 1.
24 T. P. C. Kirkpatrick, *Ernest Reginald McClintock Dix (1857–1936), Irish bibliographer* (Dublin, 1937).

material of Irish interest took place over the following decades, to a significant degree driven by budgetary constraints.

The hitherto unfinished East Wing was completed in 1925/6. An exhibition room was opened in September 1927, and exhibitions of Irish material were regularly mounted. The separation of the printed-book collection into two distinct sequences, Irish and General, took place in 1928/9. This arrangement continued to 2001, when the Dewey sequences were closed, and a sequential numbering system was adopted.

The *Industrial and Commercial Property (Protection) Act*, 1927 gave the NLI legal deposit status for the first time, entitling the Library to material published in the Irish Free State. A growth in the newspaper and periodical collection is evident from this date. (The *Copyright Act*, 1963 and the *Copyright and Related Rights Act*, 2000 subsequently amended this.) The *Trustees' Report* of 1933/4 carries an appeal from Best requesting material relating to 'The bibliography of the struggle for national independence'. This led to James Carty's *Bibliography of Irish history, 1912–1921* (1936) and *Bibliography of Irish history, 1870–1911* (1940), both based on the Library's collections and reflecting its changing emphasis. A project to microfilm Irish manuscript material in private collections and foreign archives began in the 1940s. Richard J. Hayes became Director in 1940 (the title had been changed from Librarian to Director in 1934/5). His contribution to Irish bibliography is immense. The *Trustees' Report* of 1953/4 refers to 'a national bibliography on a scale unattempted in any other country'; the results of this ambitious project are the *Sources for the history of Irish civilisation: Articles in Irish periodicals*, 9 vols. (Boston, 1970); *Manuscript sources for the history of Irish civilisation*, 11 vols. (Boston, 1965) and *Manuscript sources for the history of Irish civilisation: first supplement 1965–1975*, 3 vols. (Boston, 1979). Hayes and his colleague Brighid Ní Dhonnchadha also compiled *Clár Litridheachta na NuaGhaeilge 1850–1936*, 3 vols. (Dublin, 1938–40), a comprehensive index to Irish-language periodicals and books.

In April 1943, the Office of Arms became part of the National Library, and was renamed the Genealogical Office, though it remained in Dublin Castle until 1981. The ancient title of Ulster King of Arms was changed to Chief Herald, a position held *ex officio* by the Director of the Library from September 1995 to August 2005.[25] The first Chief Herald was Edward MacLysaght, author of *Irish families* (Dublin, 1957) and other standard works.

The *Trustees' Report* of 1953/4 refers to the 'critical' problem of housing the collections. The preferred solution was a move to new premises. In 1959,

---

25 S. Hood, *Royal roots – Republican inheritance: the survival of the Office of Arms* (Dublin, 2002).

Hayes proposed (to Éamon de Valera, then Taoiseach)[26] a sharing of resources with the nearby library of Trinity College Dublin, including the construction of a new block, in Trinity's grounds, in which both libraries would have independent reading rooms, but access to each other's collections. The proposal, supported by A. J. McConnell, Provost of Trinity, but not made public, was abandoned in 1960, after the Roman Catholic Archbishop of Dublin, John Charles McQuaid, expressed his disapproval to Seán Lemass, who had become Taoiseach. The idea of basing a national cultural institution in Trinity College, popularly perceived as a bastion of Protestant privilege in a predominantly Catholic state, was never likely to meet with widespread approval. However, the episode concentrated attention on the problems of the two libraries, perhaps the real intention of Hayes and McConnell.[27] In 1960, TCD announced an international architectural competition for a new library, and a site was acquired at Morehampton Road in Dublin for a new National Library building in 1961/2. The *Trustees' Report* of 1964/5 notes a plan to build a new National Library at Northumberland Road. The Library, however, remained in Kildare Street, and the severe shortage of space was the main problem which faced Patrick Henchy, who succeeded Hayes as Director in 1967.

In 1968/9 Dr Kenneth Humphreys, Librarian of the University of Birmingham, was appointed by the Minister of Education, on Henchy's recommendation, as consultant 'to undertake a thorough survey on the functions and requirements of the National Library'.[28] In April 1971, his report, which presented an alarming description of the Library's premises, was submitted to the Minister for Education. Recommendations included considerable improvements in staffing and funding, the compilation of catalogues and the national bibliography (retrospective and current), and the provision of new premises:

> It is recommended that *either* (a) a new building for the Library should be erected as soon as possible on a site as near as possible to the centre of Dublin . . . *or* (b) the buildings in the vicinity of the present Library, i.e. the National College of Art and Design and the buildings in Kildare towards

26 The Taoiseach is the head of government in the Republic of Ireland, equivalent to the Prime Minister of the United Kingdom.

27 J. Bowman: 'The wolf in sheep's clothing: Richard Hayes's proposal for a new National Library of Ireland, 1959–60', in R. J. Hill and M. Marsh (eds.), *Modern Irish democracy: essays in honour of Basil Chubb* (Blackrock, 1993), 44–61. B. Grimes: '"Will not be heard of again": a proposal to combine the resources of the National Library and Trinity College Library', *Long Room* 46 (2001), 18–22.

28 *Trustees' Report* 1968/9, 7. See also P. Henchy, *The National Library of Ireland, 1941–1976: a look back* (Dublin, 1986), esp. 22–25. Dr Humphreys's report was never formally published, but there is a copy in the National Library's archives; the section quoted is on page 57.

> Nassau Street should be evacuated and demolished. On the resultant area cleared the National Library should be expanded with full modern library facilities... This is the most urgent of all the Library's problems.

It met with a sympathetic response, and further premises in the vicinity – nos. 2–5 Kildare Street – were acquired and a commitment was made to develop the Library at the Kildare Street site. (The *Report* also recommended that the contents of the State Paper Office and all public and private archives of historical interest in state custody be transferred to the Library, and that the title be changed to 'National Library and Archives'. This did not happen. The State Paper Office and the Public Record Office amalgamated in 1988 to form the National Archives of Ireland.)

Patrick Henchy's greatest achievement as Director was to ensure additional accommodation for the Library. This, however, did not happen immediately; the problem of insufficient accommodation and storage, and the inadequate purchase grant, were the constant concerns of Alf MacLochlainn, Director from 1976 to 1982, and his successor Michael Hewson, Director 1982–88.

In July 1986, the Library was transferred to the Department of An Taoiseach. The Department of Arts, Culture and the Gaeltacht (later Arts, Heritage, the Gaeltacht and the Islands) was established in 1992, and assumed responsibility for the Library until June 2002, when it was moved to the newly founded Department of Arts, Sport and Tourism. Dr Patricia Donlon became the first woman Director in 1989 – this was also the first time that the post was filled by open competition. In the same year, the Library took over responsibility for the compilation and publication of the *Irish Publishing Record*, the national bibliography. The last published issue is for the year 1994: since July 2004, the Library distributes monthly legal deposit accessions lists by electronic mail. The Manuscripts Reading Room at 2–3 Kildare Street (previously part of the premises of the Kildare Street Club) was formally opened in 1991.

In 1992, the Library published its *Strategic Plan 1992–1997*,[29] indicating key objectives in the areas of access, acquisitions, services, implementation of a technology programme, and the building programme, and noting that 'The strategy outlined in this plan leading from the mission statement centres on three pivotal points – collections, services and buildings.' Dr Donlon retired in February 1997, having made a significant contribution to the development and modernisation of the Library. Subsequently, Seán Cromien, formerly Secretary of the Department of Finance, held the post of Director on a part-time acting capacity, and in September 1997 Brendan O Donoghue, formerly Secretary

---

29 National Library of Ireland, *Strategic plan 1992–1997* (Dublin, 1992), 28.

of the Department of the Environment, was appointed Director. During his six years as Director, the Library underwent a transformation. Staff numbers and funding for acquisitions both increased significantly. The National Photographic Archive, housing the Library's photographic collections, opened in Meeting House Square, Temple Bar, in October 1998. The main part of the Leinster Lane premises, formerly the National College of Art and Design, has been converted to provide additional reading rooms, an exhibition space and a lecture theatre. Future phases of the building programme will include refurbishment of the main library building and the construction of a large repository building. Since 1999, the Library has published a quarterly newsletter.

In 2002, the Library acquired the personal libraries of William Butler Yeats and Seán O'Casey. In the same year it was able to purchase previously unknown James Joyce manuscript material for £8 million; these manuscripts were the centrepiece of a major exhibition on Joyce's novel *Ulysses*, marking the opening of the Library's new exhibition space on 14 June 2004 (two days prior to the centenary of 'Bloomsday' in the novel). Other significant accessions include the papers of the playwright Brian Friel, and an extensive collection of material by and relating to Harry Clarke, the stained glass artist. Brendan O Donoghue retired as Director in September 2003. Aongus O hAonghusa was appointed Director in January 2005, having already held the position in an acting capacity.

The National Cultural Institutions Act dealing with the National Library and the National Museum (and to a lesser extent the National Gallery), originally passed in 1997, was finally implemented in May 2005.[30] The Act alters the statutory and administrative framework of the Library, giving it more autonomy, and allowing for the broadening of its legal-deposit privileges. The Council of Trustees has been replaced by a Library Board, with expanded powers which will lead to new developments, while continuing the tradition of 128 years since the Library's foundation. Through times of tribulation and vicissitude, and through times of progress and prosperity, it has done its utmost to sustain the vision of the National Library as the best manifestation of a country's characteristics.

---

30 'O'Donoghue announces National Library is to be Independent Semi-State Body' (press release from the Minister for Arts, Sport and Tourism, Dublin, 22 April 2005).

PART IV

*

THE NATION'S TREASURY: BRITAIN'S NATIONAL LIBRARY AS CONCEPT AND REALITY

23

Introduction: Britain's national library as concept and reality

GRAHAM JEFCOATE

The process of defining the role and functions of a national library for the United Kingdom has been a long and complex one and it should not surprise us if the British Library, founded in 1972 as the result of long deliberations, remains 'a work in progress'. A characteristic feature of its work today is its close links – and often active co-operation – with national libraries abroad, grouped as they are in such bodies as the Conference of Directors of National Libraries (CDNL) and Conference of European National Libraries (CENL). Through such contacts it has become clear that each national library has assumed its own peculiar role within each nation state, a role based on local traditions and current cultural policy. There is no template for what a national library is or does; one of the few criteria laid down for membership of CENL, for example, is the maintenance of a national bibliography, but even this seems to be a rule that is not universally applied.

Many national libraries, including the British Library, acknowledge a particular responsibility for the national documentary record, the written (or sometimes spoken) heritage recorded in a variety of ancient and modern media. The Library of the British Museum, however, was conceived from the beginning as a scholarly research collection that would not confine itself to the record of British publication and achievement. As reconceived by Anthony Panizzi, it aspired to be universal in its range and scope, its collections of print especially representing all significant topics, polities and cultures. In its great Reading Room, the mind of the scholar should range unconfined by barriers of space, time and language, forging new knowledge, connecting the previously unconnected. Few other national libraries have had this ambition; soon after Panizzi's death, as the Museum's finances began to feel the strain of government expenditure cuts, his legacy was already proving difficult to maintain.

The modern type of a 'universal library' is essentially an invention of the seventeenth century, at a time when the European community of scholars was much more homogeneous than today and when the record of scholarly discourse was contained almost exclusively in the media of manuscript and print. A national library claiming, as the modern British Library does, to provide access to 'the world's knowledge' will need continually to state an increasingly difficult case for the resources it needs to fulfil its vision. In purely organisational terms, it will need to define its role in the context of the so-called 'copyright' libraries, those libraries with an acknowledged national status and a legal right to request the deposit of new publications (the National Libraries of Scotland and Wales, the Bodleian Library and Cambridge University Library; Trinity College Dublin continues to be included in this select group). Similarly it will need to define its position *vis-à-vis* subject-specialist libraries with rich collections based on particular topics (the Wellcome Library for the History of Medicine, in close proximity to the British Library's St Pancras headquarters, is often cited as an example). It will also need to explain the need to continue to collect foreign imprints when projects such as The European Library (TEL) enable the exchange of documents on demand via electronic networks. It is above all the British Library's response to the challenge of networked information and the Internet that will define its future. If the Library proves able to rise to these challenges and to redefine its role, this will be at least in part because the past has provided it with a plausible vision for the future.

24

The British Museum Library 1857–1973

P. R. HARRIS

When Antonio (later Sir Anthony) Panizzi was promoted from Keeper of the Department of Printed Books to Principal Librarian (i.e. Director) of the British Museum in 1856, the role of the British Museum Library as the national library (in fact, although not in theory) had been established.[1] This was the result of his work as Keeper since 1837, and of the work of Sir Frederic Madden as Keeper of Manuscripts since the same date. Although he kept a close eye on his old department, Panizzi had to spend much of his time during his ten years as Principal Librarian dealing with the antiquities and natural history departments of the Museum, and with the accommodation problems of the institution as a whole. He also improved the morale of the staff by obtaining for them in 1860 the benefit of retirement pensions. This had the additional advantage of increasing the efficiency of the Museum, because hitherto the Trustees had been reluctant to dispense with staff who were past their best, because of the financial hardship which this involved.[2]

John Winter Jones, who succeeded Panizzi as Keeper of Printed Books (and in 1866 followed him as Principal Librarian), was his devoted disciple and had every intention of continuing on the lines which Panizzi had laid down. So he successfully campaigned for the restoration of the purchase grant for printed books to the figure of £10,000 per annum which Panizzi had achieved in 1846 (and which had been cut in the 1850s, because of the lack of space to house books until the new Reading Room and Iron Library were completed in 1857). He also pressed on with the preparation of the new general catalogue which had taken up so much of the staff's time since 1839, and he continued Panizzi's policy of refusing to print this until the whole work had been prepared in manuscript. Winter Jones was the first Keeper who made considerable efforts

---

1 Archival authorities for the statements in this article are to be found in P. R. Harris, *A history of the British Museum Library, 1753–1973* (London, 1998).
2 E. Miller, 'Antonio Panizzi and the British Museum', *British Library Journal* 5 (1979), 1–17.

to obtain the official publications of Britain's colonies because he was convinced of their importance as evidence of the history of the Empire.[3]

The opening of the new round Reading Room in May 1857 provoked much favourable comment, and the number of persons using it rose rapidly. The previous Reading Room had dealt with about 220 readers each day; in the latter part of 1857 the number rose to over 400, and went on increasing until the figure of 450 was reached in 1861. This was too many to cope with, so in 1862, the Trustees excluded persons aged under twenty-one, and during the next ten years the average attendance each day was about 350. The superintendent of the new room, Thomas Watts, was a person of very wide knowledge and his appointment to the post revived the tradition (which had existed until 1824) that a senior member of the staff should be available in the Reading Room to assist readers.

Soon after becoming Principal Librarian Winter Jones persuaded the Trustees to set up a separate Department of Maps, Charts, Plans and Topographical Drawings, with Richard H. Major as Keeper. This department only existed from 1867 until 1880 when Major was retired after a dispute with E. A. (later Sir Edward) Bond, the Principal Librarian, and the maps were returned to the care of the Keepers of Manuscripts and of Printed Books. Winter Jones was also responsible for the appointment in 1867 of a second Keeper in the Department of Manuscripts, to take charge of the oriental manuscripts. While the Department of Maps failed to survive, the Sub-department of Oriental Manuscripts developed in 1892 into the separate Department of Oriental Printed Books and Manuscripts.

When the Library Association was set up in 1877, Winter Jones took a prominent part in its activities. Other members of the staff (including Richard Garnett) were also involved, and the tradition continued. Arundell Esdaile was very active in the Library Association in the period after the 1914–18 War, and at a later date so were Cecil B. Oldman, Principal Keeper of Printed Books, and F. C. (later Sir Frank) Francis, Director of the British Museum.

Madden retired from the Keepership of Manuscripts in 1866. During his twenty-nine years in the post, he had greatly increased the collections, had supervised the repair of the Cotton Manuscripts damaged in 1731, and had begun the series of printed *Catalogues of additions to the manuscripts*. His successor was E. A. Bond, a man of vision and drive. In 1878 he succeeded Winter Jones as Principal Librarian, and in the next ten years introduced many

---

3 R. Garnett, *Essays in librarianship and bibliography* (London, 1899), 314–24.

reforms.[4] At the urging of Richard Garnett (and despite the opposition of George Bullen, the Keeper of Printed Books) he forced through a plan to print the catalogue of printed books, which in its manuscript form was occupying a larger and larger proportion of the space in the Reading Room. He arranged for the installation of electric lighting in the Museum (gas had never been used because of the danger of fire and pollution). As a result the Reading Room and the Manuscripts students' room could be kept open for longer periods each day. In the early 1880s Bond supervised the construction of the White Wing in the south-east corner of the Museum (named after William White who bequeathed the funds which paid for it), which provided the Department of Manuscripts with a proper students' room and better working space for the staff. The Department of Printed Books also benefited because it was then possible to provide a special reading room and extra storage space for the growing collection of newspapers; the collection had increased greatly since 1869 when newspapers were first claimed under the deposit provisions of the Copyright Act. (Previously the Museum had been given newspapers which had been deposited in the Stamp Office.)

Richard Garnett, one of the Assistant Keepers in the Department of Printed Books from 1875 until 1890 (when he became Keeper of the department) was an able lieutenant to Bond.[5] He gained a high reputation as superintendent of the Reading Room from 1875 until 1884, and during the latter part of this time he supervised the printing of the *General catalogue of printed books*. This was published between 1881 and 1900, with a supplement produced between 1901 and 1905 containing entries for books acquired since 1881 which had not been included in the main catalogue. The total number of works recorded in the catalogue was about 3,735,000. A considerable amount of space was saved by transforming the catalogue from manuscript to print.[6]

Garnett also produced a temporary solution to the perennial problem of the Library – lack of space to hold the constantly growing stock of books. When the Iron Library surrounding the Reading Room had been finished in 1857 it was thought that it would accommodate the intake of printed books for the rest of the century, but within twenty-five years more space was required. Garnett suggested the use of movable presses hanging in front of the existing presses. Bond supported this solution, and after a detailed scheme had been

---

4 Garnett, *Essays*, 335–9.
5 B. McCrimmon, *Richard Garnett* (Chicago, 1989), 78–97, 115–21, 141–5.
6 B. McCrimmon, *Power, politics and print: the publication of the British Museum catalogue 1881–1900* (Hamden, Conn. and London, 1981), 95–149.

worked out by Henry Jenner (who was in charge of arranging the books in the library) a programme of installing such presses was begun, and continued for the next forty years.[7]

There was considerable growth of the collections of manuscripts in the second half of the nineteenth century. The outstanding acquisition was the Stowe collection which was purchased from the earl of Ashburnham in 1883. Important additions were also made to the collections of older printed books, partly from the major sales which were held during this period, such as those of Blenheim Palace and Hamilton Palace.

Attention was also given to oriental printed material, such as the Japanese and Korean books acquired from the collection of Ernest Satow. Two important new sources of material were exploited from the 1880s. Since the enactment of a revised Copyright Act in 1842 the British Museum had been entitled to the deposit of publications from British possessions overseas, but it had not been possible to enforce this right. However, from 1885 various colonies made regulations requiring local publishers to make deposits, and this provided an important source of material for the Museum.[8] The other new type of intake consisted of official publications from overseas which arrived as a result of exchange agreements between Great Britain and foreign governments.

Under such notable superintendents as Thomas Watts, Richard Garnett and George K. Fortescue, the Reading Room became a very famous institution in the second half of the nineteenth century. A popular author such as Jerome K. Jerome could refer to it in his well-known *Three men in a boat*, secure in the knowledge that his readers would be well aware of its reputation. In 1885 *Punch* printed a cartoon showing some well-known readers there, including Algernon Swinburne, Dean Frederic Farrar, Sir Leslie Stephen, William Lecky and Charles Bradlaugh. Despite the growth in the number of libraries of learned and professional bodies, public libraries and university and college libraries, the Reading Room was still the prime resource for research.[9] However the move of the natural history departments of the British Museum to South Kensington between 1881 and 1885, and the setting up of specialist libraries there, as well as the growth of the Patent Office Library (from 1855) and of what was to become the Science Museum Library, led to scientists using the Reading Room less and less. On the other hand, the increased call for rare books

7 Garnett, *Essays*, 262–71.
8 I. Sternberg, 'The British Museum Library and colonial copyright deposit', *British Library Journal* 17 (1991), 61–82.
9 P. R. Harris, *The Reading Room* (London, 1986), 17–26.

led to the development of the Large Room (later called the North Library) as a specialist reading room for those using such material.

The growth of the newspaper collections by the end of the nineteenth century provoked a crisis. The Trustees were so concerned that, in response to pressure from the Treasury, they agreed that a Bill should be introduced into Parliament to enable them to hand over provincial newspapers to the care of local government authorities. When the Bill was debated in the House of Lords there was such public opposition that it was abandoned. So, with great reluctance, the Treasury agreed to the construction of a repository at Colindale, on the north-west outskirts of London, for a large proportion of the collection of newspapers. This was in operation by 1906, and newspapers required by readers were brought to Bloomsbury by van each week, where they were consulted in the Newspaper Room which had been opened in the White Wing in 1885.

This development took place when Fortescue was Keeper of Printed Books (1899–1912). When he had been superintendent of the Reading Room from 1884 until 1896 he had realised that there was an urgent need for subject access to the collections. He was a very practical man, who realised that while there were endless arguments about the ways to provide classified catalogues, the most used part of any classified catalogue was the alphabetical index. So he compiled catalogues in which the subjects were arranged in alphabetical (rather than classified) order. The initial volume (compiled in his own time) covered the years 1880 to 1885 and was published in 1886. It was the first in a series of *Subject indexes* which continued until that for the period 1971–5, by which time the total number of entries since 1880 was 3,127,000. This very down-to-earth system had many advantages over more elaborate subject catalogues, but it was never widely adopted by the rest of the library world.[10]

Another innovation when Fortescue was Keeper had a considerable impact on the world of scholarship. This was the *Catalogue of books printed in the XVth century now in the British Museum*, the first volume of which appeared in 1908 and, with eleven volumes printed, still awaits the volume dealing with British incunables. The foundation of this catalogue was laid by Robert Proctor, who joined the staff in 1893. Soon after Fortescue became Keeper in 1899 he reported to the Trustees on the need to bring together the Museum's collection of incunables. Proctor, who had a great knowledge of early typography, was

---

10 F. J. Hill, '"Fortescue": the British Museum and British Library Subject Index', *British Library Journal* 12 (1986), 58–63.

entrusted with this task, and he arranged the collection in chronological order, grouped by countries, towns and presses. He died in 1903 before he had quite finished this task, and the work was completed by Alfred W. Pollard and Henry Jenner. Pollard (a considerable scholar, who was Keeper of Printed Books from 1919 until 1924) began work on the catalogue in 1906. This concentration on the incunables stimulated attempts to fill gaps in the collection, and 1,173 were acquired between 1899 and 1914, by which time the total number in the library was 9,501 (excluding duplicates).

The Department of Manuscripts began to make material in its collections available to a wider public by publishing facsimiles. This process began in the 1870s and 1880s when facsimiles of charters, of Latin and Greek manuscripts, and of the Codex Alexandrinus were printed. The programme was continued with facsimiles of illuminated manuscripts in the early twentieth century. The Director of the Museum during part of this time was Sir Frederic Kenyon, who had until 1909 been in the Department of Manuscripts where he had specialised in papyri, of which he had published catalogues. He wished to widen the appeal of the Museum to the general public and so he set up a bookstall which sold postcards showing items in the collections, and other printed material. He also appointed a guide-lecturer to explain the items on display in the galleries.

Apart from the large numbers of papyri acquired from 1888 onwards, the Department of Manuscripts added to its collections outstanding items such as the Buckler topographical drawings, Nelson's memorandum on the eve of the battle of Trafalgar, the 930 volumes of the Hardwicke papers and the tenth-century Bosworth Psalter. The department also received part of the bequest of fifty important volumes from Alfred H. Huth in 1910. The remainder of the bequest went to the Department of Printed Books and included a Caxton, a Shakespeare first quarto and two volumes containing seventy-five Elizabethan ballads. Other bequests of major importance to this department were the Thomas K. Tapling collection of postage stamps (1891), and the Henry S. Ashbee collection, which included 1,715 volumes of Cervantes as well as erotica and other material (1900). The Department of Printed Books was also affected by the passage of a new Copyright Act in 1911, because the clause relating to the deposit of publications in the Museum led to the receipt there of material of minor importance (such as bottle-labels), which had previously been registered at Stationers' Hall. Acts of 1915 and 1932 gave the Trustees power to exempt such material from the deposit requirement.

The establishment of the Department of Oriental Printed Books and Manuscripts in 1892 led to increased attention being given to material of this type.[11] Acquisitions increased, a special oriental students' room was opened in 1898, and by 1914 the department had published the remarkable total of thirty-one catalogues. Several of these were produced by Lionel D. Barnett, who joined the department in 1899, became Keeper in 1908, and held this post for twenty-eight years. He was a notable scholar in the field of Indian languages, and was re-employed to deal with material of this kind in 1947 when the department was very short of staff. He continued with this work until his death, aged 89, in 1960.

The staff of the Library have of course always been distinguished for their linguistic skills. Thomas Watts, who worked in the Department of Printed Books from 1838 until 1869, selected for purchase books in Spanish, Portuguese, modern Greek, Dutch, Swedish, Danish, Russian, Polish, Hungarian, French, Italian and German.[12] Considerable emphasis was placed on the acquisition of Slavonic material from Panizzi's time onwards. The selection of oriental language material was often dealt with by Jewish scholars, several of whom in the nineteenth century came to the British Museum from the Continent. One such was Emanuel Deutsch, born in Silesia, who was on the staff from 1855 until 1873, and was well known for his article on the Talmud in the *Quarterly Review*.[13] A knowledge of Greek and Latin was of course expected of most of the senior staff, particularly those in the Department of Manuscripts.

The construction of the King Edward Building, to the north of the existing Museum, between 1906 and 1914 made it possible to increase the size of the Large Room, which was the reading room for rare books. It was then renamed the North Library. The new building also provided accommodation for the office where books and periodicals were deposited in accordance with the provisions of the Copyright Act (hitherto in the White Wing), the Map and Music Rooms, and ultimately for a reading room dealing with the official publications of British and foreign governments.

Much of this accommodation was not in fact occupied until the end of the 1914–18 War. The war of course interfered considerably with the operations of the Library, because many members of the staff were called up for service in the armed forces, or transferred to work for government departments. The war also caused a breach of the normal rule that none of the collections should leave the building except in response to a demand from a court of law. In

11 H. J. Goodacre and A. P. Pritchard, *Guide to the Department of Oriental Manuscripts and Printed Books* (London, 1977), 9–10.

12 C. Thomas and B. Henderson, 'Watts, Panizzi and Asher', *British Library Journal* 23 (1997), 154–75.

13 B. McCrimmon, 'W. R. S. Ralston, 1828–89', *British Library Journal* 14 (1988), 184–5.

view of the national emergency, thousands of books and maps were loaned to government departments to provide them with essential information. (Such loans were also made during the 1939–45 War.)

Fortunately the air raids which became more frequent as the war progressed resulted in very little damage to the building, and virtually no damage to the collections. Even so, the threat had to be taken seriously and in 1918 some of the most valuable books and manuscripts were evacuated to the National Library of Wales at Aberystwyth and to a country house in Worcestershire.

When the war ended the perennial problem of lack of space for the constantly growing collections came to the fore again. The difficulties were made worse because it became apparent that the movable presses, which had provided much of the expansion space since the 1880s, were straining the structure of the Iron Library round the Reading Room. By the mid-1920s no more could be installed, and some of those in use had to be dismantled and re-erected, fixed to the floor, in the basement of the King Edward Building. In another attempt to solve the problem of lack of space, an additional floor was constructed on the top of the south-east quadrant of the Iron Library. But this too put a strain on the structure and the plan to extend the extra floor over the remainder of the Iron Library had to be abandoned.

The lack of space had become so acute by 1927 that the Trustees sent a deputation to the Prime Minister, Stanley Baldwin, to lay the problem before him. Not surprisingly, he expressed sympathy but said that the financial difficulties of the country prevented any immediate solution. He did however set up a Royal Commission to look into the problems of the national museums and galleries. Much to the relief of the Trustees this Commission recommended that urgent action should be taken to deal with the British Museum's accommodation difficulties, and to provide a remedy for the fact that the open-plan nature of the Iron Library made it an immense fire risk. The four bookstacks of the Iron Library round the Reading Room should be rebuilt in steel and concrete, separated from the Reading Room and from each other by fire-proof walls. It was estimated that the rebuilt bookstacks would allow for fifty years of growth – not for the first time such an estimate was falsified by events. The Royal Commission was also in favour of extending the newspaper repository at Colindale to house all the Library's newspapers, with space for twenty-five years' expansion, and providing a reading room there so that volumes would no longer have to be transported to Bloomsbury to be consulted by readers.[14]

14 Royal Commission on National Museums and Galleries. *Interim Report* (London, 1928) (Cmd. 3192), 30–4.

The Government accepted these recommendations, and the developments at Colindale were carried out between 1930 and 1932. Work also began on constructing mezzanine floors in the north wing of the British Museum building to provide decanting space for the books from the stacks which were to be rebuilt, and enlarged staff working areas. By 1937 this work was complete, as was the rebuilding of the rare books reading room (the North Library). The demolition and rebuilding of the north-west quadrant of the bookstacks round the Reading Room was carried out between 1934 and 1937. In 1938 work began on the north-east quadrant of the stacks and the new structure was completed by 1940. Because of the outbreak of war in 1939, the shelving and other interior fitments took a long time to complete.

Apart from the problem of lack of space the other main concern of the Department of Printed Books in the inter-war period was the compilation of a revised edition of the *General catalogue of printed books*, to replace that printed between 1881 and 1905. This first edition was out of print by 1918, and in the 1920s a revision of the cataloguing rules was carried out in preparation for a new edition. Attempts were made to co-ordinate these rules with those of the other five libraries which enjoyed the privilege of copyright deposit, but no positive responses were received – indeed both the Bodleian and the Cambridge University Library made it clear that they were not prepared to change their rules at that time. By 1928, in view of outside demands for a new version of the General Catalogue, Robert F. Sharp, the Keeper of Printed Books, was instructed to draw up plans for a new edition. His calculations proved in the event to be far too optimistic, because he thought that without any extra cataloguing staff the work could be completed in about 165 volumes in seven or eight years. As financial assistance was offered by the Rockefeller Foundation the Trustees agreed that work could begin.

After Sharp's retirement at the end of 1929, his successor Wilfred A. Marsden prepared more detailed plans. The expected output had already been reduced from twenty-four volumes per annum to twelve, but soon after the first batch of copy was sent to the printers early in 1930, Marsden informed the Trustees that he doubted whether even this revised figure could be achieved. The first volume was published in 1931, but by 1933 complaints were being received from subscribers about the slow progress of the project. The Trustees therefore asked the Treasury for permission to recruit temporary staff to help with the work, and in October 1933 the Treasury approved the employment of twenty Assistant Cataloguers. The first of these began duty in February 1934, but recruitment had to be spread over three years because of the need to give the new staff proper training. Despite all efforts, production could not be raised above four or five volumes per annum, and by the end of 1939 only twenty-nine volumes had appeared, bringing the work to the end of the letter B. Then the war slowed progress even further.[15]

In the early 1920s a very useful series of short-title catalogues of early books in the collections had been begun. The first of these was published in 1921 and dealt with Spanish books up to 1600; another, dealing with French books appeared in 1924. Both of these were compiled by Henry (later Sir Henry) Thomas, who was Keeper of the Department of Printed Books from 1943 until 1947. Further volumes concerned with Portuguese, Spanish-American, Italian, German and Dutch books were produced in the period up to 1965.

The Department of Manuscripts experienced cataloguing problems in the period between 1918 and 1939. The *Catalogue of additions to the manuscripts* fell increasingly into arrears. While the volume for the years 1906–10 had appeared in 1912, that for 1911–15 was delayed until 1925 (partly of course because of the war), and that for 1916–20 until 1933. The next volume, for 1921–5, was not published until 1950. The main reason for these delays was lack of staff to catalogue the large collections of modern historical papers (such as those of Sir Robert Peel and the earl of Aberdeen) which the library acquired.

Funds for acquisitions either remained static or diminished in the inter-war period, and the Department of Printed Books had in consequence to cancel some subscriptions to foreign periodicals. It proved impossible to buy the original manuscript of Lewis Carroll's *Alice's adventures in Wonderland* when it was auctioned in 1928, and it went to the USA, as did many of the choice printed books from the Britwell Library rather earlier. (The Lewis Carroll manuscript was presented to the British Museum in 1948 by a body of American subscribers as a tribute to Britain's efforts during the 1939–45 War.) At the time of the Britwell sales Pollard, the Keeper of Printed Books, expressed his fear that in future all important pre-1640 books coming up for sale would go to the USA.

Special efforts did enable the Department of Manuscripts to buy the Luttrell Psalter and the Bedford Book of Hours, with the help of the National Art-Collections Fund. The fourth-century Greek Bible known as the Codex Sinaiticus was bought from the Soviet Government in 1933 for £100,000 with a Treasury grant and over £53,000 subscribed by the public in answer to a special appeal. The Department of Oriental Printed Books and Manuscripts bought Moses Gaster's collection of about 1,230 manuscripts (mainly Hebrew and

---

15 A. H. Chaplin, *GK: 150 years of the General Catalogue of Printed Books* (Aldershot, 1987), 101–19.

Samaritan). In 1937 the Department of Printed Books purchased the Ashley Library from the widow of Thomas J. Wise for £66,000; it had to forfeit the £1,500 per annum which it normally spent on antiquarian books for the next six years as a contribution towards the purchase price.

One of the recommendations of the 1927 Committee on Public Libraries (of which Kenyon, the British Museum Director, was chairman) was that the Central Library for Students, which since 1916 had provided a loan service, should become a department of the British Museum and arrange inter-library loans in Britain. After consideration, the Trustees decided that it would be better if the new organization had its own Trustees, but worked closely with the British Museum Library. So when the National Central Library began operations in 1931, British Museum Trustees and staff were on its governing body.[16] If this failure to take full responsibility for the National Central Library was open to criticism on the grounds that it illustrated the Museum's tendency to be insufficiently outward-looking, three other developments showed the opposite tendency. Special temporary exhibitions to appeal to the general public were begun in the 1880s, and the number of them greatly increased after 1920. In 1924 an Act gave the Trustees power to lend material from all the departments of the Museum for exhibition at institutions within the United Kingdom. (The number of loans increased very considerably after 1963 when an Act enabled the Trustees to lend for exhibitions abroad.) The third development which made it possible for the Library to assist those who found difficulty in visiting the reading rooms was the great increase in photographic work after the 1914–18 War. By 1923 the Keepers of Manuscripts and of Printed Books were concerned about the wear and tear on the collections which this caused, and so the Trustees decided to appoint an official photographer who would be required to treat the collections with great care. (Previously outside firms had dealt with photography.) As time passed more and more of the Library's collections were made available at a distance, not only by photographs but also by photocopies and microfilms.

The 1939–45 War of course interrupted the normal work of the library, and the buildings and collections of the Department of Printed Books suffered severely from German air-raids. As early as 1933, because of instructions from the Government, the staff of the Museum had started preparations for evacuating and otherwise safeguarding the collections in the event of war. These plans were put into effect on 24 August 1939. Material from the collections of the Departments of Manuscripts and of Oriental Printed Books and

---

16 S. P. L. Filon, *The National Central Library* (London, 1977), 29–38.

Manuscripts was sent to the National Library of Wales at Aberystwyth, as were considerable numbers of rare and valuable items from the Department of Printed Books. Material which remained in the Museum building was, as far as possible, moved to more secure locations. The reading rooms were closed while staff concentrated on this work, but the main Reading Room reopened in the middle of September, and a joint students' room for the Departments of Manuscripts and of Oriental Printed Books and Manuscripts operated from January 1940. As in the 1914–18 War, members of the staff were called up for the armed forces or moved to work in Government departments. Ultimately the library staff was reduced to about half its pre-war complement.

The first air-raid damage to the buildings and collections occurred in September 1940. A bomb exploded in the King's Library, but fortunately only about 1,500 volumes of the library of George III were affected, and about two-thirds of these were repairable. On 23 October the original building of the Newspaper Library at Colindale was bombed. About 40,000 volumes of English provincial and Irish newspapers (mainly of the nineteenth century) were affected, and several thousands of these were destroyed. More material was evacuated from the British Museum building, and additional space to accommodate it was found in country houses, and in a disused stone-quarry in Wiltshire. The combined Manuscripts and Oriental Printed Books and Manuscripts students' room was closed from September 1940 until after the end of the war. Because of the danger from the great amount of glass in the Reading Room, readers were moved to the North Library in October. A few days later an oil bomb pierced the dome of the Reading Room, but most of the oil remained on the exterior, and the resulting fire was quickly extinguished.

The real disaster for the Library came on the night of 10/11 May 1941, when many incendiary bombs hit the Museum, severely damaging the southern part of the building and destroying the south-west quadrant of the Iron Library. Between 200,000 and 250,000 volumes were lost, most of which dated from after 1857 when the Iron Library was built. Further evacuations took place and these continued until 1944. In 1943 the 65,000 volumes of the King's Library were sent to the new building of the Bodleian Library. Fortunately no more bombs fell on the Museum building after 1941, and luckily it escaped the V1 flying bombs and the V2 rockets which were targeted on London in 1944 and 1945.[17]

When the war ended in the summer of 1945, there was much to be done to put the Library back into full operation. The evacuated books and manuscripts

17 P. R. Harris, 'Acquisitions in the Department of Printed Books and the effects of the war', *British Library Journal* 12 (1986), 119–44.

were brought back between the autumn of 1945 and November 1946. (The return of some was delayed because of lack of space to house them in the damaged Museum building.) The Reading Room was repaired and the readers moved back there in May 1946 from their temporary quarters in the North Library. The students' room of the Department of Manuscripts reopened in December 1946, but that of the Department of Oriental Printed Books and Manuscripts remained closed until March 1948, because of shortage of staff. Some building work was carried out at the Newspaper Library, and the bomb damage in the King's Library was repaired by 1951. This gallery was then used for an expanded programme of exhibitions for the general public. The problem of providing space for acquisitions was temporarily solved by the rebuilding of the destroyed south-west quadrant, which was finished in 1954.

Although the acquisition of printed books had continued on a reduced scale throughout the war, it was of course impossible to obtain material from enemy countries (and from the countries overrun by them). So urgent steps were taken from 1945 to rebuild the network of agents abroad which had since Panizzi's time helped the library to achieve (as far as possible) its aim of obtaining material of research value from the whole world (bearing in mind of course that the intake of foreign publications in the field of the natural sciences had been considerably reduced since the end of the nineteenth century). The other major task, as regards acquisitions of printed books, was to replace the books and periodicals destroyed in May 1941. This replacement programme took up a considerable proportion of the department's acquisitions budget for several years.

The collections of the Department of Manuscripts received some important additions, including the Helmingham Hall Orosius and the Yelverton manuscripts (both in 1953), the Salvin Hours (1955) and the Gorleston Psalter (1958). In 1957 the Benedictional of St Ethelwold was acquired from Chatsworth, having been accepted with other items by the Treasury from the Duke of Devonshire in lieu of death duties. The Department of Oriental Printed Books and Manuscripts received as a bequest from Charles W. Dyson Perrins (who had made other generous gifts to the library) the splendid Khamseh of Nizami, illuminated by Indian artists for the Mughal Emperor Akbar in 1595–6. As far as routine acquisitions were concerned the department suffered when India (after it became independent in 1947) ended the legal deposit of Indian publications in the British Museum. The annual grant of the department then had to be increased in order that it could buy such material.

The Department of Printed Books acquired the music library of Paul Hirsch (1946), books from Holkham Hall (1950) and from Chatsworth (1958), and the

J. F. Dexter collection of works of Dickens (1968). In 1957 Queen Elizabeth II presented the Royal Music Library (which contained manuscripts as well as printed books); this had been on loan to the Trustees since 1911. There was massive increase in the number of foreign official publications acquired as a result of international exchange agreements which were concluded, and considerable quantities of items in Slavonic languages were obtained by arranging barter exchanges with the countries of Eastern Europe. As British colonies achieved independence the intake of material from them by copyright deposit diminished steadily and ended almost completely in the 1960s. So arrangements had to be made to buy books and periodicals from these countries.

The continuing outflow overseas of rare books and manuscripts (mainly to the USA) led to the setting up of an export control system, which enabled the library to secure some of these items. When the funds to purchase such books and manuscripts could not be raised, the losses were often mitigated by obtaining microfilms of the material in question. The increased use of microforms to add to the collections was a marked feature of the post-war period. The Department of Manuscripts obtained in this way material such as microfilms of the Hatfield Manuscripts, and the Department of Printed Books acquired many newspapers on microfilm (or transformed original sets into microfilm), and bought some of the large collections of microfilmed material which were published, such as the *Early American Imprints* series.

Cataloguing the collections presented those in charge of the library with major problems. The greatest of these concerned the revised version of the *General catalogue of printed books* (known as GK II) which had been in progress since 1931. By 1945 thirty-nine volumes had been published, bringing the work to the middle of the letter C. As staff returned from war service and new staff were recruited, more were allocated to the revision of the catalogue, but the project still progressed far too slowly. In 1953 it was calculated that without extra staff the work would take 270 years to complete. Because of the quantity of new accessions which would arrive during this time it would occupy 540 volumes. Obviously this was an impossible situation, and the chances of persuading the Treasury to authorise the extra forty-two staff needed to complete the work in forty-five years were negligible.

It was now that one of the most notable persons ever to serve in the Library took the lead. Frank C. Francis (knighted in 1960) had joined the staff of the Department of Printed Books in 1926, and in 1946 and 1947 he was seconded to the Director's Office to act as Secretary of the Museum. From 1947 until 1959 he was one of the two Keepers of Printed Books (under Oldman, the Principal Keeper), and then from 1959 until 1968 he was Director of the Museum. As

Keeper one of his responsibilities was the cataloguing work of the Department of Printed Books, and he decided that GK II must be brought to an end, and a new method of producing a printed version of the catalogue devised. He recommended that the existing entries in one of the working copies of the catalogue should be rearranged in proper order, with the entries for accessions since 1905 interfiled with those of the original printed catalogue (published between 1881 and 1905), and then printed by photolithography. Revision, such as had been been carried out in GK II, would be abandoned. Against much opposition he forced this plan through, and GK II ended in 1955 with volume 51 (covering DEO to DEZ). A new type of camera to photograph the entries in correct order was produced by Messrs Balding and Mansell, and in 1957 the Trustees agreed to award the contract for printing the catalogue to them. Legal negotiations over the terms of the contract delayed the start of the work until 1959, but it then proceeded with great speed and the new version of the catalogue (known as GK III) was published in 263 volumes between 1960 and 1966. The whole edition sold out and made a handsome profit.[18]

This was only one of Francis's contributions to the library. He always advocated co-operation with other parts of the library world, both at home and abroad, and was active in the Library Association, the Standing Conference of National and University Libraries, the International Federation of Library Associations and the Bibliographical Society (in which members of the Library staff had played a prominent part since its foundation in 1892). He was a key figure in the creation of the *British National Bibliography*, which began publication in 1950. Francis was chairman of the committee set up in 1948 which brought the *BNB* into existence, and he arranged for the new organisation to be accommodated in Museum premises, and to have access to the books deposited in the Copyright Receipt Office of the Museum.[19] He also was the person who revived the nineteenth-century tradition that the British Museum Library covered not only the humanities, but also the natural sciences. From 1951 he was involved in discussions about the improvement of library services to scientists, and he succeeded in having the National Reference Library of Science and Invention set up as part of the British Museum Library. In 1960 the various government departments involved agreed that such a library should be created by developing the Patent Office Library, and the new organisation became part of the Department of Printed Books in 1966.

During his period as one of the Keepers of the Department of Printed Books Francis had wrestled with the problem of cataloguing backlogs which derived

18 Chaplin, *GK*, 120–50.
19 A. Stephens, *The history of the British National Bibliography* (London, 1994), 6–7, 20.

partly from the influx of large quantities of purchased and presented material in the post-war period, and partly from the great increase of books and periodicals published in this country and deposited in the Museum in accordance with the provisions of the Copyright Act. This was one problem which Francis did not solve, and one with which the British Library is still struggling at the beginning of the twenty-first century. The Department of Manuscripts also had problems with cataloguing which dated back to the inter-war period.

However, as so often in the history of the Library, one of the most intractable problems in the post-war years was the lack of space to house the collections. Pending the construction of a completely new building for the library departments (plans for which dated back to 1944) the Trustees reluctantly concluded that some of the printed collections would have to be outhoused. They were granted power to do this in the 1963 British Museum Act, and in 1964 the first material was moved to a building in the former Woolwich Arsenal in southeast London. Much of the original outhoused material consisted of foreign official publications, the intake of which had vastly increased since the end of the war, and which was less used than the material in the general library. Later other buildings were used to outhouse parts of the collections, including the rapidly growing holdings of the National Reference Library of Science and Invention.

In the long term however a new building for the Library was essential.[20] A site for this, immediately south of the British Museum building, had been designated in the London County Council development plan in 1951, which was approved by the Ministry of Housing and Local Government in 1955 after a public enquiry. Preliminary planning then took place, and after Francis became Director in 1959 he urged the project forward. Architects were appointed in 1962, and by 1965 plans were submitted to the local authority (first to Holborn Borough Council, and then to its successor Camden Borough Council). Camden accepted the plans in general but wanted some details altered. Then in 1966 Richard Crossman, Minister of Housing and Local Government, expressed hostility, and was supported by Mrs Lena Jeger, the local Member of Parliament, who objected to the loss of housing accommodation and historic buildings on the site. Then local residents joined the opposition. In October 1967, without any prior warning to the Trustees, the Government of Harold Wilson announced that the plan to construct a new

---

20 Colin St John Wilson gives a convenient account, from the architect's standpoint, of the long-drawn-out plans for expanding the Library in *The design and construction of the British Library* (London, 1998), 9–14.

library adjacent to the British Museum had been abandoned.[21] The Trustees' sense of outrage[22] received much public support, and debates in both Houses of Parliament clearly demonstrated this.[23] The government set up a committee to consider the contributions of the British Museum Library, the National Central Library, the National Lending Library for Science and Technology and the Science Museum Library in providing national library facilities and to recommend whether these facilities should be brought into a unified framework. This committee, chaired by Dr (later Lord) Dainton, reported in June 1969,[24] and as a result the British Library (incorporating the British Museum Library and other bodies) came into existence in 1973.[25]

The period between 1967 and 1973 was a very difficult one for the British Museum Library. There was complete uncertainty about the future (which harmed staff morale), and projects such as planning for the introduction of automatic data processing into the Library were frozen until the future structure was known. Then there was an episode in 1971 which led to a breakdown in health of the Principal Keeper of Printed Books – the discovery that the Assistant Keeper in charge of the philatelic collections had stolen material loaned to the Museum by the Crown Agents for Oversea Governments and Administrations.

So the final years of the British Museum Library were not a happy time. But overall, when the Library was incorporated into the British Library, those who had worked in it could look back on a history of great achievements. Since 1857 the collections of the Department of Printed Books (excluding those of the National Reference Library of Science and Invention) had grown from 550,000 volumes to 8,500,000 and of the Department of Manuscripts from 35,000 volumes to 100,000. In addition, in 1973, the Department of Oriental Printed Books and Manuscripts had 250,000 printed volumes and 35,000 manuscripts. In the early 1970s (excluding those who used the National Reference Library of Science and Invention) well over 400,000 visits were being made each year to the various reading and students' rooms (in the 1860s the figure had been just over 100,000). The catalogues of the Library were of very good quality, although there had been problems in keeping up with the constantly

---

21 Department of Education and Science, *Principal documentary evidence submitted to the National Libraries Committee*, 2 vols. (London, 1969), vol. 1, A88–9.
22 Lord Radcliffe, *Government by contempt: a speech in the House of Lords* (London, 1968), 15–32.
23 *Parliamentary Debates (Hansard), House of Commons*, vol. 754, no. 13 (16 November 1967), 725–76; *Parliamentary Debates (Hansard), House of Lords*, vol. 287, no. 22 (13 December 1967), 1114–1240.
24 *Report of the National Libraries Committee* (London, 1969) (Cmnd. 4028) (Dainton Report).
25 For the development of the British Library see chapter 25 below.

increasing intake of acquisitions. These catalogues reflected the good academic qualifications of the staff. Since 1952 the main Reading Room had been equipped with an enquiry desk where staff were available to give more help to readers than the superintendents had had time to do. Facilities had been provided for readers who wished to use typewriters, or to consult microfilms. There were special reading rooms for maps, music and official publications. The Manuscripts students' room had been increased in size in 1957, and the students' room for Oriental Printed Books and Manuscripts was much larger than the one which had existed up to 1938. Despite the growth of other libraries in the country, that of the British Museum was still the prime resource for those carrying out research in the humanities and the social sciences. For the general public a greatly increased number of exhibitions were provided, and many more publications were produced. The setting up of the National Reference Library of Science and Invention as part of the British Museum Library in 1966 provided for many of the needs of the natural scientists.

Only after the creation of the British Library in 1973 did Britain officially have a national library, but in fact the British Museum Library had largely fulfilled this role for a century and a half. It could have done more if it had been given increased financial resources and accommodation, and the fact that it had its own cataloguing and subject index systems which were not in use elsewhere limited its usefulness as far as other libraries were concerned. It did however provide for those who used it a very large and well-selected stock of foreign material, a high proportion of the printed archive of Great Britain (mainly received by legal deposit), general and specialist reading areas, and a knowledgeable staff.

The British Library and its antecedents

JOHN HOPSON

Introduction

The British Library, the national library of the United Kingdom, is one of the world's greatest libraries. It was formed comparatively recently, in 1973, when a number of existing organisations were administratively combined by the British Library Act of 1972, but its history dates back over 250 years to the foundation of the British Museum in 1753. The British Library collection, inherited from the former library departments of the British Museum and elsewhere, has been much augmented in the past thirty years and now contains more than 150 million items, in over 400 languages, with a further 3 million items added every year. Many of these additions arrive through the privilege of legal deposit, also inherited from the British Museum, whereby the British Library receives one copy of almost every printed item published in the United Kingdom and Ireland, but significant numbers are acquired through purchase, donation or voluntary deposit arrangements. The collection is as diverse as it is large and includes books, manuscripts, maps, music, newspapers, prints and drawings, photographs, patents, sound recordings, stamps and philatelic items, electronic publications and websites. The oldest items – oracle bones that carry the earliest surviving Chinese writing – are about 3,500 years old. Among the Library's greatest treasures are two versions of Magna Carta, regarded by many as the foundation of civil liberties; the Lindisfarne Gospels, a magnificent example of Anglo-Saxon artistry; the Diamond Sutra, the world's earliest dated printed document; and the Gutenberg Bible, the first major book printed in Europe from movable type.

The British Library operates from two main locations, in London and at Boston Spa, 200 miles further north in West Yorkshire. The London operations are centred on the reading rooms and exhibition galleries in the new building at St Pancras, with an additional site at Colindale in north London where the Newspaper Library is located, and two further storage buildings in Islington and Woolwich. The Boston Spa site, acquired in 1958 for the National Lending Library for Science and Technology, houses the British Library's main lending and document-supply operations. The legal-deposit intake and other acquisitions are now also handled at Boston Spa, linked to the cataloguing and other bibliographic services on the same site, which also houses personnel, finance and computing functions.

This account of the history of the British Library concentrates on how and why the Library was created, and how it has developed and evolved since 1973 as an organisation with the vision of helping people advance knowledge to enrich lives.

The approach to a national library

In April 1965, following the introduction of the Public Libraries and Museums Act 1964 and the transfer of certain functions from other government departments, the Department of Education and Science (DES) became responsible for almost all library functions in England and Wales, including a number of bodies that provided library services of one sort or another at a national level. The Department had, for many years, been responsible for the Science Museum Library and it now acquired a number of new functions. It was given responsibility for the grant-in-aid to the British Museum, whose library – which included the National Reference Library of Science and Invention (NRLSI), formed in 1962 and since 1966 incorporating the Patent Office Library – was generally considered to be the national reference library. It took over the administration of the government grant to the National Central Library – created in 1916 as the Central Library for Students – which operated as a national centre for inter-library lending in the humanities. With the break-up of the Department of Scientific and Industrial Research, it was also given responsibility for running the National Lending Library for Science and Technology (NLLST), at Boston Spa, created by Donald Urquhart amidst much controversy in the library world and triumphantly successful from the commencement of operations in 1962. Added to these bodies, the Office for Scientific and Technical Information (OSTI) was formed within the DES in 1965, to promote research in new techniques and systems for information services, to stimulate training of scientists for information work and to co-ordinate information activities both nationally and internationally.[1]

1 *OSTI: the first five years* (London, 1971), 1.

It has been widely assumed that the concept of the British Library as it was established in 1973 began with the University Grants Committee's *Parry Report* of 1967, which as well as considering 'the most effective and economical arrangements for meeting the needs of Universities and Colleges of Advanced Technology and Central Institutions for books and periodicals' stepped outside its strict terms of reference to recommend setting up a national library, based on the library collections of the British Museum.[2] However, even before the Parry Report was published, officials and ministers in the Department of Education and Science had started to look into the national library system in the United Kingdom, had identified the need for radical change, and had begun to draw up plans.

Within the DES responsibility for libraries was divided between various branches, and it was evident at an early stage that some co-ordinating mechanism was urgently required. Many of the national bodies were now seeking to diversify and expand. The piecemeal nature of these developments was the cause of concern, and fundamental questions were being asked, for example about the need for expanding reference services in central London. Another concern was cost: rough calculations within the Department showed that more than £50 million was spent on library services annually – and the conviction was growing that the nation was often asked to pay twice for the same thing.

In September 1966 Harry Hookway, then an official in the DES, put forward a formal case for a departmental committee. The first meeting of the Departmental Committee on Policy for National Libraries was held in January 1967 to consider a paper which proposed one form of 'ideal' national library service and was intended to stimulate critical analysis and alternative proposals.[3] While the proposed framework assumed the continued existence of separate reference and lending services, it was more adventurous in other areas, notably with suggestions that the Department of Printed Books should be detached from the British Museum and that the National Central Library should cease to exist as a separate institution.

In March 1967, as the proposals for a new national library service were being refined, the DES was also giving urgent attention to the British Museum's plans to build a massive extension for the library on a site to the south of Great

2 University Grants Committee, *Report of the Committee on Libraries* (London, 1967) (The Parry Report).
3 'Possible framework for a national library service', British Library Archives, file sI/16/18 pt I.

Russell Street. These were strongly opposed by the local borough council and a campaign to preserve the historic environment of Bloomsbury, led by Mrs Lena Jeger MP, rallied popular support.[4] In the face of these protests the government was persuaded that the plans should not be permitted to proceed, but the DES recognised the need for expansion in the context of wider needs. Arising from Hookway's report, a recommendation was made for a committee to investigate the whole question of a national library. The results were far-reaching.

The National Libraries Committee and the creation of the new Library

Dr Frederick (later Lord) Dainton, Vice-Chancellor of the University of Nottingham and an eminent scientist, was selected to be the Chairman of the National Libraries Committee. Dainton accepted the post subject to certain conditions: the committee was to be small in number; its members would between them cover the main subject areas for which the national libraries had holdings; and above all they were to be appointed on the basis of competence not representativeness.[5] The Committee's remit was to 'examine the functions of the British Museum Library, the National Central Library, the National Lending Library for Science and Technology, and the Science Museum Library in providing national library facilities; to consider whether in the interests of efficiency and economy such facilities should be brought into a unified framework; and to make recommendations'.[6]

The Committee worked swiftly and well and took only about fifteen months to complete its work. During this time it visited all the libraries included in the terms of reference and also took evidence from more than sixty university libraries, as well as many other interested bodies. Its report, published in June 1969, contained 132 recommendations, involving all aspects of the work of the national libraries.[7] The Committee's main recommendation was for the establishment of a new body, a National Libraries Authority, incorporating the library departments of the British Museum, the NLLST, the National Central Library and the British National Bibliography.

---

4 The plans, and the protests, are discussed in the preceding chapter on the British Museum Library.
5 F. Dainton, *Doubts and certainties: a personal memoir of the 20th century* (Sheffield, 2001), 185.
6 National Libraries Committee Report (London, 1969), 1 (Cmnd. 4028) (Dainton Report).
7 National Libraries Committee Report, 146–61.

Not surprisingly, reactions from the four bodies to be assimilated into the National Library Authority varied. To the Trustees and staff of the National Central Library the Dainton report was, according to Sidney Filon (Librarian of the NCL 1958–71),[8] 'a most disagreeable shock'; the Committee had taken 'an adverse view of almost every aspect of the Library's work' and furthermore recommended the early transfer of its loan services, including its bookstock and its union catalogues, to Boston Spa. In contrast, the Committee regarded the NLLST as a great success, and of all the heads of organisations recommended for assimilation into the National Libraries Authority Donald Urquhart had most reason to be satisfied with its recommendations. For the Council of the British National Bibliography there was some disappointment that the case for continued independence had been ignored, but it was not implacably opposed to assimilation into the new body. Lastly, the reaction of the Trustees of the British Museum to the Dainton Report was essentially one of relief: they had already resigned themselves to losing control of the library departments, and the recommendation that the newly defined National Reference Library should be located in central London, preferably on the Bloomsbury site, was regarded as a positive outcome.

In January 1971, following a general election and a change of Government, a White Paper was published setting out government plans.[9] It was Lord Eccles – Chairman of the British Museum Trustees until the general election, and the cabinet minister responsible for libraries after it – who rejected the name National Libraries Authority for the new organisation and came up with the alternative, simple name, the British Library. The White Paper accepted the main proposals of the Dainton Committee, including the need for a new building on the Bloomsbury site, and set out three stages for the development of the British Library: first setting up an organising committee, second the passage of legislation and third the establishment of the Library.

The British Library Organising Committee was established in January 1971 – with Lord Eccles, the Paymaster General, as chairman and Dr Hookway as vice-chairman – to prepare plans for the organisation, staffing and accommodation of the British Library, to co-ordinate action between the Department of Education and Science and the organisations involved, and to frame a conception of the role and needs of the British Library as these might develop over twenty-five to thirty years. The Committee was made up of representatives of the institutions to be combined – at Eccles's insistence permanent officials

---

8 S. P. L. Filon, *The National Central Library: an experiment in library co-operation* (London, 1977), 117.

9 *The British Library* (London, 1971) (Cmnd 4572).

rather than Trustees or governors – together with members chosen to reflect the needs of other libraries and interested bodies. A Planning Secretariat was set up and detailed work was carried out by a series of planning groups.

The Organising Committee was also responsible for drafting the necessary legislation, and in July 1972 the British Library Act became law.[10] The Act provided for the establishment of the British Library as the national library of the United Kingdom, 'consisting of a comprehensive collection of books, manuscripts, periodicals, films and other recorded matter, whether printed or otherwise', to be managed by the British Library Board 'as a national centre for reference, study and bibliographical and other information services, in relation both to scientific and technological matters and to humanities'. The British Library Act is brief and rather non-specific – of the bodies to be included in the new organisation only the British Museum Library is actually mentioned – but this is entirely deliberate. Writing in 1977 Sir Harry Hookway said that the Act was 'designed to provide great flexibility so that future, and as yet unforeseen, developments which may cause radical changes in the methods of operation of the new library can be accommodated'.[11]

The Organising Committee was conscious that it should avoid decisions on issues that were properly the responsibility of the proposed British Library Board. One controversial decision that the Organising Committee did make related to the operation of the lending services. The White Paper had left open the possibility of having two lending services, one for humanities and social sciences and one for science and technology. To Sidney Filon this option was rather attractive and allowed for continuing operation of the National Central Library as a separate unit within the British Library, albeit under a new name. Filon wanted the matter to be left for the British Library Board to consider, whereas Donald Urquhart, who strongly opposed the idea of separate lending services, wanted the issue resolved by the Organising Committee. Urquhart prevailed and it was decided that the staff and stocks of the National Central Library should be transferred to Boston Spa, with the NCL and the NLLST integrated under a single management structure.[12] The implementation of this decision also incidentally simplified inter-lending procedures for libraries that had been using both institutions.[13] (Urquhart also proposed that the British Library Board headquarters should be located at Peterborough,

10 *The British Library Act 1972* (London, 1972).
11 H. Hookway, 'The British Library: introduction', in W. L. Saunders (ed.), *British librarianship today* (London, 1976), 39.
12 Filon, *National Central Library*, 141–2.
13 Cf. Antonia Bunch's chapter 44 on inter-library co-operation, below.

roughly halfway between London and Boston Spa; his concern was that the British Library might become too London-centred and that the Boston Spa operations would lose out as a result. On this occasion, however, he failed to win over his colleagues on the Organising Committee and the proposal received no support.)[14] The relationship between Filon and Urquhart, and therefore between the NCL and the NLLST, was never easy, but when Sidney Filon retired in autumn 1971, and was replaced by Maurice Line, matters improved considerably.[15] Line – Librarian of the University of Bath and Director of the National Libraries ADP Study – was already a member of the Organising Committee, and he and Urquhart shared a strong mutual respect.

Probably the most difficult problem facing the British Library Organising Committee was to bring together the staff from a number of institutions, each with its own system of pay and conditions, to produce a single team. The Organising Committee saw a unified pay and conditions system, covering all staff, as essential if this objective was to be realised. In this it had the support of the DES and most, though not all, of the trade unions and staff associations involved in the negotiations. The Civil Service Department, however, was determined that a new system should not cost the taxpayer any more money and proposals which increased costs, even with the prospect of improved efficiency and later savings, were not attractive. Negotiations continued until the last minute and vesting day – the day the British Library was to begin operating – was postponed by a month in an unsuccessful attempt to obtain agreement. When the British Library did commence operations most of its staff were still on secondment from their original employer, an unsatisfactory situation that continued for many years, with further difficulties at the British National Bibliography which delayed the formation of the Bibliographic Services Division by more than a year after the Reference and Lending Divisions.

The British Library – early years, growth and expansion

The British Library Board was established on 1 April 1973 and the British Library commenced operations four months later on 1 July. An early problem facing the Board was the absence of a Chairman and despite increasing anxiety among Board members it was not until December 1973 that Lord Eccles was appointed.

---

14 D. Urquhart, *Mr Boston Spa* (Leeds, 1990), 212.
15 Urquhart, *Mr Boston Spa*, 209.

Harry Hookway's position as Deputy Chairman and Chief Executive had been ratified at the first meeting of the Board on 27 April 1973, which also discussed arrangements to fill three director-general posts, to head the three main functional units of the British Library: the Reference Division, based on the library departments of the British Museum; the Lending Division, merging the National Lending Library for Science and Technology and the National Central Library; and the Bibliographic Services Division, made by combining the functions of the British National Bibliography and the Copyright Receipt Office from the British Museum. Although it was not a statutory requirement, it was planned that the director-generals would be ex-officio members of the British Library Board, in addition to having responsibility for the day to day management of their respective divisions. Donald Urquhart was the first Director-General of the Lending Division, but from the outset it was planned that Maurice Line would succeed to the post when Urquhart retired in 1974. Donovan Richnell – Goldsmith's Librarian of the University of London and a member of the Organising Committee – was selected for the post of Director-General of the Reference Division, and A. J. Wells – who had been Managing Editor of the British National Bibliography from its establishment in 1949 – was asked to take the post of Director-General of the Bibliographic Services Division for six months, to allow for a long-term appointment to be made. Richard Coward, Head of the Systems Development Branch of the British Library, succeeded Wells in February 1975.

To these three divisions were added two smaller units, or departments. Central Administration dealt with accommodation, personnel, finance and other common services. The Research and Development Department (later the Research and Innovation Centre), created when the OSTI was transferred to the British Library from the Department of Education and Science in April 1974, was intended to promote and sponsor research and development related to library and information operations in all subject fields, and had a major effect in supporting this important aspect of library work country-wide.

The years immediately following the creation of the British Library were characterised by consolidation – much needed after a period of upheaval – and also by growth, particularly in the period before 1979. Grant-in-aid rose from about £16.5 million in the year 1975/6 – the first complete year of the Library being fully operational – to almost £45 million in 1983/4, and over the same period receipts from other sources grew from £2.5 million (about 12% of total receipts) to £11 million (nearly 20%). The importance of not relying solely on grant-in-aid became particularly evident after 1979 when, for the first time, the Library suffered cuts in its budget.

Under the Act the British Library had inherited the legal deposit privilege held by the British Museum under the 1911 Copyright Act, a provision tacitly confirmed in later legislation. This gave the Library the right to one copy of every printed item published in the United Kingdom, ensuring a strong base for its collections and confirming its status as the national library for the whole country – but no provision was made, initially or later, for an expansion in the number of copies to match the British Library's extended role.

New and innovatory services were introduced. In April 1977, the British Library Automated Information Service (BLAISE), the first online bibliographic information service in the UK, became operational; future developments confirmed the British Library's role as the national bibliographic service, providing electronic catalogue data for use by other libraries in the United Kingdom and further afield. In later years the computerisation of the British Library's own catalogues (of manuscripts as well as printed books) and their eventual launch as an effective web-based resource for the whole world gave a completely new sense of access to the collections. Exciting new projects were started, which continue today: also in 1977 the *Eighteenth-century short-title catalogue* (ESTC) commenced; in 1983 NEWSPLAN, a collaborative project for recording and microfilming local UK newspapers, was initiated; and in 1984 the National Preservation Office was set up to provide a UK focus for good preservation practice.

It was clear that the new institution was setting out to be a partner (albeit with a leading role) in the wider library community, in a way that had been less apparent in earlier years. In a move demonstrating its new commitment to that community the British Library even assumed responsibility for the library of the main professional body, the Library Association, in 1974, though the much-appreciated special service to LA members and to the profession at large could not easily be continued after the move to St Pancras, when the collections were merged with the Library's own holdings.

Of course, not all projects came to fruition; one notable failure was MER-LIN, the ambitious Machine Readable Library Information Network, which was cancelled in 1979 (to the great disappointment of many in the library world) when the British Library's budget was cut by nearly £600,000.

Other organisations were welcomed into the British Library fold; in 1982 responsibility for administering the India Office Library and Records passed to the Library from the Foreign and Commonwealth Office, creating with the Library's existing Oriental collections a vast resource for the history of much of Asia. In 1983 the British Institute for Recorded Sound joined the Library as the National Sound Archive, a pioneering venture into the world of non-book materials which was to figure ever more largely as electronic information became widespread later in the century.

Most significant of all was the progress on a new building for the Library. As mentioned earlier, the original scheme for a new building for the British Museum Library in Bloomsbury was abandoned in 1967, at the same time as the National Libraries Committee was set up. However, having examined the issues relating to the siting of a new building, the Dainton Committee concluded that the new library should, after all, be located in central London and suggested that the Bloomsbury site was the most suitable. A change of government in June 1970 had cleared the way for a revival of the plans and Colin St John Wilson – who with Sir Leslie Martin had designed the previous scheme – was commissioned to undertake a new design. Predictably, the campaign to 'save' Bloomsbury was relaunched: Lena Jeger MP was again prominent, with Frank Dobson, leader of Camden Council and a Bloomsbury resident, as a staunch ally. In January 1974 Camden Council published *Bloomsbury: the case against destruction*, a large booklet, beautifully produced and well illustrated with nostalgic views of the area under threat. The British Library responded later the same year with its own booklet, *The Bloomsbury site for rehousing the reference collections of the British Library*, much smaller and lacking the visual appeal of Camden's publication. There were other problems. The site area had been reduced by the requirement to preserve in full the west side of Bloomsbury Square. At the same time estimates of the amount of space needed had risen dramatically. Even after a number of functions were deleted from the brief, the resulting design was, according to the architect, massively overcrowded and the site had no scope for future expansion.[16]

In December 1974 the British Library Board agreed to examine with Government the feasibility of siting the proposed building on a $9^1/_2$ acre site in Somers Town, St Pancras, which was being vacated by British Rail. This was one of the two sites suggested by Camden Council – the other being Covent Garden – in its defence of Bloomsbury. A feasibility study was carried out by Colin St John Wilson and in August 1975 the Board accepted the Somers Town site for the construction of the new building, albeit with much regret at 'the loss of a unique opportunity to create in Bloomsbury a cultural complex of museum, library and university institutions unrivalled in the world'. The eventual success of the new building should not obscure the real sense of loss at the removal of all library functions from the British Museum site – especially

---

16 C. St John Wilson, *The design and construction of the British Library* (London, 1998) gives an account of the earlier schemes and the controversies, as well as of the final design.

the abandonment of the Round Reading Room with its historic associations, but also the loss of convenient access to the library collections for Museum curators.

The St Pancras site was purchased in 1976 and design of the new building work began. In 1980 government approved the first stage of construction, in 1982 the foundation stone was unveiled by the Prince of Wales at a ceremony at the interim headquarters of the British Library Board in Novello House in Soho, and in 1984 excavation of the basements and work on the superstructure started. It would be a further thirteen years before the new building was opened, after a painful and controversial gestation.

Sir Harry Hookway retired on 31 August 1984 after more than eleven years as Chief Executive. Together with Lord Eccles and Lord Dainton – who took over from Eccles as Chairman of the British Library Board in 1978 – Sir Harry had been hugely influential in determining the shape and direction of national library provision. All three had been involved with the British Library project, one way or another, from the earliest days and latterly they had provided the stability that allowed the new organisation to settle and then to grow and develop. Sir Harry's retirement, followed a year later by the retirement of Lord Dainton, was a signal for another period of change.

The middle years, 1985–1997

Kenneth Cooper took over as Chief Executive on 3 September 1984. Like his predecessor he was not a librarian; he had wide experience in both public and private sectors and quickly made a number of changes. He set about improving relations with the Office of Arts and Libraries, which had become somewhat strained, and persuaded the British Library Board to invite an observer from the parent department to all Board meetings; he introduced an executive Management Committee comprised of himself, the three director-generals, and the directors of Research and Development and of Central Administration. He also introduced, for the first time, a strategic planning process, with the primary aim of enabling the Library to discharge its duties in the most cost-effective manner. This led in 1985 to the publication of *Advancing with knowledge: the British Library strategic plan, 1985–1990*. This gave a statement, for the first time, of the Library's central aim, defined as:

> To preserve, develop, exploit and promote the combined resources of its collections and its facilities for reference, document supply, bibliographic research, and other services for the best benefit, both now and in the future,

of scholarship, research, industry, commerce and other major categories of information users.[17]

Advancing with knowledge heralded the first major changes to the Library's structure since its creation some twelve years previously. The Lending Division was renamed the Document Supply Centre (BLDSC) and combined with the former Science Reference Library, renamed the Science Reference and Information Service (SRIS), to form a new division for Science, Technology and Industry (even though the BLDSC now included the former 'humanities' functions of the National Central Library). The remainder of the Reference Division was renamed Humanities and Social Sciences and was reorganised to reflect cross-division responsibility for services that had previously been the responsibility of each department. The old British Museum Library departments of Manuscripts and of Oriental Manuscripts and Printed Books were reduced to sub-department level, while the Department of Printed Books was abolished, its responsibilities distributed across the five new departments of Humanities and Social Sciences: Collection Development; Preservation Service; Planning and Administration; Special Collections; and Public Services. The thinking which lay behind these radical changes was the need for greater integration of the Document Supply Centre into the Library and a desire to bring some of the Boston Spa management style and dynamism – which had particularly impressed Kenneth Cooper – into the Library's London operations.

The ongoing strategic planning process also initiated a review of the Library's acquisition and retention policies, carried out by a small team of British Library staff led by Dr Brian Enright, Librarian of the University of Newcastle upon Tyne. The report was published in 1989 as *Selection for survival*, and contained a number of recommendations, both general and specific, to enable the Library to deal with the growth of published material and to maintain the quality of the Library's collections.[18] Not surprisingly, the concept of the national library's treating its collecting responsibilities 'selectively' aroused controversy within both academic circles and the professional library world, but many of the principles recommended came to be accepted in later years.

Also in 1989 came the second strategic plan, *Gateway to knowledge*, some two years earlier than expected.[19] The main reason for the premature appearance of this plan was the Library's altered circumstances, brought about by a reducing

---

17 *Advancing with knowledge: the British Library strategic plan 1985–1990* (London, 1985), 1.
18 B. Enright, L. Hellinga and B. Leigh, *Selection for survival: a review of acquisition and retention policies* (London, 1989).
19 *Gateway to knowledge: the British Library strategic plan, 1989–1994* (London, 1989).

amount of money from Government; *Advancing with knowledge* was written in expectation of level funding for the Library, whereas *Gateway to knowledge* was written against a background of reducing support. In *Gateway to knowledge* the British Library gave a declaration of purpose, the first paragraph of which reads: 'The British Library has to be leader – for the cause of books and for the love of learning, for other libraries and for information services.' It also includes, in red and in capital letters, the Library's first mission statement – 'Our purpose is to advance knowledge' – and goes on to set out the Library's aspirations for the year 2000. As Alan Day remarked in 1994: 'as a cultivated expression of the "vision thing" this could hardly be bettered'.[20]

Throughout Kenneth Cooper's time as Chief Executive, progress on the new building at St Pancras was a source of much concern, both to the Library and to the government. The problems were partly the result of the funding arrangements for the project, which meant that the construction timetable could only be planned year by year. In 1988, in a determined effort to control costs, the government announced an overall cash-limit of £300 million for Phase 1A and plans for a scaled-down building, with phases 1B and 1C combined into a Completion Phase and stages 2 and 3 of the original building abandoned.

The reduction in size of the building meant that the number of reader places planned was reduced from more than 3,000 to just under 1,200, representing only 7% growth on existing provision. Storage facilities too were drastically reduced. The original plans had made provision for storage needs until about the year 2030; by the early 1990s it was expected that the building would be operationally full by the time of its completion in 1996, with low-use material outhoused at Boston Spa. The scaled-down building also meant that it was impossible to house all the Library's existing London activities in the new building, and in 1989 the British Library Board approved a plan to remove all activities that did not have to be carried out in London to Boston Spa. Relocation started in December 1990, and the activities that were ultimately moved north included cataloguing and acquisitions, most IT functions and much of the administration, finance and training.

In March 1991, shortly before his retirement, Kenneth Cooper publicly attacked the cuts of £4.5 million in the Library's grant-in-aid for 1991/2. He called for an additional £6–7 million a year to cover St Pancras's running costs and automation, and warned that if the Library was not given 'a margin of extra resources we shall be in rather serious trouble when we open up operations in the new building'.[21] The following financial year, 1992/3, the British Library

20 A. Day, *The new British Library* (London, 1994), 43.
21 *Focus: the British Library Staff Newsletter* 62 (May 1991).

received an additional £2 million grant-in-aid, described by Brian Lang – who succeeded Kenneth Cooper as Chief Executive on 1 July 1991 – as an 'important boost to our finances'.

Dr Lang very quickly identified his top priority: 'to get St Pancras up and running as a first class library', but a series of technical difficulties were to frustrate him. In July 1991, in his first month in office, problems with the custom-made mobile shelving were identified and the move of books into the new building had to be postponed. Then there were faults with the cabling; these had been spotted as early as 1989, but the nature and scale of the problem only became apparent in November 1993, leading inevitably to further hold-ups. And as delays became longer, costs went up, to the consternation of all.

Not the least of the problems was the public perception that the Library itself was responsible, through incompetence and ineptness, for the escalation of costs and for the delays to the new building, whereas the building project was actually in the hands of the Public Services Agency. In an effort to correct this misunderstanding, and to counter the widely held belief that the whole project was misconceived, Sir Anthony Kenny – Chairman of the British Library Board since 1993 – produced a pamphlet setting out the Library's case cogently and with notable clarity.[22]

In 1994 the National Heritage Committee, chaired by Gerald Kaufman MP, examined the British Library project and in its report famously described the new building as resembling 'a Babylonian ziggurat seen through a fun-fair distorting mirror'.[23] The Committee heard evidence from the British Library and the Department of Culture, Media and Sport, and also from the Regular Readers Group, a pressure group set up in 1990 in response to anxieties over the future of the Library. The Group suggested that the Library should see St Pancras 'as an "outhouse" while holding on to Bloomsbury for its Reading Rooms and substantial storage'; the National Heritage Committee agreed and strongly recommended that the Round Reading Room should be retained in perpetuity. The Government however ignored the recommendations.

In June 1996 the Public Accounts Committee again looked at progress. They found 'a dismal story of incompetence and wasted taxpayers' money', and said that the further delays and the increased costs were 'unacceptable'. In a memorandum to the Committee, dated 15 June 1996, the Regular Readers Group again criticised the management of the project, quoting Keith Waterhouse

---

22 Sir A. Kenny, *The British Library and the St Pancras building* (London, 1994).
23 National Heritage Committee, *Fifth report: the British Library*, House of Commons Paper 550 (London, 1994).

of the *Daily Mail* – 'If a camel is a horse designed by a committee, then the British Library is an edifice that appears to have been planned by a committee of camels' – and restating its belief that storage and reader facilities should be retained at Bloomsbury.[24] As part of the preparations for the move to St Pancras, in July 1995 the Library initiated a restructuring of the organisation, intended to establish a more homogeneous corporate culture, with management appropriate to optimum service delivery and placing greater emphasis on meeting the needs of users in industry, the universities and other libraries. A little over a year later, in August 1996, the Library announced major changes in its senior management, described by Dr Lang as 'a strategy to provide more focussed services from fewer directorates, increasing efficiency and reducing bureaucracy'. The number of directorates was reduced from thirteen to eleven, with plans for a further reduction to nine once the move to St Pancras was complete.

The move to the new building and beyond

The construction problems ultimately delayed the Library's move to its new building for five years. Occupation of the new building eventually started in November 1996, when a small group of staff was based there permanently. A few days later the first books arrived and the biggest book move in history had begun; it continued for many months. Staff were moved into the new building in a phased occupation and the first reading room opened in November 1997. The official opening by Her Majesty the Queen on 25 June 1998 was a hugely important, and successful, occasion and probably the highlight of Brian Lang's term at the British Library.

When the last reading rooms opened in 1999 the building was at last fully operational. The public response to the building was overwhelmingly positive – particularly to the hugely impressive entrance hall. The inspired location of the King's Library in a glass tower dominated the interior and preserved the long tradition that George III's library should be on view to the general public.[25] While critics of the building, and defenders of the Round Reading Room, were not wholly silenced, appreciation of the facilities available to readers and visitors, and of the new services (despite teething troubles), heavily outweighed negative reactions.

24 Committee of Public Accounts, *Second report: progress in completing the new British Library,* House of Commons Paper 38 (London, 1996).
25 For the architect's comments on the symbolic role of the King's Library see Wilson, *Design and construction,* 28–30.

It would be wrong to see Brian Lang's term as Chief Executive solely in terms of the new building. There were major acquisitions of rare books and manuscripts, of which the Tyndale Bible in 1994 and the Sherborne Missal in 1998 are perhaps the most important. Other significant achievements include development of the Library's interactive display software, 'Turning the Pages', which gives visitors the 'virtual' facility to turn the pages of a medieval manuscript, enhancing the already hugely impressive experience of the new exhibitions suite. However, for the whole of his period as Chief Executive, the new building was the Library's main preoccupation, and Dr Lang himself regarded preparation for the opening as his main task: the task was now complete. Dr Lang had always said that he would move on when this had been achieved, and it came as no real surprise when he announced, in the autumn of 1999, that he would retire as Chief Executive in May 2000, with a year of his contract still to run.

On 1 July 2000 Lynne Brindley took over as Chief Executive of the British Library. Mrs Brindley had wide experience in a number of senior management posts in the libraries of major academic institutions, notably at the London School of Economics and at Leeds University, as well as a spell as a senior management consultant with KPMG. However, her appointment was most significant because, unlike her three predecessors, she had trained as a librarian; not only that, she already had extensive knowledge of the British Library itself, having spent the early years of her professional career there in a number of posts, including a spell as head of the Chief Executive's Office during Kenneth Cooper's period of office. She had also worked previously with the then Chairman, John Ashworth, during the early 1990s at LSE, when he was Director and she was Librarian and Director of Information Services there.

In September 2000 Lynne Brindley commissioned Hay Management Consultants to undertake a review of the top structure of the British Library, charged with producing a structure that would:

support the Library's strategic aims;
promote cross-boundary working;
strengthen project management;
enable the Library to be more outward-looking and relate more closely to customers;
focus the top team on strategy.

After implementation of the recommendations put forward by Hay – with a few minor amendments – and the resounding support of the British Library

Board, the new top tier is smaller, with the senior executive body – Exec Team – made up of the Chief Executive and the six directors.

During its short lifetime the Library has made many plans – not all of which have come to fruition – seen many changes and dealt with many challenges, but the need to develop strategies for the future is as great now as it has ever been. It is perhaps fitting that this chapter on the history of the British Library should finish on one of the undoubted high points. In October 2003 the Legal Deposit Libraries Bill – a Private Member's Bill sponsored by Chris Mole MP – received Royal Assent and passed into law, bringing CD-ROMs, electronic journals, websites and other non-book materials within the scope of legal deposit. The Library had campaigned for many years for new legal deposit legislation and in particular for this extension of coverage, to recognise the increasing importance of non-print information in the modern world. The new Act still requires detailed implementation and there will be new challenges as this is worked out, but it will bring the British Library into line with national libraries in many other countries where electronic publications are already covered by legislation.[26] It must be seen as one of the most significant developments in the Library's recent history.

26 P. Hoare, 'Legal deposit of electronic publications and other non-print material: an international overview', *Alexandria* 9 (1997), 59–79.

PART V

*

THE SPIRIT OF ENQUIRY: HIGHER EDUCATION AND LIBRARIES

26

Introduction: Higher education and libraries

PETER HOARE

The development of a modern concept of higher education can, in much of Europe, be traced back to the Enlightenment, and the British Isles are no exception. The foundation of new universities and colleges in the early nineteenth century was a result of the growing awareness of the need to open up the world of the mind (including the natural world in all its manifestations) to a wider audience. The establishment later in the century of the colleges which developed into the civic universities took up the same theme, adding a new element, the practical and technical application of thought. Newer foundations in the twentieth century followed the same path, with refinements being added when expansion was fostered by government first in the 1960s, following the Robbins Report of 1963, then in a much greater degree towards the end of the century.

University and college libraries in this country are integral parts of their institutions (not, as in some countries, a parallel but separate state-supported system). As such, they inevitably reflect the same philosophies, and to a large extent the fortunes, of their parent bodies. While state funding has become a fundamental part of university financing (and so of library budgeting), it was for long felt that they should be left to manage their own affairs without much state interference, and while this has changed drastically in recent years the principle of semi-independence affected the ways libraries were treated in different institutions. The statement of the University Grants Committee that the library was 'the power-house of the university' became a touchstone for librarians and others pressing their claims for resources.

The differences in universities explain the structure of this section of the volume, which separates the pre-Robbins period (covered in the first three chapters) from the later years. The ancient universities in England, Scotland and Ireland, all founded before 1600, had much in common despite differing national traditions, and their centuries of history affected and still affect their libraries' development. Despite the dominance of Oxford and Cambridge – on the world stage as well as in this country – they have all therefore been treated together. The newer foundations have again different characteristics and defining philosophies: the libraries of the University of London, with the advantages of their location in the capital but also with the problems of a federal structure, are dealt with in one chapter; the Civic universities, the means for the spread of higher education throughout the country (especially in the industrial cities of the midlands and the north of England), also led the way in many aspects of library provision and again have their own chapter. With the move towards mass higher education in the 1960s university libraries found themselves more and more facing common problems and the (perhaps) more unified picture is accorded a chapter covering the last forty years of the twentieth century: but this chapter also deals with the new institutions founded in the 1960s, the growth of the polytechnics and their transference to the university sector at the end of the century – and the increasing *dirigisme* from government.

University libraries, along with their purely academic functions, have in many cases sustained intellectual enquiry and information use for a much wider circle than their own members. Their collections are a major part of the national stock; they serve industry and commerce and, in varying degree, the general public – at the same time coping with the tensions of conflicting demands for research-level and student-level provision within their own institutions. They have also been in the forefront of developing innovative methods, from their early espousal of inter-library loans to the introduction of automated library systems and electronic information. Their appearance at the heart of this volume indicates that they are without any doubt at all a crucial element in the national provision of library services: but the routes they have taken are diverse and enlightening in their variety.

27

The libraries of the ancient universities to the 1960s

PETER HOARE

Introduction

By the mid-nineteenth century Oxford and Cambridge had lost their age-old monopoly of higher education in England and Wales, with the founding of universities in London (1826) and Durham (1833), and on a smaller scale at St David's College in Lampeter (1827). Further competition followed with the establishment of the Civic universities later in the century and further expansion of higher education in the twentieth century, but Oxford and Cambridge continued to dominate the library scene as well as the academic world, at least in size and richness, and in popular perception. (Surprisingly, however, they play only a small part in the two most influential library reports at the end of our period: the University Grants Committee's *Report of the Committee on Libraries* (1967) (the Parry Report), and the *Report of the National Libraries Committee* (1969) (the Dainton Report).)

The existence of a number of other universities in Scotland and Ireland, dating from the fifteenth and sixteenth centuries, must not be overlooked, since they share some characteristics of their English counterparts, including the impact of new foundations. The four (or five) ancient Scottish universities at St Andrews (founded 1411), Glasgow (1451), Aberdeen (1495/1593)[1] and Edinburgh (1584) came to face competition, though rarely in library terms, from professional colleges and younger institutions such as Anderson's Institution in Glasgow (1796). In Ireland Trinity College Dublin was established as a Protestant bulwark by Queen Elizabeth I in 1599; the non-denominational Queen's Colleges founded in 1845 and the Catholic University of Ireland of 1854 had developed by the early twentieth century into the federal National University of Ireland and the independent Queen's University in Belfast. All

---

1 The two universities of King's College (founded 1495) and Marischal College (1593) remained separate institutions until their 'fusion' into the present University of Aberdeen in 1860.

these drew their students very largely from Ireland, whereas Trinity College Dublin continued also to attract students from England and Scotland.

As with Oxford and Cambridge in England, it was the older university libraries that played by far the major role in scholarly library provision in Scotland and Ireland until well into the twentieth century, and they remain among the largest libraries in the British Isles. Many of the ancient universities, and the major libraries in them, have been the subject of comprehensive historical studies, usually based on archival sources (the best of these place the library firmly within the academic context of its institution), and the present chapter does not attempt to repeat or summarise those histories.[2] Rather, the growth and the various activities of the libraries are here considered alongside similar developments in the other ancient institutions and their libraries.

There is some logic in treating all these pre-seventeenth-century foundations together, even in the modern period. They never formed a coherent group as did the 'Civic' universities of the late nineteenth century or the new universities of the 1960s, but they had much in common, not least a perception of their own individual importance. By the mid-nineteenth century all their libraries had substantial collections, which formed in some ways a dispersed complement to the British Museum's developing role as a national library; this is a position which in many ways they still hold, certainly in respect of their historic collections.

Most of the universities had, as well as a pre-eminent university library, a host of other libraries which made up the total provision within the university, though this was often uncoordinated. At Oxford and Cambridge (and historically at St Andrews) the college libraries were an important element;

2 For Oxford: *The history of the University of Oxford*, vols. 6–7, ed. M. G. Brock and M. C. Curthoys (Oxford, 1997), on the nineteenth century, and vol. 8, ed. B. Harrison (Oxford, 1994), on the twentieth century; Sir E. Craster, *History of the Bodleian Library 1845–1945* (Oxford, 1952).

For Cambridge: *A history of the University of Cambridge*, vol. 3, *1750–1870*, by P. Searby (Cambridge, 1997), and vol. 4, *1870–1990*, by C. N. L. Brooke (Cambridge, 1993); D. McKitterick, *Cambridge University Library: a history*, vol. 2 (Cambridge, 1986), on the eighteenth and nineteenth centuries; P. Fox (ed.), *Cambridge University Library: the great collections* (Cambridge, 1998).

For Scotland: J. R. Pickard, *A history of King's College Library, Aberdeen*, 3 vols. (Aberdeen, 1987); J. R. Guild and A. Law (eds.), *Edinburgh University Library 1580–1980* (Edinburgh, 1982); A. L. Brown and M. Moss, *The University of Glasgow 1451–1996* (Edinburgh, 1996); R. G. Cant, *The University of St Andrews: a short history*, 3rd edn (St Andrews, 1992).

For Dublin: R. B. McDowell and D. A. Webb, *Trinity College Dublin 1592–1952: an academic history* (Cambridge, 1982); P. Fox (ed.), *Treasures of the library, Trinity College Dublin* (Dublin, 1986); V. Kinane and A. Walsh (eds), *Essays on the history of Trinity College Library, Dublin* (Dublin, 2000).

Articles on the libraries of all the ancient universities except Aberdeen appear in D. H. Stam (ed.), *International dictionary of library histories*, 2 vols. (Chicago and London, 2001).

at Edinburgh and Glasgow, as at Oxford and Cambridge, a large number of libraries for faculty or class use existed almost independently of the university library. Many of these smaller libraries have not been studied in their historical context, though there are a number of important exceptions.[3] The libraries of museums such as the Ashmolean at Oxford and the Fitzwilliam at Cambridge (both libraries essentially nineteenth-century creations) also play an important part in each university's total provision in their specialised fields; the Fitzwilliam's riches in medieval and later manuscripts, for example, make it of national importance.

All the universities faced somewhat similar problems in accommodating old practices to a new world of higher education from the time of the nineteenth-century reforms and the social upheavals of the twentieth century, which in turn affected their library policies. Royal Commissions examined all the old universities from the 1840s onwards and their reports contributed to reform of the ancient institutions – notably of their finances (an essential factor in library development) but also of their administration and educational practices. All of them, as major repositories of knowledge, played their part in the growth of scholarship, especially but by no means solely in the humanities, and they played a major role in the convergence of the history of libraries and of scholarship.[4] Such vast projects as the *Oxford English Dictionary* and the great series of *Cambridge Histories* initiated by Lord Acton would have been much more difficult to achieve without the resources represented in these ancient libraries, and it is significant that even today many such projects are associated with the universities with the richest collections.

The differences between these universities, however, are as significant as their similarities; even Oxford and Cambridge have distinct characteristics. Perhaps the most notable example of differing working patterns relates to access to the shelves and borrowing: Cambridge has given readers a generous measure of access to the collections, and also allows senior members to borrow. This has been suggested (by a Cambridge historian) as a major element in

3 B. C. Bloomfield (ed.), *A directory of rare book and special collections in the United Kingdom and the Republic of Ireland*, 2nd edn (London, 1997) gives useful historical information about many such libraries in all the ancient universities. G. Barber, *Arks for learning: a short history of Oxford library buildings* (Oxford, 1995) includes a number of smaller libraries; for fuller coverage see P. Morgan, *Oxford libraries outside the Bodleian: a guide*, 2nd edn (Oxford, 1980). A. N. L. Munby, *Cambridge college libraries: aids for research students*, 2nd edn (Cambridge, 1962) is valuable but does not deal with departmental and other non-college libraries. The 'very large number' of such libraries at Edinburgh are described in M. D. Bell, 'Faculty and class libraries', in Guild and Law (eds.), *Edinburgh University Library*, 163–81.

4 I. R. Willison, *On the history of libraries and scholarship* (Washington DC, 1980). Cf. also B. C. Bloomfield's chapter 38, below.

Cambridge's having been 'the best research library in Europe' and one which 'fundamentally altered the place of Cambridge in the arts'.[5] The Bodleian, on the other hand, follows the more common pattern for research libraries of ensuring that all its books remain in the library and are not borrowed. The practice was examined by the 1852 Royal Commission, when strong arguments were adduced for and against the practice of lending books: 'Such a promiscuous and extensive liberty . . . would upon the whole, I think, tend to defeat the great objects of such an institution'[6] – though the same professorial witness considered that it would be safe to lend books to professors. In the following decades there was some relaxation: an ambiguous statute of 1873 'empowered the Curators to borrow, not to lend', but the principle was decisively rejected in 1887.[7]

While the Scottish university libraries have much in common with each other (notably their greater *local* significance) they are also individual institutions with their own peculiarities; their part in the development of modern librarianship and higher education is perhaps closer to that of the English civic universities. (This was prefigured in James Lorimer's Association for the Expansion of Scottish Universities founded in 1853.[8]) Trinity College Dublin, which in library terms is often rightly aligned with Oxford and Cambridge, is coloured by its Irish dimension but has close parallels with Britain.

Royal Commissions and university organisation

The investigations and recommendations of the various Royal Commissions into the universities, which were such a feature of the nineteenth-century educational world, are among the earlier manifestations of government concern for libraries in the British Isles. Their reports, and the accompanying minutes of evidence, give remarkable detail of the state of libraries at the time, and of the concerns of their users and other members of the university concerned. The first, the 1831 enquiry into the Scottish universities,[9] was followed by the Scottish Universities Act of 1858, then by further enquiries into progress and

5 C. Brooke, 'The University Library and its buildings', in Fox (ed.), *Cambridge University Library: the great collections*, 215.
6 Oxford University Commission, *Report* (London, 1852), 117–18.
7 Craster, *History of the Bodleian*, 80–2.
8 R. Anderson, 'Ideas of the university in 19th century Scotland: teaching versus research?', in M. Hewitt (ed.), *Scholarship in Victorian Britain* (Leeds, 1998), 1–26.
9 *Report by a Royal Commission of Inquiry into the state of the universities of Scotland* (London, 1831).

another Royal Commission in 1876.[10] Meanwhile the other three universities had also been studied in detail in 1849–52,[11] and further reports were made in later years.

That the Commissions' recommendations were, everywhere, never fully implemented is not surprising in the light of the independence and strong-mindedness of the academic community at large – though this very independence was one of the reasons for their establishment. A motion presented in Parliament on 23 April 1850 noted *inter alia* that 'better laws are needed . . . to diminish the exclusivity of the university libraries' and called for a Royal Commission on Oxford, Cambridge and Dublin 'with a view to assist in the adaptation of those important institutions to the requirements of modern times'.[12]

The Royal Commissions also sought to regulate the universities' financial affairs, particularly in respect of government funding. Early reports give detailed breakdowns of income (including endowments, rental income, etc.) for each university or college, and in more or less detail explore expenditure patterns. The 1922 Commission on Oxford and Cambridge Universities clarified the level of government support for the libraries of these universities, with the recommendation of annual grants of £10,000 to the Bodleian and to the University Library at Cambridge, in addition to the recurrent grant to the university itself.[13] From 1923/4 the University Grants Committee included Oxford and Cambridge in its annual statistics, though the state subvention was for many years seen only as a supplement to those universities' endowment income (particularly that of the colleges, which were also called on to support – sometimes reluctantly – central functions in teaching and research). Library funding remained a matter for the university itself, with little or no earmarked government funds. For the Scottish universities a small annual grant had been paid by the Crown for 200 years until it was transferred to a parliamentary vote in 1832; from 1889 they were brought into the national system of support later administered by the University Grants Committee, but at an

---

10 *Report of the Royal Commissioners appointed to inquire into the universities of Scotland*, 4 vols. (London, 1878) (Command paper C. 1935).

11 Royal Commission to enquire into the state, discipline, studies and revenue of the University and Colleges of Oxford, *Report* and *Minutes of Evidence* (London, 1852) (Command paper 1482), and similar reports for Cambridge (Command paper 1559) and for 'the University of Dublin and of Trinity College' (Command paper 1637). Cited as: *Oxford University Commission, Cambridge University Commission, Dublin University Commission*.

12 E. Leedham-Green, *A concise history of the University of Cambridge* (Cambridge, 1996), 152.

13 *Royal Commission on Oxford and Cambridge Universities* (1922), 250 (par. 159). Cf. Craster, *History of the Bodleian*, 261.

institutional level, again without any earmarking of the library as a separate entity.[14]

Reforms in the wake of the Royal Commissions of 1849–52, at both Oxford and Cambridge (as after the Scottish Universities Act of 1858), encouraged expansion in the range of disciplines; for example the Cambridge Commission of 1852 recommended new faculties for Modern Languages, Law, Engineering and Theology, and also proposed degrees in Natural Sciences and Moral Sciences.[15] This in turn opened the door to the provision of library services in new subject areas. Specialist libraries came into existence to serve such areas, going beyond the services provided by the central university library and the colleges. In Oxford the Radcliffe (Science) Library had already begun to establish itself as the university's major collection in the natural sciences in the early nineteenth century; its model was followed by the Taylor Institution for modern languages opened in 1847.[16] Similar central provision was made at Cambridge: in 1881 the University Library took an interest in the Philosophical Society's library (founded 1819), which later became the Scientific Periodicals Library, rather as the Haddon Library of anthropology and archaeology, established as such only in 1936, incorporated the collections of the Cambridge Antiquarian Society, presented to the university in 1883.[17] Provision for medicine and law is dealt with in later chapters of this volume, but other faculties and departments also built up important collections outside the university libraries. This is also true of the other ancient universities, though usually with a greater degree of central management. An example of this can be found in two music libraries, the Reid at Edinburgh, begun about 1850 as a class library and since 1947 part of the University Library, and the Pendlebury at Cambridge, which is still run by the Faculty of Music though in liaison with the University Library.

In Oxford and Cambridge the relationship of all these other libraries, and of the expanding provision in colleges, to the university libraries has perhaps not yet been fully resolved, despite major developments towards the end of the twentieth century. An early proposal for a 'university library system' at Oxford was put forward to the international conference of librarians in London in 1877 by C. H. Robarts, librarian of All Souls: he suggested that his own college's

14 C. H. Shinn, *Paying the piper: the development of the University Grants Committee 1919–1946* (Lewes, 1986), 22–3.
15 *History of the University of Cambridge*, vol. 2, 507–44.
16 H. C. Harley, 'The Radcliffe Science Library', and G. Barber, 'The Taylor Institution', in *History of the University of Oxford*, vol. 6, 692–3 and 631–40.
17 J. D. Pickles, 'The Haddon Library, Cambridge', *Library History* 8 (1988), 1–9.

buildings should largely be turned over to the Bodleian, with a great widening of access, but his 'grandiose scheme' found no favour with the University.[18] Five years later, in his presidential address to the Library Association's 1882 annual meeting at Cambridge, the University Librarian Henry Bradshaw could say:

> I look upon the small library attached by gift to the Divinity School and now preserved there, the old library of the Modern History School and the more recent Political Economy collections of Professor Pryme, together with the equally special libraries of the Antiquarian and Philological Societies . . . as capable, one and all, of a wide development for the use of special students, after the model of the recently organised Philosophical Library . . . a scientific library thrown open to all who are engaged in those branches of study which display to the utmost the vitality of Cambridge work. Only let the others be worked on the same principle and in the same spirit, with the University Library as a centre and feeder of the rest.[19]

Some at least of Bradshaw's hopes bore fruit, as noted above; his explicit vision is noteworthy, though in other respects his antiquarian view of a great library was outdated. According to his biographer he regarded it 'in the light of a museum of literary and typographical records quite as much as, perhaps even more than, that of a collection of practically useful books'.[20]

The 1931 report on *Library provision in Oxford* (following the Royal Commissions of 1852, 1877 and 1922) examined the Ashmolean and Taylorian libraries (as centrally funded institutions) in considering the need for expansion of the Bodleian, and also recommended bringing together the English, Modern History and Philosophy libraries in new accommodation with links to the Bodleian; but the role of the college libraries was not addressed in any detail.[21] Similar reports appeared in all the universities through the twentieth century, with greater or lesser impact, until the opportunities for co-ordination presented by electronic systems allowed a much more realistic approach at the end of the century.

18 Craster, *History of the Bodleian*, 50 and 250–1.
19 H. Bradshaw, 'Address at the opening of the fifth annual meeting of the Library Association', in his *Collected papers* (Cambridge, 1889), 371–409; reprinted in part in J. L. Thornton (ed.), *Selected readings in the history of librarianship* (London, 1966), 128–39. Cf. also McKitterick, *Cambridge University Library*, 754–5.
20 G. W. Prothero, *A memoir of Henry Bradshaw, Fellow of King's College, Cambridge, and University Librarian* (London, 1888), 374.
21 *Library provision in Oxford*. Report and recommendations of the commission appointed by the Congregation of the University (Oxford, 1931).

The collections: acquisitions and catalogues

Size is not the only criterion for judging a library, but the extent of its collections is undoubtedly a major factor in the ability of a university library to fulfil its purpose. In the case of the ancient universities these collections go back through the centuries, and are continually upgraded by new acquisitions, whether by purchase, donation or bequests, or for the favoured few by legal deposit.

Sir Edmund Craster refers to 'that first duty of all libraries, the increase of its resources by buying in the book market' (this was in respect of the failure of his forerunner E. W. B. Nicholson to increase purchasing for the Bodleian in the 1880s).[22] And in its annual report for 1923/4 the University Grants Committee (writing of course of *all* universities not only the ancient ones, though these were included in UGC statistics for the first time that year) referred to 'the obligation of building up and maintaining a really good and comprehensive collection of books and periodicals' from which not even the poorest institution could be absolved.[23]

Book purchasing, either through local suppliers or using specialist book-sellers in London or other centres, needs no special comment. Books were selected variously on the recommendation of academic staff (whose word ran most strongly in departmental collections and college libraries) or by library staff using published reviews and bibliographies to supplement personal knowledge of particular fields – or sometimes by booksellers with special expertise such as Bernard Quaritch, who was a regular partner in the development of collections at Cambridge from 1870 to the end of the century.[24] Henry Stevens of Vermont, an American antiquarian bookseller active in London in the later nineteenth century, is known particularly for his purchases for the British Museum and for his American clients.[25] He was also used heavily by Oxford and Cambridge both to strengthen their collections of American books and of early printing (Stevens's speciality) and to dispose of duplicates or other unwanted material to mutual profit – a practice which would now perhaps be considered more controversial than it was then.[26]

In the case of the legal deposit libraries, purchasing of current literature was most significantly of foreign publications not received under the Copyright

22 Craster, *History of the Bodleian*, 163.
23 University Grants Committee, *Report including returns from universities and university colleges in receipt of Treasury grant, academic year 1923–1924* (London, 1925), 22.
24 McKitterick, *Cambridge University Library*, 667ff.
25 W. W. Parker, *Henry Stevens of Vermont, American rare book dealer in London, 1845–1886* (Amsterdam, 1963).
26 McKitterick, *Cambridge University Library*, 635–47.

Act (including American publications not also published in Britain), but they were also able to survey their collections and fill historic gaps. All libraries are liable to such shortcomings, deriving from past underfunding or missed opportunities; and the challenge to make one's library fully representative (if not wholly comprehensive) faced all libraries alike, not only those benefiting from legal deposit – though for them the urge towards universality was that much stronger.

Many of the ancient universities benefited from the deposit or gift of institutional libraries *en bloc*. Some of these, such as the many parochial libraries deposited at Oxford and Cambridge (in both the university libraries and in colleges), are now largely of historical interest.[27] The 'Bibliotheck' of 300 volumes bequeathed by William Baikie in 1683 'to the ministers of Kirkwall successivelie for a Publick Liberarie' (one of the first in the British Isles) moved from Orkney to Aberdeen as a gift from the town in 1914, no doubt reflecting the greater accessibility of such a historic collection within a university library.[28] Elsewhere in Scotland the close connection with the Presbyterian churches has remained a feature. New College Edinburgh (founded 1843 after the Disruption which established the Free Church of Scotland, and with a handsome building of 1850) was transferred to Edinburgh University in 1962, where it now forms a divisional library for Divinity with both historic and current material. Similarly Glasgow acquired the rich library of Trinity College Glasgow on deposit in 1974; like New College, this Free Church college, dating from 1855, incorporated remarkable riches from other institutions and private collectors, now given new life in a wider context. Such 'institutional' acquisitions continue today, indicating perhaps a new dimension in the relationship of university libraries to the wider world.

In fact the libraries of all the universities had from their earliest days relied heavily on donations (usually of books and manuscripts but also including a wide variety of artefacts), many of them discussed in earlier volumes. In the modern period this continued, though the contribution of gifts was with some exceptions less fundamental to a library's total strength. The celebratory volumes on Dublin's and Cambridge's great collections,[29] from the earliest donations to the most recent and encompassing manuscripts and archives (even

---

27 M. Perkin, *A directory of the parochial libraries of the Church of England and the Church in Wales*, revised edn (London, 2004), *passim*.

28 J. B. Craven, *Descriptive catalogue of the Bibliotheck of Kirkwall* (Kirkwall, 1897; see also P. Kaufman, 'Discovering the oldest public bibliotheck in the Northern Isles', *Library Review* 23 (1972), 285–7.

29 P. Fox (ed.), *Treasures of the library: Trinity College Dublin* (Dublin, 1986); Fox (ed.), *Cambridge University Library: the great collections*.

Chinese oracle bones and papyrus fragments) as well as printed books, make it clear how these gifts enriched – and continue to enrich – even an already well-provided library. In 1969 Oxford mounted an exhibition in the United States which then continued in Oxford, demonstrating the importance of its friends and their gifts.[30] Similarly, though more modestly, Glasgow celebrated the quincentenary of the first recorded gift of books to the university in 1476 with an exhibition which again illustrated the range of material acquired by this route.[31]

Among the largest single collections of printed books to be added to any of our libraries was Lord Acton's phenomenal library of 70,000 volumes, acquired by Cambridge University Library in 1903.[32] It has been noted that Acton 'left behind him a tradition of awareness of the work of contemporary continental historians and a library of largely continental books to supply what would otherwise have been a woeful deficit in the holdings of the University Library'.[33] None the less the collection presented a real challenge: its riches were partly duplicated elsewhere in the Library and proper accommodation was impossible to find until the opening of the new University Library in 1934. In that respect the Acton Library is a typical example (but writ large) of the way in which donations can be mixed blessings for the recipients.

Even the best-known libraries may not be donors' first choices, and some collections came by circuitous routes, like the parochial libraries already referred to. The Dugald Stewart collection, containing much of the libraries of two eighteenth-century Edinburgh professors as well as more modern works, was left in 1852 to the United Services Club in London but was transferred to a more logical resting place in Edinburgh University Library in 1910. William Euing left his collections of Bibles and early printing to Glasgow University Library,[34] but his rich musical library was 'bequeathed to Anderson's University, Glasgow (now called Anderson's College)' in 1874.[35] It was transferred to Glasgow University, along with a large number of bound copies of the idiosyncratic 1878 catalogue, in 1936. The 4,000 volumes of George Hay Forbes's theological library were held by the Episcopal Church in Edinburgh from his death in 1875

---

30 The Bodleian Library and its friends: catalogue of an exhibition held 1969–1970, 2nd issue (Oxford, 1970).
31 Glasgow University Library, 500 years of donations (Glasgow, 1976).
32 O. Chadwick, 'The Acton Library', in Fox (ed.), Cambridge University Library: the great collections, 136–52.
33 Leedham-Green, Concise history, 197.
34 J. Lymburn, 'Notice of the Euing collection of Bibles', in W. P. Dickson, The Glasgow University Library: notes on its history, arrangements, and aims (Glasgow, 1888), 72–87.
35 The Euing Musical Library: catalogue of the musical library of the late Wm. Euing, Esq. (Glasgow, 1878).

until they were deposited at St Andrews in 1969. John Johnson's great collection of printed ephemera, established at Oxford University Press while Johnson was Printer, came to the Bodleian from the Press only in 1968, after many years when it was not considered appropriate material for a research library.[36] Even Lord Acton's library reached Cambridge after having been through the hands of Andrew Carnegie (who had bought it to save it from dispersal) and John Morley.[37]

Donations are by their very nature usually arbitrary and however welcome cannot be counted on to develop the basic stock of a library. Throughout our period and beyond, current purchasing has represented a large part of every library's budget (staff costs being relatively low), even for those with legal deposit. Periodical publications came to take an ever-higher proportion of the budget, despite the opportunities for exchange negotiated by institutions with scholarly publications, and the struggle to maintain collections at appropriate levels (not least through two World Wars) affected all libraries, however well endowed.

The pattern of catalogues to provide access to the collections had been similar in most institutions for many years, with printed catalogues the norm. Marked-up copies of the Bodleian's printed catalogue, one of the most comprehensive bibliographical records in existence, had long been used by others as a substitute for a library's own catalogue. Trinity College Dublin used the 1843 Bodleian catalogue in this way until its own catalogue appeared in 1872; at All Souls College an interleaved Bodleian catalogue remained the college's sole means of access from 1844–5 until a card catalogue was introduced nearly a century later.[38]

From the mid-nineteenth century the guard-book or page catalogue became a common form, with pasted-in slips adjusted from time to time to accommodate new entries in the right place. This was laborious but adequate for relatively low levels of use in a single location. It continued to be a familiar tool in the older university libraries until late in the twentieth century, though card catalogues were often used alongside the guard-book and were also seen in less traditional libraries. G. H. Bushnell, Librarian at St Andrews and noted for his unusually broad professional views, characteristically referred in 1930 to the 'terrific onslaught of the card catalogue'.[39] He remarked that scholars found the 'page form' of the guard-book more convenient than cards – just

36 *The John Johnson Collection: catalogue of an exhibition* (Oxford, 1971).
37 Chadwick, 'The Acton Library', 136.
38 Sir E. Craster, *The history of All Souls College Library*, ed. by E. F. Jacob (London, 1971), 93.
39 G. H. Bushnell, *University librarianship* (London, 1930), 58.

as later scholars lamented the replacement of their familiar card catalogues by the arrival of microfiche in the 1970s and online catalogues in the 1990s. These developments also led to the final demise of guard-books. At Trinity College Dublin the guard-book based on the 1872 printed catalogue remained in use for many years, alongside card catalogues and supplementary printed lists, until in 1972, under Peter Brown, Librarian 1970–84 but formerly Keeper of Catalogues at the Bodleian, Dublin introduced the first computer-produced catalogue of any major library in the British Isles.[40] Glasgow and Cambridge, like many libraries elsewhere, followed suit and abandoned their guard-books in the 1980s and 1990s, the delay being largely due to the formidable problems of converting catalogue records for large collections going back over the centuries.

Attempts to create union catalogues, to cover all libraries in one university, were mooted everywhere from time to time but proved largely impracticable until the application of computer technology. (There were exceptions such as catalogues of special categories of material, like H. M. Adams's magisterial catalogue of sixteenth-century continental printing.[41]) The reasons were not always simply technological: in 1935 the Court of Edinburgh University rejected – on grounds of principle – a proposal from students that details of all departmental libraries should be included in the Main Library catalogue.[42] At Oxford, the Radcliffe Science Library, while part of the Bodleian, had a slip catalogue (later typed cards), complicating still further the multiplicity of catalogues having to be consulted for a comprehensive view.

Catalogues of manuscripts were no less important, and remain of continuing significance (perhaps more so than catalogues of printed books since they deal, usually in great detail, with unique items). In the ancient universities, libraries small and large published catalogues of their medieval and later manuscripts, which have facilitated innumerable scholarly enterprises. Cambridge University Library took the lead in issuing a four-volume catalogue of its own western manuscripts in 1856–67, extended half a century later by the great series by M. R. James, encompassing thirteen Cambridge college libraries as well as the Fitzwilliam Museum. (James's efforts also extended to Aberdeen University Library, Eton College, Lambeth Palace and the John Rylands Library.) At Oxford, H. O. Coxe had begun the series of Quarto catalogues later continued by W. D. Macray; but slow progress led to a decision in 1890 that a summary

40 Fox (ed.) *Treasures of the library*, viii.
41 H. M. Adams, *Catalogue of books printed on the continent of Europe, 1501–1600 in Cambridge libraries*, 2 vols. (Cambridge, 1967).
42 Guild and Law (eds.), *Edinburgh University Library*, 112.

catalogue should be prepared. Falconer Madan's work led to the publication of this comprehensive listing covering western manuscripts acquired up to 1915.[43] The manuscripts of Trinity College Dublin were described in T. K. Abbott's catalogue of 1900, based in part on J. H. Todd's work on the Library's incomparable Irish manuscripts.[44] Special materials elsewhere also called for expert treatment, as with Adolf Neubauer's work in 1868–86 on the Hebrew manuscripts at Oxford,[45] or the many Cambridge scholars who worked to catalogue such diverse collections as the Cairo Genizah or the papers of Charles Darwin.[46]

Legal deposit

The privilege of legal deposit produces great benefits but also some of the same dilemmas as donations for those libraries entitled to it. New publications rapidly fill the shelves and necessitate additional accommodation; the very principle has been used as an argument for unrestricted public access; and the quality of publications received under comprehensive legislation can vary widely, from the most valuable and expensive material to 'trash' (which may still have historical importance in years to come).

From a wider perspective, however, there is real value in a spread of libraries acting as effective extensions of the national library, helping to preserve and record the output of the nation's presses.[47] In the words of a memorandum from Trinity College Dublin in 1911, copyright privilege ensures that there is 'a comprehensive collection, representing the actual facts of publication rather than the judgement of individual librarians or committees'.[48] The shelves of twentieth-century novels still in their dust-jackets, preserved almost uniquely

43 F. Madan and others, *A summary catalogue of western manuscripts in the Bodleian Library at Oxford*, 7 vols. in 8 (Oxford, 1895–1953). Vol. 1 (1953) includes a historical introduction by R. W. Hunt.

44 G. O. Simms, 'Early Christian manuscripts' and G. Mac Niocaill, 'The Irish-language manuscripts', in Fox (ed.), *Treasures of the library*, 38–56 and 57–66. This book also includes chapters on other groups of manuscripts and their catalogues.

45 R. S. Kohn, 'A treasured legacy: Hebrew manuscripts at the Bodleiana', *Library History* 20 (2004), 95–116.

46 S. C. Reif, 'The Genizah fragments: a unique archive?' and Frederick Burkhardt, 'The Darwin papers', in Fox (ed.), *Cambridge University Library: the great collections*, 55–64 and 118–35.

47 I. Willison, 'Legal deposit: a provisional perspective', *Publishing History* 45 (1999), 5–34. The standard work is R. C. B. Partridge, *The history of the legal deposit of books throughout the British Empire* (London, 1938).

48 Quoted in V. Kinane, 'Legal deposit, 1801–1922', in Kinane and Walsh (eds.), *Essays*, 120–37 (citation p. 120).

at Cambridge, are a further reminder of the remarkable value of these legal deposit collections.[49]

Three university libraries, Oxford, Cambridge and Dublin, as well as the Advocates' Library in Edinburgh, had retained 'copyright deposit' under the Copyright Act of 1836. The act had removed the privilege from the Scottish universities and from King's Inns in Dublin, though they were compensated with fixed grants calculated from an estimate of their copyright intake. This loss was not an unmitigated disaster for the Scottish universities, initially at least, since the grants were earmarked for acquisitions and a wider range of material could be acquired, including continental printing for which little money had been available in earlier years.[50] On the other hand in 1878-9 Oxford argued strongly against any change, in the face of proposals from the Copyright Commission that it should receive a grant of £1,200 in exchange, making the point that 'the preservation of a single copy in London was insufficient protection against loss' (a precaution borne out by the British Museum's losses in 1940-1).[51] Cambridge too rejected the Commission's suggestion that the Library could well afford to lose the privilege: 'the University Library has by virtue of this right a catholicity of character which it would not possess were the choice of books governed merely by considerations of a practical utility'.[52] These appeals were successful in averting the threat, and no new Copyright Act was forthcoming for another thirty-two years.

Antonio Panizzi had tightened up very considerably the British Museum's claims on publishers to send in their entire production in the 1830s and 1840s, but resistance to the demands of the other copyright libraries continued through successive Copyright Acts of 1842 and 1911.[53] Unlike the British Museum the other copyright libraries had to request the books they wished to receive, and the practice of using a London agent became the normal method of ensuring compliance, though provincial publications were more difficult to track down. Problems with their incompetent agent at the Stationers' Company, Joseph Greenhill, meant that the university libraries were dissatisfied with the

---

49 Fox (ed.), *Cambridge University Library: the great collections*, plates 118–19.
50 C. M. Miller, 'The effect of the loss of copyright privilege on Glasgow University library, 1790–1858', *Library History* 7 (2) (1985), 45–57. Glasgow had the largest grant, of £707, which continued at the same cash level well into the twentieth century.
51 Craster, *History of the Bodleian*, 63–4; P. R. Harris, *A history of the British Museum Library 1753–1973* (London, 1998), 554–8.
52 McKitterick, *Cambridge University Library*, 752.
53 V. Kinane, 'Legal deposit, 1801–1922' gives a good summary of the situation, not restricted to an Irish perspective.

acquisition process and faced even greater obstruction from publishers.[54] The threats of the Royal Commission in 1878 gave impetus to reforms, and, with the active encouragement of university librarians like Nicholson of the Bodleian, agents after Greenhill's retirement in 1883 streamlined procedures and greatly improved the libraries' acquisitions by this route. So successful were Nicholson's efforts that in 1895 the Bodleian Curators, alarmed by the flood of new books, actually sought 'to diminish the quantity of books received under the Copyright Act' and approached other libraries for support in this cause.[55]

Fortunately the other copyright libraries failed to agree, and when threats were renewed in 1910, in the bill which led to the Copyright Act of 1911, they combined their efforts under the energetic leadership of Francis Jenkinson of Cambridge. They were successful in resisting further proposals to remove the privilege from all libraries except the British Museum, and in the 1911 Act the newly founded National Library of Wales was added with no reduction elsewhere. Trinity College Dublin faced additional danger since Ireland too now had a National Library which might have claimed copyright status, but it was able to argue successfully for the retention of the *status quo* and the National Library of Ireland had to await the 1927 Industrial and Commercial Property (Protection) Act of the Irish Free State. Remarkably, the establishment of the Free State in 1922 (and of the Irish Republic in 1945) did not remove the British copyright privilege from Trinity, thanks to a 'firm ruling' from the Colonial Office.[56] It is now almost unique in benefiting from legal deposit under foreign legislation as well as under later Irish Acts. There was however in 1941 a threat to remove Trinity's privilege in respect of Irish publications, owing to the 'disorganized state' of the Library under the long-serving but inefficient J. G. Smyly (librarian 1914–48).[57] Trinity also faced special difficulties in coping with restrictive censorship laws in the new state, strongly influenced by the Roman Catholic hierarchy: a great many legal deposit books from Britain had to remain locked away and inaccessible until more liberal attitudes prevailed late in the century.

The receipt of legal deposit material continued through the twentieth century with no new legislation; even the radical Copyright, Designs and Patents

---

54 S. Eliot, '"Mr Greenhill, whom you cannot get rid of": copyright, legal deposit and the Stationers' Company in the nineteenth century', in R. Myers, M. Harris and G. Mandelbrote (eds.), *Libraries and the book trade: the formation of collections from the sixteenth to the twentieth century* (New Castle, DE, 2000), 51–84.

55 Craster, *History of the Bodleian*, 173–4.

56 K. C. Bailey, *A history of Trinity College Dublin 1892–1945* (Dublin, 1947), 166.

57 P. Fox, 'The librarians of Trinity College', in Kinane and Walsh (eds.), *Essays*, 11–24 (specifically p. 13).

Act of 1988 made no changes to legal deposit. Attacks from the publishing trade continued but successive agents for the copyright libraries (now acting for the National Libraries of Scotland and Wales as well as the three universities) showed increasing efficiency in collecting material. However, much locally published material and the output of small presses failed to reach the agents, and could not easily be monitored by the libraries themselves. In any case legislation covered only printed material, and as alternative formats – not least electronic media – increased in importance through the century it became clear that a distributed national archive of all published material was imperfect in concept and difficult to achieve.[58] Proposals for expansion of coverage, at least for some electronic publications, have been made in the early years of the twenty-first century but seem likely to benefit the British Library rather than the three universities. How far this will fundamentally change the nature of the collections of the ancient university libraries it is too soon to say.

The personal touch

Impulses towards modernisation in the later nineteenth century came from many librarians and curators. It was normal for such officers to have a strong academic background, sometimes even to hold a professorial chair as well as a library position, and the senior staff of a university's library would normally be dominated by its own graduates well into the next century. (Very occasionally there were exceptions, as when H. R. Creswick moved from the post of Bodley's Librarian to Cambridge in 1949.) The same was even more true of Oxbridge college libraries, where the Fellow Librarian would be first and foremost a senior academic member of the governing body, though many such achieved much in their libraries with or without the aid of professional staff.[59] At Trinity College Dublin the tradition of a Fellow Librarian, with a professional Deputy, continued until 1965, since when all its Librarians have had professional experience elsewhere.[60]

Major names among nineteenth-century librarians, such as J. E. B. Mayor and Henry Bradshaw[61] at Cambridge, Henry Octavius Coxe and

---

58 Willison, 'Legal deposit', 20–1.
59 An example of a sequence of strong librarians (Sir William Anson, Sir Charles Oman, Sir Edmund Craster), albeit in an atypical college, is given in E. F. Jacobs's chapter on the nineteenth century and after, in Craster, *History of All Souls College library*, 92–101.
60 Fox, 'Librarians of Trinity College'.
61 McKitterick, *Cambridge University Library*, 62–57 on Mayor, 658–764 on Bradshaw (cf. also Prothero, *Memoir*).

E. W. B. Nicholson[62] at Oxford, and James Henthorn Todd[63] at Trinity College Dublin all helped to establish their libraries as major players within the university and on the national stage. Relationships with university committees could be difficult, and the continual angling for advantage could affect outcomes and even personal health; but the influence of the librarian could often be crucial in carrying things forward (as negotiations for new buildings in the twentieth century would often prove). In the case of college libraries and in most specialised institutes relationships were, on the whole, less formalised and less prone to personality clashes; but perhaps less was at stake.

It is however clear that in Scotland at least some librarians appointed a century ago were not viewed as fully senior members of the university. At Glasgow and Edinburgh a senior professor was appointed Curator with explicit responsibility for the library, effectively overseeing the Librarian. In fact both William Purdie Dickson at Glasgow (1866–1901) and Julius Eggeling at Edinburgh (1900–13) contributed significantly to their libraries' development – even though the post of university librarian was for a while suspended in Edinburgh (1900–5) and Glasgow (1915–25).[64]

Individual librarians made their mark in different ways. Some were responsible for the creation of new catalogues of their libraries (for example Coxe at the Bodleian and Dickson at Glasgow, both of whom left catalogues behind them that continued in use for many years). F. C. Nicholson's printed catalogue at Edinburgh was almost the last of its kind.[65] Catalogues of manuscripts (Coxe again at Oxford, and J. H. Todd and T. K. Abbott at Dublin) or of other special collections can also stand as their memorial. Others are known for the expansion of the library's buildings or collection; some endowed their libraries with their own collections, as did Henry Bradshaw with his Irish books at Cambridge.[66]

Some left their mark in other ways. E. W. B. Nicholson, as well as leading the reform of legal deposit, sought to increase the Bodleian staff economically in 1882 by introducing 'library boys' recruited straight from school: many of these went on to high positions in the Bodleian or other great libraries. This system was continued in the Bodleian for many years and was taken up with

62 Craster, *History of the Bodleian*, 31–151 *passim* on Coxe, 152–7 on Nicholson (and later on Nicholson's controversial career). Cf. also K. A. Manley, 'E. W. B. Nicholson and his importance for librarianship', unpublished DPhil thesis, University of Oxford (1977).

63 G. O. Simms, 'James Henthorn Todd', *Hermathena* 109 (1969), 5–23.

64 Guild and Law (eds.), *Edinburgh University Library*, 104–5; P. Hoare, 'The librarians of Glasgow University 1641–1991', *Library Review* 40 (2/3) (1991), 27–43.

65 *Catalogue of the printed books in Edinburgh University Library*, 3 vols. (Edinburgh, 1918–23).

66 *A catalogue of the Bradshaw collection of Irish books in the University Library, Cambridge*, 3 vols. (Cambridge, 1916).

success in London and some of the civic universities.[67] (In many of the old universities, however, young graduates were recruited as junior staff even for quite routine positions.)

Such innovative staff management had, perhaps, something to do with Nicholson's background at the London Institution and his involvement in the Library Association, the infant professional body which he had worked energetically to establish before moving to Oxford. The ancient universities were represented on the Association's first committee in 1877 by John Small from Edinburgh, with Coxe from Oxford and J. A. Malet from Dublin as vice-presidents. Coxe, like Henry Bradshaw from Cambridge and J. K. Ingram from Dublin, was among the early presidents of the Association.[68] It is true that as time went by and public libraries came to dominate its business the professional body was perceived as less relevant; Library Association qualifications were often seen as inappropriate for research libraries, and disputes over their imposition led to further distancing of the ancient universities from the Association. (There were exceptions: G. H. Bushnell, Librarian at St Andrews 1924–61, whose manual *University librarianship* spoke warmly of 'our representative body'[69] and defended the Association's lack of interest in the university sector, and R. O. MacKenna (Glasgow 1951–78), who also cautioned in the 1950s against too strong a separatist line.) The ancient universities however were more actively involved in SCONUL, founded in 1950, where common ground could be found with national libraries and other historic foundations.[70]

Undergraduate provision

The term 'research' is largely a twentieth-century innovation, and as late as 1931 it could be said at Oxford that 'Post-graduate study does not form part of the ordinary educational routine of the University, as it does in America, where Master's degrees are awarded on rudimentary theses.'[71] It has been pointed out that research was not at the heart of the universities' purpose until the late nineteenth century, when economic competition increased.[72] None the

---

67 S. Gillam, 'The Bodleian Library in the nineteen thirties', *Bodleian Library Record* 18 (1) (2003), 16–31 (Gillam's account of life as a 'Bodley Boy' includes a note on Nicholson's innovation).
68 W. A. Munford, *A history of the Library Association 1877–1977* (London, 1976), 30.
69 Bushnell, *University librarianship*, 30.
70 T. Bowyer, 'The founding of the Standing Conference of National and University Libraries (SCONUL)', in J. Thompson (ed.), *University library history: an international review* (New York and London, 1980), 208–28.
71 *Library provision in Oxford*, 52.
72 Anderson, 'Ideas of the university in 19th century Scotland'.

less, the great historic strengths of the libraries were crucial to their role in scholarship, and their collection-building was consequently directed largely at the needs of senior members of the university. Students at a lower level had different needs, though many benefited from the vast range of resources available (if not always very freely) for extra-curricular study. Special provision for their needs, however, varied greatly.

The report of the 1852 Cambridge University Commission noted 'a considerable deficiency of modern books for the use of students'[73] and found a wide variety of practice in colleges on the provision of library resources for undergraduates. This ranged from Trinity's well-established collection with 5,000 loans a year to Peterhouse where junior members might not use the library unless accompanied by the Master or a Foundation Fellow.[74] This situation was not unique to Cambridge: the parallel report of the Oxford Commission remarked more briefly that 'in some colleges . . . [undergraduates] are still excluded',[75] though at Christ Church a reading room specifically for undergraduates was created in 1884.[76] At the university level Oxford proved more liberal: after 1861 the Radcliffe Camera rapidly became the principal undergraduate reading room; additional seating had to be provided as early as 1888 and 'the books on the shelves were selected specifically to meet their requirements'.[77] At Edinburgh increasing student numbers (doubling between 1854 and 1878) put pressure on the Students' Reading Room, which additional bookstock did little to alleviate since students were not granted free access to the shelves and had to rely on overworked assistants to obtain their two permitted titles.[78]

The situation was not very different in the other ancient universities. Access to the main university library collections was often restricted to graduates and academic staff; the access permitted to undergraduates was seen as a privilege on reaching a certain degree of seniority (sometimes, as at Glasgow, preceded by a personal interview with the University Librarian). In Scotland class libraries, notably for the use of students in the large Ordinary Degree classes, were a common feature alongside departmental libraries serving teaching and research staff.

---

73 Cambridge University Commission, *Report* (London, 1852), 113.
74 McKitterick, *Cambridge University Library*, 615–18.
75 Oxford University Commission, *Report* (London, 1852), 119.
76 M. Chichester, 'The later development of Christ Church Library, Oxford', *Library History* 5 (1980), 109–17 (specifically 114–15).
77 S. Gillam, *The Radcliffe Camera* (Oxford, 1992), 31.
78 S. M. Simpson, 'The history of the library 1837–1939', in Guild and Law (eds.), *Edinburgh University Library*, 100–1 (including an account of the insalubrious conditions in 1880).

The needs of students were often supposed to be restricted and predictable, in line with educational philosophies which did not encourage independent intellectual enterprise or exploration on the part of more junior students. The Librarian of Edinburgh University, John Small, gave evidence to the 1876 Commissioners that the reading room was provided as 'an adjunct to study as far as possible', and that his Committee aimed 'to limit the supply of books to such subjects as will be really useful to the students while attending class'.[79] The bishop of Meath, Dr J. H. Singer (formerly Regius Professor of Divinity at Trinity), explained to the Dublin University Commission in 1851 that 'it is injurious to the Student to have an unlimited range of books at his command' and that he therefore supported the creation of a select lending library.[80] As late as 1899 the Curator of Glasgow University Library, the generally enlightened Professor William P. Dickson, argued against admitting students to the stacks of the university library with the words: 'Why should he be brought into contact possibly not merely with rubbish, but with garbage? Why should he have to run the risk of being distracted, perplexed, and, it might be, led astray amidst the possibilities of a large and miscellaneous aggregation?'[81]

The continuing need for special provision in Glasgow was highlighted in 1938 in a report on the (public) Mitchell Library: 'The Mitchell Library stands out as an example of an efficient reference service greatly used by the people. It has come to be looked upon by them as a place for research and study, and so good is the service that students at the University make more use of it than of their own University Library.'[82] The remark is a testimony as much to the quality of the Mitchell's services as to the difficulties faced by the university library in its sixty-year-old accommodation (its new round reading room opened only in 1939). Positive relationships with the public library were the exception rather than the rule and there is little evidence of mixed town-and-gown use of the public libraries in Oxford or Cambridge; in Edinburgh on the other hand the opening of the public library in 1890 relieved peak-demand pressure on the university library which had had a measure of public access.[83]

Specifically student-orientated reading rooms continued to develop in the twentieth century: by the end of that century, as undergraduate curricula

79 Simpson, 'History of the library 1837–1939', 100.
80 Dublin University Commission, *Report: comments, suggestions and evidence* (Dublin, 1853), 304.
81 W. P. Dickson, *Statement by the Curator as to the bearings of a proposal to grant 'free access' to selected students* (Glasgow, 1899), 8.
82 A. S. Cooke, in L. R. McColvin (ed.), *A survey of libraries: reports on a survey made by the Library Association* (London, 1938), 29.
83 Guild and Law (eds.), *Edinburgh University Library*, 97.

widened and independent research was encouraged, they were coming to be seen as obsolete, though there has been something of a revival in the form of short-loan collections and electronic course-packs (a return to the utilitarian view of students' reading as restricted and predictable).

Expansion and buildings

At the beginning of our period many libraries still occupied ancient buildings. Expansion of the universities themselves, as well as of the libraries' stocks, necessitated change and development at an ever-increasing rate through the later nineteenth and twentieth centuries.

In the nineteenth century Oxford retained, as it does today, the medieval Duke Humfrey's Library and its later accretions forming the Bodleian quadrangle, and from 1860 the Bodleian also had the use of the Radcliffe Camera (1749), together with the new Radcliffe Science Library from 1901. Cambridge remained in the Old Schools, the university's central building which the library had gradually taken over since the fourteenth century; the majestic extension by C. R. Cockerell of 1840 had substantially increased its space but the plan for it to encompass the whole University Library was never completed.[84] Both English universities also boasted a variety of college libraries, many of them fine examples of early library design, some like Trinity College Cambridge's Wren Library and All Souls' Codrington Library of the greatest splendour. While these remained in use, the needs of the universities centrally were increasingly difficult to meet and major developments became necessary in the twentieth century at both Oxford and Cambridge, as discussed below.

Edinburgh had the magnificent Playfair Library of 1834, whereas Glasgow's library of 1744 was becoming increasingly insufficient for its stock despite expansion in 1784 (even though the Hunterian Books and Manuscripts, received in 1807, had been accommodated in a separate new building). St Andrews had a library building of 1643, much remodelled and expanded in 1764, while Aberdeen still had libraries in both King's College and Marischal College. At Trinity College Dublin the 1732 Long Room already suffered from overcrowding, relieved by structural changes in 1859 which allowed extra shelving in the gallery (the colonnades under the library remained open until 1890 when they were enclosed to provide still more storage space). Like the adjustments made elsewhere, these were not sufficient to cater for future needs.

---

84 McKitterick, *Cambridge University Library*, 486–9.

Change came at varying speeds. Most dramatically Glasgow abandoned the Old College, its home for 400 years, and moved to a new site overlooking Kelvin Grove in 1870, where a complete set of new buildings for the university was erected to the design of Sir George Gilbert Scott. This placed the library at the heart of the university, with space for expansion; an estimate of 1888 referred to 'provision probably sufficient at the present rate of increase for the next fifty years'.[85] A reading room forming part of the original design proved unsatisfactory and was replaced by the lower hall of the University Museum (until a new circular reading room was erected in 1939, in an inflexible closed-access design). The Gilbert Scott building remained the increasingly constrained home of the library until 1968, when the first stage (only) of a towering new library opened, with a radical design juxtaposing reading areas, bookstacks and subject staff.

A similar delay was suffered in Edinburgh, where the Playfair Library and other library accommodation in the Old College remained in use until 1967. The new library in George Square, near other new university buildings, was built in one stage, avoiding the pitfalls of Glasgow's staged design, and was comfortably big enough for the whole library. It was the first library building in Britain to be fully air-conditioned – however inadequately – and was hailed as a triumph of architectural design.[86]

Plans for a shared building in Dublin, to ease pressure on both Trinity College and the National Library, were proposed to the government in 1959 by Richard Hayes, librarian of the NLI, with the support of the Provost of Trinity; but they aroused the suspicion of the Roman Catholic hierarchy and were abandoned.[87] It was 1967 before the college opened what is now the Berkeley Library, complementing the Long Room and the adjacent Memorial Reading Room of 1937 in an uncompromising modernist idiom.[88]

The 1960s and 1970s saw widespread investment in new academic library buildings across the country.[89] The examples of Edinburgh, Glasgow and

85 W. P. Dickson, *Glasgow University Library: notes on its history, arrangements, and aims* (Glasgow, 1888), 46. Dickson included a list of relatively minor complaints about the building and its furnishing.

86 E. R. S. Fifoot, 'From Old College to George Square', in Guild and Law (eds.), *Edinburgh University Library*, 130–9.

87 J. Bowman, 'The wolf in sheep's clothing: Richard Hayes's proposal for a new National Library of Ireland, 1959–60', in R. J. Hill and M. Marsh (eds.), *Modern Irish democracy: essays in honour of Basil Chubb* (Blackrock, 1993), 44–61. Cf. Gerard Long's chapter on the National Library, above.

88 Dan Cruickshank, 'Berkeley Library: Trinity College Dublin 1967–1997', *RIBA Journal* 104 (10) (1997), 69–75.

89 R. S. Smith, 'The history of academic library buildings', in Thompson (ed.), *University library history*, 128–46.

Dublin were followed elsewhere and modern design came to be expected in universities old and new. Aberdeen had erected a new Science Library in 1965: this later came to serve the whole university under the name Queen Mother Library, but space in the old buildings of King's College was retained for its special collections. The last of the old Scottish universities to have new accommodation was St Andrews, which in 1984 moved into a long-overdue modern building. In all these buildings, to a greater or lesser extent, the dominant pressure was for accommodation for students, a consequence of the change in the very nature of universities, though unlike some more modern institutions the ancient universities had both to provide for very substantial bookstocks and to cater for the special needs of large holdings of manuscripts and early printing.

This change in the nature of universities can also be observed, though to a lesser degree because of their earlier date, in two great undertakings each side of the Second World War, remarkably both by the same architect Giles Gilbert Scott. Cambridge, more radically, abandoned its ancient home in the centre of the town and erected a completely new library across the river; Oxford built on a similar scale but retained its old buildings as well as the New Bodleian. Both enterprises were controversial and aroused passions – and admiration.

Both universities had long been considering how best to house their growing collections. Oxford had built extensive underground stacks in 1909–12, but it was Cambridge which took the first step towards a major building, with a Senate vote in 1921 on a new site for the University Library. The bold scheme to abandon the Old Schools and the Cockerell Building[90] was led by Sir Hugh Ker Anderson, Master of Caius and a member of the Royal Commission, who not only persuaded his colleagues to accept the plan but won over the Rockefeller Foundation to find half the cost.[91] Giles Gilbert Scott's elegant original design was amended at Rockefeller's request but traces remain in the simple post-classical styling of the present building with its dominant bookstack tower (largely open access), opened in 1934. Subsequent extensions have increased the accommodation without removing the impressive nature of this landmark, visible from far away across the fens. Other new university building west of the river in recent years has reduced its isolation from the

90 The Cockerell Building was later used by the Squire Law Library and the Seeley Historical Library (cf. *History of the University of Cambridge*, vol. 4, 224–5), and has now been taken over by Gonville and Caius College.
91 C. N. L. Brooke, 'The University Library', in *History of the University of Cambridge*, vol. 4, 370–87, is very largely concerned with the new building; cf. also his 'The University Library and its buildings', in Fox (ed.), *Cambridge University Library: the great collections*, 211–27.

main routes of academic activity: there are new colleges such as Churchill (founded in 1959) and faculty buildings with new libraries such as those on the Sidgwick Site, and the controversial building (1964–8) by James Stirling for the History Faculty and Seeley Library, which was threatened with demolition only twenty years later.[92]

Oxford by 1930 had begun an investigation of possibilities – a completely new building, or an adjacent extension, or a compromise such as an extensive repository elsewhere in the city. All found favour; but the report of the commission appointed that year was almost unanimous in recommending the creation of the New Bodleian a few yards away across Broad Street, essentially a huge bookstack.[93] A minority report by H. R. F. (later Sir Roy) Harrod reflected the generation gap between old and younger scholars, proposing *inter alia* that the stack should be opened up, with reading spaces and even carrels throughout.[94] Harrod's idea of wider access won favour, and limited space for readers was incorporated into the design. Building began in 1936 (again with help from the Rockefeller Foundation) and was far enough advanced by 1940 for transfers of stock to begin despite the war, though it was not fully opened until 1946. Restoration of the medieval buildings followed, with dramatic discoveries about the fifteenth-century library by Bodley's Librarian J. N. L. Myres. [95]

Like Cambridge, Oxford developed new areas for teaching and study (with libraries) in the early 1960s, such as the St Cross Building, and both universities have continued to expand their library facilities at both central and college level. So have the other ancient universities, addressing the issues of mass higher education (which Oxford and Cambridge remained somewhat aloof from for many years). The greatest expansion, however, both of new buildings and conversion of old ones, and of facilities in the form of automation, has come in the last forty years and is covered in later chapters.

---

92 C. Brooke and R. Highfield, *Oxford and Cambridge* (Cambridge, 1988), 322–3.

93 *Library provision in Oxford* (1931) gives considerable detail of the proposals. Craster, *History of the Bodleian*, 329–37, describes the new library as it was built.

94 D. Besoni, 'Roy Harrod and the committee of enquiry into the Bodleian Question 1930–31', *Bodleian Library Record* 17 (1) (2000), 36–44.

95 J. N. L. Myres, 'Recent discoveries in the Bodleian Library', *Archaeologia* 101 (1967), 150–68.

28

The libraries of the University of London to the 1960s

BERNARD NAYLOR

The beginnings of the university

Following the end of the Napoleonic war, London was pre-eminent among the capitals of Europe. This pre-eminence, however, had been secured, above all, by the exercise of military, maritime and financial power. For the liberal and progressive groups in the city, victory in war was not in itself enough. In England, at that time, higher education was monopolised by the ancient universities of Oxford and Cambridge, which were traditional, complacent, and socially and religiously exclusive. Further afield, most of the great cities of mainland Europe had long had universities, for example Amsterdam (since 1632), Lisbon (since 1288), Madrid (since 1508), Rome (since 1303) and Vienna (since 1365).

During the 1820s, the poet Thomas Campbell and the politician Lord Brougham led an initiative which raised enough money to buy the site in Gower Street on which University College (henceforth UCL) was founded in 1826. Conservative opposition to this development was led by the archbishop of Canterbury, the duke of Wellington and Sir Robert Peel, and led to the founding of the rival King's College (henceforth KCL) in 1829. The inevitable controversy as to which of the two institutions should be accorded a royal charter, entitling it to award degrees, was resolved by the establishment of 'the University of London' in 1836, through which each of the colleges was required to present its students for graduation.

The formal establishment of the university should not be allowed to obscure the fact that some facilities did already exist in London for the pursuit of higher learning, including the Inns of Court (for law) and the ancient teaching hospitals, such as St Thomas's and St Bartholomew's. The 'umbrella' university, created to resolve the dispute between UCL and KCL, was later to offer a hospitable environment to a number of institutions of learning which began their lives before or after 1836.

Libraries in the nineteenth century

An account of libraries in the nineteenth-century university can safely be concentrated on four institutions, the university itself, the two founding colleges and the British Museum. So far as the university and the colleges are concerned, the story is by no means distinguished.

At UCL, things did begin with a flourish. In the first designs for college accommodation, approved by the College Council in 1826, 'the whole of the first floor of the southern half of the main block was devoted to the Library'.[1] There was to be a 'Great Library' and a 'Students' Library'. A Library Committee was established in 1828. A Librarian (Dr Francis Augustus Cox, a Baptist minister) was appointed. Four months after classes began, the Library opened its doors to users on 19 January 1829. Cox himself produced the first catalogue of the Library in 1829.[2] College annals record the establishment of a law library and a medical library, both in 1829. Unfortunately, these auspicious beginnings were not sustained. Though the Students' Library was fitted out, lack of money meant that the Great Library could not be and, following a fire in 1836, the Great Library was converted into classrooms in the next year. Cox himself also departed, another victim of the lack of money, in 1831, and, for decades, beadles (college security staff) took on responsibility for the Library. In 1838, the Library Committee also lapsed. As for acquisitions, Newcombe records that 'the donations nearly always greatly exceeded the number of books purchased'.[3] The philosopher Jeremy Bentham donated 4,000 books in 1833 and his papers were also added to the college's holdings in 1849, shortly after the deposit of the manuscript minutes, letters and accounts of the Society for the Diffusion of Useful Knowledge.[4]

As the century wore on, some improvements were achieved. In 1848–9, the Donaldson Library was built. In 1868, the College Committee of Management decided it must appoint a Librarian and recruited Arthur Bleeck from the British Museum Library in the same year. Though his tenure of office was brief, it was followed by a further Librarian appointment, Adrian Wheeler, in 1871. One of the Library's outstanding collections (the Graves) was bequeathed to it in 1870: its strengths are in mathematics, physics and chemistry. The foundation of the Slade School of Art in 1872 led to the establishment of a

---

1 L. Newcombe, 'The Library of University College', unpublished typescript (1926), 1.
2 Newcombe, 'Library of UCL', 57.
3 Newcombe, 'Library of UCL', 17.
4 B. Naylor, 'The libraries of London University: a historical sketch', in J. Thompson (ed.), *University library history: an international review*, (New York, 1980), 229–49 (quotation from p. 231).

Fine Art Library and in 1877 the College Library Committee was reborn. Newcombe however does emphasise that throughout the nineteenth century the library resources available to the students or even the staff of the college were extremely meagre.[5]

Information about KCL Library during this period is thinner. F. J. C. Hearnshaw records that the original college building (opened in 1831 in the Strand) contained 'two large rooms divided by a corridor, designed to accommodate the libraries of the institution'.[6] The collections grew more slowly than at UCL, though one of the important early benefactions dates from this period: the Marsden collection of some 3,000 books, given in 1835 by Dr William Marsden, a former Secretary to the Navy. A catalogue of books in the Library 'published up to 1839' survives. A Library Committee was established in 1871 and has met uninterruptedly since then; its Minutes for the period 1871–1927 are in the Library's files.

There is not much more to tell about the beginnings of the University of London Library (henceforth ULL). On the face of it, one might wonder why there should be a 'university library', considering that the university was established as a 'concept' to manage the situation following the foundation of UCL and KCL. However, the first gifts of books arrived not long after the 1836 Charter, and in 1839 a committee was appointed 'to take into consideration the subject of books which may be required for the use of the University'. Progress was inevitably slow, not least because the Library lacked both accommodation and a Librarian. The first of these deficiencies was remedied in 1870 when the Library was housed in Burlington Gardens, but the second remained a factor for a further three decades. The Library appears to have functioned mainly as a source of books for loan to the colleges. The concept of a collection adjacent to a study space, which might be thought an essential characteristic of an academic library, seems not to have featured.

An early member of the Library Committee of UCL was an Italian teacher, Antonio Panizzi, later Sir Anthony Panizzi. The report of the College Council of 24 February 1830 recorded (p. 7) that 'the vicinity of the British Museum, and the facilities of access to the noble collections in that establishment, render it unnecessary to buy rare and expensive books'. It was the same Panizzi, already a senior member of the British Museum Library staff, whose evidence to a Parliamentary Committee in 1834–6 stirred the British Museum Library from its relatively somnolent state and ensured that it would be the

5 Newcombe, 'Library of UCL', 37.
6 F. J. C. Hearnshaw, *Centenary history of King's College, London, 1828–1927* (London, 1929), 66.

serious resource for the new University of London envisaged by the UCL elders.

While this section has concentrated on a few institutions, it is worth noting that the university had already embarked on expansion, most notably with the foundation of three colleges for women, Bedford (1849), Westfield (1882) and Royal Holloway (1886), all three becoming formally part of the university in 1900–2. The University of London was the first British institution to admit women to degrees.

The emergence of the academic library

Circumstantial evidence suggests that the founding of the London School of Economics and Political Science (the LSE) and the British Library of Political and Economic Science (BLPES) in 1895 was a defining moment in library provision in the university. (The present name of the library dates from 1925.) Like UCL in its day, the LSE was founded by public subscription, under the leadership of Sidney Webb (later Lord Passfield; 1859–1947), who took a continuing interest in the Library. From the beginning, the Library was intended to be 'a new laboratory of sociological research'.[7] The School's initial prospectus envisaged that 'the new library will of course be open freely for use by public officials of every kind, researchers and investigators upon its special subjects, and all serious students'. The value of the collections of the British Museum Library was admitted, but the founding fathers of the new institution pointed to lacunae, for example in 'municipal and other official documents issued elsewhere than in London', and also drew unfavourable comparisons with library provision in such United States institutions as Johns Hopkins University and Columbia University.

In 1903, the Library began systematic receipt of US Federal documents. In 1904, an arrangement was reached for the deposit of nineteenth-century Parliamentary Blue Books which were underutilised at the London Institution. By then, a Library Committee was already in operation and Minute X of 6 December 1912 records a proposal for a 'Current Bibliography of Works on Economics and Political Science' – though a marginal note records that the proposal was 'postponed', and it was 1925 before the idea was brought to fruition under

---

7 A. H. John, *The British Library of Political and Economic Science: a brief history* (London, 1971), 4.

B. M. Headicar, Librarian from 1910.[8] By 1909, Book Selection Committees were in operation in different subject fields such as Geography, Law, Transport, Economics and Statistics, and Finance and Accounting. Accommodation for the Library was a more difficult matter and it was not until 1933 that the present main buildings of the LSE were completed. They incorporated special accommodation for the Library, including a catalogue hall thought to be the first of its kind in England.[9]

The vigour demonstrated by the founders of the LSE and BLPES may have been the factor which galvanised ULL and UCL in this same period. At UCL, R. W. Chambers, then Quain Student in English, addressed a memorandum to the College Management Committee about the Library's accommodation and catalogues.[10] He had a powerful ally in the Provost, Sir Gregory Foster, who according to Chambers himself 'had simultaneously the keenest sympathy with the claims both of central administration and of departmental libraries'.[11] Chambers was still conscious of the proximity of the British Museum, and in his report on the libraries of UCL which was read to the College Committee of Management on 24 April 1901 he observed that: 'there is a limit to the accumulation of books which is desirable. Selection and ready access rather than omnivoracity, should be our aim.' He also feared that growing pressure for the establishment of subject libraries would lead to 'the ultimate disintegration of the College Library into a number of unconnected fragments'.[12] Chambers's opportunity arose when University College School decamped to Hampstead in 1907, releasing the South Wing of the college buildings, and enabling him to realise his plan for a series of open-access seminar libraries leading off a corridor, a pattern of provision which, in considerable measure, still persists. In 1926, John Wilks succeeded Chambers (after a short interregnum by Luxmoore Newcombe), and it was he who took receipt of the magnificent bequest of Sir John Rotton, 30,000 volumes on the literature and history of England, France and Italy, the classics, economics, law and fine art. This period also saw the deposit of further learned-society libraries including the Geologists'

8 *A London bibliography of the social sciences: being the subject catalogue of the British Library of Political and Economic Science* was first published in 3 vols. (and author index) in 1931–2 and continues to the present day.
9 John, *British Library of Political and Economic Science*, 11.
10 J. Wilks, *The influence of R. W. Chambers on the development of university libraries* (London, 1953), 5 (The 2nd Chambers Memorial Lecture, 1953).
11 R. W. Chambers, in an extended contribution to H. H. Bellot, *University College London 1826–1926*, (London, 1929), 421.
12 Wilks, *The Influence of R. W. Chambers*, 9.

Association and the Folk-Lore Society to join the first of these (the Philological Society Library, deposited in 1887).

The defining event in the history of ULL, which took place in this period, was undoubtedly the acquisition of the Goldsmiths' Library of Economic Literature. The collection of 30,000 volumes on economics (broadly interpreted) had been assembled by Professor H. S. Foxwell. Though he held his chair at Cambridge University, he also taught at UCL, and at LSE. In 1901, he sold the collection to the Worshipful Company of Goldsmiths. He is known to have been hostile to the possibility that the collection might be added to the BLPES collection, but, in any event, the decision was taken (in 1903) to donate the books to ULL.

The acquisition of this major resource raised the important issue of the management of ULL itself. In 1903, a visiting group of members of the University Convocation (former students) found 'the books . . . in hopeless confusion, having been placed anywhere out of the way'.[13] The first serious response to this state of affairs was the appointment of Lawrence Haward as Librarian, in February 1904, but his tenure was shortlived, and he resigned in November 1906. He was succeeded by Reginald Arthur Rye, recruited from University College, where important developments in library provision were already under way. Rye was given the title of Goldsmiths' Librarian on his appointment. He was to lead the Library for almost forty years (until 1944) and under him it became a university resource of prime importance.

The accommodation of the Library underwent some vicissitudes, though they eventually led to a most fortunate outcome. Already, by the end of the century, the central university and library were outgrowing their accommodation in Burlington Gardens. The remedy adopted in 1900 was to transfer them to the Imperial Institute in South Kensington. Negley Harte, however, characterised this as 'a flit that was to prove disastrous over the next thirty years',[14] and even in 1910 the Principal of the university, Henry Miers, could remark that many students might be 'ignorant of the existence of a library in the University Building'.[15] Despite delays occasioned by the First World War, a debate on the university's future, initiated in 1909 by a Royal Commission, resulted in a decision to relocate the central offices and the Library once again, this time to Bloomsbury. On a large site, one of the most prominent architects

13 R. Steele, Unpublished manuscript history of the University of London Library [c. 1995], 8.
14 N. Harte, The University of London 1836–1986: an illustrated history (London, 1986), 160.
15 In his preface to the second edition of R. A. Rye's The libraries of London: a guide for students (London, 1910), x.

of the day, Charles Holden, led the construction of the massive buildings which still serve the central university and the University Library. Although Rye had been a colleague of Chambers at UCL, with its emphasis on specialist open-access collections, the splendid premises he was provided with envisaged a library of traditional form, with handsome reading rooms (including special accommodation for the Goldsmiths' Library), but most of the stock on closed access in a large central tower. Notwithstanding the limitations inherent in the design, the University Library's Senate House premises are among the most distinguished in a university which, it has to be admitted, is not notable for library buildings.

Further proof of the increased importance attached to library provision was the founding of the Senate Institutes. The Institute of Historical Research, founded in 1921, had as its central element a library organised specifically to support the main research interests of the university in that discipline. The School of Oriental Studies, founded in 1917 and from 1938 the School of Oriental and African Studies, was another example of an institution which from its earliest days placed a heavy emphasis on the central role of a library. On the other hand, at Imperial College, founded in 1907 in South Kensington on the basis of three older institutions, the proximity of the Science Museum Library was found sufficient reason for not providing a central college library until 1962.

The BLPES also took an early lead in the important matter of staff training. Here again, unfavourable comparisons with prominent US institutions, such as the University of Illinois, were a powerful motivating factor. In 1902, the Governors of LSE considered a report on 'Courses of Instruction in Library Administration' and appointed a committee to prepare a scheme of instruction, the aim being to provide 'an educational and genuinely cultivating course'.[16] James Duff Brown, Stanley Jast and Douglas Cockerell (on bookbinding) were among the prestigious contributors to the programme. By 1911, the LSE's continuation of the programme had become dependent on a guarantee by the Library Association to provide at least sixty students per session. Only a year later, there was concern that the Library Association's guarantee was not being fulfilled and, by 1915, the belt-tightening necessitated by the demands of the First World War caused the arrangement to be terminated, even though some effort had been expended by the LA in negotiations with the Carnegie Trustees for the provision of dedicated accommodation for the classes. Whatever the

16 N. Webber, 'The first library school in the United Kingdom: the London School of Economics, 1900–1919', *Library History* 12 (1996), 142–54.

difficulties being experienced at the LSE, UCL responded positively in 1917 to overtures from the Library Association about the provision of professional education.[17] In February 1919, the University College Committee of Management received the report of a joint UC/LA Committee and recommended the desirability of instituting 'a School of Librarianship in co-operation with the Library Association'. The recommendation was put into effect later that year, thus establishing the UK's first school of professional education.

UCL Library is also indelibly associated with another development in professional education, namely the so-called 'library boys system'. Once again, the evidence is that, in London at least, LSE was the originator, though following the system established at the Bodleian by E. W. B. Nicholson in the 1880s. Writing to the Library Organization Committee in July 1902, the Director of the LSE, W. A. S. Hewins, said:

> The Director hopes to obtain as assistants young men and women who have distinguished themselves in their school curriculum, but, for various reasons, economic or other, are not in a position to proceed to University. The training given during their engagement in the Library of this School will be distinctly one of University type with the added advantage of the practical work of library administration.

Whatever the origins, it was R. W. Chambers, the retired Librarian of UCL, who was able to write to Wilfred Bonser, Librarian of the University of Birmingham, in December 1941: 'The one thing I am proud about in life is the way that I have sent Newcombe [to the National Central Library] and Offor [to Leeds University Library] and you out from the Library at U.C.L. to spread the light in other libraries.'[18] This UCL 'gospel' spread throughout the UK university library world through much of the twentieth century.[19] In 1953 John Wilks had cited nine university libraries where he saw the chief librarian as being in the 'library boys tradition'. He named them as the University of London Library, Leeds, Glasgow, Nottingham, Belfast, University College Dublin, BLPES, Queen Mary College (London) and Birkbeck College (London). The most significant nodes were developed at Birmingham, Leeds (which under Offor's successor B. S. Page supplied librarians to most of the new universities of the 1960s) and Glasgow (where R. O. MacKenna, formerly also at Leeds, sent nearly a dozen chief librarians to other universities in the 1960s and 1970s).[20]

---

17 W. A. Munford, *A history of the Library Association 1877–1977* (London, 1976), 147–8.
18 Wilks, *The influence of R. W. Chambers*, 12.
19 Naylor, *Libraries of London University*, 237
20 M. McIlwraith and E. Rodger, 'Robert Ogilvie Mackenna: an appreciation', *Library Review* 40 (2/3) (1991), 5–8.

The early years of the twentieth century also saw increasing concern about the need to achieve a rational development of the entire library resources of the university. In July 1907, Rye obtained the approval of the University Library Committee for a 'descriptive handbook of the libraries of the University', the first edition of which was published by the university in 1908 under the title *The libraries of London: a guide for students*. In 1908, there was discussion in the Committee about rationalisation of periodical subscriptions, and, on the initiative of the Provost of UCL, about 'some regular means of communication between the Library Committee at South Kensington and the Library Committee at Gower Street'. Next, it was decided, at the Library Committee meeting on 27 April 1908, to establish a sub-committee 'to consider and present a reasoned report on the question of the organisation according to some systematic plan of the libraries belonging to the University'. By the end of the year, it had been agreed to appoint a 'Board of Librarians', membership of which comprised the Goldsmiths' Librarian of the University and the Librarians of BLPES, KCL and UCL 'and others as invited'. Eighteen months later, Rye completed the second edition of his handbook, expanding it to include libraries outside the university likely to be useful to students.[21] BLPES had already decided in 1908 that 'in the event of a central catalogue of the libraries of the University being undertaken, the Library of the School should supply duplicate entries of the catalogue for this purpose'.[22]

Despite these favourable auguries, the initiative ran into the sand. The authors of a KCL report in 1910 took an impartial view of the causes impeding the development of inter-collegiate co-operation between UCL and KCL, and referred in their report to

> the policy either of the Colleges or the Professors to cover the whole of the necessary ground in their own institutions. In various cases it has been stated 'Your men may come to us, but we have no need to send our men to you because we cover all the ground.' If this is allowed to continue, the inter-Collegiate system must fail.[23]

A more partisan line was taken by Professor Sir John Laughton of KCL: 'the real difficulty was that University College wished to get all they could and give nothing'.[24] By June 1914 BLPES was terminating its collaboration with

---

21 R. A. Rye, *The libraries of London: a guide for students*, 2nd edn, illustrated (London, 1910).
22 Minute VII of the BLPES Library Committee meeting of 17 May 1911.
23 Report [dated 25 November 1910] of the Professorial Board on Intercollegiate work and on co-operation with University College (KCL archives K/RPTI/16 p. 4).
24 Memorandum [dated 24 June 1910] on the development of King's College. First Report. Appendix II Opinions of the Professors (KCL archives K/RPTI/15 p. 15).

Rye's union catalogue because it was not retrospective, it excluded important reports and other official publications received from various foreign countries, and it was located at South Kensington only. In effect, it would be sixty years before such an agenda of collaboration was again seriously contemplated.

The Second World War and its aftermath

By the beginning of the Second World War, the university consisted of thirty-three institutions, including thirteen medical schools (some of which, as previously indicated, had been in existence since long before the foundation of the university itself), thirteen other schools (some general such as UCL and KCL, others special such as LSE and the School of Oriental and African Studies) and five Senate Institutes. Although the collection of statistics was still far from systematic, both ULL and UCL claimed a stock of between 300,000 and 400,000 volumes. The University Library added 14,000 volumes in 1938, and UCL spent over £4,000 on non-staff expenditure in the academic year 1936–7.

Because of the threat of bombing, the Second World War was much more serious in its implications for the libraries of the university than the first had been. UCL suffered the most. One hundred thousand volumes were lost in a fire started by an air raid on 24 September 1940. The remainder of the collection was then evacuated, which proved to be a wise decision because a subsequent raid on 16 April 1941 devastated the remainder of the Library's accommodation.[25] Barely 200 yards away, and an obvious target because of the size of the Senate House building, ULL escaped almost unscathed, though the Goldsmiths' Collection had, in any case, already been evacuated to Oxford. KCL, under Robert Hutton, its Librarian from 1931, took the precaution of moving their collections to Bristol, where they nevertheless also suffered from enemy action which resulted in the loss of 7,000 volumes in the fields of the arts and law. Normal library services inevitably ceased to function, though the LSE's collection in particular, with its riches in international economics and politics, was seen as an important resource for the war effort.

The post-war period was one of both reconstruction and development. A whole cohort of mature librarians (Headicar, Hutton, Rye and Wilks) made way for a new generation, represented by Kenneth Garside (KCL from 1958), J. H. P. Pafford (ULL from 1945), Joseph Scott (UCL from 1954) and Geoffrey Woledge (BLPES from 1944). Collections were now growing steadily through

---

25 Wilks's organisation of the evacuation of the library and its return, as an entity, to the college's war-damaged building 'was a model for such exercises' (W. A. Munford, *Who was who in British librarianship 1800–1985* (London, 1987), 84).

systematic purchase. Both the ULL collection and the UCL collection doubled in size in the period between 1938 and 1960. The acquisition of special collections also continued to feature significantly. In 1953, UCL purchased the Ogden Collection, the third and greatest of its major special collections. It was built up by C. K. Ogden (1889–1957) and is devoted to 'orthography', but a central component is a collection of 50,000 letters addressed to Lord Brougham (1778–1868). In 1956, the University Library received as a gift from Sir Louis Sterling (1879–1958) his rich collection of English literature.[26] However, it should also be noted that, because of the university's multi-institutional character, an important contribution to overall library provision – bookstock, study places and services – was being made collectively by a large number of smaller libraries. Together, they represented an immensely strong and diverse provision, the great strengths in research support of some being balanced by the particular commitment of others to the support of taught courses, and the general libraries equally being balanced by specialist libraries of considerable distinction.

In service terms, this period saw the triumph of the concept of open access to the shelves by library users. This had been an established policy at UCL since the days of Chambers, but it was also given emphasis by Pafford at ULL, despite the inflexibilities of Charles Holden's library building, through the introduction of the Open Lending Library of 60,000 heavily used volumes and the Periodicals Reading Room, both developments of the fifties. It also saw the beginnings of a more developed reader service based on the concept of the 'subject librarian'. Scott claimed that, while Chambers had invented the subject library, he (Scott) could reasonably take credit for the invention of the subject librarian, as he organised UCL's graduate professionally qualified staff on subject-specialist lines, and gave this much greater importance than the more traditional functional staff structure.[27]

For two decades after the end of the war, the centre of the university in the Senate House was at the height of its power and influence, the role of Sir Douglas Logan as Principal being undoubtedly a critical factor. It was he who steered through an important development, at once symbolic and practical, which addressed the inevitably growing accommodation requirements of the university's libraries. In the late 1940s, planning began for the construction of the University of London Library Depository, the object of which was

26 *The Sterling Library: a catalogue of the printed books and literary manuscripts collected by Sir Louis Sterling and presented by him to the University of London* (London, 1954).

27 J. W. Scott, 'The library of University College' in R. Irwin and R. Staveley (eds.), *The libraries of London*, 2nd rev. edn (London, 1964), 191.

to provide low-cost accommodation for low-use library stock in a purpose-built building in the grounds of Royal Holloway College at Egham, some 22 miles from the Senate House building. Construction of the first stage, to hold 250,000 volumes, began in 1959. Rapid take-up of the space in the first three stages proved that it was meeting a practical need. The symbolic significance of the Depository Library lay in the concept of the federal university finding a collective solution to a problem which was at once particular to each of the many libraries of the university from time to time but over the course of time common to them all.

The other significant 'federal' development was the founding (1955) of the Standing Conference of Librarians of London University Libraries (SCOLLUL), a conscious imitation of the Standing Conference of National and University Libraries (SCONUL) founded in 1950. SCOLLUL encouraged the compilation of some specialised union lists of periodicals and in 1959 began a newsletter aimed at disseminating information and breaking down the possible isolation of some of the smaller libraries, an interesting revival of the Provost of UCL's proposal of 1908. In this renewed general commitment to collaboration and co-operation, it is fair to single out the role of *primus inter pares* played by the University Librarian J. H. P. Pafford, and later continued by his successor (and at one time his Deputy) D. T. Richnell. But it must also be acknowledged that the leadership role exercised from the University Library was not to be a permanent feature even though its decline lies outside our period.

Despite these initiatives, the disaggregated nature of library provision inevitably encouraged thoughts that, if only greater co-ordination could be achieved, the substantial resources being spent by the university on libraries could be put to better effect, or possibly reduced. It was these two contradictory feelings of 'strength through diversity' and 'diseconomy through dispersal' that the university was to bring into the environment of investment and expansion initiated by the Robbins Report.

29

The Civic universities and their libraries

F. W. RATCLIFFE

Why these universities or colleges should be only at Cambridge and Oxford, I know no reason . . . doubtless it would be more suitable and more advantageous to the good of all the people, to have universities or colleges, one at least, in every great town or city in the nation, as in London, York, Bristol, Exeter, Norwich and the like: and for the state to allow these colleges an honest and competent maintenance, for some godly and learned men to teach the tongues and arts, under a due reformation. And this the state may the better do, by provision out of every county, or otherwise, as shall be judged the best, seeing then there will be no such need of endowment of scholarships; inasmuch as the people having colleges in their own cities, near their own houses, may maintain their children at home, whilst they learn in the schools; which would indeed be the greatest advantage to learning that can be thought of.

William Dell, Master of Gonville and Caius College, Cambridge, 1653[1]

Much has been written about the spread of education in England before, during and after the industrial revolution. Many of the publications touch on the emergence of the Civic universities and a few deal directly with their origins, birth and early development.[2] Inevitably, much that has been published has implications for their libraries but, apart from occasional comparative studies and references in the history of individual universities,[3] these have rarely been considered in a general library context. University libraries are essentially corollaries of their universities and their *modus vivendi* and *modus operandi* are to a very large extent determined by them. In the case of the Civic university libraries, this is specially important, for their distinctive origins and

---

1 W. Dell, *The right reformation of learning, schools and universities (1653)*, quoted in S. C. Roberts, *British universities* (London, 1947), 39–40.
2 Such as W. H. G. Armytage, *Civic universities: aspects of a British tradition* (London, 1955).
3 Such as H. B. Charlton, *Portrait of a university, 1851–1951: to commemorate the centenary of Manchester University* (Manchester, 1951); P. H. J. H. Gosden and A. J. Taylor (eds.), *Studies in the history of a university, 1874–1974: to commemorate the centenary of the University of Leeds* (Leeds, 1975), etc.

early history set them apart from the libraries of Cambridge, Oxford and the ancient Scottish universities, and also from most of the later foundations.

It is important to understand that the term 'Civics' refers to some of those universities commonly called 'redbrick' which were established as a result of local ambition and patronage in the late nineteenth and early twentieth century. Some developed from colleges founded by individuals, others from colleges formed as a result of local pressures. They comprise two groups – those achieving university status before the First World War and those achieving it before the arrival of the 'new universities' which, in this context, include Keele and Sussex.[4] In order of college foundation date[5] the first consists of Manchester (Owens College 1851), Leeds (Yorkshire College 1874), Birmingham (Mason College 1875), Bristol (University College 1876), Liverpool (University College 1879) and Sheffield (Firth College 1879). The second group embraces Southampton (Hartley Institute 1862), Nottingham (University College 1877), Reading (University College 1892), Exeter (University College 1901), Leicester (University College 1922) and Hull (University College 1926).

The University of London, made up of the 'godless' University College on Gower Street and the Anglican-based King's College, pre-dates the Civics, being founded in 1836. It differs in its origins, neither of its founding institutions being the product of local aspiration or ambition, and is not classed with them. The ancient Scottish universities, St Andrews, Glasgow, Aberdeen and Edinburgh, though having much in common with the Civics are hardly of them, nor do they readily come to mind as 'redbrick', although Sampson includes them as such.[6] Even University College Dundee, which was founded expressly on the model of Owens College in 1880,[7] would not usually be included in the Civics. The term generally refers only to certain English universities. The three Welsh University Colleges at Aberystwyth, 1872, Bangor, 1883, and Cardiff, 1883, which led to the federal University of Wales, received state funding like the universities in Scotland but they too, like Dundee, are today essentially civic in character.

Of the other nineteenth-century foundations, the University of Durham, an ecclesiastical foundation of 1832, was cast in the Oxbridge mould and still shows some of their characteristics but today resembles the Civics in almost all

---

4 Keele received its charter before Southampton, Hull, Exeter and Leicester. Sussex was established in 1961, before the 'new' universities.

5 The dates of foundation given here are generally accepted but some colleges also relate their foundation to earlier institutions.

6 A. Sampson, *Anatomy of Britain* (London, 1962), 207.

7 P. J. Hartog, *The Owens College, Manchester, founded 1851: a brief history of the College and description of its various departments* (Manchester, 1900), 21, note 2.

respects.[8] Its College of Science, later named Armstrong College, established in 1871 in Newcastle upon Tyne, developed entirely on the lines of the Civics and today belongs in their ranks as the University of Newcastle upon Tyne. The Queen's University of Belfast, founded as Queen's College in 1845, also differed clearly from the Civics in its origins and funding, receiving state support from the start, although it, too, is now hardly distinguishable from them. All the Civics grew out of locally based university colleges, although for a while University College, Liverpool, and Yorkshire College, Leeds, became with Owens College constituent colleges of the Victoria University of Manchester. It was the dominant route to university status until the appearance of the 'new' universities in the 1960s.

The importance of the local origins of the civic universities cannot be overstated. Sampson observed that many were 'founded by the mayors and corporations as the product of local pride, many of whom still maintain a town-hall attitude, regarding students' frolics as an affront to civil dignity'.[9] They have maintained strong official links with their cities and include city and other representatives from the locality on their university councils. Many local personalities are also graduates of the local university. The implications of these ties, which Oxbridge does not have and would probably resist,[10] have been crucially important in the development of the Civics and their libraries. In the creation of the latest batch of new 'new universities', civic pride continues to be for many of them an important factor. It is significant that where a second university has been created in a city in which an old Civic already exists, the civic relationship is highly valued by the later foundation, although from the beginning dependent on state funding.

The antiquity of the universities of Oxford and Cambridge, the copyright deposit status of their university libraries traceable to the beginnings of the seventeenth century, their extensive holdings and quasi-national status, might suggest to the layman, even to many 'information professionals', that, outside London and the ancient universities, libraries and books in the rest of England were a post-industrial revolution development. The extensive literature on the industrial revolution highlighting the plight of the working classes and similar

---

8 University Grants Committee, *Returns from universities and university colleges, 1920–21* (London, 1922), 71: 'The seven major civic universities are Birmingham, Bristol, Durham (with King's College, Newcastle), Leeds, Liverpool, Manchester (with College of Technology) and Sheffield.'

9 Sampson, *Anatomy of Britain*, 7.

10 The Wass Syndicate established to report on the government of the University of Cambridge included in its 1989 report a recommendation to include laymen on university bodies. This was rejected by the university.

well-known themes, not least the novels of Dickens, all serves to aid and abet such thinking. In fact, as so many economic historians have demonstrated, this was far from being the case. Rather, the appearance of the Civics is to be seen either as the beginning of a new chapter in English higher education or the beginning of the end of an old one which has, in the shape of the 'new' new universities, only recently finally run its course. Before the Civics appeared there is much evidence of significant traditions of learning, in particular of scientific and technological learning, especially in and around those thriving industrial and commercial centres which later nurtured them.

This learning was a major, even essential factor in the industrial revolution which generated so much wealth and power in these provincial cities. It conferred on them new standing at national level and this in turn stimulated local pride. One expression of this was the founding of 'their' university, such as those in Scottish or continental cities. Paradoxically, the cities of Oxford and Cambridge had and still have little real influence in the life of the universities which bear their name, whilst the Civics were and are essentially of the cities in which they were born. Such is the importance of this that any discussion about the libraries of the Civics would be lacking a basic dimension without some understanding of their background and the role and influence of their founding fathers. Many of their policies and practices today, such as collection-building, admissions, co-operative arrangements, were influenced by them.

Manchester, the earliest of the Civics, set an example for those that followed for more than half a century and for that reason features more prominently in this chapter. It was an example not only in the way it advanced to university status but also in its attitude to its city and region. It is well known that as early as 1640, Henry Fairfax, brother of Lord Fairfax, petitioned the Long Parliament to establish a Northern University based in Manchester, so the desire to have universities outside of Oxbridge pre-dated the Civics by a good many years. There were petitions for a University of York, for a Western University at Shrewsbury, proposals to establish a University in London, and even, from a Dr John Ellis, rector of Dolgallan, for a Welsh university based at Ludlow.[11]

The Master of Caius, in the prefatory quotation, was clearly expressing a view widely held outside Oxbridge. Fairfax's petition was unsuccessful, as were all the others, but Cromwell established a university at Durham at the end of the Civil War which survived until the Restoration. It is of more than passing interest that the Chetham's Library and Hospital in Manchester, founded

---

11 Armytage, *Civic universities*, 105, 111, 116, etc.

in 1655, occupies the site and medieval buildings in which Fairfax proposed locating the Northern University. Today, despite past occasional sales of rarities to preserve its independence, this oldest 'Free Public Library' can be compared directly and favourably – in that its medieval buildings and interior have remained largely unchanged – with some of the older Oxbridge college libraries.

It is instructive to look at some of the bodies established in Manchester prior to the founding of Owens College in 1851. These include: the Literary and Philosophical Society (1781); the College of Arts and Science (1783); the Manchester Academy (1786); the New College (1793, in which year John Dalton was appointed its 'Professor' of mathematics and natural philosophy); the Natural History Society (1821); the Royal Manchester Institution (1824); the Mechanics' Institution (1824); the Royal Medical College (1824); the Manchester Statistical Society (1833) and the Manchester Geological Society (1836). As early as 1718 a Mathematical Society held meetings in the town. The first course of medical lectures was given in 1783 in the premises of the Literary and Philosophical Society whilst the earliest 'apprentice apothecaries' dated back to the founding of the Publick Infirmary in 1752. The teaching of clinical medicine began formally in 1827 when Thomas Turner's medical school in Pine Street was recognised by the Royal College of Surgeons.[12]

The libraries formed by most of these bodies can be traced in the holdings of the University Library, in the case of the Medical, Natural History and Geological Societies in their entirety. These were rich in the literature of the sciences and laid the foundations for what were to become strong university holdings in these subjects. Important for the arts was the large German immigrant community established in early nineteenth-century Manchester. It founded both a Goethe-Gesellschaft and a Schiller-Anstalt, the latter with Friedrich Engels as its sometime president. Their libraries formed the basis of the fine German collections now in the University Library.

Manchester was in no sense alone in such developments. Similar societies are to be found in most provincial cities. Literary and Philosophical Societies, with occasional variations in title, appeared in Newcastle upon Tyne in 1793, Liverpool 1812, Leeds 1820, Sheffield 1822 and Hull 1822. Though founded by the middle class to promote science and the applied sciences they soon became of wider cultural interest through their public lectures and their interest in museums, libraries and laboratories. They also formed fine libraries. Those societies which survive today, often in spite of financial difficulties, are still

12 J. Thompson, *The Owens College: its foundation and growth and its connection with the Victoria University, Manchester* (Manchester, 1886), 435.

centres of intellectual activity and the importance of their libraries may be judged from that of the Newcastle 'Lit and Phil'. Many of the other local societies were often inspired or promoted by them and all played some part in establishing the colleges which later became the Civics.

Of particular importance in the pre-history of the Civics were the medical schools which, of necessity, developed libraries. Six of the provincial towns which later had universities established such schools. They met an obvious and increasing need, since seventy-nine hospitals had been founded in England by 1825. These included Liverpool 1749, Newcastle 1751, Manchester 1752, Leeds 1767, Leicester 1771, Birmingham 1779, Nottingham 1782, Hull 1784, Durham 1793 and Sheffield 1797, all future homes of Civic universities. No less important in the early nineteenth century were the mechanics' institutes. By 1850 there existed some 700 across the towns of England with a total membership running into hundreds of thousands.[13] Aimed at 'tradesmen' of the working class in the first instance, they quickly attracted a wide variety of users from the 'working' to professional classes. Many formed libraries of considerable size. The Yorkshire Union of Mechanic Institutes acted in 1849 for 113 'with 8,500 members and 83,000 books in its libraries'. James Hole, Secretary of the Yorkshire Union, proposed in 1853 'that mechanics' institutes should be assisted by government grants, and become constituent colleges of the proposed industrial university which had been mooted'.[14]

Of the greatest relevance to the founding of the Civics were the Dissenting Academies which, though much earlier, pioneered the way the Civics were later to take. A direct result of the imposition of religious tests at Oxbridge, the Academies provided not only for the training of nonconformist ministers but eventually for the education of any nonconformist and others besides. The roll-call of 'graduates' from these institutions is impressive. They were so successful as to pose a threat to what has to be seen as the monopoly of Oxbridge in England and lead to the Schism Act of 1714, the primary aim of which was to close them down. They survived, ironically, on the teaching of subjects which lay outside religion and remained focal points in nonconformist education. Priestley, Malthus, Dalton, among many other luminaries, left their mark both in these institutions and on the scholarship of the nation. Eventually, they were absorbed into other local institutions but remained a powerful, if indirect force in the eventual establishment of the Civics. It is of interest that Manchester College, now Manchester Harris College, Oxford, began life in

13 G. W. Roderick and M. D. Stephens, *Education and industry in the nineteenth century* (London, 1978), 54–61, etc.
14 Armytage, *Civic universities*, 178 and 207.

1757 as the Warrington Academy, the 'Athens of the North', and reached Oxford via sojourns in Manchester, York, Manchester again and London.

Apart from the many societies and institutions which flourished in the birthplace of the Civics there is also much further evidence to suggest that the appetite for learning and education, for libraries and books in the country at large was widespread long before they and their founding colleges appeared. The provincial press, the beginnings of which can be traced to 1701, expanded to such an extent that 'Dr Johnson could write in 1758 that "now almost every large town has its weekly historian, who regularly circulates his periodical intelligence". In fact, in this year twenty-eight towns had at least one "weekly historian"; five of them – Liverpool, Manchester, Nottingham, Coventry and Bath – had two, and Newcastle and Bristol had three.'[15] By the mid-nineteenth century, although illiteracy was rife and has rightly engaged the attention of educationists and historians, it is clear that there was also a sizeable literate public for the majority of which there was no university option in England.

There were also various other libraries, long before circulating libraries were born in the mid-eighteenth century, in cathedrals, parish churches and the old grammar schools. It can also be no coincidence that the Civics took root in the cities which were the homes of some of the oldest and most famous grammar schools – Manchester Grammar School, King Edward VI Birmingham, King Edward VI Sheffield, Bristol Grammar School, the Royal Grammar School Newcastle upon Tyne, among others. Of later origin but certainly significant were the Sunday schools, adult schools and Lyceums providing for unskilled working men, and similar enterprises, which flourished in the early nineteenth century in these centres. All formed collections of books: all pointed to the need. In Scotland, ancient universities provided for such a need in four cities. In Germany, there were at least twenty-four institutions before 1800, a further seven before 1850, all among the many old-established German universities of today. England seemed to lack the kind of co-ordinated intellectual tradition of Germany, so that Luther's early call to educate the young or the School Regulations of Weimar of 1619, establishing compulsory attendance at elementary schools as a civic duty, just two of a number of examples, found no positive echoes here. Fichte's promotion of education in the early nineteenth century[16] contrasts sharply with the views of Gladstone and the English establishment.

---

15 I. Jackson, *The provincial press and the community* (Manchester, 1971), 3.
16 Johann Gottlieb Fichte (1762–1814, German philosopher), *Reden an die deutsche Nation*, 1807–8.

Much that is highly relevant to the birth-pangs of the Civics can be traced in such comparisons.[17]

In many provincial cities voice was often given to the need, and strong cases were made out by individuals and institutions for local universities. The Manchester Statistical Society, the first of its kind in England, published in 1836 a paper by H. L. Jones, sometime Fellow of Magdalene College, Cambridge, entitled *A plan of a university for the town of Manchester*. He insisted not only that a university should be established but, more significantly, that it should reflect its Manchester origins. In addition to the traditional academic subjects 'great encouragement should be given to the study of mathematical science, of political and social history, and of the practical application of mathematics and calculation to the affairs of banking and commercial operations'. In Leeds the objectives of Yorkshire College were even more clearly expressed:

> to supply an urgent and recognized want, viz., instruction in those sciences which are applicable to the Industrial Arts, especially those which may be classed under Engineering, Manufacturing, Agriculture, Mining and Metallurgy. It is designed for the use of persons who will afterwards be engaged in those trades as foremen, managers or employers; and also for the training of teachers of technical science.[18]

Statements like these had obvious consequences for the curricula. The implications for the civic libraries were clear and are still reflected in their holdings.

Much the same sort of evidence can be produced for the other Civics. All reflected their local industries and needs, which became formative influences in the libraries of the Civics. In Birmingham, Josiah Mason, a local industrialist, founded Mason College to 'provide enlarged means of scientific instruction on the scale required by the necessities of the town and district'.[19] The purpose of benefaction was, not surprisingly, often openly directed at the benefactor's interests, so that the Department of Brewing in Birmingham was established by a grant from local brewers. In Sheffield, Mark Firth, a local steelmaster, endowed Firth College, and coal mining and subjects of value to the local industries were pursued. Sheffield was competing strongly with Leeds to be seen as the Yorkshire University and this was an incentive to local benefactors. University College Liverpool, like Manchester, benefited greatly from its local

---

17 See M. E. Sadler, 'The history of education', in C. H. Herford (ed.), *Germany in the nineteenth century: a series of lectures* (Manchester, 1915), 101–27.
18 Gosden and Taylor (eds.), *Studies in the history of a university, 1874–1974*, 2, quoting the inaugural prospectus of the Yorkshire College (1872).
19 Armytage, *Civic universities*, 223.

community, which included many wealthy merchants. In both Liverpool and Newcastle naval architecture was introduced.

The role of Oxbridge in the founding of the Civics was important if unintentional. They had a vested interest in maintaining the *status quo* but the establishing of London University had already weakened their hold. Their exclusion of so much potential graduate material on the grounds of religion was as much a factor in the promotion of the new universities as it had been in the case of the Dissenting Academies. Nonconformity was a prominent feature of many provincial towns, not least among leading figures in the community. Many of the trustees of John Owens, founder of Owens College, were dissenters like Owen himself, 'thoroughly representative men . . . Tory and Liberal churchmen, Independents, Baptists, Unitarians and Moravians'.[20] Most, again like Owens, were involved in the industrial, commercial life of the Manchester region or the political. It was a powerful combination. In his will Owens stipulated that no one involved with the college should be 'required to make any declaration as to, or submit to any test whatsoever of, their religious opinions' and that preference in admission should be given first to those living within Manchester, secondly to those residing in south Lancashire. The former meant that when a Faculty of Theology was established it was non-sectarian and this was reflected in the library's theological holdings. As for the latter, home-based students still comprise a significant proportion of the student numbers in Manchester and other Civics and are likely to increase in the context of present funding arrangements.

For a model Owens trustees looked to Scotland and observed that its universities 'are intended and well fitted to embrace the education of youth of the highest ranks of society, their institutions have in no respect been framed or modified with reference to the means, or pursuits, or habits of the aristocracy: their system is that of a general plan of education by which persons of all ranks may be equally benefited'. Their libraries reflected the needs of both teaching and research and special provision for undergraduates was made at a very early stage in their history. The reference to the aristocracy was clearly made with Oxbridge in mind which served as a kind of finishing school for many of the rich and privileged. In addition to traditional university subjects, the trustees included subjects relevant to interests of the area, so that chemistry, for example, 'a branch of science of so much local importance as well as of general interest', found a place in the curriculum and in the library from the start. An early donation to Owens in 1885 was the 4,000 volume Angus Smith

---

20 Thompson, *The Owens College*, 51.

Memorial Library on chemistry and physics which laid the foundations for the fine holdings of the future.

The birth of the Civics was not attended by government enthusiasm. A large deputation to the Prime Minister, Benjamin Disraeli, on 24th March 1868, promoting the Manchester Owens College cause, included no less than thirty-five MPs, many distinguished scholars, clerics and representatives of the Learned Societies in addition to the Manchester/south Lancashire contingent. In declining their wishes Disraeli observed prophetically and perceptively: 'But if her Majesty's government, in the exigencies of the state, should be unable to comply with your request, I am quite certain that the public spirit and generosity of Lancashire will not allow the interests of the College to suffer.'[21] The failure to secure the grant of £100,000 from government in 1868 towards an extension at Owens College must have stimulated the appeal, which brought in a then massive sum of £106,706, entirely from local sources.

William Ewart Gladstone succeeded him as Prime Minister and met a similar powerful deputation on 18 February 1869. As, in his own words, 'an out and out inequalitarian' he was predictably less sympathetic. His views on universities, as expressed in one of his speeches on the Irish University Bill in February 1873, were shared by many in the establishment:

> The great bulk of . . . matriculated students, or at least, a very large portion of them, are simply professional students, and are not students in Arts. But when we speak of University education as an instrument of the higher culture, we mean University education in Arts. Schools of law, schools of medicine, schools of engineering, and I know not how many other schools, are excellent things; but these are things totally distinct and different from what we understand by that University training which we look upon as the most powerful instrument for the formation of the mind.[22]

The protectionist voice of Oxbridge spoke loud and clear in Gladstone. It is easy to forget that in these subjects, in themselves essential ingredients in current university life, it was the Civics which pointed the way forward. It was to be many years before medical studies in the fullest sense, such an important component in the identity of the leading Civics, were established at Oxbridge.

Despite his unenthusiastic approach to the foundation of new universities, Gladstone did much to promote the cause of libraries, even writing in 1890 an article on librarianship when the profession was struggling for an identity in

---

21 Thompson, *The Owens College*, 330.
22 A. T. Bassett, *Gladstone's speeches: descriptive index and bibliography* (London, 1916), 434–5. Cf. F. W. Ratcliffe, 'Mr Gladstone, the Librarian, and St Deiniol's Library, Hawarden', in P. J. Jagger (ed.), *Gladstone, politics and religion* (London, 1985), 65.

Britain.[23] Moreover, in 1889 the first government grant of £15,000 was made for distribution among the eleven 'new' colleges which by then existed in England and Scotland. Increased to £25,000 in 1896, it was made explicitly to 'supplement and encourage local effort', not as a substitute for it. This marked the beginning of regular government grants which culminated in the establishing of the University Grants Committee in 1919. It is significant that Oxbridge, too, applied for government grants from 1915. Some thirty years after the first, reluctant government grant, the oft-quoted statement of the UGC appeared in its report of 1921: 'The character and efficiency of a university may be gauged by its treatment of its central organ – the library. We regard the fullest provision for library maintenance as the primary and most vital need in the equipment of a university.'[24] In quoting this in 1967, the Parry Report also recommended a proportion of 6% of the total income of the parent institution as a realistic guideline for library funding.[25] This figure has been reached by Oxbridge but never by any of the older Civics in the terms referred to by the Report. The individual incomes of the universities and of their libraries are an important statement on their changed circumstances. Sampson noted that by 1960 the first grant of 1889 had been multiplied by 4,000 times. Less spectacular but by no means less important are the student numbers, which almost doubled between 1937 and 1957, and almost trebled by 1962. Today, both are very much higher and it is tempting to see the continental influence in the growth of the Civics' student numbers.

From the moment that government conceded its first grant to the Civics – which in itself marked official recognition of the necessity of national support for a university system – and through subsequent funding developments, their establishment was manifestly justified, even inevitable. Apart from the local and religious considerations, there were other factors which shaped their identity. Their attitude to women students had not only repercussions on the future of the new colleges, but an impact at national level. Courses for women began in 1874 in Owens College and a Department for Women was established in 1883; women were admitted to all university degrees. In Leeds women were admitted from 1896, and the other Civic foundations followed suit. In Cambridge religious tests were abolished in 1871, by which time the

23 'On books and the housing of them', *The Nineteenth Century* 27 (1890), 388. Gladstone resigned from his fourth administration in 1894 and died in 1898.
24 University Grants Committee. *Report, etc.,* 1921. Quoted here from the Parry Report, p. 9 (see note 25).
25 University Grants Committee, *Report of the Committee on Libraries* (London, 1967) (The Parry Report).

potential of the new civic colleges was clear: but the full recognition of women followed much later.

The new universities were well ahead of their time in this and other respects and quite out of tune with Oxbridge. In fact, in looking to Scotland and the Continent for models the colleges virtually turned their backs on the Oxbridge system. In 1885, Sir Edward Baines, MP, proprietor of the *Leeds Mercury*, in reference to the breadth of Yorkshire College's academic interests, observed that 'a fuller curriculum could scarcely be found in a German university'.[26] It is no accident that the continental system of lectures rather than the Oxbridge tutorial system was preferred, financial considerations apart. Later, in 1917/18, in introducing the new English degree, the Doctorate of Philosophy, PhD, Manchester openly pointed to the influence of Germany and the United States. It was later taken up by Oxbridge.[27] Such developments affected the libraries of the Civics fundamentally in terms of stock, staff and funding, and, it should be added, status. Their support role for research was now explicitly recognised.

Nevertheless, at the founding of the Civics any comparison between them and Oxbridge must have looked bleak. In terms of their libraries it could hardly have been worse. The copyright deposit privilege alone made any comparison otiose. In terms of university politics, however, the libraries of the Civics had one modest, important advantage – there was no competition from other libraries of the university for 'library money' or for benefactions. It was many years before the Public Library in Cambridge, as the University Library was often called, established its absolute primacy among the other libraries of the university, notwithstanding its status as a legal deposit library. This applied not solely to the acquisition funding of the library but also to its staffing and its accommodation. Apart from the college libraries some twenty faculty/departmental libraries date to before 1900 and are of significance.

No less important was the attitude or loyalty of the university academic staff to the university library. In the Civics, certainly at the outset, the central library was the only library. The financial constraints were such that there was never any possibility of considering introduction of the institute libraries found in many of the older German universities operating in tandem with the main university library. The departments depended on the central library for both teaching and research, so that it was incumbent on their academic staff to ensure that these were as good as possible. The university library was 'their' library and the level of their involvement in it has never been equalled by Oxbridge. As a result, book selection in the Civics is influenced more directly

26 Gosden and Taylor (eds.), *Studies in the history of a university, 1874–1974*, 11.
27 Charlton, *Portrait of a university, 1851–1951*, 93.

by the academic departments than is the case in Oxbridge, where it is still very much a recognised library staff responsibility.

Just how significant this academic input is may be seen from the disposal by the late Professor Ralph Leigh of his fine collection of eighteenth-century materials on Rousseau. When it was offered to Manchester in 1979–80, it was declined not on grounds of cost, but because of the seriously heavy duplication its acquisition would have involved. In Cambridge in October 1980, the University Library purchased the collection because the element of duplication was much smaller than in Manchester. French studies were among a number of subjects in which Manchester maintained a high degree of excellence during the greater part of the twentieth century and the commitment of the department's academic staff to the library was reflected in the university library's holdings and in its decisions on purchase.

The librarian of the Civic has, however, always been less likely to be aware of these modest advantages than of the comments on the library's shortcomings as expressed by academic staff imported from Oxbridge or by visiting scholars from overseas. Moreover, whilst the civic university library, like the Scottish, aims to meet the needs of all users, the Bodleian and Cambridge University Library are primarily research libraries, and enjoy the inestimable benefit of copyright deposit. The annual total published output in Britain has passed the 100,000 mark and in Cambridge, in 1993/4,[28] over 76,500 selected items came into the library under the Copyright Act. It took Leeds University fifty years to amass its first 100,000 volumes and the UGC *Returns* for 1938/9 record Liverpool with 200,000 volumes, Leeds with 210,000, Birmingham with 213,000 and Manchester, after almost ninety years, with 380,000. The UGC returns for 1964/5 underline how fundamental the copyright privilege has been in distancing Oxbridge libraries from those of the Civics. It not only enriched the library in British publications but also released 'accessions money' to purchase materials from overseas. The Parry Report noted that 'mere magnitude is obviously no indication of excellence'[29] but the size of a library's holdings, rightly or wrongly, has generally become an accepted marker of its scholarly importance and a guide to the standing of its parent body.

Large as the difference between Oxbridge and the others is, it is important to remember that the holdings of the Civics were brought together almost entirely in the context of their institutional teaching and research needs. Oxbridge libraries have a national dimension which is reflected in both

---

28 The year of my retirement from the office of University Librarian.
29 University Grants Committee, *Report*, 8 (The Parry Report).

the copyright deposit and its funding. It comes as no surprise that in 1964/5 the total catalogued stock of Birmingham, Bristol, Leeds, Liverpool, Manchester and Sheffield (3,072,000) fell short of the combined total of Oxbridge (3,215,000), excluding the holdings of the other Oxbridge libraries. Nevertheless, even accepting that in the Civics there must be a fair degree of duplication in teaching materials, it is clear that their libraries comprise important scholarly resources in regions where organised collections of material for higher education were entirely wanting a century earlier. At the same time it is also clear that, even with inter-library lending services, researchers in the Civics – certainly in the humanities – have been at a serious disadvantage when compared with their colleagues at Oxbridge.

Although financial support from local sources dwindled rapidly in the context of government grants, the Civics remained rooted in their locality. They were established for local students, and their library policies, their role in the city and wider region, their attitudes to external users, were and will continue to be influenced by this. They also owe to this source not only their original funding but also significant parts of their holdings. The list of benefactors in the Owens College library, later the university library, is virtually a roll call of those Manchester and regional worthies who first founded, then later supported it. They also governed many of the institutions which were eventually amalgamated with it. Many had built important specialist collections which they donated. These brought with them the scholarship of the lifetime during which they were formed. Such collections undoubtedly influenced the subjects taught in the college, providing ready-made subject bases. It is of interest that the merger with the John Rylands Library in 1972 met with the unanimous approval of the city authorities as an entirely natural solution to the Rylands's problems.

Similar patterns of development can be traced in all the Civics. They were the creation of the cities where they were born and have remained essentially 'their' universities. The benefaction of their founding years developed into a tradition of giving which both enforced their local characters and enriched them, so that much of local interest is to be found in them. For example, the archives of Joseph, Austen and Neville Chamberlain are in Birmingham University Library along with collections associated with Baskerville, Bishop E. W. Barnes, and the Birmingham and Midland Institute among others. Much material relating to the Brunels is in Bristol with collections like the Somerset Miners' Association; the Knowsley pamphlet collection and the T. G. Rylands collection of early Lancashire and Cheshire cartography are in Liverpool University; the Trevelyan (Wallington) Papers, and the Robert White and Pybus collections are in Newcastle upon Tyne; the D. H. Lawrence and other similar archives are in Nottingham; the Sir Charles Firth collection is in Sheffield. The Brotherton Collection in Leeds University Library more than makes up for rather moderate support received from the locality in its early days.[30] Such collections put an indelible local stamp on their libraries. The entries for the Civics in the Library Association's *Directory of rare book and special collections* underline the vital role benefaction from the locality has played in their birth and development.[31]

There are numerous examples as the Civics became the obvious repository for locally generated collections. It is reasonable to ask what would have become of these without the development of the Civics and their libraries. The new public library movement was largely not motivated to acquire such materials and the regional Record Offices arrived much later. Such collections have contributed significantly to the national and international standing of the libraries whilst preserving for the nation items of real heritage value which could well have been lost. The tradition of depositing or giving archives and libraries to local university libraries has never been healthier than it has been in the post-World War II period. If the copyright libraries are the keepers of the nation's printed archive, many of the Civics can claim to be the keepers of those of their regions.

The birth of the Civics coincided with the development of the public library system. This was not mere coincidence but another witness to the striving for self-improvement and education which characterised that age; but it was hardly to the advantage of the fledgling university libraries. The Public Libraries Act of 1850 was a landmark in British librarianship. The free town libraries which followed Ewart's Act are an astonishing index of the demand for, and spread of, education in the second half of the nineteenth century. Manchester Public Library was founded in the same year as Owens College, 1851. An appeal for funds to buy books for the new free library produced £10,000, of which £800 was raised from some 20,000 members of the working class.[32] The tremendous activity in the public library field makes the establishing, survival and flourishing of the libraries of the Civics that much more remarkable.

---

30 M. Sanderson, *The universities and British industry, 1850–1970* (London, 1972). The chapter on 'The Civic Universities, 1850–1914' traces their endowment and local support in some detail.

31 B. C. Bloomfield (ed.), *A directory of rare book and special collections in the United Kingdom and the Republic of Ireland*, 2nd edn (London, 1997).

32 R. D. Waller and C. D. Legge, 'Adult education in the Manchester area', in *Manchester and its region: a survey* (Manchester, 1962), 227; M. Hewitt, 'Confronting the modern city: the Manchester Free Public Library, 1850–80', *Urban History* 27 (2000), 62–88.

The libraries of the Civics, a mere handful still in the early years of this century, have to be seen, therefore, in the light of the numerous free public libraries established following the Act and of the undoubted influence which these had on them. Gladstone, when opening the Free Public Library of St Martin-in-the-Fields, stated that from 1850 to 1886 '133 places had availed themselves of the benefits of the Act'. He then pointed to the surge which took place between 1886 and 1890 when no less than seventy more were founded. The speech was reported at length by both the *Library Journal* and *The Library*,[33] along with news of other library developments. The 'Notes and News' section of the *Library Association Record*, established in 1899, contains important evidence of the growth of the public library movement. There is, however, very little amidst these frequent reports which relates to the Civics, understandably, given the huge difference in numbers, but also because of their lack of a clear library identity.

When there is mention it is rarely to the advantage of its library. The 'Notes and News' entry for Nottingham in 1909 is instructive:

> The Public Library and the University College work hand in hand in many ways. The latest development is the preparation by the City Librarian of 'The University College of Nottingham Book Lists', of which two have recently been printed. These lists are of books on 'Japan' and 'Printing' respectively, which are available in the Reference Library and Central Public Library, both of which are located in the University College buildings. A 'Dante' book list was issued last year. It has recently been decided also to grant to students of the College who do not reside in Nottingham the privilege of obtaining tickets enabling them to borrow books other than fiction from the Central Library on obtaining the usual guaranty.[34]

Civic pride can be very single-minded and in some of the Civics such as Birmingham or Nottingham the presence of a strong public library in the immediate vicinity inhibited, initially, development of the university's own library. Only the relocation of the universities away from the city centre resolved this problem. Being quite different in their aims and, inevitably, in their stock, the libraries of the new Civics constituted a very different library concept from that of the public library.

---

33 'Gladstone on the growth of public libraries in England: speech delivered at the opening of the Free Public Library of St Martin-in-the-Fields', *Library Journal* 17 (1892), 200; *The Library* 3 (1891), 109–15.
34 *Library Association Record 1*, Notes and news (1899), 602. University College Nottingham did not have its own professional librarian until 1931, after its move out of the city centre, when G. Ellis Flack was appointed from Birmingham University Library.

The Public Libraries Act had significant implications for all university libraries, both old and new. It brought in its train professional librarianship and, with the founding of the Library Association in 1877, initiated a wrangle about professional status which lasted for almost a century, and which, in the early days at least, was very much between the university and the public library.[35] The personnel who ran the Civics' libraries in their formative years were a hybrid breed, a curious mixture of the new public and traditional academic librarians, part would-be professional, part 'black letter men', often just clerical assistants. At first the libraries were administered by academics with hired hands to do the work, but the latter eventually gained control. They had evolved into the library staff we recognise today by the early thirties, although in some instances a university professor remained as executive head into the post-World War II period. By then, the Assistant Librarian staff were usually well-qualified graduates in traditional university disciplines, sometimes with a higher degree, sometimes with a professional qualification, often with neither, but academic respectability had become the norm in recruitment. The Library Association's insistence on a professional qualification, i.e. *their* qualification, caused much friction between the LA and the university and national libraries. Along with the frustration at belonging to a public-library-dominated association, this was a major factor in the establishing of the Standing Conference of National and University Libraries in 1950.[36]

The individual character of the Civics led to uncoordinated developments in their libraries. Dr Moses Tyson, Librarian of Manchester University 1935–65, a stout advocate of the 'scholar librarian', successfully secured full academic status for his graduate staff as early as 1935, achieved on the basis of their academic stature, not professional standing. His advertisements angered the Library Association, but his achievement was of major importance in assisting other libraries to secure similar conditions. Across the Pennines, first Richard Offor then B. S. Page, as successive Librarians of Leeds University, were establishing a veritable dynasty of university librarians and exporting them across the country, much as Wilfrid Bonser did at Birmingham in the 1930s.[37] The

---

35 F. W. Ratcliffe, 'Professional librarianship and the university library' in A. Jeffreys (ed.), *The art of the librarian* (Newcastle upon Tyne, 1973), 140–56; J. M. Smethurst, 'University library staffing in the United Kingdom', in J. Thompson (ed.), *University library history: an international review* (London, 1980), 56–76.

36 T. H. Bowyer, 'The founding of the Standing Conference of National and University Libraries', in Thompson (ed.), *University library history*, 208–28.

37 J. Thompson, *A centennial history of the library of the University of Birmingham 1880–1995* (Birmingham, 2000), 74–8. Page had himself been one of Bonser's 'very strong team of senior staff'.

influence of such men and their numerous colleagues and successors in steering the development of university librarianship in the country and in achieving the high status now accorded to academic librarianship has yet to be assessed in depth, but it will certainly be seen to have been decisive. They had a leading part in determining its profile, as even a brief perusal of the professional literature show.

The library school of University College London, for so long the sole means of obtaining a recognisable university qualification in librarianship, must also figure highly in any such assessment and, less happily, in the conflict with the Library Association. The funding in the post-World War II period of more library schools in universities with undergraduate and postgraduate degrees in librarianship forced a change in LA attitudes to professional qualification, resulting in an all-graduate profession. Perhaps one measure of the success of the Civics can be read into the appointment of the present writer as the first non-Oxbridge product to head one of the ancient English university libraries in all the centuries of their recorded history and, some seventeen years later, of R. P. Carr as Bodley's Librarian. Both are products of the scholar-librarian tradition of Manchester University.

It was not only in staffing that the Civics were to forge new library identities. In the timing of their arrival they, like the public libraries, were caught up immediately in all the library innovations of the time – open access, lending systems, classification and subject catalogues, and eventually Dewey, Bliss, Cutter, even Ranganathan, all of which distinguished them from the Oxbridge libraries' traditional practices. From the start they were geared to admit readers to their shelves with minimal degrees of closed access, to systems for lending books and to promoting procedures which made the most of their limited stock through classified sequences and subject lists. What was good for the new public libraries was also put to good use by the infant Civics. They recognised the virtue of the undergraduate provision in Scotland and were free to examine and introduce American practices. There were some distinct advantages in being born into the contemporary educational movement without the baggage of centuries of library tradition. Oxbridge's inflexibilities, borne of centuries of practice, left innovation in university librarianship very much in the hands of the Civics. The growing body of literature on university librarianship prior to 1960 reflects their numerous contributions on library theory and practice.[38]

38 For example the influential *Manual of university and college library practice* (London, 1940), by G. Woledge and B. S. Page, at the time the librarians of Queen's University Belfast

The limited resources of the Civics' libraries contained, ironically, the seeds of the library progress. They determined that their librarians 'made virtues out of necessities' and subsequently all university libraries benefited from their efforts to eke out their modest means. After World War II, when student numbers began to grow rapidly, not only did the Civics lack the riches of Oxbridge but many of the students came from backgrounds where books were virtually absent and school libraries were an unknown quantity. Library instruction in the shape of introductory talks and tours, longer opening hours, undergraduate and short-term loan collections, so much of what is now taken for granted, reflect efforts to exploit resources for the benefit of the students. They were indispensable to the 'new' universities which followed.

The Civics saw at an early stage that inter-library lending could become an important means of supplementing their sparse resources. The formal history of such lending, a fine example of self-help, now extends over nearly eighty years. In January 1925 the Association of University Teachers – itself founded in Manchester – arranged for its Library Cooperation Committee and a number of university librarians to meet with a view to formalising inter-library lending. This was clearly of great potential importance to the Civics and an enquiry or clearing office was established in Birmingham University.[39] This operated until the National Central Library was set up in 1931. Supported by the nine Regional Library Systems formed between 1931 and 1936, the NCL became the forerunner to the British Library Document Supply Centre, one of the most important initiatives in the post-World War II library scene: the Civics can take much credit for their early part in it. They were also much in evidence at the foundation meeting of SCONUL in 1950, which was formed not only to give academic librarians a voice in the library affairs of the nation but also to meet some of the exigencies of the post-war expansion of higher education. Of the nineteen institutions represented there, sixteen were from England. Of these, four were from national London-based bodies, two from Oxbridge, two from London University and eight from the Civics (and two more Civics sent apologies for absence).[40]

Today, almost 150 years after the first Civic was founded, their success after a somewhat stumbling start and never overgenerous funding is a matter for congratulation rather than commiseration. From very modest, unpromising

and King's College Newcastle respectively. Woledge moved to the London School of Economics in 1944, Page to Leeds in 1947, and both played a major part in post-war university librarianship.

39 Thompson, *Centennial history*, 68.
40 Bowyer, 'The founding of the Standing Conference', 227–8.

beginnings they had become by 1960 an important, indeed indispensable component in university library provision nationally, whilst losing little of their
attachment to the locality. Individually and collectively they comprised forces
to be reckoned with in the field of scholarly librarianship. Despite being now
major players in university library scholarship at home and abroad, their
regional role has continued to grow and this is nowhere more obvious than
in their libraries, where the presence of scholars external to the university has
greatly increased with the years. Only the costs of such liberality are likely
to inhibit further growth. Though part of the story of the Civics and their
cities, the sharing of resources with the community of local scholars needs
funding and this may well be sought in looking afresh at the support from
the local communities on which, at one time, they were entirely dependent
and which today are often so vocal and possessive about the achievements
of 'their' university. Cambridge may assert that Rutherford split the atom in
Cambridge but Mancunians would insist that it occurred whilst he was in
'their' university. Achievements such as the Atlas computer or Jodrell Bank are
seen as Manchester's achievements, so closely is the university identified with
the city.

Reading the accounts of Manchester's formative years, when the cotton
famine was fresh in everyone's mind and yet so much money was raised
locally, can lead to questioning the wisdom of ever accepting funding from
government. This is an issue which not only Oxbridge but some of the larger
Civics will certainly consider in the years ahead. Hartog, in his history of
Owens College, could have been speaking for all the Civics when he stated
that, unlike the universities of Oxford, Cambridge and London, the college
was

> really the creation of a city, conscious, like the medieval cities of Italy, of its
> own individuality, and desiring University teaching and University work of the
> highest kind to form part of the city life. The Owens College created a new
> type. Eight other University Colleges have since been established in as many
> large towns of England and Scotland. Each college forms an integral part of
> a great commercial and industrial community, to whose needs it must ever
> respond, on whose support its future must eventually depend.[41]

This rather idealistic vision pre-dated the creation of the UGC and state
funding. Today, it would well serve as the 'mission statement' of the Civics
and their libraries in the light of decentralisation and the growth of regional
power and influence.

41 Hartog, *The Owens College*, 21.

30

Academic libraries and the expansion of higher education since the 1960s

IAN R. M. MOWAT

Introduction[1]

There are two broad approaches to the writing of history: thematic or narrative. The former may allow for a more rigorous analysis, while the latter permits a more even flow and an easier understanding of the broad picture. The more contemporary the history, the more difficult it becomes to be objective: to see issues in their proper perspective or to give due weight to one aspect of life against another in the continuous flow of development. With that in mind, this chapter will look at the issues thematically. If objectivity is difficult for events through which one has lived, it is all the more difficult when the writer has been a participant, even if in a minor fashion, in many of the events to be related. While an attempt has been made in this chapter to present a balanced review, there can be little doubt that partisan opinions will, from time to time, have broken through. It is to be hoped that this will help to enliven the discourse, rather than distorting the reality.

The year of the Robbins Report[2] is taken as the starting point for this chapter as the report is often represented as being the beginning of the development of mass education in this country. It was, of course, no such thing. There was a significant growth in the numbers of students in the post-war period before Robbins, with a 46% growth from 1953 to 1963. Even by 1973, ten years after Robbins, the number had risen only to 239,000, although this represented more than 100% growth during the previous decade.[3] As the century approached its close, governments of both persuasions took pride in the level of coverage which had been achieved. In 2000 22% of the eighteen-year-old age cohort

---

1 Ian Mowat died in an accident while hill-walking in Glencoe in September 2002. This chapter has been edited and revised since his death by Peter Hoare, as a tribute to many years' friendship and to his work for the library profession.
2 *Report of the Committee on Higher Education* (London, 1963), (Cmnd. 2154) (The Robbins Report).
3 W. A. C. Stewart, *Higher education in postwar Britain* (Basingstoke, 1989), 268.

attended higher education institutions in England – though the attitude, purpose and coherence of such institutions had changed dramatically in the period since Robbins. Even then, as revealed by the figures from Scotland – where 32% of the equivalent age group were identified as attending higher education – there was scope for further growth in a UK context, although, at the turn of the millennium, statistics indicate that the number of UK graduates now exceeds the number of graduates in the United States: a position which would have been regarded as inconceivable only a decade previously.[4]

Nevertheless, it is probably true that Robbins marks the point at which there was public recognition that university education was no longer to be the preserve of a class elite leavened by the occasional intrusion of the brainy and deserving poor. Even if the middle classes continued to dominate university entrance, first-generation students with no family experience of university life became commonplace (perhaps for the first time since the first early days of universities).

However, Robbins can also be seen to represent another milestone. Governments for centuries have taken an interest in universities and what they do; and government funding of higher education has been a long-standing commitment. In previous generations the government–university interface was limited and occasional in nature, and the creation in 1928 of the UGC, intended to act as a buffer between government and the universities, can be taken as representative of a long-term relationship.[5] The government response to Robbins was a significant ratcheting-up of the role of government in higher education and, in retrospect, can be seen to be the start of a period in which government interference in the higher education process became much more frequent and much more direct. From the 1960s, the increase in the corporate state, which was evident in society as a whole, made its impact on universities. Although the so-called Thatcherite revolution was supposed to set society free from the reins of government, the rhetoric frequently exceeded reality, and nowhere more so than in the university sphere. Through the 1980s and 1990s government interference in university life actually became more rigorous. Governments indeed attempted to cut back on their financial contribution to higher education and to reverse the pattern set by Robbins. The Conservatives abandoned any attempt to relate maintenance payments to the cost of living when they introduced a loan scheme in 1996, while the Labour government

---

4 G. Kerevan, 'A revolution too far', *The Scotsman* (31 January 2001), 8; W. Woodward, 'Britain tops US in degree league' *The Guardian* (17 May 2000), 5.
5 University Grants Committee, *University development from 1935 to 1947* (London, 1948), 6–9.

elected in 1997 went a step further and introduced direct tuition fees charged to individual students.[6]

During the second half of the twentieth century universities proliferated as part of the government strategy to increase participation. Following some growth in the immediate post-war years, the Robbins era saw the arrival of the so-called plate-glass universities, followed by the promotion of the Colleges of Advanced Technology in the 1960s; and of the creation of the 'binary divide' resulting from the foundation of the polytechnics in 1970 (established on the basis of existing colleges, and initially supposed to have a more vocational role than the universities), which finally vanished with their elevation to university status in 1992.[7]

Government involvement

If government intervention was a principal theme for universities as a whole over the period, such involvement has also been of primary importance in determining the shape and development of academic libraries. Following from the Robbins Report, a Committee on Libraries[8] was set up in July 1963 by the University Grants Committee (UGC) with the following terms of reference:

> To consider the most effective and economical arrangements for meeting the needs of the Universities and the Colleges of Advanced Technology and Central Institutions for books and periodicals, taking into account expanding staff and student populations, the possible needs of other users, the growth of research, the rising cost of books and periodicals and the increasing capital cost of library accommodation; to assess how far greater use might with advantage be made of shared facilities, both between the institutions themselves and between them, outside library systems and other institutions, and of modern methods of reproduction; and to report.[9]

The committee, working under the chairmanship of Dr Thomas Parry, Principal of University College, Aberystwyth, produced its report in March 1967. Although certainly not the most successful report on libraries within the

---

6 M. Salusbury, *Thatcherism goes to College: the Conservative assault on higher education* (London, 1989).
7 H. Perkins, *New universities in the United Kingdom* (Paris, 1969); Stewart, *Higher education*. The first breach of the binary divide was in 1984 in Northern Ireland, when the New University of Ulster (founded in Coleraine in 1967) merged with Ulster Polytechnic to form the University of Ulster, with four campuses across the Province.
8 University Grants Committee, *Report of the Committee on Libraries* (London, 1967) (The Parry Report).
9 Parry Report, 1.

period, it did, in many respects, set the tone for the remainder of the century. Despite the failure of the terms of reference to cover automation, the report itself was remarkably prescient on the future. While recognising that the 'practical implementation of these possibilities lies in the future',[10] the report forecast (from existing American research) all the major developments in automation. In the areas that were included in its remit, the Committee reported wisely, and its recommendations, within the context of the time, were sensible. It is all the more to be regretted that, although the recommendations certainly informed the practice of librarians during the subsequent decade, they did not produce as much response from government or from the university system as might have been hoped.[11] The report's first main recommendation, that a Libraries sub-committee of the UGC be established, was not adopted.[12]

More successful was another leading recommendation: the creation of a national library. Following the Dainton Report,[13] the British Library came into being in 1973. Parry took a national view of library provision, being conscious of the benefits of co-operation both within and outwith the higher education sector. Throughout the world in varying degrees relations between national and academic libraries are marked by factionalism, disputation and competition. Where both national and academic libraries are strong the opportunities for dispute are correspondingly larger. It is remarkable, therefore, not that there has been some disagreement between the British Library and longer-established academic institutions, but that some valuable co-operation has taken place. A perhaps partial assessment would point to the schizophrenic approach of the British Library as the most likely cause of both the relative harmony and the lack of progress. The British Library has attempted endlessly to foster co-operation, often through its research programmes, inherited from OSTI and run under the auspices of what eventually became the British Library Research and Development Centre before passing, at the end of the century, to the Library and Information Commission and its successor Re:Source (renamed the Museums, Libraries and Archives Council in 2004).[14]

10 Parry Report, 135.
11 Parry Report, 157.
12 F. W. Ratcliffe, 'After Atkinson', *Library Review* 35 (1986), 73.
13 *Report of the National Libraries Committee* (London, 1969) (Cmnd. 4028) (The Dainton Report).
14 British Library, *Annual Report 1973–4–* (London, 1974–); N. Moore, 'Meeting the costs of development: the role of the British Library (Research and Development Department)', *Journal of Librarianship* 16 (1984), 188–98; D. Greenwood, 'The BNB Research Fund: cutting across the boundaries', *Journal of Librarianship* 21 (1989), 246–59.

The next key milestone in government intervention in libraries was the Atkinson Report of 1976.[15] As it was primarily concerned with library buildings its outcomes will be dealt with in the relevant section. It is worth recording here, however, the mixed inputs to the report and the responses it evoked. The report was generally felt to be in tune with contemporary government thinking to ensure a more cost-effective approach to university expenditure and received a generally hostile reception from librarians who saw it as an attempt to restrict plans for infinite expansion. This reaction probably says less about the merit of the report itself than about the continuing belief of many in the academic community, even into the 1970s, that it was still possible to aspire to create a new Bodleian in every university in the country. Indeed, one of the report's authors, Dr Brian Enright (himself a distinguished academic librarian), believed that the common response represented a singular failure of imagination on the part of the academic community. He held that the recommendations laid out a sensible path for the future expansion of university libraries in the United Kingdom.[16] Whether or not he was correct, the impact of the Atkinson report was limited in respect to overall library development, and university libraries ceased to be a central concern of government for a decade and a half thereafter.

This did not mean that government initiatives did not impact upon academic libraries: merely that the impact came tangentially, rather than as a purposeful attempt to address library issues. The most significant example of such practice can be seen in the efforts of the University Grants Committee and its successor, the Universities Funding Council (UFC), to rationalise the structure of academic departments across the country in the late 1980s. A recognition of the higher costs of small departments coincided with the evidence of the research assessment exercises, by which departments were judged on their research performance, to suggest that weaker departments should be closed, with the transfer of active staff and other resources to stronger departments in other universities.

Amongst the resources affected were the relevant library collections. It appears that the UFC hoped that the appropriate subject collections would transfer with the staff to new universities. But while it may have wished the end, the UFC made very little effort to provide the means. Some small reimbursement was provided to cover the specific costs of moving stock but even

15 University Grants Committee, *Capital provision for university libraries: report of a working party* (London, 1976) (The Atkinson Report).
16 Personal communication from B. J. Enright. See also I. Winkworth and B. Enright, 'Relevance and reality in libraries', *Library Review* 35 (1986), 79–90.

that was minimal. It certainly did not cover all the costs of identification and deselection, although it did meet the cost of actual transport. There was no provision for compensation to the universities which had built up the collections. Nor was there any rational guideline for the division of spoils when academics moved to more than one university – as frequently happened. Unsurprisingly, the net outcome was a damp squib. A few universities took a positive approach: Lancaster reacted to the closure of its Slavonic department by dispersing the library collections to those universities that were accommodating the displaced staff.[17] Librarians know that there are no friends to be won within a university by suggesting the discard of stock. At a time when the universities losing departments were feeling threatened anyway, the academic community was less likely than ever to look kindly upon the dispersal of library collections. Amazing interest was shown in collections which had been relatively little used, even when the appropriate department had been functioning. The fact that residual teaching in a closed department often continued, at least for an interim period, was used as an excuse to delay or prevent the transfer of relevant stock. The net result was little more than to increase the irrelevance of many university library collections to the research interests of home-based academic staff.

After a fairly sorry saga of inappropriate or inadequate government intervention in library affairs throughout the greater part of the period, the twentieth century closed with what, almost certainly, will be seen as the most valuable government contribution to academic libraries for many decades. The elevation of the former polytechnics to university status in 1992[18] occasioned a great deal of thinking – positive, negative, and often ill-informed – about the purpose and practice of universities. Once again, initially, the government wished the end without providing the means. However, significant student protest at the inadequacy of provision in the newly created universities provided the impetus for a rethink.[19] The protesters had made poor library provision one of their main issues. The government finally did appreciate that something had to be done to cater for actual need.

That something was the creation of the Follett review. A panel, under the chairmanship of Sir Brian Follett, a distinguished academic with interests

---

17 University of Lancaster, *Report of University Librarian, 1986–87*, 3–4; *1987–88*, 4; *1988–89*, 4. Care was taken to direct appropriate subject collections to appropriate institutions; for example, the Czech literature went with the lecturer in Czech (an obvious outcome, perhaps, but one that was far from universally practised).

18 *Higher education: a new framework* (London, 1991) (Cmnd. 1541).

19 M. Anderson, 'Access to research collections in the UK: the Anderson Report updated', *Library Review* 47 (1998), 262–6.

in publishing in the biological sciences and subsequently Vice-Chancellor of Warwick University, produced a report in 1993 that revolutionised the British academic library scene.[20]

The report was successful not only because of the wisdom of its recommendations but because its recommendations were agreed by government and implemented. Anecdotally, Sir Brian reported that this was because there was regular interaction between the review panel, especially Sir Brian himself, and the Civil Service. As he put it, on each issue he would go to the civil servants responsible for implementing the outcomes and indicate the sort of financial sum needed to address the issue the panel was currently discussing. If the reaction from the civil servant was positive, that sum would go forward as a recommendation. If the reaction was negative, discussion would take place on what sum might be acceptable and, after the necessary horse-trading, that sum or a variation upon it would appear as a recommendation. In effect, the report had already been accepted before it was published.

The successful outcome was all the more remarkable because of the report's recommendations. The review, it should be remembered, was set up in response to a perceived problem relating to teaching and learning and its terms of reference related to that area of university activity. Although teaching and learning were indeed seriously addressed in the report, the Follett Committee clearly did not feel limited by this constraint. The recommendations on research were just as far-reaching and significant.[21] To some extent, the criticism might be levied that research interests had hijacked a review that was intended to concentrate on teaching and learning. Cynics might see it as all of a piece with the tendency of the older and larger universities to absorb funding at the expense of newer and smaller institutions.

In practice, however, even if research interests took a larger slice of funding than might have been expected from the original remit, the gain was for the higher education sector as a whole. The report identified three main areas for action: automation, building and collections. With regard to automation, the main outcome was the creation of the electronic library programme under the auspices of the Joint Information Services Committee of the Higher Education Funding Councils (JISC).[22] A longer-term assessment of the value of Elib may indeed question the merit of many, if not most, of the programmes funded for

20 Report [of the] Joint Funding Councils' Libraries Review Group: a report for the HEFCE, SHEFC, HEFCW and DENI (London, 1993) (The Follett Report).
21 Follett Report, 8.
22 Follett Report, 73–4; J. W. T. Smith, 'A review of the use of networking and related technologies by the UK academic library and information sector', IASLIC Bulletin 41 (1996), 49–69.

their contribution to the information needs of the academic sector. The specific projects supported, certainly in the initial phases of the project, produced very little in the way of practical outcomes. But there can be no question that the swift learning experience produced by partnership involvement in projects changed the whole mind-set of a generation of librarians, while the associated work of JISC in its Committee on Electronic Information led to the development of national collections of electronic material. It is possible that a few other countries have surpassed the achievements of JISC in this area – Finland is an obvious example[23] – but the enormous benefit which the programme brought, in terms of reduced costs and wider access to electronic material, cannot be denied.

The outcomes relating to library buildings are discussed in the section of this chapter which deals with buildings. All that needs to be said here is that Follett money provided the largest input of resources to library buildings in the academic community that has ever been experienced in this country.

Automation and buildings were areas which could have been anticipated from the setting up of the review. Identification of resource for research collections was rather more unexpected. Astonishingly, something in the order of £50 million was found to support a programme to support research collections (see below).

As the century drew to a close there remained a last twist to government intervention. The election of the Labour government in 1997 astonishingly led to the implementation of a policy on devolution which had been in and out of Labour manifestos for a century and more. New assemblies were set up for Scotland and Wales, and power, at least for the time being, was restored to a Northern Ireland assembly. Within England there was also a renewed emphasis on regional co-operation and development. By the end of the century it was too early to say how important these constitutional and administrative changes would be in their impact upon academic libraries but there was already some indication of effect. In Yorkshire and the north-east of England, for example, existing co-operation between academic institutions and cross-sectorally between universities and other regional bodies was strengthened by the new position. The establishment of a Museums, Libraries and Archives Council (MLAC) in each of the English regions in 2002–3 developed this further. The Welsh Assembly had very limited powers of decision making and the Northern Ireland Assembly tended to follow the English lead in higher

23 I. Saonharju, 'Country licensing by the Finnish electronic library programme', *Helsinki University Library Bulletin* (1999), 10–12.

education matters, but in Scotland political devolution, following many years of administrative devolution, had an immediate effect on, for example, the distribution of funding to universities. Perhaps more significantly, the ease with which cross-sectoral approaches could be tackled within a smaller-scale environment was already beginning to manifest itself as the century ended.

Automation

If government initiatives were important in driving change and development in the higher education library sector, the change with the greatest impact was undoubtedly the introduction of automation. Although the Parry Report was optimistic about an (undefined) automated future there should be no doubt about the boldness with which the pioneers in library automation embarked upon an adventure with no clear end. Visionaries have always pointed the way to the future but the future has not always materialised quite as expected. In the 1930s miniaturisation in the shape of microform was being pushed as the answer to library problems.[24] Its exponents would be disappointed at the limited, if important, impact which microform has had on academic libraries. User-resistance has proved too strong except where the case has been overwhelmingly strong or no suitable economic alternative has existed. But miniaturisation has indeed won out with the advent of automation and digitisation and even the 1930s enthusiasts for microform could feel an element of justification. If they were not able to envisage the means, they certainly forecast the end.

The pioneers in library automation in the 1960s deserve credit for having the vision to see that there was a useful future in a product which, at the time, arguably was less efficient than existing systems. Even as late as the early 1970s IBM were offering a batch-process circulation system at a cost in the region of £250,000 to the university library sector: it provided no modules on cataloguing or acquisitions and no public catalogue, and its circulation-control was so limited that there were lengthy periods when the previous day's loans could not be known to either users or library staff.[25] Yet, by the end of the century, automated housekeeping systems at much lower prices were offering very sophisticated management of and access to information.[26]

24 S. J. Teague, *Microform librarianship* (London, 1977), 4–5.
25 The author was involved in discussions with IBM on such a system for a small university library in 1972 when a price of £250,000 was quoted.
26 Prices for new systems tend to be commercially in confidence but the author is aware of one estimate of under £70,000 for one of the leading commercial systems, received by a small university in 2002.

Automation as a broad issue is considered elsewhere in this volume and it would not be sensible to duplicate the more general treatment by merely repeating it in an academic context. However, as academic libraries have led in the introduction of automation, and as automation has determined the development path of academic libraries, the issue cannot wholly be ignored. Indeed, academic libraries can take pride in their ready and early adoption of automated techniques. Despite increasing financial restrictions they have been quick to exploit new technology: apparently well ahead of more high-profile industries.

Early experiments in automation took place in the 1960s in a number of libraries, of which Southampton and Newcastle were amongst the leaders.[27] The early emphasis was on housekeeping systems, designed to make the process of handling discrete physical items of information in the library's ownership easier and faster. Batch processing was the norm and there was relatively little access by end-users to the new technology. More mundane experiments, such as the automated production of a serials list at Glasgow University in 1968, were fairly widespread and, of course, there were failures, now long forgotten. An automated order-system introduced to Edinburgh in the early 1970s proved so traumatic that it delayed further forays into library automation in that institution for several years.[28] The inevitable failures and lack of progress explain why the onward progress of automation was neither as rapid nor as welcome as might, with hindsight, appear to have been inevitable.

Since commercial suppliers were still finding their way in a new market, much of the early effort was in-house development. There was, in consequence, a lack of common standards or general applicability. To counter this, the traditional tendency of librarians to co-operate came to the rescue and a number of collaborative projects emerged in the 1960s and early 1970s. The most successful of these was the Birmingham Libraries Cooperative Mechanisation Project (BLCMP),[29] which started life as a shared cataloguing database but transformed itself over the years to become a standard library software supplier serving a wide market of academic and other libraries. Apart from a brief foray into Europe by BLCMP, British-based consortia remained

27 R. O. MacKenna, 'University library organization', in J. Thompson (ed.), *University library history: an international review* (New York, 1980), 104. For the work of other libraries in this area, see P. Havard-Williams, 'University libraries', in P. H. Sewell (ed.), *Five years' work in librarianship, 1961–65* (London, 1968), 34–5.

28 Edinburgh University Library, *Annual report 1972–73*, 7; *1974–75*, 3; *1975–76*, 3.

29 J. Thompson, *A centennial history of the library of the University of Birmingham 1880–1995* (Birmingham, 2000), 179, 191.

single-country organisations, though their later development into commercial enterprises expanded their market.

A significant advance in automated provision took place at the start of the 1980s with the arrival of commercially developed, stand-alone systems of a far higher calibre than the existing collaborative models. Although there were a number of strong competitors the standard was set by GEAC – a Canadian company whose principal business was in providing automation for banks, which, it had been noted, had similar needs to libraries. Although GEAC's strength was in its highly functional circulation system, it offered one of the first user-friendly automated catalogues designed for the end user rather than library staff.[30]

Commercial systems increased in sophistication as the century drew to a close but it was only in the last few years of the millennium that the next major shift begin to take place: the move from systems acting as guides to finding texts, to systems providing on-line access to the texts themselves. America, as ever, led the field but there were specific areas in which the United Kingdom proved to be a market leader: more particularly in the area of digital preservation.

One consequence of increased automation, and greater use of electronic information in many areas of academic activity, was the ever-closer relations between libraries and university computing centres. From the mid-1980s a growing number of universities combined their libraries and computing centres (often along with other academic services) into a 'converged' information services unit. Although in part a response to the need for budget cuts, the trend was also a genuine response to changing conditions. The pattern was set initially by the newer and smaller institutions (Salford was one of the earliest), but by the end of the century even larger universities such as Birmingham and Bristol were following the same path, with the title 'Director of Information Services' often replacing the traditional 'University Librarian'.

Buildings

Judged solely by the most obvious physical manifestation of libraries, the buildings in which they are housed, the second half of the twentieth century was probably the most successful in the history of British academic libraries. The

---

30 T. W. Graham, R. Lane and K. M. Richards, 'Keyword and Boolean searching on GEAC at Hull University', *Vine* 48 (1983), 3–7. The author had the privilege to be present in City University New York on the day the first GEAC online catalogue system was launched there and shared in the excitement at the ease with which library users took to the new provision.

number and size of the buildings erected has been without parallel. Though the architectural quality has not always been of a high standing, that is a truism that applies to all periods of construction and, in practice, the lack of monumentality in most of the libraries erected since the 1960s has almost certainly been a great advantage in terms of efficiency of use.[31]

It would be wrong to imply that aesthetic quality was entirely missing and tribute should be paid, in particular, to the work of Harry Faulkner Brown, a Newcastle architect. Faulkner Brown's practice designed new libraries or major extensions across the country, from Cambridge in the south to Cardiff in the west and Dundee in the north. At their best, as in Nottingham, his libraries represented the idea of calm, well-ordered flexible buildings, fitting well into their environment and an aesthetic pleasure as well as a utilitarian success.[32]

Traditional fixed-purpose buildings were still being built into the early 1960s, as at the University of Sheffield.[33] Fortunately, the concepts of the great American practitioner Keyes Metcalf were introduced to good effect in many of the libraries of the new universities founded in the Robbins era.[34] Although the libraries of universities such as East Anglia, Essex, Lancaster and Warwick were designed and built over a period of more than a decade from the early 1960s, each with individual features, they all represented the triumph of flexibility over fixed purpose.[35] Despite being designed in an era when automation was in its infancy, they accommodated to change over succeeding decades.

The University of Edinburgh Main Library, completed in 1967, represented a particularly striking example of 1960s library design at its best.[36] It was designed, like the library of the University of Sussex, by the firm headed by Sir

31 R. S. Smith, 'The history of academic library buildings', in Thompson (ed.), *University library history*, 128–46 (specifically 143–4).
32 H. Faulkner-Brown, 'Some thoughts on the design of major library buildings', in *Intelligent library buildings: proceedings of the 10th seminar of the IFLA Section on Library Buildings and Equipment* (The Hague, 1997), 9–24.
33 University of Sheffield, *Report of the Librarian, 1958–9*, [1]. The new library was opened by T. S. Eliot.
34 K. D. Metcalf, *Planning academic and research library buildings* (New York, 1965); B. E. Moon, 'Building a university library: from Robbins to Atkinson', in B. Dyson (ed.), *The modern academic library: essays in memory of Philip Larkin* (London, 1989), 20–31; A. Vaughan, 'The ideology of flexibility: a study of recent British academic library buildings', *Journal of Librarianship* 11 (1979), 277–93.
35 G. Thompson, *Planning and design of library buildings*, 2nd edn (London, 1977); University of East Anglia, *Annual Report of Librarian*, 1967–8, [1]; University of Leicester, *University Library Annual Report, 1974–75*, 3; 1975–76, 3–4. P. Havard-Williams, 'University library buildings', in H. A. Whatley (ed.), *British librarianship and information science, 1966–70* (London, 1972), 181–91.
36 Edinburgh University Library, *Annual Report, 1966–67*, 3; 1967–68, 3; 1970–71, 6–7.

Basil Spence. Complete flexibility proved a chimera because of the high costs associated with making each part of a building capable of adaptation to serve all possible functions, but Edinburgh stood the test of over thirty years constant adaptation remarkably well.[37] Indeed Edinburgh illustrated very clearly the strengths and weaknesses of architects to provide suitable library buildings over the period. A relatively bland, though not undistinguished exterior concealed an element of monumentality in the entrance hall which might equally have served for an airport lounge. The remainder of the building was largely utilitarian, with bare floors and unadorned concrete pillars. Succeeding years saw attempts to humanise the interior with the introduction of carpets and paint.

In Edinburgh, as in most library buildings of the period, there was a singular failure by architects and engineers to resolve problems of air conditioning. There is, of course, a conflict between the conditions which best suit books and those which are most appropriate for human beings. The designers of later twentieth-century libraries appear to have addressed the conflict by resolving to satisfy neither need. Temperatures above 90 degrees Fahrenheit were recorded in Glasgow in the years immediately following its opening in 1968, and in Sheffield attempts to increase reading space by providing tables and chairs in the stack areas were for many years rendered ineffective because of the high temperatures and low quality of air in these areas.[38] It is possibly an inevitable consequence of the dominance of automation at the end of the twentieth century that research or investigations into many traditional aspects of library activity such as buildings has very significantly diminished. Yet the need for improvements in building design remains and seems likely to continue to be required.

As with almost every other flat-roofed library building constructed in the second half of the twentieth century, Edinburgh was beset by constant leakages. Leicester stands out as a partial exception to the general pattern. Although a flat-roofed building, the architects had the superficially mad idea of placing a huge tank of water on the roof of the building. In practice, so long as the tank remained, Leicester bucked the trend and avoided water leakages. Only when the water was removed did the roof start to leak. Future generations

37 At a SCONUL Buildings Sub-Committee meeting in 1973 the Librarians of Glasgow and Edinburgh Universities compared their libraries. The former suggested that his building (which was inflexible) had been open for five years and had not required change. The latter reported that his had been open for six years and had been changed every year since it opened!
38 University of Glasgow, *Report of the Library Committee for Senate*, 1969–70, 1; University of Sheffield, *Report of the Librarian*, 1959–60, [1]; 1989–90, 11; 1990–91, 16.

should be aware of the substantial element of staff time which was spent in university libraries in dealing with copious amounts of water ingress, whether through the roof, rising from under the floor or flowing from burst pipes, or leaking or blocked taps. In the main, major disasters to stock were avoided from water-initiated problems, although Glasgow University was able to fund the installation of a conservation unit to deal with one major flood from the insurance cover.[39]

The high costs of Edinburgh's new library were such a drain on UGC finances that it is believed that the UGC was persuaded by them to adopt a new approach to library building.[40] Whatever the real reason, the new policy meant that, instead of long-term planning, the UGC limited itself to a ten-year horizon and determined to fund new buildings or extensions to meet only the requirements of that short-term requirement. No doubt, even in the late 1960s, the potential impact of automation was being considered by the UGC but the immediate outcome of the change of policy and the way it was handled was disastrous for Glasgow, the first University Library to be built according to the new principles. Funding was available for only half of the original design. Thereafter, small sums became available at irregular intervals, with no clear indication that further funding would be forthcoming. As a consequence, instead of the original, well-considered design, a hotchpotch of a building was constructed over thirty years with constant disruption as each phase of building impinged upon what had gone before.[41]

The Atkinson Report, although a blow to expansionist ideals, at least made very clear to all concerned the basis on which new building would be permitted. Its formula of allowing $1.25m^2$ per student, plus an allowance for growth and for special collections if necessary was used in the succeeding period to argue the case for new build or extensions to existing libraries in many universities.[42]

Where government funding was not central to the university's effort a more generous approach could be adopted. At Cambridge, for example, the university, with access to private funding, was able to add major extensions to its 1930s library building that were not constrained by Atkinson norms.

If Atkinson was at best a mixed blessing, the end of the twentieth century saw what was almost certainly the biggest boost for British academic library buildings in history. The Follett report recommended an investment of

39 Glasgow University Library, *Annual Report, 1983–84*, 6.
40 M. Smethurst, 'Henry Heaney: an appreciation', *Library Review* 47 (1998), 256–61.
41 E. M. Rodger, 'Who wins – the architect or the librarian? Academic library building in Britain 1984–1989', *Library Review* 40 (1991), 74.
42 Atkinson Report, 16.

£140 million for new library buildings and the outcome was startlingly success-ful.[43] Many new libraries and extensions to existing buildings were constructed to imaginative designs, with proper account taken for the needs of automation and for the extended opening hours that were increasingly a feature of univer-sity life at the end of the century. Cranfield University Library might stand as an exemplar for the period – though at Cranfield, as so often elsewhere, the architect (Sir Norman Foster) was unable to match the need for quiet against the competing demands of other specifications. A similar problem did not stop Abertay University using its new library of 1998 as a symbol of the whole university. A rather more distinctive design, also of iconic value, was the new Ruskin Library at Lancaster.

Collections

Throughout their history libraries have existed primarily as collections of infor-mation. The aim of librarians was to have the largest and most comprehensive collection possible to provide for the needs of the community the library was intended to serve. Almost certainly at no time has the goal of having every-thing relevant in the one library been achieved, and by the twentieth century there was not the slightest prospect of resources being available to any aca-demic library in the United Kingdom to get anywhere near comprehensiveness except in very narrow areas of endeavour. Nevertheless, the dream of compre-hensive acquisition continued to dominate professional thinking for most of the century. Dr F. W. Ratcliffe, a leading force in British academic librarianship for most of the period covered in this chapter, advocated that collection should take precedence over cataloguing or otherwise processing material since the opportunity to buy, once missed, might not easily recur.[44]

In practice growth was variable, depending upon such factors as the age of the library, its level of funding and the spread of subjects. A sample table of libraries for which data exist at the beginning and end of the period reveals some startling differences (Table 30.1).[45]

The fact that the two dominant universities in England, Oxford and Cambridge, both had legal deposit privileges which entitled them to a copy of every book published in the United Kingdom and Ireland led to rapid

43 Follett Report, 83.
44 F. W. Ratcliffe, 'The growth of university library collections in the United Kingdom', in Thompson, *University library history*, 5–32; F. W. Ratcliffe 'Collections, collectors and collection building', in C. Harris (ed.), *The new university library: issues for the '90s and beyond* (London, 1994), 4–18.
45 Parry Report, 172–3; SCONUL, *Annual library statistics 1993–4* (London, 1995), 9–11.

Table 30.1. *Growth of university libraries 1964/5 to 1993/4*

Library	Hull	Birmingham	Leicester	Cardiff	Aberdeen	York
Volumes 1964/5	237,000	657,000	194,000	207,000	404,000	69,000
Volumes 1993/4	630,926	1,917,000	1,073,867	523,384	784,069	546,729
Increase 1964–5 to 1993–4	166%	192%	454%	153%	94%	692%

expansion, as publishing output increased over the decades.[46] This gave further academic respectability to size of both collections and acquisitions as a benchmark for excellence in other institutions. The attitude persisted until the end of the century and it was a ground-breaking decision of the Follett Committee to set out to avoid creating another fifty research libraries for the former polytechnics by encouraging a more strategic approach to collaboration.[47]

Polytechnics were far less tied to this belief in size, emphasising the usefulness of the stock instead.[48] Polytechnic librarians were perfectly happy to dispose of unwanted material where most university librarians held firm to the just-in-case philosophy: someone, sometime might want a book even if it had never been opened or even had its pages cut.[49] The Atkinson Report undermined the traditional perspective somewhat, and the increasing gap between theory and reality as the end of the boom years in funding of higher education in the 1960s gave way to steady-state funding and then to actual cuts in the 1980s and 1990s moved the profession further away from adherence to such beliefs. If it is true for farmers that most years are bad years and the rest are perfectly disastrous, a similar belief might hold true of those who chose to read the annual reports of university librarians with their reiterated complaints that budget increases were signally failing to keep pace with inflation or demand.[50]

Inflation was possibly an even greater problem than small increases or cuts in funding. Robert Maxwell, who made his fortune as a publisher of academic journals, was well known as a shady character by librarians well before the

46 By way of comparison, the British Library's intake of legal deposit material increased from 273,400 items (including periodical parts) in 1973–4, to 507,762 in 1997–8, a rise of only 86%, although in a shorter period (British Library, *Annual Report*, 1973–4 and 1997–8).
47 Follett Report, 48–52.
48 Winkworth and Enright, 'Relevance and reality in libraries'.
49 As an undergraduate in Aberdeen the author had the joy of coming across in the library stacks a volume received on legal deposit in the eighteenth century with the pages still uncut. There has been savage criticism of those who discard print-on-paper too easily: see N. Baker, *Double fold: libraries and the assault on paper* (New York, 2001).
50 J. Thompson, *Redirection in academic library management*, 2nd edn (London, 1991), 12–40.

exposures of his later years.[51] His Pergamon Press was one of the first to realise that universities were a captive market and that the price of journals could be increased year after year without any reference to true cost. Librarians and their academic masters stand accused in equal measure of supine failure in standing up to barefaced robbery. Elsevier – a publisher of great distinction and age – purchased the Maxwell stable of journals and took over the same policy on pricing until the end of the century. Against these exorbitant price increases libraries could not compete and budgets continued to trail behind, despite strong efforts by many universities to recognise the higher-than-average costs of library materials.[52]

The final nail in the coffin of collection growth was the development of electronic information. Publishers took the opportunity to tighten their hold on the market by licensing access to electronic information, rather than selling it outright.[53] Most such information was accessed remotely, rather than being held in the subscribing institution. This was particularly true for journals (the market for electronic books was only tentatively being opened up as the century ended). By the end of the century, university libraries were spending about a quarter of their materials budgets on electronic information and this figure was rising rapidly.[54] In the new century the concept of libraries as service centres, rather than collection centres, has become common, with some, such as the influential American commercial co-operative OCLC, envisaging libraries without significant collections as a norm.

Even when growth was still the expectation, the realisation that funds did not match aims led libraries to collaborate on purchasing schemes. Some of the schemes in the early part of the period were, in retrospect, quite absurd. One scheme in the 1960s and 1970s parcelled out publishing dates between universities and all-but-arbitrarily assigned two separate decades to each library participating in the scheme. The library concerned was expected to purchase as many items as it could of those published within the specified decades, irrespective of the relevance of the items to the local community (or anyone else).

---

51 R. Davies, *Foreign body: the secret life of Robert Maxwell* (London, 1995).
52 CURL, *Scholarly communications crisis* (n.p., 2001); Follett Report, 19–25.
53 C. Johnston, 'Electronic technology and its impact on libraries', *Journal of Librarianship and Information Science* 30 (1998), 7–24.
54 An electronic poll of SCONUL libraries in March 2002 revealed, from a response of twenty-three libraries, that, on average, these libraries spent 24.5% of their materials budget on electronic materials in year 2001–2. It is likely, from the detailed comments received, that this was a conservative response.

The dream of 'rational' shared collecting continued to bedevil the scene even longer than the belief in growth. It may seem inconceivable to future generations that academic libraries, whose primary purpose was to serve their local communities, communities constantly in transition in the range of interests studied, could aspire to rational policies of collecting. By the end of the century no scheme had yet been devised which sensibly took account of long-term retention and preservation as well as acquisitions, and yet it was clear that the search for such a scheme and the likely wasted expenditure of considerable sums of money would continue.

More sensible was the belief that better knowledge of strengths and weaknesses would assist scholars to make efficient use of scattered collections. Unfortunately the tools available were not up to the job. The *Aslib Directory* for many years gave subjective, locally derived descriptions of collections from each library listed, which all claimed equal excellence despite vast discrepancies in relative size.[55] Henry Heaney, Librarian of Glasgow University, took the lead in persuading some Scottish university libraries[56] to undertake a Conspectus exercise, using the mapping technique devised by the Research Libraries Group in the United States.[57] Whatever the merits of Conspectus, it was an incredibly costly scheme to administer and was devised for a society where expenditure on collections was substantially larger than in the United Kingdom. Inevitably, staff costs reduced the objective elements of the exercise and the end result again betrayed the subjective weaknesses (if not to the same extent) of the *Aslib Directory*.[58]

Preservation of collections was a continuing concern throughout the period but reached a peak of heightened awareness with the publication of the Ratcliffe Report in 1984.[59] While the report had some long-standing significance, leading, amongst other things, to the creation of the National Preservation Office within the British Library, the largest injection of money for preservation in academic libraries came from the programme for Non-Formula Funding of Special Collections in the Humanities, another success of the Follett Report. A large element of the approximately £50 million from this programme was

55 *Aslib directory*, 3rd edn (London, 1968–70).
56 R. Milne, 'Conspectus at the coal face', *British Journal of Academic Librarianship* 3 (1988), 89–98.
57 N. E. Gwinn and P. H. Mosher, 'Co-ordinating collection development', *College and Research Libraries* 44 (1983), 128–40.
58 Smethurst, 'Henry Heaney: an appreciation', 259.
59 F. W. Ratcliffe, *Preservation policies and conservation in British libraries: report of the Cambridge University Library Conservation Project* (London, 1984).

dedicated to conservation projects, with most of the remainder going to ret-rospective cataloguing.[60]

Staffing

If collections and the buildings which enclose them were two of the main com-ponents of the traditional library, the third was staff. It is possible that library staff may be the main surviving element of libraries in the future. It is appropri-ate, therefore, that during the second half of the twentieth century academic librarianship finally ceased to be an adjunct of mainstream academic life and developed an identity of its own. There were, of course, librarians running aca-demic libraries in a managerial fashion for many years before the Second World War but a perception lingered well into the 1960s that academic librarianship, unlike public librarianship, was the haunt of the scholar and that scholarship was valued at least as much as any competence in management skills. The foundation of new departments of librarianship in the 1960s, exemplified by Sheffield in 1964, gave a boost to the professional standing of librarians.[61] Stu-dents doing the postgraduate course at Sheffield were explicitly enjoined to eschew thoughts of undertaking PhDs in their undergraduate disciplines and instead encouraged to consider the delights of research in library-related top-ics. In a decade when the social sciences were highly popular, social-science concepts and precepts – surveys, statistical analysis and sociological perspec-tives – were all adopted by aspiring library researchers to demonstrate the intellectual validity of their undertakings.[62]

Inevitably, the older universities stuck longest to traditional patterns. Size, comparative wealth and intellectual prestige meant that these universities had specific requirements of their library staff not always so evident in smaller and newer institutions. In particular, skills in the handling of older books and manuscripts and the very specific linguistic accomplishments required to service departments teaching relatively uncommon languages such as Chinese led to the recruitment of staff whose primary qualifications were specific to the post. The newer universities took a new look at what was expected of library staff.

---

60 Follett Report, 72; Accessing our humanities collections: a guide to specialized collections for humanities researchers (London, 1998).
61 R. Staveley, 'Professional education', in Sewell (ed.), Five years' work in librarianship, 1961–65, 604–6.
62 M. B. Line, Information requirements of researchers in the social sciences (Bath, 1971).

Although universities, especially in the 1960s, prided themselves on collegiality and some element of democracy (at least amongst academic staff), most academic libraries were traditionally hierarchical in their organisational structures. Some of the new universities, such as Sussex and East Anglia, introduced a degree of participative management and, even in the long-established institutions, pressure from the Association of University Teachers (in which librarians were often active) or a more general recognition of trends led to at least some consultative mechanisms being set up. But, in general, the traditional pyramid of control reigned, with a small group of senior staff (usually designated sub-librarians) answering directly to the Librarian and with sub-sets of professional and non-professional staff answering to the sub-librarians.

For most of the period being reviewed, there were two principal arrangements of library staff. The first was a traditional division between technical services (procurement, cataloguing and classification) and reader services (circulation, shelving and other public functions). Increasingly, in the 1960s, an alternative approach stressing the subject-librarian or subject-group was adopted. One of the earliest models was that introduced by Dr Willi Guttsman at the University of East Anglia. Some variants of this model gathered most of the functions of the library in a subject grouping rather than in traditional functional departments, although other activities, such as circulation, tended to remain centralised unless the distribution of library sites approximated closely to subject division.[63]

The growth of liaison librarians undermined the traditional dominance of the cataloguer in academic libraries, and with the growth of automation other specialists began to appear.[64] Towards the end of the century there was an increase in the number of appointments drawn from outwith the library or scholarly areas. However, there was a reversal of the earlier trend as reductions in the number of academic-related staff led to a decline in subject-librarians and the rise of computer databases gave new emphasis to the role of cataloguers. Professional personnel officers, fund-raisers and accountants, for example, made their appearance because of the increased complexity of legislation and university administration.

63 P. A. Woodhead and J. V. Martin, 'Subject specialization in British university libraries: a survey', *Journal of Librarianship* 14 (1982), 93–108; J. V. Martin, 'Subject specialization in British university libraries: a second survey', *Journal of Librarianship and Information Science* 28 (1996), 159–69; MacKenna, 'University library organization', 92–108; B. Prince and P. F. Burton, 'Changing dimensions in academic library structures: the impact of information technology', *British Journal of Academic Librarianship* 3 (1988), 67–81; D. Baker, 'Structures for the 1990s', *British Journal of Academic Librarianship* 5 (1990), 159–63.
64 G. A. Muirhead, 'The role of the systems librarian in libraries in the United Kingdom', *Journal of Librarianship and Information Science* 25 (1993), 123–35.

It would be quite unfair to accuse earlier generations of a lack of management skills, although it might seem odd to later generations that Glasgow only introduced a management team meeting in the mid-1980s (and may not have been the last to do so).[65] Hindsight has identified many areas where tighter purse-strings have forced later generations to find more cost-effective ways of doing things, and the adoption of management styles and techniques was more evident as a consequence of both the professionalisation of activity and the greater attention paid to managements within the university sector as a whole. In the last two decades of the twentieth century management courses specifically targeted at senior academic librarians were arranged.[66]

Although parallel salary structures existed between academic staff and senior library staff it was only in the mid-1970s that a nationally negotiated structure for academic-related library staff came into being. Even then, there were variances which allowed different interpretation from one institution to another. The link was much weaker in those universities which had formerly been polytechnics, which retained quite different salary scales. An uneasy balance was maintained in the older universities throughout the period of this review but the Bett Report again questioned the link between library and academic salaries – identifying academic librarians as well paid in comparison to other librarians.[67]

In the 1960s the typical gender balance was that women dominated, almost to exclusion, the bottom level of the pyramid of control, while male numbers increased as the pyramid narrowed. (This was not atypical of the period and reflected the various social restrictions in equal conditions for women.) While several of the former university colleges had had women as chief librarians,[68] the presence of women at that level was rare in universities until the 1980s. The polytechnics were quicker to correct the imbalance, and a typical SCONUL meeting today (since the merger with COPOL in 1994) has what appears to be a balanced distribution between the sexes, whereas standard SCONUL sessions up to the 1980s had been almost exclusively male.[69] Given women's numerical

65 M. B. Line, 'Library management styles and structures: a need to rethink', *Journal of Librarianship and Information Science* 23 (1991), 97–104; M. Heery, 'New model librarians: a question of realism', *Journal of Librarianship and Information Science* 25 (1993), 137–42.
66 S. Corrall, 'Management development in academic libraries and the Joint Funding Councils' Libraries Review', *British Journal of Academic Librarianship* 9 (1994), 220.
67 *Independent review of higher education pay and conditions: report of a committee* (London, 1999). (The Bett Report)
68 For example Hull, Leicester and Southampton.
69 The official photographs of SCONUL meetings from the 1960s onward reveal the male dominance of that period and the gradual increase in female participation, which accelerated after the merger with COPOL.

domination of professional librarianship, however, it may have proved easier (or slightly less difficult) for women to fight their way to the top in librarianship than in many other professional arenas.[70]

The 1960s was a decade of expansion, and library staff increased significantly in number, but the proportion of library expenditure on staff remained broadly similar throughout the period: 53% in 1964–5, 52% in 1973–4, 57% in 1981–2 and 56% in 1991–2. It is less easy to identify patterns of change in numbers of staff or in the distribution between professional and non-professional staff because of inadequate data: library annual reports and other sources do not always distinguish between part-time and full-time staff and record the distinction between professional and other staff in different ways. The author, as a practising librarian, would have a firm view that total numbers of staff employed in libraries were in decline and that this was most noticeable amongst professional staff. However, a randomly selected sample of libraries from which data are available does not bear this out. Indeed, between 1993–4 and 1999–2000, the mean figure for library staff numbers in SCONUL institutions increased from 65.85 to 77.5 although the percentage of professionals fell from 40% to 35%.[71]

Co-operation

Libraries themselves represent a collaborative solution to the problems of access to information. For centuries the concept of the wandering scholar, visiting archives and libraries, has been a leading theme of intellectual life, and in the twentieth century this was joined by the concept of the wandering book – or the inter-library loan.[72] The creation of what was known, for most of its existence, as 'Boston Spa' was a step-change in the inter-library loan process in the United Kingdom.[73] Requests to the National Lending Library for Science and Technology in 1962 totalled 217,000; requests to its successor, the British Library Document Supply Centre, reached 1,832,000 in 1973–4 and 4,271,374 in 1997–8. Its success diminished the demand both for large local holdings of scientific journals and for sophisticated inter-library loan systems. Oxford and

70 C. Steele and M. Henty, 'A woman's place is in the – library? A review article', Journal of Librarianship 19 (1987), 121–32; N. Moore and E. Kempson, 'The nature of the library and information workforce in the United Kingdom', Journal of Librarianship 17 (1985), 137–54.
71 SCONUL, Annual library statistics, 1993–4, 64–5; University Grants Committee, Statistics of education, vol. 6: Universities (London, 1974), 148.
72 Encyclopedia of Library and Information Science, vol. 12 (New York, 1974), 197–211.
73 D. Cox, 'Cooperation among university libraries in the United Kingdom', in Thompson, University library history, 170–86 (at 173).

Cambridge came to serve as back-up libraries to Boston Spa and the largest research libraries continued to lend significant numbers of monographs either through direct enquiry or by participating in regional inter-lending schemes. But with over 90% of the average academic library's inter-library loan requests being satisfied through BLDSC there was little need for British university libraries to develop sophisticated inter-library lending schemes.[74] Libraries and their parent institutions were reluctant to commit significant sums from local budgets to support collaborative effort, while at the same time complaining quite strongly about the level of top-slicing of government education grant for official collaborative ventures. Much of the most successful co-operation has been government-led, or at least the result of government funding.[75]

Collaboration independent of government directive did, of course, take place, with the central body for university libraries during the second half of the twentieth century being SCONUL.[76] Originally created in 1956 as a consequence of dissatisfaction with the Library Association's attitude to university libraries, SCONUL quickly became the formal voice of the academic library community. In its early days it was seen as an elitist club but by the late 1960s it had settled down as the main forum for the interchange of ideas and information between university chief librarians. It flourished principally as an ideas exchange, as British academic libraries lacked the initiative or enthusiasm to go on to create a collaborative organisation capable of delivering services.

Indeed, SCONUL at first lacked any professional staff and was run on a voluntary basis by the Librarian of Birmingham University, Dr K. W. Humphreys. The appointment of Henry Heaney as the first full-time Assistant Secretary in 1969 gave it new impetus and a number of successful initiatives can be attributed to the body, such as the SCONUL graduate trainee scheme, and more formal training courses for specialist areas, such as rare-books librarianship, where SCONUL felt that existing provision was inadequate.[77] In addition, SCONUL organised overseas visits allowing British university librarians an opportunity

74 A local perspective is given in A. F. MacDougall, H. Wheelhouse and J. M. Wilson, 'Academic library cooperation and document supply: possibilities and consideration of cost-effectiveness', *Journal of Librarianship* 21 (1989), 186–99.

75 This is not to ignore but to attempt to place in proper perspective the work of regional co-operatives; cf. J. Blunden-Ellis, 'Looking to the future: the Consortium of Academic Libraries in Manchester (CALIM)', in Harris (ed.), *The new university library*, 45–54.

76 T. H. Bowyer, 'The founding of the Standing Conference of National and University Libraries (SCONUL)', in Thompson, *University library history*, 208–28.

77 T. Bainton, 'SCONUL and research libraries', *Library Review* 47 (1998), 267–70; B. Loughridge, 'The SCONUL Graduate Trainee Scheme as preparation for professional education in librarianship and information work', *British Journal of Academic Librarianship* 2 (1987), 191–203.

to compare and contrast UK performance with others, at a time when the opportunities for broadening perspective by professional foreign travel were more limited.

The creation of the polytechnics led to the formation of a similar body to SCONUL for their librarians – the Council of Polytechnic Librarians (COPOL). With its smaller and less well-funded constituency, COPOL could not afford professional staff and remained true to the original SCONUL concept of voluntary effort. In some ways this led to a more energetic body, concentrating on spreading best practice through the publication of a range of excellent reports.

Despite its successes, SCONUL somehow never appeared to match the sum of all its parts. When the decision was made in 1994 to merge SCONUL and COPOL, following the redesignation of polytechnics as universities, there was some hope that a new vigour would be injected into the enlarged organisation. It was not clear, as the century ended, whether the sclerosis of the older SCONUL or the vigour of COPOL would triumph in the longer term.

However, there were some consequential dramatic changes, around the time of the merger (as well as the change in gender-balance referred to earlier). The emphasis of SCONUL activity swung very sharply away from research towards the support of teaching and learning. In part, this change was encouraged by the creation, in 1983, of the Consortium of University Research Libraries (CURL).[78] A self-selected group of seven research libraries began to meet for reasons very similar to those which led to the creation of SCONUL in the first place. Although initially dubbed, irreverently, the Consortium for University Rich Lunches – on account of the *bon-viveur* proclivities of some of the participants – CURL quickly began to concentrate on the creation of a joint database and union catalogue – COPAC. To further this activity it obtained funding from JISC and formed a close alliance with the Research Libraries Group in the United States. By the end of the century, CURL had grown to include over twenty institutions and continued to develop its international links as well as to deepen the connections between the members.

Conclusion

At the start of this chapter note was made of the difficulty of maintaining perspective in contemporary history. With all due regard to the fact that events through which participants live always seem more dramatic than those of past

78 R. Carr. 'Research collections in the digital age: the role of CURL', *Library Review* 47 (1998), 277–81.

generations, it seems probable that future commentators will see the second half of the twentieth century as a major turning point in the development of libraries. After centuries of growth, interrupted only by occasional financial crises, British academic libraries in the later twentieth century reached an unsurpassed pinnacle of grandeur in terms of collections, buildings, services and staffing. The post-Robbins era indeed saw growth that was exceptional by the standards of preceding eras. But, as it is always possible to see the seeds of decay at the height of success, so in the achievements of the later twentieth century it is possible to detect, if not the end of libraries, at least the first major indicators that traditional libraries, as physical spaces housing physical objects, may decline rapidly in the twenty-first century. The extension of automation from processing to information creation, while possibly the most important single factor, may have helped to hide other contributing issues, such as the role of government control in forcing changes in academic behaviour leading to a reduction in library use and importance. Only the passage of another half-century will tell how far the indicators at the end of the twentieth century have pointed to significant change in the new millennium.

PART VI

*

THE RISE OF PROFESSIONAL
SOCIETY: LIBRARIES FOR
SPECIALIST AREAS

31

Libraries and information for specialist areas

JACK MEADOWS

Introduction

The creation of libraries to cater for specialist interests has a long history. As early as the mid-sixteenth century cathedrals received royal orders to start theological libraries. Access to specialised libraries was, indeed, a valuable aid to all the traditional professions – law and medicine, as well as the church. Thus, the Inns of Court had rudimentary libraries from early in their career, while the library of the Royal College of Physicians of London soon developed from an existing private collection. As knowledge expanded in subsequent centuries, so did the variety of professional interests. Hence arose the need for new types of specialised libraries. By the end of the eighteenth century, for example, the Foreign Office had recognised the need not only for a departmental library, but also for a librarian to manage it. Alongside professional developments, new intellectual interests led to the formation of societies devoted to specific subjects. Both the Royal Society in the seventeenth century and the Society of Antiquaries in the eighteenth century began to build collections soon after their foundation.

Although these two strands – the growth of professions and of organised interest in specific topics – therefore existed prior to the nineteenth century, it was during that century that they began to develop rapidly, and specialisation became the norm. Engineering, for example, came to be recognised not only as an important new profession, but as one that increasingly required its practitioners to specialise in one branch of the subject only. Consequently, in the latter part of the nineteenth century, a range of new engineering societies (for gas engineers, mining engineers, and so on) were created to cater for these growing bands of specialists. This fragmentation was a necessary response to the ever-widening range of knowledge covered by engineering. It involved, and was supported by, the growth of new employment opportunities that required specialist practitioners. A similar tale can be told of other subjects.

This is only part of the story. Interest in specialisms that offered few job opportunities expanded at the same time. This interest, too, was catered for by a range of new societies. In terms of membership, such societies often had a greater number of members than those dealing with more practitioner-orientated topics. For example, at the end of the 1860s, the Anthropological Society had over five times as many members as the Chemical Society.[1] The difference reflects the growth of amateur interest in specific topics during the nineteenth century, again encouraged by the new knowledge that was appearing, as well as by increasing leisure and prosperity.

All this was backed by changes in the educational scene. By the end of the nineteenth century, the reform of school education was creating a demand for specialist teachers across a range of subjects. The new universities that sprouted at this time could therefore afford to provide more specialised degrees – in English as much as in Chemistry. The dominant model of specialisation accepted then by British universities came from Germany, where it was linked to developing research in all disciplines. In Britain, the development of specialisation was less professionalised and systematic than in Germany, but the trend was in the same direction, with research becoming increasingly important.

The nature of special libraries

The concept of 'special libraries' in our modern sense emerged from this growth of specialisation in the latter half of the nineteenth century. By the 1870s, the term had come to mean 'a collection in a specified, limited subject field, sponsored by an institution or society, by a private individual, or by a department or college in a university'.[2] (A modern definition would exclude collections belonging to private individuals or universities, which are treated elsewhere in this volume.)

In view of the variegated way in which specialisation developed in Britain, this diversity of ownership is hardly surprising. The early development of special libraries often depended on individual initiatives. This could be true even in commercial and industrial enterprises. Thus the library of the twentieth-century giant, ICI Dyestuffs Division, originated in an individual initiative in the nineteenth century in one of its constituent firms.[3] This rather haphazard approach to collection development differed from the more systematic

---

1 L. Levi, 'On the progress of learned societies', *British Association Report*, Norwich (1868), 169–73.
2 A. W. Johns, *Special libraries* (Metuchen, NJ, 1968), 13.
3 W. Ashworth, 'Information in Britain', *Aslib Proceedings* 23 (1971), 635–44.

approach often taken by American or German companies, who typically attached greater value to the acquisition of information. Ludwig Mond moved to England from Germany, and became a major power in the British chemical industry. At the end of the nineteenth century, he provided funding for the expansion of the Royal Institution. According to one of his sons, a significant factor in this decision was the value he attached to the Royal Institution's library for research.[4]

The growth of commercial and industrial libraries, in particular, led to the recognition that the requirements for running a special library often differed from those for traditional (more especially public) libraries. The formation of the Department for Scientific and Industrial Research (DSIR) during the First World War, and its subsequent support for a number of industrial research associations, provided a focus for an examination of these differences. Partly as a result of observing special library activities in the United States, directors of two metallurgical research associations, J. G. Pearce and R. S. Hutton, decided to arrange a conference on special libraries. This was organised by A. F. Ridley (the librarian at Hutton's establishment) in Hertfordshire in 1924. As Hutton later explained:

> we had prominently in mind two vital problems which faced industrial research associations but which appeared to us to be common to both scientific and humanistic enterprises however diverse their individual professional interest might be. These twofold tasks were: how to make as complete as possible a survey on some special subject from world-wide sources, and how to bring the more important results of the survey to the attention of members of the organisation, however unwilling or inexperienced they might be, at first, to utilize the knowledge so gained.[5]

The first point here is noteworthy. Though the instigation of the conference came from the industrial side, it was recognised that special libraries could cover any topic. They were distinguished more by their method of operation than by their subject matter. Hutton then suggests two ways in which their operations differed from those of traditional libraries. The first was that they were more concerned with information than with the material form in which that information appeared. Public libraries concentrated on collecting books, more especially those published in Britain. Special libraries had broader interests, particularly in what came to be called the 'gray literature'. If their

4 I. M. McCabe, 'The Royal Institution and its library', *Royal Institution Proceedings* 61 (1989), 283–90.
5 R. S. Hutton, 'The origin and history of Aslib', *Journal of Documentation* 1 (1945), 6–20.

specialism was of interest world-wide, then they sought relevant information from abroad, as well as from home. A second characteristic was that special libraries had a greater concern with dissemination. A public library, on this picture, was a general depository from which readers selected what they wanted. Special librarians searched for, evaluated and selected material themselves. Then they were typically involved in the dissemination to their clients of the information they had acquired.

The Hertfordshire conference proved to be highly successful. It soon led to the formation of an Association of Special Libraries and Information Bureaux. (Its acronym, ASLIB, was subsequently written in the form 'Aslib'.) The conference had received financial support from the Carnegie Trust, and the Trustees provided Aslib with further backing during its early years. One result of their funding was the appearance of the *Aslib directory: a guide to sources of specialized information in Great Britain and Ireland*. This was the first time that special libraries in the British Isles, along with their resources, had been listed.

Where the boundary occurred between special libraries and information bureaux was far from clear, though collections involving humanities material were normally considered to be special libraries. The confusion is reflected in a contemporary comment by an American librarian: 'Before everything else, it [the special library] is an information bureau. The main function of the general library is to make books available. The function of the special library is to make information available.'[6] The understanding of how special libraries differed from traditional libraries continued to be refined. At the end of the 1940s, E. M. R. Ditmas, General Secretary of Aslib for many years, quoted approvingly an American writer concerning those characteristics of a special library which distinguished it from other libraries:

> Its primary functions are: (1) to maintain a continuing survey and evaluation of current publications, research in progress, and activities of individual authorities, on behalf of its clientele; (2) to organise the sources of both written and unwritten experience and knowledge from the specialist viewpoint; (3) to assemble from within and without the library both publications and information as required by the activities of its clientele, disseminating these on the initiative of the library as well as on request, often in abstract or memorandum form oriented for immediate application to any individual's work.[7]

6 E. Johnson, 'The special library and some of its problems', *Special Libraries* 6 (1915), 158–9.
7 E. M. R. Ditmas, 'The literature of special librarianship', *Aslib Proceedings* 2 (1950), 217–42.

Although it was generally agreed that special libraries could exist in any subject, Aslib had mainly commercial and industrial libraries as members from the beginning. The preceding description of special librarianship reflects primarily the requirements of these kinds of libraries. Special librarians in areas remote from commerce or industry might find difficulty in identifying with all the activities specified. For example, to what extent are (say) cathedral librarians involved in the active selection and dissemination of information to their clientele? Yet clearly there are some factors in common between the different types of special library. One is the spread of material that such a library embraces. Cathedral librarians may not have to cover report literature to the same extent as their colleagues in industry, but they do have to look after such additional items as illustrations, music sheets and archival material.

A significant requirement, automatically assumed in many definitions of special libraries, is that special librarians need to be subject specialists. This may mean that they have previously worked as a practitioner in the field covered by the library. In the early days of industrial libraries, for example librarians were often recruited from R & D staff in the firm. In recent years, the training of prospective special librarians has become more organised, but employers still typically look for some background knowledge relevant to the specialism. This identification with the subject leads special librarians on to a greater degree of involvement with their clientele. Cathedral librarians – to use them again as an example – may not need to be highly proactive. They are certainly expected, however, to discuss readers' needs with them, and to advise readers on the use of material in the cathedral library.

Librarians and information specialists

Evidently, there are common themes applicable to most types of special library despite their diversity. One confusing factor is that specialist librarians in general libraries (such as university or national) may often act in rather similar ways. As this indicates, the distinction between a specialist librarian and a special librarian is still not entirely clear-cut; so it is hardly surprising that it took some time to be drawn. When a Special Libraries Association was formed in the United States not long before the First World War, most of its founding members were actually specialist librarians, rather than special librarians in the present sense. Correspondingly, the meeting that initiated the new association was held at a conference of the American Library Association.[8] This

8 R. V. Williams, 'The documentation and special libraries movements in the United States, 1910–1960', *Journal of the American Society for Information Science* 48 (1987), 775–81.

may be contrasted with the situation in Britain. Although the founders of Aslib held amicable discussions with the Library Association in London during the 1920s, it was concluded that the aims of the two bodies were too different to allow for any formal linkage. In effect, the Library Association found it easier to embrace specialist librarians, than special librarians. It should be added that the designation 'special librarian', which seems to have originated in the United States, was not particularly popular either among the practitioners themselves, or among other librarians. It continued in use for want of a better term.

The differing approaches in Britain and the USA can also be discerned in the development of training for special librarians. Up to the second half of the twentieth century, special librarians in the USA were a good deal more likely to have had a library training than their counterparts in Britain. British special librarianship was based more on the amateur tradition of *ad hoc* adaptation, with all its defects and virtues. For example, the Librarian of the Royal Geographical Society in the latter years of the nineteenth century had a background in theology. He simultaneously acted as an editor for the publisher, Macmillan, and as a staff writer on a range of topics for *The Times*.[9] Nevertheless, there was already a growing perception that supervision of special libraries required some previous acquaintance with the way they operated. In 1899, the Library Committee of the Architectural Association protested to its General Committee when the latter nominated as honorary librarian a person who had no previous connection with the work of the Association's library.[10]

The primary defect of this tradition was that new recruits to special librarianship in the early days were usually ignorant of what had already been achieved in general librarianship. The corresponding virtue was that they could undertake new initiatives to meet the specific needs of special libraries unencumbered by past experience in other types of library. Librarianship, as taught between the two World Wars, was essentially an arts-orientated activity. The concentration was particularly on books, and on the importance of conservation. Both these aspects were of minor importance in most special libraries (outside the humanities), where the concern was rather with current information. The difference in orientation of the two groups led to a continuing debate over the relative value of library knowledge and subject knowledge. From the viewpoint of traditional librarians, the debate was exacerbated by the

9   H. R. Mill, *The record of the Royal Geographical Society, 1830–1930* (London, 1930), 106.
10 'The Architectural Association Library 1862–1978', *The Architectural Association Annual Review* (1979), 15–70.

fact that the special librarians' lack of formal training was often accompanied by higher salaries.

So far as training was concerned, the Library Association introduced elements of special librarianship into the syllabus from the 1930s onwards. Similarly, the new School of Librarianship at University College London tried to provide subject training for candidates across the board – for the sciences as well as the humanities.[11] In both cases, take-up was limited. Special libraries in industry and the Civil Service expanded rapidly after the Second World War, and this helped increase the urgency of the training question. The debate became intense in the 1950s. Aslib and the Library Association set up a joint working party which made some progress in agreeing what were the core topics of special librarianship. Aslib was reluctant itself to become an examining body. A group of members therefore decided to establish a new body – the Institute of Information Scientists – with the prime objective of establishing standards and qualifications in the subject. This was in 1959, and by 1961 an IIS-approved course was under way at Northampton College of Advanced Technology (now City University). Meanwhile, the Library Association, at a rather more leisurely pace, introduced its own new syllabus for special librarianship. By the end of the 1960s, special librarianship was consequently becoming an activity involving both formal training and qualifications of its own.[12]

'Information science' was not the term initially used to describe the interests of special librarians. A commoner early description of their activities was 'documentation'. So, when Aslib set up a journal in 1945, it was named the *Journal of Documentation*. Similarly, the pioneering text on the topic by S. C. Bradford in 1948 was simply called *Documentation*. It is symptomatic of the confusion existing between traditional librarianship and special librarianship that there were widely divergent views as to what exactly the term 'documentation' meant. In essence, three possible viewpoints existed.[13] The first saw documentation in very broad terms. Documentation on this definition was the collection, arrangement and distribution of documents of every sort in all fields of human activity. On this view, librarianship was a sub-division of documentation. The second viewpoint saw librarianship and documentation as complementary activities: librarians look after collections, while documentalists exploit them. Finally, the third view saw documentation as a sub-division of

11 W. Ashworth, 'Special libraries', in W. L. Saunders (ed.), *British librarianship today* (London, 1976), 272–96.

12 Ashworth, 'Special libraries'.

13 T. P. Loosjes, *On documentation of scientific literature* (London, 1967).

librarianship. Documentation in this case was simply bibliography and library information work suited to the situation in special libraries. Substituting 'information science' for 'documentation' has not resolved this debate. An analysis of changes in the names of library schools in the UK suggests that, by the last decade of the twentieth century, information work was increasingly being seen as the dominant activity, with library work as one of its facets. A major factor in this change was the growth in use of computers and networks for information handling.

The use of the word 'documentation' in connection with special library work can be traced back to the Belgian bibliographer, P. M. G. Otlet, at the beginning of the twentieth century. Its use in this context is reflected in the name of the international body often associated with special libraries, the Fédération Internationale de Documentation (FID). It remained the preferred term for such work on the Continent, and in French-speaking countries more generally, after 'information science' became common usage in the UK and other English-speaking countries. (For example, the American Documentation Institute was founded in 1937. It changed its name to the American Society for Information Science in 1968.) However, by the end of the twentieth century, 'information science', 'informatics', or parallel terms in other languages, were widely used.

Differences and similarities

The name 'documentalist' with its variety of meanings sat reasonably happily with special library work in any field. For example, Theodore Besterman, who helped establish the *Journal of Documentation* at Aslib, specialised in the writings of Voltaire. 'Information scientist' was a less congenial term to special librarians in the humanities. Its use in the latter part of the twentieth century was therefore particularly common in special libraries with a science base. Correspondingly, librarians dealing with special collections in the humanities were more likely to find traditional library training and qualifications helpful. One reason was that they were much more concerned with the need to conserve old publications than their peers in science-based libraries. Humanities libraries have typically commanded a lower level of funding than other special libraries. Funding for conservation has therefore been a continuing problem for them. Some relief for specific collections was obtained in the latter part of the twentieth century as a result of the central provision of grants for conservation administered by the British Library. For example, Lambeth Palace

Library received a grant in the 1980s to rebind sixteenth- to eighteenth-century books.

Older collections that had been exposed to the dual hazards of nineteenth-century acid paper and nineteenth-century library conditions were particularly at risk. As a member of one provincial society explained concerning the state of the books in its library at the end of the nineteenth century:

> I do not allude now to the minute ravages of the book-worm or the extensive dilapidations of the professional book-borrower, but rather to what the law calls 'the act of God', to wit, damp, gas fumes and the like. The binding of the books was suffering greatly from the products of the imperfect combination of poor coal gas. When you took a book off the higher shelves it would generally act like a hermit-crab and leave its outer covering.[14]

Even in the first half of the twentieth century, when electric lighting had generally replaced gas, conservation was often not a prime consideration in many special libraries. A member of one society noted sourly in 1931:

> the problem of keeping the books in the shelves free from dust [should] be tackled in real earnest and that – failing any other – as a concrete suggestion the committee considers the minimum quarterly dusting of them by a vacuum cleaner – resulting certainly in a considerable saving of soap and towels – and better health – after any reference to the shelves in their present state.[15]

At the same time, the tendency of books to wander seems to have been more noticeable prior to the Second World War. One librarian commented to members of his association in 1920:

> In the matter of [donating] books architects are generous, but have short memories. The Association has had its own books bequeathed to it by deceased members, on more than one occasion, but the Librarian hopes this method of returning books will not be considered as a precedent to be followed.[16]

Public libraries or university libraries have sufficient in common within their respective categories for some generalisations to be made about them fairly easily. Given all the different categories, it is less obvious that useful generalisations can be made regarding special libraries. A survey carried out in the latter part of the 1990s indicates some of the differences and similarities between

---

14 R. S. Watson, *The history of the Literary and Philosophical Society of Newcastle-upon-Tyne (1793–1896)* (London, 1897), 193.
15 T. Barringer, 'The rise, fall and rising again of the Royal Commonwealth Society Library', *SALG Newsletter* 41 (1994), 15–22.
16 'Architectural Association Library 1862–1978', 49.

them.[17] One difference relates to the level of penetration of special libraries into different sectors. For example, whereas all government departments were found to have libraries, this was true of only just over half of voluntary associations. Even within sectors, there were major variations. In the industrial sector, almost all firms in the pharmaceutical industry had libraries, but only a small minority of firms in the food industry. Though there was a fairly indiscriminate use of the terms 'library' and 'information centre/unit' for what we here call a 'special library', some sectors showed a preference. Government, law and professional associations used the term 'library', while pharmaceutical firms and consultancies preferred 'information centre/unit'. Most special libraries in the latter part of the twentieth century catered for a few hundred users, though the figure was ten times higher for professional associations. Most sectors showed either steady, or increasing levels of staff recruitment, but government libraries provided an exception, with reductions in staff.

Resources

Differences between special libraries depend, in the first instance, on the nature of the body that owns the library – government department, industrial firm or whatever. However, the most powerful factor at work has often been the libraries' resources – in terms of finance, accommodation and staff. The level of such resources often depends on external pressures and trends. Hence, some parallels can be drawn, even between special libraries in different sectors, in terms of the influence of these external factors.

To illustrate this point, consider the history of the Royal Commonwealth Society library.[18] The Society was established in central London in 1868 as the Colonial Society. Its subsequent changes in title – to Royal Colonial Institute, then Royal Empire Society and, finally, to Royal Commonwealth Society – reflect the changes in the political environment over the past century and a half. The Society's charter specified that it would 'establish a Reading Room and Library in which recent and authentic intelligence upon Colonial and Indian subjects may be constantly available'. Until the Second World War, the library expanded, and, allowing for the effects of the Depression, was reasonably well resourced. It was unfortunate enough to be bombed during the war, but the main post-war headache was the diminishing role of the society. Meanwhile, relevant material appeared in large amounts: it increasingly had

17 D. Spiller, C. Creaser and A. Murphy, *Libraries in the workplace* (Loughborough, 1998).
18 Barringer, 'The rise, fall and rising again of the Royal Commonwealth Society', 15.

to be purchased, rather than being donated. Selected material from the library was therefore sold to try and make ends meet. By the end of the 1980s, external consultants were advising that the library should be sold off. An appeal was launched to try and keep the library together. One of the problems had been that much usage of the library had come from non-members of the Society. This now proved to be an advantage: the media, which had made considerable use of the library, now publicised its plight. By 1993, the £3 million required to save the library had been donated, and the library was deposited in its entirety at the Cambridge University Library.

Clearly, there are factors here that are specific to the institution. An obvious example is the decline in the clientele for whom the Society was originally designed. At the same time, the library's history provides a number of themes that can also be found in the development of various other special libraries. An obvious one relates to financial difficulties after the Second World War. Post-war, special libraries (especially those in science-based fields) grew in both number and importance. At the same time, the amount of information being produced in many fields grew even more rapidly. Special librarians found they had to run fast in order to remain on the same spot. How to support special libraries therefore became a matter of increasing debate as the second half of the century progressed. Another theme suggested by the story of the Royal Commonwealth Society is the growth in usage of the library by non-members often for historical purposes, rather than fulfilling its original function of current awareness for members. A further theme is disposal of some, or all, of the library stock as part of the survival strategy for the host institution, often supplemented or replaced by a public appeal for funds.

These themes are reflected across a variety of special libraries.[19] A range of examples might be quoted. By the 1970s, the Liberal Club could no longer afford its accommodation overlooking the Thames. It decided to sell its library to the University of Bristol. A few years before, the Royal Anthropological Institute faced a crisis when the lease on its premises expired, and the rent demanded was increased by a factor of ten. In this case, the Institute kept its library in central London by putting it on temporary deposit with the Ethnographic Section of the British Museum. The Royal Statistical Society changed its address a number of times after the Second World War. As part of its need to economise, it disposed of much of its older library material, either by sale or donation (for example, to the Department of Industry). Part of the

19 Sir F. Francis and V. Bloomfield, *Independent libraries in England: a survey of selected institutional, proprietary and endowed libraries* (London, 1977).

problem for these bodies was the cost of space in central London. Where the accommodation was owned by the body, this was less of a difficulty, though costs (e.g. of rates) rose rapidly after the war. Some institutions decided to move out of London altogether, despite the increased problems this posed for would-be visitors. Others economised on staffing (though independent special libraries typically paid their staff less well then universities or industry in any case).

It is interesting to compare this picture with the development of special libraries in industry. Such libraries were boosted by the impact of the Second World War, just as they had been by the First. After the war, many expanded further, though their cost came under increasing scrutiny. This expansion is reflected in the membership of Aslib, which, helped by a government grant-in-aid, increased sixfold in the twenty years after the war. The initial post-war emphasis on research aided this expansion, since research is an information-intensive activity. However, economic depressions, which led to cutbacks in research, also led to cuts in special library expenditure. During the 1970s, there was a net decrease in the number of special libraries operating (though this was partly offset by a slight increase in the overall number of posts available).[20] In some cases, firms closed their information units and made the staff redundant. Simultaneous government encouragement of small and medium-sized enterprises was of little help, since these firms were generally too small to afford a library and trained personnel. In consequence, industrial libraries as a group, like independent special libraries, came under increasing financial pressure in the latter part of the twentieth century, though for different reasons.

The post-war years were far from proving restrictive for all types of special library. For example, libraries for legal practitioners were still essentially confined at the end of the Second World War to such institutions as the Inns of Court, law societies and universities. Then law firms started to create their own libraries, to allow them to keep abreast of the ever-changing legislative scene. The British and Irish Association of Law Librarians was established in 1969. By the end of the century, it had some 670 members, half of whom worked for law firms.[21] Looking backward in time, it is possible to see how particular types of special library have flourished or decayed as the information environment has changed. Law libraries flourished: music libraries provide a good example of decay. These libraries, which collected and circulated music for use at

20 H. East, 'Changes in the staffing of UK special libraries and information services in the decade 1972–81: a review of the DES census data', *Journal of Documentation* 39 (1983), 247–65.

21 D. J. Way, 'BIALL: the first 30 years – a personal view', *The Law Librarian* 31 (1999), 122–4.

home or in small groups, flourished throughout the nineteenth century. As the interest in this kind of activity decreased, so the libraries disappeared in the early twentieth century. Only a few in this category still operate.[22]

Besides their differences in subject matter, special libraries have always had differences in their outreach, ranging in scope from the international to the strictly local. Libraries at the top end of this scale – such as the Science Museum Library – occupy positions of world-wide significance in their chosen fields. (These national collections are covered elsewhere in this volume.) At the other end of the scale are small, local bodies that nevertheless maintain a limited collection of publications. Thus, an examination of local societies affiliated to the British Association in the latter part of the nineteenth century suggests that about a third then claimed to have libraries. The problem is that such small bodies are more liable to rapid change. A good example of this comes from an examination of libraries in Northern Ireland.[23] In 1975, there were four major historical societies, together with a few smaller ones, in the province. By 1990, this had grown to some sixty local history societies, all involved in document handling. Changes can also occur in the scope of a special library as time passes. For example, the Linen Hall Library in Belfast started life as an independent subscription library covering a wide range of subjects. As the result of a major financial crisis in 1980, a campaign was launched to keep the library open. This successfully emphasised its important holdings of Irish publications, and the library came to be seen as a centre for Irish and local studies.

Control of the literature

Special libraries have always been concerned with co-operation. Originally, this was primarily with other libraries in the same or adjacent fields. In the latter part of the twentieth century, wider involvement became increasingly common. Libraries in the medical and health care sector provide an obvious example. A wide variety of special libraries, in such bodies as government departments, hospitals, learned and professional societies, cater for medical staff. At the same time, other libraries – university and public – have long been involved in the needs of staff and patients. The development of co-operation across these various bodies can be traced, in part, in the history of Library

---

22 A. H. King, 'The history of music libraries in the United Kingdom', *Fontes Artis Musicae* 15 (1978), 201–4.
23 Library and Information Services Council (Northern Ireland), *Library and Information Plan for Northern Ireland* (Belfast, 1990).

Association sections. The Medical Section (formed in 1947) merged in 1978 with the Hospital and Handicapped Readers Group (formed in 1962) and ultimately became the current Health Libraries Group, which brings together librarians from all sectors.

Special libraries have always had a particular concern with inter-library loans. One reason relates to their specialised interests. This has meant that they may lack literature in borderline areas. Voluntary networks for such loans were already operating between special libraries in the first half of the twentieth century. It has been estimated that, in the period before the establishment of the National Lending Library, the volume of inter-library loans between special libraries was as large as all the loans made by the National Central Library and the regional library systems combined.[24]

Co-operation with other types of library was less common in the earlier years. Indeed, services might sometimes be seen as in competition. For example, the Library Association helped inspire the creation of municipal commercial and technical libraries during and after the First World War. The formation of research association libraries was widely seen as creating an alternative, competing service. In the humanities, co-operation was commoner. A topic such as local history is supported by special collections – often complementary – in public libraries and universities, as well as by special libraries. In the latter part of the twentieth century, co-operation has become commoner, not least in response to financial pressures. For example, though deposit of special library collections in university libraries has a long history (University College London accepted its first deposit in 1887), it has grown in popularity. An alternative approach has been to co-ordinate access and acquisition between different libraries. Newcastle upon Tyne offers an example. The Literary and Philosophical Society there reached a reciprocal agreement in the early 1970s with both the University and the Polytechnic (as it then was).

The characteristic features of special library operations – such as the variety of their contents and the need for active assistance to readers – resulted in a concern with the bibliographic control of specialist material from early on. An example is the crusade of the inter-war years, led especially by S. C. Bradford at the Science Museum Library, for the use of the Universal Decimal Classification in special libraries. It was argued that the UDC provided better access to documentation than other systems then employed elsewhere.

Amongst the various kinds of documents handled by special librarians, major emphasis has always been laid on the periodical literature. This emphasis

24 W. Ashworth, 'Special libraries in the UK in recent years', in K. Barr and M. Line (eds.), *Essays on information and libraries* (London, 1975), 17–27.

has led to significant contributions to bibliographical control of the literature. The obvious example is the development of abstracts journals. Although the practice of producing abstracts of documents goes back for centuries, the first abstracts journals in the modern sense appeared in Germany in the first half of the nineteenth century. In the UK, the key period was the latter half of that century, when learned societies, especially in the sciences, took the lead in producing abstracts.[25] For some societies, the cost and effort of producing abstracts was found to be excessive. For others, the increasing competition from the USA in the twentieth century proved too much. One British abstract journal of international importance that survived through the twentieth century was *Physics Abstracts*, started in the 1890s. Even so, it had to be rescued in the early years of the last century by financial assistance from the Institution of Electrical Engineers. (This has had the odd result that the main physics abstracts journal in the world is associated with electrical engineers rather than physicists.)

Information studies

Interest in active control of the literature led some special librarians to examine more closely the ways in which information could and should be handled. Thus, in the 1930s, S. C. Bradford investigated how well the existing indexes and abstracts journals covered the literature. His findings led him to formulate his law of scattering. The same question intrigued information users. Just before the Second World War, the physicist J. D. Bernal published *The social function of science*. This devoted considerable attention to communication, including bibliographical aspects. After the Second World War, this common interest of researchers and special librarians in the problems of information handling led to the organisation of a major conference involving both groups. The Royal Society Scientific Information Conference was held in London in 1948. It proved to be a landmark meeting, with significant implications for the future of special library work. This was less for its specific suggestions than for its wider implications. In particular, it emphasised the importance of special libraries, of carrying out research into information handling, and of planning for the future.

As after the First World War, so after the Second, much of information needs came under the auspices of the DSIR. In the 1960s, however, this Department

25 A. J. Meadows, 'Access to the results of scientific research: developments in Victorian Britain', in A. J. Meadows (ed.), *Development of science publishing in Europe* (Amsterdam, 1980), 43–62.

was broken up. One of the fragments to which it gave birth was the Office for Scientific and Technical Information (OSTI). The Office was instructed to encourage, and assist financially, four types of information activity – research, development, education and co-operation. After a few years of independent existence, OSTI was incorporated into the new British Library in 1974, becoming the British Library Research and Development Department (BLRDD). OSTI's original brief, despite its name, covered the social sciences, as well as science-based subjects. When it was incorporated into the British Library, this brief was extended to include the humanities.

Initially, a number of research projects were aimed at the needs of special libraries. By the early 1980s, Aslib was running some ten such BLRDD-supported projects. However, in 1985, Aslib ran into major financial problems. As part of the restructuring to cope with this, its R & D Division was closed down. The removal of Aslib as a co-ordinator reduced the coherence and level of research activity in the special library sector. Useful work was carried out within specific sectors. In the learned society sector, for example, the Royal Society was involved in two major surveys of the scientific information system in the UK during the latter decades of the twentieth century. In the commercial sector, the information needs of small and medium-sized enterprises were examined in some detail over the same period. Nevertheless, these efforts were typically *ad hoc* and isolated, rather than forming part of an overall research scheme for special libraries.[26]

Computerisation

At the end of the 1970s, there was a meeting between BLRDD and representatives from the Confederation of British Industry (CBI) and Aslib to discuss what industrial information activities were currently raising queries. One major concern was the handling of electronic information. Special libraries were interested in the possibilities of such handling from early on, and, by the mid-1990s, virtually all were using computers. Part of their interest related to internal library operations, but here special libraries differed little from other types of library in terms of development. Partly the concern was with readers' use, and here special libraries played a pioneering role, both in providing and in disseminating electronic information. For example, *Physics Abstracts*, as noted previously, has always been a major source of information in physics. By the

26 A. J. Meadows, *Innovation in information: twenty years of the British Library Research and Development Department* (London, 1994).

1970s, its publisher (now labelled 'INSPEC' – 'Information Services: Physics, Electrical and Electronics, and Computers and Control') was providing the information in three different forms – print, microform and magnetic tape. The electronic version could be used to provide tailor-made services based on the information profile of users. This could be run through the database at intervals to provide selective dissemination of information (SDI). In a similar way, the Chemical Society set up the United Kingdom Chemical Information Service (UKCIS) in the same period, which provided an SDI service from a number of databases. Special libraries wealthy enough to purchase the tapes could carry out the process for themselves; SDI fitted in well with the way they worked.

Microform had been used for storage purposes in special libraries since before the mid-twentieth century. It proved particularly valuable for archival material in humanities libraries. For shorter-term storage – the main concern in many special libraries – electronic storage rapidly displaced microform as the preferred medium in the latter decades of the last century. Similarly, as better electronic storage media were devised, magnetic tapes were consigned to oblivion. The significant development, however, was the growth of networking. Special libraries, not least those in defence-related fields, were involved early on in this. By the end of the century, the great majority of special libraries in all sectors (except the voluntary) were connected to the Internet.[27]

The change from stand-alone to networked computers led to new developments in information handling. One result, for example, was that SDI in its established form declined. More importantly, networks allowed much wider access to electronic information. Yet such developments reflected the continuing changes which the handling of electronic information required. These had major resource implications. For example, some special libraries enthusiastically embraced CD-ROM databases when they appeared, only to find that Internet services were soon overtaking them. Indeed, the extension of networking could underline existing organisational problems. For example, incompatibilities were found between information handling in different regions of the NHS.

The growth of electronic information handling had an increasing impact on all kinds of libraries. One consequence was that the activities expected of librarians and information staff, and the skills they needed to have, began to converge. This was clearly reflected in the frequent changes in the training they received in the last two decades of the century. It also appeared in the policies

27 Spiller, Creaser and Murphy, *Libraries in the workplace*, 201.

of their professional bodies. Towards the end of the 1980s, the LA, IIS and Aslib discussed the possibility of closer co-operation. These talks foundered, in part because Aslib was a different kind of organisation from the other two. In the late 1990s, talks aimed at a possible merger were restarted between the LA and the IIS. The seriousness of these talks reflected the changed outlook of the two bodies on the nature of librarianship since the mid-twentieth century. In 2002, after much agonising over possible names, the LA and the IIS merged to form CILIP (the Chartered Institute of Library and Information Professionals).

From the viewpoint of special librarians, the growth of information technology offered both a promise and a threat. On the one hand, information handling was becoming increasingly central to all the organisations in which they worked. The range of expected activities was correspondingly expanding – reflected, for example, in the introduction of the term 'knowledge management'. On the other hand, the growing importance of information handling brought in many who had no background in special library and information work. A key question at the end of the twentieth century was whether special libraries in the traditional sense would become more or less central to their host organisations.

32

The scientist and engineer and their need for information

JACK MEADOWS

Introduction

A variety of factors have affected the development of science and technology libraries over the past century and a half. The most important have been related to the growth in the number of publications appearing and in the number of people wishing to read them. Complaints about the proliferation of publications were heard well before the nineteenth century, but it was scientists in that century who had most reason for concern. Scientific knowledge was agreed to be cumulative. New research must always be built on the basis of what had gone before. This implied absorbing the relevant information in the literature before adding one's own contribution. By the nineteenth century, the growing number of scientific publications was making this ideal unattainable. Even so conscientious a researcher as Faraday was driven to complain: 'It is certainly impossible for any person who wishes to devote a portion of his time to chemical experiment, to read all the books and papers that are published in connection with his pursuit.'[1]

It became apparent during the nineteenth century that scientists' demands on libraries differed from those of most other readers. In good part, this was due to their emphasis on reading journals. Another difference was that scientists often required good subject-based catalogues, rather than the customary author-based catalogues. Moreover, the flood of publications meant that scientists had to become increasingly specialised in their interests in order to keep up with the research front. Libraries serving scientists, correspondingly, had either to become large, or to specialise. Inevitably, the typical library catering for scientists in the twentieth century has concentrated on acquiring those titles most required by its clientele. This has left the need for a back-up service

---

1 Quoted in J. G. Crowther, *British scientists of the nineteenth century*, vol. 1 (Harmondsworth, 1940), 113.

for those titles not taken. It was clear from the beginning that such a service would need to be national in its scope.

The Science Museum Library

The institution which carried this vision forward in the first half of the twentieth century was the Science Museum Library. The Science Museum – originally the South Kensington Museum – opened in 1857 as one of the numerous bodies established at South Kensington in the wake of the 1851 Great Exhibition. It soon acquired a collection of books for educational purposes. In 1883, this was enhanced by books transferred from the then Museum of Practical Geology (just off Piccadilly), and the Science Museum Library was officially inaugurated. Members of the Royal College of Science, another of the South Kensington institutions, became accustomed to using the Library as their college library. When, in the early years of the twentieth century, the Royal College of Science became the Imperial College of Science and Technology, this relationship was formalised. Indeed, the Science Library – as it was usually called – moved into new accommodation provided by the college.

It was after the First World War that the Science Library began to play a wider role in the provision of information. The Library was by now lending material to a number of neighbouring institutions. Moreover, it was acting as a reference library on science and technology for anyone who wished to use the Reading Room. Despite inadequate funding for acquisitions, it was decided in 1923 to extend the loan service to all government departments. A much more important step was taken three years later, in 1926, when the loan service was extended to all *bona fide* scientists and engineers. The service was taken up immediately. By the early 1930s, the number of postal loans per year was well over 10,000, and the number of readers using the Reading Room was double the 1920 figure.[2]

The Science Library was now well on the way to becoming the national focus for scientific and technological information. This was certainly the intention of S. C. Bradford, the head of the Library during this period. His twin aims were to develop the Library as a national resource, and to create a comprehensive index of scientific literature. These ambitions, and especially the first, were supported by the Museum. The Board of Education was much harder to convince. A Departmental Committee set up by the Board in the latter part of the 1920s

---

2 A discussion of the development of the Science Museum Library can be found in D. Follett, *The rise of the Science Museum under Henry Lyons* (London, 1978), 125–36.

suggested a major increase in the Library's acquisitions budget. At about the same time, a Royal Commission on Museums and Galleries also investigated the Library, and made similar recommendations to somewhat greater effect. By 1931, the acquisitions budget had risen to £3,000. This constituted a major achievement at the height of the economic depression.

The Board, however, had by now become disturbed by the Library's ambitious plans. It was not simply a question of funding acquisitions, but even more of funding additional staff. The number employed in the Library had more than doubled in the period from the early 1920s to the early 1930s. The Board was especially worried by the open-ended commitment implied by the provision of a loan service. It therefore referred the matter of the Library to the Standing Committee on Museums and Galleries. The Standing Committee's report was a good deal less supportive of the Library's ambitions than earlier reports. The rebuff was more apparent than real; for, despite the worries of the Board of Education, the Library's policy remained unchanged up to the Second World War. Indeed, by 1939, the Library housed one of the largest collections of science journals in Europe. Bradford, at least, never had any doubts about what was happening. He placed a plaque – totally unauthorised – outside the entrance, proclaiming that it was the 'National Science Library'.

Though the Science Museum was closed for much of the Second World War, its Library remained open. Demand for scientific and technological information grew, and the loan service was considerably expanded. By 1947, nearly 80,000 requests a year were being received. One consequence of this was that long waiting lists began to build up for journals in high demand. This latter problem was alleviated by introducing the newly developed technology of 'photostatting'. Predictably, the more efficient fulfilment of requests led to a further increase in demand. By 1954, there were new complaints about the efficiency of the loans service.

This growth in the loans service put severe pressure on the Library, not least because the number of staff was only about half that of the 1930s. Hardly surprisingly, there were increasing complaints about the effect of the loans service on other library services. In 1950, a new Director was appointed to the Science Museum whose main concern was with strengthening the historical aspect of the Library's work. The time was now ripe for a new initiative in terms of the central provision of contemporary scientific and technological literature. One of the people most involved in this new initiative was D. J. Urquhart, who started his career in the Science Library just prior to the war. In 1948, he transferred to the DSIR (Department of Scientific and Industrial

Research). In the aftermath of the war, DSIR was charged with the task of assisting the development of civilian science. As part of this, it was suggested in 1947 that the information unit in the Intelligence Division of DSIR should be expanded to provide a national advisory service on technical information sources.

Meanwhile, the scientific community had its own worries about the provision of information in the post-war period. The Royal Society took a number of soundings, and then, in 1948, organised (with government backing) a major conference on scientific information. The conference put forward a number of recommendations concerning the provision of national reference and lending facilities. These were backed by the Advisory Council on Scientific Policy (ACSP) which, in 1950, suggested the need for a central reference library in London and a national lending library that might be situated outside London. The Royal Society conference and, subsequently, the ACSP both saw the Science Museum Library as providing the basis for the proposed science lending library, whilst the Patent Office Library was suggested as a basis for the science reference library.[3]

By the mid-1950s, it had been agreed that the DSIR would take responsibility for a new National Lending Library for Science and Technology. In 1956, Urquhart was put in charge of the project.[4] He strongly supported the idea that the library should be outside London, not least because London was already better catered for in terms of scientific and technological literature than any other part of the country. He found that a number of disused Royal Ordnance factories existed in the north of England, and finally selected one at Boston Spa to form the basis for the new library. Work started there in 1958, boosted by concerns about lack of knowledge of Soviet science and technology after the launch in 1957 of the first artificial satellite.

The new library opened officially in 1962. Some of its stock came from the Science Museum Library, but the majority was newly acquired. It was soon evident that the library provided for a growing need. Loan requests increased from fewer than 120,000 in 1962 to over 375,000 in 1965. By the end of the 1960s, the number of staff employed had risen to well over 200 (at which point its history is taken up elsewhere in this volume). The Science Museum Library meanwhile concentrated on assisting historians of science and members of Imperial College.

---

3 For a detailed analysis of the development of the National Lending Library, see P. G. Watson, *Great Britain's National Lending Library* (Los Angeles, 1970).
4 For a personal view of events, see D. Urquhart, *Mr Boston Spa* (Leeds, 1990).

The British Museum (Natural History) Library

If the Science Museum Library encountered difficulties in its development, the library of the British Museum (Natural History) endured even more. The British Museum originally covered all areas of knowledge, but it soon became apparent that the natural history collections were particularly demanding in terms of space. The idea of transferring them elsewhere arose quite early on, but matters were brought to a head in 1856 when the Zoological Society donated the contents of its own museum to the British Museum. A scheme was therefore proposed for the removal of the natural history collections to South Kensington – the obvious place for a scientific institution in the latter half of the nineteenth century. The proposal for the move was put forward by the Trustees in 1860, but rejected by the House of Commons on the grounds of expense. However, the site of the 1862 Exhibition in South Kensington was subsequently acquired, and at long last, in 1881, the British Museum (Natural History) was opened. On its new site, the museum complemented the nearby Science Museum, which concentrated on the physical sciences and technology.[5]

At Bloomsbury, each natural history department had received an annual grant for the purchase of publications. Staff depended on the main collection, especially the library donated by Sir Joseph Banks in 1820, for material not covered in their departments. The Trustees of the British Museum decided that only material in departmental libraries could be transferred to South Kensington; the Banksian collection, in particular, would be retained at Bloomsbury. It was hoped that the Treasury would provide additional funds to purchase the publications required for the move. The hopes long proved to be in vain: it was not until the actual year of the move that the Treasury, under pressure from the scientific community, relented. Expenditure of £5,000 a year for five years was authorised. Some alleviation was also provided by the agreement that duplicate copies of natural history titles at Bloomsbury could be transferred to South Kensington.

Money was not the only problem. The final plans for the new building failed to allow any space for a general library: indeed, they did not explicitly include space for departmental libraries. A general library was essential because many publications contained material that overlapped the interests of more than one department. The Trustees appointed B. B. Woodward, who had previously worked at Bloomsbury, to take charge of the library, though his domain was

---

5 The move and its aftermath are described in W. T. Stearn, *The Natural History Museum at South Kensington* (London, 1981). For a discussion of the library, see pp. 319–28.

mainly confined to the corridors and the basement. The effort to build up the Museum's depleted collections extended throughout the 1880s. (It is said that Quaritch's bookshop developed its interest in scientific literature as a result of servicing the Museum's requirements.) By the end of the decade, the general and departmental libraries in the Museum had a sufficiently good coverage for Woodward to embark on the construction of a general catalogue, and this continued to be produced long after his retirement in 1921.[6]

The departmental libraries remained independent, making their own purchases and doing much of their own cataloguing until after the Second World War. In 1946, the Trustees decided to centralise these activities into the general library, but the attempt by the then Librarian to gain overall administrative control of the departmental libraries failed. It took another thirty years before all the library administration was centralised, at which point the post of Museum Librarian was relabelled Head of Library Services. Meanwhile, in 1958, space was finally found for a proper library, though it was only after the building of an extension fifteen years later that all the library stock was brought together. New accommodation was also provided for some of the departmental collections. Though the libraries of the Natural History Museum were originally built up to assist staff, their importance as a national resource had long been recognised.

The Patent Office Library

One science library of national importance was not situated at South Kensington, though its creation resulted in part from the events of 1851. This was the Patent Office Library. By the mid-nineteenth century, there was growing dissatisfaction with the bureaucratic problems of obtaining patents, something that became particularly debated in the run-up to the Great Exhibition. In consequence, patent law was amended in 1852 to allow the setting up of a Patent Office. This was established at Chancery Lane, the legal focus of London. Bennet Woodcroft, previously a professor at University College London, was appointed Superintendent of Specifications (and subsequently the head of the Patent Office). He immediately embarked on a programme of codifying and publishing all patents both past and present. These specifications were widely distributed free of charge to bodies ranging from learned societies to the new public libraries (whose existence they helped to stimulate). In 1855,

---

6 The viewpoint of one of the staff concerned is presented in A. E. Gunther, *A century of zoology* (London, 1975), 355–8.

Woodford opened a library at the Patent Office, intended to provide not only patent specifications, but also a wide range of scientific and technical literature. Pressure for this came from the Prince Consort, who urged that both a museum and a library of scientific books should be set up. He was backed by a memorial from the Institution of Mechanical Engineers, and signed by many of the leading British engineers.[7]

The Patent Office building had not been designed to hold a library, so it was initially housed along a narrow corridor known as the 'drain pipe'. Readers found they had 'to manage matters by resting books on our knees [and] making notes on paper placed on top of our hats'.[8] Hardly surprisingly, the Commissioners were soon pressing for more library space, but there followed the usual political prevarication. By the mid-1860s, the Patent Office Library was being described as superior to any other technical library in Europe or North America in terms of holdings, but certainly not in terms of easy access. A purpose-built library only materialised in 1902, by which time the holdings exceeded 100,000 volumes.

For much of the first half of the twentieth century, the great strength of the Patent Office Library in the physical sciences and technology was not as widely recognised as it deserved. This situation changed after the Second World War. At the same time that the Science Museum Library was being discussed as the focus for a national science lending library, the Patent Office Library was seen as providing the basis for a national science reference library. After much debate, it was recommended at the end of the 1950s that the Patent Office Library should be linked to the British Museum. The rationale for this was that the British Museum Library possessed an excellent science collection that was very underused. Adding this to the stock of the Patent Office would create a major new science collection, to be known as the National Reference Library of Science and Invention. (These were the days when the Prime Minister, Harold Wilson, was talking of 'the white heat of the technological revolution'.) The development of this new national resource in the 1960s was an important step towards the subsequent appearance of the British Library. The development of the British Library is treated elsewhere in this volume. However, it is worth noting that planning for the new building at St Pancras tried to take account of past experience. For example, it differentiated between the ways that researchers in the sciences and the humanities used information.

7 For a detailed discussion of the founding of the Patent Office with some mention of its library, see H. Harding, *Patent Office centenary* (London, 1953).
8 J. B. Tooley, 'London scientific libraries in the 19th century, II: government intervention', *Library History* 3 (1974), 129–39.

Despite this, the move to St Pancras was not universally welcomed. Patent agents, in particular, regretted the change of location.

Summary

In looking at the history of these three major science libraries – at the Science Museum, the British Museum (Natural History) and the Patent Office – some parallels can be discerned. All were in London, and all were adjuncts of other activities (museums or patents). Because of their ancillary nature, they were not initially allotted high priority in terms of accommodation. Though they acquired strong support from users and their own institutions, it proved difficult to convince the providers of funds – especially civil servants – of their importance. Indeed, it was not until well into the twentieth century that most such people accepted both that scientists had special information needs, and that it was important to cater for them.

The learned societies

The nineteenth century was *par excellence* the time for creating learned and professional societies. Their appearance reflected the increasing move towards specialisation that characterised the intellectual world in that century. There were differences that had some effect on the libraries. A learned society was essentially concerned with developing its subject. Professional societies (for engineers, doctors, etc.) were also concerned with protecting the status of practitioners. In some subjects (e.g. chemistry, physics) which involved both pure and applied aspects, separate societies were established for researchers and practitioners.

The nationally important societies, with their headquarters in London, were typically concerned with a well-defined subject (e.g. the Zoological Society). Societies outside London were often broader in their scope. The various Literary and Philosophical Societies, for example, mixed science with non-science in their activities. One characteristic they had in common was a desire to support a library: the ability to consult specialist publications was a significant advantage of membership.

The oldest society of them all – the Royal Society – dated back to the days before specialisation. It had long possessed a library. In fact, its library committee had the distinction of being the first in-house committee set up by the Society. Yet even the Royal Society was experiencing problems in acquiring publications across all the sciences by the end of the nineteenth century. The problem was nicely encapsulated in the Society's project to create a *Catalogue of scientific papers*. This was intended to provide a record of all scientific papers published in Europe or North America throughout the nineteenth century. From the appearance of the first volume in 1866 to the end of the century, the amount of space required for coverage of each decade rose inexorably. The work continued up to the First World War, after which financial problems led to its discontinuation.[9]

Finance

Finance was often a problem for society libraries. If a society experienced a lean period, cutting the library budget often seemed to offer an easy way out. For example, the mid-nineteenth century was a period of financial depression which affected many societies and their library acquisitions. The Linnean Society could only afford twelve guineas a year for library purchases during the 1850s,[10] while the Royal Dublin Society almost ceased making purchases.[11] The Horticultural Society (the 'Royal' was added in 1861) carried such cuts to their ultimate extreme by selling off its entire library.[12] Once the crisis was past, the Society had to start again from scratch, which involved expending more money than had been obtained from the sale. (This experience led to the Society setting up a trust scheme for its library to ensure that it was never sold off again.)

Societies tried many and varied methods to obtain extra financial support for their libraries. The Royal Geographical Society did well during the 1850s by negotiating an annual government grant of £500 in support of its collection of books, periodicals and maps.[13] In return, the maps, but not the library stock, had to be made available to the general public. The Cambridge Philosophical Society also encountered financial difficulties in the mid-nineteenth century.[14] These were overcome by soliciting Cambridge University to provide accommodation. In the 1880s, the university not only made more library space available, it also paid the librarian's salary. In return, the library was managed by a joint committee and its stock could be accessed by any member of the university teaching staff.

---

9 See Sir Henry Lyons, *The Royal Society 1660–1940* (Cambridge, 1944).
10 A. T. Gage, *A history of the Linnean Society of London* (London, 1938), 129.
11 J. Meenan and D. Clark (eds.), *The Royal Dublin Society 1731–1981* (Dublin, 1981), 80.
12 H. R. Fletcher, *The story of the Royal Horticultural Society* (Oxford, 1969), 411.
13 H. R. Mill, *The record of the Royal Geographical Society 1830–1930* (London, 1930), 67.
14 R. J. Wyatt, 'The development of scientific and technological libraries in Great Britain', *IATUL Quarterly* 5 (1990), 70–8.

During the First World War, the library of the Chemical Society was much used by government departments to access chemical publications not readily available elsewhere. After the war, the Chemical Society explored whether there was a continuing external demand for use of its library. As a result, it set up a scheme which offered reading rights to external bodies in return for financial contributions.[15] At the end of the same decade, the 1920s, the Linnean Society became an outlier library of the National Central Library. This brought it a grant of £2,000 from the Carnegie Trust to spend on books.[16]

As these examples suggest, one of the standard ways of obtaining additional funds was to make the library accessible to new groups of users. That such groups existed reflects the importance achieved by the societies as providers of information in their various disciplines. Perhaps the largest development of this kind in the latter part of the nineteenth century related to the government provision of space in Burlington House for several of the learned societies. In the original plans, it was suggested that the societies should have a common library. This proposal was dropped when the move actually took place, but it was agreed that Fellows of any one society could use the libraries of the other societies, and that they could also propose non-Fellows as library users.

Funding was required not only for acquisitions, but also to pay for library staff. The post of librarian was often seen as part-time: attractive as much for the cachet it gave as for the salary (perhaps £100–£150 p.a. in the nineteenth century). As both the library collection and the society membership grew, so did the demands on staff, and the work became increasingly full-time. Looking after the library now required appropriate accommodation for the librarian plus any assistants. In the nineteenth century, such space often consisted of a table in the reading room. Despite its inadequacy, this arrangement sometimes survived long into the twentieth century.

Accommodation

The reason staff were given so little room was the other major headache for societies, alongside finance – the insatiable demand for more library space produced by the continuing growth in scientific publications. In 1885, the Chemical Society commented: 'the enormous amount of scientific literature which is being published relating to chemistry and allied subjects is causing some little anxiety as to where the books are to be placed in the future'.[17]

15 T. S. Moore and J. C. Philip, *The Chemical Society 1841–1941* (London, 1947), 111–12.
16 Gage, *History of the Linnean Society*, 131.
17 Moore and Philip, *The Chemical Society*, 64.

By the 1930s, the matter had become considerably more urgent. The Society was:

> faced with the problem of storage, the more acute because of measures previously taken – the conversion of the basement into a book store, the erection of a gallery with bookcases in the Council Room, the erection of bookcases in the old 'tea room', and double banking of books whenever possible . . . In 1938 the situation seemed so desperate that plans were under consideration for adapting the Meeting Room to library use, which would have made it impossible for the Society to hold any of its meetings in its own rooms.[18]

Data on the Society's library acquisitions illustrate the scale of the problem. In terms of bound volumes, the Chemical Society possessed, in 1880, nearly 2,000 books and 3,000 periodicals. By 1940, these figures had risen to more than 13,000 and 31,000, respectively. In the event, alleviating measures were taken, and it was not until well after the Second World War, when the Chemical Society took over the Royal Society's apartments in Burlington House, that appropriate library accommodation became available. It was primarily this problem of information growth that led British societies in the physical sciences and engineering to become pioneers in the handling of information in electronic form (under the acronyms of UKCIS and INSPEC).

Library activities

Substantial amounts of material were occasionally donated or bequeathed to societies, so that several acquired special collections alongside their main libraries. Periodicals and serials were often obtained by exchange. The society would provide copies of its own publications in return for those of other societies. This was a common method of avoiding cash transactions throughout the nineteenth and twentieth centuries. For example, in the 1930s, the Linnean Society library took some 600–700 journal titles, over 500 of them by exchange or gift. In the mid-1970s, the Zoological Society library received about a thousand journal titles, more than half of which were still by exchange. The interconnection between publishing and acquiring was underlined in the nineteenth century, when society librarians were frequently expected to have some involvement in the publishing side. Their duties might even go further. Thus, in the latter part of the nineteenth century, the Secretary of the Institution of Electrical Engineers was also its librarian and the editor of its journal.

18 Moore and Philip, *The Chemical Society*, 170–1.

Devolving the library

Though the librarians came from a variety of backgrounds, it became apparent to all, sooner or later, that their expanding libraries required cataloguing. This sometimes led to pioneering work on subject classification, but could also reveal a lack of appreciation of the practical aspects. For example, the Zoological Society adopted the 'fixed location' system of giving each shelf a number, and then writing this number in the book and the catalogue. This worked satisfactorily when there was plenty of space, but the Society failed to change the system as journal output increased. By the 1960s, 'a situation had been reached where space was so short that whenever a delivery of bound journals was received from the binder an intricate game of musical chairs was necessary to shelve them'.[19]

In the latter half of the twentieth century, the problem of providing library accommodation (especially where it was at high cost in central London) was clearly affecting a number of societies. Consequently, the reason for having society libraries became a matter for debate. Such libraries had been important when members had little access to publications on their specialist topic elsewhere. Now members were frequently professionals with satisfactory libraries in their own institutions and good access to inter-library loan facilities. In some instances, the most assiduous users of a society library had become those with historical interests, who might not even be members. This led some societies to the conclusion that it would be better to get rid of part or all of their library, and to concentrate on providing other information services. Thus both the Mathematical Association and the Physical Society deposited their collections with the University of Leicester. It is noticeable that moving or dispersing libraries has been less popular where societies have a large amateur membership. Witness, for example, the debate during the 1990s in the Royal Horticultural Society on moving its library out of central London.

The most interesting example of such a move involved the Royal Society of Edinburgh.[20] The Society was much concerned with the need for more library space in the 1960s, especially because of the expansion of its journal holdings. The preferred solution that emerged was to amalgamate the foreign journal holdings with the scientific publications held by the National Library of Scotland to form a new Scottish Science Reference Library. Negotiations

---

19 Lord Zuckerman (ed.), *The Zoological Society of London, 1826–1976 and beyond* (London, 1976), 246.

20 N. Campbell and R. M. S. Smellie, *The Royal Society of Edinburgh 1783–1983* (Edinburgh, 1983), 141.

went slowly, as always, but agreement was finally reached in 1980. The Society received £500,000 plus some funding for research fellowships by way of compensation, as well as gaining space.

This was almost the reverse of what had happened in Ireland a century before. The Royal Dublin Society had been created in the eighteenth century to aid agriculture and manufacturing, and immediate provision was made for a library. In 1877, much of the stock of the library was taken over to help form the basis for a National Library of Ireland. The main exception was learned society publications, which the Society was allowed to retain. Since a building for the new National Library was not available for some time, this led to problems. As was commented in 1880: 'The present plan of having two perfectly distinct libraries mixed together on the same shelves is most inconvenient and gives rise to great complications and confusion.'[21]

Other libraries

Apart from museums and societies, a variety of other libraries have been set up for specific groups of scientists or engineers. Two, in particular, deserve mention – research associations and research institutes. (Libraries and information centres attached to industrial enterprises are discussed in an earlier chapter.)

As a consequence of problems of industrial development and supply encountered during the First World War, the government decided to encourage industrial research. It therefore collaborated with industry to set up jointly funded centres to cater for the particular needs of each branch. Some twenty research associations were established between the wars, mostly for manufacturing industry. With time, however, the idea spread more widely. For example, a Bee Research Association was established, which acquired the most significant collection of literature on apiculture in Europe. The main problem for the libraries, as for the research associations, themselves, has been uncertainties regarding funding. This has been affected by fluctuations in both governmental and industrial support.

As is noted elsewhere in this volume, the Association of Special Libraries and Information Bureaux was set up in 1925 as a result of an initiative from two of the research associations. During the twentieth century, Aslib developed a number of co-operative ventures of interest to a wide variety of special libraries. These ranged from the creation of a panel of technical

21 Meenan and Clarke (eds.), *The Royal Dublin Society*, 83.

translators, through microfilm copying of enemy publications during the Second World War, to the provision of specialised training courses for information officers.[22]

Another variegated group of institutes typically concentrate on research that is less immediately tied to applications than that at the research associations. Most have received government funding, either directly or indirectly: a number, for example, receive support from the Research Councils. Some have developed libraries of international significance in their fields. A good example is the earliest research institute of them all – the Royal Observatory established at Greenwich in 1675. Unfortunately, the late twentieth century has not been a happy time for some research institutions. This certainly applies to the Royal Observatory. After the Second World War, the Observatory moved to Herstmonceux Castle in Sussex in order to get away from the bright lights and pollution of London. This advantaged the library since it provided more satisfactory accommodation. But then, financial support decreased; Herstmonceux Castle was sold, and the Observatory moved to Cambridge only to be disbanded there in the 1990s. The library, meanwhile, had been attached to the Cambridge University Library, where it now essentially forms a special collection. Other research institute libraries have been affected by moves, amalgamations and privatisation over the same period. For example, the Geological Survey, after a century and a half in London, moved into Nottinghamshire. Though this has been a good move for the library in terms of accommodation, it is dubious whether visitors to the collections find it always as convenient.

Some institutions have flourished – an example being the leading botanic gardens. The most famous of these, the Royal Botanic Gardens at Kew, owes its library to the almost simultaneous acquisition of an appropriate building and the donations of two major collections in the early 1850s.[23] By the end of the 1960s, its stock had reached 100,000 books plus even more pamphlets, and it was taking some 1,500 serials. The library of the Royal Botanic Garden in Edinburgh also began with a donation of books. In this case, the Botanical Society of Edinburgh offered its collection, at least in part because it could not afford the continuing upkeep.[24] Even successful research institutes, however, face continuing financial pressures on their libraries.

---

22 'Forty years of Aslib', *Aslib Proceedings*, 16 (1964), 381–2.
23 R. King, *Royal Kew* (London, 1985), 201.
24 H. R. Fletcher and W. H. Brown, *The Royal Botanic Garden Edinburgh 1670–1970* (Edinburgh, 1970), 119–20.

Conclusion

The growth of special science libraries can be dated to the nineteenth century. The rapid expansion of science with its concomitant specialisation of research interests meant either that large libraries must be built up to cover several fields of science and technology (as with the institutions treated first in this chapter), or that smaller libraries must concentrate on a particular field (as with learned society libraries). Libraries with a national outreach were typically situated in London, with smaller clusters in Edinburgh and Dublin. Besides the obvious social reasons, these cities were easy to access via the expanding railway network.

Many of the older libraries show a somewhat similar pattern of development. They started in the nineteenth century and, often despite inappropriate accommodation and inadequate funding, grew quite briskly. In consequence, questions of organising the collection became increasingly important. The first half of the twentieth century was often a period of consolidation, although the continuing growth of the literature ensured that accommodation problems continued. The second half of the twentieth century saw a new period of change. The burgeoning cost of accommodation, especially in central London, led to moves out of the city, or to the sale or transfer of library collections.

These developments can be related to the library users involved. In recent decades, professional scientists and technologists have mostly acquired adequate local collections for them to consult. Hence, for them, the national collections often represent libraries of last resort. For amateurs, the situation can be different: so societies with many amateur members have found it less easy to leave a central location or disperse their collections. However, all science libraries have expanded their services to members, so that they are increasingly becoming purveyors of information, rather than purely repositories of publications.

33

Information in the service of medicine

ANTONIA J. BUNCH

From ancient times until the present day, the written, the printed and, more recently, the electronic word has played an important part in the communication of information in medicine. Thus by 1850 there was a large legacy of medical literature, both manuscript and printed, in addition to several well-established medical libraries many of which continue today.

Possibly the oldest extant medical 'text' is a Sumerian cuneiform clay tablet dating from around 2100 BC, but the most significant survivor from the ancient world is the Egyptian *Papyrus Ebers*, written about 1550 BC and discovered in a tomb at Thebes in AD 1860. It is generally accounted the oldest medical book.

The most important medical practitioners of the classical world were Greek: Hippocrates (*c.*460–*c.*370 BC, the 'Father of Medicine') and Galen (AD 130–200), born at Pergamon but active in Rome. Their writings influenced medicine in Europe for over 1,500 years and copies of their works were to be found in practitioners' libraries for many centuries. Galen, for example, advocated blood-letting for the treatment of fevers and this practice continued until well into the nineteenth century.

Among the medieval universities, the teaching of medicine took place most notably at Paris, Bologna, Montpellier and Padua, attracting students from all over Europe. Medicine was also taught at the universities of Oxford and Cambridge and, by the early sixteenth century, in Aberdeen and Glasgow. Hippocrates, Galen and the writers of the Arabian schools of medicine, Rhazes (AD 865–925) and Avicenna (AD 980–1037), were the principal authors studied, but there was also a growing corpus of indigenous texts. The advent of the printed book in Europe from the mid-fifteenth century onwards not only made it possible to reproduce existing works in greater numbers, it also encouraged the writing of new material and facilitated the wider diffusion of learning.

Individual practitioners would certainly have possessed some medical texts as part of the tools of their trade and, undoubtedly, there would have been medical manuscripts and books in the libraries of the universities which taught medicine. It was not, however, until the foundation of corporate bodies that specifically medical libraries came into being, and indeed the earliest of these contained much that was not medical.

The Royal Colleges

From the late medieval period onwards, practitioners sought to regulate and license the profession by founding examining bodies and colleges, sometimes in direct conflict with the universities. One of the earliest was the College (later Royal College) of Physicians of London founded by King Henry VIII in 1518, largely upon the prompting of the scholar and physician Thomas Linacre, who had spent several years in Italy graduating MD in Padua. Undoubtedly Linacre was impressed by the existence of Colleges of Physicians in many Italian cities and there was added pressure in the form of the rival surgeons, who had become powerful by forming an alliance with the London Barbers Company at the end of the fourteenth century. Linacre donated property to the College of Physicians as well as his own collection of medical and other books in order to found the library. Throughout succeeding centuries, the library continued to grow and important additions were made, including several bequests. Later, other colleges were established, sometimes initially as trade guilds: The Royal College of Surgeons of Edinburgh (1505); The Royal College of Surgeons of England (1540 as the Barber Surgeons Company); the Royal College of Physicians and Surgeons of Glasgow (1599); the Royal College of Physicians of Ireland (1654); the Royal College of Physicians of Edinburgh (1681); and the Royal College of Surgeons of Ireland (1784). In the twentieth century, among new foundations were the Royal College of Obstetricians and Gynaecologists (1929) and the Royal College of General Practitioners (1957). All these institutions have established libraries, although not always immediately on foundation. The collections have grown over the centuries and all are providing important information services to their members. They are also usually willing to co-operate with other libraries in the field.

Medical societies

The Royal Colleges were founded principally to control and regulate the practice of medicine and surgery, but medical practitioners in common with other professions have always wanted to meet with their peers for discussion, and sometimes publication. Initially, they met with other scientists, forming societies that were of a more general scientific nature. The United Kingdom's leading scientific society, the Royal Society of London, for example, numbered fourteen medical men among its founding Fellows in 1660. Gradually these groups became more specialised, until, in modern times, every branch of medicine is represented by its own society. Many accumulated libraries, some of these becoming quite substantial collections. Most were at their zenith in the eighteenth and early nineteenth centuries. Subsequently many of these collections were dispersed, sometimes by auction, but also by being merged with university or Royal College libraries. Two of the most important, however, have survived to the present day, albeit in a different format, and are among the most significant medical libraries in the United Kingdom.

In 1832 Charles Hastings formed the Provincial Medical and Surgical Society in Worcester 'for the advancement of medical science and to promote intercourse among its members'. In 1856 it became the British Medical Association and in the following year its *Transactions* became the *British Medical Journal*. The Association is concerned with anything connected with the profession, including medical reform, professional ethics and public health. The library, now known as the Nuffield Library after Lord Nuffield a benefactor, was formed in 1887 and incorporates the collection made by Sir Charles Hastings, the founder.

In 1907 eighteen medical societies amalgamated to form the Royal Society of Medicine (RSM). The most important of them was the Royal Medico-Chirurgical Society (founded 1805), which possessed an extensive library. Throughout most of the twentieth century the RSM has been the largest single medical library in the United Kingdom. Although a private library primarily for its members, it acts as a back-up for the British Library Document Supply Centre and will co-operate with other libraries, on request.

Bibliographical control

If published material is to be useful as an information tool, and in particular once it proliferates, some form of organised access needs to be created. Medicine was one of the very first disciplines in which such an attempt was made, and undoubtedly the structure of medicine, and the sciences in general, lends itself easily to the approach of the indexer. Medical bibliography has a long pedigree, and indeed two of the greatest general bibliographies of the past were compiled by medical men. Conrad Gesner (1516–65), known as 'the father of bibliography', studied medicine at Montpellier and Basle and produced his *Bibliotheca universalis* . . . in three volumes with an Appendix, between 1545 and 1555. Medicine was not included, although Gesner later published other medical bibliographical works.

Robert Watt (1774–1819), after working as a ploughboy, stone-dyker and cabinet-maker, eventually studied philosophy, divinity and anatomy at Glasgow and Edinburgh universities. After becoming a Licentiate of the Glasgow Faculty of Physicians and Surgeons he set up medical practice in Paisley. His monumental *Bibliotheca Britannica* (1819–24) commenced life as an attempt to list all medical books published in the United Kingdom. Watt then added law, divinity and 'miscellaneous' subjects making the bibliography more universal and one of the most important works of its kind.

The first generally accredited medical bibliography was produced by Symphorien Champier (1472–1539) and entitled *De medicine claris scriptoribus* (Lyons, c.1506). The most significant, however, were the series on anatomy, botany, surgery and medicine published by Albrecht von Haller between 1774 and 1778. Haller was a professor at the University of Göttingen and his own library consisted of about 20,000 volumes.

Important though these bibliographies of books undoubtedly were, the increase in periodical literature in the nineteenth century brought about its own, rather different, problems of bibliographical control. Richard Neale (1827–1900) began work on *The Medical Digest* whilst still a student and edited it for over fifty years. First published in 1877 by the New Sydenham Society, subsequent editions were issued in 1882 and 1891 with appendices in 1886, 1895 and 1899; it was not itself a periodical publication as are indexes and abstracts today. It was selective in its coverage and arranged in classified order with an index. It is to the United States, however, that we must look for the most important contribution to medical bibliography.

John Shaw Billings (1838–1913) graduated in medicine from the Medical College of Ohio in 1860. He joined the United States Army in the Civil War, and in 1864 was assigned to the Surgeon-General's Office in Washington where he took charge of the library. Eventually he developed this into the most important medical library in the world, purchasing books from Europe and preparing the first *Index-Catalogue of the Library of the Surgeon-General's Office* (16 vols., Washington, DC, 1880–95). Subsequent series were issued in 1896–1916, 1918–32 and 1936–55. Perhaps more importantly, he inaugurated in 1879, together with Bristol-born Robert Fletcher (1823–1912), the *Index Medicus*. In 1896, Billings became Director of the New York Public Library, building that famous institution into a comprehensive system serving a wide community. Fletcher worked as Principal Assistant Librarian in the Surgeon-General's Office for almost thirty-five years and a colleague was Fielding Hudson Garrison (1870–1935), author of several works of which perhaps the best known is the original check-list which formed the basis of *Garrison and Morton's Medical bibliography: an annotated checklist of texts illustrating the history of medicine* (1943 with subsequent reprints), usually referred to as *Garrison-Morton*.

A detailed account of the bibliographical history of the *Index Medicus* is beyond the scope of the present chapter[1] but its role as an information tool in the latter part of the twentieth century has been paramount. Originally a private monthly publication and later financed by the Carnegie Institute, it has also been issued under the auspices of the American Medical Association and finally, since 1960, by the National Library of Medicine, the successor to the library of the Surgeon-General's Office. During the sixties, the print issues were compiled using a computerised information retrieval system known as MEDLARS (Medical Literature Analysis and Retrieval System). This paved the way ultimately for a full online retrieval system, MEDLINE, which initially was available only through libraries. Subsequently published in CD-ROM format, *Index Medicus* is now available on the Internet and provides some abstracts.

Although indexing services are vitally important in accessing periodical literature, the information they provide covers only author, title and source. Many searchers would prefer to know something more about an article before seeking it out, and therefore abstracting services, providing précis of articles, have always been popular. One of the most important of these in medicine is that provided by the Excerpta Medica Foundation, based in Amsterdam. From 1947, this publication has appeared in sections devoted to specific branches of medicine, enabling the smaller, perhaps more specialist, medical library to subscribe only to those parts that are relevant to its users. It is now available electronically under the title EMBASE.

University libraries and medical education

Until the eighteenth century, the practice of medicine in Western Europe was based on the principles enunciated by Hippocrates, Galen and the medieval Arabian schools. Only Andreas Vesalius (1514–64) with the publication of his important work on human anatomy, *De humani corporis fabrica* (1543), and William Harvey (1578–1657) with his influential study of the circulation of the blood, *Excercitatio anatomica de motu cordis et sanguinis in animalibus* (1628), had advanced significantly the study of medicine. The nineteenth century

---

1 For a fuller account see J. L. Thornton, *Medical books, libraries and collectors*, 2nd edn (London, 1966), 252–4, 256–7.

saw the start of a more scientific approach to pathology, especially in Paris where François Bichat (1771–1802) had been encouraging students to leave their textbooks and get into the laboratory or dissecting theatre. Paradoxically, the new scientific medicine gave rise to an increase in the output of medical papers, the medical journal becoming the primary means of communication.

By the beginning of the nineteenth century, medical education at the universities of Oxford and Cambridge had become thoroughly discredited. English students requiring a medical degree had to study either at Leiden in the Netherlands or in France, Italy or Scotland. An alternative means of qualification for English students was attendance at lectures in either a private school of anatomy, the most famous of which in eighteenth-century London was that established by the Scotsman William Hunter (1718–83), or in the hospitals. Most medical practitioners, and especially those with pupils, amassed libraries of varying sizes. Some were quite small working libraries; others became very important collections consisting of much more than medical textbooks. William Hunter, for example, perhaps under the initial influence of the physician Sir Hans Sloane (1660–1753), whose great collection eventually formed the basis of the British Museum Library, collected extensively in other fields, including examples of fine printing. He bequeathed his library to Glasgow University.

By 1815, with the passing of the Apothecaries Act, London had restructured its medical teaching. All apothecaries (i.e. general practitioners) had to possess the Licentiateship of the Society of Apothecaries. Candidates therefore had to attend lectures on anatomy, botany, chemistry, materia medica and the theory and practice of physic. The demand for clinical training increased dramatically and the London hospitals were forced to expand their teaching facilities. University College London was established in 1826 specifically to counter the traditionalism and religious and social exclusion of Oxford and Cambridge. Together with King's College (founded 1829), it became part of the University of London, when this establishment received its Charter in 1836. Ultimately, the teaching departments of the London hospitals became incorporated as medical schools of London University.

Advances in medicine, the introduction of the powered printing press and greater control in regulation of education meant that a well-stocked library was becoming even more important to the study and practice of medicine. By the middle of the nineteenth century, most of the London teaching hospitals had started libraries: St Bartholomew's (1800); King's College (1831); Charing Cross (1834); Middlesex (1835); St George's (1836); St Thomas's (1842); London (1854); St Mary's (1854); Royal Free (1874). The libraries of Guy's, University College and

Westminster were founded in 1903 (refoundation), 1907 and 1938 respectively. In the early 1990s, some of these amalgamated, with ensuing problems for the relocation of their, by then, extensive libraries. Within London University also, several postgraduate institutes covering such disciplines as, to name only a few, Hygiene and Tropical Medicine, Cancer Research, Child Health and Diseases of the Chest were established during the twentieth century and these support highly specialised libraries.

Throughout the nineteenth century, university medical education continued to develop in the English provinces. Cities such as Leeds, Manchester, Bristol, Birmingham, Newcastle, Liverpool and Sheffield all established medical schools. In most cases medical books would originally form part of a general library but gradually separate medical libraries came to be developed, frequently incorporating the libraries of local medical societies; for example, the University of Leeds Medical Library incorporates the library of the old infirmary founded in about 1767, and of the Leeds and West Riding Medico-Chirurgical Society (1875). Major new medical schools were established in the 1960s at Nottingham, Southampton and Leicester, with some fine new buildings housing their medical libraries. More recently further medical schools have been founded, many of them relying heavily on the electronic information sources which have been so successful in the field of medicine.

In Scotland, although there had been some teaching at Aberdeen and Glasgow in medieval times, medical schools in the modern sense were not established until 1685 (Edinburgh), 1704 (Glasgow), 1860 (Aberdeen) and 1898 (St Andrews/Dundee). Libraries followed in their wake, some incorporating older, donated material, and in the latter part of the twentieth century these libraries were playing an important role in the provision of medical information throughout Scotland.

The University of Wales College of Medicine, originally established in 1893, has libraries located at the University Hospital of Wales, Cardiff and in other local hospitals. In Belfast, the medical school library at Queen's University was part of the main university library until 1954, when a separate library for clinical medicine was created. The library of Trinity College Dublin, founded in 1598, has had legal deposit privileges since 1801 and incorporates a large medical collection. The three constituent colleges of the National University of Ireland at Dublin, Cork and Galway, founded at the beginning of the twentieth century, all have medical schools. Again the pattern is of medical material being available initially in a general library, with specialist medical libraries coming later.[2]

2 I am grateful to Beatrice Doran for her helpful response to my plea for information on Irish medical and health libraries, about which there is little in print.

Special libraries

In the twentieth century, many well-established libraries continued but new ones were established to meet ever-changing needs. Government health departments in the United Kingdom and Ireland instituted library and information services, initially for internal use, but more recently some of these have become available to a wider group of users. The Medical Research Council (MRC) is responsible for the library of the National Institute for Medical Research, at Mill Hill in London since 1950, but founded at Hampstead in 1920. In 1970, the MRC opened a new Clinical Research Centre with an extensive library at Harrow in Middlesex. Industry has always recognised the importance of information derived from recorded research, and pharmaceutical firms such as Boots, Glaxo and ICI Pharmaceuticals all established extensive libraries, some of them among the best medical libraries in the country.

Of an entirely different nature, the library of the Wellcome Institute for the History of Medicine is based on the collection formed by Sir Henry Wellcome between 1895 and his death in 1936. It is now the largest and most comprehensive collection in Europe on the history of medicine. Historical material continues to be acquired, including libraries of societies, for example the Medical Society of London, the Royal Society of Health and some older volumes from the Royal Society of Medicine.

Libraries for nursing

Until the middle of the nineteenth century, nurses received virtually no training and were merely assistants to physicians. Often they were of dubious character and Dickens's Sarah Gamp in *Martin Chuzzlewit* is probably not an exaggeration. Florence Nightingale changed nursing forever when she introduced formal training in 1860. By the turn of the century a high standard of nursing care was to be found in most hospitals. World War I brought into high relief the importance of good nursing care and a movement for the registration of nurses led to the passing of the Nurses Registration Acts for England and Wales, Scotland, and Northern Ireland in 1919. With the emergence of nursing as a profession came the establishment of the College of Nursing (afterwards Royal College) in 1916 and its library in 1921. As Gillespie observes, 'at that time it had a stock of 178 books, listed in the committee minutes as "one textbook for nurses, four for midwives and 173 on medical and surgical subjects". The only textbook on nursing was *Notes on nursing, what it is and what it is not*, written by

Florence Nightingale in 1859.'[3] The Royal College of Nursing Library is now the most important library of nursing in the United Kingdom. It has published retrospective bibliographical guides to nursing literature and was responsible for the production of the important monthly *Nursing Bibliography* from 1972 onwards. Together with a number of other institutions, it now produces the *British Nursing Index* (1994–).

For most of the twentieth century, systematic training for nurses was carried out in nurse training schools attached to major hospitals. The publication of the Briggs report in 1972[4] was probably the most significant agent for change in nurse training since Florence Nightingale. It led to the greater integration of nursing and midwifery and the education for these professions. This in turn had implications for the provision of library services, which were almost universally considerably improved. The 1960s had been a period of a few nursing textbooks and periodicals in locked cupboards. The 1980s were characterised by increasingly well-stocked libraries with professionally qualified library staff. By the end of the century, the education of nurses had moved into the universities and the stocks of the nursing college libraries were merged into those of the parent university library.

Although provision for nurses in training was ultimately improved, once qualified it was more difficult for a nurse to obtain information in the workplace. Emerging medical libraries in hospitals and postgraduate centres were just that – medical libraries for doctors. Often the source of funding for the library would militate against its use by other professions. As late as 1997 the journal *Nursing Standard* was conducting a campaign to increase library access for nurses, and by the end of the century there was a heightened awareness of the needs of all health service staffs for information. Recent directives from the central authorities are making it clear that access to information is for all.[5]

The National Health Service

Arguably, the most important development in twentieth-century medicine was the establishment in 1948 of the National Health Service (NHS). Unique in the Western world, it offered, for the first time anywhere, access to medical services by rich and poor alike, without payment at the point of delivery. During the fifties, the new service progressed steadily, despite the continuing austerities

3 S. Gillespie, in M. Carmel (ed.), *Medical librarianship* (London, 1981), 22–3.
4 A. Briggs (Chairman), *Report of the committee on nursing* (London, 1972) (Cmnd. 5115).
5 NHS Executive, *Health Service Guidelines, library and information services* (HSG(97)47) (London, 1997).

imposed after World War II. By the end of that decade, an increasing population and the recovery of the economy led to a reassessment of the delivery of health care.

In publishing the *Hospital plan for England and Wales (1961)* and the *Hospital plan for Scotland* (1962), the government created the concept of the district general hospital, and announced a major programme of hospital building over the following ten years. The district general hospital's role was to provide at local level some, although not all, of the facilities that had hitherto been available only at the big teaching hospitals in the cities. In turn this led to a greater need for improved library facilities for clinicians working at some distance from university medical libraries in the teaching hospitals. Until the 1960s most medical library services were in the universities, the Royal Colleges and major societies such as the Royal Society of Medicine and the British Medical Association. Additionally, from the early 1960s considerable emphasis was placed on continuing postgraduate medical education. Postgraduate centres were established, often in association with the district general hospital. Parallel with this development, more advanced training standards were being introduced for nurses and other professions related to medicine, all of which required improved access to information, not only during training but subsequently in the workplace.

This period also saw the development of patients' libraries in hospitals, many being provided by the local authority library service and staffed by professional librarians.[6] As hospital managers began to recognise the need for improved services for staff, the concept of the 'integrated' library was born – 'integrated' not in the sense that medical texts and works of fiction were kept in the same room, but in that there was a realisation that it made economic sense to employ one professional to supervise both. The concept caused great controversy, especially among an older generation of medical librarians, who argued, quite reasonably, that the qualities required for a good medical librarian were not those that made a good patients' librarian. Many other librarians, whilst not disagreeing, felt that good professional skills could overcome other possible shortcomings, and the success of many librarians who did fill both roles testifies to this argument. Many of these, together with colleagues in the library schools and in national institutions like the King's Fund Centre and the Scottish Hospital Centre, whose libraries were established in the 1960s to provide information services to Health Service

6 For the vicissitudes of the Hospital Library Council, founded in Dublin in 1937 to provide books for patients and finally closed down in 1977, see chapter 21 on Ireland by C. Moran and P. Quinn, above.

managers, were in the forefront of the movement to promote the growth of libraries and better access to information for all health care professionals. This was done principally through holding meetings and conferences, publishing papers and bringing pressure to bear on government departments. The Library Association issued *Recommended standards for libraries in hospitals* in 1965, revised in 1972 and reissued as *Guidelines* in 1978. In Scotland, a survey undertaken by Bunch and Cumming[7] led to some improvements, most notably in schools of nursing. So great was the enthusiasm for an apparently developing area of librarianship that, for a time, specialist courses were on offer in the library schools, most notably at the College of Librarianship Wales, at the Polytechnic of North London and in Aberdeen and Manchester. Ultimately, changes in library education generally, with a move away from specialisms, caused the curtailment of these courses.

It did not take long to realise that, given the wealth and availability of printed literature, and its cost, no district general hospital library could possibly hope to hold a comprehensive, let alone an exhaustive, collection, nor indeed would it be desirable for it to do so. The future seemed to lie in some form of regional and national co-ordination. It was the Sheffield Regional Hospital Board which first proposed the concept of a regional system in 1965,[8] but the honour of establishing the first service fell to Wessex, which appointed a professional librarian in 1967. Other regions in England followed suit, although by no means all of them immediately. Although boundaries have been changed by subsequent reorganisations of the NHS, there are currently twenty-eight Strategic Health Authorities in England, each with co-ordinated library services. These networks are of paramount importance in the delivery of information to health care professionals today, with the university medical library often playing a substantial role.

One of the most helpful stimuli to improving the flow of information at local level was the creation in 1973 of the British Library. Earlier, there had been some discussion in the profession about the desirability of establishing a National Library of Medicine in Britain; Thornton[9] was a particularly strong advocate for this, fearing that rising costs would force the United States National Library of Medicine to restrict its stock, and therefore the *Index Medicus*, solely to North American publications. Clearly, at that time, and indeed at any time in the twentieth century, the very high costs of such a venture

7 A. J. Bunch and E. E. Cumming, *Libraries in hospitals: a review of services in Scotland* (Edinburgh, 1969).
8 Sheffield Regional Hospital Board, *Working party on medical libraries: final report* (Sheffield, 1965).
9 Thornton, *Medical books*, 232, 263.

precluded the establishment of a British National Library of Medicine. Today, with electronic networking and the availability of library catalogues online, the need for the giant repository, except for purposes of conservation, has been superseded. For a time, the library of the Royal Society of Medicine as the largest holder of medical journals in the United Kingdom acted more or less in lieu of a national medical library. Something more akin to the National Library of Medicine came about, however, when, in 1973, the British Library was created by amalgamating several existing libraries, including the British Museum Library, the Science Reference Library, the National Central Library and the National Lending Library for Science and Technology (NLLST). The NLLST became the British Library Lending Division and later the British Library Document Supply Centre (BLDSC). It has one of the largest collections of medical and scientific literature in the country, including, journals, conference proceedings and report literature. It provides an extensive loan and photocopy service and can call upon other back-up libraries when necessary. The service was hailed as a major breakthrough, but ultimately ever increasing charges forced many librarians, especially in the smaller hospital libraries, to fall back on more local schemes of co-operation within and between regions. The British Library was also responsible for the promotion of the MEDLINE database in its early days and, setting up a medical information service, undertook searches on behalf of libraries which did not have direct access.

The term 'information' is capable of many different interpretations, and to a Health Service manager in the sixties and seventies it meant either press and public relations 'information', or the statistical data that could be extracted from, for example, patients' records or epidemiological studies and which in turn would be used to plan services. Librarians had an uphill struggle to convince managers that other formats, especially the journal article, could also provide 'information'.

The last two decades of the twentieth century saw many changes in the provision of medical or, as it is now more appropriate to call it, health care information. In the eighties, the financial constraints imposed on the National Health Service by the government of the day placed great strains on the maintenance of existing library services, and in many areas development was curtailed. A culture of competition rather than co-operation developed, through the imposition of the 'internal market'. For the same reasons, university library services, including those to medicine, experienced similar difficulties. Librarians had to grapple with such concepts as performance indicators, accreditation and quality control. Simultaneously, rapid advances in information technology dictated that librarians would have to adopt new approaches to the provision of information. Indexing and abstracting services became available, online and then in CD-ROM format, enabling direct end-user searching. Increasingly, information of value to clinicians has become available on the Internet. Some feared that this would rob the librarians of their traditional entrepreneurial role. This seems not to have happened, and indeed the introduction into the NHS of evidence-based practice, in which clinicians need access to the results of primary research or quality reviews of research results, has opened up new opportunities for librarians and information specialists. Among many new databases in this area, one of the most significant is the Cochrane Library. The NHS's new national electronic library for health, NeLH, is available on the Internet. Additionally, the move in health policy towards a primary-care-led NHS is blurring the boundaries between health and social care. The largest growth area in health care information has been in the area of health information for the patient and the general public. There are welcome indications that central authorities are recognising the importance of library-based information services by, for example, the appointment of an NHS Libraries Adviser in England, and the review of NHS library services in Scotland undertaken by the Scottish Library and Information Council at the suggestion of the Scottish Health Information Network (SHINE). The appointment of a Scottish Health Service Libraries Adviser had been first proposed as early as 1969.[10] New NHS guidelines on library and information services aim to ensure that all health libraries and information services will be multi-professional, that is open to all staff, not only doctors.[11]

Not all information in the service of medicine, however, is concerned with current clinical practice. In the final year of the twentieth century, the Wellcome Trust organised an important conference in London focusing on preservation for posterity.[12]

Organisation of the library profession

The earliest medical librarians were frequently medical practitioners, but with increasing numbers of professionally qualified librarians working in medicine during the twentieth century, it was natural that they should wish to associate formally in some way.

Currently, the main group in Great Britain is the Health Libraries Group (formerly the Medical, Health and Welfare Libraries Group) of the Chartered

---

10 Bunch and Cumming, *Libraries in hospitals*, 38.
11 NHS Executive, *Health Service Guidelines, library and information services*.
12 Wellcome Trust, *A healthy heritage: collecting for the future of medical history* (London, 1999).

Institute of Library and Information Professionals (CILIP). The Medical, Health and Welfare Libraries Group was itself a merger, or perhaps more correctly a federalisation, in 1978, of the older Medical Section and the Hospital Libraries and Handicapped Readers' Group.

The Medical Section was formed in 1947 and was responsible for the publication of the *Directory of medical libraries in the British Isles* (10th edn 1998), and a useful bibliographical tool, *Books and periodicals for medical libraries in hospitals* (5th edn 1978). It published a *Bulletin* from 1951, has convened annual conferences, and has sponsored a prize essay in memory of C. C. Barnard and an annual lecture in memory of W. J. Bishop, both distinguished medical librarians.

The Hospital Libraries and Handicapped Readers' Group was founded in 1962 with the aim of uniting those interested in library services to the sick and the handicapped. From the mid-sixties on, as non-teaching hospitals sought to develop better library services for both staff and patients, librarians increasingly found themselves in charge of two rather different types of library. Additionally, at this time, the development of professional library services to health service management, planning and design teams introduced a new but very much related subject interest. Increasingly, articles in the Group's publication, *Book Trolley* (1965–73), and its successor, *Health and Welfare Libraries Quarterly* (1974–5), reflected the widening responsibilities. Most librarians found it necessary to belong to both groups in order to be able to associate more fully in all relevant professional activities. For a number of years, each group had a representative on the other's committee. Eventually there was a sufficient groundswell for a merger to be proposed. This went ahead in 1978 in spite of the opposition by several senior members of the Medical Section who felt, quite strongly, that medical librarianship was a distinct specialism within librarianship. The united group has, however, ably demonstrated the old adage about strength in numbers, although there are sub-sections within it catering for the diversity of services that now comprise 'health libraries'. The Group's official journal is *Health Information and Libraries Journal*, previously *Health Libraries Review* (1984–) and it issues a quarterly *Newsletter*.

Librarians responsible for services at regional level have formed the NHS Library and Knowledge Development Network (formerly the NHS Regional Librarians Group), a forum for chief librarians in this sector. They aim particularly to improve the quality of NHS library services, to inform and influence policy makers and to ensure the best possible access to the knowledge base of health care. They have been involved in training initiatives and continuing professional development. Informal networking among university medical librarians eventually coalesced into the University Medical Schools Librarians Group and the University Health Sciences Librarians Group.

In Scotland, the differences in health care provision led to the establishment, in January 1975, of the Association of Scottish Health Sciences Librarians (ASHSL), with a constitution that specifically required representation from medical, nursing, health management and patients' services. It has always remained independent of other bodies, although links are maintained with the CILIPS and the Health Libraries Group. ASHSL meetings are held usually twice a year and an occasional newsletter, *Interim*, is issued. A major achievement of this group has been the compilation of a Union List of Periodicals held in member libraries. As a result of a seminar on consumer health information organised by the group, the Health Education Board for Scotland established a patients' information service. In 1998 the group's name was changed to SHINE (Scottish Health Information Network) to reflect the increasing diversity amongst its membership.

In Wales, the creation of a small working party, Welsh Information and Library Services for Health (WILSH), led eventually to the formation of the Association of Welsh Health Librarians in 1981 with the aim of improving the conditions and career structure of those working in health information in Wales and of raising the standards of library and information services offered to health professionals. In 1988 a section for health sciences libraries was formed within the Library Association of Ireland. It has created an active inter-library loans network among Irish hospital libraries based on a union list of holdings. In 1993 this group produced standards for Irish healthcare libraries.

Conclusion

At the start of the twenty-first century, many of the long-established and distinguished medical libraries continue to serve their users alongside newer institutions. For 4,000 years, 'information in the service of medicine' has meant manuscript and printed texts in the form of books, pamphlets, treatises, journal articles, conference proceedings. In the twenty-first century, health care librarians are facing many new challenges in meeting their users' needs. Information comes in many different formats. Significantly one of the reasons that the Association of Scottish Health Sciences Librarians changed its name in 1998 to Scottish Health Information Network was that many of its members are increasingly working in specialised information units and are no longer titled 'librarian'. It has been a long journey from *Papyrus Ebers* to medical information on the Internet.

34

Lawyers and their libraries

GUY HOLBORN

The bar and its libraries in England and Wales

The bar has traditionally regarded itself as the learned branch of the profession and the provision of libraries has accordingly loomed large in its history. In England the barristers' profession has centred on the four Inns of Court,[1] collegiate bodies dating from medieval times. Lincoln's Inn, Inner Temple, Middle Temple and Gray's Inn are independent, unincorporated bodies, each having had a library from early in their history.[2] An obvious resemblance to the colleges of Oxford and Cambridge is not a mere visitor's impression of the Inns of Court and their libraries. The Inns of Court were indeed regarded and described as 'The Third University of England' until the English Civil War.

The mid-nineteenth century was a period of significant expansion for the Inn libraries, one reason being the large increase in the output of law from the numerous jurisdictions of the Empire. In 1859 it was estimated that Inner and Middle Temple each had about 15,000 volumes while Lincoln's Inn had 30,000 volumes.[3] Between 1831 and 1861 all the Inns invested in new buildings for their libraries. New buildings were not only the result of the expansion of the collections but also a cause of it. The profiles of the libraries were raised both with the benchers, who authorised expenditure, and with the members, whose donations of books had always been a significant source of acquisitions. Apart from meeting a practical necessity, the new buildings

---

1 At the opening of our period there was also still in existence Doctors' Commons, the home of the advocates (Doctors of Civil Law) who practised in the ecclesiastical and admiralty courts. Its fine library was sold in 1861 when it was disbanded. See G. D. Squibb, *Doctors' Commons: a history of the College of Advocates and Doctors of Law* (Oxford, 1977), especially chapter 6, 'The library', 88–97.
2 See references cited under entries for each in B. C. Bloomfield, *A directory of rare book and special collections*, 2nd edn (London, 1997); W. C. Richardson, *A history of the Inns of Court* (Baton Rouge, [1977]), 469–73; D. S. Bland, *A bibliography of the Inns of Court and Chancery* (London, 1965), 51–3.
3 'The libraries of the Inns of Court', *Law Magazine and Law Review* 8 (1859), 131–42; 'The Library of the Middle Temple', *Law Magazine and Law Review* 7 (1859), 67–82.

were also a significant opportunity for the Inns to display their Victorian self-confidence and prosperity to the outside world. The best architects of the day were employed, resulting in striking buildings; indeed at Lincoln's Inn Edwards considered that 'few collections in the world are more handsomely housed'.[4] The growth of the libraries in turn dictated the appointment of librarians to manage them, rather than leaving it to benchers or servants, and this new breed of professional librarian was naturally assiduous in developing the collections. For example during the tenure of William Ralph Douthwaite from 1867 to 1903, the collection at Gray's Inn doubled in size.[5]

Furthermore, rapid growth dictated fresh catalogues. This was the great age of the printed catalogue. Middle Temple produced their first catalogue for more than a hundred years in 1845; Lincoln's Inn followed suit in 1859 and Gray's Inn in 1872 (all with later supplements or new editions). Interestingly, Inner Temple took a different view. An article in the *Solicitors' Journal* in 1907,[6] complaining that Inner Temple had not produced a printed catalogue since 1833, elicited a swift and sharp letter from the Librarian in reply.[7] He had advised his library committee against preparing a new printed catalogue as far back as 1889. The disadvantages were: '(1) Its limited usefulness. (2) The short time that it exists as a trustworthy guide . . . (3) The large cost of printing. (4) The fact that it must consist in a great degree of titles of books that everybody would take for granted were there.' The rationale of the fourth ground may not be immediately apparent, but of course Inner Temple's logic otherwise proved unassailable and no printed catalogue was issued by any of the Inns after the Middle Temple catalogue of 1914.

The nineteenth century was perhaps the heyday of the Inn libraries – in 1850 Lincoln's Inn Library was the largest in the common law world. Their history during the twentieth century centres on the catastrophes of the Second World War. The Blitz destroyed the library buildings at Inner Temple, Middle Temple and Gray's Inn; Gray's Inn lost all its books as well, and there was substantial damage to Inner Temple's collection. Only Lincoln's Inn was spared. Apart from the enormous costs of rebuilding, the Inns' finances were perilous, largely owing to the policy, only reversed in the 1980s, of providing chambers at meagre rents, when rent was virtually their only source of income. Salaries of library staff even by the profession's standards were low. In 1897 the salary

4 E. Edwards, *Memoirs of libraries*, vol. 1 (London, 1859), 731.
5 P. C. Beddingham, 'Gray's Inn Library 1555–1973', *Law Librarian* 5 (1974), 3–5.
6 'Concerning law libraries', *Solicitors' Journal* 51 (1906/7), 205–6.
7 J. E. L. Pickering, '[Letter to the editor in reply to the article] "Concerning law libraries"', *Solicitors' Journal* 51 (1906/7), 227.

of the Librarian of Lincoln's Inn had been the same as that of the Librarian of London University;[8] in the 1950s, 1960s and 1970s it was barely more than that of a Senior Library Assistant. By the end of the twentieth century, however, the Inn libraries had recovered something of their former status. With the bar operating in an increasingly competitive environment, and having doubled in size between 1985 and 1999, the importance of having a modern legal information service could gain more ready recognition.

The Inn libraries were primarily for reference – only benchers had borrowing rights (sometimes a source of resentment for the ordinary member).[9] Before 1983, when the Bar Library in the Royal Courts of Justice became the main lending service for the bar, funded largely by the Court Service (until then it was for reference only and was funded by the four Inns), to borrow books for use in court or in chambers the bar had to resort to self-help or private enterprise. Self-help took the form of the Probate Library (founded in 1831 – its name came from its location not its content).[10] Though given houseroom in the courts, it was independently constituted and paid for by its users – in 1968 a subscription for a set of chambers was four guineas a year.[11] Private enterprise took the form of a rather remarkable commercial lending library, the Law Notes Lending Library Ltd. It was a venture of Arthur Weldon, joint proprietor of the private law tutorial firm Gibson and Weldon and of the periodical *Law Notes*.[12] It opened in 1886 in Chancery Lane. It was originally a service for subscribers to *Law Notes*, but after only four months it was made generally available and must have been a commercial success since it only closed its doors in the 1990s.

There also existed another institution called the Inns of Court Lending Library. This was not in fact a law library for barristers at all but a lending library of general literature for barristers' clerks. As such it affords a vivid and possibly previously unrecorded illustration of such libraries in the Victorian age – particularly the paternalistic morality underlying them. It was founded in 1866 and it was said to have been formed because 'barristers' clerks have much time on their hands, and it is desirable that they should have ready

---

8 R. Walker, 'Lincoln's Inn Library', *Law Librarian*, 8 (1977), 3–4.

9 For public expressions of such resentment see the preface to C. G. Addison, *A treatise on the law of contracts* (London, 1845): cited in *Law Times* 149 (1920), 27, and 'The libraries of the Inns', 138.

10 T. Hort, *History and progress of the Chancery Library, now called the Probate Library* (London, 1895); K. W. Best, 'The Supreme Court Library', *Law Librarian* 10 (1983), 13.

11 W. W. S. Breem, 'Professional law libraries in Great Britain', *Law Library Journal* 64 (1971), 282.

12 R. H. Kersley, *Gibson's 1876–1962: a chapter in legal education* (London, 1973), 11.

means to employ it usefully'.[13] The *Law Journal* considered that it must be a great boon to its members since 'doubtless many of the junior clerks especially were prevented by its influence from reading the really injurious literature, in the form of illustrated numbers, which was now published in such quantities for boys'.[14]

The libraries described above catered for the barrister based in London. At the beginning of the nineteenth century the provincial bar was virtually non-existent. By 1830 there were about eighty barristers (perhaps 7% of the total) practising in the main commercial cities and the number continued to increase thereafter. Today there are about 3,700 (35%).[15]

The provincial barrister would originally have had virtually no library resources at his disposal, other than his own. The same problem had been recognised by provincial solicitors, who during the nineteenth century had been active in establishing local law societies, many of which had libraries. The barrister had no equivalent, other than the circuit mess, whose main collective action for mutual benefit was the bulk purchase of wine. However, many local law society libraries came to open their doors to barristers as well (for the extra subscriptions were welcome). This did not extend to barristers being *members* of the local law societies, and only in 1974 were the rules of professional conduct relaxed so as to allow a barrister to serve on the library committee of a local law society.[16] In recent years, with the advent of photocopiers and faxes, the Inn libraries have been able to help, and today the Court Service does give local practitioners access to court libraries where the physical location of the collection in the building allows it.[17]

The bar and its libraries in Ireland and Scotland

The organisation of the legal profession both in Ireland and Scotland had significant differences from that in England, which is reflected in the history of their law libraries. Scotland, a distinct jurisdiction whose legal system is based on Roman civil law rather than English common law, most obviously stands

---

13 *Law Times* 41 (1865), 195.

14 *Law Journal* 12 (1877), 163. See also *Solicitors' Journal* 25 (1880), 476.

15 Richard L. Abel, *The legal profession in England and Wales* (Oxford, 1988) and recent annual reports of the General Council of the Bar.

16 See General Council of the Bar, *Annual Statement* 1922, 8; 1952, 23; and *Annual Statement of the Senate of the Inns of Court and the Bar* 1974–5, 39.

17 For an unsuccessful attempt by BIALL to achieve this back in 1972 see *Law Librarian* 6 (1975), 22–4.

separately. But Ireland too, despite following English common law and having 'barristers' and 'solicitors', has its own particularities.

In looking at the Irish bar and its libraries, English eyes will naturally first turn to King's Inns (plural only in name, a single society), assuming a direct parallel in Dublin with the four Inns of Court in London. It certainly has comparable antiquity, but there were a number of constitutional differences, notably that until 1866 attorneys and solicitors were not merely permitted but were compelled to join, whereas the exclusion of attorneys and solicitors was a defining part of the London Inns' history. There were also some practical differences, not least that it had no library until 1788, when it purchased the library of the late Mr Justice Robinson.[18]

Although the initial nucleus of the library consisted of law books, the character of the library, which it still retains, was heavily determined by the Deputy Librarian Bartholomew Duhigg, an eccentric barrister, pamphleteer and antiquarian appointed in 1794.[19] Like the Advocates' Library and Signet Library in Edinburgh, the newly founded King's Inns Library endeavoured to become a general learned library. An opportunity arose when the Copyright (Ireland) Act 1801 was being debated in parliament. Without consulting his benchers, Duhigg entirely of his own accord prevailed upon the Speaker to secure an amendment to the bill giving King's Inns Library copyright deposit status. Perhaps fortunately, given the difficulties of having such a privilege that were to be experienced by the Advocates' Library, this only lasted until 1836. Duhigg's successors continued to build up the library's non-legal collections, which include a fine collection of Irish-language manuscripts. In 1972 a series of sales generated high controversy.[20] Nevertheless about 40% of the library's 96,000 volumes are still today non-legal. That King's Inns Library should in Ireland retain a highly regarded place as a scholarly resource is perhaps to the good. Though an excellent law library, from its start it suffered from the handicap of its location (more than half a mile from the courts) and, unlike the libraries of the English Inns, it is not the place of first resort for the practising bar.

The practising bar instead adopted the arrangement, peculiar to Ireland (though later to be followed in Scotland), whereby its principal library and its principal place of work are one and the same, namely the Law Library at

---

18 C. Kenny, *King's Inns and the kingdom of Ireland: the Irish 'Inn of Court' 1541–1800* (Dublin, 1992), 193. On the Inn and its library see also D. Hogan, *The legal profession in Ireland 1789–1922* (Dublin, 1986), especially 23–6; M. J. Neylon, 'King's Inns Library, Dublin', *Law Librarian* 4 (1973), 3–4.

19 C. Kenny, 'Counsellor Duhigg: antiquarian and activist', *Irish Jurist* 21 (1986), 300–25.

20 C. Kenny, *King's Inns and the battle of the books, 1972: cultural controversy at a Dublin library* (Dublin, 2002).

the Four Courts. The magnificent Four Courts building, designed by James Gandon at the end of the eighteenth century, originally had no library, but one was provided in 1836 when the building was extended. This gradually became the meeting and working place of barristers. It was far from salubrious. A report from an engineer in 1894 stated that it ought to be at least twice its then capacity to meet the minimum requirements of ordinary sanitary condition, and *The Times* reported that 'a number of cases of typhoid fever, one of which proved fatal, have recently occurred amongst the members of the Irish bar'.[21] The result was the Four Courts Library Act 1894, which 'for the purpose of promoting the health and convenience of the members of the Bar of Ireland' authorised funds for a new building on the site. The library built as a new east wing was opened in 1897, and functioned without incident for twenty-five years. Then there were the catastrophic events of 1922. Having been occupied by the Irish Republican Army, the Four Courts building was recaptured only after bombardment by the forces of the provisional government; the building and much of its contents were destroyed. A temporary law library with the salvaged remains was set up in Dublin Castle. The Law Library resumed functioning at the rebuilt Four Courts in 1934. The Bar Library in Belfast, set up after partition in 1922, operates in a similar fashion.

The Library of the Faculty of Advocates in Edinburgh occupies a central place in the intellectual and cultural history of Scotland. Fuelled by its tercentenary in 1989, it must be one of the best-documented libraries discussed in this work. How a small professional society of lawyers,[22] whose total membership when at its largest in the mid-nineteenth century barely exceeded 400, should have created and maintained a national library which eventually, when it did become the National Library in 1925, was to contain three-quarters of a million volumes is indeed a remarkable story, which is covered more fully elsewhere in this volume.[23] From 1925, it reverted to being solely a law library, and since the 1970s it has functioned as the main professional base for the bar, like the Law Library in Dublin.[24]

21 Hogan, *The legal profession in Ireland*, 64–5.
22 For a history of the Faculty see *The laws of Scotland: Stair memorial encyclopaedia*, vol. 13 (Edinburgh, 1992) paras. 1239–1300. The Faculty's connection with the Juridical Library, yet another Edinburgh law library, is mentioned at 1287 and 1294; see further *History of the Juridical Society of Edinburgh* [edited by William Reid] (Edinburgh, 1875), and *The Society of Writers to His Majesty's Signet* (Edinburgh, 1936), 404–7.
23 For more information see Ian McGowan's chapter on the National Library of Scotland, above.
24 C. John, 'The Advocates' Library three hundred and ten years on', *Law Librarian* 23 (1992), 111–14.

Libraries for the courts and judiciary

Unless one counts the House of Lords Library (originally created as a law library in 1826),[25] the establishment of organised court libraries is very much a recent phenomenon. Even at the Royal Courts of Justice, a formal structure in the form of the Supreme Court Library was established only in 1968 and then only in a rudimentary fashion to begin with.[26] Before that date there were only small pockets of organisation. For example, there were collections for both the High Court of Admiralty and the Queen's Bench Division that were sufficiently developed for printed catalogues to be officially published by HMSO, in 1861 and 1879 respectively.

One reason for the late development of court libraries, apart from official parsimony, was that the needs to be met were generally much more limited than those of the bar or of solicitors – a few standard works that might need to be referred to during the course of a hearing or be needed by court officials in the discharge of their duties. Although it was later to have a rather more substantial collection, we get the picture from what was available at the Old Bailey at the end of the eighteenth century. Outside the courtroom was a small closet containing inkstands, some recent Acts of Parliament, the *Statutes at Large*, Coke's *Institutes*, Foster's *Crown law*, Hale's *Pleas of the Crown*, six Testaments and a Hebrew bible.[27] Another factor was that under the English concept of the judicial role judges do not conduct their own independent legal research – it is the job of counsel to do that. Historically, therefore, there were not really any libraries specifically for judges alone, other than small collections of books in their rooms. And of course judges, being wealthy men and having previously been successful practitioners, would often have had extensive private libraries.[28]

Solicitors and their libraries in England and Wales

Solicitors (or attorneys as they were also known until 1875) as a profession are as old as barristers. The number of solicitors has also always far exceeded the

25 C. Dobson, *The Library of the House of Lords: a short history*, rev. edn (London, 1972); D. L. Jones. 'The House of Lords Library', *Law Librarian* 29 (1998), 105–7.
26 Best, 'The Supreme Court Library', 13.
27 'Inventory of furniture, Sessions House 1781', City of London Record Office, Misc. MSS 5.10; cited in A. N. May, *The bar and the Old Bailey, 1750–1850* (Chapel Hill, 2003), 19.
28 The most remarkable private law library was that maintained by the Lee family: *Catalogue of the law books in the Library at Hartwell* (London, 1855); W. H. McAlpine, *A catalogue of the Law Library at Hartwell House, Buckinghamshire* (London, 1865); H. A. Hanley, *Dr John Lee of Hartwell* (Buckingham, 1983).

number of barristers. That the first law library for solicitors in London did not open until 1831 thus requires some explanation.

A prerequisite for a library is some form of professional organisation.[29] The bar had the Inns of Court, which controlled admission to the profession and professional conduct and discipline. Attorneys had no equivalent bodies. The development of professional organisation, and of libraries for solicitors, in fact proceeded at a greater pace out of London than in. Country practitioners were more ready to co-operate with each other than were London practitioners. Starting with Bristol in 1770, eleven local law societies were formed before 1827, when the deed of settlement for the Law Society in London was drawn up. Some of them originated merely as social clubs or as benevolent societies for 'distressed members of the profession'. The promotion of 'fair and liberal practice' – i.e. professional respectability and self-interest – was also a prominent object. In these respects, as Robson points out,[30] there are strong parallels with the early Chambers of Commerce, which were founded at around the same time by similar sorts of men. But, interestingly, others were explicitly founded as law libraries. For example when the society at Bristol was relaunched in 1819 it was as the 'Bristol Law Library Society', only becoming the 'Bristol Incorporated Law Society' in 1870. In this there are also strong parallels with the provincial medical societies, many of which were founded as book clubs during the same period.[31]

Histories of the Law Society and its library have tended, understandably, to make much of the evidence given by Robert Maugham, its first secretary, to the House of Commons Select Committee on Legal Education in 1846: 'What are the special objects of the Society? – The first and principal object is the formation of a library.'[32] But the subject of the Select Committee's enquiry may have coloured his reply and the energy with which the scheme for the Law Society was promoted would not have been forthcoming had it not been for more immediate advantages. One was the pressing need for a larger and more powerful voice in regulating the profession. Another was the purely practical matter of having premises in central London, where lawyers could meet to transact business and for social reasons. None the less, a library was a

29 M. Birks, *Gentlemen of the law* (London, 1960); H. Kirk, *Portrait of a profession: a history of the solicitor's profession, 1100 to the present day* (London, 1976); D. Sugarman, *A brief history of the Law Society* (London, 1995).
30 R. Robson, *The attorney in eighteenth-century England* (Cambridge, 1959), 51; and see generally, 38–49.
31 A. B. Shaw, 'The oldest medical societies in Great Britain', *Medical History* 12 (1968), 232–44.
32 Select Committee on Legal Education, *Report and minutes of evidence*, Parliamentary Papers (1846) vol. 10, 224 (para. 2082) (H.C. 686).

prominent feature of the original design of the new body and its new building. A library would be provided in the Hall,

> To contain a complete collection of books in the law, and relating to those branches of literature which may be considered more particularly connected with the profession, such as . . . county and local histories; topographical, genealogical and other matters of antiquarian research, etc.[33]

Having raised sufficient funds, the building on Chancery Lane was opened in 1831, with the Library occupying handsome and lofty rooms along the entire first floor.[34] The Society was granted a Royal Charter and became the authorised body under the Solicitors Act 1843 for maintaining the official roll of attorneys and solicitors. From the point of view of the library, this was a matter not simply of status but also of funds – payments for practising certificates came to the Society, not into government coffers.

The Law Society Library flourished. A journal article of 1867 points out that, having installed gaslight, it was able to open from 9 a.m. to 9 p.m. throughout the whole year, whereas the Inn libraries still used candles and had to close at 4 p.m. in the winter months.[35] Printed catalogues were issued from 1851 to 1906. By 1970 its collection amounted to 81,654 volumes, a similar size to the Inn libraries at that time.[36] Today it operates very much as one would expect the library and information service of a major professional body to do.

However, their professional body is no longer the sole resource for many solicitors. At the end of the nineteenth century solicitors started looking at what is nowadays called 'practice management' – the efficient running of their offices. An early article on the subject in 1884 even has a section, 'The solicitor's law library'. It paints a sorry picture:

> It is little short of amazing what small regard is paid by a large number of solicitors, who are not within immediate reach of a library, and are not restricted as to their pecuniary ability, to the matter of law books. Over and over again we have come across solicitors – and solicitors in good practice – whose book-shelves have been furnished with an incredibly meagre supply of books.[37]

---

33 F. P. Richardson, 'The Law Society Library: a short historical description', *Law Librarian* 1 (1970), 15.
34 F. Allibone and L. Quiney, *The Law Society's Hall: an architectural history 1823–1995* (London, 1995).
35 'Our law libraries', *Law Times* 44 (1867), 76.
36 Breem, 'Professional law libraries', 278.
37 'The organization of a solicitor's office', *Solicitors' Journal* 29 (1884), 22–3.

Tellingly, the writer adds: 'Economy – false, because to the professional man time and money are synonyms – may have something to do with this.' And it was ultimately business sense that led law firms to invest not only in adequate libraries, but also in law librarians to run them. In the United States the first law firm librarian was appointed in 1921, and by 1950 there were sixty.[38] The main reason that law firm librarians were not appointed in the United Kingdom until the 1970s was the firms' size.[39] Servicing the multinational commercial needs of an expanding City of London, such firms as Slaughter and May and Freshfields had by 1965 grown sufficiently to have a total staff of about 300.[40] But by law they could have no more than twenty partners. The repeal of that restriction by the Companies Act 1967 opened the floodgates, and led to the creation of the modern city law firm, with global offshoots, and fee income measured in hundreds of millions. By 1984 there were thirty-four law firm libraries listed in the main directory; the edition of 2002 has 180.[41]

Although the history of legal education and university law libraries is largely beyond the scope of this chapter, mention should be made of the Institute of Advanced Legal Studies in the University of London, founded in 1947, because of its relationship with the profession.[42] Today its library is one of the three major academic legal research libraries in the country (the others being at Oxford and Cambridge) and is the nearest we have to a national law library.

The main avenue for academic research is comparative law. The development of this discipline received a particular impetus with the Second World War owing to the influx of distinguished European legal scholars as refugees, and the arrival of able postgraduate students from the Commonwealth countries. The time was thus ripe for the establishment of a national institution, which would promote legal research and provide a research library with the requisite width and depth of coverage of legal materials from other jurisdictions. Its holdings of foreign material now far outstrip anything the Inns or the Law Society can provide, so it also operates – since 1989 on a subscription

38 L. N. Gasaway and M. G. Chiorazzi (eds.), *Law librarianship: historical perspectives* (Littleton, Colo., 1996), 79.
39 The first edition of E. M. Moys (ed.), *Manual of law librarianship: the use and organization of legal literature* (London, 1976) has a single paragraph on law firm libraries under the heading 'Miscellaneous libraries' in the introductory chapter of 27 pages.
40 B. Abel-Smith and R. Stevens, *Lawyers and the courts: a sociological study of the English legal system* (London, 1967), 435.
41 British and Irish Association of Law Librarians, *Directory of law libraries in the British Isles*, 2nd edn (Yeovil, 1984); *Directory of British and Irish law libraries*, 7th edn (Warwick, 2002).
42 W. A. Steiner, *The Institute of Advanced Legal Studies of the University of London 1947–1976* (London, 2000).

basis – as a back-up resource for practitioners, particularly solicitors from the city firms with multinational practices.[43]

Solicitors and their libraries in Scotland and Ireland

Although not concentrated in a single body, this branch of the profession had a sophisticated formal organisation in Scotland long before it did in England. Coupled with an appetite for learning, fostered by the Scottish Enlightenment in the eighteenth century, such organisation encouraged the foundation of libraries that, if not quite as large, could respectably stand next to the Advocates' Library.

The earliest body was the Society of Writers to His Majesty's Signet, formally created in 1532.[44] The Library, founded in 1722, started out as a working law library. However, members looked enviously at the provision made at the Advocates' Library for non-legal works and in 1778 the decision was taken to form a general library on a large scale. The library grew apace. A cycle of influences similar to that described at the Inns of Court ensued – the appointment of assiduous official librarians, new buildings, and, as both cause and effect of these two factors, ever greater expansion. By 1879 it contained about 65,000 volumes and in 1904 a new wing was necessitated to accommodate in excess of 100,000 volumes.

Very much in emulation of its friendly rival, the Advocates' Library, the library came to regard itself for the purposes of scholarly research as a public library and indeed officially describes itself as such in 1853. And like the Advocates' Library, but without even the benefit of free copyright deposit, the maintenance of such a general library on such a generous scale out of the funds of a relatively small professional body was eventually to become a liability. By the end of the Second World War the writing was clearly on the wall. The decision was eventually taken to dispose of valuable parts of the non-legal collection to raise cash. A series of auctions were held from 1959 to 1979. A large amount of money was raised and a very large number of books went. The collection was reduced to about 60,000 volumes, and largely reverted, as it was in origin, to being a working law library.

Founded in 1784 to represent practitioners in the higher courts who were not Writers to the Signet, the Society of Solicitors in the Supreme Courts of Scotland is another professional body. And it too has a library, which dates

43 J. Winterton, 'The Institute of Advanced Legal Studies Library', *Law Librarian* 31 (1999), 129–30, and references cited there.

44 G. H. Ballantyne, *The Signet Library, Edinburgh and its librarians 1722–1972* (Glasgow, 1979).

from 1809.[45] That its library did not by any means languish as the poor relation to the Signet Library is indicated by the fact that in 1935 the latter was more than happy to secure the services of the SSC Librarian, Charles A. Malcolm, as its own Librarian. Remarkably, Malcolm, who was sixty at the time of his new appointment and had already served for thirty-five years at the SSC, was to be the Signet Librarian for a further twenty-six-years.

Practitioners in the lower courts outside Edinburgh were known as procurators (though in Aberdeen they were confusingly called 'advocates'). Having locally based practices, they organised themselves into local 'faculties' and some, like the English local law societies, had libraries.[46] The two largest local faculties, which date from the seventeenth century or earlier, are the Royal Faculty of Procurators in Glasgow[47] and the Society of Advocates in Aberdeen.[48] The former has had a proper library since 1817. It is no surprise to learn that it functioned as a general learned (and lending) library as well as catering for its members' immediate professional needs. An attempted change in policy in 1887 to 'restrict the Library as much as possible to books on Law' met with only limited success since also to be collected were 'cognate subjects such as history, biography, antiquities, and economics'.[49] It will also be no surprise to learn that in modern conditions much of the non-legal books had to go.[50] The Aberdeen library was rather smaller, but it too had non-legal books, which were sold in 1977.

In Ireland, as has been mentioned, King's Inns retained formal control over the solicitors' branch of the profession until 1866. But even before that date there were a number of independent societies, eventually leading to the founding in 1841 of the Society of Attorneys and Solicitors of Ireland. As with the Law Society in London, two of its main objects, going hand in hand, were finding premises and forming a library. With the help of funds and surplus books from King's Inns it was able to achieve them.[51] The society in due course became the professional body for solicitors.[52] It is also noteworthy that

45 J. B. Barclay, The S.S.C. story 1784–1984 (Edinburgh, 1984), 108–25.
46 See, for example, Catalogue of the law books in the Library of the Society of Procurators and Solicitors of Forfarshire (Forfar District) (Forfar, 1896); Constitution and rules of the Society of Procurators of Mid-Lothian . . . with catalogue of books in the Library of the Society (Edinburgh, 1900).
47 'The Royal Faculty of Procurators in Glasgow', Journal of the Law Society of Scotland 14 (1969), 295–7.
48 'The Advocates of Aberdeen', Journal of the Law Society of Scotland 14 (1969), 325–6.
49 J. Muir, Catalogue of the books in the Library of the Faculty of Procurators in Glasgow (Glasgow, 1903), vii.
50 G. H. Ballantyne, 'Scottish law society libraries', Law Librarian 9 (1978), 12.
51 Hogan, The legal profession in Ireland, 101 and 116.
52 M. Byrne, 'Law libraries in Ireland', Law Librarian 21 (1990), 53–8.

the two main local law societies, the Southern Law Association founded in Cork in 1859 and the Northern Law Club founded in Belfast in 1843, both had a library as the reason for their formation. After partition in 1922 the latter became the Law Society of Northern Ireland.

The content of law libraries and the information needs of the profession

In looking at the history of the content of law libraries, one striking fact that has already emerged is that many of them did not exclusively, or even predominately comprise books on law. The Inns of Court, the Law Society, the great Scottish law libraries all had extensive non-legal collections, and such non-legal collections were regarded not as luxuries but as necessities to the man of law. It is true that some of the material occasionally had tangential relevance to legal matters, but an explanation must also lie in the character of the Victorian professional classes. The belief in the law as a learned calling accorded with a more general belief in the virtues of scholarship and self-improvement. A striking statement of this sentiment is provided in a printed catalogue of the Hardwicke Society library, a collection of trials and biographies housed at Middle Temple: 'Behind the Library of Advocacy is the thought that the profession of the Law is more than a business. If an advocate does not enlarge life beyond his fees . . . he will be an inferior form of lawyer.'[53] That almost all the non-legal collections have gone, or at least been drastically reduced, with only isolated outcry, is one small but clear illustration of the change in the character of the profession.

The history of the legal content of law libraries is inextricably linked with the economics of law publishing. Law publishers and lawyers have always relied on each other – whether the relationship is one of symbiosis or of parasitism rather depends on one's views of a market economy. No more clearly is this illustrated than in the history of law reporting.

Even before the days when an action for professional negligence was a threat ever lurking in the lawyer's mind (as it would in the doctor's), the fear of missing some important new decision of the courts was a natural condition – and as the reporting of cases was entirely a matter of private enterprise of commercial publishers that fear was readily preyed upon. The consequence was

---

53 *A catalogue of the books in the Library of Advocacy of the Hardwicke Society, comprising the seventeenth annual report* (Oxford, 1935), 5. See also W. Latey, 'The Hardwicke Society', *Law Times* 206 (1948), 335–6.

a multiplicity of law reports. The establishment of the Incorporated Council of Law Reporting in 1865 was intended to replace the plethora of series with a single series, to be known, with the definite article, as *The Law Reports*, produced by a non-profit-making body governed by the profession. It was blithely assumed that commercial rivals would wither away. Little did the founders of the Incorporated Council know that by the end of the twentieth century there would be well over fifty series of English law reports other than *The Law Reports*, not to mention an ever greater number of electronic services trying to muscle in on the scene. The scale of these commercial interests that have shown so little sign of being dislodged is not to be underestimated. Throughout the twentieth century, law publishing has been dominated by the highly profitable duopoly of Butterworths and Sweet and Maxwell,[54] that duopoly being now a global phenomenon, each being part of Reed Elsevier and Thomson Corporation respectively. There are strong parallels with the development of scientific and medical journal publishing, masterminded by Robert Maxwell.

Another type of publication that was to have a marked impact on the legal publishing scene, and hence on the content of law libraries, was the loose-leaf encyclopaedia. One of the earliest experiments was a loose-leaf version of the *Encyclopaedia of forms and precedents*, first issued in 1916 by Butterworths. But it was Sweet and Maxwell who stole a march with the concept of the loose-leaf subject encyclopaedia, issuing in 1948 the *Encyclopedia of town and country planning*, followed in due course by many others. Apart from their cost, the proliferation of loose-leaf publications had two very obvious consequences for law library administration. One was that it added to the number of serial publications, with the attendant acquisition and control problems. The other was the simple matter of loose-leaf filing. A measurable proportion of the wage costs of most large law libraries remains, even in the electronic age, attributable to loose-leaf filing.[55]

Managing the information needs of the lawyer has centred in the last thirty years on the development of automated systems. The needs (and resources) of lawyers have put them at the forefront of this development generally. The project led by J. F. Horty at the University of Pittsburgh Health Law Center from 1956 to 1968, which put the text of Pennsylvania health and medical statutes

54 H. K. Jones, *Butterworths: history of a publishing house*, 2nd edn (London, 1997); Sweet and Maxwell, *Then and now 1799–1974* (London, 1974); A. J. Kinahan (ed.), *Now and then: a celebration of Sweet & Maxwell's bicentenary* (London, 1999).
55 C. L. Wilkinson, 'Legal information and loose-leaf services', *Law Librarian* 29 (1998), 249–57.

into computerised form, resulted in one of the first full-text retrieval systems in any field.[56] There was also the Ohio Bar Automated Research Corporation set up in the 1960s, which was to form the basis of LEXIS, launched in 1973. But in the United Kingdom research and development were no less advanced. In the late 1960s the STATUS software was written at the UK Atomic Energy Authority for a database of atomic energy legislation, and it was eventually to be utilised in the EUROLEX online service launched in January 1980.[57] Following hard on the heels of EUROLEX was the launch by Butterworths of LEXIS in the UK in February 1980. The rivalry was only ended by the takeover of EUROLEX by Butterworths in 1985, which caused a good deal of controversy, attracting the attentions of the Monopolies and Mergers Commission and eliciting Parliamentary Questions in the House of Commons. Controversy also surrounded the marketing of LEXIS and restrictions on its use in libraries. Its progenitor at Butterworths was later to admit: 'Relationships with law librarians had not always been easy. I wanted lawyers to use LEXIS – more hands and minds using it equalled more potential revenue for Butterworths – but they, understandably, wanted to use it themselves on behalf of their partners and assistants.'[58] Much of the market dominance of LEXIS was attributable not to its search facilities but to its coverage of transcripts of unreported cases, which otherwise, with limited exceptions, were wholly unobtainable once the shorthand writers had wiped their tapes after six years. In 1979 the Society for Computers and Law (founded in 1973) had published an influential and prescient report,[59] which concluded that the need for access to computerised legal information by the full spectrum of the legal profession (and non-lawyers) could not be satisfactorily met by purely commercial services. Only recently, some twenty years later, has the Internet, and a concomitant change in official attitudes, started to loosen the commercial stranglehold on access to court judgments and other primary legal materials.

The emergence of the professional law librarian

The Victorian and Edwardian image of librarians as scholarly or literary gentlemen can certainly be discerned in those in charge of law libraries. Most

---

56 G. Bull, 'Technical developments in legal information retrieval', *Law Librarian* 11 (1980), 34–40.
57 'Eurolex: [news item]', *Law Librarian* 11 (1980), 5.
58 K. Bosworth, 'In praise of law librarians: LEXIS in the United Kingdom 1975–1993', *Law Librarian* 24 (1993), 133–6.
59 Society for Computers and Law, *A national law library – the way ahead: a proposal for a computer-assisted retrieval system for the UK* (Abingdon, 1979).

strongly representing it are those at the great Scottish libraries and at King's Inns, and there are other examples, such as John Hutchinson, poet and teacher, who was Librarian of Middle Temple from 1880 to 1909.[60] But there began to be recognition that librarians had professional skills beyond their learning – and their ability to enforce silence. In 1883 the *Law Journal* noted the promotion of J. E. L. Pickering, 'happily endowed with the qualities which constitute the ideal librarian':

> One of the first conditions of a well-ordered library is the observance of absolute silence, and one of the most arduous duties of a librarian is to enforce the observance of the rule . . . Under the beneficent sway of the new librarian the Inner Temple Library ought to be a paradise for students, as none but the ill-conditioned could resist the unspoken reproof of a look or a shake of the head.[61]

A decade later the *Law Journal* speculated on the appointment to the post of Librarian of Lincoln's Inn, it having been rumoured that several members of the bar were among the applicants. Though it was not wholly against the selected candidate being a barrister, the more important qualification was that 'he be a skilled librarian'.[62]

From the recognition that librarians were professionals in their own right, eventually grew the recognition that law librarians were also specialists in their own right. Perhaps one of the earliest references to there being such a speciality as law librarianship was an article in the *Library Association Record* in 1948, which pointed to the complete dearth of literature on the subject in this country.[63] Law librarians as they grew in numbers began to identify themselves more comfortably with their subject rather than conventionally, as elsewhere in librarianship, with the type of library in which they worked. This followed the pattern already set in the United States. In 1906 the American Association of Law Libraries was founded in order to fulfil a need not met by the American Library Association.[64] In England in 1968 Leeds Library School ran a workshop on law librarianship, which seems to have been the first of its kind. It proved a success and led directly to the establishment of the British

---

60 R. C. B. Oliver, 'John Hutchinson: teacher, poet and librarian, 1829–1916', *Radnorshire Society Transactions* 50 (1980), 34–55.
61 *Law Journal* 18 (1883), 44.
62 ['Obiter dicta' editorial], *Law Journal* 29 (1894), 625. The skills were not defined.
63 A. R. Hewitt, 'Law librarianship', *Library Association Record* 50 (1948), 91–7.
64 S. B. Kauffman, 'Law libraries', in W. A. Wiegand and D. G. Davis (eds.), *Encyclopedia of library history* (New York, 1994), 332–6.

and Irish Association of Law Librarians (BIALL). The first thirty years of this Association have now been chronicled.[65]

The dearth of literature on the subject of law librarianship noted in 1948 was swiftly remedied with the establishment of the Association's journal, *The Law Librarian*, in 1970 (in 2001 renamed, significantly, *Legal Information Management*). Derek Way, one of the founders of BIALL, had published in 1967 the first book on what would now be called legal research,[66] but by 1976 the subject had developed sufficiently for a substantial treatise of over 700 pages on it to be published under the auspices of the Association.[67] BIALL had seventeen founding members; today it has over 800 members, the majority of whom, it should be added, in complete contrast to the position in the profession in 1850, are of course women.

The increase in the number and the skills of law librarians doubtless reflects to some extent a more ready recognition of the value of organised legal information to the legal profession. But it would be a Whiggish view of history to conclude that this is the result of the inevitable march of progress. The fact is that there has always been an ineluctably strong tie between the law and books (which survives in their modern surrogates). While the scientists have their laboratories and the doctors their clinics, the lawyers have always had and valued their libraries.

65 M. Blake, *A history of the British and Irish Association of Law Librarians 1969–1999* (Warwick, 2000).
66 D. J. Way, *The student's guide to law libraries* (London, 1967).
67 Moys, *Manual of law librarianship* (1976); followed by a second edition (London, 1987), with a successor publication, again significantly renamed, *Handbook of legal information management* forthcoming in 2006.

35

Spreading the Word: religious libraries in the ages of enthusiasm and secularism

ALAN F. JESSON

'In the beginning . . .'

Proper understanding of the period since 1850 requires a beginning at least in the eighteenth century, latterly a time of political unrest. All levels of society feared that the revolutionary fervour publicly recognised in America in 1776, and in France thirteen or so years later, would lead to anarchy in England. It was also a period of rapid social change, and these twin influences had profound impact on the nature of British society throughout the next century.

Acquisition of reading skills was one eagerly espoused change. Initially this was one major result of the Evangelical Revival of the eighteenth century, and the Lancasterian (or 'Circulating') schools. The former inculcated a desire for personal reading of the Scriptures, and the latter provided the means to acquire the skills. But this led to a dearth of reading materials and to the foundation of organisations such as the British and Foreign Bible Society (1804).[1] The BFBS perceived a need to supply Scriptures in English and Welsh and throughout the world, and their methods were to change the book trade dramatically throughout the century. It is not too far fetched to claim that the demands laid on the printing and book trades by the BFBS stimulated the reading habit in Britain:

> Supplying Bibles, however, did not satisfy the whole public thirst for reading matter. After Bibles, newspapers were popular, and it was the need to print ever quicker, ever cheaper, ever more copies that drove the change from flat-bed to rotary presses, capable not of hundreds of copies an hour but thousands. By 1908 it took the very latest rotary presses just one hour to produce 50,000 copies of a thirty-two page weekly journal.[2]

1 One notable publisher of Bibles and religious tracts, the Society for Promoting Christian Knowledge, is omitted from consideration here as it was founded in 1698.
2 A. F. Jesson, *The impact of the Word on the world* (Rome, 2000), 19. This point is also discussed in, e.g., L. Howsam, *Cheap Bibles, nineteenth century publishing and the British and Foreign Bible Society* (Cambridge, 1991).

From its beginning the BFBS decided that it needed its own library, so – runs the Committee minute – 'the Society might never be at a loss for a standard edition and the means of collation whenever an occasion should arise for printing an edition on its own account'. By December 1804 it possessed an embryo library of some thirty-nine volumes, all Scriptures. As the library grew, however, non-Scripture materials were added, mainly reference materials to aid the process of translation. By the time of Bullen's catalogue[3] in 1855 the Scriptures Library had grown to over 5,000 volumes with more than 150 languages represented on the shelves.[4]

Of course the BFBS was not the only significant theologically related library available then. The Church Missionary Society (CMS) established a reference library in 1800, a year after its foundation, but it was not until 1891 that a 'circulating' library was formed as an independent entity by a group of supporters. In 1906 the two collections were amalgamated. Sion College Library, established in 1630 was a copyright deposit library between 1710 and 1836, and the Society of Friends' Library (1673), Dr. Williams's Library (1729) and the Library of the British province of the Moravian Church (after 1738) were all available to their respective members.

Theological libraries, unsurprisingly, paralleled the range of libraries in other disciplines. There were the specialist sections in general collections – such as those of *inter alia* the older colleges of Oxford and Cambridge, St Andrews University and Winchester College. There were the denominational libraries. Many of these owed allegiance to the Church of England or its missionary societies, but there was a surprising number of others. Some theological libraries were established – like those of the BFBS and CMS – as a function of and to assist the main work of the organisation. Parochial libraries, often with a more specifically theological content than some of the older ones, continued to be founded through the nineteenth century, by the Associates of the late Dr Thomas Bray as well as by private individuals.[5] The last main category is the private library, the collection by an individual or organisation, not primarily intended for public use but which, with the goodwill of the owner, may offer limited access to those outside. Many country clergymen formed a collection for their own use but then making it available to the parish. Of course, these are broad categories. On closer examination many libraries are seen to fall

---

3 G. Bullen, *Catalogue of the library of the British & Foreign Bible Society* (London, 1857). Bullen later became the Keeper of Printed Books at the British Museum.

4 Currently more than 35,000 volumes of Scripture in more than 2,500 languages.

5 M. Perkin (ed.), *A directory of the parochial libraries of the Church of England and the Church in Wales*, revised edn (London, 2004) gives details of many of these later foundations, which were not covered by Neil Ker's original survey published in 1959.

into more than one category, and on occasion the distinctions between categories will disappear. But together the categories show the main strands of theological librarianship during the first half of the nineteenth century.

The rise . . . 1850–1950

By 1850 there was a sizeable market for theological books and hence theological libraries. The bishop of Chester founded St Bees' College for training non-graduate clergy as early as 1816, the CMS established a college for non-graduate missionary candidates at Islington in 1825, and Anglican theological colleges continued to be founded into the twentieth century. Chichester, the oldest of the graduate colleges, opened in 1839, and others followed: Wells (1840); Cuddesdon (1854); Lincoln (1874); Ely (1876); Kelham (1891); Mirfield (1902). Without exception the Anglican theological colleges followed the 'party line' – Evangelical, Anglo-Catholic, Liberal:[6]

> The object of the Catholic is to produce a good priest, one who will speak as the mouthpiece of the Church; the object of the Evangelical is to produce an evangelist and preacher, one who will be able to win souls; the object of the Liberal is to produce the teacher, one who will be able to instruct his people and lead them to fresh fields of knowledge.[7]

In theory, all the colleges taught across the spectrum of Anglicanism, but inevitably there was a bias to their own position on that spectrum, and equally inevitably their book stocks reflected that bias. Nevertheless, it was possible for some of the colleges to build up comprehensive collections of a reasonable size over the century.

The nineteenth-century revival of religious orders in the Anglican Church was one of the perhaps unexpected results of the Oxford Movement (c.1833–45), which idealised the High Anglicanism of the seventeenth century. At first women's communities were promoted, notably by Edward Bouverie Pusey, who founded his first community in 1845 at Regent's Park. Men's communities had a slower start, the first, the Society of St John the Evangelist established by R. M. Benson at Cowley, being founded in 1865. The Community of the Resurrection, founded in 1892, migrated in 1898 to Mirfield in Yorkshire, with a library now grown to over 55,000 volumes. The library of the Society of

---

6 It should be noted that my usage here is intended to reflect that of the time and not that of today. Over the last century and a half there has been a considerable convergence in the middle of the spectrum of churchmanship, paralleled by a greater divergence at the extremities.

7 L. E. Elliot-Binns, *Religion in the Victorian era* (London, 1936), 451–2.

the Sacred Mission ('Kelham Fathers'), founded in 1893, located at Kelham in Nottinghamshire 1903–74 then at Willen Priory near Milton Keynes, is another notable collection, though this was formed from the old theological college library on the latter's closure.

Nonconformist theological colleges were largely founded earlier than the Anglican, primarily because until the foundation of the newer, secular universities nonconformist ordinands had no access to university-level education. By 1858, for example, the Congregational Church had no less than ten fully fledged colleges, and a greater number of private academies (the exact number is hard to determine): and additionally certain of their pastors were authorised to receive students for training. For the Baptist churches, the Bristol Baptist College, although founded in 1679, started its library proper only late in the eighteenth century. A Baptist college was founded at Bradford in 1804[8] and another – which became Regent's Park College – at Stepney in 1820.

Didsbury College, Manchester, a Methodist foundation, was established in 1842, and Headingley College, Leeds, in 1868. In 1968 the two colleges merged and moved to form Wesley College in Bristol, with a library of over 18,000 volumes and around 100 current periodicals.

In Ireland Maynooth Seminary was founded with a government grant in 1798.[9] In England the Roman Catholic hierarchy was not restored until 1850, though there were seminaries and other educational establishments active earlier: Ampleforth Abbey and College (founded 1802), for example, or Stonyhurst College, which moved from Liège to Lancashire in 1794. The Order of St Benedict established Belmont Abbey, Hereford, in 1859 to provide a seminary for monks. The library at St John's Seminary at Wonersh, near Guildford (founded 1891), grew to over 30,000 volumes of general theology, naturally with a Roman Catholic bias.

Scotland was well supplied with theological libraries, with around forty extant at the end of the nineteenth century, some of ancient foundation. The oldest of the four ancient universities, St Andrews, was founded in 1411. The largest separate theological college in the UK is New College Library, founded 1843, but administratively a part of Edinburgh University since 1962.[10] The substantial collections of Trinity College Glasgow, including the library of Constantin Tischendorf, were deposited in the University Library in 1974.

---

8 P. Shepherd, *The making of a Northern Baptist College* (Manchester, 2004).
9 A. Neligan (ed.), *Maynooth library treasures: from the collections of Saint Patrick's College* (Dublin, 1995).
10 Further details of Scottish theological libraries may be found in J. V. Howard, 'Libraries (Church, Theological, etc)', in N. M. de S. Cameron (ed.), *Dictionary of Scottish church history* (Edinburgh, 1993), 482–3.

The early part of the twentieth century saw a number of private subscription theological libraries founded, notably the Evangelical Library (1928), originally known as the Beddington Free Grace Library. In a way these continued the earlier tradition of collections being speculatively made available by booksellers. General circulating libraries such as those begun in London and the spa towns in the early eighteenth century were well patronised, as were the more exclusive subscription libraries for the serious student such as those founded at Liverpool (1758), Leeds and Birmingham. In London in the early 1740s the Revd Samuel Fancourt founded a circulating library for the learned professions, particularly nonconformist clergy. A similar, later foundation was Darling's Clerical Library established in 1839 by the Scottish bookseller and publisher James Darling. For an annual subscription of one guinea theological students could borrow one volume at a time and use the reading room. Alas, many of the twentieth-century foundations, like their earlier forerunners, had little or no long-term funding in place and therefore did not long survive. Darling's Library was put up for sale in 1853–4, victim of his parlous financial state.

Of the major non-Christian religions, the Jewish community established the Jews' College in 1855, though its renowned library collection was not established until 1860. The college is responsible for the training of Orthodox rabbis and cantors: congregations of one or other of the Orthodox groupings make up about 80% of the British Jewish community. The remainder, the Progressive section, is divided into Reform and Liberal Judaism, the latter of which, despite strong similarities with the Reform movement, is more radical in its ideology. Reform and Liberal rabbis are trained at the Leo Baeck College, whose library was founded in 1956. The Jewish Historical Society of London opened the Mocatta Library in 1905. It contained literature on hermeneutics, the philosophy and history of Judaism, liturgy and pietistic writings. A large part of the collection was destroyed in 1940, but it reopened in 1954 and is now deposited in the library of University College London.[11]

In addition to the publicly accessible collections, there are a number of more restricted libraries, such as the Beth Hamidrash Library and the B'nai Brith Hillel Foundation Library, both in London, where access is strictly limited to male, Jewish, bona fide scholars.

Buddhism became established in Britain in the early 1920s. Formal organisation began in about 1923 and the Buddhist Society established its collection

---

11 R. Irwin and R. Staveley (eds.), *The libraries of London*, 2nd edn repr. with corrections (London, 1964), 186–8.

in 1924. The Buddhist Vihara Library was formed in 1926 on the foundation of the British Mahabodhi Society. A notable modern collection is the Amaravati Library, founded at Great Gaddesden in 1985.

The Islamic community in Great Britain has changed radically during the last half-century. In broad terms, up to the middle of the Second World War the majority of Muslims in Britain were of Arab origin, mainly sailors from the Yemen and Aden working on British ships and residing in the major port towns. There was also a significant but small population of students and businessmen from British India. At the end of World War II many soldiers from the African colonies and the Indian sub-continent were demobilised in Britain and opted to settle here. Migration from South Asia increased heavily with the partition and Independence of India in 1947.

Although the first attempts to build an Islamic study centre started in 1900, it was not until 1944 that the Islamic Cultural Centre, including the London Central Mosque, was officially opened by King George VI. Then this was considered sufficient: the Islamic community was too diffuse to require any significant library provision, but 'it is only as the migrants became immigrants and settlers, and as their children grew up in Britain that parts of those communities began to re-establish their Muslim identities in the new circumstances'.[12]

Before 1960 there were nine mosques registered as places of worship. By the end of 1985 there were 329. Since Islam shares with Judaism and Christianity not only its monotheism but a great corpus of religious literature, most if not all of these mosques, not just the major ones, would have a theological library attached, however basic.

The 1850 Public Libraries Act permitted, but did not compel, local authorities to establish libraries funded from the general rates, but with limitations. It was not popular legislation and, with a few notable exceptions, was not enthusiastically adopted by local authorities. Nevertheless, as new public libraries opened, new collections of theology were established, if only in a vain attempt to counter the provision of popular fiction. This is not the place for a detailed review of the public library system, but no consideration of theological collections is complete without acknowledgement of their presence. Some, like King's Lynn, had complete collections deposited with them, either from private individuals or from the remnants of parochial libraries. Some, like Fulham in London, actively collected in the subject area as part of a local co-operative scheme such as those organised before national co-operation was established.

---

12 J. S. Nielsen, 'Islamic communities in Britain', in P. Badham (ed.), *Religion, state, and society in modern Britain* (Lewiston, 1989), 225.

Some public libraries – the Mitchell Library in Glasgow or Birmingham Central Library are just two examples – formed large and important collections across the whole spectrum of theology, Christian and non-Christian, and even allocated specialist staff to run them. It must be noted, however, that this was relatively uncommon, even in what was something of a Golden Age for theological librarianship.

'Golden Age' is, of course, both a subjective and an emotional term. For theological libraries it meant that – at least for a while – collections were being built and cared for; funding was adequate, though rarely generous; and the collections were being used. Once again, however, there was a spectrum of experience. Some libraries were endowed generously whilst others had little or no income, only a diminishing fund of goodwill. Thus there was simultaneously a significant number of professional specialist librarians caring for theological collections, but important collections were still in the care of enthusiastic but untrained volunteers. The part played by these latter should not be denigrated or diminished: many a collection was kept intact and in reasonable order by their care and concern, some to be deposited in larger collections, some to remain independent and flourish for some years more.

The Second World War brought an end to this particular Golden Age. Many collections suffered damage and loss either as a direct result of bombing or by the efforts to preserve them. Some collections were dispersed to safer parts of the country and were reunited after the hostilities. Some collections, alas, fell victim to salvage drives 'to help the War effort' and there was a considerable and deliberate destruction of both printed books and archives, especially those which were old enough to be of limited current use, but not yet old enough to be 'historic'.

In the reconstruction of the post-war years theological collections were not high on the list of priorities. It is almost impossible now to imagine the controls on building work, the continuation of rationing and the other petty restrictions of daily life. Nevertheless there were signs of hope. The Library Association offered examination papers in theological librarianship from 1945 as a sub-set of its 'Literary Criticism and Appreciation' series: in 1963 it became 'Paper 301 – Theology'. Robert L. Collison noted in 1957 that there were at least fifty libraries in London specialising in theology and philosophy, including five public libraries responsible for parts of these subject areas under the Metropolitan Special Collections Scheme, one of the local co-operative schemes. However: 'nearly all of them were in difficulties owing to the post-war inflation. Nevertheless, between them they constituted probably the finest resource of research material in the world.'[13] The formation of the Standing Conference of Theological and Philosophical Libraries in London (SCOTAPLL) was intended to assist the student or researcher in tracing sources of theological information; to unveil the hidden strengths of collections, such as the strong collection on Islam in the Church Missionary Society Library; and to avoid duplication in purchasing, thus making, Collison writes, 'money available for those items which no library is buying at present – a consideration of especial importance with regard to expensive reference works and foreign periodicals'.[14]

. . . and fall? 1950–2000

The devastation of the war meant that avoiding another such conflict was eagerly pursued, and international co-operation was seen as a high priority. In 1954 the World Council of Churches Study Department convened a meeting in Paris under UNESCO auspices. A strong need was perceived for dissemination throughout the world of information about theological libraries, librarianship and literature. IFLA, the International Federation of Library Associations founded in 1927, proposed at a meeting in Brussels in 1955 that an International Association of Theological Libraries[15] should be set up, and the Association of British Theological and Philosophical Libraries (ABTAPL) was founded as the British representative of the IATL. Unfortunately IATL did not survive for long, but many of its aims and objectives are now carried out by the Bibliothèques Européenes de Théologie (BETH), of which ABTAPL is a full member.

ABTAPL was formally established on 25 October 1956, with members of SCOTAPLL providing all the preliminaries. The first committee of ABTAPL included representatives from Christian libraries – with more than seven denominations represented – and non-Christian libraries, and covering public, special, university and government libraries. For its time it was a remarkable spread of interest and talents. (Most of the associations in continental Europe were formed strictly along denominational lines.)

The first issue of the *ABTAPL Bulletin* appeared in November 1956 and contained *inter alia* articles on the founding of the Association and an account

---

13 R. L. Collison, 'SCOTAPLL', *Bulletin of the Association of British Theological and Philosophical Libraries* 2 (1957), 3.
14 Collison, 'SCOTAPLL', 3.
15 An editorial note on the foundation of IATL and its ethos is in *Libri* 6 (1955), 65.

of the recataloguing project being undertaken at Dr Williams's Library. In succeeding years articles on member libraries were a regular feature, together with the occasional specialist book review. (A rather scathing review of the Central Council for the Care of Churches' report on the preservation of parochial libraries issued in 1959 appeared in *Bulletin* 14 (March 1961): from the beginning reviewers have been often devastatingly honest!) SCOTAPLL, now deeming that its work was being solidly undertaken by the national association, dissolved itself in 1964 after its sixteen years establishing a new mood of cooperation, including an interchangeable admissions ticket and an embryonic co-operative purchase scheme, amongst its members.

ABTAPL attempted on a national scale what SCOTAPLL had done locally, but the times, the nature of librarianship as a profession, and society at large were changing. The number of ordinands for the Church of England began to decline and with it the need for theological colleges. Ely, an early casualty, closed in 1964; St Aidan's, Birkenhead and Bishop's College, Cheshunt both closed in 1969. Some colleges amalgamated: Wells (founded 1840) and Salisbury (founded 1860) amalgamated in 1972 at Salisbury. Further financial constraints meant that the Salisbury and Wells Theological College finally closed in 1994 (it was refounded as an independent organisation, Sarum College, providing a wide spectrum of theological education, but not ministerial training). Lincoln Theological College's library went to Sheffield University and has now been transferred to Norwich Cathedral Library. Some of the libraries were completely dispersed through the trade; some were deposited in their entirety with other institutions, and some retained a nucleus and dispersed the rest. In almost every case action was taken independently, with little or no consultation within the profession.

Not only the Church of England was constrained: a number of the nonconformist theological colleges closed or merged: for example the Handsworth College (Methodist) merged with Queen's College (Anglican) in Birmingham. Notably the Northern Baptist College, Hartley Victoria Methodist College, and the United Reformed Church and Unitarian Church Colleges in Manchester formed a federation in 1984 for joint ordination training.

As a result of the pressures ABTAPL became moribund: it was difficult to arrange meetings and to issue the *Bulletin*. There was a long period when it even became impossible to arrange an AGM. However, in 1974 it was refounded largely through the efforts of John V. Howard, librarian of New College in Edinburgh. Acting as both chairman and editor of the *Bulletin* for the best part of a decade, he enthused others to take on the roles of secretary and treasurer, and conferences were arranged, well attended and written up. Accounts of individual, often recondite, theological libraries and reviews of major resources, bibliographies and other theological reference works once again appeared and became essential reading.

In 1973 R. J. Duckett wrote with conviction about the 'parlous state' of theological librarianship.[16] Few of the librarians in charge, even of major collections, were qualified librarians, working full-time and subject specialists. During the 1980s and 1990s a reinvigorated ABTAPL became more of a voice for theological librarians. Its conferences, whilst recognising that the social element was important for people working mostly in single-staff situations, were more focused on professional training. The 1989 Conference, for example, concentrated on conservation and disaster planning; this was considered a rather controversial decision at the time, but was justified within a few days when one member's library was partially flooded by a burst water pipe. The skills and immediate action she learned at the conference greatly minimised damage to the book stock.[17] Other conferences covered topics like strategic planning, various aspects of management, and the use of volunteers. Since theological colleges were beginning to realise the value of properly stocked and well-organised libraries when competing for students (and especially the funding they brought with them), ABTAPL issued another special enlarged issue of the *Bulletin* setting out *Guidelines for Theological College Libraries*.[18] One of the most important of ABTAPL's publications, given the original aim of increasing co-operation across the speciality, was the publication in 1986 of *A guide to the theological libraries of Great Britain and Ireland*,[19] which surveyed and listed 397 theological collections. Some libraries co-operated fully, others did not, and the results are reflected in individual entries. It contains as an introduction an exhaustive and important review of theological librarianship, which, though a second edition (1999) has superseded the *Guide*,[20] remains definitive still.

16 R. J. Duckett, 'The parlous state of the librarianship of religion', *Library Association Record* 75 (1973), 21.

17 *Bulletin of ABTAPL*, new series 2 (6) (November 1989), normally a periodical of 16–20 pages, devoted 82 pages to the reports of both the ABTAPL conference and the Cathedral Libraries conference on the same topic.

18 *Bulletin of ABTAPL*, new series 2 (8) (June 1990), 2–31.

19 E. R. M. Lea and A. F. Jesson, *A guide to the theological libraries of Great Britain and Ireland* (London, 1986).

20 D. A. Kerry *A guide to theological and religious studies collections of Great Britain and Ireland* (London, 1999) now updated and available at the ABTAPL website: http://www.abtapl. org.uk/database/contents.html.

The late twentieth century saw a continuation of the 'highly fragmented and complex picture' that Duckett depicted in 1977.[21] Some collections, notably the university libraries, have enhanced their theological holdings by the acquisition of collections, which could no longer be supported by their owners. These deposits are not always on a small scale. The BFBS historical collections, the Scriptures Library and the Archives, and parts of the non-Scriptures collection, were placed on deposit at Cambridge University Library, beginning in 1984. Through grant aid from public and private sources many cathedral and private libraries have been able to refurbish and catalogue their stocks. Co-operation between specialist collections has been enhanced both by traditional methods such as the *ABTAPL Union List of Periodicals*, published every other year since 1996, and by the new, such as the World Wide Web. E-mail is proving a quick, efficient and – most importantly – inexpensive method of exchanging information and is available to more of the smaller libraries. In 1986 the *Guide* reported that, other than collections in or affiliated to university libraries, none of the independent theological libraries had an automated catalogue or access to online retrieval services; five of them, however, were planning automated catalogues. By 2000 there were seventy-two members on the ABTAPL mailing list, and the use of the computer for all aspects of stock-control including cataloguing is now commonplace, though not universal. On the other hand the closure of Sion College's library, despite widespread protests, and the dispersal of its collections to Lambeth Palace and King's College libraries must rank as a national scandal.[22]

It seems reasonable to predict that the picture will continue to be complex since, although amalgamation, deposit and outright closure reduce the numbers of special theology collections, others have been opening: the Henry Martyn Centre for the study of missiology, based at Westminster College, Cambridge, for example, or the Jain Centre Library in Leicester. Indeed, there has been a growth in the number of non-Christian theological libraries in the last decade, often funded from overseas sources to support the local faith community.

There are grounds for cautious optimism. Although, with few exceptions, theological collections are chronically underfunded, there is a new interest in the subject, and there are new opportunities for 'marketing' the collections.

21 R. J. Duckett, 'Theological libraries and librarianship', in H. A. Whatley (ed.), *British librarianship and information science 1971–75* (London, 1977), 258.
22 Events are still too close for an objective study of this sad episode: it is to be hoped that someone more removed from the events will soon provide a definitive study of a campaign which raised high passions in a normally sedate section of society.

Although specialist full-time staff are still rare, there are sufficient people coming along to replace those who are retiring, though not yet in sufficient numbers to be able to offer a proper career progression. Most promising of all, the growth of the Internet suggests that as their existence becomes more widely known the specialist libraries will find their public profiles higher and usage increasing.

36

Government and parliamentary libraries

CHRISTOPHER MURPHY

In terms of academic and historical study the Civil Service is like a painting, a small part of which is brilliantly lit, but the rest barely perceived among the shadows. Great attention has been paid to the policy advice role played by senior 'mandarins', while the much vaster administrative and support functions underpinning the edifice remain largely ignored. Peter Hennessey's magisterial *Whitehall* has only two extremely incidental references to government libraries in over 850 pages.[1] Not a single article on departmental libraries (which must be distinguished from the centrally funded 'national libraries') has appeared in the journal *Library History*. Until much more research is undertaken the conclusions and even some of the facts given below must remain rather tentative. There is at present little evidence on some important issues, such as the extent to which posts were professionalised before 1939 or the entry of women (who formed some 70% of professional staff by 1993) into government libraries.

Another major difficulty arises from the frequent reorganisation of Whitehall departments (e.g. the Ministry of Public Buildings and Works was renamed five times in thirty years) and their complex internal structures (thus the Ministry of Defence had some seventy individual libraries in the early 1990s). The sheer diversity of experience between government libraries thus prevents more than the crudest analytical generalisation in the space available. Likewise our evidence as to the deployment of technology and levels of service provision is often contradictory. For example, the Foreign Office (FO) librarian preferred to use a quill pen until his death in 1943, even though steel tipped ones had been available from the 1820s.[2] Yet the same man devised a 'current awareness' service as sophisticated as any later model.[3]

---

1 P. Hennessey, *Whitehall* (London, 1989).
2 A. Seldon, *Foreign Office: an illustrated history of the place and its people* (London, 2000), 200.
3 FCO Historians, Library and Record Department, Foreign and Commonwealth Office, *Foreign and Commonwealth Library and Records 1782–1995*, History Notes 8 (London, 1995).

In contrast, parliamentary libraries enjoy much better coverage and a far simpler institutional setting and thus will be dealt with separately, later in the chapter.

Government libraries

There were just under 40,000 civil servants in 1850, clustered round a small number of ministries. Early officials did not distinguish between the archives, working documents and textbooks they used in performing their duties. Books were not originally centrally housed in 'libraries', but held as retention copies by individual civil servants or groups of officials. Indeed, the use of 'permanent loan' copies of material was to be an enduring feature of civil service information provision. William Blathwayt, the Secretary for War, established the first apparent example of a 'library' as a discrete collection at the end of the seventeenth century.[4] The East India Company (which governed British India until 1858) appointed a librarian in 1800 and had dedicated accommodation for its collection when this was opened for use in the following year.[5]

This was an exception. In the FO library, also established in 1801, the volumes were housed in any available space throughout the cramped passages of its overcrowded building. The collection was not brought together in a purpose-built 'library' setting until 1868. Over the course of the second half of the nineteenth century 'libraries', in the sense of collections of published material held together and arranged on a systematic basis, did become more widely available to officials. The Board of Trade (BOT) had a statistics collection from 1832 and a departmental librarian by 1843. Catalogues started to be compiled.[6] Whitehall reformer Sir Charles Trevelyan arranged for Her Majesty's Stationery Office (HMSO) to catalogue the Treasury's holdings in 1858. Catalogues were also compiled by the BOT (1866) – although this was of poor bibliographic quality[7] – and the FO (1886).

A 'Whiggish' uninterrupted advance in the standing of government libraries should not be inferred from these developments. The BOT abolished the post of librarian in 1870 and would have sold much of its collection for scrap had not

---

4 H.M. Treasury Organisation and Methods Division, *A guide to government libraries* (London, 1952), 94.
5 A. J. Arberry, *India Office Library: a historical sketch* (London, 1967).
6 H.M. Treasury, *A guide*, 34, 86, 89.
7 K. A. Mallaber, 'An early Wheatley Catalogue: the 1866 catalogue of the Board of Trade library', *The Indexer* 7 (1970), 42–5.

the FO hastened to take charge of it. Nevertheless, the growth of the residual BOT library led to the restoration of a board librarian by 1895.[8]

These libraries were managed by academics or administrators, 'librarian' being then the title of a post, not the name of a profession. Thus the first East India Company Librarian was Charles Wilkins, the 'father of Sanskrit studies' in England. Horace Wilson, Professor of Sanskrit at Oxford, succeeded him at the later India Office, and an American and then a German orientalist continued this scholarly line. A later example was Sir Stephen Gaselee, who was persuaded to leave his chair in Coptic at Cambridge to head the FO's library from 1920 to 1935.[9] A prominent non-academic was Lewis Hertslet, FO Librarian 1810–57, appointed sub-librarian aged fourteen in 1801. His son Edward, who succeeded him, joined the library when only sixteen. A less distinguished appointment was that of the proto-librarian of the Prince Consort's Army Library in Aldershot, a corporal of the Royal Engineers. With huge scandal he was unmasked as a deserter from another unit only days before the library was due to be officially opened by Prince Albert in 1860.[10]

As the nineteenth century drew to a close, a minimalist, 'nightwatchman' model of government was still firmly dominant. There was an increase in the number of civil servants over the last half of the nineteenth century and some new departments: Scottish Office (1885) and Boards of Agriculture and Education (both 1899) were created, but the increase in state activity was quite modest. The first significant enlargement came with the arrival of 'New Liberalism', imbued with Lloyd George's economic and social activism, to government in 1906. From 116,00 civil servants in 1901, the headcount soared to 282,00 in 1914 as new recruits were brought in to staff innovations such as labour exchanges and the National Insurance scheme.

The unprecedented demands of fighting the first 'total war' in 1914–18 led to a massive short-term extension of state control of industry and the development of a huge administrative machine. But when peace returned the overwhelming political impulse was to return to 'normality', with the restoration of pre-war institutional arrangements the easiest way of seeming to achieve this. Very soon much of the governmental apparatus created during the conflict was dismantled. However, some of the new bodies created during the war survived. Thus the Ministry of Labour, the Cabinet Office and the Department

8 J. Fawcett, 'History of the Board of Trade Library', unpublished BA dissertation, Birmingham Polytechnic (1985), held by Department of Trade and Industry Library and Information Service, 1 Victoria Street, London SW1H 0ET.

9 W. A. Munford, *Who was who in British librarianship 1850–1985* (London, 1987).

10 E. Roberts, 'The Prince Consort's Library, Aldershot', *State Librarian* 24 (1976), 24.

of Industrial and Scientific Research (all created in 1916) and the Ministry of Transport (1919) were added to the Whitehall firmament.

An important post-war outcome for civil servants was the acceptance of the Whitley system in 1919. This involved a joint council of employers and trade unions meeting regularly to exchange views. Although public service staff associations existed towards the end of the Victorian era, the Treasury always ignored them. Now it had to negotiate with the Whitehall unions, thus marking the creation of a unified civil service, with common rates of pay and conditions.

Although Whitehall was now a single body in employment terms, depart-mentalism was still strong. Library services had developed independently with-out common aims, procedures, classification schemes or mechanisms of co-ordination. The first firm evidence of library co-operation is the participation of half a dozen government library chiefs in the Panizzi Club of 1914. This failed to survive the First World War. A later informal grouping, the Circle of State Librarians (CSL), brought together heads of government libraries and had forty-two members by 1935. Meetings were held three times a year, but the Circle was a forum for discussion rather than an instrument of collective action.[11]

Most of those employed in government libraries were executive or clerical officers on temporary secondments intended to help them 'get to know the ministry'. An internal review of the BOT in 1920 found thirteen staff working in the library, printing and stationery section. The services offered included main-taining the collection of books and parliamentary papers, answering enquiries, circulating some one hundred daily newspapers and providing translations. The review recommended upgrading the librarian post from clerical to execu-tive level.[12] Although professional librarians started entering the Civil Service from the beginning of the twentieth century, they were few in number until the Second World War. By 1935 large collections of books had been built up (100,000 in the BOT, 80,000 in the FO, 76,000 in the Board of Education), yet library staffing levels remained modest. There were only two library profes-sionals among the eleven library staff in the BOT and four out of a total of nine at the Colonial Office.[13]

---

11 C. Rogers, paper on 'Cooperation activities of the Committee of Departmental Librar-ians' given at 1980 Circle of State Librarians conference on government library and information networks, *State Librarian* 29 (1981), 8.

12 Board of Trade, *Reorganisation: Intelligence and Parliamentary branch* PRO File BT 13/41 (1920).

13 Royal Mail Archives, Appendix to *Headquarters Library: Report of the Committee* POST72 (1935).

The Second World War led to the temporary recruitment of a larger number of qualified staff, especially in the new ministries created to cope with another 'total war'. One of these was the Ministry of Food. The main function of its library was 'to purchase and circulate journals' and some 250 titles were taken. Most of the Ministry's books were retention copies held by officials rather than kept in the library, and a rapid response service was available for works needed urgently. Publication orders placed by 16.00 could be fulfilled by 09.30 the following day, despite the disruption produced by war. The Library also provided a reference service for Ministry staff, the main categories of query being (a) statistical, (b) Parliamentary Questions, official announcements and press or journal articles and (c) minor legal research.[14]

Although the size of the government machine contracted again as wartime ministries were abolished and the economic controls of the post-war 'austerity' period gradually relaxed, there was no attempt to return to pre-war 'normality' as in 1919. To support the vast new public edifice of a welfare state, major nationalised industries and large-scale armed forces deployed in the Cold War some 643,000 civil servants were in post by 1960.

The war left Whitehall librarians with a legacy of wrecked buildings, stocks depleted during the Blitz and a patchwork of collections located on numerous sites. Reconstruction of a service able to meet the demands of 'big government' was going to be a formidable task. In 1946 the CSL was revived and took on a new role negotiating on behalf of departmental libraries with the Treasury and Stationery Office. The Institution of Professional Civil Servants (IPCS), the union representing librarians, pressed the Treasury for their recognition as a distinct occupational category within the Civil Service. Initial resistance from both management and the union representing non-professionals serving in government libraries was finally overcome in 1949 when the class of professional 'Librarians' gained separate status.[15]

New blood in the form of ambitious, qualified, career librarians was now injected into government departments. For example, 1950 saw Ken Mallaber and Frank Hirst become the first professional Librarians of the BOT and Ministry of Agriculture and Fisheries respectively. Much of the impetus for the ongoing professionalisation of library posts came from these types of forceful leader, as well as from the IPCS Librarians Group, chaired from 1950 to 1965 by the redoubtable Derrick King. He battled hard to have vacant or newly created posts staffed by qualified librarians. The professionalisation of scientific

---

14 C. Bennett, 'The Library of the Ministry of Food', *Library Association Record* 44 (1942), 184–6.
15 H.M. Treasury, *Establishment circular Ec 40/49* (1949).

libraries proved particularly difficult, with librarians only beginning to replace experimental officers after the abolition of the Department of Scientific and Industrial Research in 1964. King also served as secretary of the CSL from 1952–7. When its negotiating role was taken over by the newly formed Committee of Departmental Librarians in 1954, he effected the transformation of the Circle, opening its membership (hitherto restricted to library chiefs) to professional librarians from every grade.[16]

During the long post-war economic boom the scale of government library provision mushroomed. For example, Mallaber led forty staff (none of them professional librarians) at the Board of Trade in 1950; by 1976 this had grown to 147, including forty-six librarians and twenty-two translators.[17] In 1974 the first review of central government library services as a whole was published. Commissioned from P-E Consulting Group, this covered thirteen departments. A user study found that 'the libraries are providing a high level of service and are much used'. The consultants recommended that departmental libraries have formal statements of aims and that Chief Librarians act as 'heads of profession' advising on regional libraries where these were under local management control. They also wanted greater subject specialisation to avoid duplication of titles, supported by heavier use of inter-library loans, along with a reduction in binding and more vigorous weeding of stock.[18]

The departmentalist legacy still exerted a strong influence on classification schemes. Before the war the BOT and the Board of Education used the Dewey classification scheme (or a variant of it), while the FO and Colonial Office arranged their books by 'size and number as acquired'.[19] By the 1970s most government libraries used UDC. The Library of Congress scheme was also commonly employed, although the Home Office preferred the Moys classification and the Department of Health and Social Security (DHSS) used Bliss. The BOT replaced their rough and ready Dewey-based scheme with Library of Congress in 1951, but returned to Dewey in 1979. The Anglo-American Cataloguing Rules were more universally adopted and a common microfiche catalogue, 'Interlib II', despite the failure of an earlier scheme, was eventually generated by the British Library

A powerful unifying feature was the 'trawl' system of notifying library vacancies to all members of the librarians group. Likewise, the preservation of

---

16 J. Andrews, 'Obituary: Derrick King', *State Librarian* 28 (1980), 41–2.
17 W. Pearson, 'Kenneth A. Mallaber, F.L.A.: a valediction', *State Librarian* 24 (1976), 25.
18 P-E Consulting Group Limited, Summary of 'Study of central government departmental libraries: final report', *State Librarian* 23 (1975), 2–4.
19 Consignia Archives, Appendix to 'Headquarters Library: Report of the Committee'.

united 'common services', including libraries, when 'super ministries' such as the Departments of Trade and Industry (DTI) or Environment were broken up in 1974, helped mitigate the disruptive effects of changes in the machinery of government.

An abrupt change of course took place with the election of the Thatcher government in 1979. Faltering economic performance and widespread industrial unrest over the 1970s led to the breakdown of the post-war political consensus. Margaret Thatcher sought a more limited role for government and was determined to cut Civil Service numbers, which had risen by 15% in the white collar grades since 1970. A recruitment freeze was imposed and the reduction in staff levels had some impact on libraries, with the DHSS service closed one day a week and library hours reduced at the Civil Service Department.

The Prime Minister and her efficiency adviser Sir Derek Rayner believed the many previous attempts at fundamental reform of Whitehall had foundered because they were too broadbrush and lacked detailed focus. Rayner's solution was rapid 'scrutinies' of specific functional units, seeking opportunities to end, privatise or streamline existing activities. In 1985 the DTI library service was examined and broadly favourable conclusions were reached. It was found to make a valuable contribution to the Department's work, although there was concern that many officials lacked awareness of the services it could offer or even of its existence, and there appeared to be little scope for privatisation. The scrutineers also advocated 'out-bedding' librarians (seconding them to other functional areas) as a way of both spreading library 'presence' within the DTI and broadening librarians' skills and experience, a reversal of the earlier 'get to know your ministry by working in its library' idea.[20]

Other Rayner studies of accommodation costs led to reductions in the floor space allocated to the Home Office and Department of Employment libraries. From 1991 the government introduced 'market testing' whereby government librarians had to compete against external service providers.[21] There were few instances of wholesale privatisation of library services, but some ministries outsourced specific functions such as acquisitions.[22] Despite the atmosphere of retrenchment there was actually a small increase in the total professional complement. Although the number of Assistant Librarian level posts was cut, this was balanced by a number of promotions from this grade to Librarian among officers running libraries in the regions. Likewise the deployment of

20 R. Upson and R. Hobbs, *Scrutiny of library services in the Department of Trade and Industry* (London, 1985).
21 Cabinet Office, *Competing for quality: buying better public services*, CM 1730 (London, 1991).
22 I. Snowley, 'Managing the market', *Serials* 7 (1994), 129–32.

computer technology, which started with the provision of online facilities to search external databases in the late 1970s and was then extended to acquisitions and cataloguing in the early 1980s, failed to result in the heavy job losses that many had feared.

Promotion prospects by the end of the 1980s were nevertheless bleak, with Assistants typically taking five years to reach the grade of 'Librarian' and then facing a one in three chance of advancement to Senior Librarian after a further five to ten years' service. Unsurprisingly, there was a high wastage rate within the Assistant grade and a growing skills shortage was met by the employment of casual labour. Sir Derek Rayner observed that 'the greatest waste I found in government is that so much talent at the service of the nation . . . is not being harnessed'.[23] Symptomatic of this profligacy were a number of departures to the private sector, even at more senior levels. A highly symbolic example was Dorothy Smith, a DTI librarian, who left for a post at the London Business School, Britain's foremost pedagogic proponent of the 'enterprise culture' in 1987.

Where local mandarins were of inferior intellectual calibre, librarians were treated with scant respect. In the Department of Energy, characterised by the eminent political commentator Peter Jenkins as 'our nearest equivalent to a Siberian power station',[24] a large part of the collection was thrown away – to provide a snooker room. More generally, the conversion of many parts of government into autonomous 'agencies',[25] along with the scrapping of the trawling system, reversed the trend towards a more unified Civil Service and increased the sense of occupational isolation.[26] A survey of professional staff in 1993 found that while three-quarters were glad to be librarians, barely half felt the Civil Service was definitely the right choice, and there was a general mood of anxiety and uncertainty about the future.[27]

There was also concern that services to the public had deteriorated. Government libraries traditionally focused on serving Ministers and officials and, with a few exceptions such as the BOT's Statistics and Market Intelligence Library created in 1962 to serve exporters,[28] did not admit outsiders. However, state librarians applied their subject expertise to benefit a wider clientele,

23 P. Hennessey, 'Whitehall talent "wasted"', *The Times* (28 August 1981).

24 P. Jenkins, *Mrs Thatcher's revolution: the ending of the socialist era* (London, 1987), 175.

25 Efficiency Unit, *Improving management in government: the next stops: report to the Prime Minister* (London, 1988).

26 S. Burge, 'Much pain, little gain: privatisation and UK government libraries', *Inspel* 22 (1999), 10–19.

27 S. Burge, *Broken down by grade and sex: the career development of government librarians* (London, 1995).

28 M. Collins, 'Statistics and Market Intelligence Library', *State Librarian* 32 (1984), 13–14.

particularly through listing government publications not published by HMSO and selling current awareness services such as the DTI's 'Contents of Recent Economic Journals'. A prominent individual example was Ernie Bush, who won the Besterman Medal in 1974 for his monumental bibliography of agriculture.[29] Another instance of the willingness of state librarians to be involved with the wider world was the creation in 1978 of a Government Libraries Group within the Library Association.[30]

By the early 1990s there were complaints that collections were diminished, information from government was harder to trace and a keener appetite for cost recovery was excluding those unable to pay for access to public data.[31] More recently the grudging progress towards more 'open government' and the powerful opportunities for low-cost distribution created by the Internet are beginning to counteract this fragmentation of government information sources.

Parliamentary libraries

Library support for MPs themselves has a longer history than that for the departments that MPs have managed once in government. The Clerk of the House of Commons maintained a small collection of books and papers at Westminster and in 1780 it was suggested these should receive special accommodation. In 1800 a house was leased in Abingdon Street for the Clerk of the Journals to hold this material. Charles Abbot became Speaker in 1802 and, dismayed by the disordered state of parliamentary papers, arranged for them to be collected together, bound and indexed. This collection formed the nucleus of the Commons Library when it opened in 1818, in a room 17 feet square over the lobby of the House, with Benjamin Spiller as its first Librarian. The House of Lords established a separate library in 1826. Sir John Soane designed its chamber in a rich Renaissance style and a Lords Clerk, J. F. Leary, was appointed Librarian.

The Commons Library rapidly expanded, with Soane creating enlarged accommodation in the Gothic style in 1826. It was extended again in 1833, when the Library had ten times its original floor area. Lack of space was also

29 E. A. R. Bush, *Agriculture: a bibliographic guide* (London, 1974).
30 V. T. H. Parry, 'The Government Librarians Group of the Library Association', *State Librarian* 6 (1978), 6–7, and 12.
31 F. Humphrey, 'Fragmentation of government sources of information', *Refer* 10 (1994), 14–15.

a problem in the Lords. When its French counterpart, the Chambre des Pairs, donated nearly 1,900 books (mostly on genealogy) in 1834 they could not be accommodated. Thus the destruction by fire of most of the Old Palace of Westminster in that year created an opportunity to provide the legislature with a purpose-built, logically organised and spacious new building designed by Sir Charles Barry. This was to include a suite of fine rooms occupying the ground floor overlooking the Thames to serve as libraries for the two Houses. The new Lords Library, whose collection had been saved from the fire, was opened in 1848. The Commons, which had lost many of their books in the disaster, moved into their new Library four years later.

A catalogue of the Commons collection was compiled and subject indexes to it provided from the 1860s. However, the Library developed little for nearly a century. It was strong in historical and constitutional works, but also contained a great deal of material more fitted to the library of a country house than to a working legislative facility. The MP Sir George Benson described his first encounter with it in 1930: 'I was appalled to find the House . . . served by a library which hardly progressed since 1850 . . . Latin and French classics still . . . in the exact positions . . . they had been originally placed in 1852.' Other Members shared his dissatisfaction, and the provision of a modern library service was one of the reforms called for by the constitutional expert Sir Ivor Jennings in 1934. Although the Speaker appointed an unofficial parliamentary advisory group on the Library in 1922, no significant changes came until after the Second World War.

The War led to profound questioning of existing institutions and a zeal for reform once peace returned. The general election of 1945 brought a large proportion of new MPs into the House and it was recognised that the existing Library was ill-suited to meet their demands for an efficient working tool rather than an agreeable leisure facility. Consequently a research service for Members was established in 1946, with four researchers, two of them statisticians, and two secretaries.

Because the Law Lords were peers, the Upper House's Library built up a strong legal collection, but also shared the 'country house' ethos of its Commons cousin. House of Lords Librarians tended to remain in post for very long periods, staying on into old age. James Pulman became Assistant Librarian in 1838, was appointed Librarian in 1861 and did not retire until 1897 when seventy-nine years old. William Thoms took up the post of Assistant Librarian when he was sixty and stayed until he was 77. Sir Edmund Gosse, Librarian from 1904, was shocked to be compelled to stand down in 1914 when he reached sixty-five. Charles Clay began as Assistant Librarian in 1914, became Librarian in 1922 and served until 1956. His successor, Christopher Dobson, held the post until his retirement in 1977.

It was traditional practice for Librarians of both Houses to be distinguished scholars or administrators rather than being drawn from the library profession. Gosse had been a lecturer in English at Trinity College, Cambridge and Thoms was a noted antiquary. Strathearn Gordon, Commons Librarian from 1950, a Sandhurst graduate, transferred from the Clerk's Department. His successor in 1977, David Menhennet, a scholar of French literature, held an Oxford doctorate.

In 1967 the Commons Library, hitherto part of the Speaker's Department, was given administrative independence following a Treasury review. A contemporary study of MPs' information needs found that 72% of Members used its facilities at least once a day.[32] The range and scale of library provision was extended to meet the growing pressure of business upon MPs. Constituents were far more likely to write to their Member than previously, time horizons shrank, and the volume of Parliamentary Questions soared from around 5,000 per session in 1900 to over 30,000 during the mid-1970s.[33] The introduction of an allowance for MPs to hire research assistants in 1971 was another major factor fuelling the demands placed upon the Library.

From fewer than thirty staff in 1954, numbers rose to about seventy-five in 1976, 173 by 1990 and 200 in 2000. The Commons research service now numbered twenty-four, fielding over 11,000 questions per year and producing over eighty research briefs on matters of current political interest. Until the mid-1950s the Library had only one phone, housed in a broom cupboard. Technological progress remained leisurely until the 1980s, when computerisation was undertaken and the 'POLIS' database of parliamentary questions and papers set up. In 1977 the creation of a Public Information Office was approved, to handle external requests for information on the Commons and its work and produce a 'Weekly Information Bulletin' outlining the progress of legislation and other parliamentary business. In 1991 most Commons Library staff were rehoused in 1, Derby Gate, just along Whitehall, providing them with more comfortable, if less atmospheric, accommodation. The Lords Library evolved at a much slower pace, still having only two research staff by 1990. There was

32 A. Barker and M. Rush, *The Member of Parliament and his information* (London, 1970).
33 The Clerks in the [House of Commons] Table Office, *Questions in the House of Commons*, House of Commons Public Information Office Series No. 1 (London, 1979).

some discussion of the merits of a joint library for both Houses, but this idea was rejected by a working group of peers in 1977.[34]

An historically profound change in the composition of the Lords took place when the great majority of hereditary peers lost their right to attend the House in 1999. This change had little impact on demand for the services of the Library, however, as the bulk of this came from working peers, virtually all of these being holders of life peerages. By 2002 the number of research Clerks had increased to five and, given that the continued need for a second legislative chamber (although now based upon some form of non-hereditary selection) remained unchallenged, the Lords Library looked likely to survive the ejection of most of the House's members.

The creation of assemblies in Scotland and Wales in the late 1990s added a new dimension to parliamentary library provision, drawing upon the experience of the Dublin and Belfast legislature libraries as well as the Westminster ones. The Oireachtas Library in Leinster House, Dublin serves both the Dail (lower house) and the Senate. Since 1976 the 'club-like atmosphere . . . fostered by the sympathetic ambience of the reading room's refined Palladianism' has been augmented by a research service for members.[35] Irish state library history, on both sides of the border, remains largely uncharted territory.[36] However, the formation of a Government Libraries Group in 1984[37] demonstrated a desire to mitigate the restrictive legacy of departmentalism, while the Strategic Management Initiative[38] of the early 1990s included improved library facilities as part of its prescription for Civil Service reform in the Republic.

34 Working Group on the House of Lords Library Service, *Report* (London, 1977).
35 I. R. M. Mowat, 'The Oireachtas Library, Leinster House, Dublin', *State Librarian* 26 (1978), 40–1.
36 'Government libraries in Northern Ireland', *Northern Ireland Libraries* 9 (1974), 44–6.
37 M. Doyle and O. Marshall, 'Government libraries', *Library Review* 34 (1985), 79–82.
38 M. Wallace, 'Issues for government libraries', *An Leabharlann* 12 (1995–6), 61–5.

37

Company libraries

ALISTAIR BLACK

In 1919 the company librarian J. G. Pearce wrote that: 'The Works Library is an integral portion of the modern manufacturing organisation.'[1] Arguably this statement was more advocacy than a reflection of reality. Whereas many late nineteenth- and early twentieth-century enterprises would have been home to collections of material scattered across departments, workshops, laboratories and offices, few could have boasted an authentic company library constituted by a centralised and systematically organised unit dedicated to the collection and dissemination of information pertinent to the organisation. However, the remainder of the twentieth century saw a notable expansion in the number of company libraries and in their activities. Pearce was thus nearer the mark when later he predicted that: 'Intelligence work as an independent advisory branch of a works organisation appears to extend considerably in the course of time and will be accepted as a fundamental part of every well-planned works of any magnitude.'[2]

The origins of the company library and its development before 1950

Company libraries first emerged in parallel with developments in the late Victorian and Edwardian economy and business environment. As markets expanded and diversified, enterprises became larger, more complex and increasingly responsive to their markets. Increased competition heightened the need for, and the importance of, information. Either flowing into the organisation from external sources or generated internally, information began to play a significant role at this time in the management of companies' various activities:

---

1 J. G. Pearce, 'The works library and its relation to the public technical library', *Library Association Record* 21 (1919), 8.
2 J. G. Pearce, 'Intelligence work in a modern industrial organisation', *Library Association Record* 23 (1921), 368–9.

from research and production to marketing and workforce supervision.[3] In fact, information management — which in the late twentieth century became a commonplace term in the literature of business management, closely associated with computerised information technology — is rooted in the previous century and pre-dates the age of the computer by several generations. Under various guises — works or technical library; information unit, branch, centre or bureau; research department; intelligence service — the company library became an integral part of the pre-computer information management revolution, both reflecting and supporting the emergence of 'system' in the philosophy and operations of the modern business enterprise. As conduits of formal scientific, technical, management and marketing information, company libraries contributed significantly to business growth, although this is not to deny the crucial importance of personal contact – the 'invisible colleges' of knowledge extending across companies and outside them into professional circles — in the exchange of information in relation to business.[4]

In the early twentieth century, company libraries were mostly confined to large enterprises engaged in manufacturing and extraction, in industries like oil, chemicals and engineering. By the end of the century, however, company libraries in these traditional sectors had been vastly outnumbered by units in a wide variety of firms in the service sector, in areas such as financial services, banking, law, accountancy and advertising. Similarly, although company libraries have from the outset fulfilled a range of information functions, the century saw a shift in the balance of priorities in company library work, from an emphasis on information for research and development (R & D) and production to a growing awareness of the importance of data on market conditions and opportunities.

During and immediately after the First World War, company librarians were keen to justify the continuing existence of their departments by emphasising the relative backwardness of industry in Britain – compared to Germany, for example – in its harnessing and application of science. J. G. Pearce asserted confidently in 1921 that: 'In Great Britain the handicap arising from the belated application of science to industry can be eliminated through documentation [seen as the task of collecting, indexing, cataloguing, abstracting and

---

3 A. Chandler, *The visible hand: the managerial revolution in American business* (Cambridge, MA, 1977); and J. Yates, *Control through communication: the rise of system in American management* (Baltimore, MD, 1989).

4 M. Hyde and J. Hyde, 'The industrial library: networking and cooperation', in D. Mason (ed.), *Information for industry: twenty-one years of the Library Association Industrial Group* (London, 1991), 64.

distributing information].'[5] Librarians were anxious regarding the threat posed by foreign competition. This was intensifying as a result of the major European nations having diverted their attention from the world scene during four years of war, thereby allowing trade rivals not involved in hostilities to occupy the markets that the imperial powers had neglected. Well-equipped company libraries, librarians argued, would assist reconstruction and help restore the nation's economic fortunes.

Other factors influencing the growth of the company library sector between the wars included the poverty of public provision, the growth of new industries, the rationalisation movement, the appearance of an embryonic information professionalism and an awareness of corporate library development in the United States.[6]

Although 'dedicated' technical and commercial libraries were founded in public libraries during and after the First World War, these generally did not provide, contrary to the hopes of the public library movement, the depth or breadth of service required to satisfy fully the needs of business, and certainly not the needs of medium and large enterprises which were consequently enticed to make their own provision. The same might be said of the libraries of the industrial research associations established by the Department of Scientific and Industrial Research after the war which, although they offered a useful public service, could never have hoped to provide all the information that a large corporation would have required.

The most dramatic growth in early company library activity occurred in the new, science-based industries – for example in synthetic fabrics, electrical engineering, food packaging and chemicals – where up-to-date information commanded a higher premium than in traditional, staple industries like mining, shipbuilding, steel and cotton. It was, arguably, the new industries that helped the British economy recover from the economic depression of the early 1930s. Company library activity paralleled the increasing importance of this 'new production' to the national economy. Company libraries also began to appear in banking and financial enterprises, which grew in commercial sophistication in line with the slow but perceptible modernisation of parts of the British economy.

In the business world the inter-war period was one of corporate enlargement, brought about in part by heated merger activity. The large,

5 Pearce, 'Intelligence work', 365.
6 For a fuller explanation of these factors, see A. Black, 'Hidden worlds of the early knowledge economy: libraries in British companies before the middle of the twentieth century', *Journal of Information Science* 30 (5) (2004), 418–35.

multi-divisional corporations that appeared – for example, Imperial Chemical Industries (ICI) in 1928 – commanded the financial strength to fund company library foundations or improvements. Larger and dispersed organisational structures also created the need for more efficient communication and information corporate infrastructure, of which the company library was a significant part.

As company libraries emerged they encouraged and benefited from a growing awareness of the importance of information work, distinguished from librarianship by its focus on extracting information from whole documents, its willingness to pre-empt user demands and its sympathy with new technologies for organising and disseminating information. Founded in 1924, Aslib (the Association of Special Libraries and Information Bureaux) reflected *to a degree* – for it continued to embrace traditional librarianship, albeit in special settings, and barely concerned itself with training and education – the appearance of an embryonic professionalism, to which early library work contributed much.

Finally, company library development and standards in Britain in the first half of the twentieth century were always a decade or so behind those in the United States. The idea of the company library had become embedded in America's corporate mentality even before 1914. After the First World War, therefore, companies in Britain benefited from being able to point to the efficacy of in-house library and information services in the United States and emulate patterns of provision seen there.

Early company libraries could be found in enterprises of varying size, across the sectors. During the Second World War the modest Diamond Trading Company of Holborn, in London, established a research department that was said to have 'an extensive library and technical archive' and to offer its information service 'without charge to all users of diamond tools and any interested'.[7] At the other end of the scale, the industrial giant ICI established a central technical library soon after its foundation in 1928. Other inter-war foundations included those at the General Electric Company (GEC), the food can manufacturer Metal Box, the rayon manufacturer Courtaulds, and the Bank of England. These libraries built on earlier successes during the First World War, when the electrical engineering firm Metropolitan-Vickers and the confectionery producer Rowntree and Co. both established technical repositories linked, like many that were to follow, to research departments.[8]

7 *Aslib Information* 59 (April 1944).
8 For further details of some of these, see A. Black, 'Technical libraries in British commercial and industrial enterprises before 1950', in B. Rayward and M. Bowden (eds.), *Proceedings*

But despite these developments and advances in company library activity before the middle of the twentieth century, Jason Farradane, future founder of the Institute of Information Scientists, could state as late as 1953 that: 'The majority of industrial concerns . . . remain ignorant of the full possibilities of an information service, or perhaps even of the need for information.'[9] This said, by the early 1950s between 1,200 and 1,500 British firms had established libraries or information departments, prompting the observation that 'industrial libraries now exist in sufficient numbers to be accepted as integral parts of a large concern'.[10]

The company library in the second half of the twentieth century

The second half of the twentieth century saw an extensive, although by no means evenly paced, growth in company libraries and their activities. Reflecting this expansion, an Industrial Group was established within the Library Association in 1971 and was to flourish over subsequent decades, its membership rising speedily at the outset from 250 in 1972 to 604 by the end of 1980.[11] One of the aims of the Group was to lobby for improved education and training for work in company libraries. Throughout their early history, and even beyond 1950, company libraries were often staffed by personnel *without* appropriate library or information qualifications. This occurred even at the level of librarian or unit manager, with positions perhaps being occupied by individuals who by training have been chemists, engineers or accountants first, and information experts second. But despite the fact that knowledge of the market and technological contexts of a company and its sector has always been at a premium in company library work, serious attempts were eventually made to develop a purely 'information professionalism' in company libraries, library schools responding with more appropriate optional pathways on courses from the late 1960s onwards.[12] This professional preparation was in addition, of course, to the courses in information science that began to appear in information

   of the 2002 Conference on the History and Heritage of Scientific and Technological Information Systems (Medford, NJ, in press).

9 J. Farradane, 'Information service in industry', *Research* 6 (1953), 327.

10 W. D. Piggot, 'Industrial libraries', in P. H. Sewell (ed.), *Five years' work in librarianship 1951–1955* (London, 1958), 75.

11 B. H. J. Sants, 'Industrial and commercial libraries', in L. J. Taylor (ed.), British librarianship and information work 1976–1980, vol. 2: Special libraries, materials and processes (London, 1983), 63.

12 K. P. Jones, 'Industrial libraries and information units', in H. A. Whatley (ed.), *British librarianship and information science 1966–1970* (London, 1972), 512.

curricula from the early 1960s onwards, following the establishment of the Institute of Information Scientists in 1958. Later, the growth of courses in information management in the last two decades of the century proved particularly helpful in producing a professional workforce more suited to the information needs of business and the 'emerging markets' in library and information work.[13]

Company libraries have always been sensitive to fluctuations in the economy. The enduring rule appears to be that at times of economic crisis company libraries are often among the first activities to be cut back by firms faced by a squeeze on profits. This is possibly linked to the fact that company libraries have often suffered from a lack of appreciation of their worth, if not a negative image, within organisations.[14] The work of company libraries has often been viewed merely as a clerical operation adding only marginal value, thereby rendering them susceptible to regimes of retrenchment when times get hard.[15] During economic upturns, on the other hand, the historical evidence is that support for the company library intensifies; although a period of prosperity *can* mean an increase in merger activity which, in turn, has implications for the information infrastructures of the merging enterprises in terms of the need to avoid duplicating services.

The economic difficulties of the mid-1970s and early 1980s saw a decrease in the number of company libraries, from 1,182 in 1972 to 880 in 1981.[16] Those that did survive experienced significant cuts in their budgets, thereby dispelling the myth of the company library as the rich relative in the varied library family. After the economic depression of the early 1980s, however, the number of company libraries increased rapidly, reaching around 2,000 in 1990.[17] A particular feature of this boom was the establishment of libraries in sectors that had previously showed little interest in them: in firms of architects, solicitors, chartered accountants and management consultants.[18] By 1993, Freeman was able to announce, indeed, that: 'The industrial and commercial sector of libraries

13 N. Moore, *The emerging markets for library and information workers*, British Library Research Report 56 (London, 1987).

14 M. Slater, *The neglected resource: non-usage of information services in industry and commerce* (London, 1981).

15 F. A. Graham, 'Industrial libraries', in H. A. Whatley (ed.), *British librarianship and information science 1971–1975* (London, 1977), 211.

16 J. Sherwell, 'Industrial and commercial libraries', in D. W. Bromley and A. M. Allott (eds.), *British librarianship and information work 1981–1985, vol. 2: Special libraries, materials and processes* (London, 1988), 54.

17 O. Freeman, 'Industrial and commercial libraries', in D. W. Bromley and A. M. Allott (eds.), *British librarianship and information work 1986–1990, vol. 2: Special libraries, materials and processes* (London, 1993), 73.

18 Sherwell, 'Industrial and commercial libraries', 53.

is probably the only area in librarianship where there has been any significant growth over the last decade.'[19]

Heightened activity in the late twentieth century took place across the board and was not confined to the service industries. For example, by the end of the 1980s the information service operated by the giant pharmaceutical company Beecham was receiving a massive 120,000 requests for documents each year. Around 80% of these were satisfied from the service's own stock, and over 14,000 items were obtained from the British Library Document Supply Centre.[20] At the other extreme there was an explosion in the 1980s in the number of units run by a single person, as reflected in the setting up in 1983 of a 'one-man-band' support group, with a membership of 200 by 1985.[21]

One such single-operator unit was that run by the Manchester office of the advertising agency J. Walter Thompson (JWT), an organisation which in the late 1980s had around 200 offices world-wide. The library was heavily used by many of the office's hundred or so employees, for information relating to anything from accounts management to creative design. But many enquiries had to be satisfied from outside the library's resources: from sources such as the Manchester Public Library's business department, the Manchester Business School, trade associations, other enterprises and sister operations in the JWT Group.[22]

This particular case highlights the general historical experience in company library provision. Most have been operated by very small or single-person staff establishments, with only the large (often multinational) enterprises being able to afford extensive facilities and personnel. This has placed a premium on tapping external sources. Even the most generously endowed company libraries have found it impossible to be self-sufficient and have had to look to, and co-operate with, external sources to supplement their existing services. The rapid growth of outsourcing in the late twentieth century was in many respects merely a sudden escalation in this established tradition. Ever cost-conscious, company libraries, especially small-scale operations, increasingly resorted to freelance consultants, external fee-charging services and information brokers rather than expand information provision by investing in expensive overheads, whether in the form of equipment or staff.[23]

19 Freeman, 'Industrial and commercial libraries', 71.
20 R. Brown, 'How I cope – the industrial library', *Serials* 3 (2) (July 1990), 42.
21 Sherwell, 'Industrial and commercial libraries', 54.
22 S. Frost, 'What do you mean! Insight into the working life of an advertising agency's library and information unit', *Assistant Librarian* 81 (5) (1988), 71–3.
23 Sants, 'Industrial and commercial libraries', 60.

The growth of brokering reinforced the trend in company library development away from the (near) self-sufficient, large, centralised service (the model one most closely associates with the business 'giants' earlier in the century), towards flexible and decentralised information systems which, by virtue of advances in information technology, include, crucially, the sharing of information generated internally at various points in the organisation. According to Hyde and Hyde, the function of the company library is the 'identification, acquisition and exploitation of both published and *unpublished* [my emphasis] information'.[24] Unpublished material can be either externally or internally generated. Traditionally company libraries have mostly been concerned with collecting and organising externally generated – and essentially published – information, but some have in the past assumed, or have desired to assume, responsibility for in-house information also. For example, in the 1980s the information service at Beecham served as a repository for internal company reports.[25] A similar function had been suggested in ICI in the 1930s. Earlier still, the Kaiser system of indexing that many early company libraries adopted was designed to deal with internal as well as external information.[26] In 1911 Kaiser wrote that: 'the indexes of our intelligence department must cover the entire stock of our information, including manuscripts'; such a department, he added, must 'include all reading matter used in a business, whether in manuscript, letter or book form etc, for it is essential that the information it contains, and which is useful from the standpoint of the business, should be dealt with on some uniform plan so that everything on a given subject may be available regardless of its literary form'.[27]

It is evident, therefore, that from the outset information management – which is concerned with the organisation and flow of information originating both inside and outside the organisation – was an important function, *potentially*, of the twentieth-century company library. In reality, however, only a minority of company libraries have ever fulfilled an authentic information, or records, management role, serving instead as access points for externally generated materials. In the late twentieth century, developments in information technology threatened to reduce the role and status of the company library further. The arrival of online searching in the 1970s (via services like ORBIT and DIALOG) at first enhanced the role of the library, but the proliferation

---

24 Hyde and Hyde, 'The industrial library', 63.
25 Brown, 'How I cope', 42.
26 J. Kaiser, *The card system at the office* (London, 1908); J. Kaiser, *Systematic indexing* (London, 1911).
27 Kaiser, *Systematic indexing*, paragraphs 7 and 663.

thereafter of powerful personal computers, internal databases, decision support systems, management information systems, executive intelligence systems and the electronic superhighway – encouraging the dream of the 'total', integrated information system – meant that information could be made accessible to individual employees directly. On the other hand, there remained a strong intermediary role for the company librarian, as a filter and packager of relevant data.

Despite the apparent danger posed by information management to their traditional role, company libraries began in the 1980s to embrace the concept as a means of promoting their position in parent organisations – a move reflected in the rebranding of Aslib in 1983 as the 'Association for Information Management'. It was argued that the discipline of information management, far from diminishing the professions of librarianship and information science, actually enhanced them in the context of the business organisation.[28] This said, the growth of information management has to a degree blurred the distinction between the information professions staffing company libraries. Whereas in the 1960s and 1970s a strict apartheid could be found in some organisations between librarian and information scientist,[29] in the 1980s and 1990s the roles and skills of these professions and those of the information officer or manager appeared to become increasingly shared. Indeed, such was the confluence of skills and tasks between the specialist librarian and the information scientist in the late twentieth-century company library setting, that many professionals and organisations found it convenient to adopt the single umbrella labels of 'knowledge management' and 'knowledge services' to mark out their identity. Whether these terms are intellectually defendable and can stand the test of time is another matter.[30]

28 P. Vickers, 'Promoting the concept of information management within organisations', *Journal of Information Science* 9 (1984), 124.
29 Jones, 'Industrial libraries and information units', 512–13.
30 T. Wilson, 'The nonsense of knowledge management', *Information Research* 8 (1) (2002).

38

Rare-book libraries and the growth of humanities scholarship

B. C. BLOOMFIELD

The idea of rarity

What makes a book 'rare' has been a subject of discussion since the eighteenth century when systematic enquiry into the question began,[1] when naturally the discussion was conducted in the universal language of scholarship – Latin, which was also the language of rare books. But vernacular works also became sought-after and rare, and William Oldys's *The British Librarian* (1738) was the first systematic published guide to rare books in English, followed by James Savage's periodical *The librarian, being an account of scarce, valuable and useful English books, manuscripts, libraries, public records, etc.*, 3 vols. (1808–9). By the beginning of the nineteenth century it was becoming clearer that the market value of books deemed rare had become a significant factor in this judgment. The concept of rarity necessarily implies more than one copy of a printed book, and is associated not only with book collecting, dealt with in more detail elsewhere, but also with the commercial trade in books. The defining event for Britain was the founding of the aristocratic Roxburghe Club (1812) which inspired book collectors throughout the country to collect, catalogue and display their rare books, and naturally to emphasise the rarity of books in the vernacular, as opposed to those in the previously universal scholarly language. The work of Thomas Frognall Dibdin (1776–1847), Earl Spencer's librarian, provided theoretical and practical guidance for the book collectors of his day.[2] Book collecting inevitably carried over to the public libraries established later in the century, whose collections began to emulate those of distinguished private collectors. Thus, by 1850, newly founded public libraries had begun to collect rare books for display to, and study by, their members. The exemplary survey of libraries included in Edward Edwards's *Memoirs of libraries*, 2 vols.

1 For an analysis see M. S. Batts, 'The eighteenth century concept of the rare book', *Book Collector* 45 (1975), 381–400; and the editorial by Nicolas Barker in the same issue (351–64).
2 For more biographical detail see W. Baker and K. Womack (eds.), *Nineteenth century British book-collectors and bibliographers* (Detroit, 1997).

(1859) shows that separate collections of books designated as rare were still the exception. Books thought valuable on account of their antiquity, scarcity, limited editions, valuable or esoteric knowledge, historical significance, association with famous previous owners, and other reasons, were still shelved with the normal collections, although access to them and consultation by ordinary readers might be controlled or restricted. Where rare-book collections were noted in Edwards's survey they were frequently collections of incunabula. The major public libraries in London – the British Museum Library, the library of the London Institution, the Guildhall Library of the Corporation of London, Lambeth Palace library, and the East India Company's library – all contained many rare books, but access to those libraries was usually by recommendation or membership, and rare books were not usually separately shelved or treated.[3] Similarly the libraries of the older universities, Oxford and Cambridge, and their individual colleges, while they possessed many rare and older books, did not separate them from their general collections, nor were they generally available to private scholars. The major public libraries in cities like Manchester, Birmingham and Leeds began to build up collections of rare and valuable books as a source of local pride, and many of these collections were associated with local donors and contained rare books, sometimes specifically related to the history of that locality.

From 1850 the accumulation of rare books in libraries both private and public tended to concentrate on those in the English language, since it was commonly assumed that the example provided by Great Britain and its Empire in its government, parliament, commercial success, scientific progress, political rights and liberties exemplified the epitome of liberal progress in the nineteenth century, and this progress could be paralleled in the development of its literature. The construction of an English literary canon, beginning with original charters, through the documents of the Magna Carta, the authorised translation of the Bible into English, the Book of Common Prayer, the first folio of Shakespeare's plays, Milton, Dryden and Pope, culminating in the literature of the nineteenth century exemplified by the novels of Scott, Thackeray and Dickens and the poetry of Keats, Shelley, Wordsworth and Byron, was visibly demonstrated in the exhibitions in the King's Library of the British Museum, amongst which were those commemorating the tercentenaries of

---

3 However, some of these libraries did publish guides or catalogues to their collections, e.g. *A catalogue of the library of the Corporation of London* (1840), and S. R. Maitland, *An index of such English books, printed before the year MDC., as are now in the archiepiscopal library at Lambeth* (1845).

the authorised version of the English Bible in 1911, the Shakespeare first folio in 1923, and the later permanent exhibition which, with its catalogue on sale in the bookshop, remained virtually unchanged from 1939 until the 1960s.[4]

Thus at the beginning of our period the concept of 'rarity' was already developed, and included an element of financial value as well as a recognition of a rare book's value for scholarly research. But the ideal concept of building a library of universal knowledge, Panizzi's ambition during his period at the British Museum Library, tended to preclude the separation of rare books from the main subject-organised collections.[5] Comparing Edwards's description of libraries with rare-book collections in 1859 with that provided in summary fashion in the *British library year-book 1900–1901*, edited by Thomas Greenwood (London, 1900), the only major addition is that of the John Rylands Library in Manchester, founded by Mrs Rylands on the basis of her purchase of the Spencer library and opened in 1899. The libraries of the various local Athenaeums, mechanics' institutes and other societies with their local collections were still in existence, but few had designated 'rare' sections. (The position in Europe was quite different: there the principle of separating rare books in reserves, or special collections, was recognised much earlier, and access to those collections was restricted.)

Between 1900 and 1960 there was a great redistribution of library resources and rare books, and an increased recognition of the value of rare books for scholarship. This redistribution was, in part, a product of the agricultural depression of the late nineteenth century which caused many aristocratic and large landowners to sell the contents of their houses, with works of art and libraries often the first to go, and this trend was exacerbated by two other factors: higher levels of taxation imposed after the First World War, and the increased activity of American book-collectors and university libraries during that period.[6] (The financial crash of 1926 gave added impetus to many sales and dispersals of rare-book collections.) The history of this diaspora can be studied in the biography of Dr A. S. W. Rosenbach and the catalogues and

---

4 British Museum, *A guide to the exhibition in the King's Library* (London, 1939).
5 See I. Willison, 'The creation of the concept of the rare book', *Intellectual News* 6/7 (2000), 27–36, for an extended discussion of the British Museum's influence on this topic.
6 Some rare books in country house libraries survived in the care of the National Trust, and are gradually being recorded and catalogued. For a situation report see N. Barker, *Treasures from the libraries of National Trust country houses* (New York, 1999), which also contains an essay on their architecture by Simon Jervis. A revised version of Jervis's essay appeared as 'The English country house library: an architectural history', *Library History* 18 (2002), 175–90 (in a special issue of *Library History* with seven further articles on libraries in the care of the National Trust).

histories of the two major British auction houses, Sotheby's and Christie's.[7] Concern was expressed that the nation's printed heritage was being exported at an ever increasing rate, and those complaints continued right through the twentieth century.[8]

A major participant in this redistribution of rare-book resources was the antiquarian book trade, but there is no comprehensive history of 'The Trade', although some of the flavour of the business can be gleaned from *Antiquarian books: a companion for booksellers, librarians and collectors*, edited by Philippa and Leo Bernard with Angus O'Neill, and personal memoirs like W. T. Spencer's *Forty years in my bookshop*, P. H. Muir's *Minding my own business*, George Sims's *The rare book game* and *More of the rare book game*, and Anthony Rota's *Books in the blood: memoirs of a fourth generation bookseller*.[9]

About the middle of this period came the publication of the first national directory of libraries and information sources that systematically aimed to identify special collections – the *Aslib directory: a guide to sources of specialized information in Great Britain and Ireland* (1928), now in its twelfth edition (2002) – and this was followed, after the Second World War, by the Rare Books Group of the Library Association publishing its *A directory of rare book and special collections in the United Kingdom and the Republic of Ireland*, edited by Moelwyn I. Williams (1985), with the second revised and enlarged edition edited by B. C. Bloomfield in 1997. (A supplementary study of, and guide to, the resources of the smaller libraries with special collections had previously been carried out in 1973–5 by Valerie Bloomfield under the auspices of the Council on Library Resources and published in a limited edition.[10]) The period between 1850 and 2000 saw an increasing emphasis on, and detailed description of, library resources designated rare, and an increasing recognition by scholars and librarians of the value of such collections, indicated by an increasing number of published contributions to the debate on what constitutes 'rarity',

7 British Museum, *List of catalogues of English book sales, 1767–1900* (London, 1915); A. N. L. Munby (ed.), *Sale catalogues of eminent persons*, 12 vols. (London, 1971–5); E. Wolf and J. F. Fleming, *Rosenbach: a biography* (Cleveland, OH, 1960); F. Herrmann, *Sotheby's: portrait of an auction house* (London, 1980); J. Herbert, *Inside Christie's* (London, 1990). For a view of auctions and the book trade at a less rarefied level see A. Freeman and J. I. Freeman, *Anatomy of an auction: rare books at Ruxley Lodge, 1919* (London, 1990); and O. F. Snelling, *Rare books and rarer people: some personal reminiscences of the trade* (London, 1982).

8 For example see Philip Larkin's 'A neglected responsibility: contemporary literary manuscripts', in his *Required writing* (London, 1983), 98–108; originally published in *Encounter*, July 1979.

9 There are further references in the *Cambridge bibliography of English literature*.

10 Sir F. Francis and V. Bloomfield, *Independent libraries in England: a survey of selected institutional, proprietary and endowed libraries* (London, 1977).

and consequently, what was the worth of such collections to scholarship.[11] It is also noticeable that by the middle of our period the words 'rare books' were almost always associated with the modifying terms 'special collections'.

The rise of scholarship in the humanities

Prior to the reforms of the older universities in the early nineteenth century there was no profession of university teacher or researcher. The foundation of the University of London in 1826 and its admission of those denied entry to the older universities stimulated some research, principally located in what is now University College, and its invention of the external degree system from 1858 opened the doors of university education even wider. This was followed by the Royal Commissions on the universities and colleges of Scotland (1837), the Royal Commission on Oxford and Cambridge, and the consequent reform acts of 1854 and 1856. Durham University had been refounded in 1832 and Owens College, Manchester was established in 1851 – the first of the municipal universities, which pioneered programmes of scientific and economic research closely associated with local industry. The repeal of the University Test Acts in 1871 threw universities open to all religions and this was followed by the Reform Statutes of 1881 for the older foundations. The first government grants to universities were made in 1887, and between 1851 and 1949 universities or colleges were founded in Birmingham, Liverpool, Leeds, Sheffield, Nottingham and Wales, as well as colleges in Reading, Southampton, Exeter, Leicester and elsewhere. The British Academy was founded in 1901, granted a charter of incorporation in 1902, and established to provide a centre of excellence in the humanities comparable to that provided by the Royal Society in the sciences. The University Grants Committee was established in 1919 to regulate the increasingly larger amounts of money awarded by government to subvent higher education in the growing number of universities.[12]

---

11 For example: S. Pargellis, 'Rare books and the scholar', in T. C. Blegen and others, *Book collecting and scholarship* (Minneapolis, 1954), 33–9; G. N. Ray, 'The changing world of rare books', *PBSA* 59 (1965), 103–41; G. N. Ray, 'The world of rare books re-examined', *Yale Library Gazette* 49 (1974), 77–146; G. N. Ray, *Bibliographical resources for the study of nineteenth century English fiction* (Los Angeles, 1964); G. N. Ray, *The rare book world today* (New York, 1982) among many others.

12 M. Sanderson (ed.), *The universities in the nineteenth century* (London, 1975); A. Briggs, 'Development in higher education in the United Kingdom: nineteenth and twentieth centuries', in W. R. Niblett (ed.), *Higher education: demand and response* (London, 1969), 95–116. After the Further and Higher Education Act 1992, the University Grants Committee was reorganised as the Higher Education Funding Council, with separate councils for England and Wales, and for Scotland. Northern Ireland university institutions were funded directly.

The number of university teachers continued to increase throughout the period. In the second half of the nineteenth century it is estimated there were but 800 in Oxford and Cambridge together, 500 in the municipal universities and colleges, 500 in the Scottish universities, and fewer than 250 in London. By 1900 there were probably fewer than 2,000 university teachers in total, but by 1940 there were some 5,000, by 1960 approximately 15,000, by 1980 some 40,000, and by 1998 the total, including higher education colleges was estimated at 126,000.[13]

Similarly the number of students enrolled in universities also continued to increase, from an estimated 16,700 in 1899 to 38,300 in 1929, 86,400 in 1959, 143,000 in 1974, to more than 4,237,000 in 1998, including those in higher education colleges.[14] While not all students or teachers were engaged in research, it is notable that in session 1989/90 there was an estimated total of 145,700 postgraduate students in universities, and this number had risen to 323,600 by session 1997/8. Arts and humanities students are estimated to account for 40% of student numbers during this period. Overseas students accounted for 21% of this total.

The result of this expansion of universities and research work can be gauged by the increasing numbers of postgraduate theses accepted. Prior to the late nineteenth century, most theses and dissertations followed continental models and were submitted in printed form. The first theses submitted in typewritten form date from about 1880. 'It is clear . . . that only one or two universities – London and Oxford – had as many as ten theses each year before the mid-1920s. From 1924 there were three or four times as many theses completed annually as in each of the previous years.'[15] The systematic recording of theses submitted and approved by British universities dates from an initiative by Aslib, the Library Association and others, which resulted in the publication of the *Index to theses accepted for higher degrees in the universities of Great Britain and Ireland* (London, 1953–) which recorded 2,182 titles in its first issue. The last annual sessional publication in 1992 recorded 7,988 theses, and by 1996 some 10,000 successful theses were being listed each year. (Perhaps 30–40% of the recorded titles dealt with subjects in the humanities and social sciences.) In

13 A. H. Halsey and M. A. Trow, *The British academic* (London, 1971), especially chapter 7; Loughborough University, *Library & information statistics tables for the United Kingdom 1998* (LISU, 1999).
14 A. N. Little, 'Some myths of university expansion', in P. Holmes (ed.), *Sociological studies in British university education* (Keele, 1963), 185–97. Representing an approximate annual rate of increase of 4.5%, this expansion was principally the result of the *Higher Education Report* of the Committee on Higher Education chaired by Lord Robbins (Cmnd. 2154).
15 R. B. Bilboul (ed.), *Retrospective index to theses of Great Britain and Ireland, 1716–1950*, 5 vols. (Santa Barbara and Oxford, 1975), vol.1: *Social sciences and humanities*, iii.

addition to theses, university teachers also increasingly engaged in research and publication, and both students and teachers required more intensive use of rare books and greater library resources. (The National Central Library, created in 1916 as the Central Library for Students, played a significant part in helping scholars to identify locations for rare books not in their own libraries through its union catalogues, and sometimes arranged for these books to be borrowed.[16]) How to locate these books and find these resources, how to preserve them but yet give adequate access to them, became important factors in library policies for rare books in the second half of the twentieth century. (This need was exacerbated by the introduction in 1986 of periodic Research Assessment Exercises, which attempt to measure and grade the publications and productivity of university departments and individual teachers, and to reward the successful with increased grants.)

Two other elements in the development of humanities scholarship need to be mentioned, if only in a summary fashion: first, the development of techniques of bibliographical and textual analysis during the period 1850 to 2000; and second, the importance of prevailing fashions or trends in literary and historical scholarship. Both had a considerable impact on the development of scholarship, and the ensuing history of libraries and policies designed to cope with increased demands on use and accessibility.

The supersession of eclectic editorial policies by a more systematic study of textual problems was pioneered by German scholars editing classical texts, and the techniques developed were soon applied to the surviving early texts of the Bible. In Britain similar techniques were first applied to the study of incunabula by Henry Bradshaw in the 1860s, and continued by Robert Proctor in his index to the incunabula in the British Museum Library and the Bodleian in 1898. These analytical and critical methods were then extended to the period of Elizabethan literature, and especially to the study and editing of the dramatic texts of Shakespeare's plays. This led to the founding of numerous societies which played an important part in the development of textual analysis and the editing, production and publication of many important literary texts in the established canon. The most important among these was, perhaps, the

---

16 The National Central Library maintained union catalogues of books and special catalogues for Slavonic, German and rare older books published prior to 1800, and it also promoted a scheme by the Joint Standing Committee on co-operation whereby university and some public libraries were encouraged to buy copies of books in certain periods allocated to them. See S. P. Filon, *The National Central Library: an experiment in library co-operation* (London, 1977), especially chapter 11. The NCL was absorbed into the British Library following the recommendations of the Dainton Committee.

Bibliographical Society (1892),[17] although the Edinburgh Bibliographical Society was first in actual date of foundation. The Bibliographical Society through its series of major publications and its transactions, subsequently entitled *The Library*, developed, refined and promoted techniques of bibliographical and textual analysis expounded by W. W. Greg, R. B. McKerrow and A. W. Pollard that became the accepted standard for editors of literary texts. In addition the Society published in 1926 its *Short-title catalogue of books printed in England, Scotland, Ireland and of English books printed abroad, 1475–1640*, edited by A. W. Pollard and G. R. Redgrave, which established the national bibliography for its period. (The revised edition in three volumes and edited by F. S. Ferguson, W. A. Jackson and K. F. Pantzer was published 1976–91.) Guides to literature in English proliferated but none rivalled F. W. Bateson's *Cambridge bibliography of English literature* (1940; supp., 1957) and the revised edition edited by George Watson and I. R. Willison (1969–77). The theories developed by Greg and Pollard were further refined by Professor Fredson Bowers[18] of the University of Virginia, whose Bibliographical Society was founded in 1947. The Greg/Bowers theories of textual analysis and editing were systematically extended by Professor G. T. Tanselle,[19] and what were termed Anglo-American theories and practices were generally accepted in English literary scholarship.[20] This analytical procedure reached its apogee in Professor Charlton Hinman's study of compositorial analysis in his *The printing and proof-reading of the first folio of Shakespeare* (1963), but some of his conclusions were controverted in D. F. McKenzie's 'Printers of the mind' and his 1985 Panizzi lectures.[21] French literary scholars developed a broader theory of the circumstances surrounding the publication of literary texts and these were first proposed in *L'apparition du livre*, by professors Lucien Febvre and Henri-Jean Martin (1957).[22] They projected an extended analysis of the economic and social circumstances surrounding the publication of any

---

17 See *The Bibliographical Society, 1892–1942: studies in retrospect* (London, 1945); *The Bibliographical Society, 1892–1992* (London, 1992); and P. Davison (ed.), *The book encompassed: studies in twentieth century bibliography* (Cambridge, 1992).

18 F. Bowers, *Principles of bibliographical description* (Princeton, 1949), and *Textual and literary criticism* (Cambridge, 1959).

19 G. T. Tanselle, *Textual criticism and scholarly editing* (Charlottesville, 1990).

20 Useful reviews of these developments can be found in Davison (ed.), *The book encompassed*, and D. C. Greetham, *Textual scholarship: an introduction*, corrected edn (New York, 1994).

21 D. F. McKenzie, 'Printers of the mind', *Studies in Bibliography* 22 (1969), 1–75, based on his doctoral thesis on the CUP archives, 'The Cambridge University Press, 1696–1712', 2 vols. (Cambridge, 1966); *Bibliography and the sociology of texts* (London, 1986), the first Panizzi lectures 1985.

22 English translation by David Gerard, *The coming of the book: the impact of printing 1450–1800* (London, 1976).

text, and the theoretical basis of this 'histoire du livre', as it came to be called, owed much to the French 'Annales' school of economic history.

Subsequently continental literary theorists such as Foucault, Lacan, de Man and Bourdieu developed ideas and schools of criticism loosely termed 'post-modern' or 'de-constructionist', which rejected the Anglo-American techniques of textual analysis and editorial method as well as those of the 'histoire du livre' school, asserting that the interaction of the reader with the text – any text – was the primary field of critical study. The theorists denied the importance of the explication of texts, and of methods of critical bibliographical analysis which sought to get closest to the text the author wrote. These theories spread quickly like a malignant disease through universities and departments of English literature, with potentially serious effects on libraries and rare books and special collections.[23]

In the field of historical scholarship the opening of the national archives and other repositories for serious study saw the growth of a school of constitutional history pioneered in the work of Bishop William Stubbs, and Professor T. F. Tout at Manchester. These studies attempted to construct a picture of society reflected in official legal and state papers, and gradually supplanted the work of historians primarily concerned with narrative political history, such as Carlyle, Macaulay and their successors. By the end of the nineteenth century economic and social historians were more prominent, with the founding of the London School of Economics (1895), and they relied increasingly on recorded statistical and legal documentation, as well as on survey results. But the major works of synthesis were still published in narrative political and diplomatic form in series like the *Cambridge medieval history*, 8 vols. (Cambridge, 1911–36), and the *Cambridge history of India*, 6 vols. plus supp. (Cambridge, 1922–53). Prior to the Second World War the work of Professor L. B. Namier emphasised studies of institutional history and especially the British parliament, but post-war saw the growth of a trend towards localised economic and social historical studies, sometimes referred to as 'subaltern' studies. This tendency is displayed in the *New Cambridge history of India* published as a series of separate monographic studies. Opposed to this trend was a developing school of international or global history, which grew stronger in the later years of the twentieth century.[24] These new developments in historiography presupposed

---

23 This cursory survey concentrates on literary theories that most affected the world of rare books; for a more extended survey see R. Wellek's *History of modern criticism*, 8 vols. (New Haven, 1955–93).

24 This partial and partisan survey may be supplemented by E. Breisach, *Historiography, ancient, mediaeval and modern* (Chicago, 1983).

a much greater reliance on archival resources and rare books. It is also significant that the history of science and technology became part of humanities scholarship in the latter part of the twentieth century, and rare books in those fields became increasingly sought after and valuable, with first editions of Darwin, Einstein and notable physicists being retrieved from the open shelves of academic libraries.[25] This was given added impetus by the exhibition organised in connection with the 11th International Printing Machinery and Allied Trades Exhibition in London in July 1963, with its hugely influential catalogue *Printing and the mind of man.*

The huge increase in researchers and the broadening of the range of scholarship in the humanities had consequent effects on libraries and their rare-book and special collections, how they grew and how they were administered. But there was no co-ordinated approach to the problems posed in developing rare-book collections in the humanities, and the British Academy's survey[26] carried out in 1958–60 only recommended the strengthening and development of existing arrangements without pin-pointing the deficiencies of provision or access to collections.

The libraries' response

In 1850 there was no profession of librarian or rare-book curator recognised by any qualification or examination, and those entering such a career could gain experience only by service in one of the larger or national libraries, provided they had some appropriate general education and interest in the job. The proliferation of public libraries founded after the 1850 Act produced a steady demand for experienced librarians, and the body of men so recruited, together with those employed in the national libraries, banded together to found the Library Association in 1877.[27] The new association took training for librarianship as one of its principal tasks, and was keenly interested in the problems associated with the care of rare books, many of the founders also being associated with the establishment of the Bibliographical Society in 1892.

Since in 1850 rare books were usually shelved with other books on similar subjects in encyclopaedic libraries, problems only occurred for librarians and

25 See M. Argles, *South Kensington to Robbins: an account of English technical and scientific education since 1851* (London, 1964), especially the references to library provision; but the standard text is J. L. Thornton and R. I. J. Tully, *Scientific books, libraries and collectors*, ed. A. Hunter, 4th edn (Aldershot, 1999).
26 British Academy, *Research in the humanities and social sciences: report of a survey 1958–1960* (London, 1961), especially chapter 6.
27 W. A. Munford (ed.), *Annals of the Library Association, 1877 to 1960* (London, 1965).

curators when they were required to produce items of unusual size or shape or those which necessitated the supervision of readers. The British Museum Library used its Large Room, later rebuilt and enlarged (1912) and renamed the North Library,[28] for this purpose, but other major libraries were late in providing separate accommodation for the users of rare books. The new Cambridge University Library (1934) provided its Morison Room for that purpose, the Goldsmiths' Library was built (1938) in the new University of London Library, and the Bodleian Library used Duke Humphrey's Library for readers of rare books. As these books increased in value and the numbers of readers demanding access also increased, so administrative necessity drove libraries to provide segregated facilities. But the collections of municipal universities and others founded prior to World War II were so small as to need no special provision for rare books. From 1950 onwards British university and research libraries began to grow at an accelerated rate, driven by increased numbers of students and teaching staff, and sharply rising government grants available through the University Grants Committee.[29] Collections in London University libraries rose from 2,161,000 in 1950 to 5,785,000 in 1976; in Oxford from 1,835,000 to 4,464,000; and in Cambridge from 1,750,000 to 3,572,000 over the same period. The total book collections in English universities increased from 8,469,400 to 267,260,000 during that time, while the numbers of students trebled. This huge increase in resources and bookstock drove the University Grants Committee to appoint a special committee to investigate the problems and devise a strategy for the future of university libraries. The Parry Report[30] contained little on rare books, but it did emphasise the importance for researchers in the humanities of building substantial collections of older books and representative collections of currently published indexes, union lists, location lists and reprinted material. Paragraph 165 contains the phrases that often bedevilled future development: 'The collection of research materials inevitably raises the question of acquiring rare books. It is not proper to subsidise from public funds a desire to acquire items simply because they are bibliographical curiosities. But rare books are essential for many sorts of research.' The report contains other recommendations on rare books and research collections in university libraries, but those libraries were already being overtaken by a flood of deposited and gifted material from former students, local societies whose libraries were being dissolved,

28 See P. R. Harris, *A history of the British Museum Library, 1753–1973* (London, 1998) for a
   detailed history of how the library coped with its rare books collections.
29 F. W. Ratcliffe, 'The growth of university library collections in the United Kingdom', in
   J. Thompson (ed.), *University library history: an international review* (New York, 1980), 5–32.
30 University Grants Committee, *Report of the committee on libraries* (London, 1967) (The
   Parry Report).

parish libraries and other bodies, on top of demands from teaching staff and research students to provide adequate resources for their work. Guides to what were now usually termed Special Collections proliferated.

In 1966 the Library Association formed its own special section, the Rare Books Group, of those concerned with rare books, their care, cataloguing and preservation, and this body, with a membership exceeding 1,000, achieved two editions of its *Directory*, and publishes a *Newsletter* that circulates widely.

But the expansion of rare-book and special collections funded by the increased grants following the Parry Report did not long continue. Economic difficulties forced the government of the day to reduce funding, and the University Grants Committee appointed yet another committee to review libraries since it was unable to fund the pressing demands for new buildings. The committee's report[31] recommended that universities should aim for a 'self-renewing library of limited growth' – a judgement which was almost universally derided by librarians and scholars, but it was used to restrain university library building, and the provision of specialised accommodation for rare book collections suffered considerably.

The Dainton committee report[32] had little or nothing to say about rare books, but since it led to the establishment of the British Library it had a major effect on subsequent developments in rare-book libraries, most notably in the inception in 1976 of the *Eighteenth-century short-title catalogue* (ESTC), designed to follow on from the Bibliographical Society's *Short-title catalogue . . . 1475–1640*, and Donald Wing's continuation from 1641 to 1700 based at Yale University. In November 1987 it was decided to merge all these files to create the *English short-title catalogue*, a machine-readable catalogue of all English-language titles published from 1475 up to 1800, a co-operative project between British, American, German and many overseas libraries. Beginning as a record of the material in the British Library, other records from contributing libraries began to arrive in 1978 and are still being incorporated. The records were first published in microfiche form in 1983, and two revised and enlarged editions on CD-ROM have been subsequently issued. The machine-readable file is still being edited and is now mounted and available for consultation world-wide through RLIN. The decision to begin work was taken by the then Director of the Reference Division, Donovan Richnell, and the success of the project owes much to the editors, Robin Alston in London and Henry

---

31 University Grants Committee, *Capital provision for university libraries: report of a working party* (London, 1976) (The Atkinson Report).

32 National Libraries Committee, *Report* (London, 1969) (Cmnd. 4028) (The Dainton Report).

Snyder in the United States, and to continued financial support from many sources in both countries. Without the British Library this could never have been achieved, and scholars using English-language material now have an historical record unparalleled in any other country. Similarly the *Incunabula short-title catalogue* (ISTC) owes its existence to the British Library and its first editor, Dr Lotte Hellinga. Both projects led to the issuing of commercial microfiche reproductions of important material recorded in the catalogues, with associated cataloguing data, and thus to the wider dissemination of rare material.[33]

The importance of the provision of surrogate copies of rare books can scarcely be underestimated for scholars distant from large libraries or for those working on the content of the texts, as opposed to analytic bibliographical study of the physical book. The possibilities for micro-reproduction of rare texts on a large scale had first been mooted by Fremont Rider in his *The scholar and the future of the research library* (New York, 1944), but the commercial possibilities of such reproductions were slow to be realised and were first applied to runs of scarce serials and large archival manuscript collections. In the last years of the twentieth century similar claims were made for the potential benefits of the new digital technology to store and make available to distant scholars the rarest of books and manuscripts, although the costs of capturing digital material, storing and making it available seemed to be considerable.

The importance of rare-book collections in support of research in the humanities now became the subject of much discussion, and those libraries fortunate enough to possess important collections began to realise the extra burden placed on their staff and resources in providing access to less fortunate scholars from other institutions. It was agreed that rare-book collections supported institutional teaching and research, stimulated academic curiosity, enriched readers, provided a regional repository function, and added distinction to the holding library.[34]

This discussion immediately raised the question of access to those collections. It was generally agreed that physical access to recorded rare books

33 For summaries of the history of these catalogues see F. G. Kaltwasser and J. M. Smethurst (eds.), *Retrospective cataloguing in Europe: 15th to 19th century printed materials. Proceedings of the International Conference, Munich 28th–30th September 1990* (Munich, 1992); L. Hellinga and J. Goldfinch (eds.), *Bibliography and the study of 15th century civilization* (London, 1987).

34 See for example P. Hoare, '"Loads of learned lumber": special collections in the smaller university library', in B. Dyson (ed.), *The modern academic library: essays in memory of Philip Larkin* (London, 1989), 57–66; and R. M. Auchstetter, 'The role of the rare book library in higher education', *College and Research Libraries* 51 (1990), 221–30.

was to be granted to serious scholars, including those from outside the institutional academic world. But the further question of identifying and locating rare books on any specific subject came to the fore: what is presently
termed 'resource discovery'. Guides to the location of special collections of
rare books and manuscripts were legion,[35] but were frequently in need of
revision and up-dating. Although the existence of ESTC supplied the need for
older English-language books, other languages and subject areas were lacking
in source guides.[36] Computerisation supplied the gap, and as the catalogues
of university and other learned libraries began to be available in machine-
readable form, they were mounted on the World-Wide Web or on the Joint
Academic Network (JANET) funded by the Universities Grants Committee.
Thus it was possible to search nationally, and internationally, for selected rare-
book titles and to find locations – provided those special collections had been
catalogued and the entries converted to machine-readable form and included
in general catalogues. Unfortunately this was often not the case. Three subsequent reports addressed this problem. First the report of the Joint Funding
Councils Library Review in 1993 identified the difficulties of locating rare
books and special collections for research; this was followed by the report of
a special group planning a national/regional strategy for library provision for
researchers in 1996; and by a further report on the idea of a national programme
for the retrospective conversion of those older catalogues of rare books and
special collections in 1995. A later report provided cost estimates for such a
programme.[37] These reports were followed by yet another, entitled *Full disclosure*, by Anne Chapman, Nicholas Kingsley and Lorcan Dempsey (Bath, 1999),
published on behalf of the new official Libraries and Information Commission
and sponsored by the National Council on Archives, which reinforced the conclusions of the preceding reports and reported the proceedings of a general
conference at the British Library in 1999. Meanwhile the Higher Education
Funding Councils had implemented a major programme of grants to libraries

35 For example: R. Offor, *A descriptive guide to the libraries of the University of Leeds* (Leeds,
1947); J. D. Pearson, *Oriental manuscript collections in the libraries of Great Britain and Ireland*
(London, 1954); D. Knott, *Rare book collections: a brief guide* (Reading, 1980); *Guide to special
collections* (Liverpool, [1978]); E. G. W. Bill, *Unexpected collections at Lambeth Palace Library*
(London, 1982).
36 One such is A. Weedon and M. Bott, *Book trade archives 1830–1939: a location register*,
HOBODS 5 (Oxford, 1996).
37 Joint Funding Councils Libraries Review, *Report* (Bristol, 1993) (The Follett Report);
Joint Funding Councils Libraries Review, *Report of the group on a national/regional strategy
for library provision for researchers* (Bristol, 1996) (The Anderson report); P. Bryant, A.
Chapman and B. Naylor, *Retrospective conversion of library catalogues in institutions of
higher education in the United Kingdom: a study of the justification for a national programme*
(Bath, 1995) (The Bryant report); P. Bryant, *Making the most of our libraries* (Bath, 1997).

and archives for the retro-conversion of older catalogues of rare books and special collections – its Research Support Libraries Programme (RSLP).

In support of these initiatives the Rare Books Group had sponsored and finalised its *Guidelines for the cataloguing of rare books* (1997), which recommended methods for amending standard library machine-readable cataloguing (MARC) to identify special features in specific copies in collections.[38] These guidelines were adopted by the British Library as supplementary guidance for British MARC. But texts for training rare-book librarians were still few, although Roderick Cave's *Rare book librarianship* achieved a second edition in 1982.[39] Historical bibliography was rarely taught in schools of librarianship and many librarians produced by those schools were quite unfitted to take charge of rare-book libraries. Short courses were mounted each year by the Rare Books Group dealing with some aspect of work with rare books, but the training of rare-book librarians was largely neglected, and those seeking training had little option but to seek work experience in one of the larger libraries with knowledgeable staff.[40]

Questions of access to rare books and special collections were thoroughly aired during the last ten years of the twentieth century. Older collections of rare books had often lain undisturbed until researchers learned of their existence and sought access, when it was speedily discovered that their condition after years of neglect was fragile. Bindings needed cleaning, repair or renovation; documents and paper had been attacked by damp, insects or other perils; and many rare books were in no condition to be delivered to readers – let alone borrowed or sent to other libraries. Thefts, and witting or unwitting losses, and other unrecorded dispersals were sometimes discovered. Rare-book librarians were already aware of the need for many books to be preserved or conserved, and this now became imperative as use increased. Librarians became aware, late in the day, that rare books and special collections needed special care and

38 One particular feature that demanded inclusion in cataloguing data was the history of a rare book's provenance. A major guide to the subject by D. Pearson, *Provenance research in book history: a handbook* (London, 1994) was published by the British Library.

39 R. Cave, *Rare book librarianship*, 2nd edn (London, 1982). There are useful surveys in 'Recent trends in rare book librarianship', *Library Trends* 36 (1987); S. H. Lee (ed.), *The role and future of special collections in research libraries: British and American perspectives* (New York, 1993); K. Webster, 'Research collections', in D. Baker (ed.), *Resource management in academic libraries* (London, 1997), 137–57; J. Feather, 'Institutional collections in Great Britain', in A. D. Schreyer (ed.), *Rare books 1983–84* (New York, 1984), 61–7; and B. C. Bloomfield, 'Rare book and special collections', in *Librarianship and Information Work Worldwide 1998* (London, 1998), 151–70.

40 See M. J. Crump and others, *Rare book librarians for the future: issues in training and education* (Brussels, 1996); J. P. Feather and A. Lusher, 'Education for conservation in British library schools: current practices and future prospects', *Journal of Librarianship* 21 (1989), 129–38.

protection to survive the burden of increased use and that fragile materials sometimes needed to be withdrawn from casual or scholarly use. These considerations gave more urgency to the establishment in libraries of reserved and supervised accommodation for such materials, and for more attention to be given to the conditions in which they were stored. Conservation or, as it came later to be known, preservation policies were investigated and found to be wanting in most academic libraries. Problems with the degeneration of the organic materials from which rare books are fashioned had been known for many years. But it was the damage to libraries and rare books wrought by the serious floods in Florence in 1966 that brought the problems sharply into focus for European librarians. Major problems with relatively modern books first came to light in American libraries and were studied by the W. J. Barrow Research Laboratory in a series of reports titled *Permanence/durability of the book*. Report v, *Strength and other characteristics of book papers 1800–1899* (Richmond, Virginia, 1967) tested and detected serious deterioration in papers manufactured after the introduction of chemical woodpulp in the middle of the nineteenth century; report vi, *Spot testing for unstable modern book and record papers* (Richmond, Virginia, 1969) provided guidance for identifying the extent of such deterioration. The position in Britain was found not to be as serious as in the United States, but the deterioration of paper in rare books published in the nineteenth century and after was identified as a serious problem that could be ameliorated by air conditioning and temperature controlled storage. There were also problems associated with uncontrolled use, inferior material and standards in binding, a lack of planning in cases of serious disasters by fire or flood, and the ever present and increasing danger of theft. All these problems were lumped together and included under the rubric 'preservation'. The first investigation into preservation policies in British libraries was instigated by the British Library and based in Cambridge University Library under the direction of its librarian F. W. Ratcliffe.[41] The results revealed an almost complete lack of any formal preservation plans or policies, and revealed a high proportion of library stock in a condition unfit for normal use. The report recommended action at local level in individual libraries, the provision of more training in preservation, and also the creation at national level of an advisory centre for preservation. Other recommendations applied to modern book production and, in particular, the adoption of acid-free paper by publishers and for books and journals intended for long-term retention.

41 F. W. Ratcliffe with the assistance of D. Patterson, *Preservation policies and conservation in British libraries*, Library and Information Report 25 (Boston Spa, 1984).

The Library Association established a sub-committee on Conservation and Preservation in 1982 and this body sponsored training courses in collaboration with the National Preservation Office subsequently established in the British Library, which instituted an annual series of national seminars in 1986. The Library Association devoted its entire annual conference to the subject in 1986.[42] But including the subject in the curricula of library schools remained an unfulfilled desideratum. A follow-up to the Ratcliffe report directed by Professor J. P. Feather and sponsored by the Leverhulme Trust was published in 1996,[43] and the National Preservation Office was reconstituted in 1996 with a supervisory body comprising all the British national libraries and other representative interests.

So at the beginning of the twenty-first century the world of rare books and special collections was facing development at a hitherto unprecedented rate. Rare books were being produced and identified at an increasing rate every year; knowledge of the whereabouts of rare books and special collections was increasingly being diffused world-wide through the Internet and other rapidly revised and up-dated guides; the provision of surrogate copies by photographic, electronic and digitised methods was serving those scholars interested solely in the content of those collections; but forecasts of sharply increasing use by scholars and others continue to be proved correct by statistical monitoring. Curators and librarians in future centuries will need to develop their skills to meet these challenges.

42 Library Association, *Preserving the word*, ed. R. E. Palmer (London, 1986).
43 J. Feather, G. Matthews and P. Eden, *Preservation management: policies and practices in British libraries* (Aldershot, 1996).

PART VII

THE TRADE AND ITS TOOLS: LIBRARIANS AND LIBRARIES IN ACTION

39

Introduction: librarians and libraries in action

PETER HOARE

A history of libraries needs to look not only at the libraries themselves but at the way they work and at the structures and systems that make library operations possible. Libraries do not exist in isolation but work for the communities they serve, and their history relates to the varied contexts in which they have operated. To achieve their ends libraries have developed a range of characteristics and skills which are the subject of this section of the volume.

It is one of the features of the modern age that the library world has become more self-conscious – in the best and worst senses of that word – as the sense of a profession developed. Like many other specialities, librarianship had to prove its worth in a world where other professions were also seeking to establish their position. It has developed a varied yet broadly coherent philosophy and a range of skills applicable to librarians from many different backgrounds. In building up a professional practice base, librarians have drawn on other disciplines, from office and business methods to the techniques of logical analysis as applied to classification and the structures of electronic information. Social and educational philosophies have illuminated librarians' thinking and affected the way libraries have operated. Ideas have been shared with others both nationally and internationally, and professional bodies have proliferated; training and education have developed from craft-based skills acquisition into a formal academic discipline with links to many other subjects.

That is the view from inside the profession: a positive and growing speciality requiring a wide range of skills. Outsiders have often been less appreciative, with librarians (particularly perhaps in public libraries) being presented by the media as uninspiring, with disciplinarian and conservative traits in the ascendant. The vodka advertisement with the caption 'I was the mainstay of the library until I discovered . . .' caused some concern among librarians but presumably reflected something of recognised expectations. At the same time the status of women, in librarianship as in other professions, has been a problem not only in popular image but in actual fact, despite the recognised achievements of many women in the past century or more.

This section of the volume looks at the way the profession has come to maturity and some of the particular features of modern librarianship. It is also concerned with how libraries operate: what techniques have advanced their control of information, how librarians have come together to agree standard formats or co-operative systems for supplying material to their users, how they have worked with architects and others to provide appropriate housing for their collections and services. These themes have also informed the earlier sections of this volume; here they are examined in more detail and on a wider canvas.

Fashions in architecture have changed the way libraries look, from monumentality to functionality, and the impact of the computer has been seen (in a greatly oversimplified view) to have affected their very nature, for better or for worse; but in all aspects of the work of libraries and librarians the 'outside world' has been a constant influence. Libraries after all have no purpose except to serve that 'outside world' of which they really form an essential part, and the way they have developed reflects changing perceptions and priorities in the world at large.

40

The interpretation of professional development in librarianship since 1850

IAN CORNELIUS

'Development' suggests both change and progress. Change is inevitable, but for progress to be measured we must determine what would constitute progress. Is the working experience of any practitioner better than that of a librarian in the 1850s? Are we now a different set of people, doing different things in a different world from that of our predecessors? Do we do them any better? Is the abstract entity of 'the profession' now improved or facing a more secure or more hopeful future? Do we have means of answering such questions?

There are three interpretations of the professional condition. First, the tension and fusion of idealism and utilitarianism that Black[1] claims informed British public librarianship between 1850 and 1914. Second, Winter's[2] claims about models of professional life. Third, the role Stehr[3] identifies for experts, counsellors and advisers in the information age. These offer incomplete images of the professional, so fourthly I use as models of the practitioner the icons of character of the modern age identified by MacIntyre,[4] of aesthete, therapist or manager. These are set in the context of claims about the change from one conception of a practice to another.[5]

Conditions of professional existence 1850–2000

There are three rough periods in this 150 year cycle. 1850 to 1919 marks a period of development, 1920 to 1970 a period of professional establishment, and the mid-1970s until 2000 a period of retrenchment and adaptation. The year 1850 brought the Public Libraries Act, 1877 the start of the Library Association and

1 A. Black, *A new history of the English public library: social and intellectual contexts, 1850–1914* (London, 1996).
2 M. F. Winter, *The culture and control of expertise: towards a sociological understanding of librarianship* (New York, 1988).
3 N. Stehr, *Knowledge societies* (London, 1994).
4 A. MacIntyre, *After virtue, a study in moral theory* (London, 1981).
5 I. Cornelius, *Meaning and method in information studies* (Norwood, NJ, 1996).

1898 the Charter and the start of the *Library Association Record*. The 1920–70 period began with the end of rate restriction for public libraries, the start of professional university education, the start of Aslib and the University Grants Committee and support for special and scientific and university libraries. The years 1958–80 arguably marked the high-water mark of British librarianship. The Institute of Information Scientists was founded, the new universities were set up with generous library grants, the British Library finally emerged as an independent library institution with national library responsibilities and capabilities, and the 1964 Public Library Act reached the statute book. As public library provision became compulsory, librarians became part of the local establishment of British life.

Since the 1970s changed economic social and political circumstances have forced a change in librarianship as it faced competition in information services and a less secure financial environment. First, it became possible to be various kinds of librarian, as librarianship itself changed, to present different faces to the world. In part this is not a problem; there are different kinds of lawyer, and of medical practitioner. But they tend to represent differentiated employment, surgeons or physicians, solicitors or advocates: the different kinds of librarian (bibliographers, documentalists or information scientists) were preferences for doing similar kinds of job, dependent upon institutional purpose.

Second, since World War II the techniques developed in documentation and information science have challenged and become central to librarianship. The invasion of the information machines has transformed the mechanisms and techniques, if not the objectives, of library practice, making librarians more technologised, sometimes primarily technologists. The way of doing our business depends more on methods and techniques developed outside the library world, and our world has been penetrated by those whose primary skill lies in these machines and their software and systems.

Librarians have adapted to the challenge of the new information age readily and successfully. But librarians are only a very small percentage of the total information workforce, far from the cutting edge of development of new information products. The rate of change, the sophistication of machines, the superabundance of information in a greater range of formats and the need to maximise resources for optimum performance have forced librarians to be managers, both of their own operations and of the information resource. Indeed, we present ourselves as information managers. Librarianship now wears borrowed clothes.

Black observes of the British librarian that he was, and 'he' is overwhelmingly correct in the first part of our period, as Dewey said, 'a sort of superior servant'.[6] Librarians catered for middle-class tastes, serving high literature and looking after the books, but they lacked the self-confidence of the Victorian middle class. Black comments on the poor quality of recruits to the field,[7] and concludes 'an unfortunate two-way process evolved, in that low pay attracted a sub-standard workforce which, in turn, was unable to command any higher reward than its skill level dictated'.[8] Latterly the extensive recruitment of women, who were economically exploited in a male-dominated profession, compounded the low status of library work. For some, librarianship was a gentlemanly calling, but librarianship for most did not offer the rewards of the law or the status of the church. The struggle for professional recognition was long drawn out. Black notes that 'even in the case of Edwards, the co-pioneer of public libraries and the founder of professional public librarianship, the word librarian spelt "servant" and not "partner"'.[9] This contrasts with the declaration of Dewey that the time had come when an American librarian could speak of his occupation as a profession.[10]

Professional standing brought social and occupational status and a measure of independence, giving freedom of manoeuvre in the workplace and satisfactory reward. The route to their attainment has for most of our period been professional recognition. Irritatingly, it was long in coming and the Americans always seemed one step ahead. They had a professional association before us, they produced the two most commonly used classification schemes and the most commonly used periodical indexes and subject headings lists, they started professional innovations like open access first, and in their larger libraries they developed reference service to a level almost unknown in most of our libraries. Even in closely related but separate fields like Bibliography and Information Science the lead was taken by Americans – Fredson Bowers dominated Bibliography for forty years, and American products, textbooks and authors dominated Information Science, despite early British contributions. The Americans even had the library media stars. In particular they had Melvil Dewey, who seemed central in every initiative in librarianship. Externally British librarianship exported itself around the world, but latterly those countries formerly under British influence began to look increasingly to America or Scandinavia for standards, innovations and development, even though they continued to

6 Black, *A new history*, 195.
7 Black, *A new history*, 196.
8 Black, *A new history*, 197.
9 Black, *A new history*, 198.
10 Black, *A new history*, 200.

use the one clearly internationally successful British library institution, the Document Supply Centre at Boston Spa.

One of Dewey's innovations was a college-based library school, initially based in Columbia University in 1887 but shortly forced to move because he insisted on admitting women to classes. The first British university-based library school did not appear until 1919. Although there had been an examination system in existence since 1885 the number of students was small, and large numbers of librarians had 'on the job' experience as their only training. As a rough watershed it could be said that the start of professional education with the University College London School marked the point where librarianship became a profession. Up to that time, despite the existence of the Library Association since 1877, it may be more accurate to say that librarians could and did behave professionally, but, lacking many of the classic hallmarks of older professions, that they did not constitute a profession. The period 1919–80 might be called the high professional era of British librarianship. After the 1980s librarians behaved no less professionally but the point of being a profession diminished, as many more occupations fell into some kind of professional grouping and the older-established professions became more accountable to public scrutiny. Governmental and economic developments eroded the authority and freedom to manoeuvre of all professions, even those with legal control and power over their members and practice.

The creation of formal training in the University College London School was one of the last professional pillars to be established. A professional association existed which conferred professional status through control of an examination system; that examination system and the university school tacitly admitted the existence of a body of knowledge, which it was the job of the profession to build and apply. But compared to traditional professions, librarians still did not have a code of professional ethics, had no monopoly over practice, and had no means of barring any one from practice who failed to meet the accepted professional standards. The development of a profession, measured against nineteenth-century standards, seems to have been permanently arrested. What can be said about the character of the profession in so far as it did establish itself?

Professions and professionalisation

Winter identifies three models of the profession: an early 'trait' model associated with the nineteenth-century professions, a later functionalist model, and an occupational control model. Finally he proposes a composite model sharing the advantages of all three. In the modern world the two dominant types of occupational organisation are bureaucracy and industrialism. Professionalisation, says Winter, 'is one (rather effective) way in which middle-class occupations can resist the encroachment of bureaucratic authority, counteract the moral drift of anomie, and try to protect the values threatened by industrialisation'.[11] Identifying the growth of specialised knowledge and the creation of intellectual capital for application in some occupation as the basis for the construction of professions, Winter itemises classification, indexing, and knowledge of bodies of literature as the knowledge base of librarians.[12] Admitting that librarians share their function with others who are not librarians, Winter claims 'mediating between the user and the public record of knowledge is the special province of the librarian'.[13] The importance of 'the professional association, licensing procedures and ethics codes, formal training programs, legitimate monopolies over bodies of knowledge, service orientation, and community recognition',[14] is that they legitimise and protect the professional's freedom in a professional practice incompatible with the bureaucratic discipline of the industrial organisation.

It is from the 'trait' theory that we get this model of professional characteristics, a model that applied best to the period up to 1919. The functionalist model tells us little about whether or not an occupation is a profession, but it does show the relationships of the occupation within a wider social system, including the social structure and work. The functionalist analysis emphasises the importance of the knowledge base, and of formal training within a socially accepted agency, in establishing the social authority of an occupation and legitimising it. British librarianship seems to have passed into a period in which functionalist analysis illuminates its developmental strengths in the period from 1919 to about 1980. From that date there are good reasons to think that an alternative model would have more to offer. First, as claimed above, the idea of the profession seems to be less significant for all groups since that date. No new groups acquired the independent self-regulating legal status of medicine or law, and these older professions were coming under closer public scrutiny. There seemed to be less to gain from striving to be like the older professions. Second, new social conditions – the information society and its accompanying technology – brought new working challenges.

Winter says that over a long period in librarianship, ideologies of preservation have given way to ideologies of management and control – a movement

---

11 Winter, *Culture and control*, 12–13.
12 Winter, *Culture and control*, 6.
13 Winter, *Culture and control*, 6.
14 Winter, *Culture and control*, 13.

similar to that from aesthete to manager. Winter says: 'In the occupational control model, control involves most closely the associations, the schools, and the cohesiveness or strength of shared orientations of practitioners.'[15] The knowledge base, it seems, is not given any special prominence. If we have become more like other groups in the service sector of the information society, offering a service based on some specialised knowledge, how do we compare with other groups in the category of experts, advisers and counsellors?

We should not confuse the new atmosphere that arrested the importance or social attractiveness of professions with deprofessionalisation. What underlies the new weaknesses in the professions is the opening up of their knowledge base. The assault on the knowledge base has affected librarians less drastically than it has affected medicine and law, because few others seek control over it and because librarians have always practised openness about information and knowledge. Librarians do face competition over what constitutes the basis for service: alternative knowledge bases are being used by groups offering alternatives to traditional librarians' solutions to the problems of organising and accessing knowledge. The knowledge base of librarians is in danger not of being subsumed or superseded but of being made merely a technical adjunct in a larger and more sophisticated information world. The attractiveness of the information society has been the prospect of close involvement with a larger group of information occupations, offering enhanced significance to those concerned with controlling and organising knowledge. Stehr claims the peculiar relation to knowledge of knowledge-based occupations is because knowledge itself becomes the focal point of its activity. But that activity is dependent in turn on skills not communicated but 'objectified' in the outcomes of the work that experts, counsellors and advisers do.[16]

The specialised knowledge that experts have confers a kind of power, not to be confused with more traditional political power that can restrict or circumscribe individual freedoms and enforce conformity.[17] Expert power is primarily theoretical or cognitive, and confers no ability to control society. Individually, whatever their collective power over standards and knowledge, experts may be rather powerless. But in advanced societies 'influence, authority and power are increasingly mediated by knowledge'.[18] This seems resonant with Winter's claim that an occupational control model of the professions has some

---

15 Winter, *Culture and control*, 123.
16 Stehr, *Knowledge societies*, 185.
17 Stehr, *Knowledge societies*, 168.
18 Stehr, *Knowledge societies*, 169.

explanatory force in understanding the modern professional situation, even though the relation to larger social processes is diminished in this model. The larger social processes seen in the information society are an important part of the explanation of the current state of the library profession. However, these do not characterise the practitioner or the profession for us, and they do not offer any indication of development.

Aesthetes, therapists, managers

The modern library world is a child of the Enlightenment. The medieval library caricatured by Eco[19] in *The name of the rose* guarded secret knowledge from those unequipped to handle it. The post-1850 library presupposes progress: the whole point of making information and education available through libraries is betterment and improvement – beneficial change through the application of knowledge and reason. In condemning the Enlightenment project to failure, MacIntyre[20] identifies three characters which epitomise the modern world: the aesthete, the therapist and the manager. The character is not just a role, as MacIntyre explains

> A character is an object of regard by members of the culture generally, or by some significant segment of them. He furnishes them with a cultural and moral ideal. Hence the demand is that in this type of case role and personality be fused. Social type and psychological type are required to coincide. The *character* morally legitimates a mode of social existence.[21]

Every age is partially defined by its characters. MacIntyre identifies the explorer, the engineer and the public school headmaster as partially defining the culture of Victorian England. Adaptation of MacIntyre's characters (detached from his objective) offers a typology different from those of Black or Winter, and a greater insight into professional development.

MacIntyre's aesthete struggles to avoid the enemy of boredom. For the aesthete time hangs heavy, there are unlimited means but insufficient ends to employ them on. In the library it is the entertainment literature, or the love of books for their own sake, or the provision of leisure materials, that gives effect to the aesthete in the librarian. Once the secrets of the library are unlocked, liberated from Eco's librarian, they are there for our enjoyment.

19 U. Eco, *The name of the rose* (London, 1984), 37.
20 MacIntyre, *After virtue*, 23–31.
21 MacIntyre, *After virtue*, 28.

Such a character for the librarian has always been with us: the collection builder, or the provider of light fiction and biographies.

The contrary character, one now dominant, is the manager, the librarian who constantly seeks a bureaucratic rationality, matching means to ends economically and efficiently.[22] This character we know also as the information manager, for whom means are ends. The legitimating moral force of this character is that resources are effectively employed, whatever ends those employing them might have. MacIntyre says the manager 'treats ends as given, as outside his scope; his concern is with technique'.[23] The therapist is similar, also concerned with technique, also unconcerned with ends, but focusing not on the organisation but on the person, on psychological effectiveness. We know the therapist as the outreach librarian, the bibliotherapist and the librarian who seeks well-being or personal satisfaction and development in those using the library. Neither manager nor therapist, says MacIntyre, engages in moral debate.[24] As library professionalism has increasingly emphasised organisational technique and technical competence as the identifying professional characteristics so too the library profession has lost the moral fervour and reforming zeal of both Black's idealist and his utilitarian librarians of the Victorian era. We meet the complexities of the information age without having developed a character to legitimate the profession by giving it a moral force that helps define the age rather than just accommodating to it.

Conclusion

The period since 1850 is marked by a long fight for professional standing that, ironically, may now be less relevant. The switch from librarianship to information management may be no more than a presentation and marketing ploy to secure public resources. Even if information management marks a substantive change from previous models of professional existence it still fits within the long tradition as a conception of the field.[25] The way in which librarians managed changes in name or focus or institutionalisation, and changes in relation to changes in a wider society, is a measure of success in developing the techniques to survive, either as a profession or as individual professionals. Whether librarians now are any better or happier or more hopeful than the

22 MacIntyre, *After virtue*, 24.
23 MacIntyre, *After virtue*, 29.
24 MacIntyre, *After virtue*, 29.
25 Cornelius, *Meaning and method*, 212–13.

librarians of 1850 this study cannot answer. If an analysis of the currently dominant professional character, the information manager, gives an uncomfortable comparison with our predecessors, then we may not be able to identify any professional development. Although the massive accretions of technical competence since 1850 will support the claim that there has been development, rather than just change, we must still ask if Edwards and his generation would have found it enough.

41

Education for librarianship

DAVE MUDDIMAN

1850–1939: The establishment of professional control

When they surveyed the late nineteenth-century scene of training and education in the expanding Victorian library, the founding members of the Library Association (LA) perceived an eclectic mix of written manuals, *ad hoc* classes of instruction and apprenticeship arrangements. Some practising librarians claimed that these arrangements worked well.[1] However, others argued that they failed to provide any guarantee of the competence of librarians and presented a somewhat chaotic and amateur impression of the profession to the outside world. Most senior members of the newly formed association agreed with Henry Tedder, at the annual meeting of 1882, when he urged that the LA needed to embark on a quest for status, respectability and professionalism. For this, he claimed, 'some form of preparatory examination is obligatory . . . many other bodies of professional men have taken steps in the like direction'.[2]

The association swiftly set about the erection of such an examination system. A committee on library training was established, and it soon developed a series of examinations with three levels of award. The initial preliminary examination in 1885 tempted only three candidates. However, modifications gradually attracted more, especially those of 1904, which established the intermediate level of award as the benchmark for a professional librarian. By 1906 entry levels stood at ninety-eight and by 1914 at 302.[3] In essence, despite changes of syllabus in 1920 and 1933, this system of examinations continued until World War II as the main measure of competence in the emerging library profession.

---

1 At the 1880 LA conference public librarians from Liverpool, Plymouth, Worcester and Newcastle defended their apprenticeship schemes. See R. J. Edwards, *In service training in British libraries: its development and present practice* (London, 1977), 14–16.
2 See H. Tedder 'Librarianship as a profession', in *Transactions and Proceedings of the Annual Conference of the Library Association held at Cambridge 1882* (London, 1884), 168.
3 See G. Bramley, *Apprentice to graduate: a history of library education in the United Kingdom* (London, 1981), 27.

The LA examinations gained in legitimacy and popularity primarily because the association succeeded in tying them to a quasi-legal system of professional control. In 1898, the LA was granted a Royal Charter which gave it formal and exclusive licence to 'hold examinations in librarianship' and to promote 'the position and qualifications of librarians'.[4] In 1909 L. Stanley Jast and W. Berwick Sayers successfully proposed that the charter's provisions be implemented through a linkage of the examination system to a register of professional members who would be classified into Fellows, Associates and students. Fellowship was to be conferred on those completing the diploma examination; associateship upon those completing four of its six elements. Effectively, from this point forward, to work as a qualified librarian it was necessary to join the LA and take the examinations for the diploma.[5]

Concerns about learning and instruction took second place in this formative period. By and large, the view was that 'the best training school for a future librarian is in a library'[6] and candidates had to make do with a mix of summer schools, part-time classes and correspondence courses. Summer schools were inaugurated by John James Ogle in 1893, and they ran haltingly in London and Manchester prior to 1914 and in Aberystwyth and Birmingham in the 1920s and 1930s. Part-time classes were sponsored intermittently by the association and ran in London and some regional centres like Liverpool. The classes at the London School of Economics, which began in 1902, are especially of note: perhaps the most comprehensive of the part-time training programmes, they have been labelled the 'first library school' in the United Kingdom,[7] although enrolment on them was always patchy and they were discontinued in 1914. In contrast, correspondence programmes flourished. First established in 1904 they were administered from 1930 onwards by the Library Assistants Association (subsequently the Association of Assistant Librarians). From then on, until 1965 when they were discontinued, they became the bedrock of UK part-time provision. In 1955, 993 students were enrolled on 'long' courses and 284 on revision courses.[8]

One clear exception to this uneven system of part-time tuition and correspondence was the development and relative success of the first full-time

---

4 Bramley, *Apprentice to graduate*, 29.
5 L. S. Jast and W. C. B. Sayers, 'The registration of librarians: a criticism and a suggestion', *Library Association Record* 9 (1908), 325–35.
6 T. Greenwood, *Public libraries*, 4th edn revised (London, 1894), 360.
7 See N. Webber, 'The first library school in the United Kingdom: the London School of Economics, 1900–1919', *Library History* 12 (1996), 142–54.
8 See S. W. Martin, 'The A.A.L. correspondence courses 1924–1955', *Assistant Librarian* 68 (1967), Education supplement i–iii.

school of library education at University College London. Founded in 1919, the school was supported strongly by a small number of progressive members of the LA council, and rather reluctantly by the rest. It obtained financial backing from the Carnegie United Kingdom Trust. The LA offered students completing its two-year diploma course exemption from its examination requirements, and the school also offered what was the first route to a graduate professional qualification through a one-year diploma. University College became a qualified success: although public librarians never wholeheartedly supported the venture, its diplomas undoubtedly appealed to those making a career in the expanding academic and special libraries of the inter-war period.[9] Ernest Baker, its first principal, also succeeded to some degree in inaugurating a serious scholarly approach to the study of librarianship – the school employed librarian scholars such as W. Berwick Sayers and Arundell Esdaile as part-time lecturers.

Although intellectuals like Baker argued that qualified librarians should 'possess scholarship as well as technical proficiency',[10] they were in the minority in the profession, and prior to 1939 British 'librarianship' remained largely a skills- and practice-based enterprise. The long-lasting 1904 examination syllabus consisted mainly of practical topics such as elements of practical bibliography, classification, cataloguing and practical library administration, with only 'library history and organisation' and 'literary history' designed to test broader knowledge and theory. Effectively, this syllabus focused upon the everyday skills of library work, and did little to encourage debate about the role and purpose of libraries or about their effective management. It spawned a large number of text books preoccupied with the minutiae of administration, routines, cataloguing and bibliographic techniques.[11] When attempts were made in the 1930s to enhance the difficulty and academic quality of professional examinations, the proposals attracted significant opposition from library assistants already burdened with a lengthy process of qualification. For example, at the LA conference at Scarborough in 1937, Yorkshire library assistants packed the meeting and voted down proposals for a more academic syllabus advanced by the association council.[12] The apprenticeship traditions of UK librarianship thus prevailed with some substance until 1939, and indeed, as we shall see, well beyond.

9 Bramley, *Apprentice to graduate*, 65–85.
10 E. A. Baker, 'Education of the librarian: advanced stage', *Library Association Record* 8 (1906), 579.
11 See, for example W. E. Doubleday (ed.), *A primer of librarianship* (London, 1931).
12 Bramley, *Apprentice to graduate*, 102–7.

One further exception to the generalisation about part-time provision, following the political division of Ireland in 1920, was the foundation of a school of library training based on the library of University College Dublin in 1928.[13] After 1920, education for librarianship in the Republic to some degree developed on a trajectory separate from that in the UK, although it was subject to many of the same pressures, and strong professional links with the North were maintained. As well as the school at Dublin, the Library Association of Ireland (founded in 1928) developed three-year correspondence courses resulting in professional qualifications, although like its UK equivalent, this programme was discontinued in the 1970s. University College remains the centre of education for information in the Irish Republic but it has now developed strong international links and is also a member of BAILER. Students of librarianship are supported by Irish state bursaries inaugurated under the Irish Public Library Act of 1947.

1940–1980: towards a national system of library education

As with many other aspects of British life, the pause for reflection on domestic matters which was offered by World War II proved to be a watershed for library education. In the thirty years following 1945, courses in librarianship became a permanent and well-regarded part of full-time higher education. Education for librarianship took its place alongside provision for allied professions in education, health, social welfare and the public services. It became part of a national system of vocational education in the UK, reflecting the dominant mid-century social democratic consensus, the alliance between the state and the professions, and the goal of the creation of the welfare state.[14]

The first phase of this transformation of library education was the creation, almost immediately after the end of the war, of stable institutions of full-time teaching and learning. Between 1945 and 1955, schools of librarianship were established in technical or commercial colleges at Brighton, Birmingham, Ealing, Glasgow, Leeds, City of London College, Loughborough, Manchester and Newcastle.[15] These schools prepared students for LA examinations, which were restructured to meet the needs of full-time students. The association thus

13 See J. Dean, 'Policies and programmes in library and information studies at University College, Dublin', *An Leabharlann* 7 (1978), 78–87.
14 See J. A. Jackson (ed.), *Professions and professionalisation* (Cambridge, 1970).
15 C. Bradley, 'The development of full time education for librarianship in Great Britain since the war', unpublished FLA thesis (1967). The provision at the City of London College was transferred to the North Western Polytechnic in 1951.

retained its monopoly over professional examinations, examining all students except those at University College, which had reopened its doors in 1945. In 1952, the schools formed a 'schools of librarianship committee',[16] and began to work on the development of common objectives and standards. By 1960, there were ten schools in total, employing thirty full-time staff and with 328 full-time students on roll.[17]

In the 1950s, this embryonic national system of library education ran in parallel with the part-time route to qualification which had been established prior to 1939. In 1964, however, as a result of pressure from an increasingly varied range of employers seeking specialist skills, and from the schools themselves, the LA expanded the scope and length of its registration syllabus. Two years full-time at library school would normally be required to complete this programme, and as a result part-time study became more difficult and gradually declined in popularity. A postgraduate 'diploma' route to registration was also added in 1964. The new courses proved immediately popular. By 1967 the library schools had, according to Library Association census figures, a total of 2,140 students on roll.[18]

However, in other respects, the state expansion of higher education in the sixties effectively eroded the LA's position of control. A number of universities, who had initially been hesitant about the academic credibility of librarianship courses, ventured into the field and established their own schools of librarianship and information studies. By 1970, Sheffield University, City University, Loughborough University, Queen's University Belfast, Strathclyde University and the College of Librarianship, Wales, were offering degrees and diplomas in librarianship or information science, validated and examined internally. In addition, the sixties saw the incorporation of most of the technical college schools into new 'polytechnics' with degree-awarding powers under the control of a Council for National Academic Awards (CNAA). In 1966 the CNAA set up a librarianship board, and a general move to librarianship degrees ensued. The LA examinations consequently withered in popularity until they were discontinued in the 1970s. The association gradually moved towards a less directive role in education for librarianship, based on the accreditation of courses designed and examined by the universities and colleges themselves.[19]

---

16 This later evolved into the Association of British Library Schools and eventually BAILER (British Association of Information and Library Education and Research).
17 Bradley, 'The development of full time education', 185.
18 See Bramley, *Apprentice to graduate*, 162.
19 For details see K. Wood, 'Professional education: historical review', in J. Elkin and T. Wilson (eds.), *The education of information and library professionals in the United Kingdom* (London, 1997), 20–1.

By 1980, the first edition of *Which library school?* listed a total of sixteen UK departments of library and information studies providing twenty-four under-graduate degrees and seventeen postgraduate diplomas and masters' awards.[20]

Partly as a result of these shifts, schools of librarianship began to develop a more independent and self-confident academic culture. Theoretical aspects of librarianship as a discipline of study became an issue of discussion and debate.[21] Academic journals such as the *Journal of Documentation* (1945) and the *Journal of Librarianship* (1969) were established, and the internationalisation of the literature resulted in the adoption by many library educators of American ideas and approaches to 'library science' as outlined by the academicians of the Chicago Graduate School and their successors.[22] By general agreement, the Library Association curriculum of 1964 constituted a major improvement on its predecessors: it effectively established a stable 'core' librarianship cur-riculum of bibliography, cataloguing and indexing, library management, and the library in society. It also promoted the teaching and development of a good number of specialist fields of study, such as children's librarianship, his-torical bibliography and advanced information retrieval. Such specialisation undoubtedly contributed to the beginnings of a research culture in some of the schools, especially those located in universities, such as the postgradu-ate school at Sheffield, or others, such as the North Western Polytechnic in London, which gathered together large numbers of specialist staff. Research development was encouraged by the state in the shape of funding offered by the Office of Scientific and Technical Information from 1965, and from 1974 the British Library Research and Development Department.[23]

One specific aspect of this development of academic activity in the sixties and seventies was the emergence of 'information' science as separate discipline and course of study. Ever since the foundation of Aslib in 1924, librarians in specialised libraries and information bureaux had tended to press for more specific programmes of education for this work than those embodied in the LA syllabuses. In 1958 this long-running dispute resulted in the formation of the Institute of Information Scientists as a breakaway professional organisa-tion with distinct educational aims. Three years later, under the direction of Jason Farradane, a diploma course in information science was offered at City

---

20 Association of Assistant Librarians, *Which library school?* (London, 1980).
21 See for example the discussions of the theory and philosophy of librarianship in R. Irwin, *Librarianship: essays on applied bibliography* (London, 1949).
22 See especially P. Butler, *An introduction to library science* (Chicago, 1933).
23 For a brief overview of early research in the library schools see T. Wilson, 'Research and research strategies in schools and departments of library and information studies', in Elkin and Wilson, *The education of library and information professionals*, 143–7.

University; masters programmes followed at City itself and at Sheffield University, and CNAA undergraduate degrees at Newcastle and Leeds. At one level, these courses were practical, being essentially designed to provide a toolkit for library work in science, commerce and industry. However, they quickly began to develop a theoretical discourse as a 'science of information' far broader in scope than their original roots.[24] In this respect, information science as it developed in the 1970s might with some justice claim to have been one of the original disciplines of 'information' society.

1980–2000: The information revolution and library education

The problematic impact of the information 'revolution' upon the library in general is explored elsewhere in this volume[25]. However, for library education, the most striking consequence of the 'information age' has undoubtedly been, in the course of a mere twenty years, the displacement of education for 'librarianship' by an 'information' curriculum claimed to be more relevant to these new times. In the early 1980s, this process began with a sharp rise in the information technology (IT) content of librarianship courses[26] and a small increase in the popularity of information science. In the mid-eighties, a number of schools subsequently attempted to develop integrated programmes in 'information studies', adopting the 'study of information' as an integrating theoretical and academic paradigm.[27] However, these programmes attracted uneven support in a profession increasingly concerned with skills and occupational relevance. By the 1990s, 'information management' (IM) – an eclectic mix of ideas and techniques dedicated to the improvement of the informational efficiency of enterprises – had accelerated in popularity in many former schools of librarianship and it now provides the main focus of curriculum development.[28] Courses offering a traditional focus on the bibliographic and societal aspects of library work are increasingly thin on the ground.

24 For an overview of these developments see I. Cornelius, *Meaning and method in information studies* (Norwood, NJ, 1996), 155–85.
25 See L. Chapman and F. Webster, chapter 50 below.
26 P. McGrath and P. Burton, 'Information technology in the library and information studies curriculum', in Elkin and Wilson, *The education of library and information professionals*, 83–116.
27 For illustrations of these developments see W. J. Martin, 'From library studies to information science', *Education for Information* 5 (1987), 129–37; and B. McKee 'Information studies: towards an academic discipline', *Library Association Record* 88 (1986), 236–9.
28 See D. Muddiman, 'Towards a postmodern context for information and library education', *Education for Information* 17 (1999), 8–11.

As part of this process, roughly one-half of the sixteen UK schools of librarianship active in 1980 have lost their departmental identity in a series of mergers and alliances, usually with schools of information systems or business and management. Most of the others have broadened their activities to incorporate IM programmes, and a small number of new providers (usually those with roots in the management of information systems/business information) have entered the emerging IM field. Overall, the result is a broader and more diverse pattern of institutional provision, but one that is less clearly focused on education for librarianship *per se*.

In general terms, these changes reflect an attempt by the schools to demonstrate relevance to the demands of an informational labour market increasingly shaped by global capital rather than state welfare.[29] They have been supported in this endeavour by the Library Association, which in 2002 merged with the Institute of Information Scientists to become the Chartered Institute of Library and Information Professionals (CILIP). The LA, and more latterly CILIP, has accredited most of the new IM-based educational programmes with the aim of broadening its membership base to a wider range of 'information' professionals in the private sector.[30]

More generally, the 'new vocationalist' trajectory of UK higher education has also required courses to demonstrate their relevance to the needs of these new labour markets. In the eighties, this led to a concern with the 'overproduction' of traditional librarians and with the identification of 'emerging markets' in information work.[31] In some cases new specialist areas in the curriculum such as business and health information resulted. However, in the nineties the emphasis shifted to transferable skills for general employability and the inculcation of attitudes such as enterprise and adaptability.[32] Many undergraduate IM programmes, especially, became broad, skills-based programmes designed to prepare graduates for a wide variety of 'information' work, with a dilution of their specific focus upon libraries. Ironically, the resulting vacuum in library-specific training has to some degree been filled by a state-sponsored National Vocational Qualification in Information and Library Work – a programme which echoes many of the apprenticeship principles abandoned in 1945.[33]

29 See B. Cronin and E. Davenport, *Post professionalism: transforming the information heartland* (London, 1988).
30 Wood, 'Professional education', 26–8.
31 N. Moore, *The emerging markets for library and information workers* (London, 1987).
32 D. Muddiman, 'Innovation or instrumental drift? The new vocationalism and information and library education in the United Kingdom', *Education for Information* 12 (1994), 259–70.
33 J. Arundale, *Getting your S/NVQ: a guide for candidates in the information and library sector* (London, 1996).

At the beginning of the twenty-first century, education for librarianship is thus still in print, albeit almost exclusively in an electronic format. In the United States the information age has brought with it the closure of some library schools, but this fate has not so far affected the British Isles.[34] On the contrary, optimists are able to point to the 'expansion' of the field into new disciplines such as information and knowledge management; to new instructional modes such as open learning and continuing professional development; to a developing mission to educate the 'new information professional'; and to the establishment of a significant research and postgraduate culture in some successful schools.[35] However, in reality, it must also be acknowledged that the state system of professional education for librarianship that had developed by 1980 has been fragmented and dissolved. In order to survive, its institutions have been forced to accept what Andrew Abbott identifies as 'an invasion by treatment substitution'[36] and adopt the practices, ideas and, in some cases, the governance of the newer IT and management disciplines and professions. As a result of this process, British education for *librarianship* is almost extinct, its identity blurred, its mid-century service culture out of vogue. Education for *information*, however, survives, albeit uncertainly. Perhaps, in the future information society we are so frequently promised, it will once again flourish and thrive.

34 See M. Koenig, 'Educational requirements for a library oriented career in information management', *Library Trends* 42 (1993), 277–89.

35 I. Johnson, 'Challenges in developing professionals for the "information society" and some responses by British schools of librarianship and information studies', *Library Review* 47 (1998), 52–9.

36 A. Abbott, *The system of professions* (Chicago, 1988), 224.

42

Women and libraries

JULIA TAYLOR McCAIN

Librarianship has been particularly welcoming to women and yet the careers of male and female librarians have not run in parallel. Women's role in the profession has evolved against a background of disapproval, and women librarians have found the paths of their careers hindered by a lack of parity in pay, status and prospects. A study of the history of women in libraries therefore entails an examination of both the opportunities and the obstacles they encountered along the way.

Women can justly claim to have been librarians for as long as the profession has formally existed. Their inauguration into the profession began on 5 September 1871 with an advertisement which appeared in the *Manchester Guardian*. It called for respectable, intelligent, young women to apply for the position of assistant.[1] If this advertisement had been aimed at young men, it would have elicited only a few replies. In fact, the response was huge. Twenty applicants were short-listed, and three were eventually engaged on the trial wage of six shillings a week.

The decision to employ women in this capacity was a stratagem of economy. The library movement had expanded rapidly, and had soon outgrown its base of public support and funds.[2] Moreover, at Manchester, the Library Committee was concerned at the rate at which the young male assistants were leaving to find work with greater financial rewards.[3] The experiment was successful, and by 1879 Manchester was employing thirty-one women assistants at ten to eighteen shillings a week. Seven other libraries followed this lead: Birmingham, Bradford, Bristol, Derby, Newcastle upon Tyne, Paisley and Smethwick. Only

1 'The employment of young women as library assistants in public free libraries', in *Transactions and proceedings of the second annual meeting of the Library Association of the United Kingdom held at Manchester . . . 1879* (London, 1880), 32–3.
2 K. Weibel and K. Heim, *The role of women in librarianship 1876–1976: the entry, advancement and struggle for equalization in one profession* (London, 1979), xiv.
3 H. R. Tedder, 'Librarianship as a profession', in *Transactions and proceedings of the fourth and fifth annual meetings of the Library Association of the United Kingdom held at London . . . 1881 and Cambridge . . . 1882* (London, 1884), 12.

at Bristol, however, were women employed in any number, with eleven in position at this date. The first woman chief librarian, Mrs Elliot, was employed at this time: she served as librarian of Hawick from 1879 to 1894. There followed Mrs Hannah Eteson at Blackpool from 1890 to 1891 and her successor, Miss Kate Lewtas, from 1891 to 1919.[4]

If the decision to admit women was economically calculating, it still presented them with the opportunity to engage in a congenial form of the employment. The idea had its detractors and there were many who felt that women were unsuited to the job. In 1882 the first British paper on librarianship as a profession was delivered by Henry Tedder to a meeting of the Library Association. He thought the subject of women's employment of sufficient importance to devote a considerable portion of his paper to the discussion. While apparently considering the initiative to employ women successful, he articulated some of the main objections. These included presumptions of weaker intellectual abilities, poor physical strength, a supposed tendency to distract male readers, and a disposition to marry and leave as soon as they had become 'competent' in their role.[5] In fact, termination of employment upon marriage was usually at the employer's instigation.

In America, the influential Melvil Dewey also pronounced upon the subject in an article entitled 'Women in libraries: how they are handicapped'.[6] In this he explained that the prevailing policy of library boards to offer lower wages to women sprang, not from sex discrimination, but as a result of the deficiencies of society's education of the female sex. Women, in his view, were therefore less deserving than their male counterparts. He too observed that the most serious barrier to a woman's excelling in her career was, in his phrase, 'the lack of permanence of her plans'. The idea that women should be required to choose between marriage and family, or career and celibacy, now seems indefensible, but even some women espoused this view. The professional press at this time throbs with exhortations to 'make fruitful the barrenness of human existence' and at the International Congress of Women in 1899, the woman librarian's new place in society was described in ideological language.[7] In America, Mary Ahern, a leading female librarian, maintained that the greatest gift which a woman could bring to her library was her 'womanliness'. The Editor of *Public Libraries*, Ahern offered a 'profitable field of action for a womanly woman' and assured her readers that, 'no woman can hope to reach any standing . . .

4 T. Kelly, *A history of public libraries in Great Britain 1845–1975* (London, 1977), 103.
5 Tedder, 'Librarianship as a profession', 171.
6 M. Dewey, 'Women in libraries: how they are handicapped', *Library Notes* 1 (1886), 89–90.
7 Countess of Aberdeen (ed.), *The International Congress of Women of 1899*, vol. 2: *Women in the professions* (London, 1900), 211–32.

who does not bring to it that love which suffereth long and is kind, is not puffed up, does not behave itself unseemly, vaunteth not itself, thinketh no evil, is fervent in spirit and diligent in business'.[8] The woman librarian was, it seems, entering a vocation.

By the end of the century, women were firmly established in libraries despite the recurring disapproval. The emergence of the public library carried with it a modern view of the librarian, a figure whose role it was to encourage, even entice, the public into libraries. This meant making libraries comfortable and welcoming. The public library movement was not aimed at scholars; it was pitched at ordinary citizens and increasingly became a leisure facility. Public libraries were in the service of the community, and, unlike early libraries, were not exclusive to the ecclesiastical and privileged classes. These new libraries were homely places, and librarianship acquired an element of housekeeping. Librarians exchanged tips on how to make libraries more cosy and inviting, for example, suggesting a bright carpet or a fire on dull days.[9] Women were able to consolidate their position, for by imbuing libraries with a domestic atmosphere they were performing a function already prescribed for them by society. This was underlined by the fact that the employment of women in public libraries was not reflected in academic institutions, and women librarians were a comparative rarity in the older reference libraries and those attached to colleges and universities.[10]

At the beginning of the twentieth century the public library was flourishing. Women were beginning to dominate new appointments. In fact, the new complaint was that male librarians felt overrun by women. The novelty of women being employed had now waned, and attention was no longer focused on their 'suitability'. The influence of the suffragette movement was making itself felt and an increasing impatience was surfacing. In response to the charge that women were threatening to oust men from positions in public libraries, the counter-charge was raised of how men had acquired the exclusive right to manage libraries in the first place.[11] For, with one or two notable exceptions, women still rarely progressed beyond the lower assistant ranks.

---

8 M. E. Ahern, 'The business side of a woman's career as a librarian', *Library Journal* 24 (1899), 60–2, reprinted in Weibel and Heim, *The role of women in librarianship*, 22–5.
9 L. Denis, 'How to make the most of a small library', *Library Notes* (1889), 470, quoted in D. Garrison, 'The tender technicians: the feminization of public librarianship, 1876–1905', *Journal of Social History* 6 (1972), 131–59.
10 Miss Richardson, 'Librarianship as a profession for women', *The Library* 6 (1894), 137–142, reprinted in Weibel and Heim, *The role of women in librarianship*, 18.
11 K. E. Pierce, 'Women in public libraries', *Library World* 4 (May 1902), 286–8, reprinted in Weibel and Heim, *The role of women in librarianship*, 47.

The demographic picture of women's employment is interesting. In 1897 J. D. Brown reported that, except for Manchester, Bradford, Bristol and Aberdeen, hardly any large town employed women, and London was practically closed to them.[12] This may have been because the smaller libraries were much readier to employ women for reasons of economy. In 1900–1 the number of women employed was 293, or about 12% of the total number of library staff. By 1910, the number of libraries employing women assistants had risen to 132.[13]

The First World War both expanded the available opportunities and exposed their limitations for women. Many professional male librarians were drafted into the service of government departments working on contracts to install large filing systems.[14] There was a shortage of librarians. The circumstances behind the sudden opening of opportunity created mixed emotions. One woman wrote an article in *Library World* which urged her colleagues to seize their moment and force open the doors which blocked their careers. She went on to prophesy that when the war was over the library committees who had benefited from the services of capable women assistants engaged for the period of the war would, as a result of the high quality of the work, be unanimous in their desire to retain such services permanently.[15] A storm of outraged patriotism greeted this article and the author was vilified by male and female colleagues alike for 'fighting a man when he is down' and for twisting the 'eternal rightness of things'. The author was condemned as a 'fire-breathing monster'.[16]

If anything, the situation after the war took a backward step. Male librarians, returning from active duty, were automatically given seniority even over better qualified and more experienced female candidates. The issue of pay was ever present, especially since bachelors were not retained on the same financial basis as female employees, and women with dependants were not put onto a male pay scale. Overall, the period between 1911 and 1931 saw a large increase in the recruitment of women. In 1931, 58.30% of the 3,606 professional staff recorded were female (the proportion of women in county libraries was almost certainly higher). Yet relatively few made it to the position of chief librarian.[17] In the

---

12 J. D. Brown, *Manual of library economy* (London, 1903), 87, quoted in Kelly, *A history of public libraries*, 204.

13 *Libraries, museums and art galleries yearbook 1910–11*, ed. A. J. Philip (London, 1910), 277.

14 E. Adams, *Women professional workers: a study made for the Women's Educational and Industrial Union* (New York, 1922), 360.

15 'Women assistants and the War', *Library World* 17 (1915), 197–200.

16 'Women assistants and the War'.

17 F. S. Smith (ed.), *Report on the hours, salaries, training and conditions of service in British municipal libraries 1931* (London, 1932), 10–31, quoted in Kelly, *A history of public libraries*, 309.

counties, however, the picture was different; by 1934–5 no fewer than thirty-two county authorities had women chief librarians.[18]

From the end of the Second World War until the mid-sixties, the issue of sex discrimination within the profession came under increasing discussion. In 1966 Patricia Layzell Ward was commissioned to study the untapped pool of non-working married women librarians. She concluded that it was a 'social waste' for women not to be given the opportunity to return to work, and included a series of recommendations to employing authorities which would assist married women librarians to return to work.[19] Naturally, the investigation had been prompted in the first place by the crisis of a chronic shortage of qualified librarians. In a follow-up study conducted in 1975 Layzell Ward observed that the notion that marriage put an end to a career for women librarians had now died. From an examination of statistics, she concluded that the proportion of qualified women working in the profession was high, that the issue of equal pay had been addressed, and that since 1970, three-quarters of students in UK library schools were women. However, notwithstanding these advancements she remarked:

> Preparing a detailed analysis of the exact percentages is near impossible due to the differences in labels given to similar posts in different types of libraries, but just looking through the names of chief librarians of academic, public or special libraries, few women are seen . . . It is believed that only one university, two polytechnics chiefs and three public library chiefs are women.[20]

From the beginnings of the library profession, women had formed the base of the pyramid; a strong foundation upon which the profession rested, with few individuals progressing very high. The 'glass ceiling', as it was subsequently labelled, is therefore not a new issue facing women in libraries.

---

18 *County libraries in Great Britain and Ireland: statistical report 1934–5* (1936), 28–9, quoted in Kelly, *A history of public libraries*, 309.

19 P. Layzell Ward, *Women and librarianship: an investigation into certain problems of library staffing* (London, 1966).

20 P. Layzell Ward, 'Women and librarianship in 1975', *Library Association Record* 77 (April 1975), 82–3.

43

The feminisation of librarianship: the writings of Margaret Reed

EVELYN KERSLAKE

Between 1911 and 1913, *The Librarian and Book World* published a column entitled 'Women's work in libraries'. Little is known about the author, Margaret Reed, who said her brief was to write on 'anything of interest to women librarians and assistants, from high politics to dress'.[1] A point of increasing interest at this time was women workers' equality with men. Around the turn of the twentieth century, debates about women workers shifted from a focus on their suitability for library work towards discussions of their equality with men. Margaret Reed's articles provide one articulation of the variety and extent of understandings of equality as this began to be considered in relation to library employment. Significantly, these discussions appear in a column which, for the first time, was addressed to women workers. Whilst some concerns, such as equal pay, were also pertinent to men, others more exclusively impacted on women. For example, debates about the need for women, but not men, to have uniforms or overalls are raised in several articles. The column is discussed in the latter part of this chapter which, owing to the paucity of work in this area, begins with a consideration of women's employment in libraries between 1850 and 2000 to contextualise the appearance of Reed's column in 1911.

The numerical feminisation of librarianship

There have been women library workers for as long as there have been libraries. Women worked in medieval convent libraries, seventeenth-century subscription libraries and early public libraries, yet by the turn of the twentieth century the new profession of librarianship embraced few women.[2] Routh provides an overview of library workers in the first half of the twentieth century and illustrates the increase in such workers. Until the 1970s, however, detailed

---

1 M. Reed, 'Women's work in libraries', *Librarian and Book World* 2 (1) (1911), 32.
2 E. Kerslake, 'A history of women workers in English libraries 1871–1974', unpublished PhD thesis, Loughborough University (1999), 97–8.

Table 43.1. *Librarians in the UK labour market, 1921–51, by gender* [a]

	1921		1931		1951	
	Men	Women	Men	Women	Men	Women
Librarians	1,000	1,000	3,000	4,000	5,000	11,000

[a] G. Routh, *Occupation and pay in Great Britain 1906–79* (London, 1980), Table 1.5.

data by library type rely on case studies. These show that women were most likely to work in public libraries, least likely to work in academic libraries and, regardless of the type of library, were more likely to be employed in junior or assistant posts.

As with many statistical library data more are available on the specific sphere of public libraries, but even here scant data on workers have been identified. An early estimate of women assistants, published in 1880, surveyed eighty-six of the eighty-seven UK public free libraries. Of these, thirteen employed a total of fifty-four women assistants. Two libraries – Manchester and Bristol – account for more than 80% of all these workers.[3] It should be noted, however, that by focusing on assistants and not also including chief librarians, some women, such as Hannah Eteson at Blackpool and Miss Manchip at Bridgwater, are overlooked. More detailed figures are offered by Dyer and Lloyd in their 1899 investigation which found twenty-eight women chief public librarians and 254 women assistants.[4] By 1923–4, however, the situation had changed and women outnumbered men in the library workforce with 1,450 (52%) women to 1,350 men.[5] A 1931 survey of 243 British municipal libraries reported that the proportion of men had further decreased and women now represented over 58% of the workforce.[6] This trend continued in public libraries so that by the 1970s women were around three-quarters of the workforce[7] and these proportions continued until the end of the period.[8]

---

3 H. R. Tedder and E. C. Thomas (eds.), in *Transactions and proceedings of the second annual meeting of the Library Association of the United Kingdom* (London, 1880), Appendix II.
4 B. L. Dyer and J. Lloyd, 'Women librarians in England', *Library Assistant* 1 (1899), 219–22.
5 A. Ellis, *Public libraries at the time of the Adams Report* (Stevenage, 1979), 70.
6 F. S. Smith (ed.), *Report on the hours, salaries, training and conditions of service in British municipal libraries, 1931* (London, 1932), 10.
7 Department of Education and Science, *Census of staff in librarianship and information work in the United Kingdom 1972* (London, 1974), Table 3.
8 Department of Education and Science, *Census of staff in librarianship and information work in the United Kingdom 1981* (London, 1982), 4; V. Fraser, 'Exposing the invisible ceiling in LIS', *Library Association Record* 97 (8) (1995), 434.

There are few statistical data on the employment of women in academic or special libraries. As women's colleges were established, some, such as Somerville at Oxford and Girton at Cambridge, employed their students and alumni as librarians, but others refused to employ women. Women's employment in academic libraries increased slowly and by the 1970s they accounted for around 70% of these workers.[9] A similar paucity of data is apparent for special libraries. Early Aslib conferences provide some indication that significant numbers of women workers were employed. Of the eighty-four delegates attending the first conference in 1924, fifteen were women who gave an organisational, rather than a personal, address; which may suggest employment in these organisations.[10] A small survey in the 1950s found that among the 246 employees in responding libraries 184 (75%) were women.[11] Such high levels of women's employment were not illustrated in the large studies conducted in the 1970s and 1980s, which found that special libraries, particularly certain types of special library, continued to employ proportionally more men than women.[12]

Just as throughout this period women were more likely to be employed in certain types of library, they were also more likely to be employed in certain posts. Although, as indicated above, women had been employed as chief librarians from the 1880s, they remained underrepresented in the more senior posts throughout this period. Access to such posts was significantly affected by the type of library. Academic libraries, for example, provided few women with opportunities to work in chief librarian posts. However, early exceptions include Lucy Toulmin Smith (1838–1911) at Manchester College, Oxford and Fanny Passavant (1849–1944) at Leeds University. County libraries, on the other hand, particularly in the inter-war period, were much more likely to do so. The 1938–9 county libraries' report shows that of the ninety-three county library chiefs, thirty-eight were women.[13] Significant proportions of women achieved senior posts in special libraries according to a 1950s survey. This found that in twenty (38%) of the fifty-two responding libraries the head of the unit was a woman.[14] More usually, however, women rarely occupied the more senior posts and this remained the case even towards the latter part of the period. In

9 Department of Education and Science, *Census of staff 1972*, Table 3.
10 Aslib, *Report of the proceedings of the first conference* (London, 1925).
11 Aslib, *Survey of information/library units in industrial and commercial organisations* (London, 1960), 11–12.
12 Department of Education and Science, *Census of staff 1972*, Table 3; Department of Education and Science, *Census of staff 1981*, Table D.
13 Library Association. County Libraries Section, *County libraries in Great Britain and Ireland: Statistical report 1938–9* (London, no date), 20–21.
14 Aslib, *Survey of information/library units*, 11–12.

the 1970s, men employed in public libraries were most likely to be employed in professional posts but women were more likely to hold paraprofessional posts.[15] Academic libraries in the 1970s also employed far more women than men, yet men were similarly overrepresented in the senior posts, with 81% of men employed here holding a professional post.[16] Lack of access to senior posts was not the only way in which women workers were disadvantaged in library employment. For much of the period, they also often received less pay than similarly employed men, were dismissed from work on marriage and had less access to training and career development opportunities.[17]

In summary, this overview of the sexed composition of the library workforce illustrates that from the late nineteenth century the growing library workforce was made up of an increasing proportion of women. From the 1960s, women accounted for approximately three-quarters of all library workers, yet despite this numerical domination they rarely occupied the most senior posts. As Margaret Reed began her column in 1911 the library workforce was entering a period of substantial expansion and change. From a historiographical position, her articles provide a timely insight into how library employment practices were understood.

'Women's work in libraries'

As women began to be employed in significant numbers in libraries between 1870 and 1900, public debate about them often focused on their ability to perform library work. When the proportion of women levelled with that of men, however, debates became more concerned with equal treatment at work. Richard Garnett, former Keeper of Printed Books at the British Museum, signalled this change by commenting that 'the general fitness of women for employment in libraries' was widely accepted, although the terms of women's employment were often inferior to men's.[18] Equality was conceptualised in at least two ways: first, it might be argued that women performed the same work as men and could expect the same remuneration and treatment; secondly, it was argued that women were fundamentally different from men and these

---

15 Department of Education and Science, *Census of staff 1972*, Table 9.
16 Department of Education and Science, *Census of staff 1972*, Table 3.
17 J. Liladhar and E. Kerslake, 'No more library classes for Catherine: marital status, career progression and library employment in 1950s England', *Women's Studies International Forum* 22 (2) (1999), 219.
18 'Women Librarians', in Countess of Aberdeen (ed.), *Women in the professions: being the professional section of the International Congress of Women* (London, 1900), 211.

feminine qualities equipped women, as opposed to men, for certain types of work. Margaret Reed's articles draw upon both concepts.

The first column sketches gender-based inequality in library employment. Reed writes that, 'in most cases the women assistants are labouring under considerable disadvantages', and highlights unequal pay and the limited types of work usually offered to women as examples. She advocates equal pay and suggests that, 'If women librarians and assistants do as much work as men, and do it as well, they should get as much salary; if they do not work as well, then they should not be employed as they are.'[19] Reed compares the work done by men and women and argues that if the same work is required regardless of the worker's gender then there should be equal pay. Furthermore, if women do not perform as well as men then they should not be employed 'as they are'. The persuasive force of her argument for the same treatment for men and women is achieved by focusing on the work rather than the worker, and by the sweeping approach to the subject which presents a workforce where men and women occupy similar posts, thus affording direct comparisons. This argument is constructed by ignoring both the widespread tendency to employ men in senior library posts and the different types of work required at a time when such differences were critical as the open-access debate was in full swing.[20] Some libraries had adopted open access but many continued to use indicators. By ignoring the paucity of direct comparison within the sector, Margaret Reed is able to claim that men and women performed the same work and so should receive the same pay. Later in the same article, however, she confounds her suggestion for equality based on comparable work by arguing that widespread differences in library work make attempts at comparison 'such a jumble' that it is impossible. Her argument for equality is yet more strongly qualified by the sentence which follows the claim for equal pay: 'Of course, I do not mean they [women] can do all the work a man can do, but I do think they do the work they can do as well.'[21] Margaret Reed suggests that there are fundamental differences between the types of work that men and women are able to perform, and men are constructed as more able than women. The claim for equality is weakened as women are understood as lesser workers than men. Yet a qualified equality claim is still made as Margaret Reed argues that, within a limited area, women 'do the work they can do as well' as men.

19 Reed, 'Women's work', 2 (1), 33.
20 T. Kelly, *A history of public libraries in Great Britain 1845–1975* (London, 1977), 178.
21 Reed, 'Women's work', 2 (1), 33.

Having dramatically modified her equality argument based on parity between men and women, later in the same article Margaret Reed draws on the 'difference' concept of equality. She discusses the claim that 'girl assistants flirt at the counter' and keep aside books for their men friends: 'It is quite true that a girl may keep a book for her special friend, but every girl is the friend of the young man behind the counter, with the result that *all* the new and best books would be hidden away for girl friends if it were not that the opportunities are limited.'[22] Whereas men are portrayed as socially, and possibly sexually, promiscuous, by contrast women are seen as having only one 'special friend'. Margaret Reed does not suggest that flirting and putting aside books 'is never done, but I do say it is done much less often by girl or women assistants than by youths'.[23] The difference between men and women is used here to argue that women are more appropriate for this type of work.

Margaret Reed's use of both sameness and difference concepts of equality in the same article appears contradictory: she advocates women's employment both because women are the same as men and because they are different from men. What does this suggest about understandings of equality in librarianship just before the First World War? The use of the two concepts of equality may be the result of ill-considered argument. The style of Reed's articles is sometimes informal, even nonchalant – at one point she declines to continue discussing gender-differentiated pay, a subject of enormous significance to women workers, because 'I am tired of the subject.'[24] The use of two concepts of equality could, however, indicate the circulation of a number of discourses of equality in contemporaneous debates. This has been illustrated in other sectors. Alison Oram notes that, just before the First World War, many women teachers 'endorsed the idea of a different sphere for women's efforts *at the same time* as asserting equal rights with men'.[25] Given this, the use of particular equality concepts in specific contexts may have been strategic. Thus, when arguing for equal, or the *same*, pay for men and women, Margaret Reed emphasises the sameness of men's and women's work. However, occasional hostility from men colleagues towards women library workers might be more effectively countered by defining elements of library employment as appropriate for women rather than men. Such attempts were endorsed by dominant discourses of masculinity and femininity which claimed that innate differences between men

22 Reed, 'Women's work', 2 (1), 33.
23 Reed, 'Women's work', 2 (1), 33.
24 M. Reed, 'Women's work in libraries', *Librarian and Book World*, 2 (3) (1911), 116.
25 A. Oram, *Women teachers and feminist politics* (Manchester, 1996), 115.

and women equipped them for different social roles. In this case, difference rather than sameness might be more strategically effective. Margaret Reed may not have written her articles with the strategic deployment of concepts of equality in mind, but, they may be read in this way and the interpretative resources needed to make that reading were available to her contemporaries, as Oram's work illustrates.

The limits of equality discourses in library employment are also suggested in Reed's column. One article, for example, argues that women do not need access to superannuation schemes in the same way as men, and Reed limits her advocacy of equality to immediate remuneration issues[26]. Furthermore, a discussion of black library workers in the southern USA casts some doubt about whom Reed envisions including in concepts of equality. She writes, erroneously,[27] that race issues are unimportant in the UK and wonders 'what would happen if we had negro assistants and librarians?'[28] She describes the idea of black library workers as 'Gilbertian': that is to say, ridiculous or whimsical. Her further use of dominant racist discourse allows her to express surprise that libraries managed by black women 'were quite up to the general standard of administration'. This emphasises the normativity of white library workers and marginalises black workers. If the construction of black women librarians as less able than white workers were replicated in the UK workforce, such women would also be marginalised in equality discourses. Not only, then, were there limits to the extent to which equality might be enacted, but equality might also be understood as applicable only to certain groups of workers.

Engagement with issues around equality did not hasten their widespread implementation within librarianship, and many libraries continued until the 1960s with employment practices, such as gender-differentiated pay and the marriage bar, which disadvantaged women. This subject, and Margaret Reed's column, have failed to interest UK library historians. Suzanne Hildenbrand has argued that such historiographical omissions occur because the goal of most library history has been 'profession building', that is, establishing librarianship as a true profession by aligning it with masculine traits and 'great' male leaders.[29] This goal establishes the parameters of historical significance: what is judged as worthy of inclusion in writings about the past. Measured

26 M. Reed, 'Women's work in libraries', *Librarian and Book World*, 2 (4) (1911), 149.
27 See R. Ramdin, *Reimaging Britain: 500 years of Black and Asian history* (London, 1999).
28 M. Reed, 'Women's work in libraries', *Librarian and Book World* 2 (8) (1912), 307.
29 S. Hildenbrand, 'Women in library history: from the politics of library history to the history of library politics', in S. Hildenbrand (ed.), *Reclaiming the American library past: writing the women in* (Norwood, NJ, 1996), 3.

against a profession building narrative, women library workers and many of the issues discussed by Margaret Reed may appear insignificant. Yet profession building is only one aspect of librarianship's past. As the profession embraced rising numbers of women, understandings of gender became increasingly important and Margaret Reed's articles are one opportunity for historians to engage with gendered, and raced and classed, discourses as they impact on librarianship.

44

Sharing the load: libraries in co-operation

ANTONIA J. BUNCH

From Alexandria to Antonio Panizzi, librarians have cherished the dream of containing the totality of written knowledge in one building. It is an attractive idea – a single place to 'enquire within upon everything' – but one realistically not capable of fulfilment, certainly not in the modern world. Librarians have therefore found other ways, both formal and informal, to access knowledge by sharing the resources of their libraries with each other. In the twentieth century, this practice has come to be called 'library co-operation' but it has a longer pedigree.

At the beginning of the fifteenth century, John Boston, a monk of Bury St Edmunds, compiled the *Catalogus scriptorum ecclesiae*, listing about 700 authors in English monastic libraries, a sort of medieval union catalogue. It was based on an earlier thirteenth-century Franciscan work, the *Registrum librorum Angliae*. In the seventeenth and eighteenth centuries various attempts were made, most notably at Oxford, to construct union catalogues of college library holdings, but these were largely unsuccessful.[1] It was not until the twentieth century that 'library co-operation' as such became widespread in the United Kingdom. By then, municipal public libraries had been established for half a century and were under pressure from the demands of the burgeoning adult and technical education movements, university libraries were developing but not quickly enough, and industry and the professions were recognising an increasing need to access printed information. Simultaneously, the output of printed information was growing exponentially and no individual library or library system could hope to be entirely self-sufficient. Although the national libraries had the benefit of legal deposit, even here gaps could occur, and because the collections were almost universally for reference only, accessing this material was not easy for the majority of potential users.

---

1 L. Newcombe, *Library co-operation in the British Isles* (London, 1937), 30–1.

The first proposal for a scheme of co-operation between public libraries seems to have been made by Dr E. A. Bond, Principal Librarian of the British Museum. In his presidential address to the Library Association in 1886 he suggested that the more highly endowed public libraries should 'agree on each making a particular branch of literature or science a special subject for attention . . . co-operation might be further carried out by a system of interchange of books and manuscripts on loan'.[2] In 1902 Sidney Webb, addressing the Library Association on the libraries of London, stated that 'the library service of a great city can and surely ought to be something more than a couple of hundred accidental heaps of miscellaneous volumes, each maintained and managed in jealous isolation from the rest'. He suggested that a combined catalogue should be made. Librarians could telephone and be informed which library possessed the book they were seeking. He further suggested the mutual recognition of tickets by borough libraries.[3] Subsequently, James Duff Brown in 1903 proposed a system of inter-library exchanges for non-fiction,[4] to be followed by a suggestion from J. McKillop in 1906 that a central library for students be established in London,[5] and by a proposal from S. Kirby of Hornsey Public Library in 1907 that large specialist 'store' libraries be set up in different parts of the country which would lend books only to other libraries.[6]

The first actual scheme of inter-lending appears to have been that begun in 1907 by A. J. Philip of Gravesend. This involved the libraries in London exchanging their printed catalogues and agreeing to lend books to each other. With the move to open access, printed catalogues were superseded by sheaf and card catalogues and this scheme disappeared. None the less the pressure for wider access, most especially for students, continued. In 1916 the Central Joint Advisory Committee on Tutorial Classes received a grant from the Carnegie United Kingdom Trust (CUKT) enabling it to establish the Central Library for Students (CLS). This incorporated the existing Central Library for Tutorial Classes which had been founded in 1912 by the Workers' Educational Association in collaboration with Toynbee Hall. Two of the most influential personalities in this movement were Albert Mansbridge and A. W. Pollard, the first honorary librarian. Pollard encouraged public libraries to subscribe to the

2 E. A. Bond, 'Address to the Library Association [at the Ninth Annual Meeting in London, 1886]', *Library Chronicle* 4 (1887), 1–10.
3 S. Webb, 'The library service of London: its co-ordination, development and education', *Library Association Record* 4 (1902), 193–203, 231–6.
4 J. D. Brown, *Manual of library economy* (London, 1903), 412, para. 458: Inter-library exchanges. It is possible that this is the first use of the word 'inter-library'.
5 J. McKillop, 'The present position of London municipal libraries with suggestions for increasing their efficiency', *Library Association Record* 8 (1906), 625–35, 495–7.
6 S. Kirby, 'Co-operation: a suggestion', *Library Assistant* 5 (1907), 266–9.

library and to borrow books. By 1927, the CLS was lending 35,000 books a year to public libraries, 20,000 of them going to the recently established county libraries.

After World War I, the Ministry of Reconstruction's Adult Education Committee recommended that the library should be given state aid to extend its lending activities to public libraries and to special libraries in industry which were now being created. Thus in 1923–4, three libraries (the College of Nursing, the Royal Aeronautical Society and King's College for Women) became 'outliers' of the CLS, as a result of a grant to them from the CUKT conditional upon their making their collections available through the CLS. By 1935 there were almost one hundred outlier libraries. In Scotland, the Carnegie Trust funded the establishment of the Scottish Central Library for Students in 1921.[7]

An important report on the development of public library services was published in 1927.[8] Known as the Kenyon Report, it also had far-reaching implications for the future of library co-operation. It proposed that there should be a national system based upon voluntary co-operation between all types of public library: municipal, county, county borough or urban district. It further suggested the grouping of public libraries around regional centres, generally large municipal libraries; a federation of special libraries; and a Central Library at the centre of the whole system. Implementation of these proposals would mean that for the first time there would be a formal system of national and regional co-ordination in England and Wales. The National Central Library (NCL) was eventually created four years later, in 1931. Its Librarian from 1926 (as the CLS) until his retirement in 1944 was Luxmoore Newcombe whose dedication made it, according to the NCL Annual Report for 1944–5, 'the accredited centre of the public library service in England and Wales'.[9] In 1931 the NCL also took over the functions of the Birmingham inter-library loans office, which had been founded in 1925 by the Association of University Teachers to aid the newer civic universities whose stocks could not match those of Oxford and Cambridge.[10] Special 'outlier' libraries could apply directly to the NCL but increasingly they became involved with the regional schemes that were being set up in their areas during the 1930s.

7 For a fuller account of co-operation in Scotland see W. R. Aitken, *A history of the public library movement in Scotland to 1955* (Glasgow, 1971), 133–62.
8 Board of Education, Public Libraries Committee, *Report on public libraries in England and Wales* (London, 1927) (The Kenyon Report).
9 S. P. L. Filon, *The National Central Library: an experiment in library co-operation* (London, 1977), 60–2.
10 J. Thompson, *A centennial history of the library of the University of Birmingham 1880–1995* (Birmingham, 2000), 68. Cf. also F. W. Ratcliffe's chapter on the civic universities, above.

The creation of the regional library bureaux was one of the great achievements of twentieth-century librarianship. The Northern Region was the first to be established, in 1931, followed by West Midland Region (1931), Wales (1932), South-Eastern Region (1933), East Midland Region (1935), North-Western Region (1935), Yorkshire Region (1935) and South-Western Region (1937).[11] By compiling union catalogues (Yorkshire being the notable exception), they acted as clearing houses for inter-lending, passing on to the NCL only requests that could not be supplied locally. London established its own scheme in 1934 under the Metropolitan Boroughs Joint Standing Committee, taking under its wing the London Union Catalogue commenced in 1929, but a Scottish system did not come into being formally until 1945, although a union catalogue, kept at the Mitchell Library in Glasgow, had been started in 1939.

It would appear that all ought to be well in the world of library co-operation after the creation of a national system, but a report produced in 1941 by the Library Association, which had commissioned Lionel McColvin, its honorary secretary and City Librarian of Westminster, to survey the present condition and future needs of the public library service, was fairly damning in its criticisms of the regional bureaux.[12] McColvin specifically criticised the lack of standardisation between the bureaux, suggesting that there were too many of them, resulting in duplication of effort. He commented that the number of loans was relatively small, and suggested that this means of co-operation might actually encourage some authorities to evade their responsibilities by relying on borrowing from other libraries rather than providing an adequate bookstock themselves.

On inter-library co-operation, McColvin proposed that the regional bureaux be abolished and that library authorities be allocated an area of subject specialisation relative to local interest, e.g. fishing at Aberdeen, steel at Sheffield, and that these libraries should keep a reserve stock of books in their special field which had been withdrawn from circulation. Additionally these libraries would be required to purchase all new general standard works in their special subject and retain them. Eleven city libraries, Birmingham, Bristol, Cardiff, Central London (City, Finsbury, Holborn and Westminster), Edinburgh, Glasgow, Leeds, Liverpool, Manchester, Newcastle-upon-Tyne and Sheffield, would be established as regional reference libraries for purposes of research and scholarship. In its early days, 'library co-operation' had become almost synonymous with 'inter-library lending': McColvin introduced a new concept, that of co-operative acquisition.

11 Newcombe, *Library co-operation in the British Isles*, 89–90.
12 L. R. McColvin, *The public library system of Great Britain* (London, 1942).

Clearly little could be accomplished until the end of the Second World War, but as early as 1946 the London metropolitan boroughs agreed a scheme for a joint fiction reserve, each authority being allocated certain letters of the alphabet and being required to retain fiction by authors whose names fell within that allocation. Libraries wishing to withdraw material would offer it to the requisite library before discarding it totally. McColvin's recommendation on subject specialisation was also implemented in London, each library taking responsibility for certain sections in the Dewey Decimal Classification. The South-Eastern Region followed in 1950 and later some other regions took up the idea. Scotland set up a scheme for fiction in 1951 based on the connection of an author with a particular locality, but a national arrangement in England was not created until 1962. The alphabet was divided between regions, excluding London and the South-East which already had schemes. The formation in 1948 of the British National Book Centre (BNBC), set up by the NCL with a grant from the Treasury, facilitated the exchange between libraries of discarded items. Libraries notified the BNBC of items they intended to withdraw and the BNBC then sent out lists to subscribing libraries which could request material they required.

Although it seemed that library co-operation was forging ahead in the immediate post-war period, unfortunately not all was well. The system depended almost totally on the existence of union catalogues, and these were costly and burdensome to maintain; arrears of cataloguing mounted rapidly. Doubts were expressed about the value of recording so many items that were common to most libraries. In 1949 the National Central Library and the National Committee on Regional Library Co-operation set up a joint working party to review the situation and commissioned Robert Vollans, McColvin's deputy at Westminster, to prepare a report. The publication of the Vollans Report in 1952[13] was hailed at the time as one of the most significant events in the history of library co-operation. Vollans confirmed that, in spite of the high costs of maintaining union catalogues, these were none the less highly important to the conduct of the system. The report recommended that the Yorkshire Region, which did not have a union catalogue, should establish one, and that the North-West and the West Midlands, whose holdings were incomplete, should consider how they could update them. It was proposed that from a certain date (eventually fixed as 1 January 1959) union catalogues would be completed, and thereafter records of current British material, using British National Bibliography (BNB) numbers, would be kept only at the regions; the

13 R. F. Vollans, *Library co-operation in Great Britain* (London, 1952).

National Union Catalogue would henceforth record only those books published in the United Kingdom and not listed in the BNB. From this date also, each region would be self-sufficient (or *reasonably* self-sufficient) in current British material listed in the BNB, by devising a subject specialisation scheme. Thus, the National Central Library was able to concentrate on older material and foreign literature.

Academic libraries

Although some academic libraries became involved in local schemes of co-operation, for the most part they tended to remain aloof from the public library system. Mention has already been made of the universities' loans office in Birmingham. Funded by the AUT, a grant from Carnegie and members' subscriptions, it acted as a clearing house for loans from 1925 until its merger with the NCL in 1931. Universities retained contact with other universities through the NCL but, although many participated in the regional bureau in their area, there was a feeling that, because of their specialist stocks, too great a burden was being placed upon them in lending material. Immediately after the war, the Standing Conference of National and University Libraries (SCONUL) was formed with the aim of promoting the work of national and university libraries. It has played an important role in developing co-operative arrangements between university libraries, for example initiating training schemes and convening groups to look at different aspects of library provision. It has been particularly active in the problems associated with the acquisition of foreign material, setting up its own Slavonic and East European Group, and supporting independent groups covering South and South-East Asia, Japan, the Middle East, Latin America and Africa (SCOLMA). Within the university framework also, librarians in specialist areas, for example institutes of education and medical schools, have set up their own networks.

Accessing current material was not, of course, the only problem. Scholars and researchers often require to consult much older material. In 1951, university libraries and some of the large public libraries participated in the Background Materials Scheme, intended to ensure national coverage of pre-1800 British publications. Libraries agreed to purchase material published within a certain period, allocated in accordance with existing strengths. The blocks of dates assigned were felt by some, however, to be rather arbitrary and not all librarians felt the scheme was worthwhile.

The practice of co-operative storage, which had been carried out with some success in the United States, met with little enthusiasm when SCONUL sought opinion in 1953, but in 1961 London University created a central depository for libraries within the London University federation, situated at Egham in Surrey.

In 1963, the University Grants Committee established a Committee on Libraries to consider the best means of meeting the needs of universities and other colleges for books and periodicals. The resultant Parry Report, published in 1967,[14] emphasised that the entire resources of a geographical area should be regarded as a pool from which an individual library could draw, and that libraries should investigate the co-ordination of library resources to avoid unnecessary duplication of effort. In a sense, the proposals of the Parry Report became somewhat submerged by the events of the 1960s which saw the establishment of several new universities and the transfer of colleges of advanced technology to the university sector. The librarians of this latter group formed a Standing Conference of Technological University Libraries (SCOTUL), subsequently incorporated into SCONUL, which proposed a co-operative subject-specialisation scheme combined with a current-awareness service. In 1969, thirty polytechnics were created in England and Wales (on the basis of existing colleges): their librarians formed the Council of Polytechnic Librarians (COPOL), which was able to formulate minimum standards for the widely divergent libraries under their direction. By the end of the century the so-called 'binary division' had been overcome when the polytechnics were given university status.

Information for industry

During the immediate post-war reconstruction period there was an ever-increasing need within industry for the latest technical information, especially in the form of articles in specialist journals, and a number of specialist local schemes began to be established from the 1950s on. The very first such scheme, however, and the one upon which most of the others were modelled, had been established in 1933 in Sheffield. In 1932 J. P. Lamb, the City Librarian of Sheffield, gave a paper to a conference of the Association of Special Libraries and Information Bureaux (later renamed Aslib), on the public library as an aid to industry and commerce. He commented that although the Commercial and Technical Department of Sheffield City Libraries stocked a wide range of technical journals, many libraries were bypassing this source

---

14 University Grants Committee, *Report of the Committee on Libraries* (London, 1967) (The Parry Report).

and going directly to the NCL. His suggestion was that a better and especially a quicker service could be provided by pooling local resources, with the public library co-ordinating exchange. In 1933, the Sheffield Interchange Organization (SINTO) was formally set up, with twelve founder members from industry, commerce, research and the academic world in addition to the public library. Carrying its activities beyond the inter-library loan function, SINTO compiled union lists of periodicals, an index of brand names, an index of steel specifications, locations of foreign standards and a co-operative foreign translations service. It was also instrumental in encouraging Aslib to set up a central translations index and the Patent Office to create a World Index of Trade Names.

The first imitator of SINTO was a scheme in west London, established in 1951 and called CICRIS (Co-operative Industrial Commercial Reference and Information Service). Librarianship is a profession riddled with acronyms, and as these local schemes came to be established all over the United Kingdom yet more acronyms were added to the store. This system of naming was often ridiculed but, as Jefferson has pointed out, acronyms do have a trade-name value with which industry is familiar, whereas the term 'library' has literary connotations.[15] Several schemes were established throughout the country, usually in areas with a long industrial tradition. To name but a few: HULTIS (based on Hull, 1953); LADSIRLAC (Liverpool and District, 1955); HERTIS (Hertfordshire, 1956); BRASTACS (Bradford, 1961); NANTIS (Nottingham and Nottinghamshire, 1963); and HATRICS (Hampshire, 1964). Most schemes provided enquiry services and photocopying in addition to inter-library loan, but the internal organisation of these systems varied considerably. Some produced union catalogues and union lists of serials, others had less formal arrangements. Some were centred on the public library, others around a grouping of public, college and large special libraries. In Aberdeen, for example, ANSLICS (now Grampian Information) was based on the then Robert Gordon's Institute of Technology which also had a library school. With subsequent reorganisations of local government, many boundaries changed, but most of the schemes kept their acronyms which had become well known. At national level, Aslib operated a clearing house for inter-library loan and photocopies, and published an important *Directory of information sources in the UK* (12th edn, 2002). Wider access to periodicals, on which so many industrial and other special libraries depend so heavily, was aided by the publication of both the *World*

15 G. Jefferson, *Library co-operation*, 2nd edn (London, 1977), 80.

list of scientific periodicals (1923–80) and the *British union catalogue of periodicals* (BUCOP) (1944–80).

National libraries

The information needs of science, technology and industry were being addressed not only at local level; there was also a national dimension. As early as 1926 the Science Museum Library, on the initiative of Dr S. C. Bradford, the recently appointed Keeper, began a service of direct loans to certain scientific and technical organisations. By 1946, the loan service had become its principal activity and demand was increasing rapidly as industry revived after the war. The term 'information explosion' was heard frequently during the 1950s and 1960s but it was perhaps rather more of an information 'deluge'. An important Royal Society Scientific Information Conference in 1948[16] urged the UK government to give increased support to central scientific libraries and information services, in particular the Science Museum and Patent Office libraries. Subsequently, in 1950, the Government's Advisory Council on Scientific Policy, concerned at the failure of technical libraries to keep pace with the growing number of research papers and reports, supported the recommendations of its Panel on Technical Information Services that there should be a central science reference library in London based on the Patent Office Library and a national lending library of science and technology based on the Science Museum Library. The government accepted the proposals in principle but nothing was done for six or seven years, in spite of the Advisory Council's reiteration of its recommendation in every subsequent annual report. Finally in 1960 the Patent Office Library was renamed the National Reference Library for Science and Invention and placed under the aegis of the British Museum Library,[17] and in the same year the National Lending Library for Science and Technology was created.

In 1957, the Department of Scientific and Industrial Research (DSIR) had formed a lending unit (LLU) which evolved out of its Technical Information and Documentation Unit (TIDU). The DSIR was eventually given responsibility for the establishment of the National Science Lending Library, and its redoubtable chief Dr Donald Urquhart commenced the search for a suitable location. Given that the new lending library would rely almost exclusively on postal services,

---

16 Royal Society Scientific Information Conference, 1948. *Report and papers submitted* (London, 1948). See also D. Urquhart, *Mr. Boston Spa* (Leeds, 1990), 22–7: Urquhart was an organiser of this conference and a significant contributor to it.
17 P. R. Harris, *A history of the British Museum Library 1753–1973* (London, 1998), 619–24.

the ever-practical Urquhart considered that a location more or less in the geographical centre of the UK would be more or less equally fair to those living on Shetland and in Cornwall. Thus a most unprepossessing site, the former Royal Ordnance Factory at Thorp Arch near Boston Spa in Yorkshire, was chosen for what was to become the largest and most important library of its type in Western Europe. The transfer of existing stocks to the new site was virtually complete by 1962. It was decided that the collections would be as comprehensive as possible, relying on purchase and not the rather less secure principle of legal deposit. Periodicals, conference proceedings and reports (grey literature) in particular would be covered extensively. The enormous success of the NLLST led to a demand for the inclusion of medical literature, which was added in 1963, to be joined by social sciences in 1966. In 1972 it extended its serials coverage to the humanities. The philosophy of the NLLST was one not so much of inter-library co-operation as of universal provider.[18]

The year 1973 saw the creation of the British Library.[19] This was to affect profoundly the whole structure of library co-operation. The National Central Library, which had been at the centre of the national and regional bureau inter-lending system but also had a substantial stock of its own, merged with the NLLST to form the British Library Lending Division, and the NCL stock and some staff were transferred to Yorkshire. The British Library Document Supply Centre (BLDSC), as it was later renamed, thereby became the central back-up service for the whole nation, and indeed beyond as its international activities expanded. In Scotland, although the British Library Act did not apply, the Scottish Central Library became the Lending Services Division of the National Library of Scotland.

A comprehensive overview of the state of library co-operation in the United Kingdom in 1979 is provided by a report by P. H. Sewell, commissioned by the British Library Research and Development Department. It demonstrates how complicated the structures had become.[20]

The librarians involved in national, regional and local co-operation have also formed co-operative bodies among their own numbers. CONARLS (Circle of Officers of National and Regional Library Systems) was created in 1978, evolving out of the Association of Librarians in Charge of Regional Bureaux formed in the early seventies. LINC (the Library and Information Co-operation

---

18 For a full account see Urquhart, *Mr. Boston Spa*.
19 For fuller details of its establishment see John Hopson's chapter on the British Library, above.
20 P. H. Sewell, *Library co-operation in the United Kingdom: existing arrangements, gaps in provision and research which may be needed*, BLR&D Report 5479 (London, 1979).

Council) founded in 1989, represented all the organisations promoting library co-operation in the United Kingdom and Ireland until its demise in 2002.

Some experiments in new forms of co-operation were made in the 1980s and 1990s. In an attempt to stimulate local awareness, for example, Library and Information Plans (LIPs) were created in a number of areas, usually after a survey sponsored by the British Library Research and Development Department. NEWSPLAN 2000 is a co-operative programme for the microfilming and preservation of local newspapers and making them accessible to users. It was established following the publication of ten local area reports between 1986 and 1998, all published by the British Library. It is an important and successful example of co-operation between public libraries, the British Library, the National Library of Scotland, the National Library of Wales, the National Library of Ireland and the newspaper industry. Office accommodation for the project is provided by the British Library Newspaper Library.

The electronic revolution

From the mid-1970s on, with the increasing use of computers in libraries particularly for creating catalogue records, inter-library co-operation took on a new face. Union catalogues at the regional bureaux (now renamed regional systems) were automated. ISBNs replaced BNB numbers as a means of notification. The London and South East regions amalgamated to become LASER, which took a lead in this movement. Individual libraries began to co-operate in the creation of catalogue records for new material, examples being BLCMP (Birmingham Libraries Co-operative Mechanization Project), SCOLCAP (Scottish Libraries Co-operative Automation Project) and SWALCAP (South West Academic Libraries Co-operative Automation Project). Additionally, many research libraries shared records during the retrospective conversion of existing catalogues to machine-readable format. Some of these schemes have been overtaken by events with the availability now of many library catalogues (including groups of libraries) on the Internet, creating virtual union catalogues. COPAC comprises the merged catalogues of twenty-four of the largest university and research libraries in the UK and Ireland, together with the catalogues of the British Library, the National Library of Scotland and the National Library of Wales. More recently (2002) the merged catalogues of the public and academic libraries on Merseyside became available, and in 2003 it became possible to search all the public library catalogues in London on a website entitled 'What's in London's Libraries' managed by the London Libraries Development Agency.

Conclusion

This chapter inevitably has concentrated principally on the larger schemes of co-operation, mostly formal, which have evolved during the last century. There are, however, other important and less formal methods of co-operation. The inter-availability of tickets, that is, readers being allowed to use their tickets at libraries outside their own area, has long been a feature of the public library scene. Many universities have permitted students to use the library of their home-town university whilst on vacation. Co-operative transport schemes as an adjunct to inter-library loan have been operative for many years and, despite national co-ordination, it seems that there will always be room for local initiatives. Librarians in specialist areas have set up their own schemes, for example in agriculture, law and health care. There is also what is affectionately known as 'the old boy network'. A librarian or information officer in one library could telephone, or nowadays e-mail, a colleague in another, and confidently expect to receive help with a difficult enquiry. In time, the favour would be returned. For many, this climate of mutual help and absence of competition made the practice of librarianship a very satisfying profession. Unfortunately the declaration by the British government in the 1980s that information was a 'tradeable commodity' introduced the concept of the market economy into the public service. Many libraries were forced to generate revenue by charging for information searches, which made the old system of informal networking increasingly difficult. By the end of the twentieth century the political climate had changed, and indeed new government policies of 'lifelong learning' seem set to reinvigorate library co-operation rather in the way that adult education policies at the start of the century were responsible for the establishment of the Central Library for Students. The wheel seems to have come full circle.

45

Organising knowledge: cataloguing, classification and indexing in the modern library

RODNEY M. BRUNT

The tools of the trade

The last century and a half have seen massive change in the entire sphere of the organisation for retrieval of library stock and, as a consequence, in the tools designed to provide effective use of collections as well as in those developed to fashion the retrieval devices themselves.

The degree of change is perhaps most easily measured in the move from the manuscript or printed catalogue, geared to libraries where to a great extent the librarian himself was the index, to the hypertext online catalogues of the most modern kind now available via the Internet.

This chapter examines these tools in the context of development to meet changing needs of readers and library staff, under three main heads: cataloguing (i.e. the surrogate and its known-item indexing); the subject approach (via both physical and surrogate retrieval); and indexing in special libraries.

Cataloguing

Origins

It is generally accepted that the most important development in descriptive cataloguing was the construction, publication and first use of the *Rules for the compilation of the catalogue of the printed books in the British Museum* (BM).[1] In 1839 Antonio Panizzi, in order to further his great enterprise of producing the general catalogue, established the ninety-one rules for the guidance of his cataloguers in making entries (the 'titles') for the guard-books which comprised the working version of the catalogue prior to printing.

---

1 British Museum, *Rules for the compilation of the catalogue of printed books in the British Museum* (London, 1841). Cited hereafter as '*BM*'.

The code had a profound effect on cataloguing, for it provided the foundations of modern practice. Its identification and solution of fundamental problems provided the bedrock for later codes, including the current *Anglo-American cataloguing rules*;[2] and revisiting the code today indicates that, despite the technological advances which have occurred over the past 150 years, the fundamentals identified there remain and the solutions, in essence, are still valid.

It might be argued that *BM* appeared in the right place at the right time. Many contemporary factors – including pressures of the industrial revolution and consequent commercial activity; establishment of the public library system; expansion of university and technological education – contributed to the need for more rigorous control of information presented, as it then was, in hard-copy, codex form and housed in great warehouses.

It was plain that control depended on consistent identification and indexing, and the size and nature of the collection exemplified the problems. Thus, the developing needs of the newly emergent library community (both practitioners and users) could only be met by the codification of cataloguing practice, with its consequent encouragement of consistency on a broader plain and with it (though not immediately) opportunities for co-operation.

BM addressed a number of primary cataloguing issues, including content and layout of the surrogate record (the description); headings (for indexing); and the item to be described. It was of course of its time, reflecting both social mores and the needs and activities of its narrow user-group (by today's measures) and the publication and collection habits of the times.

The catalogue for which *BM* was designed was a general catalogue allowing searching by name (personal and corporate); catchword; title (as a last resort); and form; and the rules reflect this. It is important to remember that the form of catalogue then in vogue was the printed book and this had a bearing on the rules themselves, both for description and for entry. It did not provide for access by subject and this again reflected the needs of its users.[3] The library was not yet regarded as a self-service system; the catalogue not a complete key to the stock. In this it was not unique, and libraries wishing to emulate

---

2 *Anglo-American cataloguing rules, prepared under the direction of the Joint Steering Committee for Revision of AACR*, 2nd edn, 2002 revision (London, 2002).

3 'We believe that of those who go into a place where books are collected whether to read, buy, borrow (or even steal) nineteen out of twenty know what author they want; and to them an alphabetical catalogue is all sufficient': A. De Morgan, quoted in H. B. Wheatley, *How to catalogue a library* (London, 1889), 11.

the British Museum adopted the code, or based their own on its prescriptions, e.g. Trinity College Dublin library.[4]

The years from 1840 to 1890 saw considerable interest in the development of rules in the United Kingdom. The universities produced their own: those of Cambridge University Library were based on *BM*, while the Bodleian followed those of the Library Association of the United Kingdom (LAUK) of 1878, revised at Liverpool 1881;[5] and there was interest in some municipal libraries such as Manchester.

In the United States of America, Charles Coffin Jewett at the Smithsonian Institution in Washington (who was highly influenced by *BM*) and Charles Ammi Cutter at the Boston Athenaeum[6] were active in the development of rules, as were the American Library Association (ALA) and Melvil Dewey.[7] It is interesting to note from the outset the close relationship between practitioners and theorists across the Atlantic. Quite apart from the intertwining of the respective professional associations,[8] Thomas Greenwood observed that 'In cataloguing the rules for author entries issued by the Library Association of the United Kingdom may be used, and for subject or title entries, and all questions relating to arrangement, use the "Rules for a Dictionary Catalogue," prepared by Mr. C. A. Cutter, of Boston.'[9] Cutter's rules made an important contribution to code development because of his discussion and justification of decisions.[10]

After some decades of informal cross-fertilisation a major forward-looking development took place, springing from an American initiative. Dewey among others was instrumental in establishing formal co-operation between the respective ALA and LAUK committees on cataloguing; and after a series of meetings the 'Joint code' (or AA08) was approved.[11] Given the substantial differences in library culture which had developed in the two countries, it was remarkable that of the 174 rules there was disagreement on only eleven; but that was enough to lead to separate British and American texts.[12] None the less, this represented an important stage in codification since it ultimately ensured

---

4 *Rules to be observed in compiling the catalogue of printed books in the Library of Trinity College, Dublin.* University of Dublin, MUN / LIB / 4 / 2.

5 Wheatley, *How to catalogue a library*, 46.

6 C. A. Cutter, *Rules for a printed dictionary catalogue* (Washington, DC, 1876).

7 M. Dewey, *Library school rules*, 3rd edn (Boston, MA, 1894). Cf. W. A. Wiegand, *Irrepressible reformer: a biography of Melvil Dewey* (Chicago, 1996).

8 J. Minto, *A history of the public library movement* (London, 1932), 168.

9 T. Greenwood, *Public libraries: a history of the movement and a manual for the organization and management of rate-supported libraries*, 4th edn, revised (London, 1894), 407.

10 Wheatley, *How to catalogue a library*, 47.

11 *Cataloguing rules: author and title entries*, compiled by committees of the Library Association and of the American Library Association, English edn (London, 1908), v.

12 *Cataloguing rules: author and title entries*, vi.

that the principal producers of English-language cataloguing data followed the same code. This not only enhanced the use of bibliographic machinery in the two countries and their respective bibliographic empires but opened the way to further and more ambitious international co-operation in later years.[13]

Agreement was thus reached on two central issues: the level of detail both in headings and in description (which in turn became the basis for the International Standard Bibliographic Description (ISBD) many years later); and the co-operative approach to codification which would establish the conditions for the automation of cataloguing and the MARC format.[14]

This, however, was for the future. The appearance of a new code, notwithstanding its credentials, was not immediately welcome in the UK. J. Henry Quinn, reflecting Minto, doubted its value,[15] and even in the 1930s Henry Sharp was to regret the lack of wider adoption.[16]

None the less these developments acknowledged that librarianship had moved considerably over the previous fifty years. Library collections were generally open to the public as a matter of course; stocks were larger, of greater variety and greater specialty; the card catalogue had become a commonplace. Other important influences were being felt: the Library of Congress (LC) had taken over the Library Bureau card-service in 1901 and made Jewett's (and others')[17] ideas for shared/centralised cataloguing a practicality. While of obvious greater impact on US cataloguing, some British libraries made use of the service. This had a bearing on which rules were adopted by individual libraries and how they were applied. While there was great temptation to simplify,[18] centralised cataloguing encouraged the improvement of practice. Standardisation ultimately asserted itself; and although these centralising influences were much less in the UK, which was to wait until the 1950s for similar services,[19] the strong links across the Atlantic meant that there was indirect impact on British operations.

International consolidation

The period between the two World Wars saw first a recognition that code revision was necessary, and then efforts to establish appropriate processes.

13 R. M. Brunt, 'In defence of bibliographic standards', *Aslib Proceedings* 37 (1985), 213–19.
14 E. J. Hunter and K. G. B. Bakewell, *Cataloguing*, 3rd edn (London, 1993), 6.
15 J. H. Quinn, *Library cataloguing* (London, 1913), 15.
16 H. Sharp, *Cataloguing: a textbook*, 2nd edn (London, 1937), 433.
17 Wheatley, *How to catalogue a library*, 69.
18 Examples of abbreviated codes may be found in J. D. Brown, *Library classification and cataloguing* (London, 1912), 103–36; Sharp, *Cataloguing*, 6–8.
19 A. Stephens, *The history of the British National Bibliography 1950–1973* (London, 1994), 18–20.

There were two principal driving forces: the requirements of centralised and co-operative cataloguing and the emergence of new materials and publication formats.[20] Fears were expressed on both sides of the Atlantic that 'drastic changes' were in mind and that as a result catalogues in English-speaking libraries would be thrown into chaos.[21] Opinion among cataloguers indicated that what was needed was enlargement and clarification of the code;[22] along with more and better examples for some existing rules, and new rules to cover material not already covered.[23]

The co-operation between the Library Association (LA) and the ALA which resulted in the 1908 code was renewed in 1936 with the intention of producing a revised edition, but came to an end in 1939 on the outbreak of war. The ALA continued independently, and in 1949 published *A.L.A. cataloging rules for author and title entries*, 2nd edn (a preliminary edition had been published in 1941). In 1951 the LA reconvened its cataloguing rules sub-committee on the ALA's suggested resumption of co-operation to revise the 1949 rules.

Neither of the American codes had had much bearing on UK cataloguing. With the prevailing conditions inauspicious for the introduction of new rules and the relatively slight use of centralised cataloguing, AA08 continued to be applied and its use was to be reinforced by its adoption by the *British National Bibliography* (BNB) in 1950.[24]

The new order

Even in the USA the codes of the 1940s were not to prove successful; rather, they generated an outcry.[25] The LC had commissioned a review of the rules, and in his report[26] Seymour Lubetzky heralded a departure from the enumeration of cases characteristic of codes of the previous hundred years (though he had perhaps been pre-empted in his analysis by James Duff Brown forty years earlier).[27] Lubetzky's rigorous exploration of the underlying theories governing the descriptive cataloguing of publications and the organisation for

20 R. H. Gjelsness, 'Cooperation in catalog code revision', *Catalogers' and Classifiers' Yearbook* 6 (Chicago, 1937), 65–70.
21 Sharp, *Cataloguing*, 433.
22 Gjelsness, 'Cooperation in catalog code revision', 66.
23 J. Pettee, 'Code revision – what do catalogers want?', *Library Journal* 61 (1936), 306–8, cited in Gjelsness, 'Cooperation in catalog code revision', 66.
24 J. Friedman and A. Jeffreys, *Cataloguing and classification in British university libraries* (Sheffield, 1967), 24.
25 A. D. Osborn, 'The crisis in cataloging', *Library Quarterly* 11 (1941), 393–411.
26 S. Lubetzky, *Cataloging rules and principles: a critique of the A.L.A. rules for entry and a proposed design for their revision* (Washington, DC, 1953).
27 Brown, *Library classification and cataloguing*, 102.

retrieval of the resulting bibliographic surrogates opened the way for the modernisation of cataloguing as manifested in the codes in the Anglo-American
tradition from 1967 onwards. However, it took the International Conference
on Cataloguing Principles, held in Paris in 1961,[28] to produce a code based on
the new principles, i.e. *Anglo-American cataloguing rules* (AACR) again, though
in separate texts.[29]

AACR was to be adopted in the UK with greater alacrity than its predecessor
AA08, as a survey of adoption published in 1969 indicates.[30] Factors accounting
for this included the widening acceptance of standardisation, the promised
benefits of automation, and increasing co-operation in librarianship in
general.

The Paris conference was concerned only with the problems of indexing
and retrieval of surrogates for known items. It had not addressed the problems of description; and in this respect matters had not advanced much in
theoretical terms from the days of Panizzi and Cutter. The cataloguing process still amounted to establishing the principal access point (the main entry
heading) and attaching to it an indicative abstract to characterise the work
associated with that heading. This was acceptable for manually produced and
manually searched catalogues where inconsistencies in the 'abstract' would
have little impact on the functionality of the body of the entry. However, by
1967 the Library of Congress had already made considerable strides in the
computerisation of cataloguing and this had indicated the need for greater
rigour in this aspect. MARC[31] was fully operational by 1968 and by then it
was plain that what was needed was a 'Paris conference' for descriptive cataloguing. The International Meeting of Cataloguing Experts was held under
the auspices of the International Federation of Library Associations and Institutions in Copenhagen in 1969;[32] the principal outcome was the *International
standard bibliographic description for monographs* (ISBD(M)).[33] It was intended to
support international co-operation in the use of bibliographic information by
precisely defining, organising and delineating the content of records; and the
standard specifically alluded to its contribution in the conversion of records
into machine-readable form. In 1974 ISBD(M) was incorporated into AACR.

28 International Conference on Cataloguing Principles, Paris, 1961, *Report* (London, 1963).
29 *Anglo-American cataloguing rules*, prepared by the American Library Association . . . the
   Library Association . . . British text (London, 1967).
30 'Register of adoptions of A.A.C.R. 1967', *Catalogue & Index* 14 (1969), 7–10; 15 (1969), 7–8.
31 Machine readable cataloguing formats such as US MARC, UK MARC.
32 'Report of the International Meeting of Cataloguing Experts, Copenhagen, 1969', *Libri*
   20 (1970), 105–32.
33 IFLA, *International standard bibliographic description for monographs* (London, 1971).

ISBD(M) was followed by that for serials; and then for those covering other publication formats represented in tangible collections. The latest to be established is ISBD(ER), for electronic publications, now increasingly the subject of cataloguing processes.

ISBD and MARC formed the partnership which was to facilitate both global co-operation and the commercial exploitation of bibliographic records in ways impossible to envisage in earlier eras. Further, it led to the realisation of the online catalogue accessible not only in the library itself but also via electronic telecommunications systems from anywhere in the world.

It was clear, even before publication of the 1967 code, that arrangements would have to be established to reconcile the separate texts after publication, and the memorandum of agreement of 1966 between the ALA and the LA provided the necessary machinery.[34] This included the establishment of the Joint Steering Committee for Revision of AACR (JSCAACR) in 1974, composed of representatives from the associations and the national libraries of the USA, the UK and Canada. Australian representation was included from 1981.

The second edition of the *Anglo-American cataloguing rules* (AACR2)[35] was published in 1978. It was quite radical in its presentation. The new importance of description was recognised by placing the rules in the first section with those for access in the second. Further, this reflected 'the sequence of cataloguers' operations in most present-day libraries'.[36] Of great significance was its appearance in a single text, seventy years after the first official attempts at getting agreement between the US and UK codifiers.

Before the publication of the AACR2, the decision was taken to continue the life of JSCAACR and thus establish the current regime of continuous revision. Revisions have been published in interim issues and in the consolidated editions of 1988, 1998 and 2002.

This period witnessed the adoption of the code by an ever-increasing number of countries in either original or translation.[37] Thus the influence on global operations was extended, and with it the advantages of and opportunities for widening international co-operation in cataloguing itself and bibliographic operations in general.

The early 1990s witnessed rapid developments in communications and publishing technologies, and a number of organisations were toying with local

34 *Anglo-American cataloguing rules*, 2nd edn by M. Gorman and P. W. Winkler (London, 1978), v–vi.
35 *Anglo-American cataloguing rules*, 2nd edn.
36 *Anglo-American cataloguing rules*, 2nd edn, 1 (rule 0.3).
37 *Anglo-American cataloguing rules*, 2nd edn, 1998 revision (London, 1998), xv.

solutions independent of the established revision process. In order to ensure continuity JSCAACR organised the International Conference on the Principles and Future Development of AACR in October 1997 in Toronto.[38] This 'generated a number of action items which will be dealt with by JSC . . . over the next months and years, always balancing the need for change with its impact on libraries and their catalogues'.[39] A major landmark was the publication of the code in electronic form.[40] It may now be mounted with electronic versions of other standards (e.g. Dewey Decimal Classification) on workstations to further facilitate the computerised processing of bibliographic data.

Descriptive cataloguing has moved from its almost medieval characteristics just prior to the period under review to the digital environment of today and has readily responded to the continuing developments in publication patterns and librarianship. Future tools will include document structuring standards (such as SGML, HTML, XML[41]) necessary in the World Wide Web environment, and the metadata standards now being established to control the virtual documents increasingly the subjects of bibliographic control.[42]

The subject approach

The history of providing the subject approach over the period has many strands weaving throughout each other rather untidily. While for non-fiction the catalogue is, essentially, the means of retrieval via name or title, retrieval by subject involves two possible approaches – the physical and the surrogate-based. At the beginning of the period subject retrieval depended on the former, taking a broad approach on the shelf; while the idea of a subject catalogue suffered considerable doubts about its worth, with Panizzi expressing a commonly held view that it was impossible to make a good classed catalogue as no two individuals could agree on the plan (i.e. the subject headings) of such a catalogue.[43]

38 J. Weihs (ed.), *The principles and future of AACR: proceedings of the International Conference on the Principles and Future Development of AACR, Toronto, October 1997* (London, 1998).
39 *Anglo-American cataloguing rules*, 2nd edn (1998), xvi.
40 B. Johnson, *Electronic Version of 'Anglo-American Cataloguing Rules (AACR2-E)'* added to *Library of Congress's 'Cataloger's Desktop'*, (1999). URL: http://www.loc.gov/today/pr/1999/99–013 (visited 20 April 2004).
41 F. Yergeau (ed.), *Extensible Markup Language (XML) 1.0*: W3C Recommendation 4. 3rd edn, February 2004. URL: http://www.w3.org/TR/REC-xml (visited 20 April 2004).
42 Dublin Core Metadata Initiative. URL: http://dublincore.org/about/ (visited 20 April 2004); G. E. Gorman (ed.), *Metadata applications and management*, International Yearbook of Library and Information Management 2003–4) (London, 2003).
43 *Report of the Commissioners appointed to inquire into the constitution and government of the British Museum* (London, 1850), evidence given by Panizzi, quoted in R. K. Olding (ed.),

However, by the first decade of the twentieth century detailed classification schemes were facilitating the subject approach on the shelf in public libraries;[44] and (somewhat later) even in university libraries.[45] After a period of stability in conventional classification up to the 1980s came the most recent challenge in the form of 'categorisation' for public libraries.

In the catalogue, developments responded to the debates on whether vocabulary control should use a systematic or an alphabetic approach. As special libraries (especially the scientific and technical) emerged in the 1920s and 1930s, conventional schemes of both classified and alphabetic subject-headings were found to be inadequate. This opened up the way first to the use of 'bibliographic' classification,[46] the development of the thesaurus in company with exotic retrieval devices such as post-co-ordinate indexes,[47] and the special classification scheme. Later came indexing procedures – chain procedure, rotated keyword, PRECIS, articulated indexing, and other pre-co-ordinated systems which might or might not depend on controlled vocabularies. And now the surrogate is retrieved by full-text retrieval in text databases or online catalogues; and the item itself now digitised can act as its own retrieval device, in inverted-file and hypertext modes.[48]

Physical arrangement for retrieval

This approach encompasses two main approaches: those controlling the storage systems – the presses and racks – and those controlling the individual items of stock.

By the beginning of the period the former was the norm and was represented in the shelf-classification systems found in the libraries of academic and learned institutions and national libraries, e.g. the Royal Institution and the British Museum; and in some public libraries, e.g. Manchester.[49] These provided locations for subjects at the level of the press or even the shelf, and permanent addresses for individual items of stock; but the books themselves were not given unique subject indicators. The breadth of the approach varied,

Readings in library cataloguing (London, 1966), 24–9. See also note 3 above, for opinions typical of academic users of libraries.

44 T. Kelly, *A history of public libraries in Great Britain 1845–1975*, 2nd edn, rev. (London, 1977), 184.

45 J. L. Thornton, *Cataloguing in special libraries: a survey of methods* (London, 1938), 13–19.

46 W. C. B. Sayers, *A manual of classification for librarians and bibliographers*, 2nd edn, rev. (London, 1944), 134.

47 F. W. Lancaster, *Information retrieval systems: characteristics, testing and evaluation* (New York, 1966), 36.

48 A. C. Foskett, *The subject approach to information*, 5th edn (London, 1996), 423–35.

49 J. D. Brown, *Manual of library classification and shelf arrangement* (London, 1898), 39–61.

and ranged from a small number of categories based on philosophical views of knowledge to comparatively sophisticated schemes which divided quite minutely.[50] These libraries were at first strictly closed-access and not intended for browsing, the patron having to request the required item by giving its title, or via the catalogue its call-number, for the library servant to fetch. Vestiges of this approach may be found in modern collections which include non-book materials and documentation which for security and other reasons may not be made publicly accessible. In general, however, this is a thing of the past. Its demise is due to two distinct developments: the first the invention of systematic classification for vocabulary control for subject cataloguing, the second the move towards opening up the stack to the readers.

Both emerged from United States practices.[51] To Dewey is attributed the publication of the first practicable scheme of systematic vocabulary control. Having tested it in the library of Amherst College, he then published it anonymously in 1876.[52] While it was intended as a means of organising subject entries in library catalogues, Dewey indicated from the start that it might be applied to the physical arrangement of books on shelves, with the associated advantages of collocation of books by subject.

Schemes

Dewey's *A classification and subject index for cataloguing and arranging the books and pamphlets of a library*[53] (the Dewey Decimal Classification, soon to be abbreviated to 'DDC') was not to remain for long the sole example of this approach, and from 1876 onwards others were established and developed. Cutter created his *Expansive classification*, a scheme which while not finding favour in the UK made a vicarious appearance in the *Library of Congress classification* (LCC) for which it provided the basic structure.[54] The 1890s saw British interest in development of schemes such as *Quinn-Brown*, *Adjustable classification* and *Subject classification*,[55] all encouraged by the move towards open access – led in the UK to a great degree by James Duff Brown.

In a related field, the Belgians Paul Otlet and Henri La Fontaine had launched their project to establish a universal bibliography to encompass all types of documentation and were in need of a controlling vocabulary. None of the existing

---

50 E. C. Richardson, *Classification: theoretical and practical* (New York, 1912), 45–149.
51 Kelly, *History of public libraries*, 175.
52 M. Dewey, *Classification and subject index for cataloguing and arranging the books and pamphlets of a library* (Amherst, MA, 1876).
53 Dewey, *Classification and subject index*, 3.
54 Sayers, *Manual of classification*, 150.
55 Brown, *Library classification and cataloguing*, 48–9, 75–6, 84–90.

classification schemes was considered detailed enough, and they approached Dewey to seek permission to develop his system. Thus was born the Brussels expansion of DDC, which is better known as Universal Decimal Classification (UDC).[56] Bliss devoted great energy to the development of his *Bibliographic classification* (BC), which, after a long gestation, was finally published in 1935 and in a fuller form in 1953.[57] In an attempt to make classification more suitable for the particular requirements of university libraries Garside produced his University College London scheme in 1954.[58]

Growth in the numbers of special libraries encouraged the development of special classifications capable of providing the depth of specification unavailable in the general schemes. While some classificationists followed the enumerative pattern of the general schemes, e.g. Moys for law,[59] others adopted the analytico-synthetic approach of Ranganathan[60] and produced faceted classification schemes such as those for library and information science, architecture or electrical engineering.[61] While the heyday was in the 1960s and 1970s, they still emerge.[62]

In the mid-1970s, pressures on funding, among other reasons, encouraged some public libraries to investigate ways of improving the effectiveness of stock use; and one approach selected was categorisation, a variation on the reader-interest arrangement first applied in Detroit public library in the 1930s.[63] This departure from conventional classification in branch lending libraries threw up several schemes of arrangement which included several novel and radical departures from traditional subject order based on academic disciplines.[64]

Adoption

Once DDC had been published, it was soon to be adopted in the still closed-access libraries of the United Kingdom; perhaps the earliest such adoption was by the National Library of Ireland in 1878.[65]

56 J. P. Comaromi, *The eighteen editions of the Dewey decimal classification* (Albany, NY, 1976), 225–30.

57 Foskett, *Subject approach*, 296–301.

58 K. Garside, 'The basic principles of the new library classification at University College London', *Journal of Documentation* 10 (1954), 169–92. The scheme was also later adapted for Glasgow University Library.

59 E. M. Moys, *A classification scheme for law books* (London, 1968).

60 S. R. Ranganathan, *Prolegomena to library classification* (London, 1937).

61 R. Marcella and R. Newton, *A new manual of classification* (London, 1994), 117.

62 S. Halper, 'Housing information galore', *Library Association Record* 102 (2000), 397.

63 R. J. Hyman, *Shelf access in libraries* (Chicago, 1982), 66–70.

64 P. Ainley and B. Totterdell (eds.), *Alternative arrangement: new approaches to public library stock* (London, 1982).

65 A. Mac Lochlainn, 'The National Library of Ireland, 1877–1977', *Irish University Review* 7 (1977), 157–67.

Despite its introduction in the USA in the last quarter of the nineteenth century it was some time (pioneering experiments were carried out in Cambridge and Wigan)[66] before this revolutionary idea caught on generally in the UK, and then only in public libraries. Once the battle for open access had been won, Dewey's system was to be introduced gradually over the next thirty or so years[67] (e.g. in Leeds public library, one of the later adoptions, in 1920[68]). DDC became the most widely adopted scheme in public libraries; and while other schemes such as Brown's *Subject classification*[69] were available, even patriotism was not enough to put a brake on DDC's growing hegemony. While principally to be found in public libraries, it came to be favoured by colleges, and a significant and increasing number of university libraries had adopted the scheme by mid-century.[70]

UDC was viewed as a tool for documentation or indexing rather than for shelf location,[71] although some libraries adopted UDC expansions to improve specification in DDC for shelving where it was found wanting.[72] It proved to be of interest to the librarians of special libraries, especially those in science, medicine and technology, which emerged in increasing numbers after the Great War.[73] It has also been adopted in some university libraries such as Bath.

The first adoption of LCC in the UK was by the National Library of Wales in 1913, followed by a small number of public libraries and more academic ones, once the universities had acknowledged the value of open access in the 1930s.[74] BC enjoyed some popularity in colleges of education and school libraries;[75] and while Ranganathan's *Colon classification* was to have significant impact on the development both of general schemes (such as DDC and UDC) and the majority of special schemes, its own adoption was almost negligible.

Subject retrieval by surrogate

From physical retrieval we may turn to subject retrieval dependent on the surrogates provided by catalogues and indexes. It was with some difficulty that

66 Greenwood, *Public libraries*, 41.
67 Kelly, *History of public libraries*, 246–7.
68 *Yorkshire Evening Post*, 1 September 1920.
69 J. D. Brown, *Subject classification* (London, 1906).
70 R. Sweeney, 'Dewey in Britain', *Catalogue & Index* 30 (1973) 4–6, 15.
71 S. C. Bradford, *Documentation* (London, 1948).
72 The National Library of Ireland made use of UDC (612, dated 1895) to enhance its DDC (6th edn).
73 Sayers, *Manual of classification*.
74 Friedman and Jeffreys, *Cataloguing and classification*, 5.
75 J. Metcalfe, *Information retrieval British and American 1876–1976* (Metuchen, NJ, 1976), 160–1.

librarians were convinced of the value and efficacy of the subject approach in the catalogue. The major problem was that the selection by one individual (the cataloguer) of subject headings for a book might not match the conception of the subject of the same book by others (the readers). However, an 'index of matters' could be provided to allow retrieval by subject, though it would make use of the words of the title only, and there was no concept of a controlled vocabulary (whether alphabetic or systematic).

None the less, some librarians were strong advocates of the 'classed catalogue'[76] and others showed similar enthusiasm and established index catalogues. Andrea Crestadoro,[77] in Manchester, is credited by some with inventing the keyword index[78] which computerisation a hundred years later was to make a considerable success.[79] The index catalogue was an early version of the dictionary catalogue (which was to enjoy early favour in the United States) and both of these were dependent on the catalogue itself for authority-control of headings, with new terms being established from the title words or almost arbitrarily by the cataloguer. Not until DDC was the idea of a controlled vocabulary to emerge. Even Cutter, whose *Rules for a printed dictionary catalogue* was to be the first code of rules for the alphabetic subject approach, was averse to word lists.[80]

Considerable impetus to the dictionary-catalogue approach was given by the establishment of the ALA subject headings list in 1895,[81] followed by the *Library of Congress subject headings* (LCSH) and others. Coates indicates a blossoming of subject-heading lists for special subjects,[82] pre-dating the range of special classification schemes. A further fillip was to be found in the establishment of the centralised cataloguing services, principally that of Library of Congress, which ensured that alphabetic subject headings were used by large numbers of libraries in the United States; and the method remained popular in the UK.

By the 1930s academic libraries in the UK were moving from fixed location and closed access with general catalogues to open access served by classified

76 Kelly, *History of public libraries*, 93.
77 A. Crestadoro, *The art of making catalogues of libraries* (London, 1856).
78 G. London, 'The place and role of bibliographic description in general and individual catalogues: a historical analysis', *Libri* 30 (1980), 263.
79 H. P. Luhn, 'A statistical approach to mechanized encoding and searching of literary information', *IBM Journal of Research and Development* 1 (1957), 309–17.
80 Cutter, *Rules*, rule 188.
81 American Library Association, *List of subject headings for use in dictionary catalogs* (Chicago, 1895).
82 E. J. Coates, *Subject catalogues: headings and structure* (London, 1960), 79.

catalogues.[83] Public libraries too had adopted this approach, with the classified catalogue becoming the norm from the 1920s on.[84]

The wider adoption of the classified catalogue meant that a rather more rigorous view of classification developed in the UK than in the USA, with an emphasis on minute and precise specification for both catalogue and shelf. This meant that the development of classification theory was greatly influenced by British ideas, exemplified in the interest in UDC, the formation of the Classification Research Group, and the faceted extensions of DDC in the *British National Bibliography*.[85]

Furthermore, a means had to be found to create the now necessary key to the classified sequence of the catalogue to facilitate translation of queries in natural language into their classified equivalents. Ranganathan's chain-indexing method, originally devised for the construction of pre-co-ordinated alphabetic subject headings, was found to be eminently suitable.[86] Later the chain procedure was to be mechanised,[87] but by the 1970s it had been superseded by the *Preserved context index system* (PRECIS).[88]

For some sixty years or more, the classified catalogue enjoyed its hegemony in these islands, with the many advantages offered by the systematic approach in retrieval by subject. However, with continuing developments in library automation, the online catalogue came to offer enhanced subject retrieval by means of a wider range of search techniques than was possible in manual systems. Notwithstanding the potential for classification for retrieval in the online catalogue (with research being mostly done in the USA, paradoxically),[89] the alphabetic approach has regained its former prominence.

The ability to search 'subject-rich' fields of the bibliographic record (such as title, corporate name, publication details), in addition to designated descriptor fields holding subject headings, has meant that a proto-dictionary catalogue has resurfaced, with the consequent banishment of classification to the shelf alone. However, a major weakness lies in the fact that nothing more modern

83 J. L. Thornton, *Special library methods: an introduction to special librarianship* (London, 1940), 36.

84 K. Davison, *Classification practice in Britain: report on a survey of classification opinion and practice in Britain* (London, 1966), 7.

85 British National Bibliography. *Supplementary classification schedules* (London, 1963).

86 T. D. Wilson, *An introduction to chain indexing* (London, 1971), 7–8.

87 P. Capewell, 'A computer based subject index', *Catalogue & Index* 50 (1978), 1–2, 7.

88 D. Austin, 'The development of PRECIS: a theoretical and technical history', *Journal of Documentation* 30 (1974), 47–102.

89 P. A. Cochrane and K. Markey, 'Preparing for the use of classification in online cataloging systems and in online catalogs', *Information Technology and Libraries* 4 (1985), 91–111.

than LCSH is available to control the vocabulary; and progress towards a modern alternative appears slow.[90]

Special library techniques

Special libraries (hardly acknowledged as such in early days) at first emulated the general in their techniques. At the turn of the century, though, there appeared Kaiser's *Systematic indexing*, a code of practice for the construction of alphabetic indexes to documentation rather than conventional library collections.[91] As discussed above, UDC was found to be useful in providing the required degrees of specification for the materials in special collections, first for shelving and then for indexing documentation (the original purpose of the scheme, of course). Indeed, just as classified open access became the norm for the majority of libraries, it might be said that special libraries were returning to fixed location/closed access as the dissemination of technological and scientific information meant that special libraries no longer had books to shelve.[92]

Post-co-ordinate indexing techniques[93] which came to the fore in the 1940s promoted the development of and dependence on the subject heading list in the new guise of the thesaurus.[94] Thesauri such as *Thesaurofacet* or *Inspec thesaurus* extended the concept of the simple word-list for the special subject field; their construction was greatly dependent on classification techniques (especially the facet analysis borrowed from analytico-synthetic methods). These devices ensured that the syndetic links upon which efficient retrieval depended were established along with scope-notes to clarify the meaning of each term; in this we find a return to Cutter's original ideas for the dictionary catalogue.[95] However, while the conventional subject-word headings lists were universal in scope the universal thesaurus has not appeared.

The computer offered other possibilities in the provision of alphabetical pre-co-ordinate systems such as Sharp's *Selective listing in combination* (SLIC), Lynch's articulated indexing, and keyword indexing (KWIC, KWOC).[96]

So we have come full circle. The 'classed' catalogue of the mid-nineteenth century was an alphabetic subject file, as is the approach in modern retrieval

90 M. J. Bates, 'Rethinking subject cataloging in the online environment', *Library Resources & Technical Services* 33 (1989), 400–12.

91 J. O. Kaiser, *Systematic indexing* (London, 1911).

92 Lancaster, *Information retrieval systems*, 28.

93 Lancaster, *Information retrieval systems*, 28–33.

94 B. C. Vickery, 'Thesaurus: a new word in documentation', *Journal of Documentation* 16 (1960), 181–90.

95 Foskett, *Subject approach*, 124.

96 F. W. Lancaster, *Indexing and abstracting in theory and practice*, 3rd edn (London, 2003), 50–67.

devices from the online catalogue to the World Wide Web. Despite the many clear advantages in the use of classification for retrieval it will be some time before it once again has a substantial role in subject-retrieval.

Conclusions

The period under review has witnessed a remarkable development in the equipment for the organisation of library materials for retrieval. It should not come as a surprise, since cataloguing, classification and indexing (along with bibliography) comprise the very essence of librarianship, and it is here that development ought to have provided (and indeed does provide) evidence of a healthy and dynamic field of endeavour.

While there have been many technological developments, the fundamentals of storage (and thus, in effect, hiding the item) and retrieval (providing adequate and efficient clues to reveal it) have not changed greatly over the last 150 years. New publication formats, new subjects, new readerships, new technologies have presented problems and challenges; and these have been met to a high degree by the tools and techniques created to meet the changing needs of the library community at large.

46

Storehouses of knowledge: the free library movement and the birth of modern library architecture

SIMON PEPPER

> The development of the free library movement throughout the country, and the erection of buildings to meet the requirements of the [Public Libraries] Act, have opened a fresh field and propounded a new problem for the architect. To some extent allied to museums and art schools, with which the library may be associated, the requirements nevertheless demand a distinct treatment, and as every town and village throughout the country is now promoting the erection of a free library, it may be of some practical value if we lay before the architectural reader the main principles that should be kept in view in the design of these buildings, and describe some that have been erected in the Metropolis and elsewhere – a few of which we have illustrated.[1]

With these words Maurice Adams, editor of the *Building News*, introduced to his fellow architects a lengthy series of articles on the design, planning, heating and lighting of public libraries. The introductory remarks of 1890 will serve very well as an introduction to this chapter, which also seeks to identify a number of the key issues in the architectural evolution of the modern public library.[2]

It is now possible to see the years from 1890 to World War I as critical to this process. The period represented both a construction boom and a coming together of librarians and architects – often initially in collision – in their efforts to evolve building forms that reconciled the practicalities of library management with the formal civic architecture demanded by society. The forty years from 1850 to 1890 had more than once seen towns persuaded to

---

1 *Building News* (6 June 1890), 789.
2 Many of the buildings referred to in this chapter are described or illustrated in T. Greenwood, *Public libraries: a history of the movement and a manual for the organization and management of rate-supported libraries*, 4th edn revised (London, 1894), and are usually not specifically referenced below. Similarly, most of the many references to individual libraries in T. Kelly, *A history of public libraries in Great Britain 1845–1965* (London, 1973) are not specifically identified.

adopt the Library Acts by the architectural and cultural ambitions of wealthy sponsors, and the social agenda of the free library movement relegated firmly into second place. There was a tension here that could prove highly creative, if often difficult to handle and occasionally disastrous. Philanthropists, social reformers, librarians and their architects imagined library buildings as secular cathedrals, storehouses of knowledge, or lighthouses to learning – all phrases well used in opening ceremonies – which endowed them with significance that went well beyond the efficient storage of books and the provision of controlled surroundings for different kinds of improving reading.

'Cynosure of all eyes'

The wave of British public library foundation launched in the second half of the nineteenth century represented an enormously ambitious social and cultural programme. 'In the larger towns the public library is sometimes overshadowed by a more splendid or more pretentious institution', observed the Bootle librarian John Ogle, 'but in towns with a population between, say, 10,000 and 80,000, the public library is . . . the "cynosure of all eyes", and a centre of intellectual life.'[3] Important the library was certainly seen to be, but its appearance and organisation varied enormously. The picture is a confusing one for those who seek an ordering principle in what was an essentially new Victorian building type designed to bring culture to the masses, and with it self-improvement. Unlike collegiate or subscription libraries – or even the privately supported literary or mechanics' institutes – the public library proper subsisted on municipal funds and catered for all classes of society. It needed to attract a broad social spectrum of users as well as to control their behaviour in ways that were often quite different from those employed by the earlier private institutions.

All architectural styles are represented in the early public libraries: indeed, some architects happily submitted competition plans with alternative external treatments in classical or Gothic styles, while others attached meanings to their selection and earnestly explained them to the community. Shortly before the opening in 1876 of Macclesfield's Chadwick Free Library – described by Pevsner as 'very Gothic' – the local newspaper carried a series of articles on 'Architecture – by a lover of the beautiful' which suggested that 'when one new building of a public character is about being opened, and others are in contemplation, it may be of some use in guiding and assisting public taste to

3 J. J. Ogle, *The free library: its history and present condition* (London, 1897), 242.

give . . . a brief sketch of the various features of the several distinctive styles of architecture', and went on to introduce the 'Medieval styles, or *Christian* art, in contradistinction to the ancient styles – the *heathen*.'[4] Macclesfield was not going to get a heathen building. Here the selection was made by the donor, David Chadwick MP, and his architect, A. J. Stevens, without the public debate which often accompanied open competitions. Hence the importance of an explanation.

The private sponsorship of public buildings sometimes saddled communities with expensive facilities and introduces the question of what today would be called 'procurement methods'. These included the disbursement of rate funds under the Public Library Acts, Treasury-approved civic borrowing, and public subscription of the 'widow's mite' variety, as well as spectacular examples of individual philanthropy culminating in the extensive programmes sponsored by Henry Tate, John Passmore Edwards and Andrew Carnegie, all of whom began their philanthropy in the late 1880s and 1890s. By then the public library was beginning to be seen as an end in itself, best served by a building which was not expected to cater for too many other activities. The services provided by earlier institutions varied enormously, however. One of the generalisations that can be sustained is that few of the early undertakings restricted themselves simply to a library.

The first entirely new *building* entirely funded under the Public Library Act to open its doors to the public was in Norwich, where in 1857 the combined public library, museum and art school was completed, seven years after the city had adopted the Act of 1850.[5] Before then Canterbury, Warrington and Salford had employed the Museums Act of 1845 to provide libraries as annexes to the museums which in some places commanded stronger popular support than libraries in the heyday of Victorian discovery. Liverpool's Library and Museum, which opened in 1860, was the product of a local act of parliament and a gift of £40,000 from William (afterwards Sir William) Brown, which set an example for cultural philanthropists in Britain which was not bettered until the Harris bequest to Preston of £300,000 in 1877. By the time that the Brown Library and Museum of 1860 had been joined in a single classically

---

4 *Macclesfield Courier and Herald* (20 May 1876). Illustrations in *British Architect* (27 May 1876), *The Graphic* (16 November 1878), 500, and D. Pickford, *Old Macclesfield* (1984), 6. See also B. Brill, *Macclesfield Library: the first 100 years* (Chester, 1976).

5 M. Allthorpe-Guyton and J. Stevens, *A happy eye: a school of art in Norwich 1845–1982* (Norwich, 1982), 68–9, with illustration p. 70. The Free Library and Museum shared a three-storey building with the Art School as 'unhappy bedfellows'. The photograph of 1912 shows a brick structure, with prominent classical pilasters: Roman Doric on the ground floor, Ionic on the first floor, and Corinthian on the second.

inspired complex by the Walker Art Gallery (opened 1877) and the circular Picton Reading Room with its basement lecture hall (1879), Liverpool boasted what Thomas Greenwood, one of the most energetic promoters of the Free Library Movement, called 'without doubt, the finest pile of buildings for this purpose in the whole United Kingdom and Ireland'.

Classical architecture signalled high culture in Liverpool, as it did in Sunderland's imposing domed 'Renaissance' structure of 1879 containing the new library with a museum, art gallery and music conservatory, and as it was to do in Preston's neoclassical Harris Library, Museum and Art Gallery.[6] Gothic carried meaning too, as we have seen. For the post-Pugin generation there was the 'Christian' tradition of pointed architecture, as well as the 'Britishness' of what was often represented as the native style. The Albert Memorial Institute in Dundee (1869), designed by Sir George Gilbert Scott, gave the movement one of its finest neo-Gothic monuments, as well as a sobering experience for the community which had raised £27,000 by public subscription for a library and natural history museum, and then borrowed £10,000 for an art gallery extension which saddled the committee with debt service charges that severely limited their ability to operate the facility until another private donation rescued the situation.[7] The neo-Gothic public library and museum erected at Derby in 1879 by the mayor and beer magnate Michael Thomas Bass MP was so generously funded, by contrast, that its designers were encouraged to invest in an impressive double-height central space, lit from above by a lantern, and decorated with arts-and-crafts inspired murals picking out natural forms and the names of mid-Victorian literary and scientific heroes.[8] Only the heavily stained windows presented a problem. Greenwood, who greatly enjoyed visiting the building, commented that 'Half the rooms are in a perpetual gloom, and unless the reader have the nocturnal sight of the owl or the bat, it is almost impossible to decipher print.'

Elsewhere the decoration went onto the outside surfaces. The Wedgwood Institute in Burslem (the outcome of a competition in 1859, but completed only in 1869–70) contained a lecture hall, art school and public library, all set behind elaborate terracotta façade panels advertising the products and processes of

6 *The Builder* 37 (29 November 1879), 1316–18, plans and view.
7 M. Dewe, 'H. T. Hare: Edwardian library architect', *Library Review* 27 (Summer 1978), 80–4; A. H. Millar, *Jubilee of the Albert Institute 1867–1917: a record of the work of fifty years* (Dundee, 1917).
8 *British Architect and Northern Engineer* 6 (3 November 1876), 285; 12 (11 July 1879), 16 and plate; *Builder* 34 (18 November 1876), 1128; 37 (15 November 1879), 1260–2; *Building News* 31 (10 November 1876), 468 and plate; F. J. Burgoyne, *Library construction* (London, 1897), 146–7; P. Sturges, 'Beer and books: Michael Thomas Bass, Derby Public Library, and the philanthropy of the beerage', *Libraries and Culture* 31 (1996), 247–71.

the Potteries as well as the nobility of labour and the achievements of Josiah Wedgwood.[9] One of the leading local promoters, A. Beresford Pope MP, had called for the building to 'exemplify the structural application of ceramics' and with its success helped to launch a fashion in public buildings of many kinds for highly explicit didactic sculptural decoration.[10] At the Wedgwood Institute the decorative scheme completely overshadowed a rather hesitant brick Gothic structure.

The wide-ranging facilities speak to the broad-based cultural aspirations of their founders. Books for study or home reading, and newspapers for information and job vacancies, represented just some of the means by which society could improve itself intellectually and materially. Young men in particular were to be encouraged to inform themselves, to study, to attend lectures on all manner of topics and, by occupying themselves profitably in the evenings, to avoid the temptations lurking in music halls and public houses or on the street. Museums at this time were at the cutting edge of progress in geology, geography and natural history, while art galleries and the associated schools of art raised public sensibility and provided useful skills in the burgeoning decorative industries. Museums and art galleries – possibly even more than libraries, it has been argued – also stimulated behavioural improvement for those members of the working classes who came into contact with the middle classes in a highly controlled social environment. Here everyone was on their best behaviour, and the manners of polite society as well as its cultural values could be observed and shared. Later in the century gymnasia would be included in many of the larger complexes, and were specifically provided for in the Museums and Gymnasiums Act of 1891. Gymnasia can easily be misinterpreted simply as the first public sports facilities, but the typical timetable of swimming 'classes' segregated by age and gender, boxing, and above all the parade-ground discipline of the Swedish callisthenics and other gymnastic exercises, leaves little room for doubt that here too there was a strong element of social control.

9 'The proposed Wedgwood Institute', *Builder* 21 (14 March 1863), 185; 'Wedgwood Memorial Institute Competition', *Builder* 21 (28 November 1863), 851; 22 (8 October 1864), 736–7; J. Dawson, *The Wedgwood Memorial Institute* (Burslem, 1894); A. Swale, 'The terracotta of the Wedgwood Institute, Burslem', *Journal of the Tiles and Architectural Ceramics Society* 2 (1987), 21–7. Swale establishes that the original local competition-winners had been displaced and a second competition was won by George Nichols of West Bromwich; his scheme then had imposed upon it a joint design for the sculptural façade by R. Edgar and John Lockwood Kipling (father of the famous author, and a sculptor who departed for a teaching career in India before the job was finished). Rowland James Morris, William Wright, J. M. Marsh (all from the Potteries) and Matthew Eldon (formerly of the Stoke School and a member of staff of the South Kensington Art School) executed the panels.
10 'The proposed Wedgwood Institute', 185.

Naming of parts

The core of the public library was its reading room, with walls and alcoves shelved from floor to ceiling, and often equipped with one or more galleries from which assistants could reach the higher shelves. The bigger collections reached dizzy heights, and accidents inevitably resulted when assistants were compelled to use ladders on the narrow catwalks to reach the highest shelves.[11]

The readers would be kept away from direct contact with books by a railing which corraled them in the centre of the room, and formed a race track around the outside of which the assistants scurried. While book collections were still small enough to be accommodated on the walls of large rooms, readers enjoyed the sensation of being surrounded by the treasures of the mind. Before long, however, even in the largest reading rooms, book collections had outgrown walls, alcoves, catwalks and the longest ladders. Separate extension accommodation was by then provided in what became known as bookstacks. Readers were still unable to touch the books: now they could not see most of them! In some early twentieth-century buildings the planned absence of books in the main reading rooms opened up vast areas of wall for displays of potentially instructive or improving art.

In the very smallest libraries all activity often had to take place in a single room, as in the Fitzroy Memorial Library in Lewes, an initially private foundation opened in 1862 (later incorporated into a rate-supported public library).[12] Here Sir George Gilbert Scott planned a two-storey accommodation wing fronting a large square toplit library space.[13] But the Victorian passion for classification extended well beyond the contents of book collections and museums to society as a whole, and most of the larger libraries as well as many smaller ones included different kinds of sharply segregated accommodation for what were seen as distinctly separate classes of users.

11 Greenwood, *Public libraries*, 179–80, notes that the wall-shelving in Leicester (an adapted building) rose to a height of 20 to 24 feet. 'There can be no wonder that a serious accident should have occurred some time ago, when the ladder fell while an assistant was upon it, and who was so injured that he had to be taken to the hospital. The ladder in its fall struck another assistant on the head, causing a very serious wound. It is almost criminal to place the shelving so high as this.'

12 Kelly, *History of public libraries*, 136, gives other examples of private foundations in small towns or villages which were not strictly public libraries, and which were publicised in a series of articles in *The Queen* by Lady John Manners (wife of the future duke of Rutland and leading Conservative politician). See Lady John Manners, *Some advantages of easily accessible reading and recreation rooms and free libraries* (London, 1885) and her *Encouraging experiences of reading and recreation rooms* (London, 1886). See also T. Greenwood, *Sunday school and village libraries* (London, 1892); J. J. Ogle, *The extension of the Free Libraries Act to small places* (London, 1887) and his *The free library*, 281–4.

13 D. Cole, *The work of Sir Gilbert Scott* (London, 1980), 124, and private information.

Ladies were frequently provided with a separate room – often known as a magazine room – equipped with soft furniture, a fireplace and private toilet. Occasionally, gentlemen enjoyed a conversation room (sometimes a smoking room or even games room), although such liberality did not command the support of the more serious-minded amongst the leaders of the Free Library Movement. Borrowers were usually kept apart from the readers, and made their selection of books from a printed catalogue in the 'delivery lobby' where they would wait for their requests to be delivered. Thus borrowers could order and collect their books on the ground floor (sometimes in the basement) and leave without disturbing the serious students in the reading room, or coming into contact with the users of the newspaper room who – in the rhetoric of the Movement – were amongst the principal beneficiaries of the library.

In the original newspaper room, or newsroom, the papers were fixed to tall reading lecterns and read whilst standing. A man would have to move to a vacant stand to read another paper. It was an arrangement which did not favour loiterers, or women who were not really expected to use this part of the building. Later, large tables were provided at which newspaper readers could sit, and later still separate tables for ladies appeared. Newsrooms often kept different hours from the rest of the library, opening early in the morning to assist those who needed to consult the situations vacant columns. By 1900 enlightened librarians would have these notices clipped and displayed behind glass in the lobby, or even on the pavement outside the building for the benefit of dawn job-seekers. Some were by then beginning to question the need for the segregation of serious students (implicitly men) from the ladies (with their magazines), the borrowers (heterogeneous but transient users of the building) and the working-class males who were the main users of the newsroom. Undifferentiated reading rooms and open access to the books were to become closely related concepts in the more 'democratic' twentieth-century library. By 1900, however, juveniles had been identified as a group who could benefit particularly from the library, but who needed a higher level of supervision as well as a degree of segregation. It was to be many years before the central library or larger branch achieved the open access and undifferentiated space typical of libraries in the second half of the twentieth century.

Designing the library

With user segregation came the necessity for supervision. With the rapid growth of the bookstocks, shelf-space became another key factor in library design. Fire protection, lighting and ventilation[14] also loomed large in the minds of careful librarians and their architects, but the most influential early models were chiefly shaped by the need for segregation, supervision and the ever-increasing need for book-storage capacity.

The 'panopticon' layout of Panizzi's round reading room in the British Museum, with its centrally located, slightly raised observation point for the superintendent, and clear sight-lines along the radially arranged rows of desks, was widely admired and copied.[15] The authors of Liverpool's Picton Reading Room, the United States Library of Congress, and as late as the 1920s Manchester's first purpose-built central public library, all made reference to the collaborative design of Panizzi, and his architect, the younger Smirke, who between them planned and built the Museum's round reading room between 1852 and 1857. Although not the first such solution – Oxford's Radcliffe Camera and the domed circular library of Thomas Jefferson's University of Virginia were by then already old – the fame of the British Museum reading room made it a constant reference point for central supervision, as well as for its early adoption of remote bookstack storage in the multi-storey framed 'iron library' which occupied most of what is now the Museum's Great Court.

Another influential early prototype borrowed from ecclesiastical and collegiate forms. Here the books would be stored in 'side-aisles' at two or more levels, while readers occupied the 'nave' and enjoyed potentially good daylighting from the clerestory windows, and almost certainly draughty conditions in the tall but very easily overlooked (and usually fenced-off) central space. The Astor Library in New York (1849–54) and the first Boston Public Library in Boylston Street (1858) popularised this model for public libraries in the USA. London's Corporation Library (often known as the Guildhall Library) used the same arrangement in 1870–1. It was still being employed in Britain as late as the 1890s in Manchester's John Rylands Library and in the rebuilt Patent Office Library – both of which have survived because they have never had to adapt to the changing social circumstances of municipal public libraries.

14 For these issues, rarely tackled in the modern literature, see C. Bowler and P. Brimble-combe, 'Environmental pressures on building design and Manchester's John Rylands Library,' *Journal of Design History* 13 (2000), 175–91.

15 Bentham's panopticon was of course devised for the reformed prison, but was referred to by Frederic Vinton, Librarian of the College of New Jersey, Princeton, who introduced a two-tier radial open-access scheme in the Chancellor Green Library building where, from a raised desk in the centre, 'the librarian can see no book, but he can see every person present, even the floors, being of perforated iron, presenting no great obstruction to the eye. *It is a perfect panopticon.*' ('Hints for improved library economy, drawn from usages at Princeton', *Library Journal* 2 (1877–8), 55).

Wigan's original public reference library is another rare survival from this period. Here in 1877 Thomas Taylor paid £12,000 for a library building which he hoped would persuade the citizens to adopt the Library Acts, and employed Alfred Waterhouse – the most successful commercial architect of his generation – to design it. The ground floor accommodated the lending library and newsroom, and is now a town museum. Over it was the Reference Library (now serving as the local studies annexe). Here there was a double-height central space where the readers' tables were located, with a series of iron-framed alcoves opening off each side at two levels. Only the assistants could enter the fenced-off alcoves and collect books from upper levels using the 'flying gallery'.[16]

The arrangement was almost standard in college and private libraries, where the alcoves on the main floor provided cosy corners enjoyed by the trusted readers. But the early public libraries invariably kept their readers fenced into the middle of a room that was often impressive but rarely cosy. In some key American libraries, moreover, the galleried alcoves reached far greater heights. Boston's first purpose-built library in Boylston Street had its main reading room on first-floor level (English usage) with four levels of galleried alcoves on each side, while the extension bookroom completed in 1875 for the Peabody Institute in Baltimore, Maryland, had no less than six tiers of cast-iron alcoves on each side – dwarfing the readers at the central tables in what is still one of the most spectacular library spaces in the world.

Where libraries formed one part of a complex building which might combine museum, art gallery and lecture hall – and sometimes also art and technical schools, town hall, municipal offices, public baths or a gymnasium – it was much more difficult to formulate clear models. Indeed, some of the early solutions clearly did not work very well at all. Blackburn's first purpose-built free library (1871–2) occupied the ground floor of a Gothic building with a museum and art gallery upstairs, but there was insufficient space on the ground floor for separate lending and reference libraries, or for a ladies' room and a newsroom. The lack of a ladies' reading room and a newsroom at Blackburn caused persistent rumbles of discontent until the gift of a neighbouring site permitted expansion in 1895.[17] Liverpool's original Brown Library and Museum confined itself to a reference department (an outstandingly good municipal scholarly

16 *Builder* 31 (22 February 1873), 153; *British Architect* 8 (19 October 1877), 198; Burgoyne, *Library construction*, 185–7.
17 *Builder* 29 (4 November 1871), 871; *Architect* 7 (27 January 1872), 46 and plate; *British Architect* 3; *Building News* 23 (26 July 1872), 69–70; 24 (3 January 1873), 10 and plate; 26 (19 June 1873), 685; Burgoyne, *Library construction*, 147–8.

collection) and a museum which occupied much of the space in the 1860 building.[18] The loan collection and newspaper rooms were initially provided in two separate inner-city branches – a solution which avoided the problems faced by Blackburn, but one that prevented the central complex and its various extensions from furnishing any kind of general model. The same was true of Dundee's Albert Memorial Institute (1869). The imposing hall of Sir George Gilbert Scott's original design was for public events: the reference and lending libraries occupied the ground-floor spaces under the hall – again without sufficient space for a newsroom, which had to be separately accommodated on a neighbouring site some years later when the reference library expanded upstairs to the 'Albert Hall'. The art gallery and museum were later additions by the city architect.

Sunderland's cultural facilities (1879) occupied a two-storey 'Renaissance' building, with the art gallery and museum upstairs behind a 'blind' storey with skylights. The music conservatory and public library were downstairs, opening off opposite sides of the central vestibule. Thomas Greenwood was delighted by Sunderland's 'beautiful building which is an ornament to the whole place' and was much impressed by the domed vestibule with its 'three superb models of steamers' one of which cost 'close upon a thousand pounds . . . anything finer in this line of craftsmanship is probably not to be found in the island'. Sunderland's library was a simple one-room solution.

Preston's lavishly endowed Harris Library, Museum and Art Gallery (1881–92) was planned on three main floors. The lending library, the newsroom, and a display of sculpture, architectural details and industrial machines, were all on the ground floor; the reference collection was on the first floor, together with conversation rooms, trustees' rooms and the director's suite; and the art was above in a toplit second-floor gallery. A spectacular atrium at the centre of the building rose even higher and was lit from above by a lantern.[19] The blind faces of the atrium and the upper floor of the main block allowed uninterrupted wall-space for picture hanging, as well as the top lighting favoured for galleries. They also avoided the problem in modern 'classical' buildings of window openings – which of course did not occur in the Greek or Roman temples which inspired the stricter academic exercises in the neoclassic. On the outside the blind faces carried inspirational inscriptions in both Greek and English.

18 *Builder* 14 (4 October 1856), 536–7; *Building News* 3 (2 January 1857), 12–13 (Allom's plans); 5 (20 May 1859), 463; 6 (19 October 1860), 809; Burgoyne, *Library construction*, 167–70; Liverpool City Libraries, *Descriptive handbook with illustrations and plans* (Liverpool, 1912).
19 *Builder* 43 (26 August 1882), 285 and (9 September 1882), 347 with plate; Burgoyne, *Library construction*, 181–2; Kelly, *A history of public libraries*, 119; J. Convey, *The Harris Free Public Library and Museum, Preston: 1893–1993* (Lancashire County Books, 1993).

Segregation was handled vertically at Preston. Potentially noisy visitors remained on the ground floor in the closely monitored newsroom and the lending library, or milled around the full-size reproduction sculpture and architectural fragments – among them Michelangelo's tomb of Lorenzo de' Medici, and Ghiberti's doors to the Florentine Baptistery. Scholarly readers worked above, under the scrutiny of the librarian, and above them the art lovers circulated decorously in the gallery, viewing each other as well as the paintings. Only the last two groups used the impressive flight of steps up to the portico. Newsroom and lending library both had entrances opening directly from the street.

Vertical segregation was also used in Leeds, where the library formed part of the municipal buildings complex designed by George Corson between 1876 and 1884.[20] The newspaper room on the ground floor was immediately inside the doorway. Above it was the lending department. On the second and third floors, extending into the roof, was the double-height reference library. A gallery ran around this room, housing additional reference material and giving the room the appearance of a medieval college library. All floors and basement were served by a book hoist, but after discussion it had been decided not to incorporate a 'people hoist'.[21] Patrons mounted the stairs to progressively more serious material, and those physically fit enough to do so enjoyed the most spectacular feature of George Corson's design – the great staircase which joined the library to the municipal offices, a *tour de force* of Venetian Byzantine design, complete with elaborately drilled capitals, mosaics and sculptural decoration.

Swansea's library was opened in great style by William Gladstone MP in the Queen's Jubilee year of 1887, replacing rented premises and making room not only for a much expanded bookstock, but for an important collection of paintings which had been given to the city. Although combined with the art gallery and also schools of art and science, the architect – Henry Holtom – planned all of the main library functions on one floor by concentrating the non-library facilities in a four-storey block running 160 ft along the Alexandra Road frontage. The top two floors were given over to the technical schools and

20 *British Architect* 21 (25 January 1884), 40 and plate showing the grand staircase; *Builder* 47 (30 August 1884), 305 and plates; *Building News* 37 (1 August 1879), 122 and plate.
21 The servicing systems at Leeds were advanced and included an air-handling system, lifts and lighting (it was one of the first, if not the first library in Britain to be wired for electric lighting). For details see *The Electrician* 16 (1885–6), 104–5; also Leeds City Council, Electricity Department, *Electric lighting . . . particulars . . . 1883* (Leeds, 1882–3). See also report in *British Architect* 21 (1 February 1884), 54–5, reporting the British Museum trustees' decision in favour of electric lighting. One year later the trustees of the National Gallery 'continue to resist' according to D. Grant, 'The lighting of the National Gallery', *British Architect* 23 (13 February 1885), 80.

art gallery (top-lit behind a blind upper storey), and reached from a separate entrance. Laboratories, boiler rooms and other services were in the basement. The ground floor and its differently sized rear offshoot wings housed the library.[22]

The system of library observation and control at Swansea did provide a model of its kind. Library users were separated initially in the lobby: newspaper room patrons to the right, ladies to the magazine room on the left. A corridor running the length of the building conveyed borrowers into the railed-off delivery lobby, beyond which the loan collection was shelved in a small bookstack. A doorway in the corridor controlled access to the librarian's office and the committee room. Serious readers went straight ahead from the lobby to emerge into a circular domed reading room, surrounded by a security railing and a series of galleried alcoves. Except for the shallow alcoves, it was a miniature British Museum reading room! The reference was quite deliberate, as was made clear by the report accompanying the architect's competition drawings.[23] Off the reading room opened what the 1883 competition report called a reference library, with a gallery and a very substantial reserve of book storage beyond that available in the galleried alcoves surrounding the reading room. All of the main library spaces – loan collection, reading room and reference library – projected from the back of the main block and were lit by skylights. Scarcely changed today in its essentials, the circular reading room at Swansea gives the modern visitor one of the best surviving opportunities to experience the atmosphere of a late-Victorian library.[24]

22 *British Architect* 21 (23 February 1883), 92; 22 (21 November 1884), 246 and plate. See also E. Rees and G. Walters, 'Swansea's libraries in the 19th century', *Journal of the Welsh Bibliographical Society* 10 (1) (December 1965); G. Williams, 'A brief history of the establishment of a public library in Swansea and its subsequent development to the year 1919', unpublished ALA thesis (1973), and 'A history of Swansea Public Library 1870–1974, concentrating on the years 1870–1920', FLA thesis (1981).

23 As the competition winners stated in their report: 'we adopt a plan which possesses as its most striking feature, a central Reading Room and Reference Library, arranged upon the lines of the well-known Reading Room of the British Museum . . . allowing complete supervision by the Librarian's Assistants . . . of all that goes on in the Reading Room; any irregularities or disposition to pilfer on the part of the public can thus be effectively checked'. *New public library, art gallery, and science and art schools, Swansea: report accompanying designs submitted under the motto 'Morganwg'*, 1–2.

24 Sadly, the Victorian atmosphere at Swansea also extends to the lack of publicly accessible toilets (forcing users to walk to the station, or to invade the more user-friendly Art School on the floor above). The need to supervise public WCs was, however, anticipated by the architects, whose report proposes an arrangement whereby 'the care of them may be placed in the charge of a Barber Attendant, to the comfort of the public and the profit of the Institution, a rental being payable by the said attendant in lieu of the small sums which he would be authorized to charge'. *New public library*, 2.

Swansea's opening in 1887, along with other openings that year, marked a significant change of pace in library building. It was Gladstone himself – in yet another opening ceremony speech in 1891 – who drew attention to the dramatic change before and after the Queen's Jubilee. He told his audience:

> In the thirty-six years from 1850 onward – that is down to 1886 – 133 places had availed themselves of the [Public Library] Act . . . amounting on the average to four in each of those thirty-six years . . . Now, see the change which has taken place. We have only four years from 1887 to 1890, and in those four years no less than 77 places took advantage of the Act, so that instead of an average of less than four places in the year we have an average of more than seventeen places. Now certainly that is rapid progress . . .[25]

Adoption of the Act did not, of course, always result in a new library building; but the pace of library construction certainly picked up dramatically after 1887 as communities all over the country marked fifty years of Victoria's reign with new civic buildings, and London's parishes – which up to then had lagged embarrassingly behind the northern and midlands cities – used the occasion to secure adoption of the acts by actively promoting philanthropic support for new buildings. An important question remained to be answered, however. Who was going to design all of these new buildings as the campaign got into its stride following the Queen's Jubilee?

Architects versus librarians

Before 1887 few British architects had designed more than one new library building, and even fewer could claim any real expertise. James Hibbert was an exception. The architect of Preston's Harris Library was a long-time political supporter of the Free Library Movement, had travelled extensively at home and abroad visiting libraries, and published his findings in *The Preston Guardian* in 1879 and later in a privately produced book. As an alderman from 1874 and mayor of Preston for the year 1880–1, Hibbert contrived to have himself appointed architect while still serving on the board of trustees for the Harris bequest. Totally unethical by twenty-first-century standards – and questionable even then – the arrangement allowed him to build a highly personal but unusually well-informed vision of the ideal civic cultural building. But this was a unique situation, and Hibbert built only one library. Gilbert Scott built

---

25 W. E. Gladstone at the opening of the St Martin-in-the-Fields Public Library, 12 February 1891, quoted by Greenwood, *Public libraries*, xix. See also T. Kelly, *A history of public libraries*, 16, who picks up this point.

social libraries at Lewes and Dundee, plus a number of school and college libraries which had little to offer those planning the more complex municipal institutions.[26]

During the 1860s and 1870s Britain's most experienced library architect may well have been Alfred Waterhouse, whose early northern career had given him the opportunity to design an institute centred on a reading room for his fellow Quakers in Droylesden (1858), a reading room in Cumbria for an important future client, Joseph Pease (1861), the Bingley Mechanics' Institute (1862–5), and two of the Manchester Free Library Committee's branches – those at Rusholme (1865) and Every Street (1866) – before the philanthropist Thomas Taylor commissioned him to design and build the public library which he presented to Wigan (1873–8, see above). Later, Waterhouse found time to build the public hall, library and art school complex in Alloa, Scotland (1889) – the gift of Mr J. T. Patton – and a reading room with caretaker's cottage which he built at his own expense for his country estate at Yattendon in Berkshire.[27]

Criticism of the kind articulated by William Frederick Poole (of the Boston Athenaeum and later the Newberry Library in Chicago) attacking the designs of architects such as the influential Henry Hobhouse Richardson, whom Waterhouse admired, was beginning to be heard amongst Britain's librarians as they attempted to gather material on the latest and best design developments. When the first international conference of librarians was being planned in London for October 1877, the organiser, Edward Nicholson (Librarian of the London Institution and later of the Bodleian Library), wrote to the architectural journals inviting architects to submit designs for the accompanying exhibition, and tempting them with the promise that librarians from the USA would attend:

> The organising committee will gladly give room to any designs for a library that may be sent here. Will you allow me to add that, while librarians do not yield to other people in their appreciation of architectural beauty, they set a still higher value on the provision of as much shelf-room, as much reading space, and as much light as possible, and that the designs which best satisfy these conditions will undoubtedly attract the most notice.[28]

26 Cole, *Work of Scott.*
27 C. Cunningham and P. Waterhouse, *Alfred Waterhouse 1830–1905: biography of a practice* (Oxford, 1992). Illustrations include Droylesden (plate 23) and Bingley (plate 23). Waterhouse also acted as assessor for a number of library competitions: Blackburn Free Library and Museum 1871, Nottingham 1876, Barrow-in Furness Town Hall and Library 1877, Worcester's Victoria Institute 1890, Manchester's Whitworth Institute 1892, and the Wolverhampton Library 1897.
28 *Builder* 35 (1877), 867.

A strong contingent of Americans did indeed attend the conference at the London Institution in October 1877. Poole exhibited his 'Plans for a library, chiefly circulating, without galleries'[29] and spoke on the same topic. Some years later he was to publish his ideal plan for a small public library building which featured a single-storey book-room with book-cases no higher than the reach of a library assistant.[30] Presumably the London conference received an early version of this idea. Justin Winsor (Librarian of Harvard) and Melvil Dewey (managing editor of the newly founded *Library Journal*) provided useful information on the latest heating and lighting techniques, and strongly pushed the idea of book storage in what Winsor called 'packing rooms'.[31] Why the bookstack should often be presented as an American innovation is unclear, because Panizzi's proposal for the 'iron library' surrounding the British Museum's round reading room dated from 1852 and was itself based on an earlier scheme dating from sometime in the 1840s. The Americans may not have invented the bookstack, but they energetically promoted the idea as a means of securing an efficient, flexible and moderately heated book-storage system which was separate from whatever games architects and their patrons wanted to play in the public rooms. Poole was less interested in the bookstack *per se*, than in the provision of bookshelves no higher than an assistant could reach without steps, and in the general avoidance of architectural flights of fancy.

It was a British librarian, W. H. Overall of London's Corporation Library, who introduced the conference discussion of library buildings with the observation that 'the two great enemies to libraries were architects and gas'.[32] Overall went on to declare that the

> librarian's troubles begin with the commencement of the building, the architect desiring to erect a grand hall, often without the slightest regard to its use as a library. The question of galleries, again, becomes a nuisance – the architect for the sake of appearance, wishing to keep them at a great height; whilst the librarian, for the better working of the library, desires to keep them [i.e. the bookshelves] at a height which may be reached by the attendants without ladders.[33]

---

29 E. W. B. Nicholson and H. R. Tedder (eds.), *Transactions and proceedings of the conference of librarians . . . 1877* (London, 1878), Appendix, 209.
30 W. F. Poole, 'Small library buildings,' *Library Journal* 10 (1885), 250–6.
31 Nicholson and Tedder (eds.), *Transactions*, 148.
32 Nicholson and Tedder (eds.), *Transactions*, 147.
33 Nicholson and Tedder (eds.), *Transactions*, 147–8.

Overall's Guildhall Library – mentioned earlier as an example of the nave-and-side-aisle model – had been completed by the Corporation of London's Architect and Surveyor Sir Horace Jones, only five years earlier in 1872, as just such a 'grand hall' with an upper gallery and tall shelves.[34] In the architect's defence, it should be said that the Corporation wanted the central space in the library to be available for major public events, and this is how the space is used today. But Overall was right to complain. Few architects working in 1887 – still less in 1877 – could claim any real expertise in this field.

Architects, librarians and philanthropists

Ten years later the picture had been transformed by the appearance on the scene of a number of newly minted architectural specialists, a growing body of published material on library planning, and some notably fruitful partnerships between architects and librarians. The burst of Library Act adoptions and building activity sparked off by the Jubilee celebrations contributed to this process. But the late 1880s and 1890s were also marked by the beginnings of a new pattern of philanthropy, concentrating for the most part on smaller or medium-sized library buildings, but carried out on such a scale that the building campaigns quickly dwarfed earlier initiatives. Out of this nexus of activity emerged a cadre of library architects who had been able to hone their skills on a series of projects.

In south London, Lambeth's Jubilee campaign – chaired by the vicar (an unusually influential vicar, it should be said, who would soon inherit an earl-dom) and supported by no less a figure than the archbishop of Canterbury – persuaded the voters to adopt the Act, and inspired a consortium of local phi-lanthropists headed by the sugar millionaire Henry Tate, who together in 1887 agreed to sponsor four branches and a central library. All but one of the new Lambeth buildings were to be designed by the same architect, Sidney Smith. Smith had already worked for Tate at his mansion off Streatham Common, and was later to build libraries for him at Streatham and Balham, as well as the Tate Gallery of British Art at Millbank on which his reputation is based. It was the series of commissions for Lambeth libraries which launched Smith's career, however, together with the help he received from the newly appointed Lambeth librarian, Frank Burgoyne, whose influential book helped to publi-cise his designs, all of which (save Brixton's bigger central library) allowed easy

---

34 *Builder* 28 (27 August 1870), 684–7 with plans; 30 (1872), 878–9 for opening; *Building News* 24 (18 April 1873), 441–2.

supervision by a single duty assistant, and each one of which demonstrated Smith's facility with a different style of architecture.[35]

Serial philanthropy amongst Lambeth's neighbours in south London proved highly contagious. An anonymous offer of £2,000 for a new library building helped carry the adoption vote in Clapham in 1887. Lewisham adopted the Act in 1890, aided by an offer of £1,000 with a site and the prospect of another £1,500 from a local charity. In Camberwell, William Minet was inspired to remodel a memorial hall he was already constructing on his estate at Myatt's Fields as a library, and George Livesey (major shareholder in the South London Metropolitan Gasworks) offered another building on the condition that the voters adopt the Act – which they did by a substantial majority. Livesey appointed his own architect, George Whellock, to build his library on the Old Kent Road (opened 1889) and used his influence to have Whellock commissioned to design the Camberwell central library in Peckham (1893) and another branch which was planned for Nunhead. Whellock had become another specialist. But the ambitions of Camberwell could not match the sponsorship potential of Lambeth's 'great and good', and the building programme had to be rescued by the most important of London's library philanthropists. Passmore Edwards was already supporting an extensive programme of cultural building which eventually funded twenty libraries, museums and art galleries in London and another fifteen in his native Cornwall – together with numerous special homes and cottage hospitals, amounting in all to some seventy charitable institutions.[36]

Passmore Edwards knew more than most patrons about architecture. He had made a fortune in publishing and his ownership of *The Building News* brought him into contact with some of the best architects of the day. The architectural practice of Ernest George and Peto built the South London Art Gallery in Camberwell for him in 1893;[37] Henry Hare, a future President of the RIBA, designed one of Hoxton's branches; Harrison Townsend delivered the spectacular art nouveau picture gallery at Whitechapel in 1899 next door to the free library and museum which had launched Edwards's cultural philanthropy in London in 1891. Edwards's favourite library architect was Maurice B. Adams (1849–1933), who built six libraries for him in London.[38] Adams

35 Burgoyne, *Library construction*, 218–26 for the plans of Smith's buildings in Lambeth.
36 J. J. Macdonald, *Passmore Edwards institutions: founding and opening ceremonies* (London, 1900).
37 The firm was established by Sir Ernest George (1839–1922) and Harold Ainsworth Peto (1854–1933).
38 Adams was architect for the Shoreditch (extension of 1896), Hammersmith (1895–6), Edmonton (1897), South London Institute at Camberwell (1898), and Passmore Edwards

also exercised a much wider influence through his editorship of Passmore Edwards's *Building News*. Three times as many libraries were published by *Building News* during the 1880s and 1890s as by its three chief rivals, *The Builder*, *The Architect* and *The British Architect* combined. In 1890 Adams contributed a series of articles on library planning (later brought together in a book) and for years afterwards commented critically on designs and the public exhibition of competition drawings.[39] Eighteen years before Bertram's influential notes on small library planning were circulated by the Carnegie Foundation as a 'design guide' for architects, Maurice Adams was communicating directly with the British architectural profession, promoting a doctrine of functional library planning that was welcomed by most librarians for its concentration on planning for supervision with small numbers of staff, efficient book storage, the design of reading tables and issue desks, indicators, heating systems and lighting both artificial and natural. His own designs demonstrated a 'softer' more 'domestic' approach to the design of library buildings than that of many of his contemporaries. Adams's buildings sat comfortably in London's suburbs and may well have been seen by potential users as less institutional than the previous generation of classical or Gothic 'monuments'.

Much the most important support for public libraries of course came from Andrew Carnegie, who between 1889 and 1916 gave grants for some 3,000 library buildings – just over half of them in the United States, and the remainder spread throughout the English-speaking world, with 350 recorded completions in Great Britain (and a somewhat larger number of offers).[40] Carnegie's earliest gifts to his Dunfermline birthplace and the West Pennsylvania steel towns where his steel fortune had been made were similar to the most ambitious Victorian pioneer institutions. The library at the factory town of Braddock, Pennsylvania, was the first of his libraries to open its doors in 1889 and included smoking and games rooms, baths, swimming pool, gymnasium and an 'opera house' for lecture programmes and teaching performances on the Roosevelt

libraries at Shadwell (1898), Acton (1900) and the Wells Way Library and Baths, North Camberwell (1901–02). He also built the Carnegie library at Eltham.

39 The epigraph to this chapter marks the beginning of the series, *Building News* (6 June 1890), 789.

40 The Carnegie bibliography is immense. For Britain the pioneering work is A. J. W. Smith, 'Carnegie library buildings in Great Britain: an account, evaluation and survey', unpublished FLA thesis, 4 vols. (1974). For Ireland, see B. Grimes, *Irish Carnegie libraries: a catalogue and architectural history* (Dublin, 1998). Library architecture in the USA is excellently covered in A. A. Van Slyck, *Free to all: Carnegie libraries and American culture, 1890–1920* (Chicago, 1995) and many other publications. Carnegie Endowment for International Peace, *A manual of the public benefactions of Andrew Carnegie* (1919) provides a comprehensive review of Carnegie's numerous philanthropic programmes.

concert organ (which was supplied in a separate grant programme to many communities).[41] Later the focus was narrower, and although some grants were for multi-functional institutions, Carnegie money was restricted to the library building. Library grants were extended to other American and Scottish towns during the 1890s, and to places with a special call on his generosity. They were thrown open to Britain generally in a speech at London's Guildhall in 1902 when Andrew Carnegie received the freedom of the Worshipful Company of Plumbers.[42]

A flood of applications followed the Guildhall announcement and three out of every four grant offers to British towns were made during the years 1902–4, with the bulk of the building activity reaching completion in the years 1904–7.[43] Most of the British Carnegie libraries thus pre-dated the famous *Notes on the erection of library bildings* (*sic*) first issued in 1911, and the system which was started in 1908 requiring the prior approval of the plans of all buildings constructed with Carnegie's money.[44] The *Notes* and the planning approvals were both the responsibility of James Bertram, Carnegie's private secretary, and represent one of the first successful attempts to give design guidance to architects. British architects and librarians, however, generally had to find their own way.

Liverpool received the biggest Carnegie grant for an English city – £40,000 in all – for four branches and two reading rooms, all but one designed by the city surveyor, Thomas Shelmerdine. Unusually and somewhat controversially, Carnegie offered Liverpool his first gift without receiving a request, because he had been much impressed by the branch system that the city was already constructing on their own funds when, in October 1902, he was invited to open the South End Branch. Shelmerdine had designed this and other inner city branches, like Henry Tate's architect Smith in Lambeth using a rich variety of classical and Queen Anne styles. Carnegie's money paid for a splendid 'Free Renaissance' branch at West Derby opened in 1905 with a range of facilities normally found only in central libraries. The Garston branch followed in 1909, with an unusually free use of Arts and Crafts styling. The same 'domestic' emphasis was given to the most radical of Liverpool's branches, Sefton Park, which was opened by Andrew Carnegie himself on 3 August 1911, and contained a children's library, Liverpool's first open-access loan collection, and an all-female staff (a tradition which is still maintained at this branch).

41 S. Pepper, 'A department store of learning,' *Times Literary Supplement* (9 May 1986), 500.
42 *The Times* (15 May 1902), 14 and *Library Association Record* 4 (1902), 283.
43 Smith, *Carnegie library buildings*.
44 Van Slyck, *Free to all*, 34 citing Bobinski, 57.

Shelmerdine's conversion to what was seen as a more inviting design style at Garston and Sefton Park – together with the Committee's experiment in open access – contrasts sharply with the 'Municipal Baroque' employed at the Walton branch, opened in 1911, by Briggs, Wolstenholme and Thornely. Good of its kind and typical of the time, Walton was the outcome of an open competition which had delivered a conventional 'civic' solution.[45]

Municipal Baroque, Renaissance and Queen Anne were clearly the dominant styles in the public buildings of Edwardian England, but Gothic could still be found, as well as the Scottish and Welsh vernaculars and other local styles. Libraries not infrequently employed the Collegiate Gothic, sometimes called the Free Elizabethan, which made good use of large areas of glass. A splendid example of the latter is to be found in Cardiff's Cathays branch (1906), where two halls – one a newsroom, the other a children's library – are connected by a lower wing with a lobby and delivery desk in front of a radial stack. The building is decorated with fine art nouveau low reliefs.[46]

Edwardian Britain's leading library architect was Henry Hare, who had been spotted first by Passmore Edwards, and who went on to build half-a-dozen major civic libraries between 1902 and 1908.[47] Most of them were funded by Carnegie, including Islington (1905–6) which was the best-known – if not absolutely the first – open-access library in Britain to be designed as a new building. The title of 'first purpose-built open-access library' in Britain is fiercely contested amongst buildings designed and built in 1904–5, but generally given to the Carnegie Library at Kettering, Northamptonshire by Goddard, Paget and Catlow of Leicester.[48] However, the Victoria Institute, Worcester, opened its doors in October 1896 with an open-access lending department. 'A registered borrower, on producing a card, is passed through the entrance barrier into the Library by the official in charge, and he is then at liberty to

45 *Building News* 102 (9 February 1912), 215. The firm delivered the same architecture in two other Carnegie branches at St Helens, and in their competition-winning Carnegie library at Stafford.
46 Speir and Beavan were the architects. *Building News* 89 (22 December 1905), 8 and 65 and drawing; *Library Association Record* 5 (1903), 189; *The Builder* 92 (16 March 1907), 338; and photo of the children's hall in *Library World* 26 (1923–4), 215.
47 M. Dewe, 'H. T. Hare: Edwardian library architect', *Library Review* 27 (summer 1978), 80–4; and his 'Henry Thomas Hare, 1869–1921: an Edwardian public library architect and his work', unpublished MA dissertation, University of Strathclyde (1981). Hare built the Shoreditch library (with Spalding and Cross, 1897) and the Hoxton library in east London for Passmore Edwards (1896–8), and won the competition for the Oxford municipal buildings (1897, which included a city library). His other major public libraries were Wolverhampton (1902), Southend (1903), Hammersmith (1903), Harrogate (1904), Islington (1905) and Fulham (1908). Of these, all except Wolverhampton were Carnegie funded.
48 *Building News* 87 (7 October 1904), 504, with the plan and view exhibited at the 1904 Royal Academy (and thus widely seen).

choose any book on the shelves, and, handing it to the assistant in charge to be registered, at the same time presenting his card, is allowed to pass out. The system, when fully understood, is simplicity itself.'[49]

Hare developed a particular rapport with James Duff Brown, the leading British advocate of open access. Brown pioneered the system at Clerkenwell in 1894, in a building which had been completed only four years earlier as a closed-access library[50] but was altered to allow users of both reference and borrowing sections to enter the stacks. The newspaper room disappeared, as did the separate ladies' reading room. Brown believed that the social barriers of the classic Victorian library needed to be broken down, and when he was appointed librarian at Islington in 1904 he seized the opportunity, with Henry Hare as architect and Carnegie's money in support, to build a showcase central building. In 1907, shortly after the Islington Library was opened, architect and librarian shared a stage in the lecture hall at the Royal Institute of British Architects. Maurice Adams was in the chair.[51]

Islington's Central Library did away with the newspaper room, the ladies' room and the flats commonly provided for the librarian and caretaker.[52] A much enlarged general-purpose reading room was provided on the ground floor, and the stacks opened to the readers who were checked in and out from a desk with good sightlines into both stack and reading room. The children's room was located close to the front door, 'and in this position it is well placed to prevent children from wandering about the building'.[53] The reference library was upstairs, close to James Duff Brown's office, with standard works shelved on the wall. Much of the basement was occupied by an extensive bookstore (the term 'bookstack' was carefully avoided), with a book hoist serving the other floors.

49 Supplement to *The Worcester Herald* (3 October 1896), 3. See also *Building News* 66 (6 April 1894) 463–4, 481 and plates; *The Builder* 71 (17 October 1896), 317; also A. Cotgreave, *Views and memoranda of public libraries* (London, 1901), plan and photograph.
50 View and ground-floor plan in *Building News* 59 (1 August 1890), 138–40 and plan. The 1890 building was by Karslake and Mortimer. See also J. D. Brown, *Manual of library economy* (London, 1903).
51 H. T. Hare and J. D. Brown, 'Public libraries', *Journal of the Royal Institute of British Architects* 14 (March 1907), 341–57. See also H. T. Hare, 'Libraries', *Builders' Journal* 25 (20 March 1907), 130, and for Hare's Hammersmith design, 'Some recent public libraries', *Architectural Review* 24 (2) (1908), 228–49.
52 Islington Central was published in *Architectural Review* 18 (109) (December 1905), 243–61; *Academy Architecture and Architectural Review* 29 (1906), 29; *Building News* 90 (15 June 1906), 841 and plates; *The Builder* 94 (1 February 1908), 120 with plate. See also W. A. Munford, *James Duff Brown 1862–1912* (London, 1968).
53 A. Cox, 'Islington Central Library,' *Architectural Review* 18 (December 1905), 243. Cox was architect of Kingston Library.

Hare then presented a much simplified single-storey plan for a smaller building which incorporated many of the same ideas, and was clearly based on the Islington branch at Manor Gardens (1905–6) which he had just completed. Half the floor area of Hare's model small library was occupied by a general reading room, served by a radial open stack, and a central desk. Light readers and borrowers used the same space, off which a juvenile department and a reference room opened. A single librarian could move easily through the radial stack to keep an eye on the children and help the serious students in the reference rooms, without losing sight of the main space or anyone waiting at the desk for more than a few moments. In Hare's opinion, this had more to do with standards of service than with close supervision because – in his words – it was 'easy to exaggerate the importance of supervision . . . In practice the public using the library very largely supervise themselves.'[54]

James Duff Brown told his audience that he wanted architects to continue to experiment freely, but not with the 'overbuilding' that Carnegie's millions were by then beginning to encourage – leaving many towns with 'collections of bricks rather than of books'.[55] He then reran his arguments in favour of open access, whenever possible from open shelves on the walls. An up-to-date collection, he argued, needed less storage space than was supposed by advocates of closed stacks because – if the library was working properly – much of it would be out on the bookshelves in borrowers' houses. Brown finished with unusually charitable remarks about architects whose ideas were so often thwarted by cost constraints and the ignorance of clients, which nevertheless did nothing to spare him from criticism. He concluded, 'Painters do not paint, nor do poets write, on these terms.'[56]

The librarian as designer

It would be misleading to present the harmony between Henry Hare and James Duff Brown as a final outbreak of peace between professions so often critical of each other. But it did mark a maturity in dealings between the two professions, which on both sides of the Atlantic would increasingly see those architects specialising in library design attending librarians' conferences, and librarians taking a more prominent role in library design.[57] In the United

54 Hare and Brown, 'Public libraries', 344.
55 Hare and Brown, 'Public libraries', 348.
56 Hare and Brown, 'Public libraries', 352.
57 The United States produced a number of 'specialists' who accumulated impressive totals of library buildings completed and, with them, gained enormous experience.

States William Poole's combative manner made his views more controversial and unacceptable than they deserved. Even so, Poole as a librarian played a key role in the design of two of the greatest American library buildings: the Chicago Public Library (when it was rebuilt many years after the fire which had destroyed much of the city in 1871) and the Newberry Reference Library in the same city which was based both conceptually and architecturally on specialist subject collections, housed in numerous study rooms where the books would be immediately to hand for the scholar.

The rapid development of electric lighting and ventilation systems in the early years of the twentieth century was first exploited by American library architects in the evolution of designs for what today would be called deep-floor-plate plans. Books could be stored far from windows across the full width and depth of a library, and sometimes extended far into the ground. When Baltimore, Maryland, rebuilt the Enoch Pratt Free Library in the late 1920s and early 1930s, this approach allowed the books to be housed underground and the main library spaces to open directly from the pavement. Passers-by could look directly into the library through 'shop windows'. For the first time in a major city institution the customers entered a 'democratic library' without first having climbed a monumental flight of steps.[58] Advanced developments in Britain, however, were proceeding in parallel with those in the United States, and it fell to Manchester – so long without a purpose-built central library – to take the initiative.

Manchester had been amongst the first northern cities to open a rate-supported public library in 1852. However, it was another eighty years (and an abortive architectural competition in 1910–11 for a new central library and art gallery) before the collection found a permanent home in a purpose-designed building.[59] In 1920 powers to buy a site were acquired and in 1926 an architectural competition was held for the design. Stanley Jast, Manchester's chief librarian, spelt out the strategy for the proposed new library in a lecture to University College London in December 1926 and, since he had by then also established the schedule of accommodation for the competition, it is clear that here too the librarian effectively set the agenda. He also presented a

---

58 See J. L. Wheeler and A. M. Githens, *American public library building* (New York, 1941), 324–7 for plans of Enoch Pratt.

59 Early accommodation for 20,000 books was found in the Hall of Science, Campfield (1852–77), in the old Town Hall in King Street (1877–1912), and in a temporary building in Piccadilly from 1912, with overflow storage in the old Infirmary (1916) and a YMCA hut (1919). See also 'The competition for library and art gallery, Manchester', *The Builder* 101 (15 December 1911), 707–20, and M. Hewitt, 'Confronting the modern city: the Manchester Free Public Library, 1850–80', *Urban History* 27 (2000), 62–88.

diagram of a free-standing square-plan library building with deep-floor-plate underground stacks. 'There is, of course, no doubt that all public buildings should be on island sites on esthetic [*sic*] grounds alone. A fine building deserves a fine setting. But a library demands an island site on practical grounds, and not merely because you cannot forecast its ultimate expansion.' Jast insisted on what he called a 'cross-stack', that is, a bookstack running right across the building. He contended

> that in storing books horizontal area is preferable to vertical area; that the more books you can store on one level the better; in a word, that breadth of stack is more convenient than height of stack. Instead therefore of concentrating books at the back of the building or running around the building I would run the bookstack through the building . . . across, from side to side, and from the back to as near the front as may be desirable . . . The immense convenience of it and the economy of labour it secures, may be seen, almost at a glance in the diagram.[60]

In his competition-winning design Vincent Harris proposed a circular rather than a square plan, with a round reading room in the panopticon tradition and a free-standing block as Jast had wanted. The section makes it clear that the architect had paid close attention to the librarian's ideas about book storage. American connections were clear too. Jast accompanied Harris in a tour of American libraries just after the architect had been appointed. They had visited the almost completed library at Wilmington, Delaware, designed by Edward Tilton and Morton Githens just before Tilton was commissioned to rebuild Baltimore's Enoch Pratt Free Library but embodying many of the same ideas. Wilmington, Baltimore and Manchester shadowed each other closely. In all three, deep floor plates were employed, and 'William Poole's specialist collections' were to be found in a series of small and medium-sized reading rooms. Although Manchester's main reference library was at first-floor level, above the stacks, it was reached by an internal staircase, not the monumental external steps which characterised most big city institutions in Britain and America. Entry to the popular lending library was practically at street level.

Librarians recognised immediately that Manchester was the first British big-city library with contemporary planning and social agenda: architects, not for the first time, were sidetracked by style. Harris had used the 'stripped Classical' style for his building, with low-relief decoration and simplified

---

60 L. S. Jast, *The planning of a great library* (London, 1927) gives the full text of his lecture. See also W. G. Fry and W. A. Munford, *Louis Stanley Jast: a biographical sketch* (London, 1966), 41–56, for his time at Manchester.

orders – a widely employed compromise between the full-bodied classicism of the Edwardian years and the bare surfaces and informal volumes of the emerging International Style. Sir Charles Reilly – the premier architectural critic of the time – saw, and disliked, a 'Roman' building, and in the reading room a Pantheon, not a Panopticon. Reilly was then metamorphosing into Modernism, but completely missed Manchester's modern library features and close links with American practice.[61]

Perhaps by 1934 'style' – for so long an important element in the presentation of this most didactic of building types – was beginning to obscure rather than to illuminate. If so, it was to prove only a temporary retreat from centre stage. A vigorous but difficult to classify 'style' was to return to library architecture with a vengeance in the closing decade of the twentieth century, when signature buildings like Will Alsop's Peckham Library (now a branch of the Southwark system) were presented as growth points for community regeneration as well as a new type of public information centre. Little was really new, of course. From their inception public libraries had been credited with the ability to deliver a broad range of potential social and economic benefits, and their sponsors clearly wanted to signal the importance of this mission with high-style design. Peckham, with its community facilities, Internet cafe and job centre, stands firmly within a tradition of library design that has its roots in the ambitions of Victorian philanthropists and city fathers.

61 C. H. Reilly, 'Manchester's Reference Library', *Building* 9 (1934), 44–52.

PART VIII

*

AUTOMATION PASTS, ELECTRONIC FUTURES: THE DIGITAL REVOLUTION

47

Introduction: the digital revolution in society and in libraries

GRAHAM JEFCOATE

At the beginning of the twenty-first century it is apparent that developments in information technology over the last fifty years – and the 'information revolution' these have made possible – have changed and are changing libraries and librarianship profoundly. As a term 'library automation' implies a rather mechanical process, one in which existing operations carried out manually are made more efficient by the introduction of machine-based techniques. Gutenberg's introduction of printing with movable types into Europe in the fifteenth century could also best be described as the 'automation' of a previously existing process, that is, the mass-production of identical copies of texts in medieval scriptoria. But Gutenberg's invention, by creating a new information 'platform', was to transform discourse and the exchange of ideas fundamentally. It also provided the necessary basis for the emergence of modern libraries, a process driven (though this is often overlooked) by the new medium of print. In the same way, it is now a truth universally acknowledged that the development of digital information and network services will transform both the information process and the organisation of knowledge in libraries.

Modern librarianship increasingly focuses on two aspects of library management: preservation and access. The preservation of 'legacy' collections in a variety of media (both analogue and digital) is now recognised as a primary task for libraries. Of equal importance is the provision of improved access to a knowledge base that is both analogue and digital through the development of electronic information services. British libraries, often by seizing on opportunities presented by developments in the United States, can be said to be at the forefront of such developments in Europe. Much effort has been invested in the retrospective conversion of existing data (for example library catalogues) to machine-readable form; for most significant research collections at least, this process is now largely complete. Resources are increasingly being directed to the selective digitisation of collections either as sequences of images or as full-text archives that can be searched and interrogated through specialised interfaces. Libraries are offering such services in the context of an array of commercially produced databases and online information services of varying quality available via the Internet.

The electronic future therefore presents a range of serious challenges for libraries and librarians today. Libraries will need to redefine themselves as organisational entities in physical and virtual space. In what relationship will physical library stores of print and manuscript, with their associated reading rooms, stand with virtual information archives and associated online services? What relationship will libraries have one to another? In a world of digitised images and online services what will distinguish libraries from other information providers, for example museums and archives? What role will librarians (or rather 'information specialists') play in a world where users are increasingly empowered to access data directly? Will they be able to develop and market skills as 'information mediators' or 'knowledge managers' guaranteeing quality in a world of information overload? The answers to these and other questions raised by the advent of information technology will determine the development of libraries and professional librarianship over the next decades. Will a new edition of the *Cambridge history of libraries* in a hundred years address this paradigm shift or will it acknowledge that libraries and librarians were organisations and professionals that could not be untied from the 'legacy' media of manuscript and print?

48

Automating the library process

ERIC HUNTER

First applications of computers

If one consults the third edition of the *Encyclopaedia of librarianship*, published in 1966, entries under 'Automation' or 'Computers' are conspicuous by their absence.[1] Despite this omission, although no British university library had any application of automatic data processing fully operational at that time, at least four public libraries were already producing printed catalogues by computer.[2] The reorganisation of the London boroughs meant that librarians were faced with the considerable problem of amalgamating their catalogues, and the boroughs of Barnet, Camden, Greenwich and Southwark decided to use a computer system to help achieve this. These first cataloguing systems were based on 80-column punched cards, with the resulting catalogue being produced by a line printer.[3] Once started, however, progress in implementing automated systems gathered pace. By 1970, at least thirty public library systems had automated some part of their routine work; many others were in process of implementing plans and some thirteen university libraries were using computers in systems claimed to be operational.[4]

Public libraries made use of the mainframe computers operated by their local authorities but suffered from the disadvantage that priority would very probably be given to non-library operations.[5] None the less, surveys carried out during the 1970s provide clear evidence of the growing acceptance of automation in the public library field. In 1979, the types of application with the number of operating authorities included: selection (1); ordering (16); cataloguing (55);

1 T. Landau (ed.), *Encyclopaedia of librarianship*, 3rd rev. edn (London, 1966).
2 W. R. Maidment, 'Management of libraries and mechanization', in H. A. Whatley (ed.), *British librarianship and information science 1966–70* (London, 1972), 219.
3 L. A. Tedd, *An introduction to computer-based library systems*, 3rd edn (London, 1993), 4.
4 Maidment, 'Management of libraries and mechanization', 219.
5 J. Leeves, 'Library systems then and now', *Vine* 100 (1995), 19.

subject or other printed indexes (30); accession and shelf lists (24); circulation (47); and accounting (34).[6]

In academic libraries, research funding from OSTI (the Office for Scientific and Technical Information that later became the British Library Research and Development Department) enabled university libraries to experiment with computer applications. Automation was costly; 'without OSTI's support library automation would have developed much more slowly'.[7]

Two examples of OSTI-funded projects could be found at the University of Newcastle-upon-Tyne, where the work was concerned with acquisitions, and the University of Southampton, where the emphasis was on circulation control. Both of these systems achieved some success, but many of the early computer-based library systems failed for reasons such as the lack of understanding by librarians and computer personnel of the requirements of such systems and the inadequacies of the systems themselves.[8] Woods reported that, at Southampton: 'We managed to get a few systems up and running, and we felt that each system that worked was a triumph [but] the pioneers of library automation explored new territory, and sometimes got lost.'[9]

In the sixties, librarians as a body had absolutely no experience of automation; 'a typical automation librarian would have been . . . as a computer user, totally naïve'.[10] In addition, it would be fair to describe many librarians as neo-Luddites; to them the word 'computer' was anathema. However, to the more technically aware, although the full potential of automation had yet to be appreciated, it was becoming clear that here was an administrative and management tool that could remove much of the drudgery from routine clerical tasks such as filing, a tool that could provide better control, improve efficiency and help achieve higher productivity, and a tool that could extend the service and permit increased co-operation with other libraries and information services. In addition, automated systems could generate the data that competent management and effective decision making depend upon.

Impact on staff and user perceptions

In the early days of automation it was also thought that the computer could save time, save staff and therefore save money. In the long term, staff time

6 'Computers in British public libraries: a survey', *Program* 13 (1979), 37.
7 R. G. Woods, 'How did we get here from there? Reminiscing on the early days of library automation', *Program* 21 (1987), 238.
8 Tedd, *Introduction to computer-based library systems*, 4.
9 Woods, 'How did we get here from there?', 236, 241.
10 Woods, 'How did we get here from there?', 236.

could certainly be saved but concern about staff redundancies proved to be unfounded. Indeed, staff might well be redeployed to more rewarding tasks.

Staff responses could be enthusiastic but often automation resulted in misgivings about this sudden, dramatic technological change. Dyer, for instance, notes that, apart from job security, these misgivings related to job content, the need for new skills, the use of work monitoring, health and safety issues, and stress arising from system maintenance and possible failure.[11] To counteract staff concerns, effective communication at the planning stage, participative management and adequate staff training became essential requisites when an automated system was being implemented.

One comforting thought for staff was that automated library facilities very soon became extremely popular with the user. For instance, one of the major findings of an early extensive study of the OPAC (Online Public Access Catalogue) in the United States, was that there is great user satisfaction with this form of catalogue and 94% of users preferred it to previous forms.[12] Follow-up studies have tended to confirm these findings. 'Added-value' facilities such as borrower information, reservations, circulation status, etc., are much appreciated by clients.

The more technology that is introduced, the more the image of the librarian appears to be enhanced; online catalogues, CD-ROM, access to the Internet and so on have had, and continue to have, a significant PR impact.

In many instances, the user's first impression of the library, as he or she enters, has undergone a transformation. In the writer's own Liverpool John Moores University library, for instance, the first thing that meets the eye is not the bookshelves but the rows of computer terminals which can be used to access all of the University's information services and also act as a gateway to external networks. At the enquiry desks, information and advice can be obtained not only from qualified library staff but also from computer services personnel.

Liverpool JMU is, in fact, one of those academic libraries where automation and the library's role in providing electronic and networked information have led to the convergence of the library with the computing service. Such a development is not unusual; research undertaken in the UK in 1997 revealed that over 50% of those academic institutions surveyed had converged to a greater or lesser degree.[13] Overall, user attitudes to convergence are uncertain

11 H. Dyer with A. Morris, *Human aspects of library automation* (Aldershot, 1990), 207.

12 J. R. Matthews, G. S. Lawrence and D. Ferguson (eds.), *Using online catalogs: a nationwide survey* (New York 1983).

13 L. Pugh, 'Some theoretical bases of convergence', *The New Review of Academic Librarianship* 3 (1997), 65.

but, in the case of LJMU, it has led to a significant increase in student use, and staff computer support is highly valued. Where both library and computer staff are concerned, 'convergence can generate an enormous amount of resistance' but 'staff working in most university libraries will need to develop exactly the kind of skills . . . which convergence encourages'.[14] One danger to be avoided, of course, is the possible downgrading and devaluation of the library bookstock.

The provision of computers for public use is not confined to academic libraries; they can now be found in most local libraries. These can be used not only as stand-alone machines but also to access the Internet. It has become imperative that front-line public library staff are able to use electronic sources and to navigate the Web effectively. Individual institutions hold staff training courses and there are wider initiatives. For example, a £20 million New Opportunities programme of training for public library staff was announced in 1999.[15]

Outside of the library, multi-media personal computers, with graphic user-interfaces (GUIs) such as Windows, and with modems for external access, have now become almost an essential requisite, especially in those homes with growing children. Computers are also in widespread use in schools. Children and young people are therefore more able to understand and accept computerised systems and their appreciation of libraries is thereby enhanced; 'automation attracts young researchers'.[16]

As the impact of technological advance has intensified, staff have had to respond positively to changing user perceptions and increased expectations of levels of service.

Standardisation

It was realised at an early stage in the development of computer applications that a library that acted unilaterally and used an in-house record format would be unable to receive supplied data from a central source or exchange bibliographic data with other institutions. What was needed was a communication format. This led to the development of the MARC (MAchine Readable Cataloguing) format. MARC came into being in the United States in 1966, and the following year the British National Bibliography (later to become part of the

14 P. Sykes and S. Gerrard, 'Operational convergence at Roehampton Institute London and Liverpool John Moores University', *The New Review of Academic Librarianship* 3 (1997), 84.
15 'New library training boost', *Library Association Record* 101 (1999), 499.
16 C. Strickland, 'Young users', *Wilson Library Bulletin* 62 (1988), 65.

British Library) began work on the development of a MARC system in the UK. Machine readable tapes were being distributed to libraries by 1969.

The need for standardisation had led to the development of *Anglo-American cataloguing rules* (AACR) and MARC was, and is, based upon this standard. Therefore, despite its widespread use, the MARC record remains an automated version of a manual catalogue entry. As such, some librarians question whether MARC is the most suitable format for machine-based systems. However, to date, although there are proposed metadata standards for use on the Internet such as the Dublin Core (a system in which tagged description, identification and location information is included in Web documents), no recognised new form of record has become established.

Initially, some library system developers preferred to use a more simplified record structure than MARC provided, and there were a number of non-standard schemes such as Loughborough University of Technology's Minicat, an automated 'minimum input with maximum output' cataloguing system. However, it was not long before MARC could be accessed online and it began to spread its influence across the whole spectrum of library activity, including selection, ordering, cataloguing, information retrieval and the production of bibliographies. The format became the heart of many library networks.

Networks established

Inspired by the establishment of the Ohio Colleges Library Center (OCLC; later the Online Computer Library Center) in America, in 1967, certain libraries in the UK decided that the sharing, or networking, of resources could result in greater efficiency and lower costs. The first UK co-operative automated cataloguing service was the Birmingham Libraries Cooperative Service (later BLCMP), which came into being in 1969. This Birmingham-based service was later extended to a large number of libraries of all types and sizes, and to the original cataloguing system were added other modules. SWALCAP, the South-West Academic Libraries Cooperative Automation Project (later SLS), also began in 1969. From its university roots SLS grew into a leading developer and supplier of automated library systems internationally.

Another co-operative, or network, LASER (London and South East Library Region), originated in the 1930s as SERLS (South East Regional Library System). Like other regional library systems, its main aim was to facilitate the inter-lending of books between libraries in the area. LASER was automated in 1970 and subsequently extended its services to include cataloguing and innovative technological developments.

The British Library began to develop a general-purpose automated network system in 1975. Known as MERLIN (Machine Readable Library Information), the system included online book-ordering, acquisition, cataloguing and lending modules. The library community held out high hopes for this system but unfortunately these hopes were dashed when government financial cuts resulted in the suspension of development in 1979.

A more successful British Library initiative, BLAISE (the British Library Automated Information Service) became operational in 1977. In addition to several medical databases (e.g. MEDLINE, TOXLINE, etc.), BLAISE could be used to search the UK and US MARC bibliographic databases. From its inception, BLAISE was envisaged as a complete online bibliographic service, supporting library functions as varied as cataloguing, information retrieval, acquisitions and bibliographic checking.[17] It also became possible for registered users of the British Library Lending Division to request to borrow, whilst online, any required material, a service which was well used.[18]

Linked with BLAISE was the British Library Bibliographic Services Division's Local Cataloguing Service (LOCAS). MARC-based microform catalogues were produced and maintained for each participating library. At its peak in 1983, nearly eighty libraries were receiving LOCAS catalogues[19] but batch-processed services were steadily overtaken both economically and technically and LOCAS ceased to be a mainstream British Library service in 1988.

One of the functions of the BLAISE MARC databases was to aid in the retrospective conversion of existing manual records. This was, and is, a major problem for libraries when implementing automated operations. Conversion can take many years and prove very costly. In the meantime, multiple catalogues, the new automated and the old manual, have to be maintained. There is a danger that the old catalogue may not be used and that the stock listed therein may fall into desuetude. There is no complete, ideal answer and many libraries have had to live with this situation. A range of conversion methods has been tried. They include direct keyboarding, buying in records from an external source, or using scanning and optical character recognition techniques. Bibliographic utilities such as BLCMP have also provided retrospective conversion services.

Subsequent to its inception, BLAISE established itself as one of the world's largest networks and its history has been one of continual development and

17 J. Lowery, 'Blaise of glory – twenty years of service to the online community', *Select: The Newsletter of the National Bibliographic Service, The British Library* (1997), 3.

18 L. A. Tedd, 'Computer-based information retrieval systems', in L. J. Anthony (ed.), *Handbook of special librarianship and information work*, 5th edn (London, 1982), 338.

19 *BL Bibliographic Services Newsletter* 41 (1986), 2.

innovation. From 1996 access was provided to BLAISE databases via the World Wide Web and the next year saw OPAC 1997 launched, offering free access to the British Library catalogue via the Web.

After twenty-two years of service to the online community, BLAISE was phased out in 2000; the British Library announced that, unfortunately, it was 'no longer economically viable to mount external files on the current system'.[20] A new database service had to be developed. At the same time the British Library Public Catalogue (BLPC) replaced OPAC97. Like its predecessor, this offered online access to more than 10 million records of items in the British Library collection, plus a document-ordering link. The online retailer Amazon.co.uk announced in 1999 that it was to sponsor the BL catalogue, and this support, to the relief of all librarians, meant that the BL could continue to allow free access.[21] The BL is presently implementing an Integrated Library System (ILS) that will replace the Library's main existing systems for acquisitions, cataloguing and cataloguing access within reading rooms and via the Web. This system went live in 2004.[22]

By the early 1980s, it was becoming clear that it was desirable to have some means of co-ordinating the work of the existing networks in the UK, and the British Library played a leading role in attempting to do this. A Cooperative Automation Group (CAG) was formed under its auspices. Membership included representatives from all of the major networks and nominees from other bodies. The Group decided to focus upon the possibility of creating a common database – a UK Library Database (UKLDS), which would make bibliographical records available for cataloguing purposes and provide locations for reference and lending use. However, financial support was not forthcoming, and in 1984 CAG concluded that it was no longer a realistic objective to pursue the establishment of UKLDS.[23]

CAG continued to exist but the main force shifted to a Steering Group, in which representatives of the British Library and the co-operatives continued to meet, thus providing a forum for the discussion of issues of common interest.

Further networking developments

The Joint Academic Network, JANET, inaugurated in 1984, provided links between computer facilities in universities, higher educational establishments,

---

20 *Select: The Newsletter of the National Bibliographic Service, The British Library* (2000), 5.

21 *Library Technology* 4 (1999), 27.

22 Internet web page: http://www.bl.uk.

23 Cooperative Automation Group, Press release (London, 1984).

research centres and other institutions. It could be used for e-mail, for access to computers at other sites, for example to consult online catalogues, and for the transfer of files between sites (Electronic Data Interchange or EDI). JANET permits access through gateways to the Internet and other networks. SuperJANET, a new optical fibre network, was installed on a pilot basis in 1993 and all sites had high-speed access (SuperJANET3) by 1998. A SuperJANET4 was launched in 2001 and a SuperJANET5 is currently in process.[24]

Although JANET was not intended originally for library use, it was libraries that seized hold of its potential and quickly made it an indispensable part of their operations for information retrieval and technical services.

What has been referred to as 'the dream of UKLDS revisited'[25] began in 1987 when CURL (Consortium of University Research Libraries) received funding from the Universities Funding Council to establish a project for resource sharing and exchange of data using JANET.[26] A union catalogue database was created jointly by the seven largest university libraries in the United Kingdom. This resource was available to non-CURL members over JANET.

Initially, the CURL service was only accessible to library staff but it was recognised that it could be of value to end-users too if it could be made available in an appropriate form. Thus, in 1995, a grant was made by JISC (Joint Information Systems Committee) to fund a project to produce an OPAC based on the CURL database (the CURL OPAC or COPAC), providing direct end-user access to the unified resources of the CURL member libraries.[27] Based at the University of Manchester, COPAC now provides centralised access to this online service. Currently there are some 30 million records on COPAC representing the merged holdings of twenty-six CURL member institutions.[28]

Networking developments were becoming so vitally important to libraries that a British Library press release of 1989 stated that: 'Many librarians feel a sense of frustration at the scale of the issues involved. They find it difficult to keep abreast of technical and organisational initiatives and the many developments at a national and international level.'[29] To help librarians cope with the problems as outlined, the British Library funded the setting up of a UK Office for Library Networking (UKOLN), based at the University of Bath. The aims

24 Internet web page: http://www.ja.net.
25 J. E. Rowley, 'New technology in libraries', in D. W. Bromley and A. M. Allott (eds.), *British librarianship and information work 1986–1990*, vol. 2 (London, 1993), 235.
26 S. Perry, 'The CURL database project', *Vine* 73 (1988), 4.
27 S. Cousins, 'COPAC: new research library union catalogue', *Electronic Library* 15 (1997), 185.
28 Internet web page: http://copac.ac.uk.
29 'UK Office for Library Networking established at Bath University' (London 1989). British Library Press release.

were to represent the needs of libraries to the computing and telecommunications industry and to promote the effective use of existing and developing networking infrastructure.

Seven years after CURL came into being, UK public libraries began to follow suit and investigate the networking of public libraries. It was agreed that LASER should co-ordinate and manage the project, called EARL (Electronic Access to Resources in Libraries). As with CURL, one of the aims of EARL was to facilitate information and resource sharing.[30] From its inception in 1994 EARL undertook many activities to support its partners, the number of which grew rapidly from the original six into almost 200 by the year 2000. Activities were then taking place in the context of preparation for the People's Network. The EARL Consortium for Public Library Networking revolutionised the public library landscape by offering public libraries a web presence as well as models for national networked services.

The idea for the People's Network originated in a 1997 report commissioned from LIC (the Libraries and Information Commission) by the Department for Culture, Media and Sport.[31] The government response to this report pointed to an information policy with a strong emphasis on a central role for public libraries. Subsequently, LIC appointed a Chief Network Adviser to oversee development and 100% coverage of UK public libraries was planned for 2002.[32] This initiative was part of the government's intention to give everyone in the United Kingdom the opportunity to use computers and access the Internet. At the time of writing, 4,000 ICT library centres are up and running and the government is committed to providing Internet access to all those who would like it by 2005.[33] The People's Network is the key to making this happen.

Offline to online integrated systems

The first library computer applications were offline. Computer-produced catalogues, for example, were in 'book' form. Either the computer 'print-out' itself would be used as a 'master' and then reproduced by xerography or some other method, or photocomposition would be used, the page master in this instance being a photographic negative. In the late 1960s attention first focused on the possibility of microform catalogues. Magnetic-tape output was processed into

---

30 P. Smith, 'Networking in public libraries: collaborative developments at LASER', *Vine* 98 (1995), 17.

31 Library and Information Commission, *New library: the people's network* (London, 1997).

32 Library Association, *Annual report, 1999* (London, 2000), 11.

33 Internet web page: http://www.peoplesnetwork.gov.uk.

a microform (COM – Computer Output Microform). Microform catalogues offered the advantage of being compact and easy to reproduce and they became very common in the UK in the 1970s.

Although online access to external databases had been available for some years, it was not until after 1980 that the first in-house online applications began to appear. Following developments in online real-time circulation systems and the offshoot of online public-access catalogues in the United States, the honour of being the first library in the United Kingdom to introduce online public access must probably go to the University of Hull, where a GEAC circulation system was acquired in 1980 and an associated OPAC went live in 1981.

GEAC was of the world leaders in what was called the 'turnkey' system (as easy as turning a key in a lock). Prior to this time, as noted previously, those public, academic and special libraries which developed automated housekeeping systems did so by making use of the large computers, either mainframe or mini, operated by their own local authorities or institutions.

The turnkey system was a complete package of hardware and software that could be quickly installed without the need to consider relative compatibility. Many of the systems on offer were US or Canadian in origin and in the early days most of them concentrated, as GEAC did, on circulation, that being seen as most appropriate to local control. Cataloguing was still done separately, often using a batch service such as the British Library's LOCAS or the cataloguing services of a co-operative such as BLCMP.[34]

To certain librarians, however, it was glaringly obvious that the automation of a particular process should not be undertaken in a vacuum. Records relating to material in stock, or to be added to stock, can be used for various operational functions, e.g. ordering, cataloguing, circulation and derivation of management information. What was needed was a fully integrated system.

The importance of integration was recognised by the networks and by commercial turnkey package suppliers, and during the 1980s concerns such as ALS, BLCMP, CLSI, DYNIX, GEAC, McDonnell Douglas (URICA) and SWALCAP began to offer such systems, a 'total' package including acquisition, cataloguing, circulation and statistical information. By 1986, there were nineteen suppliers of so-called integrated library systems on the market. Not all of these systems offered all of the functions, for example serials control, that a library might require, and inter-library loan modules were virtually unheard of.[35] Such modules were, however, added at a later date. The complexities of

34 Leeves, 'Library systems then and now', 20.
35 Leeves, 'Library systems then and now', 21.

serials control became an 'increasingly important aspect of library automation'[36] but the inter-library loan module was 'normally left until the very end
of the development cycle', if indeed it was ever offered.[37]

Microcomputer-based systems

At about the same time as turnkey systems were being introduced, the Apple
II and, later, the IBM PC started a boom in the purchase of smaller computers
for business purposes. The microcomputer began to put automation within
the reach of *all* libraries, large and small.

At first, libraries that wished to make use of the microcomputer had to
program and develop their own packages. Storage was a particular problem.
The Apple II had a 48K (some 48,000 characters) internal memory, extremely
small measured against library needs. The external 5-inch diameter floppy
disc might hold some 360K but this still fell far short of what was required
and multiple discs would be needed for a viable system, thus necessitating
numerous disc-changes when the system was in use. A further difficulty was
that early machines were single-user, single-task machines.

By the mid-eighties, however, dramatic increases in storage capacity and
improvements in operating systems began to make micro-based systems
a more practical possibility and commercial packages started to appear.
The University of Buckingham, for instance, used a version of Eurotec's
LIBRARIAN, with a 20 Mb hard disc which it was estimated would accommodate some 40,000 catalogue entries and 60,000 related subject index entries.[38]

Among the smaller types of library to benefit from the microcomputer were
the school library and the special library. Where the latter was concerned,
prior to 1986, it was mainly the library and information service units in the
manufacturing sector that had automated libraries, mounted on mainframes
or minis. Glaxo, for example, made use of the CAIRS package. The coming of
the microcomputer with popular packages such as MicroCAIRS and TINLIB,
suddenly enabled the smaller units to 'perform functions that they had not
had time for before and to be more professional in their approach. The major
requirements were for a simple online catalogue, online ordering, circulation
and serials control, preferably with some accounting facility.'[39] Developments

---

36 'Serials control systems: an overview', *Vine* 87 (1992), 2.
37 'Inter-library lending and document delivery: an overview', *Vine* 95 (1994), 3.
38 J. E. Pemberton, 'Cataloguing on a micro with Librarian', *Library Micromation News* 3
(1984), 7–14.
39 O. Freeman, 'Industrial and commercial libraries', in Bromley and Allott (eds.), *British
librarianship and information work 1986–1990*, vol. 2, 76–7.

in local area networking (LAN) technology further enhanced the usefulness of the microcomputer and it could be used as an intelligent terminal for online access to wide area networks such as BLAISE. Records could be selected online and processed offline, thus reducing connect time and telecommunications costs.

The microcomputer also acquired an additional facility – the CD-ROM drive. The optical disc enabled vast amounts of information to be stored in digital form. For library purposes, at that time, this provided great advantages. As an example, the British Library's *General catalogue of printed books* was launched on CD-ROM in 1989: 178,000 pages from 360 folio volumes were contained on three small (4³/₄ inch diameter) discs. CD-ROMs became very common; there was, and is, a wide range of material for use in information work. The networking of CD-ROMs further enhanced their usefulness.

It was claimed by some that CD-ROM would be a good medium for the library catalogue, but others pointed out that it is an offline medium, suffering from all the disadvantages of printout, microform and other traditional offline forms. However, many *aids* to cataloguing such as REMARC (for retrospective conversion), AACR (for cataloguing), and Dewey (for classification) have been made available on CD-ROM.

The growth of Web access has made CD-ROM less attractive for library use but multi-media and image digitisation have provided many benefits: valuable originals need no longer be handled; storage and retrieval is more effective; and search and access facilities previously unavailable may be offered.[40]

Current technological trends

Prior to the 1990s, the leading automated systems could only run on one manufacturer's hardware, but the increased use and acceptance of the UNIX operating system, which had portability in that it was designed to run on different computer architectures, helped to emphasise the benefits of an open system.[41] The trend has been towards more user-friendly interfaces based on this approach.[42] There has been a move away from the proprietary systems of the past to systems incorporating industry-standard operating systems, relational database systems and communications protocols.[43] The ANSI / NISO

---

40 J. Furner, 'Digital images in libraries', *Vine* 107 (1998), 4.
41 S. L. Mandell, *Computers and information processing: concepts and applications*, 6th edn (St. Paul, MN, 1992), 259.
42 L. A. Tedd, 'OPACs through the ages', *Library Review* 43 (1994), 30.
43 Leeves, 'Library systems then and now', 22.

z39.50 standard, for example, is a network protocol created to facilitate the searching of multiple online databases on a variety of servers in multiple locations. Many suppliers now offer products that can run on a range of platforms.

Client-server technology has become the vogue. This technology separates the software into a 'client' (which provides the interface to the user and usually runs on a PC or workstation) and a 'server' (which provides for the database management, usually on a remote computer).[44] However, financial restrictions decree that many libraries must, for the present, continue to use older products, with host-terminal architecture, implemented before client-server technology became available.

The development of the Internet, a global network of networks, and the World Wide Web during the 1990s has been one of rapid growth and widespread acceptance. Establishing a presence on the Web has become a top priority for libraries in all sectors.[45] The Web can be used not only for information retrieval but also as part of technical services with access to Web-based OPACs, shared cataloguing data, and so on. Many members of staff have authored home Web pages that contain general library information, replacing traditional guides and descriptions and providing links to external servers. 'Web-based interfaces to cataloguing, serials, acquisitions, etc. are still a gleam in the eye for most'[46] but there is no doubt that this will change.

Conclusion

The library profession as a whole has accepted the dynamic challenge of automation. Librarians have learnt to live with machines which are the latest one year and obsolete the next, and the cost of automation has forced them to co-operate.[47] At the start of the new millennium the librarian faces further changes and challenges and 'goals continue to expand'.[48] New technologies and the advent of the World Wide Web 'provide alternative delivery mechanisms on the one hand and the first real competition to libraries as organisations on the other. The basic premise that "libraries are a good thing" is now coming under question as potential users see new possibilities for information,

44 Tedd, 'OPACs through the ages', 30.
45 'The World-Wide Web in libraries: an overview', *Vine* 99 (1995), 5.
46 P. Cibbarelli, 'Library automation: today's successes and concerns', *Electronic Library* 17 (1999), 155.
47 *Vine* 54 (1984), 3–4.
48 Cibbarelli, 'Library automation', 155.

education and leisure.'[49] As more and more end-users begin to do their own searching, new concepts such as 'disintermediation' and the 'hybrid library' are being encountered in the professional literature. Demonstrating that there is clear evidence of benefit to users is recognised as being of extreme importance. Without this evidence, funding bodies will be reluctant to invest in new automation initiatives.

49 R. Adams, 'Decision support systems: an overview', *Vine* 103 (1996), 3.

Informatisation: libraries and the exploitation of electronic information services

ALISTAIR S. DUFF

The idea of informatisation[1]

Modern librarianship has been shaped by many factors, socio-cultural, political, economic and demographic, but there is a strong case – although not necessarily a technologically deterministic one – for the assertion that *technological* change has been paramount in the post-war period. Specifically, information technology, in its various manifestations as 'mechanisation', 'automation', 'IT' and now 'telematics', has transformed, albeit in differing degrees, libraries across the sectors in Britain and Ireland. The application of computers to circulation and other library routines has been explored above, and the focus will now be upon the role of information technology in the craft of information retrieval. I will suggest that in no sphere of the library world has the process of so-called 'informatisation' – a useful if ugly term referring broadly to the adoption of computerised information systems[2] – been more revolutionary than in reader services, and particularly in the facilitation of literature searching. But it may first be helpful to make a few general comments on the wider intellectual context of informatisation, and the manner in which the new IT 'paradigm' permeated library culture.

The author usually credited with coining the idea, although he never actually used the term 'informatisation', was the economist Fritz Machlup. In a classic work of 1962, Machlup propounded the startling claim that the United States of America was witnessing an unprecedented explosion of 'knowledge production', in higher education, in information and media services of many kinds, in the 'information machine' industries, and indeed throughout much

---

1 An earlier version of this chapter was published as 'Four "e"pochs: the story of informatization', *Library Review* 52 (2) (2003), 58–64.
2 'Informatisation' derives from the direct French translation of the Japanese word 'johoka': variants include 'informationisation' and 'informisation'. A detailed account of literary origins can be found in A. S. Duff, *Information society studies* (London, 2000), chapter 1.

of the economy.[3] The idea of the informatised economy has enjoyed a meteoric rise, especially since it was updated and codified in the econometrics of Marc Porat.[4] The most important sociological writer has been the Harvard sage Daniel Bell, who portrayed informatisation as part of an epochal shift from industrial to knowledge-driven societies. 'The sense was present – and still is – that in Western society we are in the midst of a vast historical change', he mused in the opening pages of *The coming of post-industrial society*.[5] Bell's eloquent statement of post-industrialism has since infused social commentary at the popular as well as academic levels, becoming a motif for pundit and politician alike.

The idea of informatisation also penetrated mainstream library thought. Admittedly, most library journals failed to review the benchmark texts mentioned above, and social theory was for a long time *terra incognita* to the average practitioner. However, as informatisation gathered pace professional librarians became increasingly attracted to the whole idea of the information age. Furthermore, certain outstanding thinkers successfully performed a mediating role, translating macrosociological abstractions into more meaningful slogans such as 'paperless society' and 'electronic library'. F. W. Lancaster's writings were seminal in this regard.[6] In 'The future of libraries in the machine age' (1966), B. C. Vickery also helped to bring home the challenge of informatisation, in this case to the orderly ranks of the Library Association. The paper began with the wry observation that 'to walk into an academic library off a busy street is to move out of a world of mechanised communication into another age'. However, Vickery then spoke of an impending information revolution programmed to overturn many of the time-honoured instrumentalities of retrieval:

> In time, there would be publications that originate in machine-readable form, are acquired and stored by the library in that form, and that never appear in visually legible form except on the screen of a user console. I do not imply that this will be the way of all printed books: Gutenberg's invention will serve man for a long time yet . . . But increasingly libraries will have to accommodate themselves to the machine handling of information.[7]

---

3 F. Machlup, *The production and distribution of knowledge in the United States* (Princeton, NJ, 1962).

4 M. U. Porat, *The information economy* (Washington, DC, 1977).

5 D. Bell, *The coming of post-industrial society: a venture in social forecasting* (London, 1974), 37.

6 See especially F. W. Lancaster, *Toward paperless information systems* (New York, 1978).

7 B. C. Vickery, 'The future of libraries in the machine age', *Library Association Record* 68 (1966), 257.

'Through the console', Vickery continued, as though contemplating the Internet of a quarter-century later, 'the user would be able to consult not only his local library resources but eventually national and even international resources.' The technological trajectory which has indeed culminated in 'end-user' access to a world-wide information network is charted below.

The electronic dispensations

It is illuminating to divide the history of library informatisation into four 'electronic dispensations'. Electronics, and latterly microelectronics in particular, has unquestionably been the core technology behind informatisation, while the metaphor of 'dispensations' – borrowed here from eschatology[8] – serves to illustrate that the major 'gifts' of electronic technology have arrived in phases, with each necessitating a unique system of 'stewardship' on the part of librarians. The four dispensations, which should not be confused with the more familiar notion of generations of computer technology, are offline, online, CD-ROM and the Internet. These are not, of course, strictly disjunctive – online and CD-ROM remain with us – nor are they exclusive, since other electronics-based technologies have been tried from time to time. Nevertheless, there now seems to be widespread agreement that these do represent the four main eras in the story of post-war library informatisation.[9]

The Offline Matrix (early 1960s to early 1970s)

Though often overlooked today, the role of offline computer processing in the development of modern reference librarianship was crucial, for it was in the exploitation of spare capacity on mainframe computers that the skills of literature searching were largely forged. Initially, however, the significance of the new information machines was not really understood, and there was a tendency to subsume them in the general category of library aids, alongside a cornucopia of ingenious, but for the most part doomed, mechanical and electro-mechanical contraptions. 'Nowhere', wrote D. R. Jamieson in 1951,

---

8 For a standard theological definition of dispensation, see W. A. Elwell (ed.), *The concise evangelical dictionary of theology* (Grand Rapids, MI, 1991), 140.

9 The primary research for this chapter comprised interviews with current academic experts in library information retrieval and professional librarians who experienced at first hand the successive waves of informatisation. Informants included John Akeroyd, Peter Dale, Andrew Dawson, Derek Law, Rennie McElroy, Gillian Martin, David Nicholas, Gillian Pentelow, Bruce Royan, Margaret Samman, and Brian (B. C.) and Alina Vickery. The author wishes to thank the Carnegie Trust for the Universities of Scotland for subsidising interviews in London and Oxford.

'is there any formulated body of opinion to guide comment on the function librarianship may eventually allot to mechanised aid.'[10] While conceding that electronic retrieval systems *might* have a role to play in highly technical special libraries, a report in the *Library Association Record* a few years later opined that they were still the 'quickest way of producing the wrong answer'; it concluded provocatively that 'perhaps after all the day is far off when the librarian changes his shiny black suit for a white coat'.[11]

By the end of the 1950s, retrieval researchers in the USA and Europe were reporting prototype indexing techniques using IBM computers,[12] but acceptance of their relevance for library-based literature searching was still not immediate. Indeed, as late as the 1961–5 edition of *Five Years' Work in Librarianship*, A. C. Foskett was suggesting that the sophisticated integrated-circuit computers then coming onto the market were better suited to the automation of library house-keeping than to information retrieval.[13] Literature searching on such computers did, however, materialise. Retrieval in the 1960s was offline and typically batch-processed, using leased time on an organisation's sole mainframe computer. Search strategies would be formulated after topic negotiation between librarian and patron, normally an engineer or scientist. Forms were handed or posted to computer personnel who encoded the strategy into computer language using 'punched' cards; the cards were then fed into the computer in batches at a pre-arranged time. Data printed onto listing paper (or sometimes microfilm) were sent back to the librarian, who passed it on to the patron after 'logging' the search. Without interactivity, modification of search strategies was difficult, with the result that relevance and recall were not always optimal. However, Selective Dissemination of Information (SDI), being an operation that could be batched, worked well with offline, and was widely used as such in special libraries.

It is generally agreed that the earliest important database was the Medical Literature Analysis and Retrieval System, better known under its acronym MEDLARS. MEDLARS had arisen when it dawned upon indexers at the National Library of Medicine, Bethesda, Maryland, that the computer files from which they were already producing the print war-horse *Index Medicus* could become retrieval tools in their own right. The service became operational in January 1964, thereby rendering 'machine-readable' the bibliographic

10 D. R. Jamieson, 'Mechanized bibliographical aid', *Library Association Record* 53 (1951), 216.
11 G. Whatmore, 'Special library notes', *Library Association Record* 57 (1955), 360.
12 See, e.g., 'Special library notes: information retrieval', *Library Association Record* 59 (1957), 173–4.
13 A. C. Foskett, 'Computers in libraries', in P. H. Sewell (ed.), *Five years' work in librarianship 1961–1965* (London, 1968), 456.

records of much of the world's biomedical literature. By definition, data in the offline dispensation could not be searched remotely: they were stored on magnetic tapes which had to be purchased or leased for running on 'in-house' mainframes. However, MEDLARS centres were established outside America to facilitate distribution, with the British headquarters located at the National Lending Library for Science and Technology in Boston Spa.[14] Other famous information databases of the pioneering period included Chemical Abstracts, BIOSIS (BioSciences Information Service) and INSPEC for physics and electrical engineering.

By the late 1960s, electronic 'A and I' (abstracts and indexes) had become *de rigueur* for a growing cohort of librarians. The 'new wave of enthusiasm . . . sweeping over the world of libraries in Britain' led to the launch in 1966 of a specialist newsletter entitled *Program: News of Computers in British University Libraries*.[15] Although *Program* was initially concerned mainly with library housekeeping, innovations in 'reference retrieval' were also noted, such as the important American experiment known as Project Intrex (Information Transfer Experiments) and, closer to home, Cyril Cleverdon's work on computer indexing at the College of Aeronautics, Cranfield.[16] It is perhaps fair to say, however, that enthusiasm for informatisation was not universal in the library world at this time. Those who were strongly in favour tended to congregate in the Institute of Information Scientists (founded 1958), while most librarians remained loyal to the more technologically conservative Library Association – a professional apartheid not seriously contested until the late 1990s.

The Online Utilities (early 1970s to early 1980s)

If magnetic tapes were the enabling technology for offline information retrieval, randomly accessible disks combined with improving telecommunication systems paved the way for the second electronic dispensation. Again the role of the national library in stewardship – particularly in sponsorship and co-ordination – should not be forgotten. One of the first online experiments took place in 1971 at the University of Newcastle under the auspices of the Office for Scientific and Technical Information, later the British Library Research and Innovation Centre.[17] This was followed in 1973 by the British Library's

---

14 See J. R. Sharp, 'Information retrieval', in W. Ashworth (ed.), *Handbook of special librarianship and information work*, 3rd edn (London, 1967), 141–232.

15 *Program* 1(1) (1966), 3.

16 R. T. Kimber, 'Computer applications in the fields of library housekeeping and information processing', *Program* 1 (6) (1967), 17–21.

17 H. A. Whatley (ed.), *British librarianship and information science 1971–1975* (London, 1977), 233.

Short Term Experimental Information Network (STEIN), a prototype service designed to bridge the gap between research and development.[18] Then, in April 1977, the British Library Automated Information Service (BLAISE) was launched as the pre-eminent subsidised dial-in utility for the British library community, a counterpart to similar initiatives in other parts of Europe. In addition to machine-readable book catalogue records, BLAISE enabled nation-wide remote access to its holdings of the National Library of Medicine's biomedical journal files, now known as MEDLINE. By 1978, polls were showing that 70% of higher education libraries in Britain were 'online'.[19]

The private sector was also instrumental in the progress of online. Dialog, the Californian database 'vendor' destined to dominate the information world for a quarter of a century, was offering world-wide dial-up access to huge data banks of journal literature from 1972; as late as 1999, it was still claiming to have data reserves fifty times the size of the entire World Wide Web.[20] Early commercial rivals included Dial-tech, ESA/IRS and Datastar.

Online made a great impression on library patrons, almost entirely favourable. A contemporary report by two of the pioneers of online retrieval at the University of London provides a fascinating collection of wide-eyed 'end-user' reactions. The following comments, of diverse disciplinary provenance, give a sense of the novelty and power of the new search medium:

'With this flexible system I discovered how limited was my knowledge of literature.' (Zoologist)

'Exceptionally useful for references in minor or foreign journals to which the library has no immediate access.' (Chemist)

'Wide range of data bases extremely important to interdisciplinary work.' (Social scientist)

'Hours of library browsing would not give such spectacular results.' (Electrical engineer)

'Excellent technique for literature search – finally brings it up to the twentieth century.' (Neuroscientist)[21]

However, the added functionality came at a price, a single online search often costing libraries as much as £20 or £30, in those days a small fortune. There

18 See P. L. Holmes, *On-line information retrieval: an introduction and guide to the British Library's Short-Term Experimental Information Network*, 2 vols. (London, 1977–8).

19 J. Akeroyd and A. Foster, 'Online information services in U.K. academic libraries', *Online Review* 3 (1979), 195.

20 http://www.dialog.com/info [March 1999].

21 A. Vickery and A. Batten, *Large-scale evaluation study of online and batch computer information services* (London, 1978), 56–7.

was also a less tangible price to pay in terms of the human cost of innovation. Alina Vickery has told a graphic story of her struggle – by no means unique – to win over bookish forces in an old-fashioned metropolitan seat of learning to the opportunities of online information retrieval.[22]

At the start of the online dispensation the databases available for remote interrogation were mainly scientific, technical and medical bibliographic files, i.e. indexes of journal articles and, later, abstracts. The first databases outside of the STM fields included ERIC (Educational Resources Information Center) for teachers and LISA (Library and Information Science Abstracts) for librarians. In the mid-1970s, service providers also began to disseminate primary financial and statistical materials. The next step was the provision of textual databases such as the legal information on LEXIS – originally targeted exclusively at end-users and actually barred to libraries – and, in 1980, the news contents of NEXIS. The importance of the transition to 'full-text' should not be underestimated. While secondary sources represented high value to 'cutting-edge' researchers, they were of little practical use to professionals or the general public. However, once share prices, case law and newspaper articles were available in self-contained data sets, albeit with arguably exorbitant 'connect-time' charges, the online dispensation became more relevant to the wider world. Public libraries thus joined in the 'migration' from print to online. Hertfordshire public library service had the distinction of being the first in Britain to provide online access to remote databases – mediated, naturally, by professional librarians – and the British Library was by 1978 funding the provision of terminals for online searching in many other public libraries.[23]

The intellectual bureaucracy was relatively expeditious in embracing the new dispensation. By the 1975–6 academic session, ten British library schools were teaching online searching.[24] The British journal *Online Review* was founded in 1977, an opposite number to the American *Online*, and the same year witnessed the first International Online Information Meeting (IOLIM), held then, as now, in London. UKOLUG, the United Kingdom Online User Group, was formed in 1978 as a special interest group of the Institute of Information Scientists; within six months it had a membership of 400.[25]

22 A. Vickery, 'The clash of interests in computer information services', *Information Processing and Management* 14 (1978), 37–43.
23 L. J. Taylor (ed.), *British librarianship and information work 1976–1980*, vol. 1: *General libraries and the profession* (London, 1982), 99.
24 B. C. Vickery, *The use of online search in teaching: an assessment of projects carried out by UK schools of library and information studies* (London, 1977).
25 Institute of Information Scientists, UK Online User Group, *Newsletter* 4 (1979).

The rapid expansion of online searching was described in an official chronicle as 'probably the major development in British library and information work' during the late 1970s.[26] Online changed for ever the skills set required of the average librarian, in the direction of greater technical know-how and also, in many cases, greater subject specialisation. There were significant indirect effects too. The high cost of online led to a reduction in library subscriptions to the venerable print sources from which many of the databases were largely derived, a major medium migration which surely represented a 'new development in library thinking'.[27] The principle of electronic information exploitation was from one point of view an egalitarian one, giving the small new library the literature-searching power of the Bodleian. On the other hand, online bequeathed troubling questions about the meaning of collection development in the 'information age', along with practical dilemmas relating to end-user charging and the balancing of budgets.

CD-ROM: user-friendly retrieval (mid-1980s to early 1990s)

While it would be inaccurate to state that no other information technology was tried out between the early 1970s and the mid-1980s, it was not until the advent of Compact Disk-Read Only Memory (CD-ROM) in 1984 that the majority of librarians became aware of an important new wave of informatisation.[28] Many libraries, including the British Library, had experimented with the teletext system Prestel after its national launch in 1979, but the range of its information resources was found to be too limited and its searching capabilities too superficial. CD-ROM, in stark contrast, achieved the feat of easy access to a deep reservoir of information. That information, moreover, was usually extremely relevant to librarians and their patrons, not least because the databases being sold in compact disk form often contained packages from the online databases with which they were already conversant. CD-ROM thus soon began to oust the older method of delivery. Indeed, this extraordinarily repellent acronym seemed for a while like the 'writing on the wall' for the vendors of the online dispensation.

A key feature of compact disks was that they were purchasable somewhat in the manner of books or print journals. Once the initial outlay had been made (including of course the requisite workstations), use could be unlimited – and

---

26 Taylor (ed.), *British librarianship 1976–1980*, vol. 1, 202.
27 Taylor (ed.), *British librarianship 1976–1980*, vol. 1, 84.
28 For an early survey, see M. P. Day, 'Electronic publishing and academic libraries', *British Journal of Academic Librarianship* 1 (1986), 54–6.

therefore uninhibited.[29] This regime was in welcome contrast to online, whose metered payment systems had always interfered with conventional library budgeting. From the library administrator's perspective, CD-ROM thus seemed to represent the acceptable face of informatisation, although the economic advantages of compact disks over online were complicated by the ensuing surge in demand for other library services, notably inter-library loans. CD-ROM's immense storage capacity – one compact disk could hold 650 megabytes of data, the equivalent of 800 'floppy' disks or 200,000 pages of text – set it apart from all previous storage systems. The compact disk was capacious enough to store digital information in sound and (to a lesser extent) moving pictures, as well as alphanumeric form; it was inherently a multimedia device. Hardly surprising, therefore, that librarians were among those who hailed CD-ROM as the 'new papyrus'.[30]

Perhaps the single most significant aspect of CD-ROM, however, was its conquest of 'user-friendliness'. Offline had been entirely a computer service-mediated amenity. Online, too, was largely administered by a priesthood-like caste of expert intermediaries, since searches were conducted in notational 'command' languages which varied according to database. Admittedly, online latterly saw some movement towards end-user searching. The success of BIDS (Bath Information and Data Service), a bibliographic information conduit housed in Bath University Library from 1991, revealed strong end-user demand, but its searching procedures were hardly intuitive, and researchers were obliged to acquire passwords – and often compulsory 'user education' – from the library.[31] It was with CD-ROM that 'disintermediation' of the electronic information chain was at last accomplished. Although the first compact disks employed command languages, the industry quickly adopted graphical user interfaces and other attributes of popular computing, and from the start marketed full-text as well as bibliographic databases. CD-ROM thus brought the information explosion to all: to librarians in general rather than just subject specialists, to the arts and humanities as well as the sciences, to undergraduates, to school-children, and eventually to the public at large.[32]

However, the new dispensation was not without its critics, even at its inception. Prominent among them was Derek Law, at the time Librarian of King's

29 Cf. J. Akeroyd, 'CD-ROM usage and prospects: an overview', *Program* 23 (1989), 370.
30 S. Lambert and S. Ropiequet (eds.), *CD-ROM: the new papyrus* (Redmond, WA, 1986).
31 On the emergence of BIDS, see D. Law, 'The development of a national policy for dataset provision in the UK: a historical perspective', *Journal of Information Networking* 1 (1994), 103–16.
32 See D. J. Brown, *Electronic publishing and libraries: planning for the impact and growth to 2003* (London, 1996), 113–32.

College London, who memorably dismissed CD-ROM as 'a young technology with a great future behind it'.[33] Precisely on account of its compact physicality it was seen by many as restrictive, essentially a reference technology, perhaps even a regressive technology.[34] However, while CD-ROM is likely to have a much shorter lifespan than papyrus, the obituary-writing is now known to have been premature. The proliferation of cognate technologies such as Compact Disk Interactive and, more recently, Digital Versatile Disk has extended the dispensation, as has the application of networking techniques to compact disks: London's South Bank Polytechnic installed the first such network in Britain, again with British Library support. In public libraries, CD-ROM still flourishes. According to the 1998 edition of a standard survey of informatisation, 'if there was ever a new application of IT which swept the public library board it was, and is, CD-ROM': the author was confident that the technology would continue to be widely used by both staff and the general public.[35]

The Internet: towards the Global Library
(since the early 1990s)

Notwithstanding the impact of the several technological breakthroughs narrated above, many commentators and library veterans assert that the Internet – and particularly its World Wide Web graphical interface – is by far the greatest revolution of all. There is a widespread sense of living at the dawn of a new electronic dispensation, at what a fashionable social theorist calls 'the rise of the network society'.[36] In spite of being generally available only since 1993, the 'Web' has already dislodged CD-ROM and the online utilities as the key information delivery mechanism at the beginning of the twenty-first century. The mystery of retrieval had been largely stripped away by CD-ROM, but it was not until the Web that searching became undeniably a popular pastime pursued in home and cybercafé. As a kaleidoscope of hardware and software incorporating many of the databases formerly offered as dedicated online utilities, in addition to innumerable personal computers and DTP (desk top publishing) systems, this new electronic dispensation has been portrayed as the consummation of previous information technologies. In a sense it nullifies

---

33 D. Law, 'CD-Rom: a young technology with a great future behind it?', *Serials* 3 (3) (1990), 34–5.

34 Cf. E. B. Brownrigg and C. A. Lynch, 'Electrons, electronic publishing, and electronic display', *Information Technology and Libraries* 4 (1985), 201–7.

35 C. Batt, *Information technology in public libraries*, 6th edn (London, 1998), 11.

36 M. Castells, *The information age: economy, society and culture*, 3 vols. (Oxford, 1996–8), vol. 1: *The rise of the network society* (1996).

them, enabling the searcher to access or manipulate data with no thought of the medium in which they are stored. For example, in many university libraries the book catalogue, the online information services and the CD-ROM network are now all Web-based. This convergence and integration phase therefore seems to allow the *information* in information technology to come to the fore.

If the Internet has at last enthroned the end-user, it has also brought librarians out of the backroom. Now concepts and skills with which the profession has been familiar for at least a generation, and in some cases helped to develop – Boolean searching, personal profiles, SDI, relevance ranking, electronic library – are talking-points in ever-expanding circles. Just as offline brought 'white-coated' computer people into the librarians' world in the 1960s, so in the 1990s the Internet thrust librarians into the midst of the technological intelligentsia and beyond. Indeed, initiatives such as the Labour government's National Grid for Learning, combined with such contingencies as the British Library's purchase of the most expensive public building in the history of Great Britain, positioned some library leaders exceptionally close to the corridors of political power.[37]

However, the invasion of the information scene by the Internet has also renewed long-standing professional concerns regarding bibliographic control. Largely unstructured and dominated by haphazard free-text retrieval, the Internet ignores a half-century of indexing advances. There are also serious issues of information ethics, particularly relating to copyright and censorship, and information economics, and again the whole question of the role of the library in the information chain. In addition, there is acute scepticism regarding the *quality* of much of the information being 'published' – which often means in this context *dumped* – on the Internet. Certainly, few librarians currently see the Internet as the new Alexandrian Library, still less as a social panacea. However, it is worth remembering that it represents an immature information environment. Without wishing here to speculate in detail on the nature or timing of the next electronic dispensation, there are major grounds for hope that the Internet is paving the way for the high-quality global reference system of librarians' dreams. [38]

37 See C. Batt, *I have seen the future and IT works* (Edinburgh, 1998).
38 For background and some futurological speculations, see A. S. Duff, 'Some post-war models of the information chain', *Journal of Librarianship and Information Science* 29 (1997), 179–87. For a discussion of broader issues of information policy, see A. S. Duff, 'The past, present and future of information policy: towards a normative theory of the information society', *Information, Communication and Society* 7 (2004), 69–87.

Conclusion

In summary, there have been four more or less distinct periods of library informatisation. The successive dispensations have not totally supplanted predecessors – arguably, even offline has returned in the form of those Web searches which report back results when one's workstation is next accessed. Each technology has, however, pushed its predecessor from the centre-stage of 'cutting-edge' library theory and practice. The new dispensation dawns and the old fades, without being wholly eclipsed. Over the post-war era as a whole, certain salient developments are discernible alongside the obvious cumulative technical advance, among them movements from local to remote delivery (although here CD-ROM represented a temporary regression), from bibliographic to full-text and now multimedia, from free to charged services, and, above all, from mediated searching to an end-user orientation. While it would be wrong to claim that post-industrial technologies have completely changed librarianship and its information-handling prerogatives, the importance of this seemingly unstoppable force of 'informatisation' can no longer be credibly denied.

50

Libraries and librarians in the Information Age

LIZ CHAPMAN AND FRANK WEBSTER

A chapter with a title such as ours unavoidably implies a review of the immediate past and a glimpse into the future. The tacit questions concern the major
direction of change and the possible role of libraries in the future. Here we will
begin by reviewing what we believe to be a popular prospectus. But we will
move on to refuse the commonplace assumption that the future holds radically
new challenges for libraries, at least from the quarters that are usually suggested. On the contrary, and notwithstanding talk of an Information Society
announced by virtuoso information and communications technologies, the
Internet especially, we shall suggest that long-established and ongoing developments in the realm of information generation and supply, though they have
accelerated in recent decades, pose deeper questions for the role of libraries
and librarians than new technologies and evocations of an Information Age.

The Information Society and libraries

In recent years it has become commonplace to suggest that we are now living
in an Information Society. Quite what this means is unclear, and scrutiny
reveals it to be a dubious and problematical concept.[1] Nevertheless, this has
not prevented commentators from presenting the 'Information Society' as a
new age which is overturning previous ways of life.

There are two particularly popular themes for Information Society writers.
The first emphasises the enormous growth in the amount of information available nowadays, and especially the technological virtuosity with which it is handled. We refer here, of course, to the plethora of articles about new media technologies, about computer communications, and the Internet. The Information
Society is frequently equated with this striking expansion of information and
communications technologies or, more generally, with 'being digital'.[2] The

---

1 F. Webster, *Theories of the information society*, 2nd edn (London, 2002).
2 N. Negroponte, *Being digital* (London, 1995).

outcome is undeniably a marked increase in the amount of information being available – round-the-clock multi-channel television, the widespread use of computers at work and at home, massive increases in book titles being published etc. In the forefront of all this is the Internet, increasingly being accessed through different agents – computers, TV, phones, personal organisers – to bring incalculable amounts of information to the public.

The second theme usually connects the Information Society to changes in the ways in which we work. Occupations in manufacture especially have declined rapidly since the 1970s, and there has been an apparent transfer of work to services. Today, in Britain, more than 70% of all jobs are in services, and data of this sort are characteristically presented as evidence of the emergence of an Information Society. Service jobs are, it is reasoned, information occupations, defined by non-tangible relations between worker and client (such as tourist guide, accountant, teacher and insurance adviser). As such they are markedly different from old-time manufacturing jobs in which people produced things, usually by using machines, by physical effort, skill and dexterity. Of course, manufacturing remains, but it is increasingly located in high-tech automated plants (so there are industrial jobs remaining) and/or production is being located far away in areas of the world such as China and Indonesia where labour costs are far lower and against which nations such as the UK cannot compete. Thus the suggestion is that, in the affluent societies at least, future job prospects are to be found in services. Though this transition is problematic for redundant coal miners and car workers, in the longer term it is more attractive for the majority of the populace, since these information jobs are better paid, people centred, white collar and professionalised.[3] The key requirement for entry into these positions is that personnel achieve the high level of education needed for work in the Information Society. This is the reason why governments in all advanced societies have promoted 'education, education, education' as their most important policy.[4] The idea is that a high-quality education system will ensure success in the Information Age.

These two themes are connected to libraries and librarians in quite direct ways. First, an explosive growth of information has major consequences for those institutions – libraries – which are information repositories. Understandably, amidst the talk of new technologies bringing about an Information Society, librarians have been keen to associate themselves with that which

3 D. Bell, *The coming of post-industrial society: a venture in social forecasting* (Harmondsworth, 1974).
4 R. B. Reich, *The work of nations: preparing ourselves for 21st century capitalism* (New York, 1991).

seems innovative and exciting. There has been a halo effect of information and communication technologies, with which many librarians have wanted to be associated. In this light, it is perhaps not surprising that some librarians have sought to recategorise themselves as Information Scientists or Knowledge Managers. Second, the librarianship profession has found itself particularly well positioned in discussions of an Information Society, because it appears to be an information occupation *par excellence*. What do librarians do, other than work with information and clients to produce an intangible, but undeniably valuable, output – the organised information which constitutes knowledge? Third, in Britain libraries have been assigned a key role in policies which endeavour to maximise social inclusion. A 1997 report, *New library: the people's network*,[5] articulated this central role for libraries. At the core was a concern that disadvantaged groups might be missing out on opportunities for success in the Information Society. Schools, of course, were assigned a primary role, but because they continue to fail marginalised groups, and because the Information Society demands ongoing adaptation and reskilling of workers throughout life, then libraries were assigned a central part in ensuring improved opportunities for social inclusion. Their convenient location, and their ready public access, suggest that libraries could be a crucial point at which disadvantaged groups might gain access to new skills.[6] The report focused on three main strategies for repositioning public libraries in the Information Society: network infrastructure, digital content development and training, or 'connectivity, content and competences'. Some further believed that those who fail in the school system and have been put off education as a result, might be drawn back into it by appropriately equipped modern public libraries, located in communities which the libraries themselves invigorate[7]. This might be caricatured as the computer-game route to success. Whatever its merits, librarians and libraries appear to have an assured place in the Information Society future. Early news reports from the New Library world, however, fail to show substantial take-up of online learning opportunities, although there are reports of librarians being heavily involved in training users how to use computers[8].

5 United Kingdom. Library and Information Commission, *New library: the people's network* (London, 1997).
6 L. Greenhalgh and K. Worpole with C. Landry, *Libraries in a world of cultural change* (London, 1995).
7 C. Batt, 'I have seen the future and IT works', *Library Review* 48 (1999), 11–17.
8 K. Henderson, D. McMenemy and F. Schofield, 'People's network libraries: comparative case studies of old and new ICT learning centres', *Library Review* 53 (2004), 157–66; and 'The People's Network: a turning point for public libraries: first findings', *Managing Information* 10 (2003), 27.

The requisite of keeping this place, of course, is that librarians and libraries welcome the Information Society and all it heralds. Above all, this means that they must *modernise*. This translates into a rejection of outdated practices such as a perceived overreverence for books and a spirited endorsement of digital materials – the vision of a 'virtual library', a 'library without walls', is at the core of what public and academic librarians are expected to create. In short, if librarians and libraries are to take up their place in the Information Society – and there is a place waiting for them – then they must make necessary changes to established ways of working.[9] Librarians need, accordingly, to continue to wire their libraries, to maintain connection with the Internet, to ensure that they have multi-media technologies, and to rid themselves of outdated and unappealing bookstock. They do this in the hope that Internet use will at least bring users into libraries, and encourage them to use books too. Unfortunately, as noted above, it is the Internet that seems to be winning in the attraction stakes.[10]

For academic libraries specifically it is proposed that the Information Age means that students and academic researchers will no longer need actually to visit the library. Scientific users, often posited as the only important users owing to the digital nature of their materials, will vote for closure.[11] This attitude conveniently forgets who pays the bills for electronic publications and spends time setting them up and providing training in their use. Others believe that academic librarians simply have to slightly enhance their skills to survive and prosper.[12]

The wider context

The scenario sketched above will be readily recognised, not least because it is frequently presented. However, we are not convinced of its validity. In our view it oversimplifies what is actually taking place in the wider society, and in the information domain itself, something which has important consequences for libraries and librarians. To put matters theoretically for the moment, our

9 I. Johnson, 'Unesco and human resource development for the information society', *Education for Information* 16 (1998), 237–42; J. Novak, 'Virtual libraries: service realities', *Australian Academic and Research Libraries* 33 (2002), 1–13; and S. Bennett, 'The golden age of libraries', *Journal of Academic Librarianship* 27 (2001), 256–8.

10 A. Pope, 'The impacts of the Internet on public library use: an analysis of the consumer market for library and Internet services in New Zealand', *New Zealand Libraries* 49 (2003), 271–9.

11 T. Hey, 'Why engage in e-science?' *Update* 3 (2004), 25–7.

12 Council on Library and Information Resources, *Diffuse libraries: emergent roles for the research library in the digital age* (Washington, DC, 2002).

view is that Information Society visions – which inform policy – are premised on two dubious notions: that technologies are the decisive factor in bringing about change and that occupational transformations can be seen in evolutionary terms. Technological determinism, and the presupposition that societies' evolution might be plotted by changing occupational types, may be challenged by highlighting wider forces in the world today which exercise a major influence on much that is taking place.

Primary amongst these wider forces must be the overwhelming triumph of what has been called *neoliberalism*. The collapse of communism in the late 1980s, and the full realisation of collectivism's economic inefficiency and political bankruptcy, meant that the West won the Cold War hands down. More than an ideological triumph, this allowed the unrestricted expansion of market civilisation into the former communist societies (China remains an enigma in this regard, marketised, yet remaining in the grip of communist authoritarians) at the same time as a more pervasive spread into Western societies. Neoliberalism has promoted its own organising principles onto a global scale, and this global reach is of great consequence in the informational realm.[13] These principles include the following.

An insistence on ability to pay as the major criterion on which to provide services (if people cannot afford to pay the going rate, then they will not be provided with the service).

Provision should come from private rather than public agencies.

Commodification should be encouraged (i.e. price valuations of relationships are to be promoted).

Profitability should be the arbiter of availability.[14]

There are many consequences of the application of these principles for the library world. Take, for instance, the shift from public to private provision of services. The effects are palpable in previously public utilities such as gas, telecommunications and electricity supply, where privatisation and liberalisation have transformed and fragmented previous services. They are evident, too, in higher education: it is increasingly self-funded, with students defined as customers who must take responsibility for their 'investment' in degree programmes. The effects are clear too in television, where subscription services advance at the expense of public service broadcasting, where digital

---

13 M. Castells, *The information age: economy, society and culture*, 3 vols. (Oxford, 1996–8).
14 F. Webster, 'Information, capitalism and uncertainty', *Information, Communication and Society* 3 (2000), 69–90.

broadcasting is to be pioneered on the basis of market criteria, and where the BBC is reinventing itself as an entrepreneur, well capable of matching the commercial competition.[15] The pressures are telling, too, in the library realm. Hence provision from taxation is deeply unpopular. Budgets are squeezed, even when the euphemisms of 'efficiency savings' and 'value for money' are preferred. The market model of information dissemination is increasingly that of the video/DVD loan chainstore: let customers determine choice of stock, supply the most popular as measured by issues, and let users pay for what they want. If not yet fully insinuated within the library world, it is this model which is in the ascendant.

The shift from public to private supply does not just influence libraries' dissemination of information; it impacts profoundly on what information is generated and made available. Growing commercialisation means that, more and more, what information is made available depends on what is saleable, and what people get hinges on what they are prepared (and able) to pay. Of course, this is not a new thing, and nor is it necessarily to be deplored outright. Publishing, after all, is a commercial activity, and we now have paperback books that are cheaper in real terms than they have ever been. Nevertheless, commercialisation has accelerated and deepened its hold over recent decades. Look here, for instance, at the demise of the UK Net Book Agreement (a protector of prices to libraries) and the resultant hike in the price of academic titles, now that the book trade is more thoroughly marketised than ever and the established habit of cross-subsidy of titles is difficult to maintain.

As commercialisation spreads the principle of private provision to just about every activity in society, so too does it pose challenging questions for institutions, such as libraries, that are organised on principles that are, if not quite antipathetic, then at least ambivalent towards it. As is well known, libraries in the UK have a long and complex history, but what is beyond dispute is that their establishment and perpetuation have been somewhat at odds with *laissez-faire* practices. Whether for paternalist reasons, or to better integrate social classes, or even to encourage educational opportunities, public libraries in particular have approached information as a *public good*, accordingly stressing that access should be uninhibited by people's ability to pay, that information should, as far as possible, be free at the point of delivery, and that commercial considerations should be minimised when it comes to handling information and knowledge. The triumph of neoliberalism asserts considerable pressure

---

15 M. Tracey, *The decline and fall of public service broadcasting* (New York, 1998).

on these principles, making traditional library practices suspect and hard to sustain.

It may be helpful to think of libraries, as several recent American commentators have done, in the same way as commons (i.e. common lands), now under threat from a second Enclosure movement.[16] The original Enclosures of the sixteenth and seventeenth centuries, it will be remembered, made private property of common lands, removing grazing, harvesting and fuel-gathering rights, as well as making trespass an offence, thereby displacing peasants from the land. In today's Information Age, Enclosure might be conceived of as the movement to commercialise information activities old and new, to ensure maximum return on intellectual property for corporate as well as individual owners, to make a business of information, and to insist that users pay the market rate even if formerly much was publically available at minimal cost. In this sense, informational resources and activities once provided from the public purse for everyone who wished and was able to participate (e.g. universities, public libraries, museums, art galleries, government statistics) are increasingly incorporated – if unevenly – into market operations.

Against this tendency, those like Lawrence Lessig[17] and David Bollier,[18] propose 'Information Commons' – to reach from public libraries as far as the Internet itself – that will be preserved for free entry, exchange and access for participants. They envisage digital libraries that include materials such as poetry and novels, political and social information, and even scientific knowledge. This advocacy resists what is considered the 'over-propertisation' that accompanies heightened market provision of academic journals, the extension of copyright that inhibits public access (since the late 1990s copyright has been raised from fifty to seventy years after death for individuals and ninety-five years for corporations following publication), and the growing corporate presence and associated commercial interests on the Internet. The proposals of Lessig, Bollier and like-minded people evoke a founding principle of libraries, that information is not something that we can afford to regard as vendible in the manner of toothpaste and tobacco.[19] Michael Gorman goes one step

16 J. Boyle, 'Fencing off ideas: enclosure and the disappearance of the public domain', *Daedalus* (Spring 2002), 13–25. Also at http://www.creativecommons.org/licenses/by-sa/1.0.

17 L. Lessig, *Code and other laws of cyberspace* (New York, 1999).

18 D. Bollier and T. Watts, *Saving the information commons: a new public interest agenda in digital media* (Washington, DC, 2002).

19 B. Hull, 'ICT and social exclusion: the role of libraries', *Telematics and Informatics* 20 (2003), 131–42.

further to envisage a new Dark Ages, if the age of print is entirely eclipsed by an electronic age.[20]

In the UK the House of Commons Science and Technology Committee Report (2004) clearly acknowledged the increasing profits of commercial publisher concentrations in the electronic age, and supports the greater spread of open-access publishing by academics.[21] Holding publications electronically in an easy access local database, known as an institutional repository, is one way to avoid costs of purchase from publishers.[22] Such open access publishing is causing publishers to seek their own version, which may involve up-front charges to authors for deposit in widely available databases. The picture is changing but it is as yet unclear which model will win out.

Challenges to libraries

An early sign of the commercialising threat came in an important document published in the 1980s, the Adam Smith Institute's pamphlet *Ex Libris*.[23] In this the state dependency of libraries was deplored on grounds of inefficiency and elitism. Libraries, because they were paid for from government revenue, were unjustly cushioned from market forces, and accordingly allocated the majority of the budget to librarians' salaries. Librarians were charged with being elitists who were insensitive to their clients' wishes and who took it upon themselves to decide which books should be stocked. Far better, said this free market think-tank, to let users pay a subscription for their library needs, and to let their choices determine stock. The librarianship community found it difficult to respond to this challenge. The report appeared at a time when the then Conservative governments (which held office from 1979 to 1997) were sympathetic to its outlook, and this contributed to a willingness to reduce public expenditure on public libraries. Some hoped that the New Labour government, elected in 1997, would reverse such policies and to a degree it has. However, the neoliberal consensus remains in place, representing the profound victory of the Adam Smith Institute's way of seeing.

Indeed, in the UK at least it is no exaggeration to say that public libraries have been attacked unremittingly – often by ostensible allies – throughout

---

20 M. Gorman, 'Human values in a technological age', *Logos* 12 (2001), 63–9.

21 House of Commons, Science and Technology Committee, *Scientific publications: free for all?* (London, 2004).

22 C. Lynch, 'Institutional repositories: essential infrastructure for scholarship', *ARL Bimonthly Report* (2003), 1–7; and M. Ware, 'Institutional repositories and scholarly publishing' *Learned Publishing*, 17 (2004), 115–24.

23 Adam Smith Institute, *Ex libris* (London, 1986).

the past twenty years, contributing to the formation of an ideological climate noticeably inhospitable to any defence of the librarian's public service role. For instance, Tim Coates, former senior executive of Waterstone's book chain and an avowed friend of libraries, lambasted the profession in 2004 for lacking managerial expertise and imagination, being overexpensive and unresponsive to customers, and generally headed for extinction unless it emulates the cappuccino cafes, low shelving, long opening hours, and appealing three-for-two deals offered by the large modern bookstore chains. Documenting a 20% decline of library users over a decade, with a 35% reduction in loans alongside a 40% increase in costs, Coates's conclusion is blunt: appoint proper library managers with clear targets for success, make substantial redundancies and redeploy existing staff (to do the work of professionals at reduced rates), and spruce up library décor.[24] With less than 10% of a £1 billion budget going on books, and these costing more than twice as much to process as in the private sector, Coates's analysis resonates with those who would blame libraries for their demise and would have them modernise with urgency. A few months earlier Cabe (Commission for Architecture and the Built Environment)[25] recommended that public libraries transform into 'living rooms for the city', with 'cafés, lounge areas with sofas, and chill-out zones where young people can watch TV and listen to CDs on listening posts'. Such criticism, meant to be helpful, starts from the presumption that libraries are outdated and dowdy, and librarians uninspiring and fusty, even – attests Demos's Charles Leadbeater[26] in a report sponsored by a large library organisation – in a 'state of denial' that keeps the service mired in traditional notions of being a book-lending centre ruled by fines for late returns, obsessive about library quiet, and run for the benefit of library staff, when they ought to be entrepreneurially and adventurously rebranding to pull in the public. No one can doubt that public libraries face severe challenges, and that they must change to address the needs of twenty-first-century users, but recommendations such as these make it impossible to continue the founding principles of a service formed, crucially, apart from (or at least on the periphery of) market relations.

We think that the neoliberal orthodoxy has more consequence for libraries than new technologies or occupational changes. Important though these are, they take second place to the inexorable and fast-acting imperatives of business

---

24 T. Coates, *Who's in charge? Responsibility for the public library service* (London, 2004).
25 Cabe (Commission for Architecture and the Built Environment), *Better public libraries* (London, 2003).
26 C. Leadbeater, *Overdue: how to create a modern public library service* (London, 2003) (Laser Foundation Report).

civilisation. For instance, we would argue that the growth in services cannot be explained simply as an evolutionary trend. There is no abstract logic of development that has led service occupations to grow. To be sure, increased affluence does stimulate expenditure on non-essentials, and this does encourage the expansion of white-collar services. But this can only be part of the story.[27] Just as crucial has been the expansion of the market system across the globe, and the resultant need to organise and manage transnational enterprises and activities. The large-scale growth of occupations in the UK in media, finance and software engineering cannot be put down to evolution. It requires situating in the milieu of a rapidly expanding and unpredictable global market system which calls for organisation and management from key locations. China is rapidly increasing its manufacturing capabilities, not because this is an evolutionary path, but because it responds to direct overtures from corporations, including publishing, located in the more developed nations, which have business strategies that see production in the Far East as the most effective economic option, although marketing and design may remain in the metropolitan regions.

Again, we need to question the commonsensical presumption that it is new technologies which are forcing the pace of change. Undoubtedly it can seem like that on the ground, and librarians do need to respond in practical ways to innovations in information and communications technologies. In truth, however, the changes accompanying new technologies may only be fully understood by placing them in the larger framework of neoliberal ascendancy. What is evident here is that there are powerful pressures encouraging the further commercialisation of information, which are working thoroughly to commodify its supply. It is worth rebutting here the frequent assertion that the Internet offers unimaginable amounts of information free to those equipped with appropriate technologies. Our point here is not that the infrastructure of Internet technologies is incomplete, since it seems undoubted that the trend is towards almost universal availability in the next decade (in at least the more affluent parts of the world), but that the key issue is the character and quality of information becoming available on the Internet. Here what is striking is that much of the most valuable information, that which extends knowledge and which has high levels of integrity, comes from non-commercial organisations such as state institutions, voluntary associations, universities and local government. We are not suggesting that these are perfect, but it is noticeable that,

---

27 K. Kumar, *From post-industrial to post-modern society: new theories of the contemporary world* (Oxford, 1995).

in the first flush of Internet development, many public service organisations have been at pains to use the new technologies to extend the availability of the information they possess. In contrast, note the massive amounts of interested information now on the net, chiefly from commercial organisations which are keen to seize opportunities for e-commerce and advertisement. This is information that is less trustworthy for the simple reason that it is motivated by the interests of the supplier, whether for monetary advantage or for ideological gain. Moreover, the pressures on public service suppliers, perhaps most importantly universities, are such that making articles and course materials freely available is becoming infeasible. Precisely because these too are subject to the commercialising pressures of neoliberalism and because they are strapped for funds from public resources owing to fiscal policies which favour market arrangements, then these too must become more willing to charge for what they develop – hence the growth in distance learning courses, e-education and restrictions of entrance to intranets that are accessible only to those who have paid the entrance fee.

In the longer term what one may see growing is an information and communications technology infrastructure which develops information supply on a basis of 'pay per piece'. Just as television is *en route* to being individuated on a basis of 'pay per view', so the logical extension will be towards payment on the basis of individual access and use of each bit of information required. With digitisation making information simultaneously more readily available and more easily tracked, there are indications of the establishment of a system of micropayments for each access. The successful launch of Internet music databases such as Apple's *iTunes*, where customers pay a few pence for each song downloaded for their personal use, suggests a future in which checking out an encyclopaedia entry, searching for a biographical sketch or details of a particular location will be charged to individuals who will be presented periodically with a personal information account, much like a credit card or a telephone bill. In university libraries there are already signs of this with regard to electronic journals. As they become increasingly available, so publishers are taking steps to ensure that subscriptions are maintained, and that there are licences and restrictions placed on those with access to electronic copy. Intellectual property rights are being vigorously asserted here to ensure that the maximum return on investment may be achieved. Ironically enough, it is effectively the academic employees of universities who have to pay to use their own intellectual production. There is some evidence that publishers bundle groups of titles to maximise profit and raise subscriptions well beyond what might be termed inflation. Libraries which work together in consortia in an attempt to negotiate better prices while guaranteeing publishers multiple sales, find that at times they are asked to sign up to new deals without even being made aware of true prices.

In the year 2000 the European Union, champion of libraries as agents to overcome social exclusion and increase lifelong learning, devised a new Copyright Directive. This could have undermined the UK and Ireland's long-held concept of 'fair dealing' which allowed those engaged in bona fide research and study to make personal copies of material found in libraries. Copying, no longer just photocopying, must now be taken to include downloading and printing from databases and the Internet, and digitising print documents. Fearful of Internet piracy where, in the case of music, items can be freely downloaded, publishers and rightsholders worked hard to curtail concessions to individual users. The Directive ironically enough referred to copyright in the 'information society' – a society which could cost libraries and their users dear, and one which seems to have no sure way to guarantee even the legal deposit of digital materials in its national collections. However, alongside the powerful publisher lobby, libraries at last banded together to lobby on their own account, and at least in the UK a spirited defence of fair dealing led to a Directive more in tune with libraries. The compulsory legal deposit of electronic publications in national libraries has had to be pursued in individual European Union nations, but with some success in the UK. This is not to say that individual libraries wishing to digitise materials to provide better access and support conservation do not face horrendous copyright problems. The electronic age should be one where libraries could for example easily provide e-versions of all items on a student reading list, whereas instead more staff have to be employed to chase up individual copyright permissions.[28]

New materials for old?

At the same time as journals are appearing in electronic form, and being stored and accessed electronically, so books too are potentially changing. The development of e-books is a modern phenomenon with, the publishers hoped, a bright future. There have been various types of e-book developed and various

---

28 S. Ang, 'Agenda for change: intellectual property rights and access management: a framework for discussion on the relationship between copyright and the role of libraries in the digital age', *Library Review* 50 (2001), 382–94.

marketing models, with no particular standard yet emerging.[29] All are based on the model of the printed book, just as printed books were themselves based on manuscripts, and cars based on carriages and horses. Several companies now sell e-books with different costing regimes, but basically starting by reselling to libraries the in-demand materials that they probably already have in print. Publishers are starting to bundle their own print titles as e-books too. The advantages offered particularly to academic libraries are: multiple use without deterioration (although one company suggests issuing e-books one at a time like print versions), full-text searching, and an ability to "use" library services day and night without having to go to the library. Another company is even suggesting sharing a small part of their profit with libraries, thus recognising the budget compromises librarians have to make when buying e-books. Retail booksellers, already vying with libraries to be the best place to read books, hoped to market hand-held e-book readers, but again a lack of standardisation has hampered development. The jury is still out on whether readers want to read substantial books on screen but some authors are beginning to work in an e-only mode, effectively on regular subscription in a new Dickensian model.

As librarians with static or reduced budgets make difficult decisions about what format they should choose for new materials, their choices may actually be narrowing.[30] Buying or taking out a licence for materials may not actually mean acquiring much new material, as so many products are now bundled together. Mainstream publishing and bookselling is concentrating in the hands of a few multinational companies, and as such the range of materials, and in particular critical materials, may be diminishing.[31] The primacy of the English language, particularly in the realm of scholarship, but also in the language used for computer systems, seems to deny the existence of important work in other languages. Librarians are left with the difficult task of balancing collections by finding and acquiring non-mainstream and foreign material.

Just as the large film companies in the USA are beginning to realise that it does not take a huge company with mountains of expensive analog equipment to make a viable movie, so individual writers, without access to major publishing houses, are using digital resources including the Internet and small

---

29 T. A. Peters, 'Gutterdammerung (twilight of the gutter margins): e-books and libraries, *Library Hi Tech* 19 (2001), 50–62.
30 L. Chapman, 'Acquisitions: the emerging electronic paradigm', *International yearbook of library and information management 2000–2001* (2000), 175–98.
31 A. Schiffrin, *The business of books: how international conglomerates took over publishing and changed the way we read* (London, 2000).

independent publishers to produce their work. Libraries have a responsibility to collect and provide access to such material, however hard it is to find. There is no doubt that the function of librarians in the Information Society still remains to find, acquire, organise and preserve material, and this includes material on the Internet. What librarians are organising here is access to materials, not necessarily physical storage, becoming guides rather than custodians, but still collectors. Paradoxically the Internet may increase the use of older materials in libraries as catalogues are made more public on the Web. The example of making movies is given here not just to illustrate a point, but to recall that libraries are involved in collecting all kinds of material, not just the printed word. The as yet unsolved question of the preservation of digital materials is not just one of physical integrity, but also a much more interesting one of content integrity. New types of material are emerging, and in the academic arena, for example, a conference or meeting may be recorded on video, it can then be replayed, annotated and digitally linked to other products such as illustrations and e-mail discussions. Librarians have to remain alert to keeping this material, and suitable equipment for access, as it will be the stuff of future research.[32]

Many will have no problem with these developments. They represent, after all, progress on the commercial side, and on the political side may be seen as simply a rigorous application of principles that are now common world-wide. As neoliberalism extends and deepens its hold over relationships, then it would be surprising indeed if its tenets did not find application. However, it is important to remember that information has long been regarded by librarians as a phenomenon that merited being treated *not* as a normal commodity. Here an important conception has been that information is, in key respects, a public good. To be sure, concerns for copyright have for well over a century indicated that property rights have some applicability as regards information, an assertion that seems on the face of it to be more pressing in the digital era. None the less, the very development of libraries as public resources has been a crucial counter-weight to this tendency.[33]

The neoliberal ascendancy seems set to swing the balance far away from the foundations of service on which libraries have operated for many years. The future, we suggest, is one in which new technologies abound in the

32 C. Lynch, 'On the threshold of discontinuity: the new genres of scholarly communication and the role of the research library' (http://www.ala.org/acrl/clynch.html, 2000).
33 G. Cornish, 'Looking both ways: the challenge to the intermediary in an electronic age', *Digital library: challenges and solutions for the new millennium* (Boston Spa, 2000), 29–37; and M. S. Dalton, 'Old values for the new information age', *Library Journal* 125 (2000), 43–6.

information arena, as it is one in which informational occupations are set to expand in the affluent societies. None the less, we hope to have convinced readers that the crucial force in change is not technology or occupational evolution, but rather the unfettered development of market civilisation, and that the basic duties of librarians, to provide a range of information, remain the same.

Bibliography

This bibliography lists all significant works cited in this volume, but ignores minor references to newspapers, etc. Library catalogues are normally included only if they contain historical material. Reports that are well known by the name of the author or committee chairman are given an additional entry under that name (e.g. Parry Report) as well as under the corporate body concerned.

Abbott, A. *The system of professions* (Chicago, 1988).

Abel, R. L. *The legal profession in England and Wales* (Oxford, 1988).

Abel-Smith, B., and R. Stevens. *Lawyers and the courts: a sociological study of the English legal system* (London, 1967).

Aberdare Central Public Library: golden jubilee 1904–54 (Aberdare, 1955).

Aberdeen, Countess of (ed.). *The International Congress of Women of 1899*, vol. 2: *Women in the professions* (London, 1900).

Accessing our humanities collections: a guide to specialized collections for humanities researchers (London, 1998).

Adam Smith Institute. *Ex libris* (London, 1986).

Adams, E. K. *Women professional workers: a study made for the women's educational and industrial union* (New York, 1921).

Adams, W. G. S. *A report on library provision and policy to the Carnegie United Kingdom Trustees* (Edinburgh, 1915).

Ahern, M. E. 'The business side of a woman's career as a librarian', *Library Journal* 24 (1899), 60–2.

Ainley, P., and B. Totterdell (eds.). *Alternative arrangement: new approaches to public library stock* (London, 1982).

Aitken, W. R. *A history of the public library movement in Scotland to 1955* (Glasgow, 1971).

Allen, M. K. E. 'Some problems of service to individual readers', *Library Association Record* 37 (1935), 61–2.

Allibone, F., and L. Quiney. *The Law Society's Hall: an architectural history 1823–1995* (London, 1995).

Allthorpe-Guyton, M. and J. Stevens. *A happy eye: a school of art in Norwich 1845–1982* (Norwich, 1982).

Altick, R. D. *The English common reader: a social history of the mass reading public 1800–1900* (Chicago, 1957).

American Library Association. *List of subject headings for use in dictionary catalogs* (Chicago, 1895).

[Anderson Report] Joint Funding Councils Libraries Review. *Report of the group on a national/regional strategy for library provision for researchers* (Bristol, 1996).

Anderson, M. 'Access to research collections in the UK: the Anderson Report updated', *Library Review* 47 (1998), 262–6.

Anderson, R. 'Ideas of the university in 19th century Scotland: teaching versus research?', in M. Hewitt (ed.), *Scholarship in Victorian Britain* (Leeds, 1998), 1–26.

Ang, S. 'Agenda for change: intellectual property rights and access management: a framework for discussion on the relationship between copyright and the role of libraries in the digital age', *Library Review* 50 (2001), 382–94.

Anglo-American cataloguing rules, prepared by the American Library Association . . . the Library Association . . . British text (London, 1967).

Anglo-American cataloguing rules, 2nd edn by M. Gorman and P. W. Winkler (London, 1978).

Anglo-American cataloguing rules, 2nd edn, 1998 revision (London, 1998); 2002 revision (London, 2002).

Apt Partnership. *The Apt review: a review of library and information co-operation in the UK and Republic of Ireland* (Sheffield, 1995).

Arberry, A. J. *India Office Library: a historical sketch* (London, 1967).

Archer, W. *Suggestions as to public library buildings: their internal plan and construction, best adapted to effect economy of space (and, hence, saving of cost), and at same time most conducive to public, as well as administrative, convenience, with more especial reference to the National Library of Ireland* (Dublin, 1881).

'The Architectural Association Library 1862–1978', *Architectural Association Annual Review* 1979, 15–70.

Argles, M. *South Kensington to Robbins: an account of English technical and scientific education since 1851* (London, 1964).

ARLIS/UK and Ireland. *Guidelines on stock disposal* (Bromsgrove, 2000).

Armour, J. 'The why and how of outreach: reach out or be forced out', in W. Martin (ed.), *Library services to the disadvantaged* (London, 1989).

Armstrong, G. 'The culture and history of South African public libraries: the experience of Durban library', *Library History* 16 (2000), 35–47.

Armytage, W. H. G. *Civic universities: aspects of a British tradition* (London, 1955).

Arundale, J. *Getting your S/NVQ: a guide for candidates in the information and library sector* (London, 1996).

Ashworth, W., 'Information in Britain', *Aslib Proceedings* 23 (1971), 635–44.

'Special libraries', in Saunders (ed.), *British librarianship today*, 272–96.

'Special libraries in the UK in recent years', in K. Barr and M. Line (eds.), *Essays on information and libraries* (London, 1975), 17–27.

Aslib. *Review of the public library service in England and Wales for the Department of National Heritage.* Final report (London, 1995).

Association of Assistant Librarians. *Which library school?* (London, 1980).

Astbury, R. (ed.). *Putting people first: some new perspectives on community librarianship* (Newcastle under Lyme, 1989).

[Atkinson Report] University Grants Committee. *Capital provision for university libraries: report of a working party* (London, 1976).

Auchstetter, R. M. 'The role of the rare book library in higher education', *College and Research Libraries* 51 (1990), 221–30.

Austin, D. 'The development of PRECIS: a theoretical and technical history', *Journal of Documentation* 30 (1974), 47–102.

Baggs, C. M. 'How well read was my valley: reading, popular fiction and the miners of South Wales, 1875–1939', *Book History* 4 (2001), 277–301.

'The libraries of the Co-operative movement: a forgotten episode', *Journal of Librarianship and Information Science* 23 (1991), 87–96.

'The Miners' Institute libraries of South Wales', in P. H. Jones and E. Rees. (eds.), *A nation and its books: a history of the book in Wales* (Aberystwyth, 1998), 297–306.

'The miners' libraries of South Wales from the 1860s to 1939', unpublished PhD thesis, University of Wales, Aberystwyth (1995).

'The National Library of Wales book box scheme, and the South Wales coalfield 1914–1939', *National Library of Wales Journal* 30 (1997), 207–29.

' "The whole tragedy of leisure in penury": the South Wales miners' institute libraries during the Great Depression', *Libraries and Culture* 39 (2004), 115–36.

Bailey, K. C. *A history of Trinity College Dublin 1892–1945* (Dublin, 1947).

[Bains Report] Department of the Environment. *The new local authorities: management and structure* (London, 1972).

Bainton, T. 'SCONUL and research libraries', *Library Review* 47 (1998), 267–70.

[Baker Report] Ministry of Education. *Inter-library co-operation in England and Wales* (London, 1962).

Baker, D. 'Structures for the 1990s', *British Journal of Academic Librarianship* 5 (1990), 159–63.

Baker, E. A. *A descriptive guide to the best fiction: British and American* (London, 1903).

'Direction for popular readers', *Contemporary Review* 89 (1906), 498–504.

'Education of the librarian: advanced stage', *Library Association Record* 8 (1906), 579.

'Standard of fiction in public libraries', *Library Association Record* (1907), 70–80.

'Wanted – a guide-book to books', *Library Association Record* 2 (1903), 89–97.

Baker, N. *Double fold: libraries and the assault on paper* (New York, 2001).

Baker, W. *The early history of the London Library* (Lewiston, NY, 1992).

Baker, W., and K. Womack (eds.). *Nineteenth century British book-collectors and bibliographers* (Detroit, 1997).

Ballantyne, G. H. *The Signet Library, Edinburgh and its librarians 1722–1972* (Glasgow, 1979).

Barber, G. *Arks for learning: a short history of Oxford library buildings* (Oxford, 1995).

'The Taylor Institution', in *History of the University of Oxford*, vol. 6, 631–40.

Barclay, J. B. *The S.S.C. story 1784–1984* (Edinburgh, 1984).

Barker, A., and M. Rush. *The Member of Parliament and his information* (London, 1970).

Barker, N. *Bibliotheca Lindesiana: the lives and collections of Alexander William, 25th earl of Crawford and 8th earl of Balcarres and James Ludovic, 26th earl of Crawford and 9th earl of Balcarres* (London, 1977).

The publications of the Roxburghe Club, 1814–1962 (Cambridge, 1964).

Treasures from the libraries of National Trust country houses (New York, 1999).

Barnish, E. 'The co-operative libraries of Lancashire, Yorkshire and Durham', in *Transactions and proceedings of the second annual meeting of the Library Association* (London, 1879), 61–4.

Barringer, T. 'The rise, fall and rising again of the Royal Commonwealth Society Library', *SALG Newsletter* 41 (1994), 15–22.

Barry, J. 'Policy of the Library Association of Ireland: a paper read at the Cavan Conference', *An Leabharlann* 7 (1940), 71–8.

Bassett, A. T., *Gladstone's speeches: descriptive index and bibliography* (London, 1916).

Bates, M. J. 'Rethinking subject cataloging in the online environment', *Library Resources & Technical Services* 33 (1989), 400–12.

Batt, C. 'I have seen the future and IT works', *Library Review* 48 (1999), 11–17.
Information technology in public libraries, 6th edn (London, 1998).

Batts, M. S., 'The eighteenth century concept of the rare book', *Book Collector* 45 (1975), 381–400.

Beckwith, F. 'The eighteenth-century proprietary library in England', *Journal of Documentation* 3 (1947), 81–98.

Beddingham, P. C. 'Gray's Inn Library 1555–1973', *Law Librarian* 5 (1974) 3–5.

Bell, D. *The coming of post-industrial society: a venture in social forecasting* (London, 1974).
'The social framework of the information society', in T. Forester (ed.), *The microelectronics revolution: the complete guide to the new technology and its impact on society* (Oxford, 1980), 500–49.

Bell, M. D. 'Faculty and class libraries', in Guild and Law (eds.), *Edinburgh University Library*, 163–81.

Bellot, H. H. *University College London 1826–1926* (London, 1929).

Bennett, C. 'The Library of the Ministry of Food', *Library Association Record* 44 (1942), 184–6.

Bennett, S. 'The golden age of libraries', *Journal of Academic Librarianship* 27 (2001), 256–8.

Berger, S. 'William Blades', in Baker and Womack (eds.), *Nineteenth-century British book-collectors*, 21–7.

Bernard, P., et al. (eds.). *Antiquarian books: a companion* (Aldershot, 1994).

Besoni, D. 'Roy Harrod and the committee of enquiry into the Bodleian Question 1930–31', *Bodleian Library Record* 17 (1) (2000), 36–44.

[Bett Report] *Independent review of higher education pay and conditions: report of a committee* (London, 1999).

Bettenson, E. M. *The University of Newcastle upon Tyne 1834–1971* (Newcastle, 1971).
The University of Newcastle upon Tyne after 1970: a selective view (Newcastle, 1987).

The Bibliographical Society, 1892–1992 (London, 1992).

Bigham, C. *The Roxburghe Club: its history and its members 1812–1927* (Oxford, 1928).

Bilboul, R. B. (ed.). *Retrospective index to theses of Great Britain and Ireland, 1716–1950*, 5 vols. (Santa Barbara, CA and Oxford, 1975), vol.1: *Social sciences and humanities*.

Bill, E. G. W. *Unexpected collections at Lambeth Palace Library* (London, 1982).

Birks, M. *Gentlemen of the law* (London, 1960).

Black, A. 'Hidden worlds of the early knowledge economy: libraries in British companies before the middle of the twentieth century', *Journal of Information Science* 30 (5) (2004), 418–35.
'Local politics and national provision', in Kinnell and Sturges (eds.), *Continuity and innovation in the public library*, 48–66.

A new history of the English public library: social and intellectual contexts, 1850–1914 (London, 1996).

'New methodologies in library history: a manifesto for the "new" library history', *Library History* 11 (1995), 76–85.

'The past public library observed: user recollections of the British public library recorded in the Mass Observation Archive', *Library Quarterly* (forthcoming).

The public library in Britain, 1914–2000 (London, 2000).

'Representations of the public library in Victorian and Edwardian fiction: assessing the semiological approach', in P. Vodosek and G. Jefcoate (eds.), *Libraries in literature / Bibliotheken in der literarischen Darstellung* (Wiesbaden, 1999), 151–66.

'Skeleton in the cupboard: social class and the public library in Britain through 150 years', *Library History* 16 (2000), 3–12.

'Technical libraries in British commercial and industrial enterprises before 1950', in W. B. Rayward and M. Bowden (eds.), *Proceedings of the 2002 Conference on the History and Heritage of Scientific and Technological Information Systems* (Medford, NJ, 2004), 281–90.

Black, A., and D. Muddiman. *Understanding community librarianship: the public library in postmodern Britain* (Aldershot, 1997).

Blake, M. *A history of the British and Irish Association of Law Librarians 1969–1999* (Warwick, 2000).

Blake, N. *Enquiry statistics: an analysis of enquiries asked at selected public and special libraries in the UK*, LISU occasional papers 11 (Loughborough, 1995).

Bland, D. S. *A bibliography of the Inns of Court and Chancery* (London, 1965).

Blegen, T. C., and others. *Book collecting and scholarship* (Minneapolis, 1954).

Block, A. *The book collector's vade mecum* (London, 1932).

Bloomfield, B. C. 'Rare book and special collections', in *Librarianship and Information Work Worldwide 1998* (London, 1998), 151–70.

Bloomfield, B. C. (ed.). *A directory of rare book and special collections in the United Kingdom and the Republic of Ireland*, 2nd edn (London, 1997).

Bloomfield, M. A. 'Sir John Ballinger: librarian and educator', *Library History* 3 (1973), 1–27.

Blunden-Ellis, J. 'Looking to the future: the Consortium of Academic Libraries in Manchester (CALIM)', in Harris (ed.), *The new university library*, 45–54.

Board of Education, Public Libraries Committee. *Report on public libraries in England and Wales* (London, 1927) (Cmd. 2868) (The Kenyon Report).

Bodleian Library. *The Bodleian Library and its friends: catalogue of an exhibition held 1969–1970*, 2nd issue (Oxford, 1970).

The John Johnson Collection: catalogue of an exhibition (Oxford, 1971).

Bollier, D., and T. Watts. *Saving the information commons: a new public interest agenda in digital media* (Washington, DC, 2002).

Bond, E. A. 'Address to the Library Association', *Library Chronicle* 4 (1887), 1–10.

'The book trade in 1984 – and after?', *The Book Collector* 33 (1984), 417–30.

Borough of Birmingham. *Opening of the Free Reference Library . . . by George Dawson* (Birmingham, 1866).

Borough of Stepney. *Public libraries committee report* (1904).

Boswell, D. 'Prisoner, seamen and military establishments', in Whatley (ed.), *British librarianship and information science 1971–75*, 297–301.

Bosworth, K. 'In praise of law librarians: LEXIS in the United Kingdom 1975–1993', *Law Librarian* 24 (1993), 133–6.

[Bourdillon Report] Ministry of Education. *Standards of public library service in England and Wales* (London, 1962).

Bowers, F. *Principles of bibliographical description* (Princeton, 1949).

Textual and literary criticism (Cambridge, 1959).

Bowler, C., and P. Brimblecombe. 'Environmental pressures on building design and Manchester's John Rylands Library', *Journal of Design History* 13 (3) (2000), 175–91.

Bowyer, T. 'The founding of the Standing Conference of National and University Libraries (SCONUL)', in Thompson (ed.), *University library history*, 208–28.

Boyd, W. (ed.). *The challenge of leisure* (London, 1936).

Boyle, J. 'Fencing off ideas: enclosure and the disappearance of the public domain', *Daedalus* (Spring 2002), 13–25.

Bradford, S. C. *Documentation* (London, 1948).

Bradley, C. 'The development of full time education for librarianship in Great Britain since the war', unpublished FLA thesis (1967).

Bradshaw, H. 'Address at the opening of the fifth annual meeting of the Library Association', in his *Collected papers* (Cambridge, 1889), 371–409.

Bramley, G. *Adult literacy, basic skills and libraries* (London, 1991).

Apprentice to graduate: a history of library education in the United Kingdom (London, 1981).

Outreach: library services for the institutionalised, the elderly and the physically handicapped (London, 1978).

Breisach, E. *Historiography, ancient, mediaeval and modern* (Chicago, 1983).

Breisch, K. A. *Henry Hobhouse Richardson and the small public library in America: study in typology* (Cambridge, MA, 1997).

Briggs, A. 'Development in higher education in the United Kingdom: nineteenth and twentieth centuries', in W. R. Niblett (ed.), *Higher education: demand and response* (London, 1969), 95–116.

Briggs, A. (Chairman), *Report of the committee on nursing* (London, 1972) (Cmnd. 5115).

Brill, B. *Macclesfield Library: the first 100 years* (Chester, 1976).

British Academy. *Research in the humanities and social sciences: report of a survey 1958–1960* (London, 1961).

British and Irish Association of Law Librarians. *Directory of law libraries in the British Isles*, 2nd edn (Yeovil, 1984); 7th edn (Warwick, 2002).

The British Library (London, 1971) (Cmnd. 4572).

The British Library Act 1972. (London, 1972).

British Library. *Advancing with knowledge: the British Library strategic plan 1985–1990* (London, 1985).

Annual report 1973–4– (London, 1974–).

Gateway to knowledge: the British Library strategic plan, 1989–1994 (London, 1989).

British Museum. *A guide to the exhibition in the King's Library* (London, 1939).

List of catalogues of English book sales, 1767–1900 (London, 1915).

Rules for the compilation of the catalogue of printed books in the British Museum (London, 1841).

Bromley, D. W., and A. M. Allott (eds.). *British librarianship and information work 1981–1985*, 2 vols. (London, 1988).

British librarianship and information work 1986–1990, 2 vols. (London, 1993).

Brooke, C. 'The University Library and its buildings', in Fox (ed.), *Cambridge University Library: the great collections*, 215.

Brooke, C., and R. Highfield. *Oxford and Cambridge* (Cambridge, 1988).

Brooks, A., and B. Haworth. *Portico Library: a history* (Lancaster, 2000).

Brown, A. L., and M. Moss. *The University of Glasgow 1451–1996* (Edinburgh, 1996).

Brown, D. J. *Electronic publishing and libraries: planning for the impact and growth to 2003* (London, 1996).

Brown, I. G. *Building for books: the architectural evolution of the Advocates' Library 1689–1925* (Aberdeen, 1989).

Brown, J. D. 'In defence of Emma Jane', *Library World* 3 (1900–1), 215–19.

Library classification and cataloguing (London, 1912).

Manual of library classification and shelf arrangement (London, 1898).

Manual of library economy (London, 1903).

The small library: a guide to the collection and care of books (London and New York, 1907).

Subject classification (London, 1906).

Brown, R. 'How I cope – the industrial library', *Serials* 3 (2) (July 1990), 42–5.

Public library administration (London, 1979).

Brown, S. J. 'The Hospital Library Service', *Irish Library Bulletin* 11 (1950), 208–10.

Libraries and literature from a Catholic standpoint (Dublin, 1937).

Brownrigg, E. B., and C. A. Lynch. 'Electrons, electronic publishing, and electronic display', *Information Technology and Libraries* 4 (1985), 201–7.

Brunt, R. M. 'In defence of bibliographic standards', *Aslib Proceedings* 37 (1985), 213–19.

Bryant, P. *Making the most of our libraries* (Bath, 1997).

Bryant, P., A. Chapman and B. Naylor. *Retrospective conversion of library catalogues in institutions of higher education in the United Kingdom: a study of the justification for a national programme* (Bath, 1995).

Bull, G. 'Technical developments in legal information retrieval', *Law Librarian* 11 (1980), 34–40.

Bullen, G. *Catalogue of the library of the British and Foreign Bible Society* (London, 1857).

Bunch, A. J. *Hospital and medical libraries in Scotland: an historical and sociological study* (Glasgow, 1975).

Bunch, A. J., and E. E. Cumming. *Libraries in hospitals: a review of services in Scotland* (Edinburgh, 1969).

Burge, S. *Broken down by grade and sex: the career development of government librarians* (London, 1995).

'Much pain, little gain: privatisation and UK government libraries', *Inspel* 22 (1999), 10–19.

Burgoyne, F. J. *Library construction: architecture, fittings and furniture* (London, 1897).

Burkett, J. (ed.). *Special library and information services in the United Kingdom* (London, 1961).

Burnett, J. (ed.). *Useful toil: autobiographies of working people from the 1820s to the 1920s* (London, 1974).

Burnett, J., D. Vincent and D. Mayall (eds.). *The autobiography of the working class: an annotated critical bibliography*, 3 vols. (Brighton, 1984–9).

Bush, E. A. R. *Agriculture: a bibliographic guide* (London, 1974).

Bushnell, G. H. *University librarianship* (London, 1930).

Butler, H. 'The county libraries: sex, religion and censorship', in his *Grandmother and Wolfe Tone* (Dublin, 1990), 50–63.

Butler, P. *An introduction to library science* (Chicago, 1933).

Byrne, B. 'Law libraries in Ireland', *Law Librarian* 21 (1990), 53–8.

Cabe (Commission for Architecture and the Built Environment). *Better public libraries* (London, 2003).

Cabinet Office. *Competing for quality: buying better public services* (London, 1991) (Cm. 1730).

Cadell, P., and A. Matheson (eds.). *For the encouragement of learning: Scotland's national library 1689–1989* (Edinburgh, 1989).

Campbell, N., and R. M. S. Smellie. *The Royal Society of Edinburgh 1783–1983* (Edinburgh, 1983).

Cant, R. G. *The University of St Andrews: a short history*, 3rd edn (St Andrews, 1992).

Capewell, P. 'A computer based subject index', *Catalogue & Index* 50 (1978) 1–2, 7.

Carleheden, M. 'Rethinking the epochs of Western modernity', in M. Carleheden and M. H. Jacobsen (eds.), *The transformation of modernity: aspects of the past, present and future of an era* (Aldershot, 2001), 83–115.

Carmel, M. (ed.). *Medical librarianship* (London, 1981).

Carnegie United Kingdom Trust. *Glimpses at the rural library problem in Ireland*, 2 vols. (Dunfermline, 1915).

Carr, R. 'Research collections in the digital age: the role of CURL', *Library Review* 47 (1998), 277–81.

Carrick, N. 'Liverpool Library in the eighteenth century', unpublished MA dissertation, University of Sheffield (1995).

Carter, J. *Taste and technique in book collecting*, 3rd impression with corrections and an epilogue (London, 1970).

Carter, J., and P. Muir (eds.), *Printing and the mind of man: a descriptive catalogue illustrating the impact of print on the evolution of western civilisation during five centuries* (London, 1967); revised edn (Munich, 1983).

Carter, J., and G. Pollard. *An enquiry into the nature of certain nineteenth-century pamphlets* (London, 1934); reprinted with additions (London, 1983).

Casteleyn, M. *A history of literacy and libraries in Ireland: the long traced pedigree* (Aldershot, 1984).

Castells, M. *The information age: economy, society and culture*, 3 vols. (Oxford, 1996–8), vol. 1: *The rise of the network society* (1996).

Cataloguing rules: author and title entries, compiled by committees of the Library Association and of the American Library Association, English edn (London, 1908).

Cave, R. *Rare book librarianship*, 2nd edn (London, 1982).

Census Returns of Great Britain 1851. *Education. England and Wales. Report and tables. 1854* (London, 1854).

Central Catholic Library (The): the first ten years of an Irish enterprise (Dublin, 1932).

Chadwick, O. 'The Acton Library', in Fox (ed.), *Cambridge University Library: the great collections*, 136–52.

Chamberlin, R. *Survival: the rise, fall and rise of the Guildford Institute* (Guildford, 1997).

Chandler, A. *The visible hand: the managerial revolution in American business* (Cambridge, MA, 1977).

Chaplin, A. H. *GK: 150 years of the General Catalogue of Printed Books* (Aldershot, 1987).

Chapman, A., Kingsley, N. and Dempsey, L. *Full disclosure* (Bath, 1999).

Chapman, L. 'Acquisitions: the emerging electronic paradigm', *International yearbook of library and information management 2000–2001* (2000), 175–98.

Charlton, H. B. *Portrait of a university, 1851–1951: to commemorate the centenary of Manchester University* (Manchester, 1951).

Chichester, M. 'The later development of Christ Church Library, Oxford', *Library History* 5 (1980), 109–17.

Chitnis, A. *The Scottish Enlightenment: a social history* (London, 1976).

An Chomhairle Leabharlanna. *The university of the people: celebrating Ireland's public libraries* (Dublin, 2003).

Christie, W. D. *An explanation of the scheme of The London Library, in a letter to the Earl of Clarendon* (London, 1841).

Cibbarelli, P. 'Library automation: today's successes and concerns', *Electronic Library* 17 (1999), 155.

Circle of State Librarians. *The State Librarian* (1948–) (published as CSL *Bulletin* 1952–74).

Ciro, J. 'Country house libraries in the nineteenth century', *Library History* 18 (2002), 89–98.

Clark, P. *British clubs and societies: the origins of an associational world* (Oxford, 2001).

Clarke, E. A. 'Dunlop Rubber Company, Ltd.: the work of the library section of the service department', *Library Association Record* 23 (1921), 371–8.

Clear, G., F. E. K. Foat and G. R. Pocklington. *The story of W. H. Smith & Son* (London, 1949).

Coates, E. J. *Subject catalogues: headings and structure* (London, 1960).

Coates, T. *Who's in charge? Responsibility for the public library service* (London, 2004).

Cochrane, P. A., and K. Markey. 'Preparing for the use of classification in online cataloging systems and in online catalogs', *Information Technology and Libraries* 4 (1985), 91–111.

Cole, D. *The work of Sir Gilbert Scott* (London, 1980).

Coleman, P. *Whose problem? The public library and the disadvantaged* (Newcastle under Lyme, 1981).

Collins, J. *The two forgers: a biography of Harry Buxton Forman and Thomas James Wise* (London, 1992).

Collins, M. 'Statistics and Market Intelligence Library', *State Librarian* 32 (1984), 13–14.

Collins, T. *Floreat Hibernia: a bio-bibliography of Robert Lloyd Praeger* (Dublin, 1985).

Collis, R., and L. Boden (eds.). *Guidelines for prison libraries*, 2nd edn (London, 1997).

Collison, R. L. 'SCOTAPLL', *Bulletin of the Association of British Theological and Philosophical Libraries* 2 (1957), 3.

Colson, J. C. 'Government libraries,' in Wiegand and Davis (eds.), *Encyclopedia of library history*, 244–8.

Comaromi, J. P. *The eighteen editions of the Dewey decimal classification* (Albany, NY, 1976).

Comedia. *Borrowed time? The future of public libraries in the UK* (Bournes Green, 1993).

Commission on the Science and Art Department in Ireland. *Report*, 2 vols. (London, 1869) (H.C. 1868–69 (4103)).

Commissioners appointed to inquire into the constitution and government of the British Museum. *Report* (London, 1850).

Committee of Public Accounts. *Second report: progress in completing the new British Library* (London, 1996) (House of Commons Paper 38).

Committee on Higher Education. *Report* (London, 1963) (Cmnd. 2154) (The Robbins Report).

'Computers in British public libraries: a survey', *Program* 13 (1979), 37.

Constitution and rules of the Society of Procurators of Mid-Lothian . . . with catalogue of books in the Library of the Society (Edinburgh, 1900).

Convey, J. *The Harris Free Public Library and Museum, Preston: 1893–1993* (Preston, 1993).

Coombs, D. *Spreading the word: the library work of the British Council* (London, 1988).

Cornelius, I. *Meaning and method in information studies* (Norwood, NJ, 1996).

Cornish, G. 'Looking both ways: the challenge to the intermediary in an electronic age', in P. Connolly and D. Reidy (eds.), *Digital library: challenges and solutions for the new millennium* (Wetherby, 2000), 29–37.

Corrall, S. 'Management development in academic libraries and the Joint Funding Councils' Libraries Review', *British Journal of Academic Librarianship* 9 (1994), 220.

Corrigan, P., and V. Gillespie. *Class struggle, social literacy and idle time* (Brighton, 1978).

Council on Library and Information Resources. *Diffuse libraries: emergent roles for the research library in the digital age* (Washington, DC, 2002).

County Libraries in Great Britain and Ireland: statistical report 1934–5 (London, 1936).

Cox, A. 'Islington Central Library', *Architectural Review* 18 (December 1905), 243.

Cox, D. 'Cooperation among university libraries in the United Kingdom', in Thompson (ed.), *University library history*, 170–86.

Cox, P. 'The Westminster experience', in M. Ashcroft and A. Wilson (eds.), *Competitive tendering and libraries: proceedings of seminars held in Stamford, Lincolnshire* (Stamford, 1992), 15–22.

Craster, Sir E. *The history of All Souls College Library*, ed. by E. F. Jacob (London, 1971).
History of the Bodleian Library 1845–1945 (Oxford, 1952).

Crawford, E. *The women's suffrage movement: a reference guide 1866–1928* (London, 1999).

Crawford, J. C. 'Denominational libraries in 19th-century Scotland', *Library History* 7 (2) (1985), 33–44.
'Historical models of library provision: the example of Scotland', unpublished PhD thesis, Glasgow Caledonian University (1993).
'The ideology of mutual improvement in Scottish working class libraries', *Library History* 12 (1996), 49–61.
'The library policies of James Coats in early twentieth century Scotland', *Journal of Library History* 22 (1987), 117–46.
'The origins and development of societal library activity in Scotland', unpublished MA thesis, University of Strathclyde (1981).
'Policy formulation for public library provision in the Highlands of Scotland', *Journal of Librarianship* 16 (1984), 94–117.

Credland, W. R. *The Manchester public free libraries: a history and description, and guide to their contents and use* (Manchester, 1899).
Manchester public free libraries: handbook, historical and descriptive, 2nd edn (Manchester, 1907).

Crestadoro, A. *The art of making catalogues of libraries* (London, 1856).

Cronin, B., and E. Davenport. *Post professionalism: transforming the information heartland* (London, 1988).

Crowther, J. G. *British scientists of the nineteenth century* (London, 1935); repr. in 2 vols. (Harmondsworth, 1940).

Cruickshank, D. 'Berkeley Library: Trinity College Dublin 1967–1997', *RIBA Journal* 104 (10) (1997), 69–75.

Crump, M. J., and others. *Rare book librarians for the future: issues in training and education* (Brussels, 1996).

CURL. *Scholarly communications crisis* (n.p., 2001).

Cutter, C. A. *Rules for a printed dictionary catalogue* (Washington, DC, 1876).

[Dainton Report] National Libraries Committee. *Report* (London, 1969) (Cmnd. 4028).

Dainton, F. *Doubts and certainties: a personal memoir of the 20th century* (Sheffield, 2001).

Dalton, M. S. 'Old values for the new information age', *Library Journal* 125 (2000), 43–6.

Darcy, B. and A. Ohri. *Libraries are ours: the public library for community groups* (London, 1978).

Davies, D. J. *Ninety years of endeavour: the history of the Tredegar Workmen's Hall, 1861–1951* (Cardiff, 1951).

Davies, D. L. *A history of Cwmaman Institute 1868–1993* (Mountain Ash, 1994).

Davies, M. Ll. *Women's Co-Operative Guild, 1883–1904* (London, 1904).

Davies, R. *Foreign body: the secret life of Robert Maxwell* (London, 1995).
   Print of a hare's foot (London, 1969).

Davies, W. L., *The National Library of Wales: a survey of its history, its contents, and its activities* (Aberystwyth, 1937).

Davison, K. *Classification practice in Britain: report on a survey of classification opinion and practice in Britain* (London, 1966).

Davison, P. (ed.). *The book encompassed: studies in twentieth century bibliography* (Cambridge, 1992).

Dawson, J. *The Wedgwood Memorial Institute* (Burslem, 1894).

Day, A. *The new British Library* (London, 1994).

Day, J. C. 'Library provision in nineteenth century Northumberland', unpublished MPhil thesis, University of Strathclyde (1987).

Day, M. P. 'Electronic publishing and academic libraries', *British Journal of Academic Librarianship* 1 (1986), 54–6.

De Hamel, C. 'Was Henry Yates Thompson a gentleman?' in Myers and Harris (eds.), *Property of a gentleman*, 77–89.

De Ricci, S. *English collectors of books and manuscripts (1530–1930) and their marks of ownership* (Cambridge, 1930).

De Vries, L. *Little wide-awake: an anthology from Victorian children's books . . . in the collection of Anne and Fernand Renier* (London, 1967).

Dean, J. 'Policies and programmes in library and information studies at University College, Dublin', *An Leabharlann* 7 (1978), 78–87.

Dell, W. *The right reformation of learning, schools and universities* (London, 1653).

Denham, D. 'Promotion', in J. Elkin and M. Kinnell (eds.), *A place for children* (London, 1997), 68–95.

Department of Education and Science. Census of staff in librarianship and information work in the United Kingdom 1972 (London, 1974).

Census of staff in librarianship and information work in the United Kingdom 1981 (London, 1982).

The libraries' choice (London, 1978).

Principal documentary evidence submitted to the National Libraries Committee, 2 vols. (London, 1969).

Department of National Heritage. *Investing in children: the future of library services for children and young people*. Library and Information Services Council (England) (London, 1995).

Reading the future (London, 1997).

Department of the Environment. *The new local authorities: management and structure* (London, 1972) (The Bains Report).

Devereux, M. 'Libraries in working class areas', *Assistant Librarian* 65 (1972), 170–2.

Devlin, F. 'Brightening the countryside: the library service in rural Ireland, 1902–1935', unpublished PhD thesis, St Patrick's College, Maynooth, 1990.

Dewe, M. 'H. T. Hare: Edwardian library architect', *Library Review* 27 (Summer 1978), 80–4.

Dewey, M. *Classification and subject index for cataloging and arranging the books and pamphlets of a library* (Amherst, MA, 1876).

Library school rules, 3rd edn (Boston, MA, 1894).

'Women in libraries: how they are handicapped', *Library Notes* 1 (1886), 89–90.

Dickinson, D. C. *Dictionary of American book collectors* (New York, 1986).

Henry E. Huntington's library of libraries (San Marino, CA, 1995).

Dickson, W. K. *The Advocates' Library* (Edinburgh, 1927).

The National Library of Scotland (Edinburgh, 1928).

Dickson, W. K., and H. P. Macmillan, with John Buchan. *A national library for Scotland* (Edinburgh, 1922).

Dickson, W. P. *The Glasgow University Library: notes on its history, arrangements, and aims* (Glasgow, 1888).

Statement by the Curator as to the bearings of a proposal to grant 'free access' to selected students (Glasgow, 1899).

Ditmas, E. M. R. 'The literature of special librarianship', *Aslib Proceedings* 2 (1950), 217–42.

Dobson, C. *The Library of the House of Lords: a short history*, rev. edn (London, 1972).

Dorling, A. R. 'The Graves mathematical collection', *Annals of Science* 33 (1976), 307–10.

Doubleday, W. E. (ed.). *A primer of librarianship* (London, 1931).

Doyle, A. I. 'Martin Joseph Routh and his books in Durham University Library', *Durham University Journal* 48 (1955–6), 100–7.

Doyle, M., and O. Marshall. 'Government libraries', *Library Review* 34 (1985), 79–82.

Drake, F. M. *A hundred years with the Devon & Exeter Institution* (Exeter, 1913), 20–2.

Dring, E. M. 'Fifty years at Quaritch', in R. Linenthal (ed.), *The Book Collector: special number for the 150th anniversary of Bernard Quaritch* (London, 1997), 35–52.

Drodge, S. 'Co-operative Society libraries and education in the nineteenth century: a preliminary assessment', *Studies in the Education of Adults* 20 (1988), 49–59.

Duckett, R. J. 'Friend or foe? The Northern Counties Library Association, 1900–1920', *Library History* 12 (1996), 155–70.

'Paradise lost? The retreat from reference', *Library Review* 41 (1) (1992), 4–24.

'The parlous state of the librarianship of religion', *Library Association Record* 75 (1973), 21–2.

'Reference libraries today', in *Encyclopedia of library and information science*, vol. 54 (New York, 1994), 305–36.

'Theological libraries and librarianship', in Whatley (ed.) *British librarianship and information science 1971–75*, 252–9.

Duff, A. S. *Information society studies* (London, 2000).

'The past, present and future of information policy: towards a normative theory of the information society', *Information, Communication and Society* 7 (2004), 69–87.

'Some post-war models of the information chain', *Journal of Librarianship and Information Science* 29 (1997), 179–87.

Dunleavy, P. 'The United Kingdom: paradoxes of an ungrounded statism', in F. G. Castles (ed.), *The comparative history of public policy* (London, 1989), 242–91.

Dyer, B. L., and J. Lloyd. 'Women librarians in England', *Library Assistant* 1 (1899), 219–22.

Dyer, H., with A. Morris. *Human aspects of library automation* (Aldershot, 1990).

Dyson, B. (ed.). *The modern academic library: essays in memory of Philip Larkin* (London, 1989).

East, H. 'Changes in the staffing of UK special libraries and information services in the decade 1972–81: a review of the DES census data', *Journal of Documentation* 39 (1983), 247–65.

Eastwood, C. R. *Mobile libraries and other library transport* (London, 1967).

Eco, U. *The name of the rose* (London, 1984).

Edwards, E. *Free town libraries, their formation, management, and history; in Britain, France, Germany, & America* (London, 1869).

Memoirs of libraries, 2 vols. (London, 1859).

Edwards, R. J. *In service training in British libraries: its development and present practice* (London, 1977).

Edwards, W. J. *From the valley I came* (London, 1956).

Efficiency Unit. *Improving management in government: the next steps: report to the Prime Minister* (London, 1988).

Ehrman, A. 'Contemporary collectors II: the Broxbourne Library', *The Book Collector* 3 (1954), 190–6.

Eliot, S. 'Bookselling by the backdoor: circulating libraries, booksellers and book clubs 1870–1966', in R. Myers and M. Harris (eds.), *A genius for letters: bookselling from the 16th to the 20th century* (Winchester, 1995).

'"Mr Greenhill, whom you cannot get rid of": copyright, legal deposit and the Stationers' Company in the nineteenth century', in Myers, Harris and Mandelbrote (eds.), *Libraries and the book trade*, 51–84.

'"Never mind the value, what about the price?" Or, how much did *Marmion* cost St John Rivers?', *Nineteenth-Century Literature* 56 (2001), 164–7.

Some patterns and trends in British publishing 1800–1919 (London, 1994).

'The three-decker novel and its first cheap reprint, 1862–94', *The Library* 6th series, 7 (1985), 38–53.

Elkin, J., and R. Lonsdale. *Focus on the child: libraries, literacy and learning* (London, 1996).

Elkin, J., and T. Wilson (eds.). *The education of information and library professionals in the United Kingdom* (London, 1997).

Elliot-Binns, L. E. *Religion in the Victorian era* (London, 1936).

Ellis, A. *Library services for young people in England and Wales 1830–1970* (Oxford, 1971).
Public libraries at the time of the Adams Report (Stevenage, 1979).

Ellis-King, D. 'Decades of aspiration: public libraries 1947–87', in An Chomhairle Leab-harlanna, *The university of the people: celebrating Ireland's public libraries* (Dublin, 2003), 43–55.

Engels, F. *The condition of the working class in England in 1844* (London, 1892).

England, L. *The library user: the reading habits and attitudes of public library users in Great Britain* (London, 1994).

Englefield, D. *Parliament and information* (London, 1981).

Englefield, D. (ed.). *Workings of Westminster: essays in honour of David Menhennet, Librarian of the House of Commons 1976–1991* (Dartmouth, 1991).

Enright, B., L. Hellinga and B. Leigh. *Selection for survival: a review of acquisition and retention policies* (London, 1989).

Evans, L. W. *Education in industrial Wales, 1700–1900: a study of the works school system in Wales during the Industrial Revolution* (Cardiff, 1971).

Everitt, J. 'Co-operative Society libraries', *Library History* 15 (1999), 33–40.
'Co-operative Society libraries and newsrooms of Lancashire and Yorkshire from 1844 to 1918', unpublished PhD thesis, University of Wales, Aberystwyth (1997).

Farradane, J. 'Information service in industry', *Research* 6 (1953), 327–30.

Faulkner-Brown, H. 'Some thoughts on the design of major library buildings', in *Intelligent library buildings: proceedings of the 10th seminar of the IFLA Section on Library Buildings and Equipment* (The Hague, 1997), 9–24.

Fawcett, J. 'History of the Board of Trade Library', unpublished BA dissertation, Birmingham Polytechnic (1985).

Fazle Kabir, A. M. *The libraries of Bengal 1700–1947* (London, 1987).

FCO Historians, Library and Records Department, Foreign and Commonwealth Office. *Foreign and Commonwealth Library and Records 1782–1995*, History Notes 8 (London, 1995).

Feather, J. *A history of British publishing* (London, 1988).
'Institutional collections in Great Britain', in A. D. Schreyer (ed.), *Rare books 1983–84* (New York, 1984), 61–7.

Feather, J., and A. Lusher. 'Education for conservation in British library schools: current practices and future prospects', *Journal of Librarianship* 21 (1989), 129–38.

Feather, J., G. Matthews and P. Eden. *Preservation management: policies and practices in British libraries* (Aldershot, 1996).

Febvre, L., and H.-J. Martin. *L'apparition du livre* (Paris, 1958); English translation by David Gerard: *The coming of the book: the impact of printing 1450–1800* (London, 1976).

Ferriter, D. 'The post-war public library service: bringing books "to the remotest hamlets and the hills"', in An Chomhairle Leabharlanna, *The university of the people: celebrating Ireland's public libraries* (Dublin, 2003), 67–77.

Filon, S. P. L. *The National Central Library: an experiment in library co-operation* (London, 1977).

Finkelstein, D. '"The Secret": British publishers and Mudie's struggle for economic survival 1861–64', *Publishing History* 34 (1993), 21–50.

Fletcher, H. G. (ed.). *The Wormsley Library: a personal selection by Sir Paul Getty* (London, 1999).

Fletcher, H. R. *The story of the Royal Horticultural Society* (Oxford, 1969).

Fletcher, H. R., and W. H. Brown. *The Royal Botanic Garden Edinburgh 1670–1970* (Edinburgh, 1970).

Follett, D. *The rise of the Science Museum under Henry Lyons* (London, 1978).

[Follett Report] Joint Funding Councils Libraries Review. *Report* (Bristol, 1993).

Foot, M. M. 'The Henry Davis Collection: the British Museum gift', in her *Studies in the history of bookbinding* (Aldershot, 1993), 355–83.

Foreman, S. *Ships and shoes and sealing wax: an illustrated history of the Board of Trade 1786–1986* (London, 1986).

Forster, G. 'Libraries for the few: the members of the Association of Independent Libraries and their archives', *Library History* 9 (1/2) (1991), 15–26.

'The subscription library in the twentieth century', *Library Review* 44 (6) (1995), 5–18.

Foskett, A. C. 'Computers in libraries', in Sewell (ed.), *Five years' work in librarianship 1961–1965*, 456.

The subject approach to information, 5th edn (London, 1996).

Foskett, D. *Information service in libraries* (London, 1958).

Fox, P. 'The librarians of Trinity College', in Kinane and Walsh (eds.), *Essays on the library of Trinity College Dublin*, 11–24.

Fox, P. (ed.) *Cambridge University Library: the great collections* (Cambridge, 1998).

(ed.). *Treasures of the library: Trinity College Dublin* (Dublin, 1986).

Francis, Sir F. C. (ed.). *The Bibliographical Society, 1892–1942: studies in retrospect* (London, 1945).

Francis, Sir F. C., and V. Bloomfield. *Independent libraries in England: a survey of selected institutional, proprietary and endowed libraries* (London, 1977).

Francis, H. 'The origins of the South Wales Miners' Library', *History Workshop* 2 (1976), 183–205.

Fraser, V. 'Exposing the invisible ceiling in LIS', *Library Association Record* 97 (8) (1995), 434.

Frazier, A. 'Magee, William Kirkpatrick', in *Oxford Dictionary of National Biography* (Oxford, 2004), vol. 36, 113–15.

Freeman, A. 'The Jazz Age library of Jerome Kern', in R. Myers, M. Harris and G. Mandelbrote (eds.), *Under the hammer: book auctions since the seventeenth century* (New Castle, DE and London, 2001), 209–30.

Freeman, A., and J. I. Freeman. *Anatomy of an auction: rare books at Ruxley Lodge, 1919* (London, 1990).

Freeman, O. 'Industrial and commercial libraries', in Bromley and Allott (eds.), *British librarianship and information work 1986–1990*, vol. 2, 271–82.

Friedman, J., and A. Jeffreys. *Cataloguing and classification in British university libraries* (Sheffield, 1967), 24.

Frost, S. 'What do you mean! Insight into the working life of an advertising agency's library and information unit', *Assistant Librarian* 81 (5) (1988), 71–3.

Fry, W. G., and W. A. Munford. *Louis Stanley Jast: a biographical sketch* (London, 1966).

Furner, J. 'Digital images in libraries', *Vine* 107 (1998), 4.

Gage, A. T. *A history of the Linnean Society of London* (London, 1938).

Garnett, R. *Essays in librarianship and bibliography* (London, 1899).

Garrett, V. 'Messrs. Rowntree's (York) technical library', *Library Association Record* 23 (1921), 369–71.

Garside, K. 'The basic principles of the new library classification at University College London', *Journal of Documentation* 10 (1954), 169–92.

Gasaway, L. N., and M. G. Chiorazzi (eds.). *Law librarianship: historical perspectives* (Littleton, Colo., 1996).

Gattie, W. M. 'What English people read', *Fortnightly Review* 46 (1889), 302–21.

Gavin, J. 'Cumbrian literary institutions: Cartmel & Furness to 1900', in P. Isaac and B. McKay (eds.), *Images & texts: their production and distribution in the 18th and 19th centuries* (Winchester, 1997), 53–64.

Gehl, P. F. 'Bertram Lord Ashburnham', in Baker and Womack (eds.), *Nineteenth-century British book-collectors*, 10–20.

Gerard, D. *Shrieking silence: a library landscape* (Metuchen, NJ and London, 1988).

Gibson, S. 'Colonel William E. Moss', *Bodleian Library Record* 5 (1955), 156–66.

Giddens, A. *The consequences of modernity* (Cambridge and Oxford, 1990).

Modernity and self-identity: self and society in the late modern age (Cambridge, 1991).

Gillam, S. 'The Bodleian Library in the nineteen thirties', *Bodleian Library Record* 18 (1) (2003), 16–31.

The Radcliffe Camera (Oxford, 1992).

Githens, A. M. 'Complete development of the open plan in the Enoch Pratt Library at Baltimore', *Library Journal* 55 (1 May 1933), 381–5.

Gjelsness, R. H. 'Cooperation in catalog code revision', *Catalogers' and Classifiers' Yearbook* 6 (1937), 65–70.

Gladstone, W. E. 'Gladstone on the growth of public libraries in England: speech delivered at the opening of the Free Public Library of St Martin-in-the-Fields', *Library Journal* 17 (1892), 200–2.

'On books and the housing of them', *The Nineteenth Century* 27 (1890), 384–96.

Glasgow University Library. *500 years of donations* (Glasgow, 1976).

Godbolt, S., and W. A. Munford. *The incomparable Mac: a biographical study of Sir John Young Walker MacAlister* (London, 1983).

Going, M. E. (ed.). *Hospital libraries*, 2nd edn (London, 1973).

(ed.). *Hospital libraries and work with the disabled* (London, 1963).

Goodacre, H. J., and A. P. Pritchard. *Guide to the Department of Oriental Manuscripts and Printed Books* (London, 1977).

Gorman, M. 'Human values in a technological age', *Logos* 12 (2001), 63–9.

Gosden, P. H. J. H., and A. J. Taylor (eds.). *Studies in the history of a university, 1874–1974: to commemorate the centenary of the University of Leeds* (Leeds, 1975).

Goulding, A. 'Libraries and social capital', *Journal of Librarianship and Information Science* 36 (2004), 3–6.

'Government libraries in Northern Ireland', *Northern Ireland Libraries* 9 (1974), 44–6.

Graham, F. A. 'Industrial libraries', in Whatley (ed.), *British librarianship and information science 1971–1975*, 209–13.

Graham, T. W., R. Lane and K. M. Richards. 'Keyword and Boolean searching on Geac at Hull University', *Vine* 48 (1983), 3–7.

Grant, D. 'The lighting of the National Gallery', *The British Architect* (13 February 1885), 80.

Grayson, L. *Library and information services for local government* (London, 1978).

Green, A. 'Digital library, open library: developments in the National Library of Wales', *Alexandria* 14 (2002), 161–70.

Greenhalgh, L., K. Worpole and C. Landry. *Libraries in a world of cultural change* (London, 1995).

Greenwood, A. *The educational department of the Rochdale Equitable Pioneers Society Limited* (Manchester, 1877).

Greenwood, D. 'The BNB Research Fund: cutting across the boundaries', *Journal of Librarianship* 21 (1989), 246–59.

Greenwood, T. *Free public libraries: their organisation, uses and management* (London, 1886).
'The great fiction question', *Library Year Book* (1897), 107–16.
Public libraries: a history of the movement and a manual for the organization and management of rate-supported libraries, 4th edn (London, 1891).
Sunday-school and village libraries: with a list of suitable books and hints on management (London, 1892).

Greenwood, T. (ed.). *British library year book 1900–1901: a record of library progress and work* (London, 1900).

Greetham, D. C. *Textual scholarship: an introduction*, corrected edn (New York, 1994).

Grenz, S. J. *A primer on postmodernism* (Grand Rapids and Cambridge, 1996).

Griest, G. L. *Mudie's Circulating Library & the Victorian novel* (Bloomington, IN, 1970).

Grieve, C. M. ('Hugh McDiarmid'). *Lucky poet: a self-study in literature and political ideas* (London, 1943).

Griffiths, L. M. 'W. H. Smith & Son's circulating library', unpublished MLS dissertation, Loughborough University (1981).

Griffiths, T. E. 'Caernarvonshire and its libraries: development of the first county library in Wales', *Transactions of the Caernarvonshire Historical Society* 33 (1972), 170–89.

Grimes, B. *Irish Carnegie libraries: a catalogue and architectural history* (Dublin, 1998).
'"Will not be heard of again": a proposal to combine the resources of the National Library and Trinity College Library', *Long Room* 46 (2001), 18–22.

Grindea, M. (ed.). *The London Library* (Ipswich, 1977).

Gross, J. *The rise and fall of the man of letters* (London, 1969).

Gruffydd, R. G. 'Wales, National Library of', in *Encyclopedia of library and information science*, vol. 41 (1986), 353.

Guild, J. R., and A. Law (eds.). *Edinburgh University Library 1580–1980* (Edinburgh, 1982).

Gunther, A. E. *A century of zoology* (London, 1975).

Gwinn, N. E., and P. H. Mosher. 'Co-ordinating collection development', *College and Research Libraries* 44 (1983), 128–40.

Habermas, J. *Structural transformation of the public sphere: an inquiry into a category of bourgeois society* (London, 1989).

Hall, J. J. 'The guard-book catalogue of Cambridge University Library', *Library History* 13 (1997), 39–56.

Halper, S. 'Housing information galore', *Library Association Record* 102 (2000), 397.

Halsey, A. H., and M. A. Trow. *The British academic* (London, 1971).

Hamilton, J. T. *Greenock libraries: a development and social history 1635–1967* (Greenock, 1967).

Hanley, H. N. *Dr John Lee of Hartwell* (Buckingham, 1983).

Hannam, H. 'Government libraries', in Whatley (ed.), *British librarianship and information work 1971–75*, 199–208.

Hansford, F. E. 'What adults read', *Library World* 38 (1935–6), 229–32.

Hanson, E. H. *An historical essay of the Ipswich Institute 1925–1987* (Ipswich, 1989).

Hanson, J. 'Free public libraries', *Westminster Review* 98 (1872), 333–77.

Harding, H. *Patent Office centenary* (London, 1953).

Hare, H. T. 'Libraries', *Builders' Journal* 25 (20 March 1907), 130.

'Some recent public libraries', *Architectural Review* 24 (2) (1908), 228–49.

Hare, H. T., and J. D. Brown. 'Public Libraries', *Journal of the Royal Institute of British Architects* 14 (March 1907), 341–57.

Harley, H. C. 'The Radcliffe Science Library', in *History of the University of Oxford*, vol. 6, 692–3.

Harley Lewis, R. *Book collecting: a new look* (Newton Abbot, 1988).

Harris, C. *The use of reference services in large city libraries: the CRUS study* (Sheffield, 1983).

Harris, J. *Ibadan University Library: some notes on its birth and growth* (Ibadan, 1968).

Harris, P. R. 'Acquisitions in the Department of Printed Books and the effects of the war', *British Library Journal* 12 (1986), 119–44.

A history of the British Museum Library 1753–1973 (London, 1998).

The Reading Room (London, 1986).

Harrison, K. C. *A librarian's odyssey: episodes of autobiography* (Eastbourne, 2000).

Harte, N. *The University of London 1836–1986: an illustrated history* (London, 1986).

Hartog, P. J. *The Owens College, Manchester, founded 1851: a brief history of the College and description of its various departments* (Manchester, 1900).

Harvey, D. *The condition of postmodernity: an inquiry into the origins of cultural change* (Oxford, 1989).

Hasson, A. 'Reaching out', in M. Kinnell and P. Sturges (eds.), *Continuity and innovation in the public library: the development of a social institution* (London, 1996), 148–66.

Havard-Williams, P. 'University libraries', in Sewell (ed.), *Five years' work in librarianship 1961–65*, 34–5.

'University library buildings', in Whatley (ed.), *British librarianship and information science 1966–70*, 181–91.

Hearnshaw, F. J. C. *Centenary history of King's College, London, 1828–1927* (London, 1929).

Heart of a London village: the Highgate Literary and Scientific Institution, 1839–1990 (Highgate, 1991).

Hedges, G. 'For those in peril on the sea: the Deal Boatmen's Rooms', *Library History* 19 (2003), 35–8.

Heeks, P., and P. Turner (eds.). *Public library aims and objectives: policy statements prepared by members of the Public Libraries Research Group* (Brighton, 1981).

Heery, M. 'New model librarians: a question of realism', *Journal of Librarianship and Information Science* 25 (1993), 137–42.

Heimann, P. M. 'The scientific revolutions', in P. Burke (ed.), *The new Cambridge modern history*, vol. 13: *Companion volume* (Cambridge, 1979), 248–70.

Hellinga, L., and J. Goldfinch (eds.). *Bibliography and the study of 15th century civilization* (London, 1987).

Henchy, P. 'The Joly family and the National Library', *Irish University Review* 7 (1977), 184–98. *The National Library of Ireland, 1941–1976: a look back* (Dublin, 1986).

Henderson, K., D. McMenemy and F. Schofield. 'People's network libraries: comparative case studies of old and new ICT learning centres', *Library Review* 53 (2004), 157–66.

Hendrick, B. J. *Andrew Carnegie*, 2 vols. (New York, 1932).

Hennessey, P. *Whitehall* (London, 1989).

Hepworth, A. 'Desert information room', *Library Association Record* 44 (1945), 175–7.

Herbert, J. *Inside Christie's* (London, 1990).

Hernon, P., and G. R. McClure. *Unobtrusive testing and library reference services* (Norwood, NJ, 1987).

Herrmann, F. *Sotheby's: portrait of an auction house* (London, 1980).

Hewitt, A. R. 'Law librarianship', *Library Association Record* 50 (1948), 91–7.

Hewitt, H. 'Confronting the modern city: the Manchester Free Public Library, 1850–80', *Urban History* 27 (2000), 62–88.

Hewitt, M. (ed.). *Scholarship in Victorian Britain* (Leeds, 1998).

Hibbert, J. (ed.). *Notes on free public libraries and museums* (Preston, 1881).

Higher education: a new framework (London, 1991) (Cmnd. 1541).

Highsmith, D. 'The long, strange trip of Barbara Gordon: images of librarians in comic books', *The Reference Librarian* 78 (2002), 61–84 (Special Issue: The image and role of the librarian).

Hildenbrand, S. 'Women in library history: from the politics of library history to the history of library politics', in S. Hildenbrand (ed.), *Reclaiming the American library past: writing the women in* (Norwood, NJ, 1996), 1–23.

Hill, F. J. '"Fortescue": the British Museum and British Library Subject Index', *British Library Journal* 12 (1986), 58–63.

Hill, J. *Children are people: the librarian in the community* (London, 1973).

Hill, K. 'Rare books as investments', *The Book Collector* 47 (1998), 342–51.

'Hints for improved library economy, drawn from usages at Princeton', *Library Journal* 2 (1877–8), 55.

Hirshberg, H. S. 'Four library buildings', *American Library Association Bulletin* 27 (15 December 1933), 732–7.

History of the Juridical Society of Edinburgh, ed. William Reid (Edinburgh, 1875).

History of the subscription library at Kingston-upon-Hull (Hull, 1876).

A history of the University of Cambridge, vol. 3: *1750–1870*, by P. Searby (Cambridge, 1997) and vol. 4: *1870–1990*, by C. N. L. Brooke (Cambridge, 1993).

The history of the University of Oxford, vols. 6–7: *Nineteenth-century Oxford*, ed. M. G. Brock and M. C. Curthoys (Oxford, 1997) and vol. 8: *The twentieth century*, ed. B. Harrison (Oxford, 1994).

HM Treasury, Organisation and Methods Division. *A guide to government libraries* (London, 1952).

Hoare, P. 'The development of a European information society', *Library Review* 47 (1998), 377–82.

'"Hungry for reading": libraries in the British zone of occupation', in A. Bance (ed.), *The cultural legacy of the British occupation in Germany* (Stuttgart, 1997), 205–22.

'Legal deposit of electronic publications and other non-print material: an international overview', *Alexandria* 9 (1997), 59–79.

'The librarians of Glasgow University 1641–1991', *Library Review* 40 (2/3) (1991), 27–43.

'"Loads of learned lumber": special collections in the smaller university library', in B. Dyson (ed.), *The modern academic library: essays in memory of Philip Larkin* (London, 1989), 57–66.

'Nottingham Subscription Library: its organisation, its collections and its management over 175 years', in R. T. Coope and J. Y. Corbett (eds.), *Bromley House 1752–1991: four essays celebrating the 175th anniversary of the Nottingham Subscription Library* (Nottingham, 1991), 1–47.

'The operatives' libraries of Nottingham: a radical community's own libraries', *Library History* 19 (2003), 173–84.

Hobson, A. R. A., and A. N. L. Munby. 'Contemporary collectors xxvi: John Roland Abbey', *The Book Collector* 10 (1961), 40–8.

Hodgson, J. R. (ed.). *A guide to special collections of the John Rylands University Library of Manchester* (Manchester, 1999).

Hogan, D. *The legal profession in Ireland 1789–1922* (Dublin, 1986).

Hogg, G. (ed.). *Special and named printed collections in the National Library of Scotland* (Edinburgh, 1999).

Holmes, P. L. *On-line information retrieval: an introduction and guide to the British Library's Short-Term Experimental Information Network,* 2 vols. (London, 1977–8).

Hood, S. *Royal roots – Republican inheritance: the survival of the Office of Arms* (Dublin, 2002).

Hookway, H. 'The British Library: introduction', in Saunders (ed.), *British librarianship today,* 37–44.

Hooton, J. 'The Hull Subscription Library closure and sale', *Library History* 4 (1976), 11–12.

Hopkins, L. 'Prison library services: the public library authorities perspective', *Public Library Journal* 9 (1994), 159–61.

Hopkins, T. M. 'A protest against low works of fiction', *Westminster Review* 149 (January 1898), 99–102.

Hort, T. *History and progress of the Chancery Library, now called the Probate Library* (London, 1895).

The Hospital Library Council, 1937–1958 (Dublin, 1958).

House of Commons, Information Office. *House of Commons Library Department,* Factsheet 50 (London, 2000).

House of Commons, Science and Technology Committee. *Scientific publications: free for all?* (London, 2004).

Howard, J. V. 'Libraries (church, theological, etc.)', in N. M. de S. Cameron (ed.), *Dictionary of Scottish church history* (Edinburgh, 1993), 482–3.

Howard-Hill, T. H. 'Enumerative and descriptive bibliography', in P. Davison (ed.), *The book encompassed* (Cambridge, 1992), 122–9.

Howsam, L. *Cheap Bibles, nineteenth century publishing and the British and Foreign Bible Society* (Cambridge, 1991).

Hudson, J. W. *History of adult education* (London, 1851).

Hull, B. 'ICT and social exclusion: the role of libraries', *Telematics and Informatics* 20 (2003), 131–42.

Humphrey, F. 'Fragmentation of government sources of information', *Refer* 10 (1994), 14–15.

Hunt, K. G. *Subject specialisation and co-operative book purchase in the libraries of Great Britain*, Library Association pamphlet 12 (London, 1955).

Hunter, E. J., and K. G. B. Bakewell. *Cataloguing*, 3rd edn (London, 1993).

Hunter, M. 'Libraries in Scottish prisons', *The Book Trolley* 2 (1968), 58–60.

Hutton, R. S. 'The origin and history of Aslib', *Journal of Documentation* 1 (1945), 6–20.

Huws, D. *The National Library of Wales: a history of the building* (Aberystwyth, 1994).

Hyde, M., and J. Hyde. 'The industrial library: networking and cooperation', in D. Mason (ed.), *Information for industry: twenty-one years of the Library Association Industrial Group* (London, 1991), 63–72.

Hyman, R. J. *Shelf access in libraries* (Chicago, 1982), 66–70.

IASLIC Bulletin 37 (3) (1992), Ranganathan centenary issue.

IFLA. *International standard bibliographic description for monographs* (London, 1971).

Independent review of higher education pay and conditions: report of a committee (London, 1999) (The Bett Report).

Insight Research. *Reference libraries and information services: technological change and financial pressure* (London, 1997).

'Inter-library lending and document delivery: an overview', *Vine* 95 (1994), 3.

International Conference on Cataloguing Principles, Paris, 1961, *Report* (London, 1963).

Irwin, R. 'The golden chain', in his *The heritage of the English library* (London, 1964), 26–42.

  Librarianship: essays on applied bibliography (London, 1949).

Irwin, R., and R. Staveley (eds.). *The libraries of London*, 2nd edn repr. with corrections (London, 1964).

Jackaman, P. 'The library in Utopia: libraries in nineteenth-century alternative communities in Britain and America', *Library History* 9 (1993), 169–89.

Jackson, I. *The provincial press and the community* (Manchester, 1971).

Jackson, J. A. (ed.). *Professions and professionalisation* (Cambridge, 1970).

Jackson, T. A. *Solo trumpet: some memories of socialist agitation and propaganda* (London, 1953).

Jamieson, D. R. 'Mechanized bibliographical aid', *Library Association Record* 53 (1951), 216.

Jast, L. S. 'The library outlook: an address to municipal library assistants', *Library Association Record* 11 (1912), 35–6.

  Libraries and living: essays and addresses of a public librarian (London, 1932).

  The planning of a great library (London, 1927).

Jast, L. S., and W. C. B. Sayers. 'The registration of librarians: a criticism and a suggestion', *Library Association Record* 9 (1908), 325–35.

Jay, E. *The Armitt story* (Ambleside, 1998).

Jefferson, G. *Library co-operation*, 2nd edn (London, 1977).

Jenkins, D. *A refuge in peace and war: the National Library of Wales to 1952* (Aberystwyth, 2002).

Jenkins, P. *Mrs Thatcher's revolution: the ending of the socialist era* (London, 1987).

Jervis, S. 'The English country house library: an architectural history', *Library History* 18 (2002), 175–90.

Jesson, A. F. *The impact of the Word on the world* (Rome, 2000).

Jobey, G. 'The Society of Antiquaries of Newcastle upon Tyne', *Archaeologia Aeliana* 5th series, 18 (1990), 197–216.

John, A. H. *The British Library of Political and Economic Science: a brief history* (London, 1971).

John, C. 'The Advocates' Library three hundred and ten years on', *Law Librarian* 23 (1992), 111–14.

Johnman, W. A. P., and M. Kendall. *Report of the commission appointed to enquire into the condition and working of free libraries of various towns in England* (Darlington, 1869).

Johns, A. W. *Special libraries* (Metuchen, NJ, 1968).

Johnson, E. 'The special library and some of its problems', *Special Libraries* 6 (1915), 158–9.

Johnson, I. 'Challenges in developing professionals for the "information society" and some responses by British schools of librarianship and information studies', *Library Review* 47 (1998), 52–9.

'Unesco and human resource development for the information society', *Education for Information* 16 (1998), 237–42.

Johnston, C., 'Electronic technology and its impact on libraries', *Journal of Librarianship and Information Science* 30 (1998), 7–24.

Joint Funding Councils Libraries Review. *Report* (Bristol, 1993) (The Follett Report).

Report of the group on a national/regional strategy for library provision for researchers (Bristol, 1996) (The Anderson Report).

Jolliffe, H. *Public library extension activities* (London, 1962).

Jones, D. L. 'The House of Lords Library', *Law Librarian* 29 (1998), 105–7.

Jones, H. K. *Butterworths: history of a publishing house*, 2nd edn (London, 1997).

Jones, K. P. 'Industrial libraries and information units', in Whatley (ed.), *British librarianship and information science 1966–1970*, 504–17.

Jones, P. H., and E. Rees (eds.). *A nation and its books: a history of the book in Wales* (Aberystwyth, 1998).

Jones, T. 'Workmen's libraries and institutes', in his *Leeks and daffodils* (Newtown, 1942), 131–40.

Jordan, P. 'Social class, race relations and the public library', *Assistant Librarian* 65 (3) (1972), 38–41.

Kaiser, J. *Systematic indexing* (London, 1911).

The card system at the office (London, 1908).

Kaltwasser, F. G., and J. M. Smethurst (eds.). *Retrospective cataloguing in Europe: 15th to 19th century printed materials. Proceedings of the International Conference, Munich, September 1990* (Munich, 1992).

Kane, B. A. *The widening circle: the story of the Folger Shakespeare Library and its collections* (Washington, DC, 1976).

Karetzky, S. *Not seeing red: American librarianship and the Soviet Union* (Lanham, NY and Oxford, 2002).

Kauffman, S. B. 'Law libraries', in Wiegand and Davis (eds.), *Encyclopedia of library history*, 332–6.

Kaufman, P. 'Coffee houses as reading centres,' in his *Libraries and their users*, 115–27.

'The community library: a chapter in English social history', *Transactions of the American Philosophical Society* new series 57 (7) (1967), 1–65 (reprinted in abridged form in his *Libraries and their users*, 188–222).

'Discovering the oldest public bibliotheck in the Northern Isles', *Library Review* 23 (1972), 285–7.

'Leadhills, library of diggers', in his *Libraries and their users*, 163–70.

Libraries and their users: collected papers in library history (London, 1969).

'The rise of community libraries in Scotland', *Papers of the Bibliographical Society of America* 59 (1963), 233–94; reprinted as 'Scotland as the home of community libraries' in his *Libraries and their users*, 134–47.

Kay, J. T. 'The provision of novels in rate-supported libraries', *Transactions and proceedings of the second annual meeting of the Library Association of the United Kingdom* (London, 1879), 42–6.

Keighley Corporation. *The public library service in Keighley, 1904–1975* (Keighley, 1954).

Kelly, J. (ed.). *The collected letters of W. B. Yeats*, vol. 3 (Oxford, 1994).

Kelly, T. *Books for the people: an illustrated history of the British public library* (London, 1977).

Early public libraries: a history of public libraries in Great Britain before 1850 (London, 1966).

A history of public libraries in Great Britain 1845–1965 (London, 1973).

A history of public libraries in Great Britain 1845–1975, 2nd edn (London, 1977).

Public libraries in Great Britain before 1850 (London, 1966).

Kennedy, M. 'Civic pride versus financial pressure: financing the Dublin Public Library Service, 1884–1920', *Library History* 9 (1992), 83–96.

'Plans for a central reference library for Dublin 1883–1946', *An Leabharlann* second series 7 (1991), 113–25.

Kenny, Sir A. *The British Library and the St Pancras building* (London, 1994).

Kenny, C. 'Counsellor Duhigg: antiquarian and activist', *Irish Jurist* 21 (1986), 300–25.

King's Inns and the battle of the books, 1972: cultural controversy at a Dublin library (Dublin, 2002).

King's Inns and the kingdom of Ireland: the Irish 'Inn of Court' 1541–1800 (Dublin, 1992).

Keogh, C. A. *Report on public library provision in the Irish Free State, 1935* (Athlone, 1936).

Kerry, D. A. *A guide to theological and religious studies collections of Great Britain and Ireland* (London, 1999).

Kerslake, E. 'A history of women workers in English libraries 1871–1974', unpublished PhD thesis, Loughborough University (1999).

'"My famous Kate Pierce": biographies of and in the archive', *Vitae Scholasticae* 19 (1) (2000), 35–58.

Kerslake, E., and J. Liladhar. 'Angry sentinels and businesslike women: identity and marital status in 1950s English library career novels', *Library History* 17 (2001), 83–90.

'"Jolly good reading" for girls: discourses of library work and femininity in career novels', *Women's History Review* 8 (3) (1999), 489–504.

Kerslake, E., and N. Moody (eds.). *Gendering library history* (Liverpool, 2000).

Kersley, R. H. *Gibson's 1876–1962: a chapter in legal education* (London, 1973).

Keynes, Sir G. *Bibliotheca bibliographici: a catalogue of the library formed by Geoffrey Keynes* (London, 1964).

Killen, J. *A history of the Linen Hall Library 1788–1988* (Belfast, 1990).

Kimber, R. T. 'Computer applications in the fields of library housekeeping and information processing', *Program* 1 (6) (1967), 17–21.

Kinahan, A. J. (ed.). *Now and then: a celebration of Sweet & Maxwell's bicentenary* (London, 1999).

Kinane, V. 'Legal deposit, 1801–1922', in Kinane and Walsh (eds.), *Essays on the history of Trinity College Library*, 120–37.

Kinane, V., and A. Walsh (eds.). *Essays on the history of Trinity College Library, Dublin* (Dublin, 2000).

King, A. H. 'The history of music libraries in the United Kingdom', *Fontes Artis Musicae* 15 (1978), 201–4.

　　Printed music in the British Museum: an account of the collections, the catalogues, and their formation, up to 1920 (London, 1979).

　　Some British collectors of music c.1600–1960 (Cambridge, 1963), 82–3.

King, D. W. 'Government departmental libraries' in R. Irwin (ed.), *The libraries of London* (London, 1949), 115–24.

King, R. *Royal Kew* (London, 1985).

Kinnell, M., and P. Sturges (eds.). *Continuity and innovation in the public library: the development of a social institution* (London, 1996).

Kirby, S. 'Co-operation: a suggestion', *Library Assistant* 5 (1907), 266–9.

Kirk, H. *Portrait of a profession: a history of the solicitor's profession, 1100 to the present day* (London, 1976).

Kirkpatrick, T. P. C. *Ernest Reginald McClintock Dix (1857–1936), Irish bibliographer* (Dublin, 1937).

Kissack, R. *Victorian Monmouth* (Monmouth, 1986).

Kissane, N. (ed.). *Treasures from the National Library of Ireland* (Drogheda, 1994).

Knott, D. *Rare book collections: a brief guide* (Reading, 1980).

Knott, J. 'A history of the libraries of Newcastle upon Tyne to 1900'. Unpublished MLitt thesis, University of Newcastle upon Tyne (1975).

　　Newcastle libraries in the early 19th century, History of the Book Trade in the North Papers (Newcastle upon Tyne, 1973).

　　Newcastle upon Tyne City Libraries: the first 100 years. (Newcastle upon Tyne, 1980).

Koch, T. *War libraries and allied studies* (New York, 1918).

Koenig, M. 'Educational requirements for a library oriented career in information management', *Library Trends* 42 (1993), 277–89.

Kohn, R. S. 'A treasured legacy: Hebrew manuscripts at the Bodleiana', *Library History* 20 (2004), 95–116.

Kumar, K. *From post-industrial to post-modern society: new theories of the contemporary world* (Oxford, 1995).

Lambert, S., and S. Ropiequet (eds.). *CD-ROM: the new papyrus* (Redmond, WA, 1986).

Lancaster, F. W. *Indexing and abstracting in theory and practice*, 3rd edn (London, 2003).

　　Information retrieval systems: characteristics, testing and evaluation (New York, 1966).

　　Toward paperless information systems (New York, 1978).

Landau, T. (ed.). *Encyclopaedia of librarianship*, 3rd rev. edn (London, 1966).

Langewiesche, D., and K. Schönhoven. 'Arbeiterbibliotheken und Arbeiterlektüre im Wilhelminischen Deutschland', *Archiv für Sozialgeschichte* 16 (1976), 135–204.

Larkin, P. 'A neglected responsibility: contemporary literary manuscripts', in his *Required writing* (London, 1983), 98–108; originally published in *Encounter*, July 1979.

Latey, W. 'The Hardwicke Society', *Law Times* 206 (1948), 335–6.

Law, D. 'CD-Rom: a young technology with a great future behind it?', *Serials* 3 (3) (1990), 34–5.

'The development of a national policy for dataset provision in the UK: a historical perspective', *Journal of Information Networking* 1 (1994), 103–16.

Layzell Ward, P. 'Women and librarianship', *Library Association Record* 77 (April 1975), 82–3.

Women and librarianship: an investigation into certain problems of library staffing (London, 1966).

Lea, E. R. M., and A. F. Jesson. *A guide to the theological libraries of Great Britain and Ireland* (London, 1986).

'An Leabhar Chumann, The Book Association of Ireland', *Irish Library Bulletin* 6 (1945), 21–2.

'An Leabhar-Chumann, The Book Association of Ireland: objects, advantages and conditions of membership', *Irish Library Bulletin* 6 (1945), 64.

Leadbeater, C. *Overdue: how to create a modern public library service* (London, 2003) (Laser Foundation Report).

Lee, S. H. (ed.). *The role and future of special collections in research libraries: British and American perspectives* (New York, 1993).

Lee, S. R. V. 'The development of libraries within the Working Men's Club and Institute Union', unpublished MLib thesis, University of Wales, Aberystwyth (1992).

Leedham-Green, E. *A concise history of the University of Cambridge* (Cambridge, 1996).

Leeves, J. 'Library systems then and now', *Vine* 100 (1995), 19.

Lenin at the British Library (London, 1990).

Lessig, L. *Code and other laws of cyberspace* (New York, 1999).

Levi, L. 'On the progress of learned societies', *British Association Report* (Norwich, 1868), 169–73.

Lewis, M. J. 'History, development, change', in J. Ryder (ed.), *Library services to housebound people* (London, 1987), 1–22.

Leyland, E. *The wider public library* (London, 1938).

Librarians speaking (London, 1974–6), 23 tapes (British Library National Sound Archive).

'The libraries of the Inns of Court', *Law Magazine and Law Review* 8 (1859), 131–42.

'The library of the Middle Temple', *Law Magazine and Law Review* 7 (1859), 67–82.

Library and Information Commission. *Building the new library network* (London, 1998).

New library: the people's network (London, 1997).

Library and Information Services Council. *Setting objectives for public library services: a manual of public library objectives* (London, 1991).

Library and Information Services Council (Northern Ireland). *Library and Information Plan for Northern Ireland* (Belfast, 1990).

Library Association. *Examination papers set for Summer 1976* (London, 1976).

Preserving the word, ed. by R. E. Palmer (London, 1986).

Transactions and proceedings of the second annual meeting of the Library Association of the United Kingdom held at Manchester . . . 1879, ed. by H. R. Tedder and E. C. Thomas (London, 1880).

Library Association, Community Services Group. 'Group rules (constitution)', *Community Librarian* 3 (1986), 18–19.

Library Association, County Libraries Section. *County libraries in Great Britain and Ireland: statistical report 1938–9* (London, 1940?).

Library provision in Oxford. Report and recommendations of the commission appointed by the Congregation of the University (Oxford, 1931).

Library Year Book (London, 1910–11).

Liladhar, J., and E. Kerslake. 'No more library classes for Catherine: marital status, career progression and library employment in 1950s England', *Women's Studies International Forum* 22 (1999), 215–24.

Line, M. B. *Information requirements of researchers in the social sciences* (Bath, 1971).
  'Library management styles and structures: a need to rethink', *Journal of Librarianship and Information Science* 23 (1991), 97–104.

Literary and Philosophical Society of Newcastle upon Tyne. *Bicentenary lectures* (Newcastle, 1994).

Little, A. N. 'Some myths of university expansion', in P. Holmes (ed.), *Sociological studies in British university education* (Keele, 1963), 185–97.

Liverpool City Libraries. *Descriptive handbook with illustrations and plans* (Liverpool, 1912).

Llanelly Mechanics' Institute. *Rules and catalogue* (Llanelly, 1870).

Lock, R. N. *Library administration* 2nd edn (London, 1965).

London, G. 'The place and role of bibliographic description in general and individual catalogues: a historical analysis', *Libri* 30 (1980), 263.

London Borough of Leyton Libraries Department. *Opportunities 1948–9* (London, 1948).

Long, G. 'The foundation of the National Library of Ireland, 1836–1877', *Long Room* 36 (1991), 41–58.
  'The National Library of Ireland', in N. Buttimer and others (eds.), *The heritage of Ireland* (Cork, 2000), 305–12.

Loosjes, T. P. *On documentation of scientific literature* (London, 1967).

Lopez, M. D. 'Books and beds: libraries in nineteenth and twentieth century American hotels', *Journal of Library History* 9 (1974), 196–221.

Loughborough University. *Library & information statistics tables for the United Kingdom 1998* (LISU, 1999).

Loughridge, B. 'The SCONUL Graduate Trainee Scheme as preparation for professional education in librarianship and information work', *British Journal of Academic Librarianship* 2 (1987), 191–203.

Lovett, W. *Life and struggles of William Lovett* (London, 1876), reprinted London, 1967.

Lovett, W., and J. Collins. *Chartism: a new organisation of the people* (London, 1841).

Lubetzky, S. *Cataloging rules and principles: a critique of the A.L.A. rules for entry and a proposed design for their revision* (Washington, DC, 1953).

Luckham, B. *The library in society* (London, 1971).

Luhn, H. P. 'A statistical approach to mechanized encoding and searching of literary information', *IBM Journal of Research and Development* 1 (1957), 309–17.

Lydenberg, H. M. *History of the New York Public Library: Astor, Lenox and Tilden Foundations* (New York, 1923).

Lymburn, J. 'Notice of the Euing collection of Bibles', in W. P. Dickson, *The Glasgow University Library: notes on its history, arrangements, and aims* (Glasgow, 1888), 72–87.

Lynch, C. 'Institutional repositories: essential infrastructure for scholarship', *ARL Bimonthly Report* (2003), 1–7.

'On the threshold of discontinuity: the new genres of scholarly communication and the role of the research library' (available at http://www.ala.org/acrl/clynch.html, 2000).

Lyons, Sir H. *The Royal Society 1660–1940* (Cambridge, 1944).

Lyons, M., and J. Arnold (eds.). *A history of the book in Australia 1891–1945* (St Lucia, Queensland, 2001).

Lysaght, S. *Robert Lloyd Praeger: the life of a naturalist* (Dublin, 1998).

Lyster, T. W. 'Great Irish book collectors: Jaspar Robert Joly', *Irish Book Lover* 5 (12) (1921), 99–101.

'The National Library of Ireland', in Department of Agriculture and Technical Instruction for Ireland, *Ireland industrial and agricultural* (Dublin, 1902), 302–3.

McAlpine, W. H. *A catalogue of the Law Library at Hartwell House, Buckinghamshire* (London, 1865).

McCabe, I. M. 'The Royal Institution and its library', *Royal Institution Proceedings* 61 (1989), 283–90.

McClellan, A. W. *The reader, the library and the book: selected papers 1949–1970* (London, 1973).

McColvin, L. R. *Library extension work and publicity* (London, 1927).

The public library system of Great Britain: a report on its present condition with proposals for post-war reorganization (London, 1942).

McColvin, L. R. (ed.). *A survey of libraries: reports on a survey made by the Library Association during 1936–1937* (London, 1938).

McCord, N. *North east England: an economic and social history* (London, 1979).

McCrimmon, B. *Power, politics and print: the publication of the British Museum catalogue 1881–1900* (Hamden, CT and London, 1981).

Richard Garnett (Chicago, 1989).

'W. R. S. Ralston, 1828–89: scholarship and scandal in the British Museum', *British Library Journal* 14 (1988), 178–98.

Macdonald, J. J. *Passmore Edwards institutions: founding and opening ceremonies* (London, 1900).

McDonald, W. R. 'Circulating libraries in the north-east of Scotland in the eighteenth century', *The Bibliotheck* 5 (1967–9), 119–37.

MacDougall, A. F., H. Wheelhouse and J. M. Wilson. 'Academic library cooperation and document supply: possibilities and consideration of cost-effectiveness', *Journal of Librarianship* 21 (1989), 186–99.

MacDougall, J. and J. M. Brittain. 'Library and information science education in the United Kingdom', *Annual Review of Information Science and Technology* 28 (1993), 361–89.

McDowell, R. B. and D. A. Webb. *Trinity College Dublin 1592–1952: an academic history* (Cambridge, 1982).

McGrath, P., and P. Burton. 'Information technology in the library and information studies curriculum', in J. Elkin and T. Wilson (eds.), *The education of library and information professionals* (London, 1997), 83–116.

Machlup, F. *The production and distribution of knowledge in the United States* (Princeton, NJ, 1962).

McIlwraith, M., and E. Rodger. 'Robert Ogilvie Mackenna: an appreciation', *Library Review* 40 (2/3) (1991), 5–8.

MacInerney, M. H. 'Catholic lending libraries', *Irish Ecclesiastical Record* 19 (1922), 577.

MacIntyre, A. *After virtue: a study in moral theory* (London, 1981).

McKee, B. 'Information studies: towards an academic discipline', *Library Association Record* 88 (1986), 236–9.

MacKenna, R. O. 'University library organization', in Thompson (ed.), *University library history*, 92–108.

McKenzie, D. F. *Bibliography and the sociology of texts* (London, 1986).

'Printers of the mind', *Studies in Bibliography* 22 (1969), 1–75.

Mackenzie, J. M. 'The Royal Commonwealth Society library', in Fox (ed.), *Cambridge University Library: the great collections*, 166–84.

McKillop, J. 'The present position of London municipal libraries with suggestions for increasing their efficiency', *Library Association Record* 8 (1906), 625–35, 495–7.

McKitterick, D. J. 'Bibliotheca bibliographici', *Bulletin of the Friends of Cambridge University Library* 4 (1983), 7–9.

Cambridge University Library: a history, vol. 2 (Cambridge, 1986).

'The Munby Collection in the University Library', *Transactions of the Cambridge Bibliographical Society* 6 (1975), 205–10.

Mac Lochlainn, A. 'The National Library of Ireland, 1877–1977', *Irish University Review* 7 (1977), 157–67.

'"Those young men . . .": the National Library of Ireland and the cultural revolution' and A. Sheehy Skeffington, 'A coterie of lively suffragists', in their *Writers, raconteurs and notable feminists: two monographs* (Dublin, 1993).

Madan, F., and others. *A summary catalogue of western manuscripts in the Bodleian Library at Oxford*, 7 vols. in 8 (Oxford, 1895–1953). Vol. 1 (1953) includes a historical introduction by R. W. Hunt.

Magee, W. K., ('John Eglinton'). *Irish literary portraits* (London, 1935).

Maidment, W. R. 'Management of libraries and mechanization', in Whatley (ed.), *British librarianship and information science 1966–70*, 219.

Mallaber, K. A. 'An early Wheatley catalogue: the 1866 catalogue of the Board of Trade library', *The Indexer* 7 (1970), 42–5.

Mandell, S. L. *Computers and information processing: concepts and applications*, 6th edn (St Paul, MN, 1992), 259.

Manley, K. A. 'E. W. B. Nicholson and his importance for librarianship'. Unpublished DPhil thesis, Oxford University of (1977).

'The Munich tramcar library', *Library History* 10 (1994), 71–5.

Manners, Lady J. *Encouraging experiences of reading and recreation rooms* (London, 1886).

Some advantages of easily accessible reading and recreation rooms and free libraries (London, 1885).

Marcella, R., and R. Newton. *A new manual of classification* (London, 1994), 117.

Martin, J. V. 'Subject specialization in British university libraries: a second survey', *Journal of Librarianship and Information Science* 28 (1996), 159–69.

Martin, L. 'The American public library as a social institution', *Library Quarterly* 7 (1937) 552.

Martin, S. W. 'The A.A.L. correspondence courses 1924–1955', *Assistant Librarian* 68 (1967), Education Supplement i–iii.

Martin, W. *Community librarianship: changing the face of public libraries* (London, 1989).

Martin, W. (ed.). *Library services to the disadvantaged* (London, 1975).

Martin, W. J. 'From library studies to information science', *Education for Information* 5 (1987), 129–37.

Martino, A. *Die deutsche Leihbibliothek* (Wiesbaden, 1990).

Matarasso, F. *Learning development: an introduction to the social impact of libraries* (London, 1998).

Matthews, J. R., G. S. Lawrence and D. Ferguson (eds.). *Using online catalogs: a nationwide survey* (New York 1983).

Matthews, P. J. 'Sir William Osler' in Baker and Womack (eds.), *Nineteenth-century British book-collectors*, 310–21.

May, A. N. *The Bar and the Old Bailey, 1750–1850* (Chapel Hill, 2003).

Mayall, D. 'The library of the London Society of Compositors, 1855–1896', *Library History* 5 (1979), 55–60.

Meadows, A. J. 'Access to the results of scientific research: developments in Victorian Britain', in A. J. Meadows (ed.), *Development of science publishing in Europe* (Amsterdam, 1980), 43–62.

Innovation in information: twenty years of the British Library Research and Development Department (London, 1994).

Meehan, C. 'An Leabhar-Chumann – The Book Association of Ireland Children's Book Week', *Irish Library Bulletin* 5 (1944), 71–3.

Meenan, J., and D. Clarke (eds.). *RDS: the Royal Dublin Society 1731–1981* (Dublin, 1981).

Menhennet, D. *The House of Commons Library: a history* (London, 1991).

Metcalf, K. D. *Planning academic and research library buildings* (New York, 1965).

Metcalfe, J. *Information retrieval British and American 1876–1976* (Metuchen, NJ, 1976).

Middlebrook, S. *Newcastle-upon-Tyne: its growth and achievement*, 2nd edn (Newcastle upon Tyne, 1968).

Middleton, R. D. *Dr. Routh* (Oxford, 1938).

Midwinter, A., and M. McVicar. *Public library finance: developments in Scotland*, Library and Information Research Report 85 (London, 1992).

Mill, H. R. *The record of the Royal Geographical Society 1830–1930* (London, 1930).

Millar, A. H. *Jubilee of the Albert Institute 1867–1917: a record of the work of fifty years* (Dundee, 1917).

Miller, C. M. 'The effect of the loss of copyright privilege on Glasgow University Library, 1790–1858', *Library History* 7 (2) (1985), 45–57.

Miller, E. 'Antonio Panizzi and the British Museum', *British Library Journal* 5 (1979), 1–17.

Prince of librarians: the life and times of Antonio Panizzi of the British Museum (London, 1967).

Miller, S. *Book collecting: a guide* (Royston, 1994).

Milne, R. 'Conspectus at the coal face', *British Journal of Academic Librarianship* 3 (1988), 89–98.

Minister for the Arts. *Financing our public library service: four subjects for debate: a consultative paper* (London, 1988) (Cm. 324).

Ministry of Education. *Inter-library co-operation in England and Wales* (1962) (The Baker Report).

Standards of public library service in England and Wales (London, 1962) (The Bourdillon Report).

The structure of the public library service in England and Wales (London, 1959) (Cmnd.660) (The Roberts Report).

Ministry of Reconstruction, Adult Education Committee. *Third interim report on libraries and museums* (London, 1919) (Cmd. 321).

Minto, J. *A history of the public library movement* (London, 1932).

Mitchell, B. R. *Abstract of British historical statistics* (London, 1962).

Mitchell, J. M. *The public library system of Great Britain and Ireland, 1921–3* (Dunfermline, 1924) (The Mitchell Report).

Moody, N. 'Fashionable design and good service: the spinster librarians at Boot's Booklover's Libraries', in E. Kerslake and N. Moody (eds.), *Gendering library history* (Liverpool, 2000), 131–44.

Moon, B. E. 'Building a university library: from Robbins to Atkinson', in B. Dyson (ed.), *The modern academic library: essays in memory of Philip Larkin* (London, 1989), 20–31.

Moore, G. *Literature at nurse, or circulating morals* (London, 1885); facsimile edition with an introduction by Pierre Coustillas (Hassocks, 1976).

Moore, N. *The emerging markets for library and information workers*, British Library Research Report 56 (London, 1987).

'Meeting the costs of development: the role of the British Library (Research and Development Department)', *Journal of Librarianship* 16 (1984), 188–98.

Moore, N., and E. Kempson. 'The nature of the library and information workforce in the United Kingdom', *Journal of Librarianship* 17 (1985), 137–54.

Moore, T. S., and J. C. Philip. *The Chemical Society 1841–1941* (London, 1947).

Moran, C. 'Fr. Stephen J. Brown, S.J.: a library life 1881–1962', unpublished MLIS thesis, University College Dublin (1998).

Morgan, P. *Oxford libraries outside the Bodleian: a guide*, 2nd edn (Oxford, 1980).

Morley, H. 'The labourer's reading room', *Household Words* 3 (1851), 581–5.

Morris, R. J. B. *Parliament and the public libraries: a survey of legislative activity promoting the municipal library service in England and Wales 1850–1876* (London, 1977).

Morrish, P. S. 'Domestic libraries: Victorian and Edwardian ideas and practice', *Library History* 10 (1994), 27–44.

'Foreign-language books in some Yorkshire subscription libraries 1785–1805', *Yorkshire Archaeological Journal* 53 (1981), 79–92.

Mosse, W. E. (ed.). *Second chance: two centuries of German-speaking Jews in the United Kingdom* (Tübingen, 1991).

Mowat, I. R. M. 'The Oireachtas Library, Leinster House, Dublin', *State Librarian* 26 (1978), 40–1.

Moys, E. M. *A classification scheme for law books* (London, 1968).

Moys, E. M. (ed.). *Manual of law librarianship: the use and organization of legal literature* (London, 1976).

Muddiman, D. 'Innovation or instrumental drift? The new vocationalism and information and library education in the United Kingdom', *Education for Information* 12 (1994), 259–70.

'Towards a postmodern context for information and library education' *Education for Information* 17 (1999), 1–19.

'World gone wrong? Alternative conceptions of the information society', in S. Hornby and Z. Clarke (eds.), *Challenge and change in the information society* (London, 2003), 42–59.

Muddiman, D. and others. *Open to all? The public library and social exclusion*, 3 vols. (London, 2000).

Muensterberger, W. *Collecting: an unruly passion* (Princeton, NJ, 1994).

Muirhead, G. A. 'The role of the systems librarian in libraries in the United Kingdom', *Journal of Librarianship and Information Science* 25 (1993), 123–35.

Mulgan, G. 'Culture', in D. Marquand and A. Seldon (eds.), *The ideas that shaped post-war Britain* (London, 1996), 195–213.

Munby, A. N. L. 'John Maynard Keynes: the book-collector', in his *Essays and papers* (London, 1977), 19–26.

Cambridge college libraries: aids for research students, 2nd edn (Cambridge, 1962).

Portrait of an obsession: the life of Sir Thomas Phillipps (London, 1967).

Munby, A. N. L. (ed.). *Sale catalogues of eminent persons*, 12 vols. (London, 1971–5).

Munford, W. A. *Edward Edwards, 1812–1886: portrait of a librarian* (London, 1963).

A history of the Library Association 1877–1977 (London, 1976).

Penny rate: aspects of British public library history, 1850–1950 (London, 1951).

'The public library idea', *Library Association Record* 57 (1955), 350.

Who was who in British librarianship 1800–1985 (London, 1987).

William Ewart, M.P., 1798–1869: portrait of a radical (London, 1960).

Munford, W. A. (ed.). *Annals of the Library Association, 1877 to 1960* (London, 1965).

Murison, W. J. *The public library* (London, 1955).

Mynott, G., D. Denham and J. Elkin. 'A place for children revisited', *Journal of Librarianship and Information Science* 33 (2001), 133–44.

Myers, R., and M. Harris (eds.). *Property of a gentleman: the formation, organisation and dispersal of the private library 1620–1920* (Winchester, 1991).

Myers, R., M. Harris and G. Mandelbrote (eds.). *Libraries and the book trade: the formation of collections from the sixteenth to the twentieth century* (New Castle, DE, 2000).

Myres, J. N. L. 'Recent discoveries in the Bodleian Library', *Archaeologia* 101 (1967), 150–68.

Nagl, M. 'Stille, Ordnung, Katastrophen: Bibliotheken im Film – Bibliotheken aus männlichem Blick?', in P. Vodosek and G. Jefcoate (eds.), *Libraries in literature / Bibliotheken in der literarischen Darstellung* (Wiesbaden, 1999), 115–26.

'The national book appeal for the unemployed. A review of the first year's work', *Library Association Record* 2 (1935), 471–3.

National Heritage Committee. *Fifth report: the British Library*, House of Commons Paper 550 (London, 1994).

National Libraries Committee. *Report* (London, 1969) (Cmnd. 4028) (The Dainton Report).

National Library of Ireland. *Strategic plan 1992–1997* (Dublin, 1992).

Naylor, B. 'British Council', in J. Feather and P. Sturges (eds.), *International encyclopedia of information and library science* (London and New York, 1997), 39–40.

    'The libraries of London University: a historical sketch', in Thompson (ed.), *University library history*, 229–49.

Negroponte, N. *Being digital* (London, 1995).

Neligan, A. (ed.). *Maynooth library treasures: from the collections of Saint Patrick's College* (Dublin, 1995).

Newcombe, L. *Library co-operation in the British Isles* (London, 1937).

    'A prisoner-of-war library', *Library Association Record* 18 (September 1919), 271–83.

    'The Library of University College', unpublished typescript (1926).

Newman, S. 'A troopship library', *Library Association Record* 42 (September 1943), 155–7.

Neylon, M. J. 'King's Inns Library, Dublin', *Law Librarian* 4 (1973), 3–4.

NHS Executive. *Health Service Guidelines, library and information services*, HSG(97)47 (London, 1997).

Nicholson, E. 'Working class readers and libraries: a social history 1800–1850', unpublished MA thesis, University of London (1976).

Nicholson, E. W. B., and H. R. Tedder (eds.). *Transactions and proceedings of the conference of librarians . . . 1877* (London, 1878).

Nielsen, J. S. 'Islamic communities in Britain', in P. Badham (ed.), *Religion, state, and society in modern Britain* (Lewiston, NY, 1989), 225–41.

Norrie, I. *Mumby's publishing and bookselling in the twentieth century* (London, 1982).

Novak, J. 'Virtual libraries: service realities', *Australian Academic and Research Libraries* 33 (2002), 1–13.

Nowell-Smith, S. 'Carlyle and the London Library', in C. B. Oldman and others, *English libraries 1800–1850* (London, 1958).

Noyce, J. *Libraries and the working classes in the nineteenth century* (Brighton, 1974).

O'Brien, M. D. 'Free libraries', in T. Mackay (ed.), *A plea for liberty: an argument against socialism and socialistic legislation* (London, 1891), 329–49.

O'Connor, F. *My father's son* (London, 1968); reprinted Belfast, 1994.

O'Dwyer, F. *The architecture of Deane and Woodward* (Cork, 1997).

O hAodha, M. 'Irish rural libraries: glimpses of the past', *Library History* 18 (2000), 49–56.

Ó Lúing, S. 'Richard Irvine Best: librarian and Celtic scholar', *Zeitschrift für Celtische Philologie* 49–50 (1997), 682–97.

Ochai, A. 'The purpose of the library in colonial tropical Africa', *International Library Review* 16 (1984), 309–15.

Offor, R. *A descriptive guide to the libraries of the University of Leeds* (Leeds, 1947).

Ogle, J. J. *The extension of the free libraries Act to small places* (London, 1887).

    The free library: its history and present condition (London, 1897).

Olding, R. K. (ed.). *Readings in library cataloguing* (London, 1966).

Oliver, R. C. B. 'John Hutchinson: teacher, poet and librarian, 1829–1916', *Radnorshire Society Transactions* 50 (1980), 34–55.

Ollé, J. G. *Library history* (London, 1969).

Opie, I. *The treasures of childhood: books, toys and games from the Opie Collection* (London, 1989).

Oram, A. *Women teachers and feminist politics* (Manchester, 1996).

'The organization of a solicitor's office', *Solicitors' Journal* 29 (1884), 22–3.

Osborn, A. D. 'The crisis in cataloging', *Library Quarterly* 11 (1941), 393–411.

OSTI: the first five years (London, 1971).

Overington, M. A. *The subject departmentalized public library* (London, 1969).

Owen, E. 'Workmen's libraries in Glamorganshire and Monmouthshire', *The Library* 8 (1896), 1–14.

Panter-Downes, M. *Ooty preserved: a Victorian hill-station* (London, 1967).

Pantry, S. 'Government libraries,' in Bromley and Allott (eds.), *British librarianship and information work 1986–90*, vol. 2, 1–9.

Pargellis, S. 'Rare books and the scholar', in T. C. Blegen and others, *Book collecting and scholarship* (Minneapolis, 1954), 33–9.

Parish, C. *The history of the Literary and Philosophical Society of Newcastle upon Tyne*, vol. 2: *1896–1989* (Newcastle, 1990).

Parker, W. W. *Henry Stevens of Vermont, American rare book dealer in London, 1845–1886* (Amsterdam, 1963).

Parliamentary returns of public libraries 1876–7.

[Parry Report] University Grants Committee. *Report of the committee on libraries* (London, 1967).

Parry, T. *Amryw bethau* (Dinbych, 1996).

Parry, V. T. H. 'The Government Librarians Group of the Library Association', *State Librarian* 6 (1978), 6–12.

Partington, W. *Thomas J. Wise in the original cloth* (London, 1948).

Partridge, R. C. B. *The history of the legal deposit of books throughout the British Empire* (London, 1938).

Paynter, W. *My generation* (London, 1972).

P-E Consulting Group Limited. 'Summary of "Study of central government departmental libraries: final report"', *State Librarian* 23 (1975), 2–4.

Pearce, J. G. 'Intelligence work in a modern industrial organisation', *Library Association Record* 23 (1921), 364–9.

'The works library and its relation to the public technical library', *Library Association Record* 21 (1919), 8–12.

Pearson, D. *Provenance research in book history: a handbook* (London, 1994).

Pearson, J. D. *Oriental manuscript collections in the libraries of Great Britain and Ireland* (London, 1954).

Pearson, W. 'Kenneth A. Mallaber, F.L.A.: a valediction', *State Librarian* 24 (1976), 25.

Pemberton, J. E. 'Cataloguing on a micro with Librarian', *Library Micromation News* 3 (1984), 7–14.

'The people's Network: a turning point for public libraries: first findings', *Managing Information* 10 (2003), 27.

Pepcroy, B. 'Tramcars as travelling libraries', *Library World* 9 (1906–7), 323–7.

Pepper, S. 'A department store of learning', *Times Literary Supplement* (9 May 1986), 500.

Perkin, M. (ed.). *A directory of the parochial libraries of the Church of England and the Church in Wales*, revised edn (London, 2004).

Perkins, H. *New universities in the United Kingdom* (Paris, 1969).

Perry, S., 'The CURL database project', *Vine* 73 (1988), 4.

Peters, T. A. 'Gutterdammerung (twilight of the gutter margins): e-books and libraries', *Library Hi Tech* 19 (2001), 50–62.

Pettee, J. 'Code revision – what do catalogers want?', *Library Journal* 61 (1936), 306–8.

Philip, A. J. 'Blacking out', *Library World* 7 (1904–5), 261–3.

Pickard, J. R. *A history of King's College Library, Aberdeen*, 3 vols. (Aberdeen, 1987).

Pickles, J. D. 'The Haddon Library, Cambridge', *Library History* 8 (1988), 1–9.

Pierce, K. E. 'Women in public libraries', *Library World* 4 (1901–2), 286–8.

Piggott, W. D. 'Industrial libraries', in Sewell (ed.), *Five years' work in librarianship 1951–1955*, 75–86.

Pollard, A. W. 'Book-collecting', in *Encyclopaedia Britannica*, 11th edn (London, 1910–11), vol. 4, 221.

Poole, W. F. 'The construction of library buildings', *American Architect and Building News* 10 (1881), 131–4.

    'The organisation and management of public libraries', in US Bureau of Education, *Public Libraries in the United States, Part I* (Washington DC, 1876).

    'Progress of library architecture', *Library Journal* 7 (1882), 130–6.

    'Small library buildings', *Library Journal* 10 (1885), 250–6.

Pope, A. 'The impacts of the Internet on public library use: an analysis of the consumer market for library and Internet services in New Zealand', *New Zealand Libraries* 49 (2003), 271–9.

Porat, M. U. *The information economy* (Washington, DC, 1977).

Powell, O. *Oral history tape*, 29th November 1973, South Wales Miners' Library, University of Wales, Swansea.

Price, R. 'The factory library', *Librarian and Book World* 30 (3) (1930), 43–4.

    'The working men's club movement and Victorian social reform ideology', *Victorian Studies* 15 (1971), 117–47.

Prince, B., and P. F. Burton. 'Changing dimensions in academic library structures: the impact of information technology', *British Journal of Academic Librarianship* 3 (1988), 67–81.

'Prohibition and propaganda', *Irish Library Bulletin* 5 (1944), 37.

'The proposed Wedgwood Institute', *The Builder* 21 (14 March 1863), 185.

Prothero, G. W. *A memoir of Henry Bradshaw, Fellow of King's College, Cambridge, and University Librarian* (London, 1888).

The Public library of our time: the President's address at the meeting of the American Library Association, Round Island, New York, August 30–September 2 1887 (privately printed, 1887).

Pugh, L. 'Some theoretical bases of convergence', *New Review of Academic Librarianship* 3 (1997), 65.

Pugh, P. *Educate, agitate, organize: 100 years of Fabian Socialism* (London, 1984).

Quinn, J. H. *Library cataloguing* (London, 1913).

Radcliffe, Lord. *Government by contempt: a speech in the House of Lords* (London, 1968).

Ramdin, R. *Reimaging Britain: 500 years of Black and Asian history* (London, 1999).

Ranganathan, S. R. *The five laws of library science* (Madras and London, 1931).

    Prolegomena to library classification (London, 1937).

'The rape of the Rylands', *The Book Collector* 37 (1988), 169–84.

Rare Books Group. *Guidelines for the cataloguing of rare books* (London, 1997).

Ratcliffe, F. W. 'After Atkinson', *Library Review* 35 (1986), 69–78.

'Collections, collectors and collection building', in C. Harris (ed.), *The new university library: issues for the '90s and beyond* (London, 1994), 4–18.

'The growth of university library collections in the United Kingdom', in Thompson (ed.) *University library history*, 5–32.

'Mr Gladstone, the Librarian, and St Deiniol's Library, Hawarden', in P. J. Jagger (ed.), *Gladstone, politics and religion* (London, 1985), 65.

Preservation policies and conservation in British libraries: report of the Cambridge University Library Conservation Project (London, 1984).

'Professional librarianship and the university library' in A. Jeffreys (ed.), *The art of the librarian* (Newcastle upon Tyne, 1973), 140–56.

Ray, C. 'United Kingdom', in his *Library service to children: an international survey* (New York, 1978), 132–9.

Ray, G. N. *Bibliographical resources for the study of nineteenth century English fiction* (Los Angeles, 1964).

'The changing world of rare books', *Papers of the Bibliographical Society of America* 59 (1965), 103–41.

The rare book world today (New York, 1982).

'The world of rare books re-examined', *Yale Library Gazette* 49 (1974), 77–146.

Rayward, W. B. *The universe of information: the work of Paul Otlet for documentation and international organisation* (Moscow, 1975).

Rayward, W. B. (ed.). *International organisation and dissemination: selected essays of Paul Otlet* (Amsterdam, 1990).

Reed, M. 'Women's work in libraries', *Librarian and Book World* (1911–13) [over 20 articles in the period 1911–13].

Rees, E., and G. Walters. 'Swansea libraries in the nineteenth century', *Journal of the Welsh Bibliographical Society* 10 (1966–71), 43–57.

Rees, G. *Libraries for children: a history and bibliography* (London, 1924).

Reich, R. B. *The work of nations: preparing ourselves for 21st century capitalism* (New York, 1991).

Reilly, C. H. 'Manchester's Reference Library', *Building* 9 (1934), 44–52.

'Report of the International Meeting of Cataloguing Experts, Copenhagen, 1969', *Libri* 20 (1970) 105–32.

Richardson, E. C. *Classification: theoretical and practical* (New York, 1912).

Richardson, F. P. 'The Law Society Library: a short historical description', *The Law Librarian* 1 (1970), 15–19.

Richardson, W. C. *A history of the Inns of Court* (Baton Rouge, [1977]).

Rider, F. *The scholar and the future of the research library* (New York, 1944).

[Robbins Report] Committee on Higher Education. *Report* (London, 1963) (Cmnd. 2154).

[Roberts Report] Ministry of Education, *The structure of the public library service in England and Wales* (London, 1959) (Cmnd. 660).

Roberts, D. M. 'The Bradford Library 1774–1974', unpublished MA dissertation, University of Sheffield (1974).

Roberts, E. 'The Prince Consort's Library, Aldershot', *State Librarian* 24 (1976), 24.

Roberts, S. C. *British universities* (London, 1947).

Robinson, L. *Curtain up: an autobiography* (London, 1942).

Robinson, L. (ed.). *Lady Gregory's journals 1916–1930* (London, 1946).

Robson, R. *The attorney in eighteenth-century England* (Cambridge, 1959).

Roderick, G. W., and M. D. Stephens. *Education and industry in the nineteenth century* (London, 1978).

Rodger, E. M. 'Who wins – the architect or the librarian? Academic library building in Britain 1984–1989', *Library Review* 40 (2–3) (1991), 72–84.

Roe, J. 'The public library in Wales: its history and development in the context of local government'. Unpublished master's thesis, Queen's University of Belfast (1970).

Rogers, C. 'Cooperation activities of the Committee of Departmental Librarians', given at 1980 Circle of State Librarians conference on government library and information networks, *State Librarian* 29 (1981), 8.

Rose, J. *The intellectual life of the British working classes* (New Haven and London, 2001).

'Marx, Jane Eyre, Tarzan: miners' libraries in South Wales 1923–52', *Leipziger Jahrbuch zur Buchgeschichte* 4 (1994), 187–207.

Rosenau, P. A. *Post-modernism and the social sciences: insights, inroads and intrusions* (Princeton, NJ, 1992).

Rota, A. 'Bookselling in a changing world' in Bernard, *et al.* (eds.), *Antiquarian books*, 1–6.

Routh, G. *Occupation and pay in Great Britain 1906–79* (London, 1980).

Rowley, J. E. 'New technology in libraries', in Bromley and Allott (eds.), *British librarianship and information work 1986–1990*, vol. 2, 235.

Rowntree, B. S., and G. R. Lavers. *English life and leisure: a social study* (London, 1951).

Royal Commission appointed to inquire into the universities of Scotland. *Report,* 4 vols. (London, 1878) (C. 1935).

Royal Commission of inquiry into the state of the universities of Scotland. *Report* (London, 1831).

Royal Commission on National Museums and Galleries. *Interim Report* (London, 1928) (Cmd. 3192).

Royal Commission to enquire into the state, discipline, studies and revenue of the University and Colleges of Cambridge. *Report and Minutes of Evidence* (London, 1852) (Command paper 1559).

Royal Commission to enquire into the state, discipline, studies and revenue of the University and Colleges of Oxford. *Report and Minutes of Evidence* (London, 1852) (Command paper 1482).

Royal Commission to enquire into the state, discipline, studies and revenue of the University of Dublin and Trinity College. Dublin University Commission. *Report: comments, suggestions and evidence* (Dublin, 1853) (Command paper 1637).

'The Royal Faculty of Procurators in Glasgow', *Journal of the Law Society of Scotland* 14 (1969), 295–7.

Royal Society Scientific Information Conference, 1948. *Report and papers submitted* (London, 1948).

Ryder, J. (ed.). *Library services to housebound people* (London, 1987).

Rye, R. A. *The libraries of London: a guide for students,* 2nd edn, illustrated (London, 1910).

Sadleir, M. 'The development during the last fifty years of bibliographical study of books of the XIXth century', in F. C. Francis (ed.), *The Bibliographical Society: studies in retrospect* (London, 1949), 146–58.

Sadler, M. E. 'The history of education', in C. H. Herford (ed.), *Germany in the nineteenth century: a series of lectures*, (Manchester, 1915), 101–27.

Salusbury, M. *Thatcherism goes to college: the Conservative assault on higher education* (London, 1989).

Sampson, A. *Anatomy of Britain* (London, 1962).

Sanderson, M. *The universities and British industry, 1850–1970* (London, 1972).

Sanderson, M. (ed.). *The universities in the nineteenth century* (London, 1975).

Sands, L. *Tuppence for the rainbow* (Bradford, 1990).

Sants, B. H. J. 'Industrial and commercial libraries', in Taylor (ed.), *British librarianship and information work 1976–1980*, vol. 2, 58–68.

Saonharju, I. 'Country licensing by the Finnish electronic library programme', *Helsinki University Library Bulletin* (1999), 10–12.

Saunders, W. L. (ed.). *British librarianship today* (London, 1976).

Saxl, F. 'The history of Warburg's library, 1886–1944', in E. H. Gombrich, *Aby Warburg: an intellectual biography* (London, 1970), 325–38.

Sayers, W. C. B. *A manual of classification for librarians and bibliographers*, 2nd rev. edn (London, 1944).

'Presidential address', *Library Association Record* 40 (1938), 291–6.

Schiffrin, A. *The business of books: how international conglomerates took over publishing and changed the way we read* (London, 2000).

Schmidt, B. Q. 'Frederick Locker-Lampson', in Baker and Womack (eds.), *Nineteenth-century British book-collectors*, 258–64.

'Henry Yates Thompson' in Baker and Womack, *Nineteenth-century British book-collectors*, 21–7.

Schofield, R. 'Dimensions of illiteracy 1750–1850', *Explorations in Economic History* 10 (1973), 437–54.

Scott, J. W. 'The library of University College', in R. Irwin and R. Staveley (eds.), *The libraries of London*, 2nd rev. edn (London, 1964), 157–96.

Seldon, A. *Foreign Office: an illustrated history of the place and its people* (London, 2000).

Select Committee on Inquiry into Drunkenness. *Report* (London, 1834) (H.C. 559).

Select Committee on Legal Education. *Report and minutes of evidence*, Parliamentary Papers (London, 1846) (H.C. 686).

Select Committee on Public Libraries. *Report* (London, 1849) (H.C. 548).

Select Committee on Scientific Institutions (Dublin). *Report* (London, 1864) (H.C. 1864).

Select Committee on Royal Dublin Society. *Report* (London, 1836) (H.C. 1836).

'Serials control systems: an overview', *Vine* 87 (1992), 2.

Sewell, P. H. *Library co-operation in the United Kingdom: existing arrangements, gaps in provision and research which may be needed*, BLR&D Report 5479 (London, 1979).

Sewell, P. H. (ed.). *Five years' work in librarianship 1961–65* (London, 1968).

Sharp, H. *Cataloguing: a textbook*, 2nd edn (London, 1937).

Sharp, J. R. 'Information retrieval', in W. Ashworth (ed.), *Handbook of special librarianship and information work*, 3rd edn (London, 1967), 141–232.

Shaw, A. B. 'The oldest medical societies in Great Britain' *Medical History* 12 (1968), 232–44.

Sheffield City Libraries. *Guide to the manuscript collection in the Sheffield City Libraries* (Sheffield, 1956).

Sheffield Regional Hospital Board. *Working party on medical libraries: final report* (Sheffield, 1965).

Shepherd, P. *The making of a Northern Baptist College* (Manchester, 2004).

Sherwell, J. 'Industrial and commercial libraries', in Bromley and Allott (eds.), *British librarianship and information work 1981–1985*, vol. 2, 53–65.

Shinn, C. H. *Paying the piper: the development of the University Grants Committee 1919–1946* (Lewes, 1986).

Shipley, S. *Club life and socialism in mid-Victorian London* (Oxford, 1971).
  'The libraries of the Alliance Cabinet Makers' Association', *History Workshop* 1 (1976), 180–4.

Silver, H. *English education and the radicals 1780–1850* (London, 1975).

Simms, G. O. 'James Henthorn Todd', *Hermathena* 109 (1969), 5–23.

Simon, B. *Education and the labour movement 1870–1920* (London, 1965).
  The two nations and the educational structure 1780–1870 (London, 1974).

Simpson, S. M. 'The history of the library 1837–1939', in Guild and Law (eds.), *Edinburgh University Library*, 94–114.

Singleton, J. W. 'The library in fiction', *Library Association Record* 20 (1918), 210–18.

Slaney, R. *Essay on the beneficial direction of rural expenditure* (London, 1824).

Slater, M. *The neglected resource: non-usage of information services in industry and commerce* (London, 1981).

Smethurst, J. M. 'Henry Heaney: an appreciation', *Library Review* 47 (1998), 256–61.
  'University library staffing in the United Kingdom', in Thompson (ed.), *University library history*, 56–76.

Smith, A. J. W. 'Carnegie library buildings in Great Britain: an account, evaluation and survey', 4 vols., unpublished FLA thesis (1974).

Smith, F. S. (ed.). *Report on the hours, salaries, training and conditions of service in British municipal libraries, 1931* (London, 1932).

Smith, J. V. 'Manners, morals and mentalities: reflections on the popular Enlightenment of early nineteenth century Scotland', in W. M. Humes and H. M. Paterson (eds.), *Scottish culture and Scottish education, 1800–1900* (Edinburgh, 1983), 25–54.

Smith, J. W. T. 'A review of the use of networking and related technologies by the UK academic library and information sector', *IASLIC Bulletin* 41 (1996), 49–69.

Smith, P. 'Networking in public libraries: collaborative developments at LASER', *Vine* 98 (1995), 17.

Smith, R. S. 'The history of academic library buildings', in Thompson (ed.), *University library history*, 128–46.

Smurthwaite, A. J. 'An occupations list of 1870', *Library History* 1 (1969), 192–4.

Snape, R. *Leisure and the rise of the public library* (London, 1995).

Snelling, O. F. *Rare books and rarer people: some personal reminiscences of the trade* (London, 1982).

Snowley, I. 'Managing the market', *Serials* 7 (1994), 129–32.

Society for Computers and Law. *A national law library – the way ahead: a proposal for a computer-assisted retrieval system for the UK* (Abingdon, 1979).

The Society of Writers to His Majesty's Signet (Edinburgh, 1936).

Spiller, D., C. Creaser and A. Murphy. *Libraries in the workplace* (Loughborough, 1998).

Squibb, G. D. *Doctors' Commons: a history of the College of Advocates and Doctors of Law* (Oxford, 1977).

St Clair, J. and R. Craik. *The Advocates' Library: 300 years of a national institution 1689–1989* (Edinburgh, 1989).

Stam, D. H. (ed.). *International dictionary of library histories,* 2 vols. (Chicago and London, 2001).

Staveley, R. 'Professional education', in Sewell (ed.), *Five years work in librarianship 1961–1965*, 604–6.

Stearn, W. T. *The Natural History Museum at South Kensington* (London, 1981).

Steele, C., and M. Henty. 'A woman's place is in the – library? A review article', *Journal of Librarianship* 19 (1987), 121–32.

Stehr, N. *Knowledge societies* (London, 1994).

Steinberg, H.-J. 'Workers' libraries in Germany before 1914', *History Workshop* 1 (1976), 166–76.

Steiner, W. A. *The Institute of Advanced Legal Studies of the University of London 1947–1976* (London, 2000).

Stephens, A. *The history of the British National Bibliography* (London, 1994).

Sternberg, I. 'The British Museum Library and colonial copyright deposit', *British Library Journal* 17 (1991), 61–82.

Stewart, J. D. (ed.). *Report on the municipal library system of London and the Home Counties* (London, 1925).

Stewart, W. A. C. *Higher education in postwar Britain* (Basingstoke, 1989).

Stimpson, F. 'Servants' reading: an examination of the servants' library at Cragside', *Library History* 19 (2003), 3–11.

Stone, L. 'Literacy and education in England 1640–1900', *Past and Present* 42 (1969), 61–139.

Strong, D. 'Services to people with mental handicaps', in J. Ryder (ed.), *Library services to housebound people* (London, 1987), 160–84.

Sturges, P. 'Beer and books: Michael Thomas Bass, Derby Public Library and the philanthropy of the beerage', *Libraries and Culture* 31 (1996), 247–71.

Sturt, R. 'Hospital libraries in England and Wales: a history', in M. Going (ed.), *Hospital libraries and work with the disabled,* 2nd edn (London, 1973), 21–66.

Sugarman, D. *A brief history of the Law Society* (London, 1995).

Sumsion, J., et al. *The CIPFA enquiry count* (Loughborough, 1994).

Supplementary catalogue of the Langholm Library (Langholm, 1900), with historical account by R. McGeorge.

Swale, A. 'The terracotta of the Wedgwood Institute, Burslem', *Journal of the Tiles and Architectural Ceramics Society* 2 (1987), 21–7.

Sweeney, R. 'Dewey in Britain', *Catalogue and Index* 30 (1973), 4–6, 15.

Sweet and Maxwell. *Then and now 1799–1974* (London, 1974).

Sydney, E. 'Adult education and the public library', *Library Association Record* 48 (1946), 275–9.

Sykes, P. *The public library in perspective: an examination of its origins and modern role* (London, 1979).

Sykes, P., and S. Gerrard. 'Operational convergence at Roehampton Institute London and Liverpool John Moores University', *New Review of Academic Librarianship* 3 (1997), 84.

Symons, J. 'These crafty dealers: Sir Henry Wellcome as a book collector', in R. Myers and M. Harris (eds.), *Medicine, mortality and the book trade* (Folkestone, 1998), 109–30.

Tanselle, G. T. *Textual criticism and scholarly editing* (Charlottesville, 1990).

The Tavistock Subscription Library 1799–1999 (Tavistock, 1999).

Taylor, J. *From self-help to glamour: the working man's club, 1860–1972* (Oxford, 1972).

Taylor, L. J. (ed.). *British librarianship and information work 1976–80*, 2 vols. (London, 1982–3).

Taylor, R. 'Of dealers and collectors', in H. G. Fletcher (ed.), *A miscellany for bibliophiles* (New York, 1979), 1–13.

Teague, S. J. *Microform librarianship* (London, 1977).

Tedd, L. A. 'Computer-based information retrieval systems', in L. J. Anthony (ed.), *Handbook of special librarianship and information work*, 5th edn (London, 1982), 338.

   An introduction to computer-based library systems, 3rd edn (London, 1993).

   'OPACs through the ages', *Library Review* 43 (1994), 30.

Tedder, H. R. 'Librarianship as a profession', in *Transactions and Proceedings of the Fourth and Fifth Annual Meetings of the Library Association of the United Kingdom held at London . . . 1881 and Cambridge . . . 1882* (London, 1884).

Theobald, R. E. 'Boot's Booklover's Library 1899–1966', unpublished MA thesis, Loughborough University (1988).

Tholfsen, T. *Working class radicalism in mid-Victorian Britain* (London, 1976).

Thomas, C., and B. Henderson. 'Watts, Panizzi and Asher', *British Library Journal* 23 (1997), 154–75.

Thompson, A. H. *Censorship in public libraries in the United Kingdom during the twentieth century* (Epping, 1975).

Thompson, G. *Planning and design of library buildings*, 2nd edn (London, 1977).

Thompson, J. *A centennial history of the library of the University of Birmingham 1880–1995* (Birmingham, 2000).

   Redirection in academic library management, 2nd edn (London, 1991).

Thompson, J. (ed.). *University library history: an international review* (New York and London, 1980).

Thompson, Joseph. *The Owens College: its foundation and growth and its connection with the Victoria University, Manchester* (Manchester, 1886).

Thornton, J. L. *Cataloguing in special libraries: a survey of methods* (London, 1938).

   Medical books, libraries and collectors, 2nd edn (London, 1966).

   Special library methods: an introduction to special librarianship (London, 1940).

Thornton, J. L. (ed.). *Selected readings in the history of librarianship* (London, 1966).

Thornton, J. L., and R. I. J. Tully. *Scientific books, libraries and collectors*, 3rd edn (London, 1971); 4th edn by A. Hunter (Aldershot, 1999).

Tobin, P. F. 'Pontypridd public library, 1890–1990', in P. F. Tobin and J. I. Davies (eds.), *The bridge and the song: some chapters in the story of Pontypridd* (Bridgend, 1991), 67–78.

Toffler, A. *The third wave* (London, 1980).

Tomlinson, O. S. 'Libraries in York', in A. Stacpoole *et al.* (eds.), *The noble city of York* (York, 1972), 969–93.

Tooley, J. B. 'Government libraries', in Sewell (ed.), *Five years' work in librarianship 1961–65*, 152–68.

'Government libraries', in Whatley (ed.), *British librarianship and information work 1966–70*, 518–35.

'London scientific libraries in the 19th century, II: government intervention', *Library History* 3 (1974), 129–39.

Topp, C. W. *Victorian yellowbacks and paperbacks 1849–1905*, vol. 3 (Denver, CO, 1997).

Totterdell, B. (ed.). *Public library purpose: a reader* (London, 1978).

Tracey, M. *The decline and fall of public service broadcasting* (New York, 1998).

Tremlett, G. *Clubmen: the history of the Working Men's Club and Institute Union* (London, 1987).

United Nations World Summit on the Information Society. *Declaration of principles. Building the information society: a global challenge in the new millennium* (Geneva, 2003).

University Grants Committee. *Capital provision for university libraries: report of a working party* (London, 1976) (The Atkinson Report).

Report including returns from universities and university colleges in receipt of Treasury grant, academic year 1923–1924 (London, 1925).

Report of the committee on libraries (London, 1967) (The Parry Report).

Returns from universities and university colleges, 1920–21 (London, 1922).

University development from 1935 to 1947 (London, 1948).

'An unusual library', *Yorkshire Observer* (20 July 1938).

Upson, R., and R. Hobbs. *Scrutiny of library services in the Department of Trade and Industry* (London, 1985).

Urquhart, D. *Mr. Boston Spa* (Leeds, 1990).

Usherwood, B. 'Public libraries and political purpose', in Kinnell and Sturges (eds.), *Continuity and innovation in the public library*, 189–209.

Van Slyck, A. A. *Free to all: Carnegie libraries and American culture 1890–1920* (Chicago and London, 1995).

'The utmost amount of effectiv [*sic*] accommodation: Andrew Carnegie and the reform of the American library', *Journal of the Society of Architectural Historians* 50 (1991), 359–83.

Varma, D. P. *The evergreen tree of diabolical knowledge* (Washington, DC, 1972).

Vaughan, A. 'The ideology of flexibility: a study of recent British academic library buildings', *Journal of Librarianship* 11 (1979), 277–93.

Vickers, P. 'Promoting the concept of information management within organisations', *Journal of Information Science* 9 (1984), 123–7.

Vickery, A. 'The clash of interests in computer information services', *Information Processing and Management* 14 (1978), 37–43.

Vickery, A., and A. Batten. *Large-scale evaluation study of on-line and batch computer information services* (London, 1978).

Vickery, B. C. 'The future of libraries in the machine age', *Library Association Record* 68 (1966), 257.

A long search for information, Graduate School of Library and Information Science, University of Illinois at Urbana-Champaign, Occasional Paper 213 (Urbana–Champaign, 2004).

'Thesaurus: a new word in documentation', *Journal of Documentation* 16 (1960), 181–90.

The use of on-line search in teaching: an assessment of projects carried out by UK schools of library and information studies (London, 1977).

Vincent, D., *Bread, knowledge and freedom* (London, 1982).

Vincent, J. *An introduction to community librarianship* (Newcastle under Lyme, 1986).

Vollans, R. F. *Library co-operation in Great Britain* (London, 1952).

Wainwright, C. 'The library as living room', in Myers and Harris (eds.), *Property of a gentleman*, 15–24.

Walker, R. 'Lincoln's Inn Library', *Law Librarian* 8 (1977), 3–4.

Wall, J. F. *Andrew Carnegie* (London and New York, 1970).

Wallace, A. 'The libraries, public, private, university and special of the city of Newcastle upon Tyne' (typescript, 1950).

Wallace, M. 'Issues for government libraries', *An Leabharlann* 12 (1995–6), 61–5.

Waller, R. D., and C. D. Legge. 'Adult education in the Manchester area', in *Manchester and its region: a survey* (Manchester, 1962), 226–33.

Walsh, A. 'The library as revealed in the Parliamentary Commission of 1853', in Kinane and Walsh (eds.), *Essays on the history of Trinity College Library*, 138–50.

Walsh, R. 'Libraries', in *Saorstat Eireann Irish Free State official handbook* (Dublin, 1932), 209.

Wardle, D. *Education and society in nineteenth century Nottingham* (Cambridge, 1971).

Ware, M. 'Institutional repositories and scholarly publishing', *Learned Publishing* 17 (2004), 115–24.

Watson, P. G. *Great Britain's National Lending Library* (Los Angeles, 1970).

Watson, R. S. *The history of the Literary and Philosophical Society of Newcastle upon Tyne 1793–1896* (London, 1897).

Way, D. J. 'BIALL: the first 30 years – a personal view', *The Law Librarian* 31 (1999), 122–4. *The student's guide to law libraries* (London, 1967).

Webb, R. K. *The British working class reader, 1790–1848* (London, 1955).

Webb, S. 'The library service of London: its co-ordination, development and education', *Library Association Record* 4 (1902), 193–203, 231–6.

Webber, N. 'The first library school in the United Kingdom: the London School of Economics, 1900–1919', *Library History* 12 (1996), 142–54.

Webster, F. 'Information, capitalism and uncertainty', *Information, communication and society* 3 (2000), 69–90. *Theories of the information society* (London, 1995); 2nd edn (London, 2002).

Webster, K. 'Research collections', in D. Baker (ed.), *Resource management in academic libraries* (London, 1997), 137–57.

Weedon, A., and M. Bott. *Book trade archives 1830–1939: a location register*, HOBODS 5 (Oxford, 1996).

Weibel, K., and Heim, K. M. (eds.). *The role of women in librarianship 1876–1976: the entry, advancement and struggle for equalization in one profession* (London, 1979).

Weihs, J. (ed.). *The principles and future of AACR: proceedings of the International Conference on the Principles and Future Development of AACR, Toronto, October 1997* (London, 1998).

Wellcome Trust. *A healthy heritage: collecting for the future of medical history* (London, 1999).

Wellek, R. *History of modern criticism*, 8 vols. (New Haven, 1955–93).

Wells, J. *Rude words: a discursive history of the London Library* (London, 1991).

West, A. J. *The Shakespeare First Folio: the history of the book*, vol. 2: *A new worldwide census of First Folios* (Oxford, 2003).

Whatley, H. A. (ed.). *British librarianship and information science 1966–1970* (London, 1972). (ed.). *British librarianship and information science 1971–1975* (London, 1977).

Whatmore, G. 'Special library notes', *Library Association Record* 57 (1955), 360.

Wheatley, H. B. *How to catalogue a library* (London, 1889).

Wheeler, J. L., and A. M. Githens. *American public library building* (New York, 1941).

Whittaker, K. 'Unobtrusive testing of reference enquiry work', *Library Review* 39 (6) (1990), 50–4.

Wiegand, W. A. *Irrepressible reformer: a biography of Melvil Dewey* (Chicago, 1996).

Wiegand, W. A., and D. G. Davis (eds.). *Encyclopedia of library history* (New York, 1994).

Wilkinson, C. L. 'Legal information and loose-leaf services', *Law Librarian* 29 (1998), 249–57.

Wilks, J. *The influence of R. W. Chambers on the development of university libraries*, The 2nd Chambers Memorial Lecture, 1953 (London, 1953).

Williams, G. 'A brief history of the establishment of a public library in Swansea and its subsequent development to the year 1919', unpublished ALA thesis (1973).
'A history of Swansea Public Library 1870–1974, concentrating on the years 1870–1920', unpublished FLA thesis (1981).

Williams, I. A. *The elements of book-collecting* (London, 1927).

Williams, R. V. 'The documentation and special libraries movements in the United States, 1910–1960', *Journal of the American Society for Information Science* 48 (1987), 775–81.

Williamson, J. 'Jungian / Myers Briggs personality types of librarians in films', *The Reference Librarian* 78 (2002), 47–60.

Williamson, W. L. *William Frederick Poole and the modern library movement* (New York, 1963).

Willison, I. R. 'The creation of the concept of the rare book', *Intellectual News* 6/7 (2000), 27–36.
'Legal deposit: a provisional perspective', *Publishing History* 45 (1999), 5–34.
On the history of libraries and scholarship (Washington, DC, 1980).

Wilson, C. *First with the news: the history of W. H. Smith 1792–1972* (London, 1985).

Wilson, C. St John. *The design and construction of the British Library* (London, 1998).

Wilson, R. N. D. *The county library service in Ireland* (Dunfermline, 1927).

Wilson, T. 'The nonsense of knowledge management', *Information Research* 8 (1) (2002), paper no. 144 [http:// InformationR.net/ ir/ 8-1/ paper 144.html].
'Research and research strategies in schools and departments of library and information studies', in J. Elkin and T. Wilson (eds.), *The education of library and information professionals* (London, 1997), 143–74.

Wilson, T. D. *An introduction to chain indexing* (London, 1971).

Wiltshire, B. 'The public library in autobiography', unpublished MPhil thesis, CNAA, North London Polytechnic (now London Metropolitan University) (1982).

Winkworth, I., and B. Enright. 'Relevance and reality in libraries', *Library Review* 35 (1986), 79–90.

Winter, M. F. *The culture and control of expertise: towards a sociological understanding of librarianship* (New York, 1988).

Winterton, J. 'The Institute of Advanced Legal Studies Library', *Law Librarian* 31 (1999), 129–30.

Woledge, G., and B. S. Page. *Manual of university and college library practice* (London, 1940).

Wolf, E., and J. F. Fleming. *Rosenbach: a biography* (Cleveland, OH, 1960).

'Women assistants and the War', *Library World* 22 (1920), 197–200.

'Women librarians', in Countess of Aberdeen (ed.), *Women in the professions: being the professional section of the International Congress of Women* (London, 1900).

Wood, J. *Account of the Edinburgh Sessional School* (Edinburgh, 1828).

Wood, K. 'Professional education: historical review' in J. Elkin and T. Wilson (eds.), *The education of information and library professionals in the United Kingdom* (London, 1997), 1–30.

Woodhead, P. A., and J. V. Martin. 'Subject specialization in British University Libraries: a survey', *Journal of Librarianship* 14 (1982), 93–108.

Woods, R. G. 'How did we get here from there? Reminiscing on the early days of library automation', *Program* 21 (1987), 238.

Wormald, J. H. 'Government libraries', in Taylor (ed.), *British librarianship and information work 1976–80*, vol. 2, 1–9.

Wormald, J. H., and S. Burge. 'Government libraries', in Bromley and Allott (eds.), *British librarianship and information work 1981–1985*, vol. 2, 1–8.

Wyatt, R. J. 'The development of scientific and technological libraries in Great Britain', *IATUL Quarterly* 5 (1990), 70–8.

Yates, J. *Control through communication: the rise of system in American management* (Baltimore, MD, 1989).

Yontz, E. 'Librarians in children's literature, 1909–2000', *The Reference Librarian* 78 (2002) (Special Issue: The Image and Role of the Librarian), 85–96.

York Subscription Library. *Celebration of its centenary* (York, 1894).

Zuckerman., Lord (ed.). *The Zoological Society of London, 1826–1976 and beyond* (London, 1976).

Index

Dates are given (where available) for librarians, but not for other persons; similarly all librarians are given full names, while others appear in the best-known form (e.g. Jast, Louis Stanley (1868–1944), but Eliot, T. S.).

Public libraries are listed under the town or city or county; other libraries (and institutions) under their own name.

Corporate bodies often referred to by acronyms are indexed under the full form, with the exceptions of Aslib (which changed its name to this form) and the various co-operative information services like BRASTACS, where the acronym was clearly thought of first! Cross-references are given from the acronyms such as SCONUL.

Institute of Information Scientists, 411, 499,
526, 631
and library education, 539
merger talks with Library Association and
Aslib, 422
see also Chartered Institute of Library and
Information Professionals
Institution of Electrical Engineers, 433
library
and abstracting services, 419
Thompson collection, 191
Institution of Mechanical Engineers, 429
Institution of Professional Civil Servants,
486
inter-library loan and document delivery, 17
automation, 622
demand driven by electronic information,
635
government libraries, 487
public libraries, 61, 559
fiction, 557
university libraries, 375, 399
Scotland, 251
Wales, 221
see also British Library Document Supply
Centre; Central Library for Students;
Irish Central Library for Students;
LASER; National Central Library;
National Library of Scotland;
Northern Regional Library Bureau;
Scottish Central Library; Wales
Regional Library Scheme
International Conference of Librarians
(London, 1877), 16, 597–8
International Conference on Cataloguing
Principles (1961), 573
International Congress of Women (1899),
544
international connections between libraries,
12–17
International Federation of Library
Associations and Institutions (IFLA),
573
and theological libraries, 477
International Meeting of Cataloguing Experts
(1969), 573
International Online Information Meeting,
633
International Standard Bibliographic Description
(ISBD), 571, 573–4
Internet, 71, 568, 625
and commercialisation of information,
648–9

and electronic information services, 636–7,
640
and public libraries, 29, 68, 616
Inverasdale, reading room, 240
Ipswich Institute, 155
Ireland
education for librarianship, 537
hospital libraries, 261–3, 447 n.6, 452
law libraries, 463
libraries, 253–65
public libraries, 26, 27, 253–65
subscription libraries, 149–50
see also Northern Ireland
Irish army training camp, Curragh, 258
Irish Central Library for Students, 257, 264
Irish Cooperative Reference Library, 256
Irish manuscripts, 271, 272
Irish Publishing Record, 274
Irish Rural Libraries Association, 254, 270
Irwin, Raymond (1902–77), 17
ISBD, *see* International Standard
Bibliographic Description
Islamic Cultural Centre, London, 475
Islamic libraries, *see* Muslim libraries
Islington public library
branches, Manor Gardens, 605
building (1905–6), 603
lectures, 80
issue systems, *see* circulation systems
Italy, immigrants from, *see* immigration and
immigrants
itinerating libraries, 239

Jain Centre, Leicester, 480
James, Montague Rhodes (1862–1936)
catalogues of MSS, 332
JANET, *see* Joint Academic Network
Jast, Louis Stanley (1868–1944), 117, 351
and design of Manchester Central Library,
606–7
and LA register, 535
and outreach, 78
and professional development, 63
as public library pioneer, 33
Jefferson, Thomas, and University of Virginia,
591
Jeger, Lena, and British Museum, 296, 302,
308
Jenkins, David (1912–2002), 231
Jenkinson, Francis John Henry (1853–1923),
and legal deposit, 335
Jerome, Jerome K., 284
Jesmond, branch library, 212